Staples, Markets, and Cultural Change
Selected Essays
Harold A. Innis
Edited by Daniel Drache

This new edition of Harold Innis's essays, published on the occasion of his centenary, assembles his most significant and representative writing. Included are many of Innis's essays on cultural issues and economic development – subjects he explored throughout his life – that have not been readily accessible before.

At the start of his career Innis set out to explain the significance of price rigidities in the cultural, social, and political institutions of new countries; by the end of his intellectual journey he had become one of the most influential critics of modernity. The essays in this collection address a variety of themes, including the rise of industrialism and the expansion of international markets, staples trades, critical factors in Canadian development, metropolitanism and nationality, the problems of adjustment, the political economy of communications, the economics of cultural change, and Innis's conception of the role of the intellectual as citizen.

Innis succeeded as few others have in providing an astute and comprehensive account of the economic and social forces shaping modernity. His abiding interest in the contradictory and unintended consequences of markets in general – the dominant structure of modern economic activity – constitutes the rich legacy of his prodigious scholarship.

DANIEL DRACHE is director of the Robarts Centre for Canadian Studies and professor of political science, York University.

Innis Centenary Series
Series Editor: Daniel Drache

Harold Innis, one of Canada's most distinguished economists, described the Canadian experience as no else ever has. His visionary works in economic geography, political economy, and communications theory have endured for over fifty years and have had a tremendous influence on scholarship, the media, and the business community.

The volumes in the Innis Centenary Series illustrate and expand Innis's legacy. Each volume is written and edited by distinguished members of the fields Innis touched. Each addresses provocative and challenging issues that have profound implications not only for Canada but for the "new world order," including the impact of globalization on national decision making; interactions among the state, social movements, and the environment; the nature of the "market" in the future; the effect of new communications technology on economic restructuring; and the role of the individual in effecting positive social change.

The complete series will provide a unique guide to many of the major challenges we face as we enter the twenty-first century.

Publication of the Innis Centenary Series is made possible by the generous support of Innis College, University of Toronto, and through private donations.

Staples, Markets, and Cultural Change

Selected Essays

HAROLD A. INNIS

CENTENARY EDITION

Edited by

DANIEL DRACHE

McGill-Queen's University Press
Montreal & Kingston • London • Buffalo

ISBN 0-7735-1299-3 (cloth)
ISBN 0-7735-1302-7 (paper)

Legal deposit first quarter 1995
Bibliothèque nationale du Québec

Printed in Canada on acid-free paper

McGill-Queen's University Press is grateful to the Canada Council for supporting its publishing program.

Canadian Cataloguing in Publication Data

Innis, Harold A., 1894–1952
Staples, markets, and cultural change: selected essays of Harold Innis

(Innis centenary series)
Centenary ed.
Includes bibliographical references and index.
ISBN 0-7735-1299-3 (bound)
ISBN 0-7735-1302-7 (pbk.)

1. Canada – Economic conditions. 2. Economics.
3. Social change. I. Drache, Daniel, 1941–
II. Title. III. Series.

HC113.I55'1995 330.971 C95-900088-7

For My Sister
Judith Rosenblatt
(1938–1994)

Contents

PART FOUR POLITICAL CULTURE, THE BIAS OF COMMUNICATION, AND ECONOMIC CHANGE

PART FIVE THE INTELLECTUAL AS CITIZEN

Acknowledgments

Many individuals have contributed to the idea of a centenary edition of Innis' collected essays. Their enthusiasm and support has made the task easier than it might have been. In no particular order, these include: Daniel Latouche, Robert Cox, Stephen Clarkson, Abe Rotstein, Marjorie Cohen, Robert Boyer, Janine Brodie, Duncan Cameron, Bill Buxton, Brian Shoesmith, Eric Mézin, Alejandro Alvarez, Teresa Gutiérrez, Dick Roman, Leesa Fawcett, Mel Watkins, Jody Berland, Roberto Perin, Matteo Sanfilippo, David Bell, Roger Kiel, Lise Gotell, Meric Gertler, Harry Glasbeek, Charles Ackland, Barbara Cameron, David Godfrey, David Cayley, Sam Lanfranco, Liss Jeffery, Terea Healey, Matthew Evenden, Gail Faurschou, Robert Lawrie, Allison Beale, Alain-G. Gagnon, Peter Penz, Shelley Hornstein, Michael Davey, Trevor Barnes, Robert Anderson, Roger Hayter, Derrick De Kerckhove, Andy Ranachan, Michael Goldrick and Leo Panitch. Special mention has to be made of the role of John Browne who, as principal of Innis College, has been a key figure in supporting this endeavour from the outset. Other timely support has come from President Susan Mann and Vice President Michael Stevenson of York University, and Dean Skip Bassford of Atkinson College. President Robert Pritchard, University of Toronto, has also contributed in important ways. Mary Cates and Anne Inis Dagg provided me with new insight into their father. Krystyna Tarkowski deserves a special thank-you for her invaluable assistance. Delwyn Higgins has helped me throughout and scrutinized the manuscript at all stages. I am very indebted to her for all her efforts. Finally, particular mention has to be made of Marilyn Lambert Drache and Charlotte Drache who have not accepted their traditional role as family members. They were not long-suffering. In the words of my daughter, "Why do you keep talking about him? You're not married to Harold Innis!" I would like to think that this project has been kept within strict limits, but evidently it has not. Mea culpa. I hope I am forgiven, but, nonetheless, I am alone responsible for any shortcomings and errors.

INTRODUCTION

Celebrating Innis: The Man, the Legacy, and Our Future

Export trade has been fundamental to the economic life of Canada since its discovery.
Harold Innis, "The Rowell-Sirois Report," 1940

Economic history is complementary to political history.
Harold Innis, *The Cod Fisheries,* 1964

Man's economy, as a rule, is submerged in his social relationships.
Karl Polanyi, *The Great Transformation,* [1944] 1957

Despite [its] much vaunted "flexibility" and capacity for easy adjustment to changing circumstances ... the market institution may reach a threshold of stress when it fails to adjust.
Abraham Rotstein, "Innis: The Alchemy of Fur and Wheat," 1977

INTRODUCTION

Harold Adams Innis remains far and away Canada's most brilliant political economist, and the centenary of his birth in 1994 is a fitting occasion on which to honour him with a new edition of his essays and articles. In his lifetime, Innis made many contributions to the study of economic geography and history, communications theory, regional development, and the history of Western civilization and technology. In his work on economic settlements and markets, he was preoccupied with the role and fate of aboriginal peoples, the development and spread of commerce, the interpenetration of cultures, the economic consequences of social disturbances, the evolution and operation of labour markets, and the power of governments to shape markets and the course of history through communications technologies. The publication of the present volume provides a unique opportunity to probe this rich legacy with depth and acuity.

In its scope and reach, this centenary edition assembles the most significant and representative writing from the early, middle, and late periods of Innis's scholarship. It includes some previously unpublished essays, as well as other material that has not been readily accessible to the public, on markets, staples, and cultural change – the primary issues and themes that preoccupied Innis in a lifetime of archival-based research. The volume covers such subjects as the rise of industrialism and the expansion of international markets, the staples trades, critical factors of Canadian development, metropolitanism and nationality, the problems of adjustment, the political economy of communications, the economics of cultural change, and, finally, Innis's conception of the role of the intellectual as citizen. To think that the later Innis was concerned strictly with cultural issues while the early Innis of the staples was narrowly focused on economic development is plainly wrong. This collection clearly demonstrates that such a division is artificial.

Like the great French historian Fernand Braudel, Innis focused on the *longue durée*, the history of events and epoch-making forces that transformed economies, states, and civilizations. The question he set for himself was to examine the complex inner dynamics of global forces that work themselves out in cycles that are endlessly renewed by the ebb and flow of commercial transactions (Braudel 1980). In fixing this goal, Innis remained faithful to his political economy origins throughout his life. He succeeded, as few have done, in providing a powerfully wide-angled account of the contradictory and cross-cutting economic and social forces that shape modernity. He believed that it was important to undertake extensive studies of a range of phenomena that were not what he called economic "success stories" (Innis, 1936a, 26). Rather, what preoccupied him as a scholar was the costly and uncontrollable effect of international markets on people and communities; it is this abiding interest in the contradictory and unintended consequences of markets in general – the dominant structure of modern economic activity – that forms the rich legacy of his prodigious output. He set out to explain the significance of price rigidities wherever they emerged in the cultural, social, and political institutions in new countries. By the end of his intellectual journey, Innis had developed one of the most powerful critiques of modernity of his generation.

INNIS: "A DIRT ECONOMIST"

That so much of Innis's scholarship concentrated on the spatial dimension of markets is not surprising. Global markets have always been highly volatile – subject to enormous swings in price and demand – as a result of technological innovation, distributional inequality, commodity shortages and investors' greed. The external market was at once more powerful and more turbulent than either the domestic market or local markets. It set the pace and direction of development for all countries, especially for frontier economies at the margin of the world order. To study this and other questions, Innis preferred to think of himself as a "dirt economist," a phrase he coined to describe the ideal economist who did not neglect the social and political side of economic life (Innis 1936a, 26). The idea of getting down to basics fitted his powerful intellect as well as his populist leanings as a public intellectual – an engaged critic of power and authority, who considered that one of his responsibilities was to think about the big-ticket items of his day. Curiously, for a man who lived through two world wars, the Great Depression, and the beginning of the Cold War, his self-definition of being a public intellectual made him antipolitical. He was not interested in politics as a calling or a profession, and he had little time or patience for the world of partisan politics, which he viewed as a world of expediency and falsehood.

On the other hand, Innis did believe passionately in the power of ideas to change what happened in the political arena and to shape the policies governments ultimately introduced. An informed public was an essential condition of democracy. Yet he had many reasons to oppose the centralizing power of a state-sponsored nationalism to ride roughshod over cultural minorities, even though he was an ardent Canadian nationalist. As will be seen in the essays in part 3, he lashed out against privilege and the exercise of power in Canada and elsewhere. He questioned business's self-appointed role as the locomotive of progress and castigated corporations for their greed and lack of planning. Above all, he was gravely concerned about the willingness of public authority to rely so frequently on force rather than reason. Yet throughout his life he remained a liberal, committed to individualism, well-being via the market, and parliamentary democracy, despite his trenchant critique of the growing authoritarianism of governments and the failure of market economics to address basic issues of growth and equity.

Innis's profound sense of social critique has confused many of his subsequent critics, who have not been able to place him in a conventional left-right view of the world. Was he a conservative-minded liberal? Was he a liberal-minded conservative on social issues? Was he a populist? A nationalist? A determinist who assigned too large a role to the environment and not enough to social actors? Or was he, in the final analysis, one of those rare scholars free of party or clan loyalties who have an uncanny grasp of the forces that have stirred up the most powerful dynamics of society and civilization? These are not easy questions to answer for the simple reason that Innis was more than an economist. Like Adam Smith, his conception of economics had a strong element of moral philosophy, and this led him to treat political economy as an integral aspect of social policy. This fact, more than any other, made Innis into an angular figure to many of his colleagues. Nor is it surprising to discover that today's mainstream economists and historians feel the same unease (Barnes 1993; and Angus and Shoesmith 1983; Clement and Williams 1989). Little has changed in this respect. Yet Innis's lifetime of scholarship has left an indelible stamp on English Canada's cultural identity. It is a testament to the richness of his vision that every generation of Canadians has been able to see something exceptional, different, and often contradictory in his theory of communications and in what he wrote about Canada in the world economy, and about nationalism. Unquestionably, this is the ultimate compliment and a mark of Innis's importance. No other Canadian scholar of standing can equal his influence across such a wide range of disciplines.[1]

There is one further reason why Innis is such a pivotal figure in Canadian social and political thought. His scholarship on Canada's conflicted commercial origins contains the most powerful psychological and social account of the nation's vulnerable place in the global economy and its relations with the United States. With Canada's weak economy dependent on US capital and with no strong national consensus on its future as a nation, Innis was one of the first to see, in the late forties, that no country stood more to lose from the new internationalism than Canada did. It ran the risk "of being boiled in the oil of international competition." As Canada moved into the American century, he predicted that it would be hard pressed to develop new national policies to withstand US influence in domestic affairs. He doubted that the fragile Canadian consensus achieved by nation-building policies during the nineteenth and twentieth centuries would be strong enough to survive the onslaught of international markets.

Innis's account of these events is of crucial significance for an understanding of the way that frontier countries, overspecialized in single staples, are battered by events and forces they cannot control. He was a strong internationalist who believed in having an international order that was stable and equitable. Narrowly based competitive strategies pushed countries to adopt beggar-thy-neighbour policies. Without adequate institutional protection, frontier economies became, in his evocative words, "storm centres to the modern international economy" (Innis 1956, 382). In the later stages of his life, he was increasingly preoccupied with the inability of Western cultural values to be a source of vigorous economic renewal. Every civilization believes in "its uniqueness and superiority over other civilizations," he wrote. "Each [has] its sacred cows." But each threatens to silence its critics. "The Middle Ages burned its heretics and the modern age threatens them with atom bombs" (Innis 1951, 139). He doubted that modern civilization, dominated by the machine industry and sophisticated information technologies, had the internal resources to reverse its own decline. It is his acerbic account of the undoing of the modern nation-state (Canada included), in a world increasingly dominated by fanaticism, new communications technologies, and powerful international bureaucracies, that continues to give Innis much contemporary relevance today. In analysing the crisis of Western civilization as a problem of values, he belonged to a select group of academic practitioners who were able to transcend their own immediate time and circumstances by the originality of their scholarship. The agenda he established for himself certainly took him far from his rural roots in southwestern Ontario.

To do justice, therefore, to Innis's lifetime work as an economic geographer, political economist, and communications theorist requires presenting the full breadth of his scholarship in a single volume. With the world economy now dominating national markets as never before, there is no better way of celebrating Innis's hundredth birthday than by retracing his multidisciplinary approach to the study of markets, economic development, and cultural change – themes that have lost none of their relevance in the closing decade of the millennium. In all, it is hoped that the appearance of this new edition will be the occasion for Canada's political, economic, and cultural communities to assess the continuing power and relevance of Harold Innis's thought.

THE MAN AND HIS IDEAS

More than any other Canadian scholar in recent times, Innis's prodigious writings on political economy shaped the views of his contemporaries, from Donald Creighton, one of Canada's most eminent historians, to Marshall McLuhan, a world figure in communications theory. As a leading university administrator, Innis was a moving force in the founding of the Social Science Research Council of

Canada and a key figure in public life while dean of graduate studies at the University of Toronto. Throughout much of his adult life, Harold Adams Innis was Canada's pre-eminent thinker and theoretician. He had the stature of a Galbraith in public policy; governments beat a path to his door for advice and counsel. As the first Canadian to be appointed chair of the prestigious Department of Political Economy at the University of Toronto, his power was without equal in Canada's small élite-based university system.

Innis's scholarship placed him at the frontier of Canadian economics. His historical research engaged the attention of Canadian social scientists because of its unifying concepts. What it offered them was the first systematic analysis of Canada's origins as an industrial nation. In the words of W.T. Easterbrook, one of his colleagues, the great virtue of the staples approach was that "it rescued Canadian economics from a one-sided preoccupation with narrowly empirical studies of trade, banking, transportation, and related problems and opened the way for sound interpretation of Canada's 'Old Industrialism' of wheat, iron and tariffs (Easterbrook 1959, 96). By the 1940s, Innis had many doubts about the new industrialism and its effect on the Canadian economy. He was one of the first to recognize the difficult problems that emerged with the changing patterns of trade and capital movements. His tough-minded critique of the new sources of power in a continental setting lent added credibility and prestige to his commanding presence both in the university and in public debate.

It is now forgotten just how much of an "insider" Innis was, even though he began life in modest circumstances, coming from a rural background. Born in Otterville, Ontario, he studied at McMaster University and took his doctorate at the University of Chicago in 1922. Thanks to graduate work there, Innis developed lifelong friendships with the leading US economists of the day, including Chester Wright and Jacob Viner. In 1946 he was elected president of the Royal Society of Canada as well as being awarded the Tyrrell Medal, the society's highest distinction for scholarship. Internationally, he was invited to give the distinguished Beit Lectures at Oxford. He received many honourary degrees throughout Canada and was a visitor to the Collège de France in 1951. During his life he was a member of three royal commissions, and at the height of his influence, in 1952, he was elected president of the American Economic Association. Innis was the first and last non-American to be accorded this highest of honours.[2]

But it was his pioneering research on economic settlement, national development, and world markets from the sixteenth to twentieth centuries that established Innis's pre-eminence as a scholar without equal among his contemporaries (Trigger 1992). His most important achievement remains his exhaustive archival research on Canada's place in the global economy. His method was as simple as it was effective; he set out to study actual economic life rather than a facile model of laissez-faire frictionless development. It is important to recall his technique. With the minimum of theory, he developed a practical approach to the larger issue of how frontier economies evolved in the international system. That his labours would result in a staple theory of development came much later and indeed somewhat unexpectedly. As an economic geographer, he was hesitant about generalizations but was fascinated by what his colleague W.A. Mackintosh described as "the broad sociological generalizations on economic development" (Mackintosh 1953, 185). This led him to do something deceptively quite conventional, namely, to understand better how the international economy operated as the motor of Canadian development in each stage of its evolution.

Innis's analytical starting point was not highly distinctive. Others had seen a similar set of forces, structures, and institutions. His spark of originality was to attempt to grasp theoretically the essential condition of a frontier economy, starting with its natural resources and the social framework that organized land, labour, and capital. Both were the determining factors that shaped the character of the Canadian economy. With development so closely tied to the production of major staples, the flow of profits was a reflection of technological advance and the exploitation of new resources. Improvements in transportation would drive costs down and profits up. Wages, too, reflected these highly competitive conditions, even though there were significant variations between different industries at different stages of development. A surplus of workers would depress wages, while workers who could restrict entry into an industry could succeed in obtaining better conditions of work and employment. The principal difficulty that Innis identified early on was that a frontier economy was subject to unpredictable shifts in technology, demand, and price. What he called the "rate of disturbance" had far-reaching consequences on "the extent of profits and losses" and on "the sharpness of the profit motive," to which Innis gave particular importance.[3]

A distinctive element of the frontier economy was its need for a continual inflow of foreign capital to pay for the infrastructure of its resource-dependent development. This meant that its development would be burdened by high debt charges, which capital would offload onto labour. Incomes would be highly variable, since producer groups would be subject to the global business cycle. Basically, a country dependent on major staples would find itself subject to pressures from the structure of capital, the technological rigidities resulting from the rapid exploitation of new resources, the price structure of transportation costs, and the inherent characteristics of highly regionalized labour markets.

Using this rather straightforward analytical framework, Innis did something highly original. As an economic historian, he started to chart the underlying currents whose larger significance only emerges over a great span of time. Beginning with furs and cod, and working his way through the staple trades of the nineteenth century – square timber, agricultural products, and wheat – to the present day energy staples of oil and gas, Innis discovered the extent to which the power of commerce left is mark on each phase in the evolution of Canada's social structure. In the process, he ascertained much about the inner workings of capitalist economies and the formation of markets. His historiography gave him a work space that stretched over more than four hundred years. Innis's grasp of the *longue durée* still remains absolutely compelling and refreshing, despite the passage of time.

Innis looked at trade as the locomotive of culture, settlement, social relations, and the organization of production in the global economy (see part 1, "Staple Trades, the Rise of Industrialism, and the Expansion of International Markets"). Why did Innis focus so extensively on trade and not simply on production? His short but compelling answer was that trade and not production had been the cutting edge of change in the international economy since the sixteenth century. Since the emergence of modern capitalism from its feudal origins, trade abetted by war had permitted the merchant to widen his scale of operations, quickening turnover and discovering new territories for exploitation. In the words of Lewis Mumford, it was trade that "developed the large scale enterprises and the administrative capacity and method that made it possible to create the industrial system as a whole and weld together its various parts" (Mumford [1934] 1963, 26). Innis, like Mumford, understood that trade was the higher authority that created new markets in the Indies and the Americas for new foods, new cereals, tobacco, furs, wheat, pulp and paper, and so on. It was also the growth of imperial trade that found outlets for the "trash" that was turned out by the eighteenth-century industrial mass-production system.

Thus, for Innis and for others of his generation, the starting point was the fundamental proposition that trade has a powerful spatial dimension which capitalism utilized ruthlessly to accelerate its penetrative powers, thanks to the extra incentive of commercial profit.[4] Thus, countries at the periphery were subject to the pervasive and destabilizing force of international commerce and the volatile condition of commodity markets. A country dependent on resources had to rely on its social and political institutions to address the many contradictory changes that accompany technological advance. Innis focused on the spatial frontier, in the largest setting possible, so that the whole history of any given topic could be revealed.

WEALTH AND DEPENDENCE: INNIS'S CONTRIBUTION TO MODERN ECONOMIC THOUGHT

Innis's theory of staple-led development is often regarded as Canada's original contribution to modern economic thought.[5] In the case of Canada, the staple theory's most powerful claim is that when Canada entered the world system as an advanced country, the backward, forward, and final demand linkages generated by export-led growth remained weak, and import penetration, foreign ownership, and the absence of an indigenous class of entrepreneurs blocked the transformation of the Canadian economy into a fully mature industrial one (Watkins 1963).[6] At the periphery, the process of capital accumulation marches to the tune of a different drummer. Exogenous forces, or what economists call externalities, set the agenda even when, as in the case of Canada, all the factors favourable for rapid and sustained development are there: a high level of domestic savings, a well-trained workforce, and its own financial institutions (Naylor 1972; Mackintosh 1923). Innis's seminal message was that Canada had a raw deal by exporting every rock and log as fast as it could. In exposing its industries to the global business cycle, Canada paid too high a price. It needed to mobilize its resources in order to build strong industries, deepen its domestic market, and create new and better employment opportunities for all. His study of staple trades came to symbolize this mega-issue of development, which bent and twisted Canada's market behaviour. The problem was structural in origin. As he noted early in the 1930s, it was difficult to find a constructive alternative to "the dangers of fluctuations in the staple commodity" (Innis 1933a, 6). Canada was caught between the strains of competitive commodity markets and the raw power of commerce. Describing this turbulent process, Innis wrote: "No country has swung backwards and forwards in response to such factors as improvements in the technique of transportation, exhaustion of raw materials and the advance of industrialism with such violence as Canada" (Innis 1933a, 82). The rapacity of powerful monopolies, the restraints on trade, and rigidities of all kinds had crippling consequences for an economy burdened with debt from railway building and subject to the backflow of interest payments from foreign investment (figure 1).

As long as Canada's orientation had to accommodate the commercial policies of the more advanced metropoles such as Britain and the United States, its development remained trapped by the conflict between local institutions and regional needs, between the intense pressures of indigenous political culture and the conflicting values of colonialism and nationalism, between the constant imposition of imperialist needs on a compliant state and the emergence of strong local markets supporting indigenous development. The story it highlights is that from early to late industrial capitalism and from one resource boom to the next, Canada's social and political arrangements reflected the role of markets in accentuating internal strains. The vast wealth generated from the staple trades went hand in hand with a crippling pattern of commercial dependency that shaped the fundamental condition of Canadian development. The wealth from resources, the revenues from markets, and the benefits from production flowed largely to others. This was because Canada's economic trajectory was subject to the decisions and strategies of states or groups within the dominant industrial countries. Development governed by such external constraints resulted in sudden overspecialization in one or two sectors of the economy while other sectors faced limited growth prospects.

Innis was not by any means the first to point out what was problematic with this strategy. It undermines the emergence of a strong national system of market institutions while supporting strong regional economies that were largely dependent on rapid exploitation of their resource base. Under such conditions, the advanced sectors are not capable of responding to national needs. Rather, they respond to the demands originating from the dominant economies: mineral or agrarian production for export; and the implantation of industries because of a shift in industrial production from the advanced bloc or because of the local strategies of multinational firms intent on capturing local markets. This essential set of circumstances highlights a much deeper problem. In an export-oriented economy, there is no compelling reason why the profits earned by selling resources will lead to investment in domestic manufacturing. In fact, the raw material exported is likely to be

Figure 1
The Staple Theory of Development: Wealth and Dependency

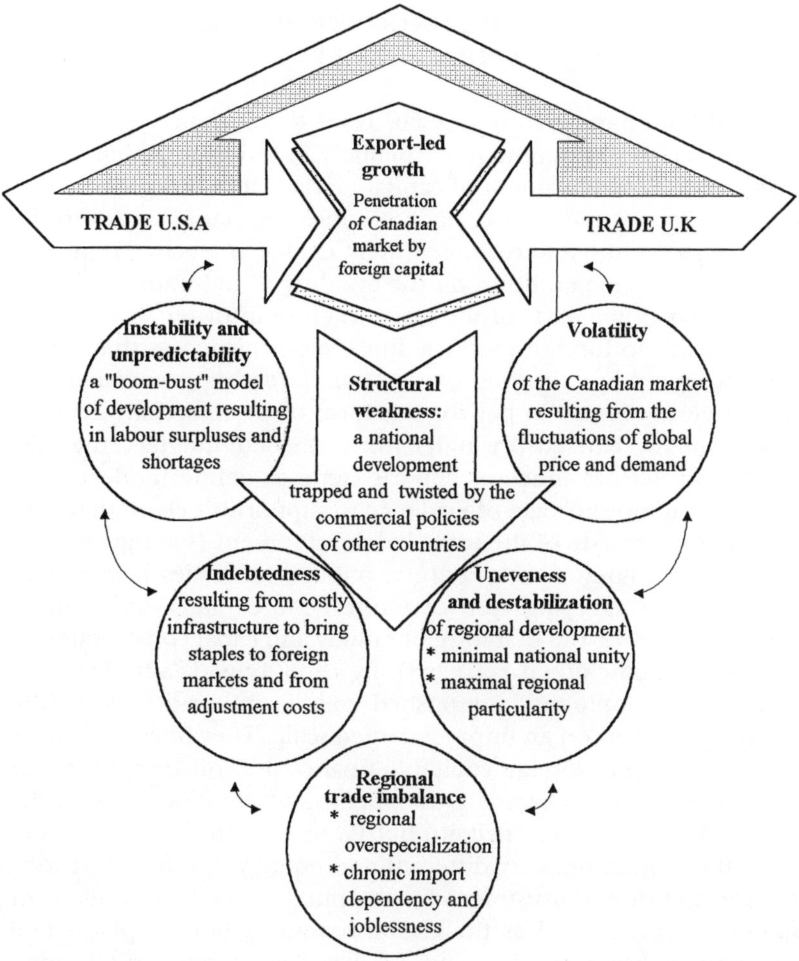

Source: Daniel Drache and Eric Mézin

processed elsewhere and then be imported back into Canada as finished products.

THE UNCONTROLLABLE UPWARD SPIRAL OF DEBT

Innis did not have to look very far to see the evidence of this kind of extroverted development, particularly in terms of capital formation and the establishment of capital markets for local growth. Foreign capital poured into Canada because the staple trades in the nineteenth century were increasingly capital intensive, requiring massive public expenditure on the building of railroads, harbours, canals, and other parts of the infrastructure in order to ship Canada's wealth to foreign markets. But the downside was that public debt mounted in a dizzying upward spiral, forcing governments to mortgage the future to pay for this form of commercially inspired development. Not surprisingly, Innis stressed the fact that the burden of debt as much as exports came to define modern Canada. He had no shortage of evidence to support his claim that debt was the reverse side of the trade-led development (see figure 2).

By the mid-nineteenth century, public authorities had already borrowed a staggering sum of money, more than $350 million dollars, to pay for the first wave of railway and canal construction in central Canada (Aitken 1961, 28). By 1898, Canada's trade-driven form of development had pushed public authorities back into financial markets on an unprecedented scale. They borrowed more than $1 billion of foreign capital to finance the construction of the Canadian Pacific Railway and the opening of the West. Most of the debt was held in Great Britain, but US investment in Canada was, from the beginning, very different and equally significant. It took the form of direct investment for the purchase of land, timber, or mineral rights as well as the establishment of branch plants and corporate subsidiaries. In 1867, US direct investment in Canada's industrial sector stood at about $15 million, and by the end of 1899 it had soared to $160 million. In the following period Canada, with its tiny population and massive resource base, absorbed another $2.5 billion of capital inflow from the United States and Britain. By 1914, total foreign capital in Canada was three times the record-high 1900 level, mostly for infrastructural development (ibid., 36).

However, the most important new development was not at all infrastructural. US capital had discovered Canada's industrial potential and had concentrated its investment frontier in Canada's nascent industries. It invested strategically in the modern sectors of the

Figure 2
The Dynamics of Staple-Led Development

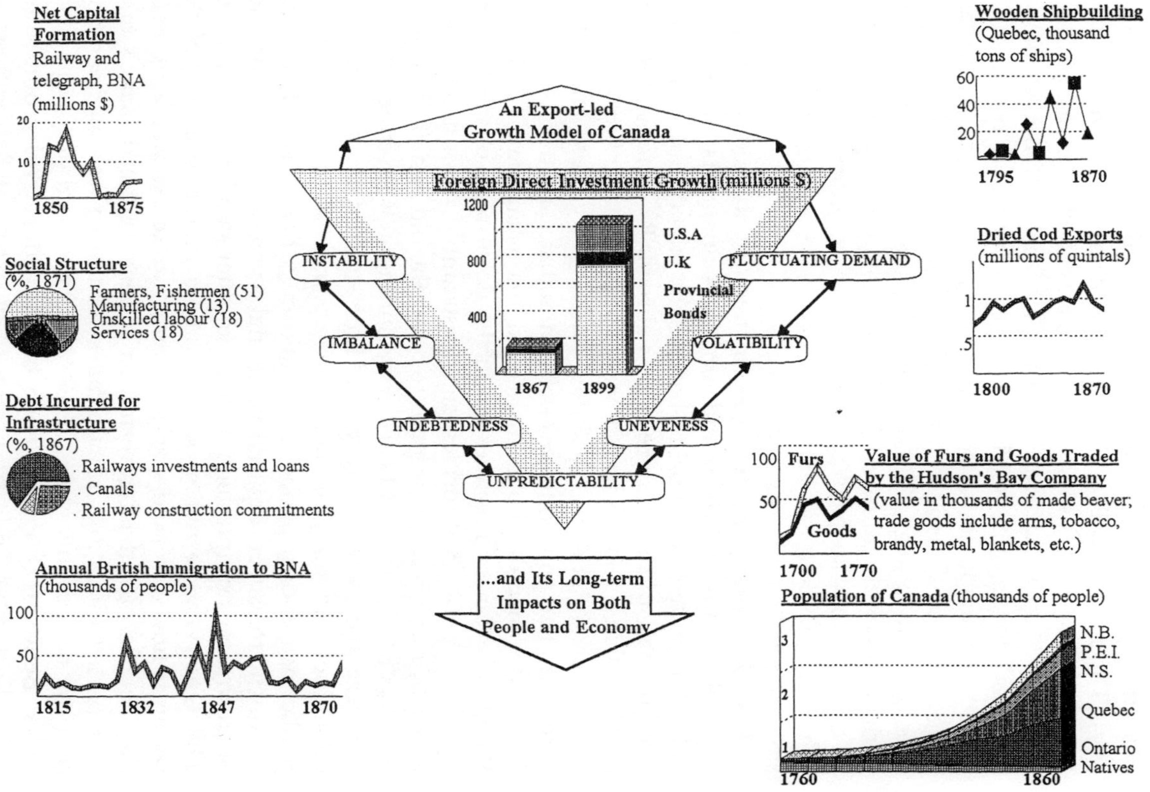

Source: Daniel Drache and Eric Mézin
Adapted from McIlwraith (1990); Aitken (1961); Norrie and Owram (1951); Rowell-Sirois Report (1940); Harris (1987), 60.

economy and in Canada's huge resource base, especially industrial minerals, pulp and paper, and oil production. Aitken writes that "Canada by 1914 had received more United States investment than any other part of the world, though Mexico was not far behind" (37). The result was that Canada, even at the height of its nation-building project, was soon to become a northern extension of the powerful US economy. Here was a classic instance of markets having intended consequences, given the persistence and power of US capital in Canadian affairs. What also struck Innis as particularly dangerous and shortsighted were the inherent risks of this export development strategy. The most problematic was the growing disparity between the burden of public indebtedness and the capacity of the economy to pay the high costs of resource development. While the problem was simple to identify, it was apparently impossible for public authority to correct.

Canada's long-term debt was financed by a fixed schedule to repay the loans to British and American financiers. Interest and debt charges had to be paid whatever the expectation of revenues from the sale of Canada's resources abroad. By contrast, the price for Canadian resources was subject to unpredictable fluctuations as world demand continually shifted and as prices rose and fell accordingly. The consequences were immediate and often dramatic. They left Canada's public finances in a constant state of disarray. When government revenues fell in the downswing of the business cycle, the public authorities had to scramble to find new funds either by negotiating new loans to cover the old (which they did as much as markets would bear) or by finding new revenues to cover the increased costs of borrowing. Money-starved governments sold off timber and mineral rights to help pay for railway subsidies, public institutions, public works, and even hospitals. Whenever a provincial treasurer required additional revenue, the commissioner of crown lands simply auctioned off another stand of timber limits. The Ontario government was not alone in this practice. Nelles recounts how it worked – and evidently worked so well as to keep the Ontario provincial government solvent: "Edward Blake's ministry parted with 5,031 square miles [of timber] in one year, and over the next twenty years Oliver Mowat disposed of 4,234 square miles. Between 1867 and 1899 bonuses, dues and ground rent from the lumber industry produced in excess of $29 million, or approximately 28 percent of the total provincial revenue. Only the federal subsidy brought in a larger sum" (Nelles 1974, 18).

Nationally, the federal government had its own response to paying the resource infrastructure bill. It imposed a consumption tax via the tariff. Since so much government revenue came from the tariff well into the first three decades of the twentieth century, the tariff became a de facto tax on consumption paid for by farmers and ordinary Canadians. It depressed their income and guaranteed huge profits for Canada's emerging industries. In an age when corporate taxation was minimal, it is not difficult to see why Innis became an outspoken critic of this clumsy tool of nation building, which put the public purse at ready for private gain. Canada found itself in an impossible position, and Innis drew the conclusion that "industrialism has provided [Canada] an abundance of goods but not the first luxury of security."

THE STAPLE TRAP AND GOVERNMENT POLICY

For Innis's generation (like the present generation), indebtedness became the public issue par excellence that constantly sapped governments' energies and taxed their management ability to the limit. More than any other issue, the debt burden came to symbolize the deep malaise of an economy organized around the large-scale production of single staples. For Innis, the blocked condition of Canada's development by an ensemble of forces, internationally and domestically, held crucial significance for an understanding of cyclical and secular disturbances, not within Canada but without. He identified countries at the margin as the "storm centres to the modern international economy," because without strong market institutions they stood little chance when "bombarded by the violent intensity of the international economy." A growth dynamic centred on paying the fixed costs of indebtedness would only push Canadian governments to do more of the same – more exports, more foreign direct investment, more public indebtedness – in the vain hope of breaking the cycle. At the end of the day, this form of government intervention could only result in greater regional inequality, because Canada's much-praised nation-building instrument, the tariff, had succeeded remarkably well in forcing US industries to set up subsidiary operations in central Canada if they wanted to have access to the market; and with a made-in-Canada branch-plant industry concentrated in Ontario for low-end manufacturing industries, all that remained for the rest of the country was to put its shoulder to the wheel and pump out world-class staples for processing abroad.

If this basic configuration begins to explain the complex process of development in Canada, Innis never thought it was the whole story. It was simply the starting point to situate local development, regional growth, the building of a transportation system, the emergence of a service economy, the establishment of a modern system of industrial relations, the broadening and deepening of labour and financial markets, the rapid diffusion of technology, and the appearance of a modern state with a full panoply of regulatory institutions, including an elaborate social policy. Innis reasoned that all these non-trade kinds of factors had to be taken into account. Later, these powerful transformative forces would modify the structures and institutions of the market and state, and would give Canada the patina of modernity, prosperity, and development. There was, however, a discernable thread of continuity in this sea of change.

Innis rejected the belief that Canada had left behind its crude laissez-faire origins. For him, there was too much evidence of continuity between the old staples order and the new industrial age. By contrast, the eminent economic historian W.A. Mackintosh held the optimistic view that export-led growth had indeed freed Canada of its colonial origins and had provided a solid basis for nation building. Writing in the twenties, he said that "nothing is more typical of colonial development than the restless increasing search for staples which would permit the pioneer community to come into close contact with the commercial world and leave behind the disabilities of a pioneer existence" (Mackintosh 1923, 4). He was so confident that Canada's economic apprenticeship as a commercial colony was virtually over and that the transition to a fully industrialized one was nearly complete that he summed up Canada's prospects in one of the most famous sentences he ever wrote: "[We were] a people facing the prosaic obstacles of a colonial existence, developing national traits, and winning through to nationhood" (15).

This judgment was wrong not because of its optimism but because of Mackintosh's inability to grasp a fundamental truth – the underlying vulnerability of Canadian expansion to sudden change in world markets. By contrast, Innis's theory of the staples cuts to the quick and explains why even when Canada was swept headlong into the age of industrialization and mass production, its development was still subject to the staples trap.

Innis and others recognized that the vast project of settling the West was not based on Robinson Crusoe methods, with pioneer settlers who were self-sufficient farm families providing for all their own needs. The truth was very far from this idyll. The family economy was embedded in all forms of market activity, much of it directly dependent on women selling all kinds of home products in local markets (Cohen 1988). Not only was women's labour expropriated for the process of capital accumulation, as modern feminist scholarship stresses, but the West became a vast frontier of capital accumulation. Goods were bought; equipment was purchased; financing of farm operations had to be arranged. Financial institutions responded to this need for a money economy. The puzzle is that Canadian governments failed to seize all the commercial and industrial advantages to build a much stronger national economy when the opportunity to do so was there. Yet Innis did not find this surprising. There was too much economic haemorrhaging as a result of indebtedness, too great a loss of out-migration as a result of viable employment, and too little consensus to build an integrated and independent economy on the northern half of the continent when all the regions and classes were pitted against one another in their efforts to gain their "alloted" share in the scramble for development.

Innis was struck by how much of Canada's old pattern of development had remained unaltered by this era of nation-building. Why had this occurred? Innis's answer remains the most prescient and powerful that Canadian scholarship has ever found. The foundations of modern Canada were weak, he reasoned, because the country was designed to fit the ebb and flow of commercialism. Wherever the élites did business, they, not geography, defined Canada's "natural boundaries." Historians, such as Carl Berger, who think that Innis was a kind of crude environmental determinist, have got it all wrong. It was not Innis's view that Canada's development was shaped by "inescapable and anonymous forces" (Berger 1976, 94). Innis had a sophisticated understanding of price rigidities and the business cycle that provides the most convincing explanation of the developmental prospects of a frontier economy in the international order (Drache 1982). Historians such as Berger have failed to understand Innis's grasp of the pivotal role of structures and agents in shaping modern economic life. To Innis, among others, geography was one such powerful structure, which constantly interacted with other principal economic forces (such as élites, technology, primary producers, labour markets, and so on). When the flow of economic life reversed direction, market structures and even the economy had to be realigned. The key to it was the way market forces had generated the need for new state forms. Innis had no shortage of examples to illustrate his basic proposition that economics, in all its many facets, had a powerful grip in setting the course of Canada's political life.

In the eighteenth century, the Hudson's Bay Company, a transnational giant, became the prototype of the latter-day Canadian nation-state, spanning a continent from east to west. The Bay succeeded, as no other monopoly had done, in inventing a structure to organize the fur trade and govern the interior of what would become Canada. Here, for Innis, was the prototypical federalist structure which Canada had adapted and inherited from its colonial past: a model of local decentralization, controlled by a small élite, spanning a continent, and run from distant London. The purchase of the HBC territories in 1870 by the new Government of Canada "was a revolution in the very nature of Canadian federation. It transformed the original Dominion from a federation of equal provinces ... into a veritable empire in its own right with a domain of public lands five times the area of the original Dominion under direct federal administration" (Martin 1938, 223). With the revenues from public lands, Canada's nascent entrepreneurs were enticed to become nation builders for the rest of the nineteenth century – and for a good part of the twentieth century as well. But in 1945, when the demand for Canada's resources pushed the economy unmistakably southwards in a continental direction, Canada's business leaders took their cue and looked again to an export-led strategy as the first choice for wealth generation. Economic nation-building was gradually put on the back burner. The problem that confronted Canadian policy makers was how to accommodate the old drive of commercialism (premised on price competition, low-cost resources, and cheap components parts destined for the American market) within the new Keynesian-style framework, which required more state regulation and a new standing for labour.

KEYNES PLUS STAPLES: THE WEAKEST LINK

The idea that the Canadian state would use its economic power for social and political purposes was hardly revolutionary. All governments shape markets to fit the demands of economic life. For Innis, the question of power – or, to be more precise, the inequality that flowed from the social relations of staples production – became central to his view of state-market relations in Canada. He realized that the market, left to its own devices, had no mechanism to correct for income inequality in a highly open economy. Individual employers were able to rely on volatile market conditions to browbeat workers into low-wage, low-benefit situations. With wages so price sensitive in an open economy, incomes rose when Canada was a price setter for its resources in international markets. But when the bottom dropped out of the business cycle, this momentum was not sustainable in a boom-bust economy. Since demand had softened, incomes fell precipitously, Declining real incomes, coupled with widespread unemployment, kept Canadian wage levels as much as 40 per cent lower than their US counterparts right into the 1950s (Drache 1984). The fallout from this deep business cycle was, of course, much broader. With workers having no institutional means of participating in a mass consumer society, wage rates were too erratic to sustain consumer demand.

For Innis, like many others, the Keynesian policy revolution seemed to depart from the crude model of staple-led growth that had been so much in evidence in the nineteenth and early twentieth centuries; but at least it offered an alternative to the traditional market model premised on universal laws of supply and demand. The Keynesian revolution proposed an alternative growth model, which arose from the ashes of the Depression and from the promises of a new order that had been made to workers during the war. The 1945 Speech from the Throne declared that "a national minimum of social security and human welfare should be advanced as rapidly as possible. Such a national minimum contemplates useful employment for all who are willing to work: standards of nutrition and housing adequate to ensure the health of the whole population; and social insurance against privation resulting from unemployment, from accident, from the death of the breadwinner, from ill-health and from old age" (Drache and Glasbeek 1992, 18).

At the same time, however, Canada's policy makers reaffirmed that there would be a continuation of resource-based strategies. The maintenance of the export of resources was the very antithesis of Keynesian notions of supply and demand control. Keynesian strategies do not depend on trade as the primary means of promoting growth. Rather, the idea is to have as many goods and services as possible produced domestically by ensuring high enough wage levels to create a strong demand for these locally produced goods and services. By contrast, export-led growth policies depend on fostering the willingness of foreign and domestic entrepreneurs to invest their capital and technological know-how in the commodities-exporting country. Development relies on being able to attract both the technology and the capital to support high levels of growth.

These two ideal types were bound to clash and vie for dominance in postwar Canada. Innis was sceptical about the prospects for renewal and a new beginning. He remained convinced that Canada's "delicately balanced economy," which had been built up in competition with the United States and had "more than once crashed through ill-designed machinery," was again in trouble. The Canadian government had too many illusions about itself and its capacity for it to read accurately and respond intelligently to the kinds of danger posed by the new international economy. Innis warned that without public leadership, Canada was "in danger of being burned at the stake of [its] natural resources" (Innis 1956).

His many different studies point to the fact that the principal market actor, the profit-maximizing corporation – the so-called engine of modernity – has a different profit-logic in the guise of a branch plant (Hymer 1975). It does not have the autonomy to be innovative independently of the home office; it is not mandated to develop economies of scale to compete for export markets; nor is it in a position to mount its own investment strategy. In sum, the branch plant is a truncated enterprise deployed by a transnational parent in order to capture local markets.[7]

What, then, is Innis's central message for economic and social development? The transcendent themes that emerge from his critique of liberal political economy are, first, the continual marginalization of the producers of wealth, beginning with Canada's aboriginal peoples in the fur trade and extending to the small individual commodity producers of the wheat economy and to Canada's resource proletariat, the rural population and the industrial working classes; secondly, the continental pressure on Canada's permeable borders, intensified by the building of the railway and the flow of commerce north-south. The continental drift from financial markets eventually undermined the prodigious efforts at nation building. In particular, this trend reinforced the growing presence of foreign investment, enabling it to play an ever larger role as Canada moved into the industrial age at the beginning of the twentieth century. Not surprisingly, powerful foreign interests retarded the emergence of a powerful class of indigenous entrepreneurs. Finally, the highly competitive and fragmented presence of labour markets also fragmented working-class solidarity and undermined labour's organizational drives.

This intense focus on the structural obstacles to development explains Innis's importance to Canada's political economy tradition. A liberal political economist, Innis wrote better than he knew.[8] His interest in the structure, evolution, and behaviour of markets transformed him into an institutional economist, who approached the study of economics from the perspective that markets had to be organized and economic space shaped by both public and private means (Boyer 1991). In conceptualizing production and social relations in this way, he provided Canadian social science with its first modern account of state policy, market logic, and economic development.

That Innis acquired this institutionalist perspective is not surprising. He belonged to a brilliant interwar generation of scientific scholars, who numbered in their ranks such pre-eminent thinkers as Sombart, Polanyi, Keynes, Kroeber, Perroux, Toynbee, Weber, Childe, Tawney, and Mumford.[9] If there was a common thread to this golden age of marxism and liberalism, it was the profound conviction that capitalism, for all its dynamism, would eventually succumb to decay, crisis, and collapse.[10]

MARKETS AND CULTURAL CHANGE: THE CORE INNISIAN LEGACY

Innis's perspective on these matters was a product of his own uniquely Canadian background. The constant factor in his thinking was his scepticism about the capacity of grand economic theory, particularly of a liberal variety, to understand complicated issues such as the way markets respond to volatile changes in price and demand. What he saw instead was that the principal mechanism of wealth creation was an incredibly complex institution, the product of history, collective practice, and social convention. Markets were not what they seemed. Buyers and sellers did not respond to market signals in the way economic theory depicted. Rather, the self-regulating market was subject to competitive, technological, and institutional pressures. It did not conform to any given set of abstract universal laws, as many conventional economists posited, nor was it a spontaneously self-regulating mechanism in the way neoclassical economics traditionally asserted. Herein lies the conundrum. Why did Innis contend that the market, the chosen instrument of wealth creation, was the storm centre for all kinds of technological, cultural, and political change?

MARKETS: THE IDEA OF DISCONTINUOUS ECONOMIC SPACE

The Interconnective and Principal Aspects of Market

The terms "market" and "market relations" are ambiguous and can be used in many different contexts (Boyer 1991). The Saturday morning farmers' market, where buyer and seller haggle one on one, has little in common with the complex structure of a modern financial market or with the organization of a modern stock exchange, where hundreds of millions of dollars are traded daily. Similarly, a highly diversified consumer market, where giant corporations compete for the consumer dollar through advertising, price competition, and service, is a world apart from a transaction undertaken by the individual consumer who goes to buy a car or a television set. Yet in liberal thought, there is no difference between them. A market is a market *tout court*, and market behaviour is a kind of black box, whose content does not need to be examined closely.

The assumption of neoclassical economists is that universal price signals serve the interests of all actors. In theory, markets are free of the taint of class, history, race, and gender, and are places where parties of equal status respond to basic price signals in the same discrete, impersonal, and neutral way. Market transactions are organized on an impartial, voluntary, arm's-length basis, which ensures optimal outcomes without fear of retribution. Yet this conventional presentation of the market logic underpinning growth and development begs an essential question; for if markets for Canada's staples operated no differently than any other market, there would be no need for any "staples thesis" or for any particular explanation of Canada's (or any other country's) developmental trajectory (Rotstein 1977, 9).

What set Innis apart from his more orthodox contemporaries was his adamant conviction that "Canada's problems cannot be answered in terms of the economics of older countries (Innis 1956, 10). His original idea was that markets are a complex response to production, business organization, technological advance, international finance, entrepreneurship, geography, religious practice, consumer spending, and public need. They are not constructed as some kind of one-dimensional space but are constituted by sets of opposite and competing characteristics: competitive or monopolistic; open or closed; fragmentary or unified; regional, national, or global; public or private; regulated or unregulated; symbolic or real; stable or highly volatile. Far from accepting the "market" as an abstract entity, Innis preferred to study the dynamics and interactivity of markets as real entities in time, which produced unpredictable outcomes under the best conditions and which were not subject to invariable universal laws of supply and demand in the worst of times.

The idea that markets have multiple, continuous, and contradictory effects and hence are unstable structures and are subject to the constant need for organization and reorganization arises from the fact that they emerge out of social relationships. Innis's main in-

Table 1
A Matrix of Market Dynamics

Factors	*Internal*	*External*
structure	competitive	monopolistic
location	national/regional	global/continental
organization	unified	fragmentary
wealth creation	public	private
mode of state regulation	high-degree intervention	low-degree intervention
trade	protected	open
commodity	real economy resources, capital, money/information, land, labour	symbol economy, foreign investment, currency flows, futures markets
price system	stable	volatile

sight is that the principal mechanism of economic life was both socially determined and historically constructed under different conditions of production in different historical circumstances (see, in particular, the following essays in this volume: "The Penetrative Powers of the Price System on New World States," "The Place of Land in North American Federations," and "Great Britain, the United States, and Canada"). Markets are like open-ended social spaces constantly subject to spontaneous countermovements by producers, consumers, owners, workers, and government, who are threatened by the price system's rapacious excesses.[11] When the price system does not work *ex mirabilis*, society relies on the state to find ways of stabilizing it and the larger economy.

That Innis turned to the language and concepts of political economy to compose his ideas may have had much to do with the fact that in Canada economic life has always had a strong institutional dimension. It is also the case that, like Keynes and others who subscribed to a larger view of economics, Innis saw the real connections between economics, culture, wealth, and welfare (Skidelsky 1992). For political economists of this persuasion, material prosperity could not be taken for granted. Business activity had only one objective: to make a quick profit, the quicker the better. By contrast, the aim of contemporary statecraft was to make society better off materially while also enhancing its social values. As a political economist, Innis subscribed to the belief that development had a higher goal than the accumulation of individual wealth. Thus, it is not surprising that he had little difficulty in shrugging off the orthodox liberal economic thought of the interwar period, which was mired in crude laissez-faire economics. His main preoccupation was to explain the way the institutional side of economic life is used to counter the highly erratic nature of market outcomes. For example, small-sale individual commodity production will by definition be competitive, fluid, and driven by price considerations, whereas large-scale industrial production, involving a handful of dominant firms that are vertically integrated, will support monopoly pricing practices and will restrict competition, engage in predatory market strategies, and seek protection from the state.

Hence, Innis had no difficulty in coming to the realization that the general dynamics that arise from exchange relations and the process of accumulation take different forms depending on the stage of development and the balance of forces between the internal and external market. This is also why commerce takes on such a central role in Innis's concept of market formation. Trade is such a megaforce because it can be conducted on liberal principles of openness or organized on a closed basis such as mercantilism. An economy without any tariff protection risks sacrificing its industries on the altar of competition, but a developmental process dominated by a set of narrowly protectionist policies without strong governmental oversight is a burden on consumers (Burton 1938; Innis 1946). National policies, too, were of critical importance to Innis because without strong and effective national measures, domestic markets cannot be integrated to serve national needs; they remain local and fragmented.

Innis's own studies confirm a basic lesson of economic history. Too open an economy enables foreign corporations to capture an ever-increasing share of local markets and to destroy indigenous Canadian firms; yet too closed an economy also has high costs, for it deprives Canada of much-needed technology transfers and foreign investment (see the essays in part 3, "Metropolitanism, Nationality, and the Crisis of Industrialism"). The answer to this dilemma, for Innis and others of his generation, was that the modern state had to have the means of creating a national system of production and exchange out of a fragmented mix of poorly integrated regional economies. (Tariffs had served this function in the nineteenth century.) Also, other policies were needed to stabilize the spatial aspects of supply and demand in the twentieth century (Hirshman 1958; see also part 3 of this volume).

The Virtues of the Domestic Market versus the Power of International Markets

Innis could not stress strongly enough that internal markets respond to a different logic and set of needs than externally based systems of exchange. This occurs because the international price mechanism is volatile and subject to violence and instability in income fluctuation. These fluctuations prove to be so detrimental to producers and the public at large that they cannot be tolerated. Even in a free enterprise system generated by the search for profits, the market needs non-market institutions to oversee it. This requires that government strengthen its regulatory norms by creating agencies, boards, and commissions to ensure that the tension between society and the economy is redressed.

Public regulation of private markets is therefore essential to protect the well-being of people and, from a long-term perspective, to shape private enterprise to conform to national needs. A strong public presence in the economy protects society against the avaricious behaviour of corporations and private actors. Public policy must have two sides to it. For the private sector, the regulatory dimension is crucial. The state has to address a basic question: Can the market operate efficiently with a low level of regulation? If the answer is no, regulatory norms must be tightened and the penalty for noncompliance increased. For public policy, it is equally important for government to tackle a second question: Does the state have sufficient regulatory instruments to correct supply-side and demand-side market imperfections as well as wielding enough power over the private sector's investment strategy?[12] Here, too, Innis saw that there was a pressing need for the state to be a counterweight to business.

His approach to economic history underscores the fact that development, in the broad sense of this term, is contingent on a mix of structural variables. At one extreme, Canadian development remains even to this day dependent on private markets for wealth creation, which is mainly organized by giant monopolies such as the CPR, a handful of corporate banking interests, mining conglomerates of all description, retail giants, food processing monopolies, and the like (Innis 1930; 1946). At the other extreme, there is the alternative model of public wealth creation, using state intervention to redress regional and distributional inequality and to compensate for the fact that all kinds of commodity markets suffer from specific injustices and abuses of monopoly and that, in a largely rural and agrarian economy organized around the needs of small commodity producers, consumers and producers soon find that the market is rigged against them. Thus, the road to economic freedom does not lead automatically to political liberty. Indeed, the reverse is true. "The development of advertising and mass propaganda masquerading as education compel the consent of the governed" (Innis 1946, 143). The central economic question for Innis was finally the problem of power. Economic liberty, he maintained, has provided "the basis for encroachment on civil liberty," and the growth of the modern state is controlled by "irreconcilable minorities" whose desire for power over others is always in the final analysis a threat to society (135).

Staples: Why This Form of Commodity Production Becomes the Flashpoint for Both the "Real" and the "Symbolic" Economies

The staples form of development is a particularly brutal example of commodity markets writ large. As a theoretical concept, the staple is usually thought of as a kind of shorthand for describing the social and economic relations of production, settlement, and commerce. It is not by chance that Innis and others chose the word. It is a precise term, loaded with historical and social importance, and dating back to fourteenth-century England. The concept has two parts, one dealing with the state regulation of the labour market and the other dealing with trade. Not surprisingly, the two market outcomes are premised on completely contradictory principles.

With respect to labour, feudal landlords, freemen, and others had been able to acquire land at cheap prices as private ownership of land spread. But when labour was in short supply after the deadly bubonic plague swept across Europe, wages rose, and the landowners believed that those working the land were asking too much. Their protests against the high labour costs bore results. Following the Black Death, the Statute of Labourers was passed in Parliament in 1351, stipulating that wages were no longer to be freely determined by supply and demand but were to be regulated by the courts and justices, the instrumental arms of the state (Pentland 1981).

On the trade front, the king had given a monopoly of wool exports to a small group of merchants of the Staple – an oligarchy of rich merchants who sold their goods through "a single mart or *Staple*," usually across the Channel. Since the trade was organized on a monopoly basis, the merchants had the exclusive right to trade the leading staple for export. The system was also advantageous to the crown, because it gave the king a steady revenue from the customs duties and ensured the loyalty of the rich traders, who could be relied on to make him large loans in time of war. But the monopoly always proved difficult to uphold, because it discriminated against local producers and, in particular, because it angered the smaller traders, who were prohibited from selling their wool locally. By 1353, merchants had obtained a new Ordinance in Parliament that permitted local trading. The once-powerful "mart of merchants" were thus forced to share their monopoly privileges with others.[13]

The central theoretical point of the term "staple" was not lost on Innis. Historically, the key export sector was organized on a monopoly footing. The contrast in norms and practices with labour markets was striking. Competitive markets for labour were harshly regulated by the state to favour owners of private property. Unions were deemed illegal for almost four hundred years; striking was a criminal activity until the twentieth century; and labour protection standards were ineffective and inadequate, and their enforcement notoriously lax for most of modernity (Hay 1975).

The generalization that Innis drew from this period taught him a singular lesson:the state and not the entrepreneur created the "prototypical market" by restricting access to it. Despite its much-vaunted flexibility and capacity for adjustment it was force, not reason, that dictated the extension of the free market. Thus, liberal society paid a high price when it imposed the market mechanism on society. Innis soon realized that the emergence of the market, in all its intricacy, drove a wedge between internal need and external demand. This insight into the interplay of forces organized around the exploitation and production of resources for external markets remains Innis's basic contribution to Canadian social science. Canada, he predicted, would find itself subject to volatile changes in international price and demand, and it would be subject to the restrictive policies of other countries. Thus, it would not be able to consolidate indigenous change when it occurred.

These different economic obstacles explain Innis's inherent scepticism about the ability of modern liberal capitalism to deliver its most appealing promise: efficiency and development.[14] As we have already seen, the shift from one staple to the next did not occur easily or automatically (see particularly the essays in part 2, "Resources and Regionalism: The Origins of Modern Canada"). Despite its "animal spirits," Innis was pessimistic about the ability of capitalism to surmount its limitations and recurring crises.

The basic problem was systemic and structural. Capitalism developed in fits and starts. It was a system of crisis, boom and bust, which rendered markets unpredictable and caused them to operate at less than optimum levels in the vast economic space of so-called new countries. In each period, this kind of stop-and-start development brought with it the disproportionate costs of adjustment: predictable job loss in the downturn of the business cycle; highly unstable labour markets in the seasonal fishing, timber, and construction industries, in particular; and, in the absence of well-developed industries, the constant out-migration of peoples (Innis 1936b).

Regional economies suffered the most from this form of development because of their narrow specialization in exporting unprocessed commodities. Destabilizing effects were magnified by the intensity and volatility of external market forces, which operated outside effective state regulation. For Innis, this last point was crucial. Market liberalism without regulation promotes imperfect competition at the expense of a model of general equilibrium.[15]

Economic theory worked out in the older industrialized countries had no adequate answer why market freedom could not easily be reconciled with economic stability. It was flawed because it did not make any distinction between the price system and other institutions in the economy. Markets could not be, and never were, closed idyllic systems of self-organizing autonomous entities. Rather, they needed the institutional muscle of the state to guarantee peaceful conditions of law and order; they required the active presence of the courts to settle disputes, enforce contracts, and protect property owners. The social and economic relations of the staple trade came to symbolize the full gamut of institutional forms of market activity. The question Innis raised remains germane today. If the market mechanism is not a functional tool for national order, how does local development take hold and flourish?

Innis's analysis of the fur trade highlights the unintended yet immediately brutal consequences of real and symbolic markets on the producers of wealth. Here is the most powerful illustration of his view of the social dynamics of markets. The fur trade exemplifies the way international markets create the preconditions for internal markets, where monopoly rather than a pure model of competition prevails and where the pattern of development is based on intense but short-lived booms of resource development.

The Social Dynamics of the Fur Trade: Luxury Consumption and Genocide

Innis described the history of the fur trade in North America as a "retreat in the face of settlement" (Innis [1930] 1956, 386). Rightly, *The Fur Trade in Canada* has become one of the classics of economic history. It illustrates Innis's great talent for historical research, field work, and the use of the most unconventional sources (Mackintosh 1953, 187). The story is one in which the control of the fur trade is an index of global rivalry and cultural change for the consumption of luxuries.

For the first two hundred years, the fur trade relied on the indigenous labour of Canada's aboriginal peoples. Natives were required to go into the interior and bring fur pelts to the trading posts. This system supported a complex set of relations between the aboriginal peoples, the settlers, and the imperial authorities. The internal trade relied on the skills and initiative of the native trader in carrying on trade with remote tribes. Canada's first peoples were its trappers, middlemen, and labourers in the transportation of bulky cargoes of furs across the length of the continent. The fur trade's organization followed the grooves of economic geography into the interior: "Trade from Quebec and Montreal with canoes up the Ottawa to Michilimackinac, La Baye, and Lake Superior could be financed with relatively small quantities of capital ... Further extension of trade through Lake Superior by Grand Portage ... to Lake Winnipeg, the Saskatchewan, Athabasca, the Mackenzie River, and New Caledonia and the Pacific coast" (ibid. 390).

From the start, the fur trade was organized as a monopoly of the English and French monarchies. Despite this, the native traders quickly learned to exploit their strategic position in it. They saw that prices for traded pelts rose when the fur barons faced tough competition from rival companies. When the Hudson's Bay Company's monopoly was broken by fierce competition from the North-West Company, prices rose and the native people bargained from a position of strength (Rotstein 1977; Trigger 1985). Conversely, their bargaining power – and thus the price paid for their furs – declined dramatically when the Hudson's Bay Company was able to establish its monopoly position by destroying its rivals (Ray 1974). However, the fact that Britain and France relied on aboriginal tribes as allies in wars against other imperial rivals, as well as for extending the lines of commerce through the interior of North America to the Pacific Coast, gave the aboriginal peoples bargaining power with the colonial authorities. Thus, the chain of dependency did not run in only one direction. While the North American natives proved to have an insatiable demand for the more elaborate goods and commodities of Europeans, the Europeans relied on the full cooperation of the different tribes, without which the fur trade could never have spread across the continent.

But wealth there was, even though "a colony engaged in the fur trade was not in a position to develop industries to compete with manufactures of the mother country" (Innis [1930] 1956, 391). Despite the absence of industry, the profits were immense. It was not uncommon in the early period for these state fur-trading monopolies to have a return of more than five fold or better on their original investments. Monopoly profits were earned, and the vast sums of money realized by the Hudson's Bay Company and other fur-trading monopolies flowed back to London, Paris, and New York.

In time, the fur trade changed markedly as the demand for high-quality beaver hats exhausted the ready sources of supply in the St Lawrence basin. Pushed by commercial rivalry, market-based relations gradually spread to the interior by the early 1800s. Other changes followed. Canadian and British interests began using local labour, thus displacing reliance on native peoples. Merchants recruited the *coureurs de bois*, the fabled Quebec small producers or landless day labourers, to travel to the interior by canoe, returning with full loads of furs.

The price mechanism of the market reflected these complex sets of relations. In this setting, the British crown was forced to sign treaties with the First Nations, treaties that exist to this day and provide Canada's aboriginal peoples with powerful legal entitlement. Unlike their American counterparts, Canada's aboriginal people did not cede their rights to the land; they were allies, not defeated peoples. The British accepted fiduciary responsibility for their well-being and agreed to provide for their future. Despite these legal and political undertakings, when the imperial authorities had no further strategic need for Canada's aboriginal nations, the native people were driven from their lands by the European immigrants who settled there. When the fur trade declined in economic importance, the native people were abandoned by their former colonial and imperial allies and were forced to migrate to the interior or to go on reserves, where the survivors were soon decimated by disease, poverty, and alcoholism.

The ensuing cultural conflict between European and aboriginal peoples stretched from the sixteenth century to the twentieth and had a genocidal impact on the original inhabitants of the New World. Their inherent right of self-government was never extinguished, but neither was it recognized in the founding of Canada. Despite this, Canada is composed of three national identities, which have continued to coexist, however uneasily: the English, the French, and the First Nations. The result is fully paradoxical. Such distinctive identifications and aspirations have had to find ways of being reconciled, but it has taken more than four hundred years for English and French Canadians to come to the fundamental realization that "the Indian and his culture were fundamental to the growth of Canadian institutions" (Innis [1930] 1956, 392).

For Innis, the story of the fur trade did not end there. He feared that Canada did not have the social traditions to overcome the deep divisions generated by its particularly brutal form of resource capitalism. He recognized that Canada remained a colony long after its colonial origins were formally behind it and that part of its failure stemmed from its inability to build on its own traditions and to accord full political rights to its founding peoples.[16] This blind spot in the Canadian political psyche was rooted in the centralization of commercial and industrial organization of an earlier period and in the imperial concept of the nation-state that is hierarchical, exclusionary, and European.

Canada was indeed marked by its commercial origins: the lure of an extra incentive for profit. Yet the fate of British North America and modern Canada was never left to the free sweep of forces determined either by the environment or by the powerful logic of markets. Canada's position in the world economy has been marked by the fact that it is simultaneously rich and underdeveloped by the dynamics of export-led growth, supporting a mature capitalist economy with many structural weakness. An institutionalist reading would stress that the principal feature of Canadian development is the drive to balance two conflicting goals: negotiating reciprocity with foreign powers and the need to expand and deepen the domestic market. This involves a complex strategy of simultaneously attempting to look outward and inward. The pressure to produce for domestic consumption is thus countered by the pull of external markets.

The legacy of staple-led development rooted in powerful regional economies explains why social cohesion Canada-wide is weak while regional identification is very pronounced. Regional oppositional agrarian movements gravitated towards populist rather than broad-visioned class-based solutions – policies that would have required a high degree of social solidarity (Drache 1984).

Innis had no doubt that these kinds of dynamics had their origins in the particularity of the way Canada had developed serving three volatile markets: one that was internal but highly regionalized; a second that was continental, reinforcing a static comparative advantage; and a third that was centred on the financial power of the more advanced economies. It is no wonder, then, that the unceasing pressure from continentalism forced him to see with unwavering clarity that the geographic unity of Canada, based on the early fur trade routes, became conspicuous by its absence in the age of industrialism. Nonetheless, he always believed that however difficult it was, a self-defensive nationalism was one of the few political instruments that Canadians had to stabilize their political system when faced with the "change from British imperialism to American imperialism" (Innis 1956, 404).

Markets and Cultural Change: Innis's Global Critique

It was Innis's work on the history of communications that finally brought together his far-ranging observations on markets, culture, and technological change. The early sixteenth century, with its wars, the renaissance, religious revolutions, the discovery of new worlds, and the immensely important invention of movable print, became a fertile terrain for his acute analytical mind.

The medieval world was closed to the outside and was authority bound by the church. Only a few people could read, and what they read was controlled by the clergy. Books were expensive to produce, and the production was controlled by Rome. The idea of a popular literature was unknown, though the oral transmission of culture was a mine of information. Just how few books existed can be gleaned from a few statistics. For instance, hardly any libraries possessed more than 300 books; some exceptions were the King of France's library with 910, and the Christ Church priory at Canterbury, with some 2,000 (Manchester 1992, 95). The movable type revolution of Johann Gutenberg in 1457–58 shook the foundations of the medieval world. Printers all over Christendom quickly copied Gutenberg's invention, and printed books began to appear in Rome (1464), Venice (1469), Paris (1470), the Netherlands (1471), Switzerland (1472), Hungary (1473), Spain (1474), England (1476), Denmark (1482), Sweden (1483), and Constantinople (1490). Like the enclosure movement, which in its brutality left a landless proletariat in its wake, or like the discovery of the steam engine, which spurred the spread of the modern factory system of mass production, the invention of printing was a seismic event that touched every aspect of life. Businessmen needed books to trade; governments quickly saw the potential of the book as a source of administrative power; people were hungry for knowledge; and the newly established Protestant movements understood the power of the printed word in evangelizing their cause.[17] The secular nation-state world was about to be born.

These events must have gripped Innis's attention as few others had. He knew better than most that modern society arose from its feudal beginnings. The print revolution came to symbolize not only the emerging world of capitalist commerce and administration but the social revolution that these new information technologies brought in their wake. Statecraft, nation-building, warfare, the organization of knowledge, the modern city with its merchants, lawyers, physicians, bankers, shipbuilders, and the dispossessed were all part of this cultural and intellectual movement. New classes were about to be born; older ones faced extinction. The constitution of public authority was about to be transformed forever. Manchester is right to focus on the humanist side of the print revolution that grew up in its wake. Modern scholarship emerged as a result or consequence of the revolutionary impact of the spread of book knowledge. The scholars who profited from Gutenberg, such as Thomas More of England and Erasmus of Rotterdam constituted "the world's first community of powerful lay intellectuals" (Manchester 1992, 107).

It would be wrong to think that Innis's sole interest in the print revolution was limited to the radical and transformative aspects of this new technology. His studies had shown him that the typographical revolution did not occur all at once. The Chinese had experimented with wooden typography four hundred years earlier. Muslims had introduced ink into Spain in the tenth century, and the discovery had quickly made its way to other European centres. In the fourteenth century, the French had begun to use discarded linen rags as a cheap source of paper. It was the social dimension of printing that arrested Innis's attention, in much the same way that he understood the staple to be a giant organizing mechanism of society in a frontier economy.

His newfound interest in communications enabled Innis to focus on the deep-seated conflict between competing centres of market power which inhere in the real and symbolic economies. His conceptual grasp of the world of good production and the world of money and information gave him a particularly powerful lens with which to capture the dynamics of cultural change in this emerging liberal society. As such, it became the crossover point between his pre-eminent early studies on the developmental aspects of political economy and his later, equally influential studies on empire and communications.

Innis's work on communications theory exhibits his growing feeling that wealth generation driven by the new information technologies was very different from the exploitation of resources. The movement of invisibles, such as money or information, both of which can be stored up, may be used to generate more money and more information. What is unique in this case is that information is a limitless resource, forever recyclable and saleable (Toffler 1990). Controlling the quantity, quality, and distribution of knowledge distinguishes information from other goods and resources that are sold internationally.

Two ideas of Innis's stand out: first, throughout history, the efficient organization of markets depends in a myriad of ways on the secular exercise of power by the élites. For Innis, control of the technology of communications is the principal lever through which this happens; hence, his concept of the "bias of communication" – the potential of every new technology to accumulate power for those who have the competence to use it. Second is his concept of "monopolies of knowledge," or the way technology increases the power of large-scale organization – be it military, religious, administrative, or corporate authority – to control social space and the social order (Postman 1992). This twofold classification permitted him to divide civilizations into two types: those that have a bias of time and are organized to enhance their social cohesion by means of powerful belief systems reinforced by family, kinship, and religious ties of all kinds; and those that have a bias of space, with a social structure that is designed to control far-flung regions of empire. For reasons that he made explicit in his essays, when each civilization reached its limits, it would be overtaken by alternative technologies. When the maelstrom of conflict erupted, he attached primary importance to the way that centralization of power, information, and force came to dominate not only the Anglo-Saxon world but classical antiquity – which is, after all, the starting point of the history of communications.

The potential presence of these two biases had dramatic implications for politics, culture, and the structure of markets. A time-bound political order is one that is loose and decentralized but has a hierarchical structure of decision making. On the other hand, a space-biased social order presents the prospect of a rigid, centralized structure, but one with the prospect of egalitarian norms and behaviour. Thus, each civilization and culture comes to depend on the existing techniques or modes of communication to acquire, store, and disseminate information. Depending on a culture's dominant system of communications technology, some will be biased in favour of time while others will be space oriented (Berland 1992).

Innis had no shortage of examples to underscore his original point. For instance, writing on clay tablets or parchment promotes continuity and hence a time bias. The Egyptian civilization used the discovery of the calendar, with the clearly established feast days, to help set up an absolute monarchy with a state-sponsored religion on the Upper Nile (Innis 1951, 34). By contrast, the printing of a newspaper encourages a space bias and present-mindedness (Kumar 1993, 2729). The nineteenth century in particular was a goldmine for all of Innis's general ideas. When the high-speed rotary "lightning" press replaced the much slower and expensive flat-bed press, publishers could see the possibilities not only of printing on both sides of the paper but of producing and selling a mass-circulation newspaper. But to take such a step, they had to have cheap paper to feed the presses, and they had to have a literate public to purchase what was written. Innis's point, which he stressed repeatedly, was that there was no technological determinism operating from on high. Rather, one invention sparked another.[18] This was the true nature of the communications revolution. It led to powerful and repeated bursts of technological discoveries, which transformed the sectors of society adjacent and dependent on it. Manchester has captured with great precision the kind of powerful cross current unleashed by the penny press:

> Vast supplies of cheap paper were required to feed these new presses. Ingenious Germans provided the answer in the 1850s: newsprint made from pulp wood. Now a literate public awaited them. W.E. Forster's Compulsory Education Act, passed by Parliament in 1870, was followed by similar legislation throughout western Europe and the United States. In 1858 only 5 percent of British army recruits could read and write; by the turn of the century the figure had risen to 85.4 percent. The 1880s had brought the institution of free libraries which was followed by an explosion in journalism and the emergence of the twentieth-century mass culture which has transformed Western civilization. (Manchester 1992, xv–xvi)

Far from being a cultural historian in the accepted use of the term, Innis used his finely honed grasp of centre-periphery dynamics, born of the battle between conflicting centres of authority in the field of communications, to examine the way that each new advance in communications technology enhanced the power of the state, the military or giant global enterprises, over the individual (Berland 1994). His sweeping studies of civilization vividly demonstrate that these worlds of time and space are bound to clash when inequities in income and wealth are maldistributed or when the territorial aims of empire produce large countermovements. In these circumstances, any redistributive struggle quickly turns into a battle for control against the powers of the dominant social and economic forces in an effort to gain control of the two strategic resources of economic life: money and information. It is this deep-seated problem of who possesses the power to control social space, be it civil or economic, that is determinant for Innis. His concern was to explore the contradictory effects of technological change on authority, power, values, public opinion, and intelligence (see part 4, "Political Culture, the Bias of Communication, and Economic Change").

Taking the case of the print revolution, Innis demonstrated how the invention of the printing press was integral to the spread of commercialism in making possible the standardization of many business practices. Yet its most important consequence was in relation to the exercise of power,[19] for the invention concentrated influence in the hands of the few who knew how to read and write. The pattern, which Innis deduced, is evident in the way élites cultivate each wave of new technology to enhance their authority and prestige by denying others access to knowledge-intensive technologies. The specialized knowledge may be used both as an economic weapon and as an instrument of power for empires, nations, and states seeking to impose their control over other people and territories.

Yet what was never clear in the early stages of a given technology's imposition onto a culture was who would gain and who would lose. This was because technological change was wildly unpredictable in its benefits and costs. Thus, when new technologies redefined what was meant by knowledge or wisdom, they inevitably altered the deeply embedded habits of a society to such an extent that they created new concepts and undermined older notions. Most important to Innis was the fact that when new technologies changed a society's culture, this occurred without anyone being fully conscious of it. The process was insidious and was dangerous for the élite and its authority, but it was even worse for the rest of us. Innis showed that history is replete with examples of traditional monopolies of knowledge being broken up by rival groups coming from the margins, where authority and power are more easily contested.

Innis was one of the first to see the way the introduction of radically innovative technologies forced a culture to conspire against itself (Postman 1992). For him, there was nothing rational in the way interests were restructured or the way the world would be radically redefined. Such changes were merely part of the process in which new technologies compete with the old for time, attention, money, prestige, and, above all else, power. World views then collide, institutions are threatened, and cultures find themselves in crisis. What he saw unfolding in history is a familiar pattern. When an old technology is assaulted by a new one, traditions, social mores, myths, and politics must fight for their lives. (Ibid.)

INNIS IN THE 1990s: IS HIS PERSPECTIVE STILL RELEVANT?

The essential question today is, What resources does a society have at its disposal to cope with the annihilation of public and private space by global markets, the compression of time by instantaneous communication, and the fragmentation of national cultures by computer and other information technologies? In present-day Canada, Innis would have seen much that would have meshed with his ideas about the imminent decline of the West and the way communications technology has, in his powerful phrase, "cut time into pieces." It is his account of this shrinking world of instant communications technology and specialized forms of knowledge that gives Innis's later work so much contemporary relevance.

The globalization of money markets and information flows provides a powerful and lasting framework for updating the Innis legacy. The current restructuring of economies has accelerated capital mobility and information flows between peoples, governments, and states, and brings with it a host of intended and unintended consequences. Purely domestic markets are increasingly a thing of the past. Trade has become the steam engine of the twenty-first century, breaking down national economies as well as redrawing the contours of the nation-state. Today, information flows function in the way the railway once did. Worldwide movements of print and electronic information accelerate the intensity and scope of social change. Communications networks link people globally as never before. But at the same time, monopolies of knowledge in private hands prevent a continuous and unimpeded two-way flow of information across national boundaries, within countries, and among communities. This interplay between markets, peoples, states, and the global trading system is creating a new global (dis)order, in which nation-states see their economic powers being radically reduced while, in the larger society, information flows irreversibly alter the social production and diffusion of knowledge.

An open economy presents unlimited investment and business opportunities for private-sector actors. But the increase in capital mobility and the growth of global markets are not without huge risks and costs. It is estimated that the average daily flow of currency movements worldwide is in excess of one trillion dollars. By comparison, the total of all currency reserves of industrial countries is just under one trillion dollars. The contrast between private wealth and public authority provides a sobering indication of the novel stresses to which all countries are subject. Information is easier to obtain than ever before. And, in theory, so is foreign investment. These open economies present unlimited investment and business opportunities for private-sector actors. With markets operating around the clock, governments face unprecedented risks from volatile prices, unregulated currency flows, and unpredictable interest rates.

How are nations coping with these new realities? What are the risks of globalized markets? What kind of public policies are needed to minimize or reduce market volatility? Can nations exist without a strong national economy? What kinds of international regulatory measures have to be established? How can new technologies in computers and communications be used to shape the future as well as serving human needs? How is money altering our perception of ourselves and our culture? Finally, what forces in modern society are transforming money into a universal *kultur* commodity form?

It would be foolish to expect Innis's works to provide answers to these tough questions. His blind spots are the obvious ones. Gender and race are absent from his analytical lexicon. Despite these shortcomings, his insights are no less valuable. He provides any scholar with a powerful multidisciplinary methodology, drawn from economics, history, geography, and environmental and cultural studies, for grappling with one of the persistent themes in Western culture, namely, structured dependency in all its manifestations. What grabbed his attention was the failure of the pure market mechanism to provide full employment and macroeconomic stability in Western industrialized countries. This inherent limitation with regard to employment and job-creation raises a series of fundamental questions about the danger of relying on markets as the most efficient way of guaranteeing society's well-being.

A return to the free-market mechanisms is likely to become a source of disillusionment in the 1990s. For even if markets do lead to political and institutional transformation, the strategic question to analyse is how market economies are forced to adapt to complex institutional settings and become socially embedded and internationally diffused. Innis always stressed the crucial role that institutional linkages play as a mechanism of adjustment. External trade reinforces competitive pressures, turning a growth cycle into its opposite. So long as this is the case, development cannot be left to the market; in the final analysis, it depends on a country's success in restructuring production and transforming consumption norms by the redistribution of income. Innis's principal conclusion was that strong governments should take the leading role in stabilizing the business cycle. Thus, relief from the costs of increased capital mobility and other structural rigidities of international financial markets can be found. His advice should not go unheeded. At a time when Canada's national government has forgotten its basic responsibility to its citizens to protect them from the uncertainty of global markets, Innis's legacy has greater relevance than ever.

CONCLUSION

Innis always conceived of markets as complex institutions and networks of behaviour that had to be shaped by state policy. He advocated a strategic, not an ideological, approach to the study of economics and cultural change. This is important to recall when thinking about the new staples of the twenty-first century: money and information. These have replaced goods and other traded commodities as the principal source of the wealth of nations. When information becomes the source of wealth and power, disturbing questions emerge about the institutional basis of the new world order. Innis once commented in another context, "And so the snake entered the paradise of ... economics. Under the stimulus of treasure from the new world the price system ate its way more rapidly into the economy of Europe and into economic thought" (Innis 1946, 145). When greed, power, and self-interest function as the motor force of history, long-term stability and economic security are the first victims of global markets, and all people run the risk of being "boiled in the oil" of international competition.

Finally, Innis believed that it was important to comprehend the way the new biases of information would be used to control what individuals do and think in contrast to the way they might enhance a people's right to know. The point he repeatedly emphasized was that everyone had to be conscious of the contradictory potential of each new technology. This is why getting access to knowledge and information has become a vast arena of struggle between businesses, communities, and nations. We have to have the means of establishing and asserting our identities, provided that we have the will to put markets back in their place. In particular, nation-states need specific kinds of cultural and economic policy instruments to protect them from the volatility of international markets. But first and foremost, they need to share Innis's deep-founded and ongoing scepticism about markets as a universal mechanism of well-being. For this, he wrote better than he knew.

Structure of the Volume

Innis produced an amazing number of articles, essays, book reviews, and comment pieces during his life.[20] Given the constraints of space limitations, I have followed three guiding principles in preparing this volume. First, I have tried to strike a balance between the early, middle, and late Innis in order to present a wide-angled view of his intellectual development as an economic geographer, political economist, and communications theorist. Secondly, I have attempted to select essays that stand the test of time and retain an interest for a contemporary reading public. This has not been an easy principle to apply. During his lifetime, many of his major economic essays were directed towards other specialists in the field. However, I have tried to select essays that are broadly representative of his scholarship and provide significant insight into the way he thought about basic issues. Finally, in order to make his work more accessible, I have lightly modified some of the titles of the essays so that they reflect their subject matter more accurately. Wherever this has been done, the reader will find a full citation to the original title and place of publication. Only the most minimal editorial changes, if any, have been made to the essays. Innis's style of writing has been left in its original form.

The Innis reader is organized into the following five sections:

1 *Staple Trades, the Rise of Industrialism, and the Expansion of International Markets.* This section addresses Innis's view of world markets and the role of empire as a force for development and global change. Because the staple trades were central to the enlargement of empire, the essays in this section analyse their social and economic effects on Canada's economic origins. They contain some of Innis's most fundamental ideas about markets, international development, and the prototypical importance of the fur trade to Canada's long-term developmental prospects, as well as the impact of the international economy in so-called new economic lands.

2 *Resources and Regionalism: The Origins of Modern Canada.* Staple-related industries have a strong regional dimension, and this is the major theme that Innis explored in this group of essays. In addition to his study of the staples, Innis wrote extensively on other factors, such as the role of land, transportation, and labour in contributing to Canadian economic development. This section highlights these three factors, not only with respect to the formation of a national economy but with regard to the pattern of regional growth.

3 *Metropolitanism, Nationality, and the Crisis of Industrialism.* The worldwide depression was a major focus of Innis, and this section contains some previously unpublished material on nationalism, the failure of markets, and the role of government and business in the

economy. In particular, it examines the impact of growing US influence on Canadian affairs, the adequacy of the Rowell-Sirois Report in addressing Canada's deep-seated structural problems, and the role of business in the economy.

4 Political Culture, the Bias of Communication, and Economic Change. The discovery of new communications technology inevitably brings sweeping social change in its wake. This section illustrates the "crossover" in Innis's scholarship from political economy to his study of communications. Innis was increasingly preoccupied with the problem of cultural change as a result of the way new communications technologies created new modes of social behaviour. The essays in this section stress his views on modernity and social conflict.

5 The Intellectual as Citizen. Innis spent much of his life as a public figure with enormous influence inside and outside the university. He defined himself as an intellectual activist promoting a democratic society rather than as a political activist advancing the special interests of any one class or region. This section collects together his writings on the responsibilities of the scholar as citizen, the role of the intellectual in Canadian social sciences, the importance of adult education, myths in the social sciences, and democracy and the free city.

Daniel Drache
York University

NOTES

Special thanks to Eric Mézin for his computer and analytical skills in producing the figures on staple trades, as well as to Delwyn Higgens for her sharp editorial eye. Abraham Rotstein and David Bell provided critical feedback at different stages, and Joe Fernandes contributed much-needed assistance in a variety of ways.

1 A measure of Innis's importance can be seen in the numerous works and articles that are indebted to his scholarship. Though not exhaustive, Matteo Sanfilippos's 1992 article contains more than a hundred references inspired by Innis.

2 In being crowned the king of the American economics profession, Innis garnered more votes than W.A. Mackintosh of Queen's University, the founder of the "other staple." The latter's name had been

proposed by Charles Kindleberger, the eminent US economic historian and trade expert (Kindleberger 1991).

3 See his short article, "Approaches to Canadian Economic History" (Innis 1936a), which captures a good deal of the way Innis thought about his methodology.

4 What Innis achieved in the Canadian archives is comparable to the kind of historical sweep and theoretical acuity that the French historian Ferdinand Braudel employed to analyse the fundamental economic structure of the Mediterranean Basin. Nonetheless, there is much that is different about the two historians.

5 Robin Neill suggests that it was Plumptre and not Innis who first tried to explain the principal characteristics of Canadian development systematically and identified the constituent elements of Canada's pattern of economic development (Neill 1991, 147). See also Plumptre 1936.

6 Gordon Laxer (1991) has brought together in one volume many of the important articles (including Watkins 1963) written by Canada's political economists in the seventies and eighties who were influenced for and against Innis's fundamental work on staple-led development.

7 For the definitive statement on the truncated nature of the firm, see Levitt 1970. This should be read along with Britton and Gilmour 1978. The late Canadian economist Stephen Hymer developed a similar perspective in a global context (Hymer 1975).

8 For Innis's place in the pantheon of Canadian political economy tradition, see Daniel Drache, "The Rediscovery of Canadian Political Economy," in Drache and Clement 1985. For a retrospective assessment of the new political economy movement, see Clement and Williams 1989.

9 Not all these social theorists were economists, but all were deeply marked by economics. They addressed a broad and pressing set of issues, such as imperialism, capitalist accumulation, the passage from antiquity to modernity, the history of technology through the ages, the founding of the city, modes of production, and the rise and decline of civilization. Innis had studied briefly with Werner Sombart in Berlin just after the war. For the extent to which he was influenced by this group of exceptional thinkers, see Christian 1980.

10 It is worth adding that this group of distinguished academics shared the conviction that politics and economics were part of a single unbroken continuum rather than being treated as two distinct, competing worlds. The linking of the economic to the political gave their individual studies a tough intellectual quality that has withstood the passage of time.

11 In a general way, there are many parallels between Innis's and Polan-

yi's views that markets were socially constructed. In fact, Polanyi knew Innis's work and visited him at least once, but Innis showed little interest in pursuing the contact. The general point should not be overdrawn because Polanyi and Innis had such different views of political economy that it is more by coincidence than anything else that these parallels emerge. See Rotstein 1977 for an excellent discussion of some of the common ground they shared.

12 There are echoes of Keynes in Innis's general critique of capitalism, but Innis did not set out to develop a systemic understanding of the limits to competitive capitalism in the same way Keynes did. For instance, there is no demand-side critique, despite the fact that Innis had read Keynes's *General Theory* (see Christian 1980).

13 Unbeknown to contemporary merchandising giants such as Wal-Mart and K mart, these aggressive retailers have their origins in the monopoly practices of the staple (see entry for "staple" in *The New Shorter Oxford Dictionary*, 1993).

14 His pessimistic views about the pending collapse of capitalism are well documented in Christian 1980.

15 The universal themes of uneven development, underdevelopment, and crisis have been the centre of much important historical writing and research in recent years. See the historical work of Fernard Braudel and the Annales School; Emmanuel Wallerstein's analysis of the origin of the world economy; in international political economy, consult Robert Cox, and in economic theory, see Robert Boyer and Samin Amin, respectively.

16 The right of Canada's aboriginal people to full political equality remained largely masked until the mid-1980s. Canada's long-simmering constitutional crisis was used by Canada's first peoples to become players in their own right and at the negotiating table (Turpel 1992; McNeil 1992).

17 These paragraphs draw heavily on William Manchester's social history of medievaldom and the origins of the Renaissance (Manchester 1992). His book can be read as a study of the revolutionary impact of the printed word on the sixteenth-century mind and political order.

18 See two important articles by Innis: "The Newspaper in Economic Development" and "An Economic Approach to English Literature in the Nineteenth Century," both in Innis 1946.

19 For instance, the written contract formed not only the basis of employment law but the development of modern property law, which facilitated the transfer of wealth from one generation of property holders to the next.

20 Robin Neill's 1972 study of Innis's economic thought contains a very useful bibliography that readers may want to consult.

BIBLIOGRAPHY

Aitken, Hugh G.J. 1961. *American Capital and Canadian Resources.* Cambridge: Harvard University Press

Angus, Ian, and Brian Shoesmith, eds. 1993. "Dependency/Space/Policy: A Dialogue with Harold A. Innis." Special Issue. *Continuum: The Australian Journal of Media and Culture* 7:1.

Barnes, Trevor, ed. 1993. "A Geographical Appreciation of Harold Innis." *Canadian Geographer* 37:4.

Berger, Carl. 1976. *The Writing of Canadian History.* Toronto: Oxford University Press.

Berland, Jody. 1992. "Angels Dancing: Cultural Technologies and the Production of Space." In *Cultural Studies,* ed. Lawrence Grossberg, Cary Nelson, and Paula Treichter. New York: Routledge.

– 1994. "Radio Space and Industrial Time: The Case of Music Formats." In *Canadian Music: Issues of Hegemony and Identity,* ed. Beverley Diamond and Robert Witmer. Toronto: Canadian Scholars Press.

Boyer, Robert. 1991. "About the Role and Efficiency of Markets: History, Theory and Policy in the Light of the Nineties." CEPREMAP 9320, Paris, France.

Braudel, Fernand. 1980. *On History.* Translated by Sarah Mathews. Chicago: University of Chicago Press.

Britton, John, and James Gilmour. 1978. *The Weakest Link: A Technological Perspective on Canadian Industrial Development.* Background Study no. 43. Ottawa: Science Council of Canada.

Burton, F.W. 1938 "Staple Production and Canada's External Relations." In *Essays on Political Economy,* ed. Harold Innis. Toronto: University of Toronto Press

Canada. 1940. Report of the Royal Commission on Dominion-Provincial Relations (Rowell-Sirois Report). Ottawa: King's Printer.

Careless, J.M.S. 1954. "Frontierism, Metropolitanism and Canadian History." *Canadian Historical Review* 35:1.

Christian, William, ed. 1980. *The Idea File of Harold Adams Innis.* Toronto: University of Toronto Press.

Clement, Wallace, and Glen Williams, eds. 1989. *The New Canadian Political Economy.* Montreal: McGill-Queen's University Press.

Cohen, Marjorie. 1988. *Women and the Development of South-Central Ontario.* Toronto: University of Toronto Press.

Creighton, Donald. [1937] 1956. *The Commercial Empire of the St. Lawrence, 1760–1850.* Reprint. Toronto: Macmillan

– 1957. *Harold Adams Innis: Portrait of a Scholar.* Toronto: University of Toronto Press.

Drache, Daniel. 1982. "Harold Innis and Canadian Capitalist Develop-

ment." 6:1–2. Reprinted in *Perspectives on Canadian Economic Development*, ed. Gordon Laxer (Toronto: Oxford University Press, 1991).
– 1984. "The Formation and Fragmentation of the Canadian Working Class." *Studies in Public Economics* 15 (Fall): 43–89. Reprinted in *Canadian Labour History*, ed. David J. Bercuson and David Bright (Toronto: Copp Clark Longman, 2d ed., 1994.
Drache, Daniel, and Clement Wallace. 1985. *The New Practical Guide to Canadian Political Economy*. Toronto: Lorimer.
Drache, Daniel, and Meric Gertler, eds. 1991. *The New Era of Global Competition*. Montreal: McGill-Queen's University Press.
Drache, Daniel, and Harry Glasbeek. 1992. *The Changing Workplace*. Toronto: Lorimer.
Easterbrook, W.T. 1959. "Trends in Canadian Economic Thought." *South Atlantic Quarterly* 58: 91–107.
Fowke, Vernon. [1957] 1975. *The National Policy and the Wheat Economy*. Reprint. Toronto: University of Toronto Press.
Francis, D., and T. Morantz. 1983. *Partners in Furs*. Montreal: McGill-Queen's University Press.
Gertler, Meric. 1993. "Harold Innis and the New Industrial Geography." *Canadian Geographer* 37:4.
Harris, Cole, ed. 1987. *Historical Atlas of Canada*. Vol. 1. Toronto: University of Toronto Press.
Hay, Douglas. 1975. "Property, Authority and Criminal Law." In Hay et al., *Albion's Fatal Tree: Crime and Society in Eighteenth Century England*. London: Allen and Unwin.
Hirshman, Albert O. 1958. *Strategy of Economic Development*. New Haven: Yale University Press.
Hymer, Stephen. 1975. "The Multinational Corporation and the Law of Uneven Development." In *International Firms and Modern Imperialism*, ed. Hugo Radice. Harmondsworth: Penguin.
Innis, Harold A. [1923] 1971. *A History of the Canadian Pacific Railway*. Reprint. Toronto: University of Toronto Press.
– 1929. *Select Documents in Canadian Economic History: 1497–1783*. Toronto: University of Toronto Press.
– [1930] 1956. *The Fur Trade in Canada: An Introduction to Canadian Economic History*. Reprint. Toronto: University of Toronto Press.
– 1933a. *Problems of Staple Production in Canada*. Toronto: University of Toronto Press.
– 1933b. *Select Documents in Canadian Economic History: 1783–1885*. Toronto: University of Toronto Press.
– 1936a. "Approaches to Canadian Economic History." *Commerce Journal*, 26.
– 1936b. *Settlement and the Mining Frontier*. Toronto: Macmillan.

– 1946. *Political Economy in the Modern State.* Toronto: Ryerson Press.
– [1950] 1972. *Empire and Communications.* Reprint. Toronto: University of Toronto Press.
– 1951. *The Bias of Communication.* Toronto: University of Toronto Press.
– 1952. *Changing Concepts of Time.* Toronto: University of Toronto Press.
– 1954. *The Cod Fisheries: The History of an International Economy.* Toronto: University of Toronto Press.
– 1956. *Essays in Canadian Economic History,* ed. Mary Quayle Innis. Toronto: University of Toronto Press.

Kindleberger, Charles. 1991. *The Life of an Economist: Autobiography.* Cambridge, Mass.: Basil Blackwell.

Kumar, Krishna. 1993. "Market Economy and Mass Literacy: Revisiting Innis' Economics of Communications." *Economic and Political Weekly* (New Delhi, India), 11 December, 2727–34.

Laxer, Gordon, ed. 1991. *Perspectives on Canadian Economic Development: Class, Staples, Gender and Elites.* Toronto: Oxford University Press.

Levitt, Kari. 1970. *Silent Surrender.* Toronto: Macmillan.

McCallum, J. 1980. *Unequal Beginnings: Agriculture and Economic Development in Quebec and Ontario until 1870.* Toronto: University of Toronto Press.

McIlwraith, Thomas F. 1990. "British North America, 1763–1867." In *North America: The Historical Geography of a Changing Continent,* ed. Robert D. Mitchell and Paul A. Groves. Savage, Md.: Rowman and Littlefield.

Mackintosh, W.A. 1923. "Economic Factors in Canadian History." In *Approaches to Canadian Economic History,* ed. W.T. Easterbrook and M.H. Watkins. (Toronto: McClelland and Stewart, 1967).
– 1953. "Innis on Canadian Economic Development." *Journal of Political Economy* 61: 185–94.

McNeil, Kent. 1992. "Aboriginal Nations and Quebec's Boundaries: Canada Couldn't Give What It Didn't Have." In *Negotiating with a Sovereign Quebec,* ed. D. Drache and R. Perin. Toronto: Lorimer.

Manchester, William. 1992. *A World Lit Only by Fire: The Medieval Mind and the Renaissance.* Boston: Little Brown.

Martin, Chester. 1938. *Dominion Lands Policy.* Vol. 2 of *Canadian Frontiers of Settlement* series. Toronto: University of Toronto Press.

Mitchell, Robert D., and Paul A. Groves, eds. 1990. *North America: The Historical Geography of a Changing Continent.* Savage, Md.: Romwan and Littlefield.

Monk, Ray. 1990. *Ludwig Wittgenstein: The Duty of Genius.* London: Vintage.

Mumford, Lewis. [1934] 1963. *Technics and Civilization.* Reprint. New York: Harcourt Brace & World Inc.

Naylor, R.T. 1972. "The Rise and Fall of the Third Commercial Empire of the St. Lawrence." In *Capitalism and the National Question in Canada,* ed. Gary Teeple. Toronto: University of Toronto Press.

Neill, Robin. 1972. *A New Theory of Value: The Canadian Economics of H.A. Innis.* Toronto: University of Toronto Press.

– 1991. *A History of Canadian Economic Thought.* London: Routledge.

Nelles, H.V. 1974. *The Politics of Development: Forest, Mines and Hydro-Electric Power in Ontario, 1840–1941.* Toronto: Macmillan.

Pentland, H. Clare. 1981. *Labour and Capital in Canada 1650–1860*, ed. Paul Phillips. Toronto: Lorimer.

Plumptre, A.F. 1936. "The Nature of Political and Economic Development in the British Dominions." *Canadian Journal of Economics and Political Science* 3: 488–507.

Postman, Neil. 1992. *Technology: The Surrender of Culture to Technology.* New York: Knopf.

Ray, Arthur J. 1974. *Indians in the Fur Trade: Their Role as Hunters, Trappers, and Middlemen in the Lands Southwest of Hudson Bay 1660–1870.* Toronto: University of Toronto Press.

– 1978. *"Give Us Good Measure!" An Economic Analysis of Relations between the Indians the Hudson's Bay Company before 1763.* Toronto: University of Toronto Press.

Rotstein, A. 1972. "Trade and Politics: An Institutional Approach." *Western Canadian Journal of Anthropology* 3: 1.

– 1977. "Innis: The Alchemy of Fur and Wheat." *Journal of Canadian Studies* 12 (Winter): 5.

Sanfilippo, Matteo. 1992. "Innis e la storiografia canadese." *Annali Accademici Canadesi* (Ottawa/CACI, Roma).

Skidelsky, Robert. 1992. *John Maynard Keynes: The Economist as Savior 1920–1937.* New York: Penguin.

Toffler, Alvin. 1990. *Powershift: Knowledge, Wealth and Power at the Edge of the 21st Century.* New York: Bantam.

Trigger, Bruce. 1985. *Natives and Newcomers.* Montreal: McGill-Queen's University Press.

– 1992. "The University and the Longue Durée." *Transactions of the Royal Society of Canada.* Series 6, 3: 57–67.

Turpel, M.E. 1992. "Does the Road to Quebec Sovereignty Run through Aboriginal Territory?" In *Negotiating with a Sovereign Quebec,* ed. D. Drache and R. Perin. Toronto: Lorimer.

Watkins, M.H. 1963. "A Staple Theory of Economic Growth." *Canadian Journal of Economics and Political Science* 29 (May): 80–100. Reprinted in *Perspectives on Canadian Economic Development: Class, Staples, Gender and Elites,* ed. Gordon Laxer (Toronto: Oxford University Press, 1991).

– 1977. "The Staple Theory Revisited." *Journal of Canadian Studies* 12 (Winter): 5.

Wright, Ronald. 1992. *Stolen Continents: The "New World" through Indian Eyes.* Toronto: Penguin.

PART ONE

Staple Trades, the Rise of Industrialism, and the Enlargement of Empire

CHAPTER ONE

The Importance of Staple Products in Canadian Development

Fundamentally the civilization of North America is the civilization of Europe and the interest of this volume is primarily in the effects of a vast new land area on European civilization. The opening of a new continent distant from Europe has been responsible for the stress placed by modern students on the dissimilar features of what has been regarded as two separate civilizations. On the other hand communication and transportation facilities have always persisted between the two continents since the settlement of North America by Europeans, and have been subject to constant improvement.

Peoples who have become accustomed to the cultural traits of their civilization – what Mr. Graham Wallas calls the social heritage – on which they subsist, find it difficult to work out new cultural traits suitable to a new environment. The high death rate of the population of the earliest European settlements is evidence to that effect. The survivors live through borrowing cultural traits of peoples who have already worked out a civilization suitable to the new environment as in the case of the Indians of North America, through adapting their own cultural traits to the new environment, and through heavy material borrowing from the peoples of the old land. The process of adaptation is extremely painful in any case but the maintenance of cultural traits to which they have been accustomed is of primary importance. A sudden change of cultural traits can be made only with great difficulty and with the disappearance of many of the peoples concerned. Depreciation of the social heritage is serious.

From *The Fur Trade in Canada*, rev. ed. (Toronto, 1956), 383–402; first appeared as "Conclusion."

The methods by which the cultural traits of a civilization may persist with the least possible depreciation involve an appreciable dependence on the peoples of the homeland. The migrant is not in a position immediately to supply all his needs and to maintain the same standard of living as that to which he has been accustomed, even with the assistance of Indians, an extremely fertile imagination, and a benevolent Providence such as would serve Robinson Crusoe or the Swiss Family Robinson on a tropical island. If those needs are to be supplied he will be forced to rely on goods which are obtainable from the mother country.

These goods were obtained from the homeland by direct transportation as in the movement of settlers' effects and household goods, involving no direct transfer of ownership, or through gifts and missionary supplies, but the most important device was trade. Goods were produced as rapidly as possible to be sold at the most advantageous price in the home market in order to purchase other goods essential to the maintenance and improvement of the current standard of living. In other words these goods supplied by the home country enabled the migrant to maintain his standard of living and to make his adjustments to the new environment without serious loss.

The migrant was consequently in search of goods which could be carried over long distances by small and expensive sailboats and which were in such demand in the home country as to yield the largest profit. These goods were essentially those in demand for the manufacture of luxuries, or goods which were not procured, or produced to a slight extent, in the home country as in the case of gold and of furs and fish. The latter was in some sense a luxury under the primitive conditions of agriculture in Europe and the demands of Catholic peoples. The importance of metropolitan centres in which luxury goods were in most demand was crucial to the development of colonial North America. In these centres goods were manufactured for the consumption of colonials and in these centres goods produced in the colonies were sold at the highest price. The number of goods produced in a north temperate climate in an area dominated by Pre-Cambrian formations, to be obtained with little difficulty in sufficient quantity and disposed of satisfactorily in the home market under prevailing transport conditions, was limited.

The most promising source of early trade was found in the abundance of fish, especially cod, to be caught off the Grand Banks of Newfoundland and in the territory adjacent to the Gulf of St Lawrence. The abundance of cod led the peoples concerned to direct all their available energy to the prosecution of the fishing industry which developed extensively. In the interior, trade with the Indians offered the largest returns in the commodity which was available on a large scale and which yielded substantial profits, namely furs and especially beaver. With the disappearance of beaver in more accessible territory, lumber became the product which brought the largest returns. In British Columbia gold became the product following the fur trade but eventually lumber and fish came into prominence. The lumber industry has been supplemented by the development of the pulp and paper industry with its chief reliance on spruce. Agricultural products – as in the case of wheat – and later minerals – gold, nickel, and other metals – have followed the inroads of machine industry.

The economic history of Canada has been dominated by the discrepancy between the centre and the margin of western civilization. Energy has been directed toward the exploitation of staple products and the tendency has been cumulative. The raw material supplied to the mother country stimulated manufactures of the finished product and also of the products which were in demand in the colony. Large-scale production of raw materials was encouraged by improvement of technique of production, of marketing, and of transport as well as by improvement in the manufacture of the finished product. As a consequence, energy in the colony was drawn into the production of the staple commodity both directly and indirectly. Population was involved directly in the production of the staple and indirectly in the production of facilities promoting production. Agriculture, industry, transportation, trade, finance, and governmental activities tend to become subordinate to the production of the staple for a more highly specialized manufacturing community. These general tendencies may be strengthened by governmental policy as in the mercantile system but the importance of these policies varies in particular industries. Canada remained British in spite of free trade and chiefly because she continued as an exporter of staples to a progressively industrialized mother country.

The general tendencies in the industrial areas of western civilization, especially in the United States and Great Britain, have had a pronounced effect on Canada's export of staples. In these areas machine industry spread with rapidity through the accessibility of the all-year-round ocean ports and the existence of ample supplies of coal and iron. In Great Britain the nineteenth century was characterized by increasing industrialization[1] with greater dependence on the staple products of new countries for raw material and on the population of these countries for a market. Lumber, wheat, cotton, wool, and meat may be cited as examples of staple imports. In the United States[2] the Civil War and railroad construction gave a direct stimulus to the iron and steel industry and hastened industrial and capitalistic growth. These two areas began to draw increasingly on outside areas for staples and even continental United States has found it necessary with the disappearance of free land, the decline of natural resources, and the demand for new industrial materials, notably rubber, to rely on outside areas as shown in her imperialistic policy of the twentieth century. Canada has participated in the industrial growth of the United States, becoming the gateway of that country to the markets of the British Empire. She has continued, however, chiefly as a producer of staples for the industrial centres of the United States even more than of Great Britain making her own contribution to the Industrial Revolution of North America and Europe and being in turn tremendously influenced thereby.

THE FUR TRADE

The history of the fur trade in North America has been shown as a retreat in the face of settlement. The strategic campaigns in that retreat include the Conquest of New France, the Quebec Act of 1774, the American Revolution, the Jay Treaty of 1794, the amalgamation of 1821, the Oregon Treaty of 1846, and the Rupert's Land Act of 1869. The struggle continues in the newly settled areas of the Dominion. The trade has been conducted by large organizations from the artificial and natural monopolies of New France to the Northwest Company and the Hudson's Bay Company which still occupies an important position. It has depended on the manufactures of Europe and the more efficient manufactures and cheaper transportation of England. Control of the fur trade was an index of world importance from the standpoint of efficient manufactures, control of markets, and consumption of luxuries. The shift from Paris to London of the fur trade was significant of the industrial growth of France and England – just as possession of Canada after the American Revolution was significant of the industrial limitations of the United States. The demands of the Indians for cheaper and greater quantities of goods were determining factors in the destiny of the northern half of North America.

The crises which disturbed the history of the fur trade were determined finally by various important factors including the geographic background and the industrial efficiency of England. These long-run factors were obscured by a complexity of causes which centred about each crisis. In the first half of the seventeenth century the Indian trading organization was essential to the trade. In the latter part of the century the French trading organization to the interior became more effective and the market became flooded with furs. Finally the geographic limits of the trade with the canoe were reached with the extension of the trade to the Saskatchewan in the first half of the eighteenth century. In the second half of the century transport became more efficient with the development of lake transport supplementary to the canoe and the trade was extended with increased capital resources and efficient business organization to the Pacific. With continued decline in the supply of beaver, the development of a more efficient transport and of a more elastic business organization from Hudson Bay, amalgamation became inevitable and the canoe disappeared as the dominant form of transport in the fur trade. Dependence on the York boat rather than the canoe was symbolic of the increasing importance of capitalism. After the amalgamation improved transport facilities from the south led to the disappearance of monopoly control in 1869 and to the reign of competition which has become increasingly severe since that date. The beaver became less important after the amalgamation and the trade more dependent on other varieties of furs. Supply decreased less rapidly and in spite of competition the trade continued on a more permanent basis. Severe fluctuations were the result, throughout the period, of the discoveries of new territory and new Indians but especially of wars. These fluctuations were more serious in the earlier period of the French *régime* and occasioned serious results for the colony and the mother country. They became less serious after the Conquest and were less disastrous to the mother country. With the disappearance of these fluctuations, business organization became more efficient. But in the long run improved transport combined with geographic advantages reigned supreme. It was significant, however, that business organization was of vital importance to the trade and, combined with geographic advantages, maintained a strong position. This combination favoured the growth of capitalism which became conspicuous in the later days of the Northwest Company and in the succeeding Hudson's Bay Company especially after 1869.

The early history of the fur trade is essentially a history of the trade in beaver fur. The beaver was found in large numbers throughout the northern half of North America. The better grades of fur came from the more northerly forested regions of North America and were obtained during the winter season when the fur was prime. A vast north temperate land area with a pronounced seasonal climate was a prerequisite to an extensive development of the trade. The animal was not highly reproductive and it was not a migrant. Its destruction in any locality necessitated the movement of hunters to new areas.

The existence of the animal in large numbers assumed a relatively scant population. It assumed an area in which population could not be increased by resort to agriculture. Limitations of geological formation, and climate and a cultural background dependent on these limitations precluded a dense population with consequent destruction of animal life. The culture was dependent on indigenous flora and fauna and the latter was of prime importance. Moose, caribou, beaver, rabbit or hare, and fish furnished the chief supplies of food and clothing. This culture assumed a thorough knowledge of animal habits and the ability of the peoples concerned to move over wide areas in pursuit of a supply of food. The devices which had been elaborated included the snowshoe and the toboggan for the winter and the birch-bark canoe for the summer. This wide area contained numerous lakes and difficult connecting waterways, to which the canoe was adapted for extensive travel. Movement over this area occasioned an extended knowledge of geography and a widespread similarity of cultural traits such as language.

The area which was crucial to the development of the fur trade was the Pre-Cambrian shield of the northern half of the North American continent. It extended northwesterly across the continent to the mouth of the Mackenzie River and was bounded on the north by the north-westerly isothermal lines which determined the limits of the northern forests and especially of the canoe birch (*B. papyrifera*). The fur trade followed the waterways along the southern edge of this formation from the St Lawrence to the Mackenzie River. In its full bloom it spread beyond this area to the Pacific drainage basin.

The history of the fur trade is the history of contact between two civilizations, the European and the North American, with especial reference to the northern portion of the continent. The limited cultural background of the North American hunting peoples provided an insatiable demand for the products of the more elaborate cultural development of Europeans. The supply of European goods, the product of a more advanced and specialized technology, enabled the Indians to gain a livelihood more easily – to obtain their supply of food, as in the case of moose, more quickly, and to hunt the beaver more effectively. Unfortunately the rapid destruction of the food supply and the revolution in the methods of living accompanied by the increasing attention to the fur trade by which these products were secured, disturbed the balance which had grown up previous to the coming of the European. The new technology with its radical innovations brought about such a rapid shift in the prevailing Indian culture as to lead to wholesale destruction of the peoples concerned by warfare and disease. The disappearance of the beaver and of the Indians necessitated the extension of European organization to the interior. New tribes demanded European goods in increasingly large amounts. The fur trade was the means by which this demand of the peoples of a more limited cultural development was met. Furs were the chief product suitable to European demands by which the North American peoples could secure European goods.

A rapid and extensive development of the trade followed accessibility to the vast areas of the Canadian Shield by the St Lawrence and its numerous tributaries and by the rivers of the Hudson Bay drainage basin. Following a rapid decline in the supply of beaver in more accessible territory and the necessity of going to more remote areas, the trade began in the Maritime Provinces, extended rapidly by the Saguenay and later by the St Lawrence and the Ottawa to the Great Lakes, and northwesterly across the headwaters of the rivers of Hudson Bay drainage basin from Lake Superior to Lake Winnipeg, the Saskatchewan, the Churchill, across the headwaters of the Mackenzie River drainage basin to Mackenzie and Peace rivers, and finally to the headwaters of rivers of the Pacific coast to New Caledonia and the Columbia. The waterways along the edge of the Canadian Shield tapped the rich fur lands of that area and in the smaller rivers of the headwaters of four drainage basins provided an environment to which the canoe could be adapted.

The extension of the trade across the northern half of the continent and the transportation of furs and goods over great distances involved the elaboration of an extensive organization of transport, of personnel, and of food supply. The development of transportation was based primarily on Indian cultural growth. The birch-bark canoe was borrowed and modified to suit the demands of the trade. Again, without Indian agriculture, Indian corn, and dependence on Indian methods of capturing buffalo and making pemmican, no extended organization of transport to the interior would have been possible in the early period. The organization of food supplies depended on agricultural development in the more favourable areas to the south and on the abundant fauna of the plains area. Limited transportation facilities, such as the canoe afforded, accentuated the organization and production of food supply in these areas. The extension of the fur trade was supported at convenient intervals by agricultural development as in the lower St Lawrence basin, in southeastern Ontario, and areas centring about Detroit, and in Michilimackinac and Lake Michigan territory, in the west at Red River, though the buffalo were more important in the plains area in the beginning, and eventually in Peace River. On the Pacific coast an agricultural base was established on the Columbia.

The increasing distances over which the trade was carried on and the increasing capital investment and expense incidental to the elaborate organization of transport had a direct influence on its financial organization. Immediate trade with Europe from the St Lawrence involved the export of large quantities of fur to meet the overhead costs of long ocean voyages and the imports of large quantities of heavy merchandise. Monopoly inevitably followed, and it was supported by the European institutional arrangements which involved the organization of monopolies for the conduct of foreign trade. On the other hand, internal trade, following its extension in the interior and the demand for larger numbers of *voyageurs* and canoes to undertake the difficult task of transportation and the increasing dependence on the initiative of the trader in carrying on trade with remote tribes, was, within certain limits, competitive. Trade from Quebec and Montreal with canoes up the Ottawa to Michilimackinac, La Baye, and Lake Superior could be financed with relatively small quantities of capital and was consequently competitive. Further extension of trade through Lake Superior by Grand Portage (later Kaministiquia) to Lake Winnipeg, the Saskatchewan, Athabasca, the Mackenzie River, and New Caledonia and the Pacific coast involved heavy overhead costs and an extensive organization of transportation. But the organization was of a type peculiar to the demands of the fur trade. Individual initiative was stressed in the partnership agreements which characterized the Northwest Company. The trade carried on over extended areas under conditions of limited transportation made close control of individual partners by a central organization impossible. The Northwest Company which extended its organization from the Atlantic to the Pacific developed along lines which were fundamentally linked to the technique of the fur trade. This organization was strengthened in the amalgamation of 1821 by control of a charter guaranteeing monopoly and by the advantages incidental to lower costs of transportation by Hudson Bay.

The effects of these large centralized organizations characteristic of the fur trade as shown in the monopolies of New France, in the Hudson's Bay Company, and in the Northwest Company were shown in the institutional development of Canada. In New France constant expansion of the trade to the interior had increased costs of transportation and extended the possibilities of competition from New England. The population of New France during the open season of navigation was increasingly engaged in carrying on the trade over longer distances to the neglect of agriculture and other phases of economic development. To offset the effects of competition from the English colonies in the south and the Hudson's Bay Company in the north, a military policy, involving Indian alliances, expenditure on strategic posts, expensive campaigns, and constant direct and indirect drains on the economic life of New France and old France, was essential. As a result of these developments control of political activities in New France was centralized and the paternalism of old France was strengthened by the fur trade. Centralized control as shown in the activities of the government, the church, the seigniorial system, and other institutions was in part a result of the overwhelming importance of the fur trade.

The institutional development of New France was an indication of the relation between the fur trade and the mercantile policy. The fur trade provided an ample supply of raw material for the manufacture of highly profitable luxury goods. A colony engaged in the fur trade was not in a position to develop industries to compete with manufactures of the mother country. Its weakness necessitated reliance upon the military support of the mother country. Finally the insatiable demands of the Indians for goods stimulated European manufactures.

The importance of manufactures in the fur trade gave England, with her more efficient industrial development, a decided advantage. The competition of cheaper goods contributed in a definite fashion to the downfall of New France and enabled Great Britain to prevail in the face of its pronounced militaristic development. Moreover, the importance of manufactured goods to the fur trade made inevitable the continuation of control by Great Britain in the northern half of North America. The participation of American and English merchants in the fur trade immediately following the Conquest led to the rapid growth of a new organization[3] which was instrumental in securing the Quebec Act and which contributed to the failure of the American Revolution so far as it affected Quebec and the St Lawrence. These merchants were active in the negotiations prior to the Constitutional Act of 1791 and the Jay Treaty of 1794.[4] As prominent members of the government formed under the Quebec Act and the Constitutional Act, they did much to direct the general trend of legislation. The later growth of the Northwest

Company assured a permanent attachment to Great Britain because of its dependence on English manufactures.

The northern half of North America remained British because of the importance of fur as a staple product. The continent of North America became divided into three areas: (1) to the north in what is now the Dominion of Canada, producing furs, (2) to the south in what were during the Civil War the secession states, producing cotton, and (3) in the centre the widely diversified economic territory including the New England states and the coal and iron areas of the middle west demanding raw materials and a market. The staple-producing areas were closely dependent on industrial Europe, especially Great Britain. The fur-producing area was destined to remain British. The cotton-producing area was forced after the Civil War to become subordinate to the central territory just as the northern fur-producing area, at present producing the staples, wheat, pulp and paper, minerals, and lumber, tends to be brought under its influence.

The Northwest Company and its successor the Hudson's Bay Company established a centralized organization which covered the northern half of North America from the Atlantic to the Pacific. The importance of this organization was recognized in boundary disputes, and it played a large role[5] in the numerous negotiations responsible for the location of the present boundaries. It is no mere accident that the present Dominion coincides roughly with the fur-trading areas of northern North America. The bases of supplies for the trade in Quebec, in western Ontario, and in British Columbia represent the agricultural areas of the present Dominion. The Northwest Company was the forerunner of the present confederation.

There are other interesting by-products of the study which may be indicated briefly. Canada has had no serious problems with her native peoples since the fur trade depended primarily on these races. In the United States no point of contact of such magnitude was at hand and troubles with the Indians were a result. The existence of small and isolated sections of French half-breeds throughout Canada is another interesting survival of this contact.[6] The half-breed has never assumed such importance in the United States.

"The lords of the lakes and forest have passed away" but their work will endure in the boundaries of the Dominion of Canada and in Canadian institutional life. The place of the beaver in Canadian life has been fittingly noted in the coat of arms. We have given to the maple a prominence which was due to the birch. We have not yet realized that the Indian and his culture were fundamental to the growth of Canadian institutions. We are only beginning to realize the central position of the Canadian Shield.

THE FOREST INDUSTRIES

Canada emerged as a political entity with boundaries largely determined by the fur trade. These boundaries included a vast north temperate land area extending from the Atlantic to the Pacific and dominated by the Canadian Shield. The present Dominion emerged not in spite of geography but because of it. The significance for the fur trade consisted in its determination of the geographic framework. Later economic developments in Canada were profoundly influenced by this background.

The decline of the fur trade in eastern Canada which followed the export of furs from the Northwest through Hudson Bay after 1821 necessitated increased dependence on other staple exports. Wheat and potash had become increasingly important but they were overshadowed by the rise of the lumber trade. The transport organization and personnel of the fur trade and its capitalistic beginnings were shifted to the development of new lines of trade.[7] An extended financial organization under the fur trade was attested by the plans for the first establishment of a bank in Canada with the strong support of Phyn and Ellice[8] and the establishment of the Bank of Montreal in 1817[9] with John Gray, an old fur trader, as president and John Richardson of Forsyth, Richardson & Company, as strong supporters. McGill University persisted as a memorial to the wealth acquired by James McGill. Edward Ellice became an important figure in London with strong colonial interests and Simon McGillivray retained an interest in colonial activities. On this basis, with the advantages of preference in England and abundant and cheap shipping after the war, the lumber exports to Great Britain increased rapidly in the face of Baltic competition.

As with the fur trade the development of the lumber trade depended on water transportation. A bulky commodity, it was restricted in the early period to the large rivers. The buoyant softwoods could be floated in rafts down the St Lawrence and the Ottawa to Quebec for shipment to England. The largest and best trees were in demand for the square-timber trade. Square timber was in demand in England for the wooden shipbuilding industry, exports of which reached a peak in 1845.[10] As the largest trees were cleared out it became necessary to go farther from the large rivers for timber and with smaller streams the long, square timber was more difficult to handle. Moreover, the cutting off of the forests and destruction by fires caused a decline in the flow of water in the streams and enhanced the difficulties and cost of transport. Decline in the use of wooden sailing vessels and increase in the use of iron steamships had an important effect on the square-timber trade. The saw-log trade developed with the improvement of sawmills which sprang into existence at an early date in response to the local demands of settlements. With decline in the size of logs, improvement of sawmill technique, and the hastening of transport in steamships, deals became of greater importance and, in the period prior to 1867, reached a peak in 1862.

The lumber industry created an important problem of overhead costs. Ships sailing from Quebec with lumber were in search of a return cargo which emigration provided.[11] "Coffin ships" suitable for the lumber trade were employed to take out emigrants. Immigration and settlement brought an increase in imports of manufactured products and in exports of potash, wheat, lumber, and other products. With agricultural development, labour and supplies were available for the seasonal prosecution of the lumber industry. With the westward movement settlement increased in Upper Canada and the middle west, the forests were cleared, and the St Lawrence and the Great Lakes became more important as a transport route. The export of commodities[12] from the territory above Niagara Falls and in Upper Canada and the western states was shown in an increase from 54,219 tons of traffic in 1836 to 1,045,821 tons in 1851 passing through the Erie Canal. Wheat exported through the Welland Canal increased from 210,105 bu. in 1831 to 1,579,966 bu. in 1841, and merchandise increased from 736 tons in 1831 to 4,051 tons in 1841. The completion of the Welland Canal made possible the export of timber from the territory above Niagara Falls. Exports of staves increased from 137,718 in 1831 to 2,776,161 in 1841, square timber (cu. ft.) from 75,992 in 1832 to 1,155,086 in 1841, lumber (ft.) 986,888 in 1831 to 3,580,911 in 1841, saw logs, 4,187 in 1831 to 11,300 in 1841.

With increase in exports and imports to Upper Canada the demand for improved communication on the upper St Lawrence became more insistent. Rafts of timber could be floated down the rapids but loads of grain and merchandise both up- and downstream became more difficult to handle. The demand of settlers for cheaper transport was an important factor in the struggle over the control of revenue to finance the construction of canals. The Act of Union of 1840 offered a solution and was followed by rapid construction of canals in the decade to 1850. Improvements of waterways were rendered obsolete through the disadvantage of water transportation, especially on the St Lawrence with its northerly direction and its long closed season, and the construction of railroads to the seaboard in the United States. Railway lines were built after 1850 to shorten the water routes as in the road from Toronto to Collingwood. The Grand Trunk was extended from Sarnia to Montreal and Portland on the open seaboard. These railways not only joined the important settlements along the waterways but provided for the settlement of territory distant from the lakes and rivers. They provided an all-year-round outlet for lumber and agricultural produce from Canada and the United States, and for the import of merchandise.

The improvement of transportation in canals and railways had important effects on the lumber trade in providing for an extension of the supply of raw material and of the market for the finished product. The increasing demand for lumber in the United States following the rapid development of settlement in the Middle West and the growth of towns, as Chicago, stimulated the production of planks and boards. Decline in the size of trees and an increase in the number of saw logs and of smaller logs facilitated the introduction of modern sawmill techniques with gang saws and band saws adapted to mass production. More recently the decline in supplies of American lumber and the rise in price of lumber hastened production on a large scale. Machine industry became increasingly important to the lumber industry. Dependence on water transportation for the raw material and the finished product, and on water power for sawing (latterly on steam power), was responsible for concentration of the industry at the mouths of large rivers as in New Brunswick. Mills were located at points accessible to large vessels along the coast and the Great Lakes as on Georgian Bay and at important waterfalls on the large rivers of the interior – the Saguenay, the St Maurice, and the Ottawa. With the concentration, railways increased the supply of raw material as in the construction of the Canada and Atlantic Railway from Ottawa to Parry Sound by J.R. Booth.

The increasing demand for paper in the United States and the exhaustion of more available supplies of pulpwood were factors responsible for the development of the pulp and paper industry especially after 1900. Machine industry in lumber production provided a basis for the pulp and paper industry with its demands for large quantities of capital. Lumber interests were in control of substantial timber limits, of large sources of power, of skilled labour especially in the woods sections, and of capital. The decline of white pine and the existence of large quantities of spruce on the limits facilitated the shift to pulp and paper production. The migration of capital, skill, and technique from the United States hastened the movement. The forest industries concentrated about the mouths of the large rivers of the Atlantic and later the Pacific coast, the pulp and paper industry being dependent on those tributaries of the Atlantic and the Pacific which furnished abundant supplies of power.

CAPITALISM AND THE STAPLES

The lumber industry of eastern Canada was largely responsible directly and indirectly for the improvement of waterways and for the construction of railways prior to Confederation. Canal and railway construction was synonymous with heavy capital investment. Capital was obtained through private enterprise and substantial guarantees and aid from the imperial and colonial governments. Heavy expenditures involved the development of a strong centralized government in Canada. Canada's financial organization had been greatly strengthened through the strains incidental to the lumber industry. The crises in Great Britain and the United States in 1825–26, 1837, 1847, and 1857 had serious effects on construction industries and on the trade of a country interested in the export of lumber. The collapse of weaker banks in these periods contributed to the centralization of banking structure which became conspicuous in the period after Confederation. The fur trade and the lumber industry contributed the basic features essential to expansion after Confederation.

Capital investment in the transport improvement of eastern Canada brought serious problems. Immigration, settlement, and agriculture were hastened by the railroads but these were not adequate to support the overhead costs incidental to the heavy initial outlay in railroad construction and early railroad finance. Railway materials had been supplied by the rapidly expanding industry of Great Britain, and English financiers, as well as the Canadian government, were anxious to promote measures increasing traffic and reducing overhead. Sir Edward Watkin with the concurrence of the Duke of Newcastle proposed to extend the Grand Trunk to the west as a means of guaranteeing the successful operation of the road and as an escape from bankruptcy. Capital expenditures on canals had been largely responsible for the Act of Union and the additional expenditures on railways were largely responsible for Confederation and its provisions for the inclusion of the area westward to the Pacific.

Grand Trunk interests[13] in 1863 acquired control of the Hudson's Bay Company in London. This step was followed by Confederation in 1867, the sale of Rupert's Land to Canada in 1869, and finally the construction of the Canadian Pacific Railway. At one stroke Imperial interests and Grand Trunk interests favourable to the new technique replaced Hudson's Bay Company interests favourable to the fur trade. The large central organization in the fur trade facilitated the transfer and the organization of the new technique over a wide area. The fur trade and its personnel[14] continued to be fundamentally important. The fur trade had not only produced a centralized organization but it had produced a succession of fur traders who were typically self-reliant, energetic, and possessed of keen bargaining ability and high organizing capacity. D.A. Smith, later Lord Strathcona,[15] was not only an important official in the Hudson's Bay Company, trained in the school of the fur trade, but he was an influential force in the construction and management of the Canadian Pacific Railway which heralded the new industry. The relationship which existed with the opening of western Canada, in which important officials of the Hudson's Bay Company were prominent in the activities of the Bank of Montreal, of the Canadian Pacific Railway Company, and of the Dominion government, was not accidental.

The superposition of machine industry on an institutional background characteristic of the fur trade was effected with remarkably little disturbance. The rapidity with which the Industrial Revolution has swept across the North American continent was a result of the centralized organization which had paved the way for immediate growth. The economic organization of the fur trade was dependent on the Canadian Shield for a supply of furs and on the development of agriculture at convenient intervals to support the heavy cost of transportation. The economic organization of modern industrial Canada has depended on these agriculturally developed areas and more recently on the Canadian Shield. Agriculture and other lines of economic activity were started in suitable territory south of the Canadian Shield under the direction of the fur trade. The organization of the fur trade occasioned the organization of other lines of trade. The forwarding of supplies to the interior and the heavy one-way, in most cases upstream, traffic of the trade stimulated the development of trade in exports other than furs. The Hudson's Bay Company shifted from the fur trade to the retail and wholesale trade as the large number of their department stores in western Canada attests. The development of transportation organization in the recent gold rush from Hudson to Red Lake along lines already opened by the Hudson's Bay Company is evidence to the same effect. Early agriculture in Red River paved the way for the extensive production of wheat on the plains following the construction of the railroads. The parallel between wheat and furs is significant. Both involve a trunk line of transportation from Montreal to Winnipeg and feeders, in the case of the fur trade, to the north, and, in the case of wheat, to the south. Both were staples dependent on industrialized Europe for a market.

The construction of the Canadian Pacific Railway to the Pacific implied a marked advance in technology such as characterized the construction of transcontinental roads in the United States, notably cheap production of iron and steel and high explosives and standardized methods of railroad construction. The westward movement in the United States which had been speeded up with the steamboat and the railroad, eventually reached the northern part of the plains area. The stretch of level and agricultural territory in western Canada was settled during the period at which industrialism had gained momentum on the North American continent. The construction of a railway across the Canadian Shield added to the overhead costs incidental to earlier construction in eastern Canada. Rapid settlement of the prairies, rapid increase in the export of wheat and in imports of manufactured products, were encouraged as a means of increasing traffic. Wheat became a new staple export demanded to an increasing extent by the industrially deficient countries and produced, transported, and manufactured on a large scale only through the efficiency of modern industrialism.[16] With the addition of other transcontinental lines the main framework of the railway system was completed and Canada came under the full swing of modern capitalism with its primary problems of reducing overhead costs.

The problems of wheat incidental to overhead costs are of primary importance. Wheat is a plant grown in a north temperate land area. Its production has increased at a rapid rate over a long period; it affords a pronounced seasonal traffic especially as it is largely dependent on seasonal navigation; it has decided variations in yield and it occasions a pronounced one-way traffic. Wheat is shipped to the elevators on Lake Superior, to Georgian Bay ports, to Port Colborne and down the St Lawrence to Montreal, and to Buffalo and New York. Shipping in the Great Lakes is suspended during the closed season and overhead costs on grain boats and elevators contribute to the general problem of the railroads.[17] Numerous devices have been followed in solution of the problem. The tariff has been invoked for the encouragement of a return traffic from the industrial east. The rapid industrial growth of eastern Canada and the growth of its metropolitan centres hastened the development of mixed farming. Heavy one-way traffic of vessels calling for wheat at Montreal provides for cheap freights on imports of raw material. The production of power on the proposed St Lawrence waterway will hasten the tendency toward increased manufactures. The wheat flow has been reduced by increasing shipments through the all-year-open port of Vancouver and the Panama Canal. Industries of the Canadian Shield including lumbering, pulp and paper, mining, power development, and agriculture have been stimulated. The tourist traffic has been fostered. At the western extremity of the railroads in British Columbia overhead costs have been reduced through the rapid increase in the production of lumber, pulp and paper, minerals, agricultural products, canned salmon and halibut, and the export of wheat. The early rapid progress of the colony resulting from gold discoveries, and its feverish later development, were stabilized through railway construction, steamship connections with the Orient, and machine industry.

In the fundamental problem of reduction of overhead costs, mining has occupied an important position necessitating the importation of large quantities of mining supplies to the Canadian Shield and providing for constant operation without appreciable seasonal fluctuations. The location of the mines within relatively short distances from the railroads has been a factor minimizing the problem of overhead charges. The pulp and paper industry has also contributed in its constant export of the finished product and its constant demands for labour and supplies. The development of surplus power, chiefly a result of the pulp and paper industry, has stimulated manufactures as in the conspicuous example of Arvida on the Saguenay. The problems consequent to a decline in the mining towns and to the exhaustion of resources will in part be solved by a shift in the use of power in these industries to manufactures. The industries of the Canadian Shield represent a direct contribution to the reduction of overhead costs – a contribution which promises to become even more important with the opening of the Hudson Bay region. The Maritime Provinces have unfortunately been outside the main continental developments although they have contributed to the main task through exports of coal, iron and steel, brains, and brawn. It is quite probable that they will become more closely linked with the movements following the opening of the Hudson Bay route.

The relation of the government of Canada to general economic growth has been unique. The heavy expenditures on transport improvements, including railways and canals, have involved government grants, subsidies, and guarantees to an exceptional degree. The budget debates on the heavy debt of the Canadian National Railways are an annual reminder of the relation between transport and government. The Canadian government has been an important contributor to the prosperity of the Canadian Pacific Railway and to the maintenance of the Canadian National Railways. The unique character of this development has been largely a result of the sudden transfer of large areas tributary to the fur trade to the new industrialism. The British North America Act, like the Act of Union, has provided for a strong central government. The prairie provinces as producers of wheat were controlled from Montreal and Ottawa as they were controlled in the earlier period as producers of fur under the Northwest Company. With the United States, residuary powers[18] were left with the states whereas in Canada they remain with the federal government or rather with eastern Canada. Canada came under the sweep of the Industrial Revolution at one stroke whereas the westward movement of the United States was a gradual development. There are no transcontinental railroads controlled by one organization in the United States. In Canada transcontinental roads are distinct entities controlled in eastern Canada. Similarly in financial institutions the branch bank system with headquarters in the east has been typical of Canada but not of the United States. No such tendency toward unity of structure in institutions and toward centralized control as found in Canada can be observed in the United States. The Canadian government has a closer relation to economic activities than most governments. The trade in staples, which characterizes an economically weak country, to the highly industrialized areas of Europe and latterly the United States, and especially the fur trade, has been responsible for various peculiar tendencies in Canadian development. The maintenance of connections with Europe, at first with France and later with Great Britain, has been a result. The diversity of institutions which has attended this relationship has made for greater elasticity in organization and for greater tolerance among her peoples. This elasticity of institutions facilitated the development of the compromise which evolved in responsible government[19] and the British Empire. Having failed in her own colonial policy England was able to build up an empire in Canada on the remarkable success of French colonial policy. The fur trade permitted the extension of the combination of authority and independence across the northern half of the continent. Moreover, the business structure shifted from the elastic organization characteristic of the Northwest Company along the St Lawrence from the Atlantic to the Pacific, to the more permanent organization from Hudson Bay. The diversity of institutions has made possible the combination of government ownership and private enterprise which has been a further characteristic of Canadian development. Canada has remained fundamentally a product of Europe.

The importance of staple exports to Canadian economic development began with the fishing industry but more conspicuously on the continent with the fur trade. The present boundaries[20] were a result of the dominance of furs. The exploitation of lumber in the more accessible areas followed the decline of furs. The geographic unity of Canada which resulted from the fur trade became less noticeable with the introduction of capitalism and the railroads. Her economic development has been one of gradual adjustment of machine industry to the framework incidental to the fur trade. The sudden growth occasioned by the production of wheat and the development of subsequent staples in the Canadian Shield have been the result of machine industry. It is probable that these sudden changes will become less conspicuous as a result of a more closely knit unity and of the constant pressure of heavy overhead costs, and that Canadian growth will proceed on a more even keel. Revolutions in transport, which have such devastating effects on new countries producing raw materials, will become less disturbing even though full allowance is made for the effects of the Hudson Bay railway.

NOTES

1 C.R. Fay, *Great Britain: An Economic and Social Survey from Adam Smith to the Present Day* (London, 1928).

2 See Charles A. and Mary R. Beard, *The Rise of American Civilization* (New York, 1927).

3 See Mrs K.B. Jackson (as M.G. Reid), "The Quebec Fur-Traders and Western Policy, 1763–1774."

4 See W.E. Stevens, *The Northwest Fur Trade, 1763–1800* (Urbana, 1928).

5 Ibid.

6 See Marcel Giraud, *Le Métis canadien* (Paris, 1945).

7 F.W. Howay, "The Fur Trade in Northwestern Development."

8 Appendix G. For an advertisement of the Canada Banking Company, see R.M. Breckenridge, *The Canadian Banking System, 1817–1890* (Toronto, 1894), 18.

9 See *Centenary of the Bank of Montreal, 1817–1917* (Montreal, 1917).

10 See A.R.M. Lower, "A History of the Canadian Timber and Lumber Trade," (master's thesis, University of Toronto, 1923).

11 H.I. Cowan, *British Emigration to British North America, 1783–1837* (Toronto, 1928).

12 See J.L. McDougall, "The Welland Canal to 1841," (master's thesis, University of Toronto, 1923).

13 See Sir E.W. Watkin, *Canada and the States: Recollections, 1851* to *1886* (London, 1887). On the problems of the period, see R.G. Trotter, *Canadian Federation* (Toronto, 1924) and "British Finance and Confederation."

14 Professor O.D. Skleton, in a review of *A History of the Canadian Pacific Railway* (*Canadian Historical Review,* June 1923), has pointed out the neglect of personality in the development of the railroad. The importance of the fur trade would appear to strengthen his contention.

15 It is an interesting conjecture that the dramatic episode in the House of Commons in which Mr. D.A. Smith was in a position to oust the Macdonald administration from the government in 1873 was in part related to his connection with the fur trade. Rumours were current that Sir Hugh Allan was engaged in promoting a rival fur company to operate in the Northwest and his position as president of the Canadian Pacific Company to whom the charter for the construction of the transcontinental road had been given made this possibility unusually alarming. Mr. D.A. Smith as fur trade commissioner of the Hudson's Bay Company may have found his task in deciding the fate of the project during the debate on the Pacific scandal somewhat easier than is ordinarily supposed. See B. Wilson, *Life of Lord Strathcona and Mount Royal, 1820–1914* (Toronto, 1915), 337. For a most suggestive biography of Lord Strathcona, see John Macnaughton, *Lord Strathcona* (Toronto, 1926).

16 For an interesting description of the importance of machine industry in the United States, see T.B. Veblen, "Price of Wheat since 1867." Canada had the advantage of a young country in borrowing directly from the experience of the United States. The extent of this borrowing has been tremendous in all lines of economic growth but wheat may be cited as an example.

17 The importance of wheat to the overhead problems of the Canadian Pacific Railway has been described in H.A. Innis, *History of the Canadian Pacific Railway* (Toronto, 1923).

18 See O.D. Skelton, *The Life and Times of Sir A.T. Galt* (Toronto, 1920), especially on Galt's place in the Confederation movement; also W.B. Munro, *American Influences on Canadian Government* (Toronto, 1929), chap. 1, and W.P.M. Kennedy, "Canada: Law and Custom in the Canadian Constitution."

19 See Georges Vattier, *Essai sur la mentalité canadienne-française* (Paris, 1928).

20 David Thompson was probably recommended by Ogilvie to help in the boundary commission; see J.J. Bigsby, *The Shoe and Canoe* (London, 1850), vol. 1, chaps. 2 and 5. J.B. Tyrrell became interested in Thompson through his work on the Dominion survey. Tyrrell bridges the gap between the fur trade, settlement (survey), and mining, the most recent development. See biography of Tyrrell by W.J. Loudon, *A Canadian Geologist* (Toronto, 1930).

CHAPTER TWO

The Political Implications of Unused Capacity in Frontier Economies

The implications of economic development on the North American continent to the economic history of Europe have been traced in detail and in general and broad generalizations have emerged to describe their character. An attempt has been made to suggest effects of concentration on specific staple products in Canadian economic expansion, particularly in the confused period of shifts to new staples. Unused capacity involved in exploitation of staples had its effect in prolonging the dominance of one staple or in hastening its decline, and contributed powerfully to the disturbance of equilibrium in Canada and in Europe. The heavy outbound cargo from Europe characteristic of the fur trade restricted immigration, and the heavy return cargo characteristic of the timber trade hastened immigration. The role of unused capacity in determining the characteristics of economic development was weakened or strengthened by peculiarities of particular staples.

North America was settled by immigrants crossing from Asia by Bering Strait. The blocking of the polar ice by this narrow gateway left the Pacific Ocean to exercise a moderating influence on the climate of the western part of the continent and to favour the migration of population to Central and South America. Aboriginal culture in North America reflected a marked adaptation to geographical environment worked out over an extended period and consequently had a profound effect on the character of relations with Europe. Migration from Europe was halted by the accessibility of the Atlantic to the Polar Sea and by the inhospitable Greenland

From *Political Economy in the Modern State* (Ryerson, 1946), 218–28; first appeared as "The Political Implications of Unused Capacity."

ice cap and the Labrador current with the result that the first approach of the Norsemen met defeat. The Pacific had its moderating influence on the vast portion of northwestern America in Arctic Felix, Alaska, and the Mackenzie River, whereas the Atlantic lowered the temperature of the eastern part of North America in Arctic Deserta. In the second effort contact was made from Spain in the subtropical areas of Europe with the highly elaborated aboriginal culture in the tropical regions of Central America. Europeans attacked aboriginal culture in areas in which it was most highly developed and brought its abrupt collapse. Reserves of precious metals were looted in Mexico and Peru and the booty taken to Europe.

Concentration on imports of precious metals brought a sharp rise in prices in Spain and the shrivelling of industry and trade. Other countries seized the opportunity to meet the demands of Spain and to secure the advantages of high prices. England with "no treasure but by trade" elaborated mercantile policies designed to attract precious metals. The fishing industry was encouraged in the New World as a means of gaining access to the Spanish market and, after the Armada, England established a foothold on Newfoundland. Early in the seventeenth century she restricted imports of sugar and tobacco from Spain in order that she might produce them in her colonies in the New World and thus secure specie rather than these commodities. Control by Spain of the more densely populated aboriginal territory in the New World compelled English expansion in the Atlantic basin to depend on the migration of English labour in Newfoundland and the northern colonies and the movement of slaves from Africa to the plantation colonies in the south and the West Indies. Trade to India was supported by exports of specie obtained through trade from Spain.

France as a country adjacent to Spain found it unnecessary to establish a foothold in the New World to prepare dried fish for the Spanish market until the latter part of the sixteenth century when the Channel ports became more directly concerned. Finding the English entrenched along the Atlantic coast the French developed the industry in the Gulf of St Lawrence, notably on the Gaspé Peninsula and thus established a base for the expansion of the fur trade up the St Lawrence and its tributaries. As Spain was profoundly influenced by her contacts with the aborigines of Central and South America through the supplies of precious metals, France was profoundly influenced by her contacts with the hunting Indians of North America through supplies of furs. France and Spain were directly concerned with the effects of contrast between aboriginal and European cultures whereas England was indirectly concerned. In France and Spain the demands of the upper classes determined the character of relations with the aborigines of North America; in England the supply of English and African labour was significant.

The vast, angular-shaped area of Precambrian formation in North America had its implications for drainage systems in the large rivers which flowed along its edge, the St Lawrence and the Mackenzie, and in the difficult shorter rivers which crossed it in flowing to Hudson Bay. In this area flora and fauna moulded the culture of the hunting Indians while in the later formations to the south soil conditions and climate favoured the agricultural Indians, the Huron Iroquois of the upper St Lawrence, southern Ontario, and northern New York. The Dutch and later the English moved from the Atlantic seaboard south of the St Lawrence approach and traded with the agricultural Indians by the Hudson River. The French were dependent first on the agricultural villages in the Georgian Bay area but with their annihilation by the Iroquois they were compelled to develop the St Lawrence areas with their own agricultural base. The English, restrained by the agricultural Indians and the Appalachians, took full advantage of the possibilities of expansion in trade with the area bordering on the Atlantic. The enormous handicaps of seasonal migration in the more northernly areas drained by the St Lawrence hastened the discovery and occupation of the Mississippi across a narrow height of land. La Salle overcame the handicaps of navigation on the upper St Lawrence, established posts on the Great Lakes, and exploited the fur trade of the head waters of the Mississippi. The flood of lower-grade furs from this area was an important cause of the development of inflation.

Attraction of the French to the south led to the establishment of a post at the mouth of the Mississippi early in the eighteenth century and to competition for trade in the interior between New Orleans and Montreal. With the success of a trade unhampered by seasonal navigation the French under La Vérendrye turned from the St Lawrence to the northwest of Lake Superior. In this direction they came into more direct competition with the Hudson's Bay Company. In New France company control broke down particularly after the destruction of the Huron villages, and after 1663 the Crown intervened with active measures hastening settlement and trade. Traders such as Radisson and Grosseilliers persuaded the English Crown shortly after the Restoration to grant a monopoly to the Hudson's Bay Company in 1670. With little possibility of agricultural development in the vicinity of Hudson Bay, posts were established at the mouths of rivers draining into James Bay and

Hudson Bay and controlled effectively from London. The problem of smuggling peculiar to commodities of small bulk and high value proved insoluable on the St Lawrence but it was solved by the highly centralized control from London as apparently it was solved in the shipment of treasure from the New World to Spain.

The interest of France in the fur trade of the St Lawrence involved dependence on a commodity which fluctuated widely in supply as a result of competition from the Dutch, and later the English, from the Hudson River, and the English from Hudson Bay; of wars between Europeans and aborigines; of geographic characteristics evident especially in the size and peculiarities of drainage basins; and of the character of aboriginal cultural traits in relation to the demand for European goods. Fur was a commodity in which not only supply but also demand fluctuated widely. As a luxury product it was exposed to the fluctuations incidental to changes of fashion in the courts of Europe and to the immediate effects of prosperity and depression. The difficulties were shown in the organization of military defence of the St Lawrence and the consequent centralization of policy in institutions of state and church, and in the inability to control the price of furs, shown in the collapse of the financial structure after 1700 through inflation. The burdens imposed by the system of defence and centralization led to the emergence of the Hudson's Bay Company in Hudson Bay, and to the failure of the St Lawrence as a base for provisions for the fishing industry on the Atlantic coast and for sugar plantations of the French West Indies. An integrated Atlantic empire became impossible and the English colonies became a source of provisions for the French in both north temperate and tropical regions.

Collapse of the French Empire in North America brought repercussions which led to collapse of the first British Empire. The extension of the fishing industry from Newfoundland to New England early in the seventeenth century was followed by competition between the west country and the colonists. Adjustments within the British colonial system were hampered by the political influence of the west country and of the sugar planters in the British West Indies. The latter resisted trade between the coastal colonies and the French West Indies and supported the Treaty of Paris, which left Guadaloupe in the French Empire and added Canada to the British Empire, thereby accentuating the disturbance in the balance, between an extended market within the British Empire for molasses and rum in the fur trade, and a narrow supply from the British West Indies. The disappearance of Louisburg and the Sugar Act made smuggling more difficult and Imperial restrictions more burdensome. Anglo-American traders reorganized the fur trade of the St Lawrence after the fall of New France and rebuilt a defence system depending on London instead of Paris. The Northwest Company solved the problem of the French régime by combining agricultural development in Ontario, to support shipping on the Great Lakes with the handling of bulk cargo, with the canoe route of the Ottawa for return shipments of furs. It extended trade from the Atlantic to the Pacific.

The second British Empire was profoundly modified by the changes involved in the withdrawal of the American colonies and the collapse of the first Empire. Flexibility was substituted for the rigidity which brought collapse of the first Empire. The supremacy of Parliament was recognized, but Lord Mansfield in *Campbell v. Hall* (1774) strengthened the position of the Assembly in the colonies, and consequently in Nova Scotia. The Colonial Tax Repeal Act (1778) further strengthened Nova Scotia by providing for control over revenues secured from taxes collected under the colonial system. Nova Scotia was able to press more effectively for revisions of the colonial system to enable her to compete with the United States, particularly as the British West Indies had suffered a decline in influence with the abolition of slavery and the competition of sugar from the East Indies. Moreover, the support of Nova Scotia brought an increase in population which enabled Newfoundland to escape the domination of the west country. On the St Lawrence, Parliament through the Quebec Act of 1774 denied an assembly to the colony and it was not until 1791 that assemblies were granted to Upper and Lower Canada. The merchants lost control of the fur trade to the northwest after the amalgamation of the Northwest Company and the Hudson's Bay Company in 1821, but the effects of the loss were offset, and along with New Brunswick the regions gained, as a result of the substantial imperial preference given to the timber trade. The struggle of Wilkes and others in securing freedom to report the proceedings of Parliament opened the door to reform and the destruction of control by vested interests. With the destruction of vested interests representing fish, sugar, timber, and ships in the colonial system the way was clear to free trade and responsible government. Whereas New England was hampered by the influence of vested interests operating from the west country in Newfoundland, and from the West Indies, Nova Scotia was able to take an active part in the defeat of those vested interests.

British North America included the French in the lower St Lawrence region who had lost their contacts with the mother country except through the Church, population which had migrated from

New England to Nova Scotia after 1713, and the Loyalists who migrated from the United States and were settled in pockets from the Atlantic seaboard to the Great Lakes. The region contained groups with the pre-revolutionary background of France steeped in the traditions of the Church in Quebec and with the loyalist traditions of the state, particularly in New Brunswick and Ontario which escaped the influence of revolutionary tradition in the United States. British North America was a young country with the oldest pre-revolutionary ideas of Europe. Expulsion of the Loyalists from the United States weakened the centralizing tendencies of the colonies and contributed to the trend which culminated in the Civil War, and, reinforced by the British military tradition, strengthened the centralizing tendencies in British North America. The military system with its division of British North America into separate colonies dominated by military power restricted the growth of responsible government. Construction of the Rideau Canal as a military route delayed the construction of other canals.

The subordination of the executive to the Assembly which characterized responsible government involved control over revenues which meant control over funds received from lands. Newfoundland with control over land and trade continuously and effectively pressed for exclusion of French, English, Canadian, and American fishermen. Responsible government was interpreted as implying "that the consent of the Community of Newfoundland is regarded by Her Majesty's government as the essential preliminary to any modification of their territorial and maritime rights."[1] From this interpretation the legislature not only waged an effective battle against the French but also resisted efforts on the part of Canada to secure control of her natural resources in proposals for admission to Confederation. Nova Scotia insisted on her rights to the extent of compelling the United States and Great Britain to concede the Reciprocity Treaty from 1854 to 1866, and of persuading Canada to adopt a permissive system, and under Confederation a compulsory system, to exclude American fishermen to the point that the United States conceded the Washington Treaty. With control over natural resources she was able to break the monopoly of the General Mining Association over coal in 1858. Confederation of the colonies left the control over land with the provinces but placed the control over the coastal fisheries under the federal government.

Competition in western Canada from the French and later the Anglo-American merchants and the North West Company from the St Lawrence with the Hudson's Bay Company from Hudson Bay assumed an intense form, characteristic of duopoly, and led to monopoly in 1821. The vast area under the control of the Hudson's Bay Company after that date included land owned by virtue of the charter granted in 1670 or that drained by rivers flowing into Hudson Bay, and regions beyond to the Pacific coast under a licence for twenty-one years. Under a monopoly, a large surplus population was moved from numerous posts to Red River and to Canada and attracted fresh competition from Americans which weakened the company on the Columbia and on the Pacific coast. The Oregon boundary was finally settled at the 49th parallel in 1846. Vancouver Island was granted to the Hudson's Bay Company in 1849, and, on the insistence of the Imperial government, an assembly was elected in 1856. On the mainland the licensing arrangement was brought to an end with the gold rush to the Fraser River and in 1858 a colony was organized. An area which had been systematically organized in defence against settlers from the United States was suddenly overrun by large numbers of people pushing northward in the search for gold. In the following year Vancouver Island was repurchased by the Imperial government. In 1864 a council was set up in British Columbia, but an assembly was refused. The character of the gold rush led Newcastle to write that "the fixed population ... is not yet large enough to form a sufficient and sound basis of representation, while the migratory element exceeds the fixed and the Indian far outnumbers both together."[2] In 1866 the government of the mainland was united with that of Vancouver Island and the Assembly of the latter disbanded. Problems of finance which arose from the sudden development of a community dependent on placer gold hastened the adoption of an arrangement involving the construction of a transcontinental railway and the inclusion of British Columbia in the federal structure. Immediately before the united colony joined Confederation in 1871 an assembly was elected and responsible government was achieved. The natural resources were left in the hands of the province.

The discovery of gold speeded up the construction of a transcontinental railway and in turn had important effects for the prairie region across which it had to be built. The territory under control of the Hudson's Bay Company by virtue of charter was organized, more effectively than that under the licensing arrangement, against encroachment from the St Lawrence across the Canadian shield but was eventually sold to the Dominion of Canada. The resistance of the Company and the delay in admitting the region to Confederation involved the defeat of efforts to secure responsible government in its full implications. Manitoba became a province but gave up land "for the purposes of the Dominion." The boundaries of Manitoba, Saskatchewan, and Alberta were determined along astronomical lines and the provinces of Alberta and Saskatchewan were created in 1905, again without control over land. The "purposes of the Dominion" having been served, and the lands largely alienated for the construction of transcontinental railways, the natural resources were given to the Prairie Provinces in 1930. Attempts to secure compensation for misuse of the lands by the Dominion have not been completely successful.

With the exception of Nova Scotia, assemblies emerged at a late stage in the second Empire and responsible government was slow to mature as a result of slowness in the adoption of parliamentary reform and of the geographic background with its emphasis on waterways and on exports of staples and the creation of vested interests centring about them. The organizations of defence in the French régime on the St Lawrence in opposition to English trade from the south and the north implied a legacy of defence in the English régime, especially after the American Revolution. Occupation of New France by conquest and the insistence on defence delayed the introduction of assemblies on the St Lawrence until 1791 and of responsible government until 1849. The organization of the Hudson's Bay Company for defence against competition from Canada and the United States in western Canada paralleled the organization for defence on the St Lawrence. Entrenchment of the Hudson's Bay Company in the fur trade and the sudden changes wrought by the gold rushes on the Pacific coast contributed to the indefinite delay of responsible government in the Prairie Provinces.

The bitterness of the struggle for responsible government on the St. Lawrence had repercussions in western Canada. The provinces which took the place of the colonies in Confederation continued with such important characteristics of responsible government as control of their natural resources. The federal government was concerned primarily with customs for revenue to support transportation improvements in railways and canals, to pay subsidies largely on a population basis and thus avoid controversies over religion, and to pay interest on debts incurred chiefly in building railways and canals and taken over from the provinces. The exclusion of the federal government from control over natural resources in eastern Canada and the dominance of the Hudson's Bay Company over a long period checked the growth of assemblies and the achievement of complete responsible government in the prairie region.[3] Land was reserved by the Dominion for the support of railway construction to carry out the agreement with British Columbia.

The use of lands "for purposes of the Dominion" was accompanied by control over competition from the United States in the tariff and in restrictions on the construction of railways to the

American boundary. Location of the Canadian Pacific Railway along the southern route left vast areas to the north to be occupied. The recovery following the long depression from the seventies to the nineties was accompanied by important new discoveries of placer beds on the Klondike in the Yukon region. As the Canadian Pacific followed the gold rushes in British Columbia, the Canadian Northern and the Grand Trunk Pacific followed the gold rushes of the Yukon in the territory north of the Canadian Pacific, but exhaustion of land led to dependence on bonds for their construction. The effectiveness with which the Dominion realized its "purposes" was evident in the enormous increase in the production of wheat in the period from 1900 to 1929. The problems which have followed concentration on wheat have been evident in western and eastern Canada in the depression and the war. Deprived of control over natural resources, the attention of the West was concentrated on federal problems such as railway rates, grain marketing, prices, tariffs, and debts.

With control over natural resources under the British North America Act and Privy Council decisions, the province of Ontario began an active policy of development by imposing embargoes on logs and pulpwood cut on Crown lands, by supporting public ownership of hydro-electric power, and by constructing the Temiskaming and Northern Ontario Railway. Cobalt, Porcupine, and Kirkland Lake poured out riches of gold and silver and hydro-electric power sites were developed. The policies were less effective in the pulp and paper industry and it was not until the demand of newspapers in the United States for cheap newsprint brought a reduction of the American tariff, and the province of Quebec and other provinces imposed an embargo after 1910, that the pulp and paper industry migrated with startling rapidity to Quebec, Ontario, and British Columbia and later to New Brunswick, Manitoba, and Nova Scotia. The problems of wheat which characterized the policies of the Dominion in fulfilment of its "purposes" in the Prairie Provinces after 1929 were accompanied by the problems of newsprint which characterized the policies of the provinces with control over their natural resources. Gold mining in Quebec, Ontario, and Manitoba offset in part the effects of the depression on wheat and newsprint. Fish, minerals, lumber, pulp and paper, hydro-electric power, and the favourable effects of the Panama Canal softened the blow of the depression in British Columbia.

In areas in which responsible government had not been achieved because of control over natural resources by the Dominion government, the position of provincial administrations reflected the maladjustment of political machinery. It has become obvious that the constitutional arrangements imposed too heavy a burden on the Prairie Provinces in that numerous makeshifts have been arranged by which the Dominion has attempted to relieve the burden and that the political atmosphere has become disturbed and confused. Manitoba, Alberta, and Saskatchewan have shown signs of achieving political maturity. In the area in which responsible government was achieved and control over natural resources was acquired at the expense of exclusion from Confederation, the problem of finance has been scarcely less acute. Newfoundland abandoned responsible government and accepted Commission government. Absence of federal control in Newfoundland has been as disastrous as excessive federal control in the Prairie Provinces.

The first Empire was concerned with the significance of land and the second Empire with the significance of trade. Gradually land has assumed increasing importance in the second Empire and the Statute of Westminster coincided closely with the return of natural resources to the Prairie Provinces. The Canadian federal structure has assumed a closer parallel to that of the United States as the feudalization of the second Empire approached the feudal character of the first. The dominance of trade in the second Empire and concentration on staples imposed heavy burdens on Great Britain until through parliamentary reform she was able to free herself from the control of vested interests in a policy of free trade and in the granting of responsible government to the colonies. The problems of trade in staples evaded by Great Britain became more acute for the colonies. But the colonies resorted to feudalism as the mother country emphasized trade. They began to concentrate on machinery designed to meet internal problems, ranging through Confederation to protection and construction of transcontinental railways. The political machinery was closely adapted to meet the severe economic demands of dependence on staples with their sharp changes in prices and income. Governmental devices stabilized in part and accentuated in part the fluctuations. Support to improvements in transportation was achieved with low interest rates secured by the government, and low costs of transportation provided a tremendous impetus with an increase in prices. The disturbances incidental to dependence on staples, including the essential importance of governmental support, created difficulties within Canada and without. Concentration on large-scale production of single staples involved sharp fluctuations in output which bombarded with violent intensity the international economy, to mention specifically the case of wheat. The study of the Canadian economy becomes of crucial significance to an understanding of cyclical and secular disturbances not only within Canada but without. In a sense the economies of frontier countries are storm centres to the modern international economy.

NOTES

1 Henry Labouchere in a dispatch of 26 March 1857.
2 Cited in A.S. Morton, *A History of the Canadian West to 1870–1* (Toronto, n.d.), 785.
3 See Chester Martin, *"Dominion Lands" Policy* (Toronto, 1938); also Morton, *A History of the Canadian West to 1870–1*, 914ff.

CHAPTER THREE

Decentralization and Democracy in the Atlantic Basin

This paper is concerned with the changes in types of power in the Atlantic basin following the discovery of America. Direct control from Europe under the French, Dutch, Spanish, and British empires has gradually changed with emergence of independent states in North and South America and of the British Commonwealth of Nations. In Canada European institutions were more strongly entrenched and feudalism continued to exercise a powerful influence, latterly, for example, in the control of natural resources by the provinces. The provinces have become landlords with great disparity of wealth varying with federal policy, technological change, and provincial policy. The changing disparity enhances the complexity of democracy in Canada.

The advantages of the British Empire in its struggle with the French Empire were in part a result of the implications of imperfect competition between drainage basins in the interior as contrasted with more effective competition between the maritime regions of the Atlantic seaboard. In the latter region, imperfect competition was reflected in the slowness with which adjustments were made between the west country in England, Newfoundland, Nova Scotia, and New England. In the interior of the continent competition was less effective in the struggle between traders of various nationalities or of the same nationality as it was carried on between drainage basins. Trunk rivers and tributaries with low heights of land between drainage basins facilitated the tapping of vast regions. The relative

---

From *Canadian Journal of Economics and Political Science* 9 (1943): 317–30; reprinted in *Political Economy in the Modern State* (Ryerson, 1946), 236–50; first appeared as "Decentralization and Democracy."

effectiveness of competition on the seaboard and in the interior of the continent had implications for the struggle of empire.

In the sixteenth century the French Empire was concerned with the extension of the fishing industry in the New World as a means of strengthening self-sufficiency with access to new supplies of food and to an industry promising naval strength. The English Empire was concerned with the acquisition of specie flowing from the New World of Spain. It concentrated on the dry fishery in Newfoundland and exports to Spain. By the end of the century the French were also influenced by the high prices of Spain only to find that the more accessible sites for the prosecution of the dry fishery were occupied by the English and that it was necessary to penetrate to more distant sites such as the Gaspé region in the Gulf of St Lawrence.

The interest of France in development of the fishery in relation to her own needs and of England in trade with Spain involved the delay of a century in penetrating the northern part of the continent. In the seventeenth century, France, after comparative failure on the seaboard, established a foothold at Quebec in the protected region of the St Lawrence, and built up connections with the Hurons of Georgian Bay by the Ottawa Route. The Hudson River was occupied by the Dutch after Hudson's voyage of 1609, and the Iroquois, driven from the St Lawrence by the Hunting Indians and the French, received support for vigorous counter-attacks. Fortifications were extended up the St Lawrence to Three Rivers, Montreal, and the mouth of the Richelieu, and trade with the agricultural Indians of the Georgian Bay region by the Ottawa route was protected. In turn the Iroquois were pressed to the interior and proceeded across the east end of Lake Ontario and north to destroy the Huron villages in 1648–9. Concentration on military activity and the restrictions on the fur trade under company control necessitated governmental intervention. The fur trade involved heavy outbound cargo and a light return cargo with the result that settlement was discouraged and that vigorous efforts by the government to encourage immigration were made. The difficulties of the fur trade stimulated the interest of traders such as Radisson and Groseilliers in the alternative outlet by Hudson Bay. The necessity of concentrating on the St Lawrence precluded the development of the route and Radisson and Groseilliers deserted to the English to assist in the formation of the Hudson's Bay Company in 1670.

The active interest of the French government in the St Lawrence was accompanied by a determined effort to build up an integrated Atlantic empire. Placentia in Newfoundland was established as a basis of the fishing industry in 1662 and attempts were made to link the St Lawrence as an agricultural base to the sugar plantations of the West Indies. The effort failed because of the increasing demands of the St Lawrence. Energy was dissipated in efforts to check competition by the destruction of English posts in Hudson Bay and by the construction of forts along the Great Lakes. Destruction of the Huron villages compelled the French to build up their own trading organization to the interior. Dissipation of resources was evident in the abandonment of Fort Frontenac in 1689 with the capture of posts on James Bay, and its re-establishment in 1694 after their loss in 1693. The uncertainty of returns from furs which followed the success or failure of military and naval activity and the changes in fashion combined, with the increasing debt incidental to expansion in the interior, to produce inflation and the disorganization of economic life in the St Lawrence. The French West Indies were compelled to rely on the English colonies and on Ireland for supplies and provisions. In the Treaty of Utrecht in 1713 France recognized defeat in retreat from Nova Scotia and Hudson Bay.

Penetration of the St Lawrence by the French involved restriction of the English to the regions along the Atlantic seaboard. In the seventeenth century, with the exception of the conquest of Quebec from 1629 to 1632, and of Nova Scotia for a short period, England confined her activities to the establishment of colonies along the southern seaboard and in the West Indies. In 1664 New York was captured from the Dutch. Mercantilist policy involved not only the export of dried fish from Newfoundland as a means of securing specie from Spain but also the production of tropical products in the British West Indies as a means of restricting the purchase of those commodities from Spain. The resources of the Atlantic seaboard enabled the colonies to provide supplies for the British West Indies and even for the French West Indies. The limitations of French integration imposed strains on an inclusive British Empire. Attempts of the west country to maintain control over Newfoundland and to check settlement facilitated the migration of labour from Newfoundland to New England. On the other hand, the increase in the production of agricultural commodities, lumber, and fish in the English colonies and restrictions on exports to the French West Indies lowered the price of exports to Newfoundland and supported the growth of settlement in spite of west country hostility. Concentration on the Atlantic seaboard emphasized the importance of naval strength and encouragement of the fishing industry and carrying trade as nurseries for seamen and reserves for ships. The construction of military fortifications was discouraged and the English Empire was never cursed with the problem of dependence on a staple commodity such as fur and the heavy burden of fixed charges incidental to the construction of forts in the interior, and the consequent devastating effects of inflation.

With retreat from Hudson Bay, Nova Scotia, and Newfoundland after 1713, France consolidated her position at Louisburg on Cape Breton and renewed efforts were made to rebuild an empire on a more solid base. But the basic problems of integration were accentuated rather than alleviated. The establishment of a settlement on Cape Breton was handicapped by the limited resources of the area, by the limitations of the St Lawrence region, and by the difficulty of attracting Acadians from the dyked lands of the Bay of Fundy to the forest lands of Prince Edward Island or of encouraging them to raise grain, rather than live-stock to be smuggled from the Bay of Fundy. The French West Indies were unable to rely on French supplies and provisions and a smuggling trade with the English colonies increased in the West Indies and in Cape Breton. Cheap supplies and provisions from the English colonies were exchanged for rum through both channels. French policy favoured consumption of French brandy in New France, and French West Indies rum was sold to the English.

The St Lawrence was handicapped by the loss of Hudson Bay, which compelled French traders to extend their trade from Lake Superior to Lake Winnipeg and the Saskatchewan under La Vérendrye and his successors. The long and difficult voyage around the arc of a circle along the edge of the Hudson Bay drainage basin, in competition with the Hudson's Bay Company on Hudson Bay at the centre of the circle, imposed heavy burdens on the colony. Moreover, the development of trade from the mouth of the Mississippi meant encroachments on the trade of the St Lawrence. Fortifications were extended along the Great Lakes to check competition from the English and the Iroquois from Albany and Oswego. In spite of efforts to encourage the iron industry and shipbuilding on the St Lawrence, France was unable to develop an agricultural and an industrial base to meet the demands of Louisburg and the West Indies and of Saskatchewan and the Great Lakes. Inflation again broke out and the Seven Years' War brought the collapse of Louisburg, Quebec, and the French Empire in North America.

Again the inability of the French to develop an integrated Empire had implications for the British Empire. Expansion of production and trade in the English colonies involved an increase in the smuggling trade to the French West Indies. Continued encouragement to the fishing industry and to shipbuilding involved a clash with British West Indies planters anxious to check trade with the

French West Indies. The influence of the planters in Great Britain secured the Molasses Act of 1733, which was designed with other legislation to create a monopoly market in Great Britain and to check the trade of surplus tropical products of the French West Indies with the surplus products of the temperate English colonies of the seaboard. The legislation stimulated the smuggling trade through Louisburg and enhanced the interest in Nova Scotia and Newfoundland. Settlement continued to increase in Newfoundland and the influence of the west country to decline. With the defeat of France it was expected that the markets of the St Lawrence would be opened to the products of the British West Indies and that more rigid control would be exercised over the trade between the English colonies and the French West Indies.

Destruction of the French Empire profoundly disturbed the equilibrium of the Atlantic and was followed by the collapse of the British Empire and the loss of the colonies. The Treaty of Versailles recognizing the independence of the United States followed the Treaty of Paris in two decades. Anglo-American traders pushed rapidly into the territory vacated by the French and quickly occupied the region northwest of the Saskatchewan. The English colonies extended the fishing industry to the Gulf of St Lawrence and participated, in spite of protests from the British West Indies, in smuggling to the French West Indies, which were no longer able to draw even meagre support from the St Lawrence. Conflicts emerged between the colonies and the British West Indies, between the colonies and Newfoundland, which under west country influence attempted to check the colonial fishery, and among the colonies themselves, since traders from Albany dependent on the Iroquois middleman organization demanded restriction of trade to the posts, and the St Lawrence region and traders from Quebec and Montreal, following the organization built up by the French after the destruction of the Huron middlemen, insisted on extending the trade among the Indians. Pallisser's Act in 1775 encouraged the Newfoundland fishery at the expense of the colonies, and the Quebec Act of 1774 enlarged the province of Quebec to extend the control of the St Lawrence at the expense of Albany. The Hudson's Bay Company in the year of the Quebec Act made its first important move inland in the construction of Cumberland House to check the encroachments of the Anglo-American traders. The complexity of an empire including the West Indies and Newfoundland with strong influential groups in England, the colonies including Nova Scotia in possession of a powerful tradition of assemblies, a conquered territory in Quebec, and a charter company in Hudson Bay, imposed too severe a strain on the constitutional resources of Great Britain, taxed by the addition of Scotland in 1707 and the corruption of Parliament under Walpole and George III. Removal of colonial fears of a major hostile power after the Seven Years' War brought disaster.

The fall of New France and the French Empire had been a result of the inadequacies of control by France with a continental background, and the dependence on military participation and consequent rigidities. The fall of the British Empire was a result of the inadequacies of control by England with a maritime background and her dependence on naval strength and consequent elasticities.

After the Revolution United Empire Loyalists followed earlier New England immigrants into Nova Scotia, and migrated to the province of Quebec in the Eastern Townships and north of the Great Lakes. The Maritimes were divided into separate colonies, Nova Scotia, New Brunswick, Prince Edward Island, and Cape Breton. Nova Scotia made a deliberate effort to establish a place for itself within the British Empire comparable to that formerly occupied by New England and the American colonies. The influence of the West Indies was weakened, particularly with legislation against slavery, as the influence of Nova Scotia became stronger. The latter opposed the re-establishment of trade between the West Indies and the region which had now become the United States, and attempted to develop her own resources, and to build up an *entrepôt* trade from the St Lawrence and from New England. Protests from the West Indies eventually led to the opening of trade with the United States. As the French had failed to build up an integrated trade between the St Lawrence, the Maritimes, and the West Indies, so Nova Scotia failed. The difficulties of Nova Scotia in relation to the West Indies were in part a result of the increase in population in Newfoundland. The American Revolution and wars between England and France weakened the control of the west country and hastened the growth of a resident population. The demands of an increasing population attracted trade from Nova Scotia and weakened her possibilities in relation to West Indies trade. The aggressive influence of Nova Scotia in the second Empire became more effective in contrast with the West Indies in the first Empire. Efforts to prevent the loss of the American colonies by such measures as the Colonial Tax Repeal Act of 1778 were exploited by Nova Scotia through an Assembly inherited from the old Empire. Whereas Massachusetts was willing to recognize the Crown but refused to recognize the supremacy of the British Parliament, Nova Scotia accepted supremacy and secured modifications in Imperial legislation enabling her to strengthen her autonomy. The dependence of Nova Scotia on the fishery, shipping, and trade was in contrast with the limited possibilities of the St Lawrence.

Anglo-American traders driven to the Northwest by the extension of immigration to the interior of the United States developed an effective instrument for the command of increasing capital which came with increasing distances. The Northwest Company emerged with the support of rum from the West Indies restricted in the American market after the Revolution, the development of shipping on the Great Lakes, the organization of food supplies, and extension to the Athabaska and the Mackenzie rivers. Organization of the American fur trade and the Jay Treaty compelled Anglo-American traders to withdraw and to penetrate the Northwest as the XY Company. Intensive competition brought amalgamation in 1804. To offset the effects of organization of trade from the St Lawrence, the Hudson's Bay Company was compelled to reorganize a structure developed in relation to the fur trade on Hudson Bay. The organization of a base for supplies of food and a determination to exact recognition of the ownership of land drained by rivers flowing into Hudson Bay provided the background for the Selkirk settlement. As on the St Lawrence the French government had been compelled to intervene to prevent retardation of settlement by companies, so on Hudson Bay competition from St Lawrence traders compelled the Hudson's Bay Company to provide a base for settlement in the Selkirk scheme. The Northwest Company extended its organization across the continent to the mouth of the Columbia River but was handicapped in the development of Pacific trade. New England, restricted after the Revolution in trade with the British Empire, became active in South America and the Pacific, and built up extensive connections with the Sandwich Islands and the Orient. While the attempt of the Northwest Company to build up trade on the Pacific failed because of the inability of Nova Scotia to build up a trading organization in relation to the St Lawrence, the West Indies, and Newfoundland, but succeeded in developing a transcontinental organization, American traders succeeded in the Pacific regions but failed to develop a transcontinental organization by the Missouri across the plains to the Columbia. The Hunting Indians of the north supported the Northwest Company but the Plains Indians of the south restricted American organization. Astoria was taken over by the Northwest Company but arrangements were made to trade with the Orient through Boston firms to avoid the monopoly of the East India Company. Limitations of the Northwest Company on the Pacific contributed to its difficulties in the competitive struggle with the Hudson's Bay Company. In 1821 the two companies were amalgamated and Hudson Bay became the dominant route with the elimination of the St Lawrence.

As in the French Empire, the St Lawrence was inadequate as a continental base to support Nova Scotia in relation to the West Indies and Newfoundland, and the fur trade to the interior. In the French Empire brandy was sold in the St Lawrence at the expense of West Indies rum, and in the British Empire settlement was followed by grain production and concentration on whiskey rather than rum. With supremacy of Hudson Bay, settlers on the lower St Lawrence and in the Great Lakes region turned to the timber trade which emerged through the efforts of Great Britain to build up an alternative supply during the Napoleonic Wars. The demands of United Empire Loyalists in the Great Lakes region and of traders in the lower St Lawrence and the importance of military strength led to the adoption of the Constitutional Act of 1791 and the division of the province of Quebec into Upper and Lower Canada. The resources of Upper and Lower Canada were in the land and of Nova Scotia in the sea. Nova Scotia developed her autonomy in relation to the trade of the Empire whereas Upper and Lower Canada were concerned with the occupation of land by settlers and the exploitation of the forests. The Crown's control over land strengthened the position of the executive, and the Assembly, without the long traditions of Nova Scotia, was less effective in its struggle for responsible government. Military control and settlement in the St Lawrence, in the British Empire as in the French Empire, strengthened the interest of Europe in finance, while naval control and trade in the Maritimes facilitated the growth of independence. Rebellion broke out in Upper and Lower Canada but Nova Scotia achieved responsible government with peace.

The Reform Act in Great Britain hastened the destruction of shelters which protected the vested interests of staple trades with long-term credit, such as sugar, thus contributing to the break-up of the second Empire. The emergence of free trade compelled realignments in the St Lawrence essential to the lowering of transportation costs to offset the loss of protection. Canals were built, the provinces of Upper and Lower Canada were united, and credit was provided to strengthen a transport system to compete with the alternative New York route. Canadian tariffs replaced the tariffs of the colonial system. In Nova Scotia, following defeat in checking trade between the United States and the West Indies, determined efforts were made to hamper the American fishery. Success was partially achieved in the opening of American markets in the Reciprocity Treaty. In the St Lawrence and in Nova Scotia advantages were gained in

American trade during the difficult period of compromise between North and South in the United States. With the success of the North in the Civil War, the Reciprocity Treaty came to an end and American tariffs were imposed. New schemes were essential on the St Lawrence to strengthen its position with the increasing difficulties of the American market and in Nova Scotia to compel a reopening of the market for fish.

In the territory under the control of the Hudson's Bay Company after 1821, monopoly was strengthened and barricades were built along the Precambrian formation against competition from the south. Signs of strain were evident in the most distant area, in the retreat from the Columbia to Victoria on Vancouver Island after the settlement of the Oregon boundary dispute. In the Red River free trade was conceded by the Hudson's Bay Company to traders from the Mississippi drainage basin to the south in 1849. A major breach in the system came with the discovery of placer gold in the Fraser River in 1857 and the rapid occupation of the Pacific coast region. The monopoly of the Hudson's Bay Company with that of the East India Company came under attack, and colonial government emerged in British Columbia and Vancouver Island. The entrenchment of the Hudson's Bay Company in the territory drained by rivers flowing into Hudson Bay, held by it under the charter from the Crown, yielded only after the joining of the provinces of Ontario, Quebec, Nova Scotia, and New Brunswick in Confederation, and the demand for a solution of their transportation problems by extension of the trunk railway of the St Lawrence. The policy of imperial defence, which created divisions in British North America after the Treaty of Versailles, successful in the War of 1812, was reversed in the interests of unity and centralization after the Civil War. The policy of division and defence after 1783 left a legacy of control by the provinces over their natural resources in the federal structure which checked the trend toward centralization.

In Newfoundland, revival of the French fishery after the Napoleonic Wars was accompanied by determined efforts to hamper it comparable to those of Nova Scotia against the United States. The struggle for responsible government brought control over natural resources and a gradual pressure for exclusion of the French by such measures as were involved in the bait legislation and later in the removal of the French from the French shore, and for exclusion of American, Nova Scotian, Canadian, and English traders and fishermen. The aggressiveness of Canada, supported by Nova Scotia, especially after the abrogation of the Washington Treaty, embittered Newfoundland and made federation impossible.

Throughout the history of northern North America the Maritimes, and especially Nova Scotia, had served as an unsuccessful base of empires. In the French régime, first in Nova Scotia and after 1713 in Cape Breton, attempts to link the St Lawrence and the French West Indies failed because of the high prices of the St Lawrence incidental to the drain of westward expansion in pursuit of the fur trade. In the British régime, Nova Scotia was again unable to take the place of the English colonies in relation to the British West Indies, but she effectively developed a position in the British Empire and assumed an aggressiveness which enabled her to enlist the support of Canada against encroachment from the United States. The price of the enlistment was recognition of Canadian tariffs and acceptance of the high price system of the St Lawrence. Higgling was evident in the free port policy in the Gaspé region and after Confederation in construction of the Intercolonial Railway and its extension to Sydney, tariffs and subventions on coal and iron, upward revisions of federal subsidies, and the Maritime Freight Rates Act.

Confederation emerged in relation to the problems of the St Lawrence and the Maritimes and of the Pacific. The resistance of the Hudson's Bay Company, weakened in Red River and on the Pacific, yielded under pressure from the Atlantic and the Pacific. But it was felt in the location of the Canadian Pacific Railway along the southern border, its extension through British Columbia by the Crow's Nest Pass line, and its monopolistic measures. The long delay which accompanied the monopoly position of the Hudson's Bay Company was followed by rapid occupation of the prairie regions. Disequilibrium as a result of resistance of the Hudson's Bay Company, characterized by large-scale migration from the St Lawrence and the Maritimes to the United States and by widening of the gauge of the Grand Trunk Railway to link up with the American system at Chicago, was followed by disequilibrium with the sudden opening of the prairies by construction of a transcontinental railway and completion of the St Lawrence canals to fourteen feet. The long depression was followed by the great boom. The monopoly position of the Canadian Pacific Railway, evident in a favourable capital structure and large dividends, was followed by the pouring in of capital into the region north of the Canadian Pacific Railway, and in the construction of two additional transcontinental railways by the Yellowhead Pass to Vancouver and Prince Rupert. These developments followed support from newly created credit instruments in the Prairie Provinces and from the interest of the provinces of Ontario and Quebec in the development of natural resources especially after the Privy Council decision of 1898. The Temiskaming and Northern Ontario Railway, expansion of the mining industry in Cobalt, Porcupine, and Kirkland Lake, exploitation of hydro-electric power, particularly in the Ontario Hydro-Electric Power Commission, fostered by protection of Nova Scotian coal, and construction of pulp and paper plants through the active intervention first of Ontario and later Quebec and the other provinces, accompanied the extension of transcontinental systems east from Winnipeg.

Rapid occupation of the prairie regions from the late 1890s to about 1930 accompanied the construction of railways and canals to the Atlantic seaboard and after the war the completion of the Panama Canal. As a result of the latter, freight rates were lowered in the areas with high freight rates to the St Lawrence and the resources of Alberta and British Columbia were developed with striking rapidity. The St Lawrence was strengthened in its struggle with the Pacific by deepening of the Welland Canal.

The depression coincided with the decline in influence of major technical developments in transportation. Regionalization became more pronounced with competition between the Panama and the St Lawrence and the development of natural resources, hydro-electric power, pulp and paper, and minerals, particularly in the provinces of Ontario and Quebec. Provincialism has paralleled the new industrialism. The increasing demands of the United States with expanding population and declining resources shifted the direction of trade from an east-west to a north-south route particularly in regions other than the Prairie Provinces.

Regionalization has brought complex problems for an economy developed in relation to the St Lawrence. It has been strengthened by the growth of automotive transport and roads in competition with coal and steam and water and rail. Confederation as an instrument of steam power has been compelled to face the implications of hydro-electric power and petroleum. Confederation has been to an important extent the creation of private enterprise represented by the Canadian Pacific Railway, supported by the federal government in a tariff and railway rate policy, and in the Canadian National Railways. The direct interest of the federal government in the Canadian National Railways cannot be separated from an indirect interest in the Canadian Pacific Railway. The burden of a political structure developed in relation to exploitation of the prairie regions has rested to an important extent on those regions and adjustment involves a struggle between regions which have become concerned with new types of power and the American rather than the European market, and regions which have suffered directly from the difficulties of the European market and costs of a system of transportation facing obsolescence from new types of transportation.

Strains on the political structure have been evident on all sides as problems of adjustment have become more acute. Demands on party organization as the basis of government have been almost insuperable. The Senate, in contrast with second chambers in Great Britain and the United States, was created in a period with limited political capacity and little effort has been made to adjust its membership to the increase in talent available. Necessities of party organization have made it a pasture for old party war horses which old age pensions render unnecessary. Regions favoured by the British North America Act with a large number of senators are able to build up powerful party organizations with the promise of tangible rewards.

With limitations of the Senate the strain imposed on the courts has not been lessened. Reform of the civil service has increased the necessity of patronage in judicial appointments. Not only has the foundation of the courts been weakened by patronage but division of authority between the Privy Council and the Supreme Court of Canada has meant lower prestige for the latter. A strong Supreme Court insistent on avoiding an attempt to follow the elections is an essential bulwark to a democracy. We are hearing far too much about peace by power and far too little about equality before the law.

In the House of Commons the exacting demands of party organization have the effect of increasing the power of the Cabinet and of a small group within the Cabinet. Patronage has been increasingly restricted to this group and taken out of the hands of the members. Not only have members of Parliament less power but they are selected from a weaker group. Decline in the influence of the press and particularly the amalgamation of newspapers since the last war precludes intense party activity and effective discussion. Editors are compelled to follow a neutral policy without endangering the interests of either party. The radio becomes more effective in the hands of a central party organization but the character of discussion is lowered because of the necessity of appealing to large numbers.[1] Discussion is restricted in the constituencies and in turn in the House of Commons. The increasing dictatorial powers of a small group in the Cabinet and the lowering of the calibre of members of Parliament have contributed to the unprecedented breaches in the British tradition of anonymity in the civil service. Members of the civil service are becoming almost as well known to the public as ministers. A new civil service has emerged with much looser responsibilities to ministers in charge of departments. Ministers are able to evade responsibility by using the pronouncements of members of the civil service as kites to test public opinion, or by throwing individuals to the wolves when the chase becomes too warm. The power of opposition has been reduced enormously during the war period. Members of the opposition oppose the government in arguments and vote with it. Union government almost prevails in fact if not in name. Opposition consequently becomes effective in separate provinces, and provincial parties[2] have emerged on a large scale, most obviously in Alberta and Quebec.

The emergence of new parties favours the growth of ideologies and the neglect of practical problems of government. These ideologies range through free enterprise, production for use and not for profit, new democracy, *bloc populaire*, and the like. Bureaucracies give rise to parties with ideologies because they prevent groups from facing immediate problems and leave them with no alternative but party activity. The economics of parties is by no means clearly understood but the supply of parties is associated with the demands of the professions, particularly the legal profession, for advertising, and the demand for parties with the inability of groups to register their views effectively. The complex problems of regionalization in the recent development of Canada render the political structure obsolete and necessitate concentration on the problem of machinery by which interests can become more vocal and their demands be met more efficiently. It is imperative that serious attention should be given to the problem of revising political machinery so that democracy can work out solutions to modern problems. The danger that bureaucracies, including Royal Commissions, will suggest legislation rather than devices by which the demands of interests can be reflected and discussed previous to the enactment of legislation has been evident.

The dangers of an obsolescent political structure cannot be avoided by patchwork solutions and plans of the bureaucracies. Each region has its conditions of equilibrium in relation to the rest of Canada and to the rest of the world, particularly in relation to Great Britain and the United States. Manipulation of a single instrument such as monetary policy implies a highly elaborate system to determine how far transfers between regions or provinces are necessary. Otherwise full employment will become a racket on the part of the central provinces for getting and keeping what they can. The provinces will require elaborate machinery to protect themselves against exploitation of haphazard federal policies. Provincial finances will reflect the influence of federal activity. The result of neglect of interrelations between the provinces and the Dominion will be evident in increasing division and greater reliance on bureaucracy.

The argument developed in this paper assumes that the end of the second thirty years' war is in sight and that the Pax Britannica will be followed by an effective Pax Americana-Britannica. It assumes that the political scientist[3] can escape from the hocus-pocus of the economist and concentrate on the extremely difficult problems of his own field. He can best make a contribution to economic development by suggested modifications to political machinery.

NOTES

1 "Then Tom Corcoran (assistant to the President) offered me a little advice. The day of the printed word, he announced, was over. 'You have no idea what a good thing it is for your soul to have to address yourself to a big radio audience. You've got to clarify your meaning, make things simple, reduce them to their ultimate essentials if you want to get them over to a big audience, because human beings are a hell of a lot stupider than you would ever think' " (Raymond Moley, *After Seven Years* [New York, 1939], 355).

2 See J.B. Crozier, *History of Intellectual Development on the Lines of Modern Evolution* (London, 1901), 3: 258–9, on parties in France.

3 "A similar revolution of ideas is very rare in the West, and indeed experience shows that innovating legislation is connected not so much with Science as with the scientific air which certain subjects, not capable of exact scientific treatment, from time to time assume. To this class of subjects belonged Bentham's scheme of Law-Reform and, above all, Political Economy as treated by Ricardo. Both have been extremely fertile sources of legislation during the last fifty years" (Sir Henry Sumner Maine, *Popular Government* [London, 1885], 146). "We Englishmen pass on the Continent as masters of the art of government; yet it may be doubted whether, even among us, the science, which corresponds to the art, is not very much in the condition of Political Economy before Adam Smith took it in hand" (ibid., 58). "Popular Government and Popular Justice were originally the same thing. The ancient democracies devoted much more time and attention to the exercise of civil and criminal jurisdiction than to the administration of their public affairs; and, as a matter of fact, popular justice has lasted longer, has had a more continuous history, and has received much more observation and cultivation than popular government" (ibid., 89–90). On the problems of government in Great Britain, and, one might add, the more acute problems of government in Canada, see the discussion of the machinery developed in the United States to check the usurpation of the Cabinet (ibid., 196ff).

CHAPTER FOUR

The Economic Development of the Maritime Provinces, 1867–1921

The economic history of the Maritime Provinces since Confederation is largely a history of the effects produced on them by economic movements in the countries of the western world and in particular those of the Atlantic Basin. These provinces have reflected faithfully the important economic changes in Canada, the United States, the West Indies, and Europe. The Civil War and subsequent industrial development of the United States, the revolution in transport by land and sea, the rapid growth of Canada since 1900, and the recent European War all left a deep impression on them.

The accuracy with which the Maritime Provinces have served as an economic seismograph is the result of geography and the remarkable adaptability of their people. Their geography has been influenced fundamentally by a geology which has been well described as one of pronounced "unconformity." The Acadian area is a subsidiary of the Appalachian region. The profound geological disturbances in this area, especially in Nova Scotia, have resulted in the shifting and folding of sedimentary rocks and in the intrusion of igneous rocks; and are responsible for scattered mineral deposits and ore bodies, diversity of topography and soil, a serrated coastline, small lakes and numerous rivers, and outlying submerged banks with their abundance of fish. New Brunswick, since it belongs more closely to the Continent, has longer rivers and greater possibilities for lumbering. As to climate, the three provinces are a part of the easterly projection of the North American Continent, and off their coast the cold waters of the Labrador current meet the warm

---

Co-authored with C.R. Fay; from *Cambridge History of the British Empire* (Cambridge, 1930), vol. 6, chap. 27.

waters of the Gulf Stream from the south. The summer flow of the St Lawrence River into the warm bays and inlets of its land-locked gulf and the relative lack of disturbance from tides make this area the fish hatchery of the north-western Atlantic; the mingling of currents on the banks to the north-east of Nova Scotia furnishes a rich supply of fish food; and the disturbed waters of the Bay of Fundy produce an abundance of fish, with a variety not found elsewhere. On land the cold north-westerly offshore winds of winter and the south-easterly onshore winds of summer, in conjunction with the Labrador current, are responsible for the prevailing cool and temperate climate. But again "unconformity" is introduced by the Gulf Stream, as witnessed by the contrast between the orchard area of Nova Scotia and the limited possibilities of agriculture in northern New Brunswick. Such in brief is the geographic background which has been responsible for the development of lumbering chiefly in New Brunswick, of fishing and mining chiefly in Nova Scotia, and of a specialised agriculture in all three provinces, but most particularly in the fertile seclusion of Prince Edward Island.

Furthermore, this background has been responsible in part for the sensitiveness of their economic activities. Situated in that part of North America which is nearest to Great Britain, and possessing numerous ocean ports open the whole year, they were subject, tariff or no tariff, to the industrial competition of the two most highly developed areas of western civilization. Their industries, like their coastline, have been beaten upon by pitiless waves. The diversified character of their raw materials has limited the development of mass production, and cheap ocean navigation has exposed them to the competition of countries in which mass production has increasingly prevailed. The result has been to compel a readjustment of economic life and a concentration upon bedrock activities. They have exploited raw materials in which they had natural advantages, and developed by specialization the distinctive resources of their soil. At Confederation the population was chiefly English, Scotch, and Irish; and apart from some increase of French in New Brunswick the racial constituents have remained, on the whole, unchanged. The population is homogeneous, highly individualistic and remarkably adaptable. Individual enterprise, acting on a variety of natural resources, is the keynote of their economic life.

The discovery and initial development of the Maritime Provinces proceeded from Europe, and their industries were developed from the sea in relation to European demands. Successively the basic industries have moved inland and since Confederation each industry has felt the increasing pull of the land. First fishing, then lumbering and mining were developed; but over the course of their history, and especially in Nova Scotia, fishing has been of primary importance in respect of age, permanence, and closeness of contact with the sea and with Europe. As late as 1891 more Nova Scotians were engaged in fishing than in any industry but agriculture; and the numbers rose until 1911. At Confederation the dry fishing in cod was still the main branch of the industry. In the eastern counties of Nova Scotia and in Cape Breton the inshore fishery, conducted from small whale boats with two to four men at distances up to five miles from shore, was of first importance. In the western agricultural counties, in addition to the inshore fishery, large vessels of 25 to 100 tons manned by at least eight men fished on the banks off the coast from 1 April to mid-June and for the balance of the season in the Gulf of St Lawrence and further north. In 1873 the Lunenburg fleet extended its activities to the Grand Banks off Newfoundland. The fish when dried were marketed, as they had been for centuries, in tropical and sub-tropical countries with a numerous Catholic population. The old triangular trade persisted, fish to the West Indies and Mediterranean, sugar and fruits to England and France, outfits and general supplies to the Maritime Provinces. Cod was at once a food for local consumption and a basic export by which necessary imports were obtained.

On the technique and capital of the cod fishery other fisheries were built up, as the market was widened by improved transportation and new methods of preserving fish. Among these was the herring fishery, which found an expanding outlet in the United States. Its product was sold in a variety of forms the whole year round. The heavy tides of the Bay of Fundy permitted intensive operations by means of brush weirs, and new uses were found for the increasing catch. Fishing from the land by the aid of brush weirs facilitated rapid exploitation. The spawning habits of the herring saved it from depletion. But another group of fish, those known as "anadromous," which spawn up the rivers, were seriously depleted. Such were the salmon, shad, and gaspereau. The ease with which these river fish could be caught, the high prices realized for the fresh product, the drying up of streams by the removal of forest, the blocking of the rivers by mill dams and refuse, led to the disappearance of some species and the rapid decline of others. Finally the herring, mackerel, and cod, which had formerly been caught inshore, when they were pursuing the fry of the river fish, moved further out. The disturbance of the equilibrium of the fisheries was among the first fruits of industrialism.

Similar tendencies have been in evidence in the lobster and

oyster fisheries. In 1867 lobsters were used as fertilizer along the Gulf shore, and the industry was limited to canning establishments at Sambro and Port Mouton for export to Great Britain, but in the 'seventies, with the exhaustion of the American fishery, districts adjoining the United States began to export live lobsters to Maine and Massachusetts. Canneries were established over a wide area; and by 1894 the lobsters provided a third of the total fish production of Prince Edward Island. With its cash return and steadiness of production and markets the lobster fishing was attractive to fishermen. As transport by steamship and rail became more regular and rapid, the wasteful process of canning was displaced, where possible, by the more profitable trade in live lobsters. By 1894 in districts adjacent to the United States canneries had been forced to close down. The oyster beds along the south of the Gulf and around Prince Edward Island have also been intensively exploited; and there has been a very serious decline in production from the high point of 1882. Overfishing, disruption of the beds by dredging for fertilizer, the introduction of disease by the importation of new oysters, poaching, and difficulties of jurisdiction between the Dominion and the province are considered to be the causes of this decline.

In recent years the status of the inshore fisheries has been profoundly affected by the introduction of motor boats and extensive plants for the handling of the product. Capital has become important in an industry which used to rest primarily upon labour. In the Bank fisheries the steam trawler has been to the fore since 1908 and threatens the operation of the inshore and Bank fisheries on the old basis. Continued winter fishing is now possible and the persistent demands of the internal market for a steady supply have been met.

The effects of industrialism are manifest in the development of new fisheries on a large scale and in the marketing of new species in large numbers. In some years the lobster has surpassed the cod in value of catch. In 1920 over and above the live lobster trade it furnished material for 512 canneries employing 2000 workers and a capital of $2,000,000. Clams, scallops, and tuna have increased in importance. By-product industries have been extended. Improved technique has shortened the time required for the catching, landing, and marketing of fish. Artificial drying plants, bait-freezing plants, and new freezing methods have made production more regular, and distribution has kept pace with production in the shape of improved express service to interior markets and improved steamship services to the West Indies. As a result, the fishing industry has been confronted with problems of depletion. The sea, the weather, and the vagaries of fish migration have resisted the encroachments of industrialism, and even the lobster has been protected by the rugged exposed coast from Port Maitland to Cape Sable. But this was not a sufficient protection, and it has been necessary to enforce a policy of conservation under the Fisheries Act of 1868 and its amendments. Differences between the Dominion and these provinces have been largely settled. The opposition of the lumber interests on the rivers has been overcome. Regulations are in force to prevent overfishing. Size limits and seasons have been established for lobsters and other fish. Hatcheries have been opened at central points and reduction plants installed to keep down the dog fish, the enemy of all fishermen. Extensive research programs have been carried out under the Biological Board of Canada at its stations in Halifax and St Andrews. Thus the technical response to industrialism has been thorough and on the whole adequate, but in the adjustment of labour less progress has been made. Excess labour has been forced into other industries; and in seasons of depression a pool of unemployment accumulates in the fisheries with results demoralising to the fishing population. The Fishermen's Union of Nova Scotia, which was incorporated in 1905, made no progress after 1909 and disappeared in 1913. The individualism of the fishermen has stood in the way of cooperative action.

The early economic development of Nova Scotia was characteristic of a peninsula with a coastline accessible to fishing grounds. New Brunswick, on the other hand, being part of the mainland, had large rivers, down which could be floated the softwood lumber of its forests. Therefore while in Nova Scotia the lines of exploitation were primarily external, in New Brunswick they were primarily internal.

Just as the fishing industry was erected on dry cod as a basic export, so the lumber industry of New Brunswick was reared on square timber of white pine. This tree was accessible, durable, and large; easy to work, free from knots, and valuable in commerce. The logs were hewn, floated down the St John or Miramichi, and exported chiefly to Great Britain. While the fishing industry was scattered along the coastline, the lumber industry was concentrated at the river mouths. The shortage by 1850 of large white pine led to the utilization of smaller species and the production of smaller grades. Increased quantities of small logs called for a rapid expansion of machine industry and the extension and improvement of saw-mills. The Crimean War raised the demand for sawn timber and especially for spruce deals, the export of which doubled between 1850 and 1860; and the trade grew with fluctuations to a high point at the end of the century. Then once again the increasing proportion of small logs necessitated a change of product, this time to small size boards, planks, and scantlings. As the more accessible forests of the United States approached exhaustion the Americans relied more on the Maritime Provinces; and the export of deals to Great Britain was replaced by that of smaller dimension lumber to America. Thus under the persistent pressure of industrialism the virgin forest was exhausted and the cutting interval was reduced to ten or twelve years. Still further encroachments on smaller trees followed the establishment of lath mills and the production of pulpwood and pulp, the raw and semi-raw material of the paper industry. The competition of Pacific Coast lumber, when this could reach eastern markets by the Panama Canal, stimulated the consolidation of the New Brunswick lumber industry and the development of pulp and paper. The lumber firms added various branches of the new industry to their existing activities, concentrating chiefly on the production of high grade sulphite pulp. The limited supply of water power was supplemented by steam power obtained from burning saw-mill refuse. But even as thus extended, the power was inadequate to meet the voracious requirements of the newsprint mills. Consequently pulpwood was exported to Three Rivers, Quebec. At Edmundston the export of sulphite pulp takes the ingenious form of pumping across the river to the paper mill at Madawaska, Maine.

The pulp and paper industry of Nova Scotia has been more seriously limited both as to power and raw material and cannot compare with that of New Brunswick. Most of the timber areas have been alienated to private hands and smaller operations have been the rule. Alienation made it impracticable to impose an embargo on the export of wood in an unmanufactured condition, as has been done in New Brunswick on the Crown lands, where most of the forest lies. And this, together with accessibility by water to New England mills, smaller streams, and the absence of large-scale organization in the parent industry of lumbering, explains why large quantities of Nova Scotia's pulpwood are exported to the United States, and why the province has confined itself to the manufacture of groundwood pulp, a product with a low and fluctuating value.

As in fishing, so also in lumbering, industrial exploitation has been conditional upon improvements in transport. The heavy bulky character of softwoods and their capacity to float made water transportation of vital importance to the industry's early growth, although in recent years there has been a trend towards land transport and the American market. When transportation was by water, the lumber furnished not only cargo, but also the square-rigged wide-beamed softwood ship on which it was conveyed. Wooden ships were built at Saint John or on the Miramichi, filled with lumber, sent to Liverpool, England, and there sold. Such for example was the business of Pollok, Gilmour and Co., merchants of Glasgow, who played a prominent part in the early development of New Brunswick and became later the steamship line of Rankin, Gilmour and Co. of Liverpool. The skill of the lumbermen, an ample supply of the various woods required for the different parts of the vessel, the foreign demand for wood and wooden ships, the experience of the New England States, and the seafaring powers of the native fishermen all played a part in the expansion of Maritime shipping. When shipbuilding spread from New Brunswick to Yarmouth, Windsor, and other ports of Nova Scotia the industry came to maturity. For Nova Scotia worked the ships which it built, drawing its personnel from the fishermen who sailed from the south-west counties to the Banks. Between 1860 and 1869 the little town of Yarmouth added 105,000 tons to its fleet; and a number of marine insurance companies established themselves there. The youth of Yarmouth County fished, farmed, or went to sea, and often they did all three. Hard-driving Blue-nose skippers, unhampered by the labour regulations of the "Limejuice" (British Merchant Shipping) Act, commanded well disciplined, well paid, well fed crews and made substantial profits for the owners. They had merchandising as well as sailing duties to perform and received a share in the profits. Sometimes they retired with a modest fortune, which it was their delight to invest in a prettily situated farm.

As the volume and quality of shipping rose, the theatre of operation was extended. Nova Scotians no longer confined themselves to the traditional trade of freighting fish and lumber to the West Indies, with return cargoes of salt and West Indian products for North American ports. They pushed out on the high seas, securing the traffic from which their American rivals were retiring as the result of the Civil War and internal expansion. They took grain and petroleum to Europe and the Orient, coal from Cardiff to Rio de Janeiro and Montevideo, guano from the Chinchas off Peru to Europe, lumber from British North American ports to Great Britain in the summer and cotton from the Gulf ports in the winter. In 1874 wooden shipbuilding was at its height, but within five years machine industry had made fatal inroads upon it. Iron-hulled barques of British make, the forerunners of tramp steamers, secured the charters for perishable and easily damaged goods; and the "windjammers" were driven to distant seas with long voyages and low-class freights. By 1885 the victory of cheap iron and steel was complete and wooden vessels were sold to the Norwegian flag, some of them returning to be used as barges for hauling gypsum to

American ports. Apart from a slight revival during the war the industry of wooden shipbuilding disappeared. The Hon. W.S. Fielding has said of this era:

In may be only a dream, but I am willing to entertain the hope, even though it be a vision, that as a result of the iron and steel industry we shall see a revival of shipbuilding in the Maritime Provinces. Nothing that has occurred in this Province for the last half century has done more to create difficulty, has been a more serious blow to the development of that section of the Dominion than the decay of the industry of shipbuilding. It was the great industry throughout this Province, not only the industry of building its ships, but the business of owning and manning them. Not only did our people build the ships, but as the result of the building of them our young men all over our provinces grew up to be mariners and sailors of every sea, and no doubt to that fact is due to a very considerable degree the large measure of intelligence that is usually credited to the people of Nova Scotia, they were indeed people who went down to the sea in ships and did business in many waters.[1]

The competition of iron and steel destroyed a magnificent achievement, an integration of capital and labour, of lumbering, fishing, and agriculture, on which rested a progressive community life. The linch pin was broken, and industrialism continued its inroads upon the people of the Maritime Provinces.

Thrown back from the sea, the lumber industry had to find new uses for its products on land. One notable extension, the pulp and paper industry, has already been described. Under this adjustment the Canadian and American markets assumed a greater importance and a larger proportion of the lumber was taken out by railroads. Saw-mills were built inland and fewer logs were floated down to Saint John despite the ocean freights and market for by-products available at this port. Drying plants and planing mills were installed with a view to reducing the weight of the product and widening the market; and hardwood areas were tapped by the introduction of small portable mills. The Restigouche has steadily overtaken the Miramichi and the shift in areas of production continues. The general result of the changes in method of production and type of product has been to bring New Brunswick more directly within the sweep of the world market. It has become increasingly sensitive to the secular and cyclical fluctuations in the building trades of North America and to changes in costs of transportation from rival sources of supply. As a protection the industry has endeavoured to diversify its production and develop by-products. Cutting regulations have been improved and an effective fire protective service has been installed, both in New Brunswick and Nova Scotia. Skill and self-reliance are still required of the lumberman, but the spread of the corporation has tended to break down the *esprit de corps* based on personal relations which was so marked when the industry was in family hands. With the increase in the practice of contracting for the delivery of logs the contact between the firm and the men in the bush has been weakened; while in the mills mass production has enlarged the field of routine. Since 1900 there have been several strikes in Saint John mills.

Like fishing and lumbering, mining began from the sea border and extended inland when transport improved. Gold, gypsum, and coal have supplied the main mineral output of Nova Scotia since Confederation. Gold was discovered in 1861 at points near the coast east of Halifax and production reached the maximum in 1898, after which date the predominance of low grade ore led to a permanent decline. On the other hand, the output of gypsum, the raw material for various plasters, has steadily increased in response to constructional activities in Canada and the United States. Growing output has been attended by concentration of quarries and shipping points and by the manufacture of some part of the semi-finished product within the province, but in the main the industry has been one of extracting a crude product for export to a foreign market. Neither gold nor gypsum can compare with coal in value of output or in influence on the life of the province.

Coal, being a heavy commodity and possessed in abundance by Great Britain and Europe, had to be sold in neighbouring markets to which there was cheap water transport, such as the New England states and Quebec. The most accessible mines lay along the west coast of Cape Breton, and during the period of the Reciprocity Treaty of 1854–66 numerous small mines were opened. But the American coal duty of 1867 and a long period of depression in Canada had so serious an effect on the industry that by 1890 only the strongest mines survived. The provincial government, as owner of the mines, assisted the reconstruction of the industry by the grant of favourable terms to lessees, looking to the Cape Breton coal industry to offset the decline in wooden shipbuilding; and thus facilitated an amalgamation of various mines under the direction of outside interests from Boston and Montreal, which formed in 1893 the Dominion Coal Company. With new capital resources modern mining equipment was installed, shipping piers were built, and the Black Diamond steamship line was established. Railway communication had been secured with the mainland in 1891 by the line from

Point Tupper in Sydney, the centre of the Cape Breton mining area; and in 1896 a further line was opened from Sydney to the all-year port of Louisbourg. Increased output and the decline of the American demand, consequent upon the Boston "Smoke Nuisance" law of 1897 (which penalized the smoky coal of Nova Scotia) and the tariff increase of the same year, hastened the formation of the Dominion Iron and Steel Company and the erection of an iron and steel plant. Ore was obtained from Wabana, Newfoundland, by arrangement with the company which, as noted below, was working that field. In 1901 the first furnaces were blown in and steel was produced in December of that year. A wire-rod mill was added in 1904 and a steel-rail mill in 1905. Difficulties over contracts made it expedient for the Coal Company and the Steel Company to unite as the Dominion Steel Corporation in 1910. All this was a case of development from without. Industrialism was late in its arrival, but once launched it developed rapidly by the aid of a technique perfected elsewhere. Community life, which depends on the control of natural resources, was weakened. In the exploitation of coal and iron outside capital met none of the resistance which fishing and lumbering with their natural diversity were able to offer. The resistance came, not from the industries as such, but from the workers to whom they gave employment.

This however was only one section of Nova Scotia's coal and iron industry. In the inland coal fields of Cumberland and Pictou development proceeded more evenly, and outside interests found it difficult to gain control. These fields had small resources and depended on a more expensive form of transport, the railroad. Some collieries close to water were in operation before Confederation, but marked expansion did not come until the construction of the Intercolonial Railway in the 'seventies. To meet the demand for railway and foundry material the Nova Scotia Forge Company and the Nova Scotia Steel Company, which made steel ingots by the Siemens process, were established; and later the two united. Difficulties in procuring suitable local ore led in 1894 to the acquisition of a deposit at Wabana on Bell Island in Conception Bay, Newfoundland. This proved marvellously rich; and in order to be closer to the new ore and to take advantage of cheaper and better coking coal, properties were purchased in 1900 in Cape Breton adjacent to those of the Dominion Coal Company. They had belonged to the General Mining Association, which before 1858 had a monopoly of coal production in the province. The Steel Company now became the Nova Scotia Steel and Coal Company. Coke ovens and blast furnaces were erected in Cape Breton and the mainland plants were extended to handle the later stages of manufacture. In 1912 an ally, the Eastern Car Company, was formed to manufacture steel railway cars at New Glasgow. The Nova Scotia Steel and Coal Company in contrast with its rival developed slowly and in response to the demands of the province. It was managed on conservative lines by Maritime interests.

As the result of improved methods of coal mining and the increased demand of the iron and steel industry, the production of coal increased from 2.6 million tons in 1899 to 7.2 in 1913. With the war railroad construction ceased but munitions took its place. In 1920 the Nova Scotia Steel and Coal Company and the Dominion Steel Corporation were merged into the British Empire Steel Corporation ("Besco") and associated with them was Halifax Shipyards Limited, formed by officials of the Canada Steamship Company with a view to using Nova Scotia steel in shipbuilding. The coming of "Besco" meant the further loss of control by local interests, and in the post-war depression the conflict between native workers and outside control came to a head. The miners had been organized since 1879, when the "Provincial Workingmen's Association" was formed. For nearly forty years the union maintained an independent existence. Its record was conservative and constructive and it helped to secure for the industry adequate protective legislation. By its support of education, temperance and provident activities it gained the sympathy of the press and the public. In 1897 practically all the miners belonged to it, but in 1898 the American Knights of Labour entered its territory and created a schism. In 1908 it was exposed to a second invasion, this time from the United Mine Workers of America, who had become active in other coal fields of Canada. For a while it held its ground, but the war, with its rising cost of living, imposed a strain on the wage agreements under which it was working, and in 1917 it joined with its first rival in an amalgamation which soon afterwards affiliated with the United Mine Workers of America. The independence of forty years was at an end. The conclusion could not have been long delayed. When there was but one employer with head office at Montreal, the logical retort was membership in a strong international Union. After 1921 prolonged labour unrest accompanied by strikes and military repression lay like a storm-cloud over the province. It was part of the painful return to post-war conditions, but to Nova Scotians its bitterness was increased by the consciousness that the province had lost control of a leading industry, with absentee ownership on the one hand and foreign labour domination on the other.

The record of consumers' cooperation (cooperative stores) in Canada is a lean one, but to this there is one outstanding exception, the British Canadian Co-operative Society Limited of Sydney Mines and Glace Bay, established in 1906. It succeeded to two earlier ventures, the second of which failed with heavy losses to the miners in 1905. The new start was due to some immigrant Lancashire miners to whom cooperation was second nature and who resented the unscrupulous treatment by local merchants of the Old Country immigrants arriving at that time. In twenty-two years the Society has distributed $1,500,000 in patronage dividend, growing from strength to strength under the guidance of one man, its devoted secretary and general manager. It has been a centre of community life in a region of bleak industrialism, a camp of democracy and cash payment confronting the bondage of the outside merchants and the unpopular company store.

The sweep of industrialism and the rapid development of new agricultural areas in the western part of the continent have exerted a profound influence on the population and agriculture of the Maritime Provinces. Within their boundaries there has been a shift of population from agriculture and fishing to other occupations, but the internal redistribution is unimportant beside the movement to the continental mainland. The population indeed has not decreased, it has grown from three-quarters of a million in 1871 to one million in 1921, but there has been throughout the period a heavy drain of native-born to the United States and to other parts of Canada; and this has not been compensated by any substantial amount of new immigration. In 1921 at least 325,000 former Maritime residents were living elsewhere, about three-quarters of them in the United States. The result on the age distribution of the population has been that, while in Canada as a whole the youthful population has been growing very rapidly, in the Maritime Provinces it has been stationary or actually decreasing. In Prince Edward Island, an almost wholly rural province, the population reached its maximum at the census of 1891.

The intensive development of lumbering and mining in this group of provinces and the vast production of wheat and cattle in the continental West for export to Eastern America and to Europe made it difficult for their farmers to compete in the principal crops. They have therefore concentrated on products for which there was an adjacent industrial demand, such as dairy produce, or on specialities for which they had peculiar advantages of soil, climate, and situation. This is most clearly seen in Prince Edward Island, which, apart from fishing and the canned lobster industry, is devoted wholly to agriculture. The Land Purchase Act of 1875 terminated the system of absentee landlordism which had disturbed the province for more than a century. Specialized agriculture began with the export of potatoes at a time when water transport by sailing ship was abundant. But the arrival of the Colorado beetle and the exhaustion of the soil through excessive cropping of potatoes and oats, the leading Maritime grain, turned attention to other opportunities. The production of factory cheese began in 1883 and of factory (creamery) butter in 1887. Progress was slow until in 1891 the Dominion Government sent down its Dairy Commissioner to organize cheese and butter factories on the cooperative method. After some years of pioneer effort the factories were strong enough to work independently on cooperative lines; and since then the range of cooperative marketing has been widened, notably in eggs and wool. The formation in 1912 of egg circles under Dominion guidance terminated a system of barter between the farmer and his local store which was incompatible with adequate returns and a high class of production. In the spring of 1914 the local circles were organized in a central sales agency, the Prince Edward Island Egg and Poultry Association. Improvement of the transport facilities between the island and mainland at the expense of the Dominion has made it possible to market perishable products on the mainland the whole year round. More recently the experience of the potato growers in the Aroostook Valley of Maine has been adapted to Prince Edward Island; and in addition to the large export trade in table potatoes a certified seed potato industry has been established to supply the demand of potato growers in the southern states for potatoes of high vitality and yield, such as Irish Cobblers and Green Mountains, the specialities of the island. But the most spectacular example of the ingenuity of the Maritime people in adapting themselves to changed conditions has been the creation of the Prince Edward Island silver fox industry. The depletion of the more valuable species of fur and the rise in the price of high grade furs stimulated an interest in the possibilities of fur farming. A long period of experiment, dating from the early 'eighties, solved the complicated problems connected with the improvement of strain, raising of young, feeding, nests, and pens. Between 1900 and 1910 exceptional prices were realized in London. In 1910 the breeders who had founded the industry began to sell the live animals and in 1911 the first fox-breeding company was formed with a charter in the United States. A period of frenzied finance ensued. Options were taken on the unborn pups and the prices of breeding pairs rose to fantastic heights. The war arrested this extravagance and the industry has again settled down to more sober lines of growth. A system of registered pedigree has been introduced and measures have been taken to protect the industry from exploitation and fraud.

The agriculture of Nova Scotia has developed similarly. The foundations have been strengthened by the extension of dairying. Between 1881 and 1921 the output of butter increased by nearly 50 per cent. Though the number of milch cows declined, the smaller herd produced more and better milk. Cheese has been largely replaced by butter, ice-cream, and fluid milk for local markets, and since 1901 there has also been a rapid increase in the production of poultry and eggs. There is no evidence for the view that the agriculture of these provinces has fallen of late years into stagnation.

The apple is Nova Scotia's speciality. The Annapolis-Cornwallis valley in which its cultivation is concentrated extends for 100 miles from Digby to Windsor, with Kentville as its centre. Commercial production began about 1880, since when a secondary crop grown for local consumption has become an important export industry, the average export rising from 30,000 barrels in 1880–5 to close on 1,000,000 in 1915–20. The apple came as a welcome substitute for the potato, the export crop on which the valley had relied until it was penalized by a heavy American duty in 1874. The climate, soil, and conformation of the valley, with its well drained sandy slopes, proved excellent for apple growing; and the improvements in ocean transport consequent upon the introduction of the steel steamer provided profitable access to the British market, which takes the bulk of the crop. As the result of long experience and of experiment by individuals, aided by the counsels of the Nova Scotia Fruit Growers' Association, which has presided over the industry from the outset, a high technique has been achieved. Varieties have been reduced and standardized. Labour for picking and packing is obtained from Halifax and Lunenburg at the close of the fishing season. Since 1900 frost-proof warehouses have been in use for the packing and storage of fruit, some of them owned by the growers; since 1910 there has been a central sales organization, the United Fruit companies of Nova Scotia Limited, to which most of the local cooperative companies belong. The short haul from the valley to the ocean port of Halifax over the Dominion Atlantic Railway and the competition of liners for first-class freight, especially after the closing of the St Lawrence, placed the growers in a favourable position for reaching their leading market. And thus, with production, marketing, and transportation improved, the industry has prospered. Furthermore, it illustrates well the way in which the activities of the three provinces are interlocked. Fertilizer comes from the Cape Breton mines, cooperage from the lumber industry, labour from the fisheries. And in its turn the beauty of the valley from blossom time to harvest has contributed to the profits of the tourist business.

The absorption of New Brunswick in its staple industry of lumbering has handicapped the growth of its agriculture. The timber trade set the pace of settlement. The timber ships brought back return cargoes of immigrants, who settled in the wild lands, selling the cleared lumber to the timber dealer and the field produce to the lumberman. Lumbering provided a cash market, as well as good wages for work in the bush during the winter season. It supplied revenue for provincial improvements, capital for industry, and the means of purchasing requirements from abroad. On the other hand it took from the farms horses and crude products such as hay and oats, with the result that live-stock was reduced in quantity and deteriorated, and the general balance so essential to mixed farming was destroyed. Young men and immigrants were drawn from the farm and the persistent attention to detail which mixed farming demands became impossible. Moreover, the dependence on an industry so speculative as lumbering exposed farmers to serious fluctuations. Agriculture, therefore, has been largely confined to the dyked marsh lands, which skirt the Bay of Fundy and extend into Nova Scotia, and to the river valleys with their adjoining uplands, especially that of the St John. As roads and railways were pushed into the forest hinterland, new land has been brought under settlement and agriculture has improved along the lines of other provinces, with orchards in the lower St John valley and intensive potato raising in Carleton and Victoria counties. A market has been found for potatoes in the West Indies, Quebec, and Ontario; and the success achieved is yet another proof of the skill with which the farmers have adjusted their agriculture to the demands of new markets in the face of intense competition in basic products and stiff tariffs in their natural market to the south. The ports of the Maritime Provinces have watched with concern the flow of wheat from the Canadian West through Montreal to the north of them and New York to the south. They cannot compete with Montreal in the summer because of the extra railway haul. In the winter Saint John handles a substantial volume, Halifax very little. New York offers to the shipper a varied mass of tonnage sailing regularly to all parts. The true interest of these provinces lies in the development of their own rich hinterland and the promotion of a trade of import and export between themselves and countries to the south.

The economic history of the three provinces since 1867 is one of prosperity so long as their face was towards the sea, and of struggle against adversity when the pull of the land increased, as happened very shortly after Confederation. The completion of the Intercolonial Railway in 1876 and of the Canadian Pacific short line from Montreal to Saint John in 1890, the selection of Saint John as a winter terminus by the Allan and Canadian Pacific steamship lines soon after 1900, and the subsequent consolidation of the railways of the provinces under one or other of the two great systems were successive landmarks in the process. *Per se* they were highly advantageous, even though the railways chiefly brought western produce in and took eastern people out, but they were part of that larger evolution in which the "Maritimes" lost control over their economic destinies. The rent made in the fabric of life by the collapse of wooden shipbuilding intensified the strain under which they laboured, as the flower of their people moved west. Though Charlottetown was the cradle of Confederation, the seat of the new Dominion was Ottawa. Nova Scotia has been a nursery of Cabinet ministers and of presidents and professors for the universities of Canada and the United States of America. Business and finance took a similar toll. Of the numerous banks which flourished in the days of wooden ships only a few of the strongest survived; and these were forced by the policies which enabled them to survive to transfer their headquarters to the mainland. The Merchants Bank of Halifax became the Royal Bank of Canada in 1901 and changed its seat to Montreal in 1907. The Bank of Nova Scotia moved its General Manager to Toronto in 1900; and its president, a Toronto financier, journeys annually to Halifax to present his address as a tribute to the days that were. In 1903 the Canadian Bank of Commerce absorbed the old Halifax Banking Company, which had been founded as far back as 1825. Such a development was doubtless requisite to a banking system which has branches from coast to coast. None the less the shock to local pride was considerable, and it contributed perhaps to a habit which has been observed in recent years, namely, tardiness to invest in local industrial enterprise.

The Dominion Government has endeavoured to join these provinces to the rest of Canada by devices which range from tariffs to the grant of "Better Terms" under the Confederation Agreement. Mention may be made of the duty placed on American coal in 1879; of the bounties to the iron and steel industry, which were granted in 1884 and continued by the Laurier Government for many years; and of the bounties paid to the fishing industry out of the moneys received from the United States under the Halifax Award of 1877. Consideration for them has been an incentive to the steps taken to increase the trade of Canada with the West Indies and Latin America. A preference was granted to the British West Indies in 1897 and agreements in 1912, 1920 and 1925 enlarged the preferences and provided subsidized steamship services. About 1900, Canadian banks, especially those of Maritime origin, began to open branches in the West Indies, including Cuba, and the chain has been extended to South America. Trade with these parts has grown rapidly since the war to the advantage of Halifax and Saint John.

The record of these provinces since Confederation is on the whole a very remarkable one. Through the individuality of their people and the diversity of their resources they have stemmed a tide of industrialism which might have submerged a less sturdy stock. Where the opportunity has offered they have struck out along new lines, and they have made contributions to the cultural life of Canada which it is beyond the province of the economic historian to appraise.

NOTES

1 Cited by R. Drummond, *Minerals and Mining* (Stellarton, NS, 1918), 233–4.

CHAPTER FIVE

The Penetrative Powers of the Price System on New World States

Economics is an older subject than statistics, but this paper is confined to the period since statistics began to leave its impression on economics and reached that stage, fatal to economics, when it came of age. Professor G.N. Clark in *Science and Social Welfare in the Age of Newton* (Oxford, 1937) has traced the background of statistics, in the growing importance of mathematics through astronomy, surveying, and book-keeping which followed the discovery of the New World, prior to its beginnings with the publication of John Gaunt's *Observations upon the Bills of Mortality* in 1662, or four years before the census of Talon in Canada. An important statistical department was set up in England under an inspector-general to collect statistics on imports and exports about 1695. The effects of the imports of treasure from North America were becoming increasingly evident and William Fleetwood, with a strong vested interest in stability in the value of fellowships, published his *Chronicon Preciosum* in 1706. And so the snake entered the paradise of academic interest in economics. Under the stimulus of treasures from the New World the price system ate its way more rapidly into the economy of Europe and into economic thought.

"A project of commerce to the East Indies, therefore, gave occasion to the first discovery of the West."[1] The rise in prices in the late sixteenth and early seventeenth centuries stimulated the flow of trade from Europe to the New World, and to the Old World from the West Indies to the East Indies.[2] With the beginning of the seven-

---

From *Canadian Journal of Economics and Policital Science* 4 (1938): 299–319; reprinted in *Political Economy in the Modern State* (Ryerson, 1946), 145–67; first appeared as "The Penetrative Powers of the Price System."

teenth century, the formation of the East India Company was accompanied by the settlement of Virginia. Dried fish from Newfoundland provided food for the fishing industry and for shipping. It was carried to Spain and exchanged for treasure, and used as food for ships going south of the line to the East Indies to exchange treasure for spices, calicoes, raw silk, and other East Indies goods. Exports of treasure from England evoked the protests of mercantilists and precipitated the discussion which became the basis of the interest shown by English economists in problems of foreign trade. It would be interesting to speculate on the history of economic thought if England had been an important producer of precious metals and not an importer and an exporter, and if large joint stock companies had not existed to be defended and to support arguments and publication. The defence of the East India Company by Thomas Mun in his pamphlet in 1621 was accompanied by the battle between divergent views of Misselden and Malynes. The rise in prices stimulated the trade described by Adam Smith: "The silver of the new continent seems in this manner to be one of the principal commodities by which the commerce between the two extremities of the old one is carried on, and it is by means of it, in a great measure, that those distant parts of the world are connected with one another."[3] Under its drive, the commercial system of England expanded in the New World and in the Old. With limited shipping facilities, the production and trade of light valuable commodities from the New World became evident in tobacco from Virginia and sugar from the West Indies. Manufactured products were sent to Africa for slaves and gold to be carried to sugar and tobacco plantations. New England was fostered by Virginia for the production of fish for exchange of specie in Spain rather than of tobacco. She expanded to produce not only fish for Europe, but also lumber, fish, and agricultural products and ships to carry these cheap bulky commodities for short distances to the English plantation colonies of the New World. I hope the historians will concede a claim to the effects of rising prices not only in the expansion of settlement in the New World but also in the Puritan Revolution, the passing of the Navigation Acts, the establishment of the colonial system, and the defeat of a powerful commercial rival in the Dutch.

While Adam Smith attacked the system which emerged, he was aware of its advantages in defence. He saw it as part of the spread of the price system which had swept aside the feudal system, and led to the discovery of the New World, and with his support, to the wiping out of the inequities of the colonial system itself. "But what all the violence of feudal institutions could never have effected, the silent and insensible operation of foreign commerce and manufactures gradually brought about."[4]

A revolution of the greatest importance to public happiness was in this manner brought about by two different orders of people, who had not the least intention to serve the public. To gratify the most childish vanity was the sole motive of the great proprietors. The merchants and artificers, much less ridiculous acted merely from a view to their own interest, and in pursuit of their own pedlar principles of turning a penny wherever a penny was to be got. Neither of them had either knowledge or foresight of that great revolution which the folly of the one, and the industry of the other, was gradually bringing about. It is thus that through the greater part of Europe the commerce and manufacture of cities, instead of being the effect, have been the cause and occasion of the improvement and cultivation of the country.[5]

His predecessor, Richardson, wrote in 1750 that "the giving trade the utmost freedoms and encouragements is the greatest and most solid improvement of the value of lands."[6]

The character of trade which emerged in relation to the growth of cities in Europe was described by Nicholas Barbon in *A Discourse of Trade* (London, 1690), who wrote:

The chief causes that promote *trade,* (not to mention good government, peace and scituation, with other advantages) are industry in the poor, and liberality in the rich.

Those expences that most promote trade, are in cloaths and lodging: in adorning the body and the house, there are a thousand traders imploy'd in cloathing and decking the body, and building and furnishing of houses, for one that is imploy'd in providing food. ... Fashion or the alteration of dress is a great promoter of *trade,* because it occasions the expense of cloaths, before the old ones are worn out: It is the spirit and life of *trade.* ... The next expence that chiefly promotes *trade,* is building ... it imploys a greater number of trades and people, than feeding or cloathing.

Beside, there is another great advantage to *trade,* by enlarging of cities; the two beneficial expences of cloathing and lodging, are increased; Man being naturally ambitious, the living together, occasions emulation, which is seen by outvying one another in apparel, equipage, and furniture of the house; whereas, if a man lived solitary alone, his chiefest expence would be food. (31–4)

External trade was an extension of internal trade. Commodities carried long distances under primitive conditions of navigation were necessarily light in bulk, high in value, and suited to the demands of the luxury class in metropolitan areas. Consumption goods, especially those involving the introduction of habits, created a steady demand. Tobacco consumption spread rapidly after the seventeenth century. Sugar was imported in increasing quantities to sweeten the tea and chocolate brought from the East especially in the latter half of the seventeenth century. Furs met the demands of fashion in clothing, and in the case of durable commodities, such as beaver hats, were passed down through various strata of society. The demands of the upper classes, encouraged by imports of specie and increasing fluidity of resources, stimulated production of luxury goods, expansion of trade, and the penetration of luxuries to lower classes.

The characteristics of production, distribution, and consumption of these commodities imposed strains on any colonial system aiming at comprehensiveness and the interests of the mother country. In the fur trade France sent vessels of goods to be traded with the hunting Indians of the Precambrian formation north of the St Lawrence, and its development involved continued penetration to the interior. Settlement and agriculture were restricted and exposed to the fluctuations in the price of a commodity determined by fashion and by uncertain supplies from the Indians. The agricultural base in the St Lawrence was consequently not adequate to the establishment of a sedentary fishery in the Maritimes and neither could be linked to the demands of the French sugar plantations of the West Indies. In the English colonial system the demands of the plantation commodities, such as sugar and tobacco, differed from those produced in the commercial colonies, such as fish and lumber for the West Indies, and those produced in Newfoundland, namely fish chiefly for European consumption. The plantations required slaves, foodstuffs to supply the slaves, lumber for buildings, and livestock to operate the mills.[7] These cheap bulky secondary commodities supplied by New England and other colonies were extremely sensitive to regulations which affected prices of luxury goods. The colonial system encouraged the plantations through monopolies of the English market and the fisheries and agriculture as a base of supply for the plantations. "To increase the shipping and naval power of Great Britain, by the extension of the fisheries of our colonies, is an object which the legislature seems to have had almost constantly in view. Those fisheries, upon this account, have had all the encouragement which freedom can give them, and they have flourished accordingly. The New England fishery in particular was, before the late disturbances, one of the most important, perhaps, in the world."[8] With the expansion of the fishery, shipping increased, larger quantities of goods were available, and protests were more vigorous against restrictions imposed at the instigation of the plantations in the interests of cheaper supplies and provisions. The colonial system had inherent contradictions stimulating production by a policy of freedom in colonies producing secondary commodities and restricting the market for those commodities by a policy of preferences for colonies producing staple commodities. New England shipping encroached consequently on the French Empire and capitalized its limitations by profitable smuggling. It supported expansion of trade from secondary bulky commodities into the luxury commodities of the New World, through the manufacture of molasses, a by-product of sugar, into rum and its exchange for furs, slaves, and fish. The difficulties of European commercial systems in North America were evident in the retreat of the French and finally in the withdrawal of the English to the St Lawrence. The effectiveness of the commercial development of New England with the advantages of freedom of trade supported by the fishery and shipping, broke down the colonial system of France and in turn of England. Shipping implied commercial strength, naval power, and defeat of European control.

The decline of the British commercial system proceeded rapidly after the American Revolution and the publication of the *Wealth of Nations*. After the War of 1812, the Colonial Trade Acts of the twenties, and admission of the United States to the British West Indies in 1830, became landmarks in the steady trend toward free trade. The attacks of Adam Smith and the group of government interventionists, who were his disciples and followers, on the vested interests of the merchant class bore fruit in clearing away the shackles of the colonial system. Decker had written in 1744, "Restraint is always harmful to trade." "Nothing but freedom can secure trade."[9] Adam Smith declared that "Of the greater part of the regulations concerning the colony trade, the merchants who carry it on, it must be observed, have been the principal advisers. We must not wonder, therefore, if, in the greater part of them, their interest has been more considered than either that of the colonies or that of the mother country."[10] "The sneaking arts of underling tradesmen are thus erected into political maxims for the conduct of a great empire; for it is the most underling tradesmen only who make it a rule to employ chiefly their own customers."[11] The slave trade was finally abolished in the West Indies, the Reform Bills destroyed the power of vested interests in Parliament, the timber preferences were reduced, the Corn Laws repealed, the Navigation Acts abrogated, and responsible government established in the colonies. The free trade system in North America was extended by the Reciprocity Treaty with the United States. The abolition of slavery in the Civil War was an important landmark in the transition from status to contract. The disappearance of the East India Company was followed by the purchase of Rupert's Land from the Hudson's Bay Company. The price system had gradually but persistently eaten out the rotting timbers of European colonial structures and as it destroyed the feudalism so it destroyed the defences of commercialism.

Commercialism left a powerful stamp on the history of the East and West. Great Britain emerged as a dominant metropolitan unit. The Americas became politically independent but continued to carry the culture of people from Spain, Portugal, France, and England. In Canada a large French population had grown up on the lower St Lawrence in response to the demands of the fur trade. Across the northern half of the continent the aborigines had felt the powerful influence of the commercial pull. Sir George Simpson wrote, "Connubial alliances are the best security we can have of the good will of the natives," and half-breeds are evidence of the policy. Religious practices detrimental to the trade were replaced by Christianity. Of one tribe Simpson wrote: "They have made a poor hunt in consequences of the death of a relation and in the agony of grief according to ancient usage rent their garments so that they are now destitute of every necessary." Again he wrote:

There may be a difference of opinion as to the effect the conversion of the Indians might have on the trade; I cannot however foresee that it could be at all injurious, on the contrary I believe it would be highly beneficial thereto as they would in time imbibe our manners and customs and imitate us in Dress; our Supplies would thus become necessary to them which would increase the consumption of European produce & manufactures and in like measure increase & benefit our trade as they would find it requisite to become more industrious and to turn their attention more seriously to the Chase in order to enable to provide themselves with such supplies; we should moreover be enabled to pass through their Lands in greater safety which would lighten the expence of transport, and supplies of Provisions would be found at every Village, and among every tribe; they might likewise be employed on extraordinary occasions as runners, Boatsmen, etc., and their Services in other respects turned to profitable account.

The Honble Committee I am satisfied will take this view of the subject and there are a few of the most enlightened in this Country who would do so likewise but there are others (and I am almost ashamed to say Members of our Council) who would condemn it as being wild & visionary and ruinous to the Fur Trade without even taking the trouble of thinking seriously thereon or looking at the question in all its bearings and important consequences.[12]

Duncan McGillivray wrote: "For the prairie Indians the love of rum is their first inducement to industry; they undergo every hardship and fatigue to procure a skinful of this delicious beverage, and when a nation becomes addicted to drinking, it affords a strong presumption that they will soon become excellent hunters."[13] With monopoly control Simpson reduced imports of spirits to a minimum. The fur trade left a framework for the later Dominion. The timber trade, based on preferences and the specific gravity of white pine, hastened English settlement in Upper Canada. The fishing industry left a region divided between four national interests, France, Newfoundland, Canada, and the United States. These divisions in northern North America illustrate the general divergent effects of commercialism.

Into the moulds of the commercial period, set by successive heavier and cheaper commodities, and determined by geographic factors, such as the St Lawrence River and the Precambrian formation; by cultural considerations, such as the English and French languages; by technology, such as the canoe and the raft; by business organization, such as the Northwest Company and Liverpool timber firms; and by political institutions peculiar to France and England, were poured the rivers of iron and steel in the form of steamships and railways which hardened into modern capitalism. Improved transportation, increasing specialization in Great Britain, the spread of machine industry in relation to coal and iron, and migration of population to urban centres involved imports, of wheat, live-stock, and dairy products from North America for foodstuffs, cotton from the United States and wool from Australia for clothing, timber from Canada and New Brunswick for housing, and raw materials for manufacturing, and exports of manufactured products. Steamships and railways lowered costs of transportation and hastened the shift to bulky imports of low value, and perishable commodities from more adjacent regions. The discovery of gold in the Pacific basin, in California and British Columbia, and in Australia and New Zealand, was followed by immediate migration of population, exports of gold and, later, of bulky commodities, and rapid extension of transportation facilities. The Suez Canal and the Union

Pacific Railway were opened in 1869, the Canadian Pacific Railway in 1885, and the routes from Great Britain via the East and the West to the Pacific drastically shortened in space and time.

The rise of industrialism in the first half of the nineteenth century was hastened by the demands of the Napoleonic Wars[14] for iron and steel and by the increasing effectiveness of the price system. It was the reverse side of the decline of the commercial system. The emergence of free trade by the middle of the century reflected and enhanced the efficiency of the price system and the growth of industrialism. The ebb of commercialism was the flow of industrialism. The establishment of responsible government in Canada marked the collapse of the colonial system and the beginnings of capitalistic development. Government was unified in the Act of Union and broadened in Confederation. The divisive trends of the United States disappeared with the success of the North in the Civil War.

Again war was followed by rapid expansion of the iron and steel industry, rapid construction of railways, and improvement of steamships. What Geddes has called palæotechnic society,[15] emerged in full bloom with its coal mines, industrialism, and urbanization. Credit facilities were improved with additional supplies of gold, completion of the Atlantic cable, development of financial structures, especially during the Civil War and after the improvement of political structures, and the improvement of the exchanges for handling commodities and securities.[16] Legislation improved the position and effectiveness of corporations, and new developments for the amassing of large quantities of capital and capital equipment, such as the trust and the holding company, were introduced. Institutions for the collection and direction of funds, such as banks, bond houses, and insurance companies, became more effective. Inefficiency was weeded out through ruthless competition, the long depression, and improved bankruptcy legislation. Marked increase in production and lowering of costs of transportation contributed to falling prices.[17] With the advantages of industrial leadership and lowering of the costs of raw material in Great Britain and the influence of mathematics and the natural sciences, the interests in the concern of Marx with the exploitation which accompanied industrial change shifted to that of Jevons, Marshall, Walras, and Pareto in the development of equilibrium analysis. The gold standard operated in the fashion familiar to all students of textbooks of economics, and the prices between countries were automatically adjusted. The price system operated at a high state of efficiency in the occupation of the vacant spaces of the earth. In countries producing cheap and more bulky raw materials, improved transportation was dependent on funds from industrial areas. They were repaid in part in areas dominated by government activity, such as Canada, by revenue from tariffs on manufactured goods from industrial areas or were avoided in part by bankruptcy in areas dominated by private enterprise, such as the United States. Competition of manufactured goods led to the protective tariff and schools of economics which traced their origins to List in Germany, Carey in the United States, and Buchanan in Canada. Canada attempted to secure revenue and to check competition from industrial countries, and to participate in the development of more extensive projects by facilitating credit expansion.

The outbreak of the Great War has been regarded as the signal for the collapse of capitalism. Sombart has traced the history of capitalism to its final stage of *hoch capitalismus.* Geddes would describe it as the rise and decline of the palæotechnic (or coal and iron) society and the beginnings of the neotechnic (or new sources of power and base metals) society. But with the shift from commercialism to capitalism, so with the shift from capitalism to what may be called later phases or whatever the war and post-war period may be designated, the ebb of one was the rise of the other. Where capitalism followed the more rigid channels of surviving commercialism or where it arrived later in a highly centralized state, it was a part of governmental machinery. In Germany,[18] Italy, and Japan and in the British Dominions the state became capital equipment. The twentieth century was Canada's; and Germany wanted a place in the sun. In Canada the federal government supported, and engaged in, railway building on an extensive scale, and the provinces, strengthened in their power by Privy Council decisions, shared in railway construction and engaged in the development of hydro-electric power and in the expansion of mining and the pulp and paper industry. In Great Britain and the United States, on the other hand, regulatory boards were conspicuous for railways and public utilities, and control was developed to combat trusts and monopolies and to meet the problems of monetary disturbance.

The war brought a marked increase in government activities in all nations.[19] The conduct of military and naval activities over a long period brought encroachment of the state on private organization, especially in the fields of banking and transportation. In Canada the federal government became an owner of railways on a large scale. Most significant developments appeared in the field of finance and in its influence on the price system through the fixing of prices of commodities by governmental bodies set up for war purposes and the floating of loans by governments on an unprecedented scale. The end of the war found the participants with debts of astronomical figures. The Treaty of Versailles riveted a debt structure on the German nation. These debts were followed by a long series of revisions and disturbances, including ruinous inflation in Germany and Austria, the Dawes Plan, the Young Plan, the League of Nations Plan, the collapse of Austria, *de facto* cancellation of debts, depreciation of sterling, the franc, and the dollar, and increasing reliance on nationalistic measures ranging through various stages of totalitarianism.

The war and post-war period to 1929 was marked by a continuation of the prosperity which had its rise in the late nineties of the last century. The state was more effectively utilized as a monetary device,[20] and political disturbances reflected economic disturbances more directly. Capital equipment begun in the war and the pre-war periods was extended and completed. Railways in Canada, the Panama Canal (opened in 1917), and the release of shipping after the war contributed to marked expansion based on accessibility to the Pacific. These extensions of palæotechnic structure were accompanied by a marked development of the neotechnic structure. Significant inventions and new sources of power were utilized and extended. Oil displaced coal in ships and vastly increased their range, especially in the Pacific. The internal combustion engine played an increasingly important role in transportation, agriculture, and industry in the densely populated areas and in the remote areas. Roads and hotels were built on an extensive scale. Hydro-electric power was developed with and without government support in the non-coal areas and contributed to a marked increase in the supply of non-ferrous metals such as nickel, zinc, lead, aluminum, and gold. Following the stimulus of the war these neotechnic developments contributed to the expansion of Russia, Japan, Italy, France, Germany, the British Dominions, and the United States. The radio and expanding newsprint production were reinforced by the nationalistic energies released by new inventions and new sources of power.

While the palæotechnic and the neotechnic developments reinforced each other in the war and carried forward the boom of the twenties they began to diverge and to conflict in the depression. The coal areas as the basis of palæotechnic industrialism were the centres of development because of the importance of coal as a weight-losing raw material[21] which attracted other raw materials. Its significance was evident to neotechnic industry in the importation of petroleum in large quantities and in the importance of iron and steel to the automobile industry. But the difficulties of the coal industry in the twenties, evident in Great Britain especially in the depressed areas, in contrast with the emergence of the light industries, such as the automobile, radio, and electrical equipment in new locations, indicate the character of the change. The railway problem in Canada and other countries followed the emphasis on heavy equipment in rails, right-of-way, locomotives, and cars, and extensive financing for handling increasingly bulky, heavier, and cheaper commodities and the consequent effectiveness of motor competition with its stress on light valuable commodities, light equipment, and ease of finance. Wheat production was rapidly extended in the war and during the twenties by intensive and extensive cultivation, with railroad construction and motor transportation, in trucks and tractors, while industrialism centred on the coal areas was in distress and the market was narrowed. Tariffs emerged with increasing nationalism to protect agriculture in the wheat markets of the world.

Hydro-electric power is less mobile and flexible than petroleum. Distance from the power site has been an important factor but the handicap has decreased with inventions and new materials. It has facilitated the exploitation of the resources of non-agricultural areas with resistant formations and broken topography distant from coal formations. The conspicuous resources have been minerals and newsprint and pulp products, but with the depression, production of metallic minerals supported by gold has become an important competitor for power and has strengthened the radio against the newspaper.

The implications of neotechnical industrialism have been evident in the growth of cities and metropolitan areas. On the one hand the skyscraper and increasing compactness of population in large apartment houses have been encouraged by developments in electrical equipment and on the other hand population has spread out over wide areas as a result of the automobile and metalled roads. Population has been released by machine industry in agriculture and has migrated to the more densely populated areas. Rising standards of expenditure and congestion have been accompanied by declining birth-rates. Building booms have characterized the sharp depreciation through obsolescence of housing equipment, and governments have attempted to encourage the construction of houses in the face of competition from more efficient apartment houses and at the expense of unfortunate individuals who have been encouraged to own their own homes. The demands of population in congested areas, under the direction of scientific work in nutrition, have shifted from carbohydrates to vitamins or from wheat to dairy products, live-stock, fruits, and vegetables. Improved transportation facilities, especially in the development of refrigeration, have increased the range of supply of proteins, fats, and vitamins. The wheat-coal economy, which involved hauling bulky commodities to the dominant coal areas, has been broken by the emergence of a large number of metropolitan centres dependent on new types of supplies and new types of transportation characteristic of recent industrialism. The strengthening of the Dominions and of the provinces in the Statute of Westminster and with the benefit of Privy Council decisions since the war reflected the decreasing importance of the metropolitan demand of Great Britain and the expansion of new metropolitan areas on the North American continent. The city has sharpened the cultural background established under the influence of commercialism.

Neotechnic industrialism superimposed on palæotechnic industrialism involved changes of tremendous implication to modern society and brought strains of great severity. The institutional structure built up on iron and steel and coal has been slow to change. Governmental machinery in those regions in which palæotechnic society developed late has been extended and government intervention in regions in which it developed earlier has been intensified as a result of the rigidities of labour organization and corporate finance. Regions which continued primarily commercial, as Newfoundland, in the export of dried fish and in which capitalism, represented by the railway and the steamship, involved heavy burdens, failed to survive the effects of the new industrialism and the impact of the depression and lost responsible government. The effects of government intervention have been less severe in regions dominated by neotechnical industrialism and enhanced in regions dominated by palæotechnical industrialism. Wheat areas and coal and iron regions have been penalized. Adjustment by tariffs, railway rates, bounties, bankruptcy legislation, and other devices which characterized palæotechnic industrialism has become inadequate and compelled the intervention on a large scale of monetary devices.

The price system has been thwarted by the burden of debt hanging over from the old industrialism and stimulated by the support of government in the growth of the new industrialism as in the Ontario Hydro-Electric Power Commission. Private enterprise has been exposed to conflict and defeat in the fields of labour and capital in the old industrialism and has been conspicuously successful in the new industrialism. The search for liquidity favoured the new industrialism. Profits from tobacco were turned into the development of hydro-electric power on the Saguenay and supported substantial profits from the production of aluminum. The Ford Motor Company has been a conspicuous tribute to individual enterprise and the use of petroleum, as has also the development of Radio City. Private enterprise has been handicapped by the inconsistencies of political decisions but it has adapted itself with amazing facility. With monetary policy the state has been compelled to concentrate on vast areas and has been less effective in major undertakings such as the St Lawrence waterways with the consequent profits which accompany disturbances on a large scale. In democratic countries with a strong labour organization or a large and vocal agricultural population, monetary policy is an important device but limited by an essentially conservative outlook.

The problem of debt in the war and the post-war period arising from the background of capitalism has had significant repercussions on the effectiveness of the price system. It was enhanced by the rise of continental economies, by the construction of transcontinental railways following the discoveries of gold on the Pacific, and by the dominance of coal and steel. Short-term credit which characterized the commercial system dominated by an island was followed by long-term credit dominated by continents. The unmanageable character of long-term credit in terms of allocation of yields in relation to costs became evident in the enormous reduction in value of railway securities in the United States, in the emergence of large fortunes through reorganizations and the formation of trusts, and in the evolution of the Canadian federal structure as an instrument capable of carrying an expanding debt. The problem of debt is the problem of Canadian federalism, as the federal structure is a credit instrument. To confine ourselves to Canada, the so-called railway problem has emerged with the problem of wheat, the competition of roads and motor transport and of new routes such as the Panama Canal, and has been evident in the disappearance of dividends on Canadian Pacific Railway stock and the continuance of deficits on the Canadian National Railways. The intensity of the problem incidental to the enormous amounts of capital involved in transcontinental railways, and the burden of overhead costs incidental to the economic, political, and geographic background has been evident in the first decade in the pronouncements of Sir Henry Thornton, and in the second decade in the pronouncements of Sir Edward Beatty. On the one hand, the Canadian Pacific Railway as the bulwark of private enterprise has shown little evidence of weakening in the struggle, and its plea for arrangements which appear to provide for operation of all Canadian railways at the expense of government is in danger of being regarded as an attempt at participation in the old game of tired businessmen in Canada. On the other hand, the Canadian National Railways are directly under the sovereign power of Parliament and should not be used to lay conduits under the name of cooperation from the Treasury to the pockets of Canadian Pacific shareholders, or be exposed to the subtle sabotage of maintaining an empty hotel in Vancouver and an empty hole in Montreal for nearly a decade in order not to injure private enterprise. It is the hope of democracy in Canada that both will continue to strive earnestly but that neither will succeed, and that the impossibility of running two competitive railways will continue. Dictatorship for the advantage of the Canadian Pacific Railway and a balanced budget is a prospect to be contemplated with concern. Those who argue for the abolition of the Canadian National deficit must suggest alternative and more effective devices for offsetting the burden of the tariff and the relief of depressed areas. Dictatorship proposed by the Canadian National in the form of a compulsory arbitration tribunal should be resisted as an encroachment on the powers of Parliament and on the rights of the Canadian Pacific. Both railways should be warned against talking nonsense about scientific rate structures and uneconomic costs in their attacks on road transport. Political agitation as to savings rather than earnings gives rise to the suspicion that the problem of efficient administration of transcontinental railways has not been solved or that administration, adapted to expansion, has been inadequate with its cessation. The public would like more indication of attempts to increase earnings rather than to be asked to make more sacrifices in the interest of savings. We may hope that the aggressiveness of the Canadian Pacific Railway will keep politics out of the Canadian National and that the aggressiveness of the Canadian National Railways will keep the Canadian Pacific out of politics and out of the Canadian Treasury, and that the results will permit the continuation of democratic government. The vested interests of the social scientist will suffer less from the attacks of Sir Edward Beatty than from the indifference of an amalgamated railway.

Organs of opinion reflect the increasing significance of regional and metropolitan growth, in demands for economies in the interests of finance or for protection against the possibilities of poorer service and discrimination which would accompany the various proposals for economic dictatorship. Montreal and Toronto have chiefly reflected the financial interests of the St Lawrence in the demands for railway amalgamation, but the exceptions and western Canada support the outlook of wheat in fears of rigidities of economic dictatorship. Interests representing the new industrialism have been evident in striking fashion in control by the pulp and paper industry of the *Mail and Empire* and then by mining and hydro-electric power in the amalgamation of the *Globe* and *Mail*. Newspapers tend to reflect to an increasing extent the influence of rapid transportation and efficient distribution characteristic of metropolitan development. The pressure of overhead costs incidental to large-scale capital equipment in newspaper plants and newsprint mills has increased the importance of large-scale circulation and of good will or the stereotype of Walter Lippmann. Dependence on advertising, particularly from department stores, has become a vital issue in policy as to news, editorials, and features.[22] The cheap newspaper is subordinated to the demands of modern industrialism and modern merchandising. Overhead costs have contributed to lack of precision in accounting, and the allocation of costs between the purchaser of goods from department stores and the purchaser of the paper, or between the purchaser of paper and the purchaser of hydro-electric power from plants owned by paper companies, is extremely difficult to determine. In paying for electric light or for groceries one cannot be certain how much is paid for newspapers. The patterns of public opinion or the stereotypes have become blurred, and amalgamations of newspapers and the fusion of editorial policies lead to demands for general programs which appeal to the business mind. Broad stereotypes are typical, such as the belief in the stability of governments, or – as social scientists, who have logically taken the place of millennialists, have been wont to put it – the dangers of civilization crashing, whatever that may mean. The Canadian variant points to the break-up of Confederation.

Periodicals emerge to meet the demands of any group whenever that group becomes sufficiently specialized to demand goods which warrant advertising on a sufficient scale to support the periodical. Specialization of this character is largely restricted to cities and regions. Such periodicals attempt to build up fresh stereotypes but are forced to compete with constantly improving technique designed to reach new and possibly lower levels of intelligence, especially those who prefer to look at photographs rather than to read. Those who prefer to read have hived off as supporters of pocket-book digests. Illustrations have reached a place of dominant importance and writers have been compelled to illustrate the illustrations including the advertisements. The difficulties which new parties experience in building up sharp stereotypes through newspapers or periodicals have been less evident in the publication of large editions of cheap books. New educational movements and reform programs make the world safe for publishers. The support of religious bodies to publishing houses has weakened and been replaced by the state with its demands for educational texts. Education comes under the jurisdiction of the provinces. A substantial publisher of textbooks is not in a strong position to publish literature other than that of a strikingly nationalistic or local character. The incipient fascism of Canadian intellectuals, the group which cannot distinguish a bar association from a trade union, in Winnipeg, Toronto, and Montreal, evident in nationalism, isolationism, and the boosting of Canadian literature in the interests of Canadian publishers, has deep roots. School texts handled on a mass production basis in an off-peak period by large organizations such as mail-order houses and providing as a by-product, advertising, reduce the volume of publishing houses and, who knows, may injure the possibility of developing Canadian poetry. Abolition of standard texts in favour of the publication of a wide variety of books increases the cost of education to the publishers, the state, and the purchaser of books, but it tends to break down broad stereotypes.

The decline in value of political stereotypes which accompanies the decline of the party newspaper has been partly a result of the increase in importance of the radio as a political weapon. Competition between newspapers and the radio for advertising, as well as in the handling of news, has been evident in the concerted attack by the press on the Canadian Broadcasting Corporation following contracts with American firms. From the standpoint of the public, it is a choice between Moon Mullins and Charlie McCarthy. The radio capitalizes the disadvantage of the large newspaper in appealing to stereotypes which refuse to be blurred, as is evident in the strength of religion in the rural areas. While it has served the dictatorship of Russia, Germany, Italy, and Japan, it has assisted in escape via the provincialism of Mr Aberhart and the federalism of Mr Roosevelt. As a new invention the radio threatens to circumvent the walls imposed by tariffs and to reach across boundaries frequently denied to other media of communication, but like the newspaper it is adapted to the demands of metropolitan areas. Saskatchewan elections may provide a rough indication of the range of the Calgary stations.

In a political entity such as Canada in which the forces of centralization are so strong, the element of size involves powerful counteracting forces of decentralization. The wheat-coal economy and the enormous burden of debt which has accompanied its decline have involved rigid interest and transportation charges supported by broad general stereotypes involving imperialism, nationalism, demands for railway amalgamation, union of the Prairie Provinces and of the Maritime Provinces, the dangers of communism, the dangers of fascism, and the like. Adam Smith might have said of capitalists as he said of merchants: "The government of an exclusive company of merchants is, perhaps, the worst of all governments for any country whatever."[23] "I have never known much good done by those who affected to trade for the public good."[24] Wide fluctuations in prices of raw materials such as furs, fish, timber, wheat, pulp and paper, and minerals involve a large element of elasticity, in marketing structures as in barter and the truck system, in the standards of living of producers, and in financial structures, as reorganizations will attest. Expanding metropolitan areas dependent on the new industries such as pulp and paper, minerals, and hydro-electric power were provided with cushions in relief, in relative financial independence, and in the more direct impact of new inventions. The exposed areas have been of the wheat-coal economy and the favoured areas have gained with the new industrialism. In spite of the hard core of rigidity of the debt structure, the monetary policies of other nations, especially of Great Britain and the United States, compelled a change in monetary structure and monetary policy in Canada. A prominent Canadian banker stated at an annual meeting of a bank largely concerned with the new industrialism, in January 1931: "For the future it is absolutely essential that means should be devised to prevent the drastic changes in the price level which have been characteristic of the period since the close of the war."[25] A representative of the same bank stated in 1938: "Experience will have taught us nothing, if as a result of occurrences of the last seven years we do not conclude that positive action from a monetary point of view is the first essential in controlling excesses of both boom and depression."[26] The effects have been evident in defaults, with and without benefit of the political success of Mr Aberhart. A monetary policy which might have softened the effects of the depression in the wheat-coal areas might have spurred on the activities of the new industrialism in the hydro-electric power, mining, and pulp and paper areas and increased the internal strain already severe as attested by the major disasters of debts necessitating the Royal Commission on Dominion-Provincial Relations. The difficulties of the wheat-coal regions are not less because of the declining sympathetic interest of the regions of the new industrialism.

The limitations of the price system in failing to overcome the handicaps of rigidities of debt burdens and in accentuating internal strains have been evident in the rise of monetary nationalism and the increasing importance of the state as a monetary instrument.

Bankruptcy is no longer accepted as an effective solvent and is no longer possible with the state as a credit instrument and the possibilities of controlling inflation. It is "unthinkable." The increasing strength and influence of institutions concerned with long-term credit, such as bond houses and insurance companies, based on the application of mathematics in the calculation of mortality tables and bond yields has left no alternative. Within the state, large-scale capital equipment and the drive to operate at capacity have accentuated the importance of alternative production and intensified competition in off-peak periods. Ridges formed by buckling under competitive pressure are conspicuous in basing point systems, intensive advertising, and monopolistic arrangements. The tendency towards fixed prices has been accompanied by more intense competition in other directions as in the case of railway service and train schedules and political agitation. The realm of intangible services assumes increasing importance and the skyscraper has become the modern cathedral. Long-term credit is the new basis of modern belief. The difficulty of competition in prices compels a shift in cost items and a realignment of accounting. The rigidity of accounting systems accentuates the importance of fixed prices with the result that the accountant is bribed to present accounts with limited value for interpretation or accuracy.[27] Accounting systems have met the demands of corporations for release from control of debt by facilitating the development of policies by which reserves and surplus have been built up, and control lost to the shareholders. Dependence on the capital market for new supplies of capital has been materially lessened, with the result that it becomes more speculative. Short-term credit and the importance of liquidity intensify speculation. Concentration of control in the hands of management, with the possibilities of interlocking directorates and the like, involves possibilities of unwise developments in large organizations, and lack of information regarding their policies. The monetary system with its mathematical implications facilitates the development of mechanical control devices, ranging from improved accounting machinery to the adaptation of automatic services to the nickel and other coins and of the Canadian nickel in size and weight to the American nickel.

The price system has stimulated minor correctives in persuading the consumer to educate himself through consumers' research organizations, societies to stop propaganda (of all things), and other devices, and still permits many of us to live in comparative peace. Its handicaps have been stressed to an increasing extent by economists who have been concerned with monopoly theory and with the decline of competition or with the rise of economic warfare and what someone has called the decline of the idea of competition. The effectiveness of the price system within the state is evident in the attempts to reinforce pecuniary by political values. The successful politician is precluded from policies which indicate class or self-interest but he is successful in so far as he succeeds in enlisting the support of the price system. He should be the orthodontist of the social sciences pursuing his way by gradual but persistent pressure, but he continues with analogies of the machine in "pulling levers" or with violent medical treatments in giving "a shot in the arm."[28]

The effectiveness of the price system has been shown in the decline of feudalism, the decline of mercantilism, the rise of palæotechnic capitalism, and the shift to neotechnic capitalism. It has stimulated the growth of inventions and the trend in the movement of goods from light and valuable raw materials to heavy and cheap raw materials, and to light and valuable finished products. It has hastened the rise of new sources of power and of new industries and accelerated the decline of obsolete regions. The drive of the price system on the economic and social structure within the state has been accompanied by continual disturbance between the states. The role of the state in assuming the burdens of depreciation through obsolescence of the wheat-coal economy and in stimulating the development of new industrialism involves rapid expansion of public debt and necessitates the continual revision of currencies in relation to other countries. The relative lack of rigid structure in the international field has probably reduced the dangers of international disturbance. The stupidity of nationalism is tempered by the chaos of internationalism. Losses through nationalism are offset by realignments of national boundaries, trade agreements, international cartels, foreign balances, world fairs, and subsidized tourists. Monetary nationalism is a reflection of the role of the state in the expansion of industrialism and the means by which the state is compelled to rely increasingly on expanded public debt and to avoid increasingly its effects. Employment and the demands for consumers' goods must be stimulated by state activity. To obtain bread we must build a gun or lay down a stone. Monetary nationalism and the constant necessity for readjustments of exchange have become normal phases of the recent effects of the price system. Responsible government in the vital sense of control over funds has disappeared in favour of secret operation of equalization funds. The automatic system which centred on London has come under divided control with the rise of North America and the opening of the Pacific. We seem destined in economics to follow the meteorologist in modifying equilibrium analysis and turning to what he has called the polar front theory in which the meeting of economic masses becomes important rather than trade between nations. There are serious weaknesses in the analogy of flowing from high to low pressure areas, and great advantages in discussing pressure groups. The economics of losses is not less significant than the economics of profits.

Economists have reflected the confusion introduced by machine industry. The decline of vested interests peculiar to the period after Adam Smith was a tribute to the economic value of the *Wealth of Nations*, but the emergence of vested interests (i.e., the legitimate right to something for nothing) under capitalism has reduced the value of economic theory based on Adam Smith and increased the value of economic theory adapted to nationalism. To extend the thesis of Mr Keynes as to the influence of rising prices on literature, it may be said that they tend to correspond with free will systems of economic thought. Jevons might have added economic systems to Acts of Parliament and sun spots. Scientific advance and the application of science to industry through inventions are characteristic of periods of prosperity. The philosophic outlook based on scientific achievement leaves its stamp on economics. Periods of prosperity may be characterized by most intensive work in economics but periods of depression have been characterized by attempts at application, particularly in the field in which mathematics provides a convenient channel between science and economics, namely money. Economics becomes a branch of physics and chemistry rather than of biology. Politics has become a method of revolt. The word political has been restored to its place with economy, and equilibrium analysis must be modified and extended throughout the social sciences. A study of the elasticity of demand for autarchies is significant to a study of the elasticity of demand for wheat.[29] Depressions produce deterministic systems and arguments such as have been advanced in this paper.

NOTES

1 Adam Smith, *An Inquiry into the Nature and Causes of the Wealth of Nations* (Modern Library ed., New York, 1937) 531.

2 See E.J. Hamilton, *American Treasure and the Price Revolution in Spain* (Cambridge, Mass., 1934); Smith, *Wealth of Nations*, 202. Bodin wrote the *Discours sur les causes de l'extrème cherté qui est aujourdhuy en France* in 1574.

3 Smith, *Wealth of Nations*, 207. "Of all the commodities, therefore,

which are bought in one foreign country, for no other purpose but to be sold or exchanged again for some other goods in another, there are none so convenient as gold and silver" (ibid., 516).

4 Ibid., 388. For an excellent account of the decline of the feudal system in Japan as a result of the introduction of money, see M. Takizawa, *The Penetration of Money Economy in Japan and its Effects upon Social and Political Institutions* (New York, 1927).

5 Smith, *Wealth of Nations*, 391–2.

6 W. Richardson, *An Essay on the Causes of the Decline of Foreign Trade* (London, 1750).

7 C.R. Fay, "Plantation Economy," *Economic Journal*, Dec. 1936.

8 Smith, *Wealth of Nations*, 544–5.

9 Sir Mathew Decker, *An Essay on the Causes of the Decline of Foreign Trade* (Dublin, 1749).

10 Smith, *Wealth of Nations*, 550.

11 Ibid., 460.

12 Frederick Merk, *Fur Trade and Empire* (Cambridge, Mass., 1931), 108.

13 A.S. Morton, *The Journal of Duncan McGillivray* (Toronto, 1929), 47.

14 T.S. Ashton, *Iron and Steel in the Industrial Revolution* (Manchester, 1924).

15 See L. Mumford, *Technics and Civilization* (New York, 1934); also E.F. Heckscher, "Recent Tendencies in Economic Life," *The World's Economic Future* (London, 1938), 97–110.

16 H.M. Larson, *Jay Cooke, Private Banker* (Cambridge, Mass., 1936).

17 "Memorandum to Royal Commission on the Depression of Trade and Industry," *Official Papers of Alfred Marshall* (London, 1926), 4–5.

18 See T. Veblen, *Imperial Germany and the Industrial Revolution* (New York, 1915).

19 See the small library on war history published by the Carnegie Endowment for International Peace.

20 See W.A. Mackintosh, "Gold and the Decline of Prices," *Proceedings of the Canadian Political Science Association*, 1931, 88–110.

21 C.J. Friedrich, *Alfred Weber's Theory of the Location of Industries* (Chicago, 1929).

22 Freedom of the press and freedom of speech have always been relative terms assuming a moderate tolerance. Newspaper space involves a substantial outlay of funds as does an hour's broadcasting. In private conversation where talk is said to be cheap, one is inclined to revise Mark Twain's dictum and to say that we have freedom of speech and freedom of the press and not the good sense not to use either of them. Small talk, bores, and other terms are in constant demand. In so-called conferences freedom of speech is paraded as a special feature, but it usually amounts to common scolding or saying things

calculated to get the conference into the newspapers – in other words, advertising space for nothing. See H.A. Innis, "Discussion in the Social Sciences," *Dalhousie Review* 15 (Jan. 1936): 401–13.

23 Smith, *Wealth of Nations*, 537.

24 Ibid., 423.

25 *Proceedings of the Canadian Political Science Association*, 1931, 122.

26 S.R. Noble, "The Monetary Experience of Canada during the Depression," *Canadian Banker*, April 1938.

27 See C.A. Ashley, "Some Aspects of Corporations," *Essays in Political Economy in Honour of E.J. Urwick* (Toronto, 1938).

28 V.F. Coe, "Monetary Theory and Politics," ibid.

29 See *The State and Economic Life* (Paris, 1934), 252–4, 289–90.

CHAPTER SIX

Liquidity Preference and the Specialization of Production in North America and the Pacific

The last half of the nineteenth century was characterized by a series of erratic outbreaks of economic activity along the Pacific coast of North America and in Australia which suddenly transformed vast, scantily populated areas into regions producing enormous quantities of raw materials for a highly industrialized Europe. Traffic to the Pacific had been restricted to commodities of high value and light bulk, such as furs, wool, and tea. The encircling movement of world trade which surrounded the globe first in the fur trade in which traders from Russia met traders from Europe and North America in Alaska was strengthened by the sudden economic cyclones which followed the gold rushes. The discovery of placer gold in California in 1848 was followed by the rush of 1849, and the opening up of other areas in the Pacific region. Possibilities of enormous wealth, the enhanced value of gold following depression and a secular decline in prices, and the uncertainty of yield, led to the immigration of large numbers, chiefly young men, with at least sufficient funds to pay the expensive passage and to buy large quantities of expensive supplies. The influx of labour and capital into regions chiefly mountainous in character, and with restricted economic development, necessitated importation of goods and supplies on a large scale. High prices as a result of sudden increase in demand and the addition of large supplies of gold provided enormous profits on imports and on shipping. The profit motive in its most intense form was in evidence in the rush of labour and supplies to new gold fields.

From *Transactions of the Royal Society of Canada*, 3rd ser., 37, sec. 2 (1943): 1–31; reprinted in *Political Economy in the Modern State* (Ryerson, 1946), 168–200; first appeared as "Liquidity Preference as a Factor of Industrial Development."

Influx of population was followed by rapid exhaustion of the accessible gold fields and the necessity of searching for new regions or of developing alternative natural resources. The return of prospectors from California, and the intimate knowledge of the peculiarities of the country which accompanied the spread of sheep-raising over wide areas in Australia, led to the discovery of gold in New South Wales and in Victoria and to an influx of immigrants in 1852. The hope of the Chief Secretary who wrote, "If this is a gold country it will stop the Home Government from sending us any more convicts and prevent emigration to California" at Sydney in 1851 was fulfilled. Population increased rapidly from 437,665 in 1857 to 1,168,149 in 1871, and gold production in the period totalled £124,000,000. Decline in the yield of the placer fields and the introduction of capitalistic methods of exploitation and displacement of labour were followed by migration, search for gold in other regions, and the rush to New Zealand (Otago in 1861, and Westland in 1865). The arrival of large numbers of young men equipped with supplies and with experience in Australian fields led to rapid exploitation.

On the Pacific coast of North America, miners pushed northward from California in search of new fields and in 1858 "about 10,000 foreign miners" were attracted to the bars of the Fraser River. Large numbers of disillusioned, among them Henry George, turned back, but others pushed up the Fraser to make the important discoveries on its tributaries in the Cariboo in the early sixties. The total yield of gold from 1858 to 1876 was estimated at $40,000,000. The population of British Columbia totalled 36,247 in 1871, when it entered Confederation.

The effects of the discovery of gold in the Pacific regions were evident in the demand of large numbers in relatively densely populated areas for ships to carry them to the gold fields. The discovery of gold in California quickened the demand for American sailing ships. Clipper ships carried passengers around the Horn for San Francisco and thence proceeded to China for a cargo of tea to be taken to London. The increasing demands for raw materials and for markets for manufactured products from Great Britain were met by the migration of ships and trade. News of the gold strike of 1851 in Australia was followed by a demand for fast, comfortable ships from England and the abandonment of the miserable emigrant ships of the forties. The Blackwallers employed from London to India were diverted to Australia. The fast sailing ships of New England and Nova Scotia were in demand in Liverpool for the Australian route. James Baines, with the Black Ball Line, purchased the famous ships of Donald McKay, a native of Nova Scotia; and his rival, the White Star Line, joined in competition for mail contracts, landing mail in Australia in from sixty-five to sixty-eight days, and for passengers. The *Marco Polo* (1,625 tons), pioneer of the Black Ball Line, built in Saint John, New Brunswick, in 1851, and her Master, Captain James Nicol Forbes, became famous in the Australian trade with a record passage by the Horn from Melbourne to Liverpool of fifty-six days, and a round trip of five months and twenty-one days. Time was reduced as a result of the theories of M.F. Maury as to wind directions and as to routes. New England and British North American ships were in demand due to larger, better sailing vessels and built of softwoods of cheaper construction. As the timber trade of British North America contributed to support industrial change in Great Britain in the first half of the century, the softwood ships of North America supported commercial change in the Pacific. But steamers to Colon, a railway thence to Panama, completed in 1855, and steamers thence to California almost displaced sailing ships by Cape Horn.

The increase in settlement along the coast of Australia, following the gold rushes, created a demand for more efficient services between the ports and from the ports to the interior. The Australian Steam Navigation Company and other companies established services in 1851 and later dates between Melbourne and Sydney, Sydney and Brisbane and Melbourne and Adelaide, and Melbourne and Newcastle. Railway mileage in Victoria and in New South Wales increased from two miles in 1854 to 171 miles in 1859 and total railway mileage in Australia to 1,042 in 1871. In 1854, a mail service was established between Melbourne and Wellington, New Zealand. Steamers ran from Melbourne to Dunedin, and Sydney to Auckland, and, after the gold rush in New Zealand, from Melbourne to Otago. New Zealand coastal steamers ran between Wellington and Dunedin, and in the gold rush to Hokitika. Steamships engaged on short runs were extremely mobile and capable of being shifted according to demands. They were taken as troopships for the Crimean War, and were engaged after 1860 in the Maori Wars in the North Island of New Zealand. Telegraph communication was established between Sydney, Melbourne, and Adelaide in 1858, and a line was opened from Perth to Fremantle in 1869. A submarine cable was laid from Tasmania via Circular Head and King Island to Cape Otway in 1859 and in the Cook Strait in 1866. In New Zealand a wooden tramway was built from the Bluff to Lake Waktipu and a railway was built from Christchurch to Lyttleton early in the sixties, and from

Invercargill to Bluff Harbour in 1867. In 1870, 1,887 miles of telegraph line had been laid.

The entrance of the steamship in the Pacific transoceanic trade was infrequent and slow to develop in spite of assistance through mail contracts. In 1853, mail was taken by the Peninsula and Oriental Company from Singapore to Sydney, but the Crimean War necessitated withdrawal of steamships and cancellation of the service. After considerable difficulty the P and O began a monthly service from England to Australia via Mauritius in 1859 but this was abandoned for connections at Galle in Ceylon. After several unsuccessful efforts, a steamship service was started from Panama to Sydney. The island of Rapa was selected as a coaling station in 1866, but the service disappeared with the completion of the Union Pacific to San Francisco in 1869 and the establishment of a line from San Francisco to Sydney in 1870.

On the American coast, steamers were employed to run from Panama to San Francisco, and to Oregon and British Columbia. Steamboats were brought up from California to be employed on the route from Victoria to Langley, and from Langley up the Fraser River to Emory's Bar. The rapidity of development of British Columbia placer mining was hastened with the plant and technique which had been developed in the California gold fields. Location of placer gold fields tended to concentrate in the upper reaches of the swift waters of relatively mountainous regions. In British Columbia, discovery of gold on the bars of the Fraser River was followed by discoveries in the Cariboo, with the result that improved land transportation was essential since navigation was not feasible. Goods were handled from Emory's Bar to Yale by smaller craft and eventually the Cariboo Road was extended to Barkerville.

The effects of placer mining on the movement of population and on transportation facilities were cyclonic in character. Rapid increase in population created demands for shipping and improved transportation, and led in the distant regions of the Pacific to the development of numerous subordinate industries. Funds brought out by immigrants from densely populated industrial areas, supplies of gold obtained from the gold fields, and a scarcity of manufactured products and provisions, led to a sharp rise in prices. The intensely speculative character of gold mining with the uncertainty of returns, the disturbances created by new discoveries, and the decline of production in relation to primitive methods, necessitated a high rate of depreciation and reinforced the trend toward high prices. The short life of a placer camp involved fabulous charges.

I

Gold mining introduced an advanced state of monetary organization which accentuated flexibility in the specialization of production. It brought a reversal in the trend of a spread of money from the centre to the circumference in the sudden emergence of money on the fringes. Mercantile systems which favoured devices increasing imports of specie and accentuated the importance of liquidity were outstripped by the production of large quantities of gold.

The demand of a large population for foodstuffs was followed by agricultural expansion. The total land under crop in Australia increased from 491,000 acres in 1850 to over a million acres in 1858: New South Wales, 223,000; Victoria, 299,000; Tasmania, 229,000; South Australia, 264,000; and Western Australia, 21,000. "All wages rose, all accessible good land was in great demand, the dealers in produce found the advantage of prices rising in the article as it passed through their hands, live stock increased in value, shipping was profitably employed."[1] The dominance of the wool trade in both Australia and New Zealand became less conspicuous. Labour was attracted to the gold fields, and wages of shepherds increased. A rise in the price of meat led to emphasis on the production of mutton. Cattle became increasingly important.

Labour was released from gold mining with the exhaustion of shallow diggings, and the displacement of primitive technique by capitalistic devices which could be adopted with the improvement of transportation. In 1861, the Victoria gold fields employed 711 steam engines (10,782 horse-power). Alternative employment was limited. Shipping in relation to gold mining implied a heavy outbound cargo and a light, highly valuable, return cargo. Ample space was available on ships returning to England and improved transportation to the gold fields facilitated a return to wool production and wool exports. Lower freights and higher prices contributed to strengthen the position of wool following the disturbances of the gold rush. But wool production did not involve a substantial demand for labour. Industries which emerged in relation to the demands of the large population of the gold fields offered greater possibilities for absorption of labour, provided new markets for manufactured products were available. In 1861, Victoria had 403 factories employing 3,830 persons. Attempts to encourage industry were accompanied by attempts to increase revenues and to stimulate agriculture development in addition to wool production.

Placer mining, with its emphasis on labour and on supplies of funds, stressed individualism, but continued exploitation necessitated capital equipment including roads which implied governmental machinery for the collection of revenue and the carrying of debt. An immediate and strong popular demand arose for improved transportation to the difficult regions of the gold mining areas. While the outlay for improved transportation was heavy, miners were extremely reluctant, as a result of high prices, to contribute to the support of transportation.

Placer mining strengthened and consolidated the trend toward democratic government. The Australian Colonies Government Act of 1850 was followed, with the stimulus of a rapid increase in population, by responsible government in New South Wales, Victoria, and Tasmania, in 1855. Self-government implied control over lands and of revenue[2] from land sales.

Following the abolition of the preference on goods from the United Kingdom in 1851, and the demands for revenue, import duties were imposed by Victoria in 1855. Under the determined and energetic leadership of David Syme, a policy of protection was adopted in 1866 and employees increased to 28,000 in 1874. This development involved industrialism, protection, and extension of agriculture. The struggle between the wool producer and the agriculturist which characterized Australian land policy became severe and was followed by the Land Act of 1862 with its emphasis on settlement.

New South Wales had been less seriously influenced by the gold rush. Population had been drained to Victoria and industrial development was weakened. In 1852 duties[3] were imposed on selected commodities. The importance of wool exports and dependence on a staple product precluded attempts to develop manufacturing by protection. The free trade policy of New South Wales was in striking contrast to the protectionism of Victoria. South Australia responded to the demands of the gold fields with increased production of wheat. With relative decline in local demand, and the introduction of agricultural machinery, particularly the stripper, exports of wheat were sent to Great Britain in 1866. The area under crop increased to 801,571 acres in 1870–1. Robert Torrens contributed to the solution of the land problem of agricultural expansion through the system which was introduced in 1858, and the Strangeways Act (1868) gave further encouragement. Tasmania, Western Australia, and Queensland increased the area under crop during the period, but the total advance was not relatively important.

The diverse economic development of the colonies of Australia involved conflicts in policies. The contrast in tariff policy between New South Wales and Victoria, and their limitations in treaty-making power, caused the failure of numerous conferences. In 1867 an agreement was reached between the two colonies, but it was not until 1873, in the Australian Colonies Duties Act, that the imperial authorities conceded the right to make trade agreements.

Agreement was conspicuous, on the other hand, in the exclusion of Chinese. Migration of Oriental labour was a result of the immediate demands for labour in the gold fields, of the high costs of labour in temperate areas of the Pacific coast with light density of population and at long distances from the Atlantic seaboard,[4] and of the existence of areas of intense population density along the Asiatic fringe.

Expansion of transport facilities and improvement of navigation, particularly the iron clippers and the beginning of regular steam traffic, supported the rapid economic growth which followed the gold rush to the distant areas of Australia. Concentration on wool as a commodity adapted to the demands of distant transportation was accentuated. Public borrowings accompanied improved transportation facilities and expansion of production. All the states had appeared on the London market to secure loans to finance capital improvements: Victoria, 1859; New South Wales, 1855; South Australia, 1854; Queensland, 1861; Western Australia, 1845; and Tasmania, 1867. Free trade in Great Britain and development of Australia through staple products in relation to the demands of that area were accompanied by financial support from Great Britain and in turn by responsible government and the institution of suitable financial machinery designed to secure adequate revenue. The geographical characteristics of Australia with its extensive coastline implied decentralization of governments and competition for labour rather than for capital, whereas in Canada concentration on the St Lawrence implied centralization and competition for capital for construction of canals and railways. Confederation appeared early in Canada as a result of competition from the United States and later in Australia as a result of difficulties between decentralized states.

The effect of the gold rush of Australia on New Zealand in the fifties was to provide a base to support the expansion which followed the gold rush to New Zealand in the early sixties. As in Australia, high prices of agricultural products stimulated production and decline in gold production released labour for the development of other industries. Canterbury and Otago, as the chief centres of sheep-raising, and the South Island generally, increased in importance with demands for provisions, supplies, labour, and shipping. The number of sheep increased from one and a half million in 1858 to nearly ten million in 1871, wool exports from nearly four million pounds to nearly thirty-eight million, and land under cultivation from one hundred thousand acres to one million, two hundred thousand acres. Grain exports declined from 118,740 bushels in 1859 to 3,238 bushels in 1863, but increased to 1,032,092 bushels in 1871. South Island definitely established economic supremacy until the end of the century over North Island which had been harassed in the sixties with the Maori Wars. In 1871 population in South Island totalled 159,918, and in North Island 96,875. The development of railways and public works followed the increase in revenue incidental to the gold rush. In 1870 the debt of the government totalled £4,543,316, and of the provinces, £3,298,575.

The effects of the gold rush in British Columbia were similar to those in Australia and New Zealand. Rapid increase in population created demands for provisions and supplies. The immediate demands and high prices of foodstuffs led not only to a rapid increase in imports, but also to local production. In spite of geographical limitations of soil and climate the colony was self-sufficient in its supply of wheat by 1866. Salmon were caught in large numbers for local consumption. Timber and planks were imported from American mills during the early building boom in Victoria, but local sawmills were rapidly introduced and by 1870 were installed on the Fraser and in the Cariboo to meet the demand of towns, and of miners for construction of flumes and sluice boxes. As placer creeks were exhausted and capitalistic methods of extraction increased in importance, surplus population moved outwards to new creeks or contributed to the more stable development in the support of new industries. Built up to meet the immediate demands of gold mining, industries served as a basis for expansion in the production of exports. As ever, gold mining involved a heavy inbound cargo and a light outbound cargo, and the lumber industry provided the raw material for an outbound cargo and for the rapid development of various regions in the Pacific. Operations begun at Alberni and Barclay Sound in 1861 were sufficient to support exports of over eleven million feet in 1862 to New Zealand, Australia, Hawaii, the Orient, South America, and even to England and Italy. Cheap lumber was essential to support the rapid transient changes in the economies of Pacific countries. The importance of industrialism as shown in the coastal steamers led to the development of the coal resources of Vancouver Island. A first shipment of 1,840 tons from Nanaimo to San Francisco in 1852 was followed by an increase of sales to a peak of 44,005 tons in 1868.

The inrush of immigrants in 1857 and 1858 led to the cancellation of the Hudson's Bay Company's licence to trade in British

Columbia in 1858. Various forms of taxation were necessary to finance local construction to the interior, and included mining licences, a head tax, a tonnage tax, an import tax, and tolls. Decline of gold mining and difficulties of taxation led to an increase in the debt of the colony. A free trade policy abandoned by Vancouver Island involved higher duties, union of the colonies in 1866, and union with Canada in 1871 in which a debt of $1,666,200 was assumed by the Dominion. Like Australia, British Columbia was faced with the Oriental problem, and as early as 1864 about two thousand Chinese were employed in the gold fields, but it was not until a much later date that restrictive legislation was enacted. The cycle of sudden immigration, exploitation and the use of capital equipment, the emergence of government and debt, and the shift to new natural resources continued in British Columbia as in other placer mining regions.

The expansion and later contraction of the gold fields of British Columbia were followed by increasing interest from the Atlantic. The long and difficult route overland began to compete with the long route by the Panama or the Horn. Milton and Cheadle crossed the Rocky Mountains in 1862 in the footsteps of fur traders and miners. Construction of an overland telegraph to Asia was brought to an abrupt stop with completion of the Atlantic cable in 1866. Alaska was added to American territory in 1867. These developments were the forerunners of the agreement by which British Columbia joined Confederation on condition that a transcontinental railway be built. The gold rush of British Columbia, the expansion of the United States, and the problem of debt in Canada precipitated the demand for political unity across the northern half of the continent and in turn for economic unity. Gold mining and its consequent economic development was a powerful factor pulling the westward extension of Empire to meet extension eastward.

II

Economic development in the Pacific prior to the completion of the Suez Canal and particularly in Australia emphasized the importance of the Cape of Good Hope and South Africa. The need of regular steam communication from England to Cape Town was increased by the internal difficulties in South Africa and by the requirements of a squadron based in Cape Town for the suppression of the East Africa slave trade. Better harbour accommodation for troop ships and passenger ships proceeding to India and Australia, and the use of Durban coal supported steamship development and traffic to the Far East. The Union Steamship Company began monthly mail service from Southampton to Cape Town in 1857. It was extended to Durban in 1865 and made semi-monthly in 1868. A telegraph was completed from Cape Town to Simonstown in 1860 and to Grahamstown in 1864. Railways were built from Cape Town to Wellington (57 miles) in 1863, and to Wynburg in 1864. The Cape Town harbour works were completed in the decade from 1860 to 1870 and the Castle Steamship Company established a line in 1872. Extension of government accompanied improvement of communications. In 1853 representative government was established in Cape Colony, but responsible government was delayed until 1872. Natal continued as a Crown colony and Basutoland came under a protectorate in 1869. As a result of the rush to the diamond fields of Kimberley in 1867–8, the British government assumed responsibility for maintaining order among the mining population in 1871, and annexed the Transvaal in 1877.

Expansion in the gold regions of the Pacific and improvement of transportation facilities strengthened extension to India and the Far East. Steamships had shortened the route to Suez, and from Suez to India. The Peninsula and Oriental Company signed a contract in January 1853 for a fortnightly service between England and Alexandria, between Marseilles and Malta, and between Suez, Calcutta, and Hong Kong with a service every two months from Singapore to Sydney. A supplementary contract in 1854 provided for a service from Suez to Bombay, but the outbreak of the Crimean War reduced a fortnightly service from Bombay to China to a monthly service. The Indian Mutiny was followed by an extension of the line between Bombay, Aden, and Suez, and with a fortnightly service from Marseilles to Alexandria and arrivals and departures alternating from Calcutta and Bombay, a weekly service was given to India. Completion of the railway from Alexandria to Cairo in 1857 and its extension to Suez facilitated the change from Marseilles to Alexandria rather than to Malta. In 1864, a telegraph line with cable was completed from London to Karachi and in 1870 a cable was completed under British control. In 1867 a weekly service was provided to Bombay, and a fortnightly service to and from China and Japan. The Suez Canal was completed in 1869 and in the same year Marseilles as the port of arrival and departure was displaced by Brindisi. With this extension of steamship service, coaling stations were established and facilities for handling steamships were developed. Coastal steamship services were extended with the formation of the British East India Navigation Company in 1857, and included the coast from Singapore to Zanzibar in 1862. Interlocking directorates with the Netherlands East India Company formed in 1866 extended a line from Singapore to the Dutch East Indies and to Brisbane, Sydney, and Melbourne by Torres Strait.

As in North America improvement of navigation contributed to the development of railways and canals in the interior, so in India, railroads extended from terminal ports, canals, and river steamships reduced costs of transportation, and involved increasing government support. The energy of Lord Dalhousie prepared the way for capital expenditures in numerous directions. Lower Burma was annexed in 1852, Jansi and Nagpur in 1853, and Oudh in 1856. The pressure of industrialism and the Indian Mutiny in 1857 were to be followed by final surrender of government control on the part of the East India Company in 1858. The Ganges Canal was completed in 1857, and the Kistna delta canals in 1855, and the Ravi Canal in 1859. The program of energetic railroad construction outlined by Lord Dalhousie in 1853 was followed, particularly after the Mutiny, by rapid progress. In 1853 a road was completed from Bombay to Lhana, in 1854 from Calcutta to Raneegunje (37 miles), and in the following year 120 miles were built in Madras. The depression in North America in 1857 and the importance of development of transportation facilities after the Mutiny led British contractors and capitalists to turn their attention to India. In 1858, Brassey began construction of a railroad from Calcutta to Khoostea on the Ganges (112 miles; completed 1862). In the following year one was built from Nulhattee to Azimgunje (27 miles) and in 1864 from Arkonam to Conjeveram (18 miles). The Delhi railway from Ghazeaabad to Umritsir (304 miles) was completed in 1870. Railway mileage in India increased from 35 in 1853–4 to 4,771 in 1870. In spite of government guarantees and other privileges, development was slow, but the serious famines of 1860 and 1866 led to active participation by the state in railway construction in 1869. The capital invested in railways in India has been estimated as follows:

	(*in thousands of pounds*)		
1858	£5,550	1864	£3,800
1859	7,150	1865	5,400
1860	7,580	1866	7,700
1861	6,500	1867	7,000
1862	5,800	1868	4,500
1863	4,750	1869	4,400

The telegraph preceded and accompanied the railroad. In the suppression of the Indian Mutiny it was said that "The electric telegraph has saved India." Before the advent of railway troops could be moved only about ten miles a day, whereas by rail they could cover four hundred miles in a day.[5]

The railway provided cheap transportation for raw materials from, and for manufactured products to, the interior. Access to the Raniganj coal fields by railway in 1854 contributed to the spread of industrialism. Wars in Russia and America accentuated the development of trade in tropical products from new sources, such as India, and had effects similar to gold in other regions. Imports of wheat in Great Britain following the abolition of the Corn Laws, and prior to the development of bulk handling, required extensive use of jute bags and the importation and manufacture of jute. The Crimean War cut off supplies of grain from Asia and necessitated increasing reliance on America for grain and on India for jute. The manufacture of jute in India began in 1855, the first power loom was introduced in 1859, and several mills were opened in the sixties. The average annual export from Calcutta from 1858 to 1863 was nearly 1,000,000 hundredweight. The cotton famine in Lancashire precipitated by the American Civil War was accompanied by high prices of textiles and increased export from Bombay and from Egypt. The value of exports of cotton from Bombay increased from £5,500,000 in 1862 to £35,000,000 in 1866. The first cotton mill was established at Bombay in 1853, but the high price of cotton during the Civil War period, and the collapse of the speculative period of the cotton boom, hampered industrial expansion. Egypt owing to her advantages in nearness and in the production of a long staple cotton could outbid India, and her exports to England increased rapidly.

Cultivation of Indian tea increased rapidly in the sixties in Assam, Bengal, southern India, and Ceylon. According to one account, a plantation of 1,876 acres in 1850 produced 216,000 pounds, and 295 plantations of 31,303 acres produced 6,251,143 pounds in 1870. After the boom of the early sixties and the crash of 1866, cultivation expanded slowly and about 10,000,000 pounds were exported to the United Kingdom in 1869. Coffee exports from the Wynaad in South India totalled nearly 20,000,000 pounds in 1860–1. In 1865, 14,613 acres were under cultivation in this region. The district of Coorg began production in 1854 and had 73,306 acres under cultivation in 1870.

As a result of the increasing consumption of coffee, 176,000 acres were planted in Ceylon from 1853 to 1869 and produced a crop valued at £4,000,000 sterling. Exports reached a maximum of 1,054,030 hundredweight in 1870. Unfortunately the spread of the coffee blight began in 1862 and eventually ruined the industry, but after a few years of sharp strain it was replaced by tea and cinchona. Cinnamon production increased in the latter part of the period but chiefly at the expense of quality. As a result of active government intervention and substantial expenditures on irrigation canals after 1856, the production of rice increased. Roads were built throughout the island and products were brought to the markets at lower costs. In 1867 a railroad was completed from Colombo to Kandy (75 miles) and in 1871 from Peradanuja to the important coffee district at Nawalapituja. Decline of coffee production in the Far East brought a shift to Brazil as at a later date decline in rubber production in Brazil followed the shift of rubber to the Far East.

Extension of steamship navigation to the Far East produced an expansion of trade. The cession of Hong Kong and the opening of treaty ports in 1842 was followed by persistent efforts to extend trade, and the treaties of Tientsin of 1858 were extended and enforced in 1860. Similarly, treaties with Japan in 1859 were extended and enforced in 1865, and supplemented by a tariff convention of 1866. The way was opened for rapid expansion after 1868. The strategic importance of Singapore and the Malay States on the route to the Far East was evinced by the creation of the Crown colony in 1867.

The extent of development of trade between the United Kingdom and the Pacific is suggested in an increase in imports of India and Ceylon from £9,094,349 in 1850 to £30,055,138 in 1860, and to £31,856,422 in 1870, and in exports from £7,874,584 in 1850 to £13,811,961 in 1860, and to £30,705,844 in 1870. British shipping entered and cleared to India and Ceylon increased from 1,081,511 tons in 1860 to 4,701,765 tons in 1870. Imports of Australia and New Zealand from the United Kingdom increased from £2,744,671 in 1850 to £16,316,853 in 1860, and amounted to £14,102,897 in 1870, and exports to the United Kingdom increased from £2,622,762 in 1850 to £12,502,378 in 1860, and to £13,343,356 in 1870. British shipping entered and cleared, exclusive of coastal trade, increased from 310,161 tons in 1850 to 2,355,399 tons in 1860 and 3,912,429 tons in 1870. British shipping entered and cleared to Hong Kong increased from 724,693 tons in 1860 to 1,649,250 tons in 1870. Imports of the Cape of Good Hope from the United Kingdom fluctuated from £1,165,624 in 1850 to £2,187,207 in 1860 and £1,956,305 in 1870, and exports to the United Kingdom from £611,817 in 1850 to £1,547,351 in 1860 and £2,123,061 in 1870. British shipping entered and cleared increased from 300,937 tons in 1850 to 388,217 tons in 1860 and 314,063 tons in 1870.

III

Attraction of the remunerative passenger traffic to the gold fields of California and Australia hastened the decline of sailing vessels and the development of the steamship in the Atlantic. The clipper ship in the United States accompanied the boom days of shipbuilding in the fifties in Quebec and New Brunswick, and of shipbuilding and shipping in Nova Scotia in the sixties. The application of steam to navigation lagged behind its application to land transport, but received a strong impetus from the demand for cheaper and faster service, the influence of invention, and government subsidies. The liberal subsidies granted by the United States to their steamships (1845–7) contributed to the breakdown of the British Navigation Acts. The repeal of these Acts in 1849 and the admission of foreign ships to the coasting trade of Great Britain in 1854 increased the mobility of shipping. Areas with advantages in abundance of shipbuilding material, and in skill and technique, responded to the demand for wooden sailing vessels. But such advantages were eventually offset by the superiority of iron, coal, and steam, and the industrial development of the United Kingdom. The pressure of industrialism based on railroads and ports was evident in the transformation of shipping. The displacement of American softwood by British hardwood, and of British hardwood by iron, prepared the way for the iron steamship. Wooden and iron steamships were at first concerned primarily with passengers and mail and superseded even the fastest clippers. The reduction in the thickness of the hull with the use of iron actually reduced the weight of ships, provided space for more cargo, involved less danger from fire, permitted the construction of larger ships to carry coal, enabled them to stand heavy driving in head seas, and overcame the handicap of spars and masts in limiting the size of ships. The increasing efficiency of marine engines, the introduction of the screw, and the decline in fuel consumption[6] widened the range of steamships. Steamships from Great Britain began to penetrate the non-coal areas of Africa, South America, and the Pacific.

The effect of the Pacific gold rushes was evident first in the rapid extension of steamship services to the West Indies and the Panama. A contract with the Royal Mail West India Steam Packet Company was extended to include a monthly service to the Brazils in 1852. Later contracts in 1857 imposed a faster schedule and development of the service to Rio de Janeiro and River Plate. In 1866 and 1868 the time from England to the Panama was reduced. The Pacific Steam Navigation Company developed a coastal trade between

Panama and Valparaiso. In 1868 a profitable monthly service was established from Liverpool via the Straits of Magellan to Valparaiso. This became a fortnightly service and was extended to Callao in 1870. Additional steamship lines were organized, particularly from Liverpool to the West Indies and the Panama with the energetic activities of Alfred Holt beginning in 1855. With the Limited Liability Act of 1862 amalgamations were formed, the West India and Pacific Steam Navigation Company in 1863, and the Liverpool, Brazil and River Plate Steamship Company in 1865. In that year a steamship of the Holt Line made an 8,500-mile non-stop trip from Liverpool to San Francisco.

Sailing ships were challenged further by completion of the Suez Canal, and of the Union Pacific Railway in 1869, which cut the continents in half and removed support from sheltered routes. The 1850's was a most interesting decade in the history of Atlantic shipping for it saw the steamer making real headway against the sailing ship, principally because iron construction and screw propulsion obtained recognition. It was, too, a period of cut-throat competition, which in addition to providing excitement for the lookers-on who did not stand to lose dividends by it, invariably meant technical development.[7] Steamship lines supported by mail subsidies were organized for regular schedules. Following the disappearance of the Collins Line, keen rivalry continued between the Cunard, Inman, Allan, and Dominion lines in the fifties and sixties. Competition for passengers penetrated to the immigrant trade. The percentage of immigrants arriving in Canada by steamships increased from 45 in 1863 to over 95 in 1869. Finally, steamships encroached on bulk cargo traffic and extended development from coastwise to ocean traffic. Improvements in navigation on the Atlantic were significant in strengthening the position of the more highly industrialized areas by lowering the costs of the cheapest form of carriage, that by water. The improvements were hastened by the advantages resulting from the increased size of the unit employed and from rapid depreciation, accentuated by losses, from mobility as to routes, and from the severity of competition between large capitalistic organizations. The early improvements were concentrated on speed and were designed to increase the mobility of labour. Improvements in relation to the movement of labour hastened the production and movement of raw materials in new areas and enlarged the demand for the manufactured products of Great Britain.

The increasing importance of iron and coal contributed to the strength of the merchant marine of Great Britain. In the depression of 1857 large numbers of American vessels[8] were sold to Great Britain, and with the outbreak of the Civil War and the ravages of Confederate cruisers half a million tons of shipping were transferred to British registry. Total shipping cleared and entered in ports of the United Kingdom increased from 24,700,000 tons in 1860 to 36,600,000 tons in 1870, and the percentage of British tonnage from 56 to 68. Shipbuilding activity in the United Kingdom was great in 1863–5, when the Civil War checked American industry, and reached its peak of 275,000 tons in 1864. By the end of the sixties the steamship had surpassed the sailing vessel in Great Britain.

	Total number of vessels		*Total tonnage*
In 1860	Sail	818	168,420
	Steam	198	93,590
In 1870	Sail	541	123,910
	Steam	433	364,860

The iron steamship capitalized the advantages of Great Britain in her possession of iron and coal and of ports accessible all the year round. Her striking competitive advantages in shipbuilding bound her formal and informal Empire more closely to her. The advantages of areas which produced wooden sailing vessels rapidly depreciated and the expansion of canals and railways to the interior of new lands was encouraged with a consequent increase in the production of raw materials and demand for finished products. The supremacy of Great Britain in shipbuilding hastened this shift of energies in the outer Empire to internal exploitation. Shipbuilding and shipping were the basis of her expansion. Thus the increasing importance of British shipping, particularly with the development of the iron steamship on the Atlantic, and the migration of about two and a half million people in each of the decades from 1850 to 1870,[9] coincided with the internal development of North America and other regions.

The Sault Ste Marie Canal, completed in 1855, gave access to the iron ore resources of Lake Superior, and the Civil War and railways created demands for iron and steel. Shipbuilding tonnage on the Great Lakes increased from 212,000 in 1851 to 547,267 in 1866, and railways extended inland from Atlantic ports to Chicago in 1852 and the Mississippi in 1854. Mileage in the United States increased from 9,021 in 1850 to 52,922 in 1870. The Homestead Act of 1862 opened up new lands for rapid occupation, and exports of wheat from the United States, particularly with rise in prices to the peak of 1867 and the increasing use of machinery which accompanied scarcity of labour in the Civil War, totalled 188,000,000 bushels in 1870. The Civil War was in part a result and in part a cause of concentration on western expansion. It involved a profound disturbance to trade. Exports of cotton were practically wiped out from 1862 and reached about three-fourths of the total of 1860 in 1870. The financial drain of the war weakened the monetary and credit structures of both North and South and contributed to the sharp upward trend of protection in the post-war period. With the end of the Civil War, restrictions on settlement in the West were removed and settlement was encouraged. Destruction of the influence of the South was favourable to an increase in the tariff in the North. Reciprocity, which had served as one of the compromises between the North and South to delay the Civil War, since Canada was expected to offset for the North the extension of slavery to Texas in the South, came to an end. Free land, loss of revenue from land sales, and war debt involved higher tariffs and protection as new sources of revenue. The South was no longer a factor restraining the tendency toward protection.

Internal expansion in the United States created a demand for capital and labour, and increased competition with less fortunate areas. These areas were consequently drawn more closely to the United Kingdom through the production of raw materials and the demand for finished products, and were forced to adopt a definite policy of encouragement of capital and labour. The Reciprocity Treaty, during its existence from 1854 to 1866, created an immediate relationship between expansion in the United States and Canada. But the Civil War marked the end of the break between the South and the North, between staple production and industrialism, and between free trade and protection, and sharpened the contrast between an economy built up around the St Lawrence, with its emphasis on water transportation, on staples and on the markets of Great Britain, and an industrialism with its emphasis on railroads, and led to the abrogation of the Reciprocity Treaty. The election of Lincoln from the marginal free soil state of Illinois marked the end of compromise and the supremacy of the North.

In Canada the improvement of transportation facilities by canals and railways was stimulated by the possibility of sharing in the rapidly expanding traffic of the Middle West and thereby reducing overhead costs. The Welland Canal and the St Lawrence canals, enabling steamships from the upper lakes to descend to Montreal, were completed by 1850, and were intended to reduce costs of transportation from Upper Canada[10] and to compete with the Erie Canal which carried traffic from Buffalo to New York.

Handicaps of seasonal navigation on the St Lawrence necessitated the construction of railways to ports on the Atlantic seaboard open all the year around. Reciprocity and the Civil War brought a marked increase in trade with the United States. A railway was built from Portland to Montreal in 1853, and from Montreal to Toronto in 1856, and to Sarnia (1855). Portage roads to offset the limitations of the St Lawrence system were built across the Welland Peninsula and to Collingwood (1855). The completion of the Victoria Bridge at Montreal in 1859 provided a through line not only to develop traffic in Canada, but also to tap the traffic of the Middle West.

The Suspension Bridge (1855) provided a shorter route for American lines to New York, and the importance of propellers on the larger vessels of the upper lakes in the sixties rendered the Welland Canal increasingly obsolete. In spite of the construction of the Welland Railway in 1858, Montreal failed to increase materially its share of traffic. In 1871, three-fourths of the tonnage could not be taken through to Lake Ontario. Shipments of flour and wheat, reduced to bushels, increased to 11,425,167 in 1869, but the total was slight compared to exports from New York. In spite of a lower rate from Chicago to Montreal, "such has been the commanding influence of that great commercial metropolis New York in drawing trade to itself and in keeping down the price of ocean transport that those efforts, though not fruitless, have not been so successful as at first anticipated."[11] High rates of ocean freight to Quebec and Montreal, partly as a result of insurance and other costs, but particularly of the inability of Montreal to provide a balanced cargo and of the seasonal character of navigation, were a serious drawback.

Inability to compete with American routes reduced long-haul traffic on the canals and railways, and necessitated increased reliance on local traffic. Revenue was reduced and the interest charges on capital invested in canals, and to a less extent in railways, were paid by increasing demands on the government. The importance of water navigation, competition from the United States for capital, labour, and traffic, and importation of skill and capital from Great Britain for construction purposes, involved government assistance on a substantial scale. The completion of the major railway systems in England by the middle decades of the century increased the demands for raw materials, and released railway contractors alert to the possibilities of guarantees from the colonial governments. The achievement of responsible government facilitated credit arrangements but involved difficulties with Great Britain and the United States.

The repeal of the Corn Laws and Navigation Acts involved the loss of preferences on colonial wheat and, coinciding with depression, led to the annexationist manifesto of 1849 and the demands for reciprocity with the United States.[12] The Reciprocity Treaty of 1854 was designed to increase trade between Canada and the United States, this is, to create a free trade area in North America, and to encourage traffic on the St Lawrence. It hastened the migration of American technique through opening a market for sawn lumber and other products. The position of the square timber trade and of wooden shipbuilding for the British market was weakened and the advantages of the St Lawrence in the production and export of white pine as square timber and wooden ships became less conspicuous with the increasing importance of the American market for sawn lumber. Removal of the preference in Great Britain, and competition from Baltic lumber and iron steamships, coincided with increasing demands for foodstuffs and especially wheat. During the Crimean War, the cessation of imports of wheat from the Black and Baltic seas, which had become important after the abolition of the Corn Laws, accentuated demands from Canada and the United States, and contributed to the rise in the price of wheat and to increasing emphasis on railroads and the steamship. The proportion of lumber and timber to total exports from land was below 50 per cent in the fifties, and the trend, with wide fluctuations, continued downward to below 30 per cent in 1870.[13] Dependence on wheat and heavy fixed charges incurred with the introduction of railways and steamships precipitated difficulties in finance. The depression of 1857 brought a sharp decline in the price of wheat which was followed by fluctuations in price and yield. In spite of the abolition of seigniorial tenure and of clergy reserves in 1854 the want of good land in Upper Canada in the early sixties was accompanied by difficulties of wheat production incidental to exhaustion of virgin soil, by the introduction of agricultural machinery from the United States, especially after the Civil War, and by increasing diversification of agriculture. The demand for live-stock and live-stock products during the Civil War and the migration of dairying technique from the United States contributed to increasing exports of dairy products (particularly cheese) to Great Britain after the abrogation of reciprocity. In the late seventies, the steamship contributed to the development of substantial exports of live-stock.

Problems of wheat and lumber exports were reflected in the crisis of 1857 in decline in imports, decline in revenue, and government deficits. The financial structure was profoundly affected by fluctuations in exports and by the shift in economic life shown particularly in the growth of towns which accompanied the railroad and the steamship. Speculation in real estate, difficulties with exports, and expansion of credit affected private as well as public finance. The more important banks of Upper Canada collapsed after 1863 and legislation restricting banks to commercial credit and to new developments followed.

An important step in meeting these problems was taken in 1858 with an increase in the tariff of 20 per cent. In 1855, Great Britain opposed negotiations for free trade between Canada and the West Indies, but a rise in the tariff was more serious.[14] Galt argued that the improvements in transportation paid for by revenue received from customs were more than sufficient through lowering of rates to offset the addition of duties and that in this sense customs duties were designed to stimulate free trade.[15]

The Tariff Act was not disallowed, nor was it adequate to meet the problem. In 1866, with a debt of $77,020,082, the government was "unable to raise more than half of a moderate loan even when offering eight per cent interest" as a result of "the disastrous effect on Canadian credit of the experience of British investors." The solution of the problem consisted in part in increasing traffic by intensive economic development, and more particularly by extensive economic development. Mr. E.W. Watkin, representing the directorate of the Grand Trunk, advised extension of the railway eastward to the Maritimes and westward to Rupert's Land. With the encouragement of the British government, he succeeded in securing a reorganization of the Hudson's Bay Company in 1863, with a view to arrangements for construction of the railway, but it was not until 1869 that the Dominion government extinguished the rights of the Hudson's Bay Company and not until 1870 that Manitoba was added to Confederation. British Columbia, seriously injured by decline in gold production, joined Confederation in 1871 on condition that a connecting railway should be built within ten years. The debts of both provinces were taken over by the Dominion, arrangements were made for the payment of subsidies to contribute to the costs of local administration, and the Canadian Pacific Railway was completed in 1885.

In the Maritimes, railways were designed as portage railways to give Halifax short connections to Windsor on the Bay of Fundy and to Pictou on the Gulf of St Lawrence, and to give Saint John a short connection to Shediac on the Gulf of St Lawrence; and totalled 365 miles in 1866 costing $15,000,000. Confederation between United Canada and the provinces of New Brunswick and Nova Scotia involved arrangements by which the debts incurred, chiefly as a result of transportation, were assumed by the Dominion. Moreover, capital was made available through a guarantee of a loan by the Imperial government for extension of the Grand Trunk Railway through British territory to the winter ports of Halifax and Saint John, and the Intercolonial Railway was completed in 1876.[16] The new Dominion served as a credit structure by which capital became available with government support, and transportation facilities were extended. The St Lawrence route, with its dependence on extensive governmental intervention in the reduction of transportation charges, and its inability to compete with American roads for through traffic, was forced to rely on fresh government support for the development of new sources of traffic. The political structure was adapted to these demands.

The establishment of fiscal autonomy in relation to Great Britain involved similar changes in relation to the United States. The competition of American manufactured products during the depression of 1857 coincided with the demand for revenue and, with the pressure of Canadian industrial interests, reinforced the trend toward higher tariffs. Protests arose from the United States against a violation of the spirit, if not the letter, of the Reciprocity Treaty. The outbreak of the Civil War brought a marked increase in trade with the United States, but the end of the war and the financial difficulties of the United States and removal of the South as a free trade influence led to increasing protests against the treaty, and to its abrogation in 1866. The Civil War, and especially the *Trent* affair and the Fenian raids, were accompanied by increasing attention on the part of Great Britain to the North American colonies, and hastened Confederation.

The trend toward centralization which characterized the economic development of the St Lawrence was in contrast to the trend towards decentralization in the Maritime Provinces, particularly Nova Scotia. Confederation was in some sense imposed by the needs of the St Lawrence. The Atlantic steamship on the St Lawrence, industrialism in Montreal, and the railroad in the Maritimes, created demands for coal from Cape Breton and the Pictou fields, while reciprocity encouraged trade, particularly from the Atlantic coast of Nova Scotia and the Bay of Fundy, to the United States. Confederation and a compromise between a high Canadian tariff and a low Nova Scotian tariff involved additional burdens to the western portion of the Maritimes which were not entirely offset by the advantages of new markets in the St Lawrence to the eastern portion. Reciprocity permitted American fishermen to fish in in-shore waters and to compete with Maritime fishermen, but the advantages to the United States were lost through the dearth of shipping during the Civil War. The fishery and settlement extended from Gaspé and from Newfoundland to the north shore of the St Lawrence and Labrador with the result that Nova Scotian vessels were compelled to search new grounds and Lunenberg vessels went for the first time on the Grand Banks in 1873. The Washington Treaty encouraged the Canadian industry.

Reciprocity between the United States and the colonies of British North America included Newfoundland and coincided roughly with the introduction of responsible government in that area in 1855. Competition from the French had effects similar to the effects of competition on Canada from the United States. Introduction of the seine in the cod fishery along the French shore and of the trawl on the banks adjacent to St Pierre and Miquelon was followed by determined efforts to restrict their operation by Newfoundland. Conservation measures and control over sales of bait to the French were designed to check French competition stimulated by bonuses and large-scale operations. A treaty of 1857 arranged between Great Britain and France as to the disposal of the Newfoundland fishery was not enforced as a result of the hostility of Newfoundland and its insistence on responsible government and the recognition of its implications by Great Britain. Control was extended through the customs to the Labrador, with the result that the position of St John's was strengthened at the expense of Nova Scotian, American, and British fishing interests. In spite of her proximity to Great Britain the effects of steam navigation were not evident until a late date. As a result of success with a submarine cable between Carleton Head, Prince Edward Island, and Cape Tormentine on the mainland completed 22 November 1852, F.N. Gisborne introduced the telegraph in St John's in the same year and planned construction of a transatlantic cable. In 1856 a cable was completed and telegraphic communication established with North America but it was not until 27 July 1866, that a permanent transatlantic cable was laid by the *Great Eastern* from Valentia to Heart's Content. In 1869 a French cable was laid from Brest to St Pierre, and in 1873 extended to Canso, Nova Scotia. Mail was carried under contract from St John's to Halifax in winter months, and direct steamship lines to Galway began in 1856 and to England under the Allan Line in 1873. Internal development was fostered by responsible government, protection, and the spread of industrialism. The steamship was introduced in the sealing industry in 1863, and improved methods of extracting seal oils were introduced in the fifties. The herring and salmon fisheries became increasingly important. Abrogation of the Reciprocity Treaty was a logical development in Newfoundland as it had been in the other colonies. Commercial credit continued of dominant importance and the Union Bank was established in 1854 and the Commercial Bank in 1857. The demand for roads and capital improvements involved insistence on the part of the Newfoundland government on the right to impose duties and collect revenue. While the Maritime Provinces had joined United Canada in spite of differences in economic and political structure, Newfoundland, less influenced by the railway, had found the differences too great to permit of political union with the continent. Capital demands were not adequate to stamp the economic life of Newfoundland in a mould adapted to the requirements of Confederation, and the dispersion of economic life, characteristic of the fishery extending along the coast, precluded political unity.

IV

The series of gold rushes hastened the trend toward increasing mobility of labour. The effects of industrialism, particularly through the steamship and the railway, contributed to expansion of free trade and responsible government in the temperate areas and to the spread of freedom of contract in the tropical regions. Further, the spread of the humanitarian movement led to protracted and finally successful efforts to suppress the transatlantic slave trade. These, however, were complicated by the decline of preferences on sugar with the adoption of free trade. West Indies planters attempted to meet the difficulties by encouraging immigration of Chinese coolies. Capital was supplied by the planters, and labour was brought out under the contract system. "By judiciously promoting emigration from China and at the same time vigorously repressing the infamous traffic in African slaves, the Christian governments of Europe and America may confer benefits upon a large portion of the human race, the effects of which it would be difficult to exaggerate." So wrote Lord Russell to Earl Cowley on 11 July 1860.[17] Chinese officials were not impressed by the advantages, and emigration to tropical countries was restricted. Emigration beginning in 1852 was checked until 1859 and carried on with numerous difficulties after that date. British Guiana brought in about fourteen thousand

Chinese in the period 1853 to 1879. For the more tropical West Indies, Indian coolies were more promising. In 1844, the East India Company granted permits to Jamaica, British Guiana, and Trinidad and in 1847 to Ceylon, to recruit coolie labour; also the British government granted similar permits in 1858 to St Lucia, in 1860 to St Vincent and St Kitts, and in 1867 to Grenada. Many liberated slaves were brought to the West Indies, especially from Sierra Leone; also a large immigration came from Madeira.

In 1851 Lagos was captured from a powerful slavery gang with heavy losses and the rightful king restored. His successor, being under the control of slaves, was deposed and in 1861 Lagos was annexed. From this beginning Great Britain checked the slave trade on the Slave Coast. Also mercantile efforts on and near the Niger secured a basis for expansion of control over Southern and Northern Nigeria.

In Cape Colony, representative government in 1853 tended to emphasize equal political rights for blacks and whites. The contrast with the policy of the neighbouring Dutch republics involved difficulties with native tribes, which forced Great Britain to assume an increasingly strong position as a means of assuring order. The shift to free trade coincided with the spread of industrialism in the coal-bearing formations of the temperate regions and with the disturbance of economic life in the tropical regions. Mobility of labour and capital which accompanied the trend toward freedom of trade was of profound significance to the relatively unpopulated areas of the temperate regions, and of serious implication to the densely populated areas of the tropical zones. The abolition of slavery through the Civil War in the United States was a part of the general trend among countries dominated by Anglo-Saxon races. The long struggle of the British Navy off the coast of West Africa to put down the slave trade, with little or no support for a long time from other powers, ended successfully in 1863–6 owing to the annexation of Lagos, to the efficiency of screw steamers in capturing slavers, and to the complete abolition of slavery in 1862 by the United States, and, later, by Brazil and Cuba. The migration of Oriental labour to the gold fields of the Pacific and of coloured labour to the tropics were indications of the far-reaching changes of the period.

The tremendous impact of the gold discoveries of the Pacific was evident in the enormous demands for capital equipment and manufactured products and also in the contributions of gold imports toward the changes of British capital structure. With increasing industrialism, the ample resources of commercial credit in Great Britain became inadequate to meet the internal and external demands for long-term credit. The crash of Overend Gurney and Company in 1865 was in part a result of the depression and in part of far-reaching changes in the financial structure. More effective organization of long-term credit facilities was evident in the extension of legislation to provide for limited liability companies in 1855 and 1862, and in the emergence of a holding company such as the International Financial Society in 1863. The completion of the Atlantic cable in 1866, the extension of cables, telegraphs, and mail steamships linked the financial structures of North America to Great Britain and to the Far East and facilitated capital movements and more direct control of economic and political development. Improvement of financial machinery hastened the decline of the East India Company and of the Hudson's Bay Company, and the development of industrialism in Great Britain and within and without the Empire. Responsible government and the realignment of political structure in the temperate and in the tropical regions provided efficient credit instruments by which shipping and transport were revolutionized with industrialism. Political control from Great Britain declined in importance, but its decline was essential to the expansion of economic control. Guarantees and bonuses were provided by colonial governments with and without the support of the Imperial government for the construction of railways; for example, the Grand Trunk Railway, under private or government construction. The weak position of Empire countries through their dependence on staple products, the timidity of capital which had suffered losses in foreign countries in the forties, and the competition of expanding industrial areas such as the United States, implied dependence on governmental support. The vested interests which characterized an Empire dependent on Navigation Acts, staple products, and commercial credit were weakened with the emergence of the Reform Acts in Great Britain, responsible government, and the progress of industrialism. The shift to navigation and land transport linked to steam was followed by the demand for, and the supply of, new staples more essential to the increasing industrialism of Great Britain, such as wheat and wool. Public finance and private finance, and political and economic institutions alike, reflected the expansion of industrialism in the Empire and the Western world.

The downward trend of duties of the period ending in 1850 continued practically to vanishing point. The British budget of 1853 abolished the duty on cotton yarn, the excise tax on soap, and the advertisement tax, and halved the duties on fruits and dairy products. In 1855 the stamp duty on newspapers was removed, and in 1860 all duties on imported manufactures. The excise duty on paper was abolished in the following year. The Cobden agreement with France was negotiated in 1860. The timber duty followed in 1866, and the sugar duty, after a series of gradual reductions, disappeared in 1874. These changes completed the movement toward free trade, and the removal of protection from the vested interests which had grown up in the colonies producing the staples, sugar and lumber, and they encouraged internal trade dependent on advertising and newspapers. With the repeal of the Navigation Acts (1849) the advantages of industrial maturity and leadership were practically unhampered by governmental restrictions.

Advantages accruing through removal of duties and taxes, and increasing efficiency of the fiscal mechanism, were supplemented by technical improvements, particularly as applied to shipping. Commodities were imported cheaply, and with improved railways, ports, and ships were carried over longer distance and at lower costs. The stream of goods and commodities moving toward and away from an enlarged metropolitan centre increased in speed and ran with less friction. The completion of a railway and canal system in the United Kingdom by the middle decades of the nineteenth century created an industrialism based on iron and coal, with the growth of an urban population, an increasing demand for raw materials, and an expanding market for finished products.

Extension of the influence of Great Britain in the Pacific and Atlantic under the impetus of technological advance, particularly in relation to navigation and transport in the Atlantic regions, and the impetus of the profit motive, particularly in the gold regions of the Pacific, implied an economic balance in which disturbances of one area were offset by advances in the other. The Civil War and the opening up of a continent in the United States involved its retreat from the sea and opened the door more widely to Great Britain. The Crimean War checked Russian exports of wheat and stimulated production and exports from Canada and the United States. The depression of 1857 in North America and the Civil War were followed by a shift of British interest to Central Africa, India, and the Pacific. The Civil War and the Crimean War forced extension outwards of empire. The shifting of interests strengthened the position of Great Britain. The possibilities of increasing traffic reduced overhead costs on expanding industrial equipment. Improved technique, such as the introduction of steel, hastened the process of expansion. The increasing efficiency of industrial Britain was accompanied by the increasing efficiency of financial and fiscal Britain. The impact on Great Britain of wide fluctuations in the economic activity of regions producing raw material, exposed to shifts from gold to wool and to variations in the yield and price of raw materials, as in the case of wheat, was softened by the balancing of regions. The costs of shifting to the more permanent base of industrialism in terms of iron and steel were borne largely by the obsolescence of areas supplying quantities of raw material, such as timber and wooden ships, and were offset in part by lower costs of transportation and the development of new staples. Agriculture in England felt the impact of competition from new areas and arable land was converted into pasture. Diversity of demands for capital as a result of the economic and political divergences of regions producing raw materials, ranging from New Zealand to the United States, involved competition for labour and capital from the aggressive, rapidly expanding, continental area of the United States, with the weaker areas of the old Empire, and the evolution of types of government and guarantees adequate to secure metropolitan growth. Canada felt more directly the effects of American expansion and of British demands for guarantees, with the result that her experiences with tariffs and political structure were destined to establish precedents for later developments in the other Dominions. The period from 1849 to 1870 was a watershed in imperial history in the spread of industrialism to new regions.

The impact of free trade and industrialism, particularly in relation to steam navigation, accentuated the emphasis on specialization of production of raw materials in new countries and on the production of finished products in more highly industrialized regions. Water transportation and the increasing distances of the Pacific stressed production of specialized raw materials. Gold production emphasized the advantages of a highly industrialized area in its ability to supply promptly and abundantly supplies of finished products. The heavy cost of production, particularly in terms of transportation of raw materials, such as wheat and wool, suited to the demands of an increasingly industrialized area, and the enormous costs involved in the shift to new staples, implied in the pressure of free trade and industrialism and of gold rushes, involved extensive government support. Free trade in Great Britain brought increasing emphasis on staple products in new countries and in turn the introduction of capital equipment, steamships, canals, roads, and railroads, and problems of finance and governmental activity along the lines of responsible government, federation, and protection. Dependence on staples involved more sweeping fluctuations of price, yield, and returns, and accentuated reliance on governmental intervention. Limited liability in its relations to the growth of corporate activity in Great Britain was paralleled by government guarantees in the regions producing raw materials. Commercialism began to give way to capitalism.

Expansion of trade brought improvement in transportation, the emergence of public debt, responsible government, and nationalism. Capital became relatively immobile and inflexible in the government securities of the Dominions. Access to bankruptcy which characterized more mature regions was denied. Political institutions were elaborated in relation to the increasing problems of debt. Dominions, provinces, and municipalities resorted to conversions and even to bankruptcies. Monetary policies were widened on an extensive scale, nationalism was intensified and capital rendered still less mobile.

The cyclonic effects of the gold rushes in the Pacific region were evident in the expansion of shipping and trade on the Atlantic and the Pacific and in the development of Great Britain as a metropolitan centre of the world. It is significant that Marshall suggested that after 1873 the economic history of one country could not be written. At a later date the gold rushes had profound effects on continental development. Transcontinental railways were built to San Francisco and in turn from Montreal to Vancouver to link up the economic areas based on the discovery of gold with the eastern seaboard of North America. Construction under private enterprise in the United States hastened railway construction with substantial government support in Canada. The Klondike gold rush had its effect in hastening construction of two additional transcontinental railways which became the basis of the Canadian National Railways. The vast resources of a continent were opened up with transcontinental lines. The discovery of placer gold reversed the basic trends of liquidity preference which favoured the growth of metropolitan areas particularly with the support of mercantilistic policies. The discovery and production of gold on a large scale shifted the impact of liquidity preference from trade to production, from established areas to new areas, and enormously widened the bounds of production and trade.

The significance of liquidity preference in economic history extends far beyond monetary policy. It was not confined to the place of gold in trade and production. Improvements in communication had the same effect. The phenomenal expansion of newspapers following the displacement of rags by wood accentuated the intensification of trade, enormously extended the sensitivity of modern economic society, and enhanced the role of liquidity preference.

The effect of liquidity preference was evident in the distortion of economic development in relation to staple production. The attractive power of gold hastened the opening of the Pacific and in turn contributed powerfully to the rapid expansion of wheat production following the construction of transcontinental railways on the North American Continent and of animal products, wool, mutton, and dairy products, in Australia and New Zealand. The pressure of agricultural products on the markets of Europe hastened industrial development and contributed to the rise of protection in industry and agriculture.

Distortion by the gold rushes of more normal trends of metropolitan development – in which improved techniques in transportation and communication gradually led to changes in types of product from the hinterlands, more easily handled products being replaced by less easily handled products, fur by timber and timber by grain – by the speeding up of transportation improvement with construction of transcontinental railways was offset in part by their effectiveness in stimulating changes in staple production. Concentration on staples implied a highly specialized economy, changes from which were accomplished with great difficulty and with distress. The Napoleonic Wars and high preferential duties brought the shift from fur to timber in the St Lawrence. The Rebellions of 1837 were in part a result of the difficulty of shifting from timber to grain.

The gold rushes hastened the shift to new staples and contributed to the difficulties of the long depression, but once the shift was made the basis was provided for the great boom. There were no gold rushes to soften the depression of the thirties, and the shift from wheat to live-stock and dairying in western Canada was accomplished with intense difficulty.

NOTES

1 Cited, *Cambridge History of the British Empire* (Cambridge, 1930), vol. 7, pt. 2, 151.

2 Licence fees were introduced in New South Wales and in Victoria, but at rates which were inadequate and which became increasingly unpopular with attempts at rigorous collection and exhaustion of the goldfields. As a result of determined protests, fees were reduced in Victoria in 1853, and following the Ballarat riots of 1854, miners' rights, conferring the franchise, displaced the licence fee, and an export duty of 2*s.* 6*d.* per ounce on gold was imposed in 1855. Local courts were established in the gold fields to settle disputes.

3 Miners were forced to pay licence fees but, with the example of Victoria, an export tax was introduced in 1857 and licence fees abolish-

ed. Wool production increased in importance, and the number of sheep increased from 5,615,054 in 1861 to 16,278,697 in 1871. The position of the squatter tended to defeat, through "dummying," the efforts of the farmer in the Land Act of 1861. Land under crop increased to 378,592 acres in 1870–1.

4 Prospects of profitable occupation induced Chinese brokers to provide capital to pay the costs of transportation (the ticket credit system) to the gold fields. It was estimated that 2,000 Chinese coolies were employed in the Victoria goldfields in 1854. The Restriction Act in 1855, prohibiting the arrival of Chinese by vessels, was followed by migration to South Australia and immigration to Victoria by land. In 1857, Chinese in the Victoria goldfields had increased to 26,370 and South Australia was persuaded to pass a restriction Act. Victoria, in the same year, imposed heavy taxation on the Chinese population. In spite of legislation, population totalled 42,000, with the result that previous Acts were replaced by legislation imposing still heavier taxation. Chinese population declined with exhaustion of the goldfields, and in 1864 restrictive legislation was repealed. In New South Wales, 12,988 Chinese were engaged in the goldfields in 1861 and a Bill similar to the Victoria Act of 1855 was enacted.

5 L.C.A. Knowles, *Economic Development of the Overseas Empire* (London, 1924), 300n.

6 The decline is illustrated by the following chart from C.E. Fayle, *A Short History of the World's Shipping Industry* (London, 1933), 241:

	Gross tons	*Coal per day in tons*	*Bunker capacity*	*Cargo capicity*
1855, *Persia*, iron steamship, paddle, simple side lever engines	3,300	150	1,640	1,100
1865, *Java*, iron steamship, screw, simple inverted engines	2,697	85	1,100	1,100
1874, *Bothnia*, iron steamship, screw, compound engines	4,556	63	940	3,000

7 F.C. Bowen, *A Century of Atlantic Travel, 1830–1930* (London, n.d.), 53.

8 In the decade from 1850 to 1860 the tonnage of the American merchant marine increased from 3,535,000 to 5,049,000, and in 1861 a maximum of 2,494,984 tons were engaged in foreign trade. As a result, the percentage of British tonnage entering and clearing United

Kingdom ports declined from 69 as an average from 1847 to 1849 to 56 in 1860.

9 W.A. Carrothers gives a total of 2,844,512 emigrants from the British Isles from 1853 to 1870 of which 61 per cent went to the United States and 28 per cent to Australia in the eight years 1853–60, and 72 per cent to the United States and 17 per cent to Australia in the ten years 1861–70.

10 Attempts to strengthen the position of the St Lawrence included a contract in 1852 with the Canadian Steam Navigation Company requiring a fortnightly service to Quebec in summer and a monthly service to Portland in winter. Difficulties led to cancellation in 1855 and a new arrangement with Messrs Allan of the Montreal Ocean Steamship Company for similar service. Weekly sailings winter and summer to Portland and Quebec respectively were begun in 1859 but it was not until 1864 that a satisfactory postal route was introduced on the St Lawrence. Lighthouses were installed on the river and on the gulf, and telegraph lines were extended from Quebec to Father Point in 1859. The channel to Montreal was steadily deepened to 22 feet in 1878. In turn, as railways were built to New York, construction of railways to Montreal to obtain a larger share of traffic was essential. Insurance charges were gradually reduced on the St Lawrence and the competitive position strengthened.

11 *Canada, Sessional Papers,* 1863, no. 3.

12 See *Cambridge History of the British Empire,* 6: 382–4; also H.A. Innis, *Problems of Staple Production* (Toronto, 1933), chap. 2.

13 A.R.M. Lower, "The Trade in Square Timber," *Contributions to Canadian Economics,* vol. 6 (Toronto, 1933).

14 The Duke of Newcastle, with the support of the Sheffield Chamber of Commerce, protested in a letter dated 13 August 1859, and Alexander Galt, the Minister of Finance, replied on 25 October 1859: "Self government would be utterly annihilated if the views of the Imperial Government were to be preferred to those of the people of Canada. It is therefore the duty of the present Government distinctly to affirm the right of the Canadian legislature to adjust the taxation of the people in the way they deem best, even if it should unfortunately happen to meet the disapproval of the Imperial Ministry ... The fiscal policy of Canada has invariably been governed by considerations of the amount of revenue required ... It is certainly ungenerous to be reproached by England, when the obligations which have caused the bulk of the indebtedness of Canada have been incurred either in compliance with the former policy of Great Britain, or more recently assumed to protect from loss those parties in England who had invested their means in our railway and municipal bonds" (*Canada, Sessional*

Papers, 1860, no. 38, cited in E. Porritt, *The Fiscal and Diplomatic Freedom of the British Overseas Dominions* [Oxford, 1922], 455–6). See also *Cambridge History of the British Empire* 6: 349.

15 "All these improvements have been undertaken with the twofold object of diminishing the cost to the consumer of what he imports, and of increasing the *net* result of the labour of the country when finally realized in Great Britain.

"If by an increasc of fivc per cent. on the duty, a reduction of ten per cent. on the other charges were produced, the benefit would accrue equally to the British manufacturer and to the consumer, and the indirect but legitimate protection to the home manufacturer would be diminished; the consumer would pay five per cent. more to the Government, but ten per cent. less to the merchant and forwarder. In this illustration lies the whole of the Canadian customs" (*Canada, Sessional Papers,* 1862, no. 23). This argument had been developed by Adam Smith. See H.A. Innis, "Significant Factors in Canadian Economic Development," *Canadian Historical Review* 18 (1937): 374–85.

16 See *Cambridge History of the British Empire* 6: 444ff, 460ff.

17 Cited, P.C. Campbell, *Chinese Coolie Emigration to Countries within the British Empire* (London, 1923), 129.

PART TWO

Resources and Regionalism: The Origins of Modern Canada

CHAPTER SEVEN

Transportation as a Factor in Canadian Economic History

Transportation has been of such basic importance to Canadian economic history that the title of this paper may appear redundant and inclusive. The paper is intended, however, as an attempt to consider the general position of transportation in Canada, with special relation to its peculiar characteristics and their relationships to Canadian development, rather than to present a brief survey of Canadian economic history.

The early development of North America was dependent on the evolution of ships adapted to crossing the Atlantic. Water transportation, which had been of first importance in the growth of European civilization, had improved to the extent that, by the beginning of the sixteenth century, long voyages could be undertaken across the north Atlantic.[1] These voyages were continued in relation to the acquisition of commodities for which a strong demand existed in Europe, and which were available in large quantities within short distances from the seaboard of the new countries. In the north Atlantic, cod was a commodity in the handling of which the advantages of water transportation were capitalized to the full. On the banks, ships from Europe caught and cured the fish in preparation for direct sale in the home market. Early in the seventeenth century, following the opening of the spanish market and the new demand for dried cod, ships from England and France developed dry fishing in Newfoundland, the remote parts of the Gulf such as Gaspé, and the New England shore.

From *Proceedings of the Canadian Political Science Association,* 1931, 166–84, and *Problems of Staple Production in Canada* (Ryerson, 1933), 1–17.

Mr Biggar has shown the relationship between dry fishing and the fur trade.[2] Penetration to the interior brought Europeans in touch with the resources of the mainland. The continued overwhelming importance of water transportation for the development of the interior warrants a brief survey of the more important waterways and their characteristics. The course and volume of the waterways in the northeastern half of North America is largely determined by the geological background of the area. The Precambrian formation is in the form of an angle, with one side pointing toward the northeast, including northern Quebec and Labrador, and bounded on the north by Hudson Straits, and the other to the northwest and bounded by the western Arctic. Hudson Bay constitutes a large portion of the territory in the angle. The resistant character of the formation and its relatively level surface have been responsible for a network of lakes and rivers. Its youthful topography following the retreat of the ice sheets is shown in the number of rapids and obstructions to the tributaries and rivers. The major water courses flow roughly along the junction of the formation with later weaker formations, as in the St Lawrence waterway which begins with the Great Lakes and flows northeast toward the Gulf, and the Mackenzie which flows northwest toward the Arctic. The St Lawrence is fed from the north by important tributaries, such as the Saguenay, the St Maurice, and the Ottawa, which are separated by low heights of land from rivers flowing to Hudson Bay. The main waterway[3] is broken by serious obstructions at Niagara and the St Lawrence rapids above Montreal, and the tributaries have numerous rapids. The drainage basins to the south, the Mississippi, the Ohio, and the rivers of New York, are separated by comparatively low heights of land.

The commodity supplied by this vast stretch of northern Precambrian territory, and demanded by Europe, was fur. The sailing ships were restricted to the mouth of the St Lawrence River, and the opening of trade on the river and its tributaries necessitated the use of pinnaces.[4] Tadoussac became the first terminus, but was displaced by Quebec after the French became more familiar with the river channel to that point. The relatively level stretch of water from Quebec to Montreal was adapted to the use of large boats, and with the improvement of the route the depot shifted from Tadoussac to Quebec, to Three Rivers, and thence to Montreal. In 1642 Montreal was established and the position of the French on this stretch of waterway consolidated. Beyond Montreal a third type of transport equipment – the canoe – became essential. The French were able to borrow directly from the equipment of the hunting Indians of the northern Precambrian area, and to adapt the transport unit, worked out by them, to their needs. With this unit French and English succeeded in bringing practically the whole of northern North America under tribute to the demands of the trade.

The canoe was adapted to the shorter Ottawa route to the upper country rather than to the longer and more difficult upper St Lawrence and Great Lakes route. The trade of Georgian Bay, Green Bay on Lake Michigan, and Lake Superior was developed from this route to Montreal. Eventually La Vérendrye and his successors extended it northwest to Lake Winnipeg and the Saskatchewan. The limitations of the birch-bark canoe, even after its enlargement and adaptation by the French, necessitated the establishment of depots for provisions at convenient points. Its labour costs were heavy.

The upper St Lawrence and Great Lakes route was never developed as a satisfactory substitute by the French, and the difficulties of La Salle with Great Lakes transportation in its initial development characterized its later history. The problems of organization of the route were enhanced by the competition of the Dutch and English through the Iroquois and the Mohawk route to Oswego prior to 1722, and through direct trade after the establishment of Oswego in that year. As a result of this competition, the St Lawrence and Great Lakes route involved a substantial drain on the trade. Posts were established at Frontenac, Niagara, and Detroit as a means of checking English competition, and the upkeep of these posts involved heavy expenses for the colony. Eventually Toronto was added in 1749 as a further check to Indian trade with the English. The shorter route to Oswego and the use of large boats on the lake were factors which seriously weakened the position of canoe transport on the Ottawa.

Only with the disappearance of the French after 1760 did it become possible to combine satisfactorily the upper St Lawrence–Great Lakes route for boats and vessels with the canoe route on the Ottawa. The lake boat became an ally to the canoe rather than an enemy. Heavy goods were carried by the lakes, and light goods were taken up and furs brought down by canoes. Cheaper supplies of provisions were available at Detroit and Niagara, and were carried at lower costs up the lakes to Grand Portage and later to Fort William. Niagara portage was organized and a canal was built at Sault Ste Marie. With the organization of Great Lakes transport it became possible to extend the trade far beyond the limits reached by the French. The Northwest Company succeeded in penetrating from Fort William to Lake Winnipeg and the Saskatchewan, by Cumberland House and Frog Portage to the Churchill, by Methye Portage to Athabaska, the Peace, and the Mackenzie, and by the passes across the Rockies to the upper Fraser and the Columbia. Supply depots were organized on the Red River, on the Saskatchewan, and on the Peace.

The efficiency of the canoe in serving as a transport unit from Montreal along the edge of the Canadian shield almost to the Arctic was dependent in part on the efficient organization of water transport along the Ottawa to Montreal, and on the Great Lakes. In 1821 this elaborate system collapsed and the canoe ceased to be a basic factor in transport. The boat again became an important factor in contributing to its failure, but from the north or Hudson Bay and not from the south. Ocean transport, in addition to supremacy of the Bay with boats in inland transport, was overwhelmingly important.

Hudson Bay was developed as a trading area over fifty years later than the St Lawrence basin, and its growth depended largely on experience acquired in the St Lawrence. Radisson and Groseilliers saw the possibility of tapping the trade from the centre of the Precambrian angle rather than from the outer edges. Accordingly ships were despatched to the mouths of the rivers flowing into James Bay and into Hudson Bay, and after the formation of the Hudson's Bay Company in 1670 the trade of the drainage basin began to flow toward the north. Ships were unable to visit the posts at the foot of James Bay because of the shallow character of the bay, and smaller boats were used to collect fur and distribute goods from a central depot on Charlton Island.[5] On Hudson Bay ships were able to visit the mouths of the Nelson and the Churchill rivers. The tributaries of the Hudson Bay drainage basin flowing from the east and the south were similar to those on the opposite side of the height of land flowing toward the St Lawrence. But the vast interior of the continent to the west poured its waters toward Hudson Bay and forced a main outlet across the Precambrian formation by the Nelson River. This outlet and its tributaries served as an entrance to the northwest from Hudson Bay. The advantages of the route were continually in evidence but were overcome temporarily by the canoe route under the French and under the English. With the use of the boat on this relatively short stretch the long line of the canoe route was cut in the centre, and after 1821 all goods for the West were taken in by York Factory, and the Fort William route was abandoned. For over half a century the York boat and Hudson Bay dominated the transport of western Canada. Brigades were organized throughout the Hudson Bay drainage basin and across to the Churchill, the Athabaska, the Peace, and the Mackenzie rivers.

Water transportation facilitated the exploitation of furs throughout the Precambrian area and beyond, but the efficiency of technique determined the routes to be used. The ocean ship to Quebec, the large boats to Montreal, the *canot de maître* to Fort William, and the *canot du nord* to the interior, assisted in the later period by the vessels on the lakes, proved unable to withstand the competition from the ocean ship to Nelson and the York boat to the interior.

The comparative ease with which the transport unit was borrowed and adapted, or devised to meet the demands of the water routes, gave the waterways a position of dominant importance in the moulding of types of economic and political structure. Rapid exploitation of the available staple product over a wide area was inevitable. Undoubtedly the character of the water routes was of fundamental importance in shifting the attention of Canada to the production of staple raw materials. It became necessary to concentrate energy on the transport of raw materials over long distances. The result was that the Canadian economic structure had the peculiar characteristics of areas dependent on staples – especially weakness in other lines of development, dependence on highly industrialized areas for markets and for supplies of manufactured goods, and the dangers of fluctuations in the staple commodity. It had the effect, however, of giving changes of technique a position of strategic importance in fluctuations in economic activity. In one year transport to the west shifted from Montreal to Hudson Bay. The St Lawrence basin flourished with the opening of trade to the west and languished when it was cut off. The legacy of the fur trade has been an organized transport over wide areas especially adapted for handling heavy manufactured goods going to the interior and for bringing out a light, valuable commodity. The heavy one-way traffic made the trade discouraging to settlement, and in turn made the trade a heavy drain on settlement. The main routes had been well organized to handle trade over vast areas.

The disappearance of fur from the St Lawrence basin was accompanied by the rise of lumber as a staple export.[6] The economy built up in relation to fur and water transport was shifted to the second product available on a large scale chiefly from the Precambrian area. Lumber in contrast to fur was a heavy, bulky commodity whether in the form of square timber, logs, deals, planks, or boards, and consequently its transport on a large scale was confined to the larger tributaries and the main St Lawrence route. The Ottawa and upper St Lawrence and Lake Ontario drained the most favourable areas for the growth of the large coniferous species, especially white pine. Rapid exploitation was limited to the softwoods which had a low specific gravity and could be floated down the rivers to Quebec. Lumber supplied its own method of conveyance, and the evolution of rafts suitable to running the rapids of the lower Ottawa in 1806, and the rapids of the St Lawrence at a later date, and finally the introduction of slides for the upper Ottawa, solved the problem of technique. Square timber was floated down the lower St Lawrence to be stored along the tidal beach at Quebec in preparation for loading on wooden ships for the protected markets of England.

The effects, on the economic development of the St Lawrence basin, of dependence on lumber as a staple product, were the opposite of the effects of dependence on fur. Whereas fur involved a heavy incoming cargo, lumber favoured a large return cargo and consequently provided a stimulus to immigration and settlement. The coffin ships of the lumber trade made an important contribution to the movement of immigrants which became prominent after 1820. The trade created a demand for labour and for agricultural products. As in the case of fur it also created violent fluctuations in the economic activity of the colony, and its position as a raw material for construction made the St Lawrence basin susceptible to an unusual extent to the effects of the business cycle.

The increase in settlement in Upper Canada after 1783 and the decline of the fur trade in 1821 raised serious problems for transportation above the Niagara Peninsula and on Lake Ontario. As early as 1801 a Kentucky boat with 350 barrels of flour was sent down the St Lawrence rapids with success,[7] and boats were used to an increasing extent to overcome the drawbacks of the route. A satisfactory outlet was obtained for goods going downstream, but upstream traffic continued a serious problem.

The limitations of the St Lawrence route were accentuated with the introduction of steam. The industrial revolution and its effects on transportation were destined to have a far-reaching influence on the economic history of Canada. Application of the new technique to a transport system adapted to the handling of raw materials on the existing waterways accentuated the influence of the waterways on the later development. The steamship was adapted first to the stretch of river between Montreal and Quebec and continued in operation after 1809. It served as a complement to the lumber trade, and immigrants were taken upstream from Quebec without the inconvenience of a long upstream pull. The pressure from improved transportation to Montreal became evident in the increasing seriousness of the handicaps of the St Lawrence rapids and the Great Lakes. Steamship communication on Lake Ontario was limited by the rapids of the St Lawrence. Under these handicaps the competition of the Erie Canal at Buffalo above Niagara, and of the Oswego route above the St Lawrence rapids, became important. An attempt to draw traffic from the upper lakes to the St Lawrence River was made in the building of the Welland Canal, with eight-foot depth, completed in 1833. This improvement made increasingly necessary the improvement of the final link of the St Lawrence rapids to Montreal. Eventually pressure from Upper Canada resulting from the handicap of high costs on the upstream traffic of manufactured goods contributed in part to the Rebellion of 1837, to the Durham *Report*, to the Act of Union, and to a determined effort to build the St Lawrence canals. These canals were completed to nine feet in the forties, and lake steamers were able to go down regularly to Montreal after 1848.

It is important to emphasize at this point the relationship between the beginnings of the industrial revolution as seen in the application of steam to the St Lawrence route, first from Quebec to Montreal, and later on the upper lakes, and the consequent pressure which led to the building of canals. These developments involved essential dependence on the government as seen in the Act of Union and the energetic canal policy of the first ten years. The Welland Canal was begun as a private enterprise, but inadequate supplies of cheap capital necessitated purchase by the government.[8] The relation between governmental activity and water transportation became an important factor in later developments.

The completion of the St Lawrence route, and the stimulus to settlement, industry, and trade which it occasioned, intensified other limitations of the route. Moreover the delay in opening the route was responsible for rapid depreciation through obsolescence. Attempts to improve the St Lawrence and compete with the Erie Canal, and to attract the export trade of the Middle West, were defeated by the construction of the American railways.[9] The problem of offsetting the handicaps of the route by land transport began at an early date. In 1727 complaints were made that contrary winds were a serious cause of delay on the journey between Montreal and Quebec, and by 1736 a road had been built along the north shore. Stage roads became necessary above Montreal and along the north shore of Lake Ontario to Toronto and west to Dundas and western Upper Canada. The numerous ports along Lake Ontario became termini for roads to the back country.

This form of land transport, however, was far from adequate to meet the demands of trade and industry. consequently the Grand Trunk was completed from Sarnia to Montreal in 1858. The old road from Toronto to Georgian Bay was abandoned with the completion of the Northern Railway from Toronto to Collingwood in 1854. Chicago and Lake Michigan traffic was captured by this route, and traffic was developed on Lake Superior by the Sault Ste Marie Canal, completed in 1855. Finally the handicap of closed seasons for navigation on the lower St Lawrence disappeared with the completion of a short line through the Eastern Townships to Portland (1853), and of the Victoria Bridge (1859). By 1860 the St Lawrence had been amply supplemented by a network of railways. After 1863 the trials of the Allan line on the St Lawrence route in the fifties were overcome and the ocean steamship became an increasingly powerful factor in the development of the route.[10] Unfortunately the location of the Grand Trunk as a line supplementary to the St Lawrence route left it exposed to competition from that route and it was brought to the verge of bankruptcy in 1857. The overwhelming importance of water transport was shown in the route followed by the Grand Trunk in tapping traffic areas built up on the St Lawrence. The completion of these early railways marked the beginning of the amphibian stage of transport history.

The cost of improving the St Lawrence route in terms of canals and railways brought new problems to the government. These problems with their solution were clearly presented by Alexander T. Galt in his reply to the Sheffield manufacturers in 1859:

> Dependence could hardly be placed upon a revival of trade to restore the revenue to its former point: but this would afford no means of meeting the future railway and municipal payments; and parliament had to choose between a continued system of borrowing to meet deficiencies or an increase of taxation to such amount as might, with economy of administration in every branch of the public service, or a revival of trade, restore the equilibrium of income and expenditure. It is true that another course was open, and that was to exact the terms upon which the railway advances were made; and to leave the holders of the municipal bonds to collect their interest, under the strict letter of the law. By these steps Canada would certainly have relieved herself from the pressure of increased taxation, and might have escaped the reproaches of those who blame the increase of her custom's duties. But it would have been at the expense of the English capitalists and legislation; and it would have been but poor consolation for them to know, that, through their loss, Canada was able to admit British goods at 15 instead of 20 per cent.

He elaborated this statement three years later in a report on the Reciprocity Treaty with the United States:[11]

The undersigned commences with two propositions which will not be denied: first that the consumer, under all circumstances, pays the entire cost of the article he uses; and secondly, that his ability to buy depends upon the net results to him of his labor after its product has gone into consumption in any form. Assuming these points as necessarily conceded, it is evident that in a new unsettled country, such as Canada was, and to a certain extent, still is, without roads, without canals, without railroads, with an uncertain, long and perilous communication with Great Britain, the cost of British goods at the early settlement of the country was enhanced by the doubtful credit of its merchants, high ocean freight, high insurance, heavy charges for lighterage, and finally after the goods reached Canada, by the enormous charges consequent on a trade conducted in the most primitive way, by the most primitive conveyances, and subject to the profits demanded by the numerous parties through whose hands it passed before it reached the ultimate consumer. Equally were the still more bulky articles produced and forwarded in payment for goods, subject to similar deduction. Consequently not very many years ago, the settler in Upper Canada, and in many parts of Lower Canada, paid the maximum for his goods and obtained the minimum for his produce.

It has been remarked that legitimate protection, which home manufacturers may enjoy, is that afforded by the cost of bringing foreign goods into competition. It must therefore be admitted that under the circumstances in which Canada was then placed, this legitimate protection was necessarily very large, and that British goods were at a very great disadvantage. In very many cases it may, with perfect truth, be stated that the cost of the goods imported was enhanced to the consumer one hundred per cent., and equally that he only obtained one-half the ultimate price, or much less, of his produce in England. At the time to which reference is made, the duty on British goods, generally, was two and a half per cent., but the price to the consumer was raised enormously by the causes referred to, and his means of purchase in an equally important degree diminished. Now, under these circumstances, it cannot admit of a doubt, that if by an increase of five per cent. on the duty, a reduction of ten per cent. on the other charges were produced, the benefit would accrue equally to the British manufacturer and to the consumer, and the indirect but legitimate protection to the home manufacturer would be diminished; the consumer would pay five per cent. more to the Government but ten percent. less to the merchant and forwarder. In this illustration lies the whole explanation of the Canadian Customs. The government has increased the duties for the purpose of enabling them to meet the interest on the public works necessary to reduce all the various charges upon the imports and exports of the country. Light-houses have been built, the St Lawrence has been deepened, and the canals constructed, to reduce the cost of inland navigation to a minimum. Railways have been assisted to give speed, safety, and permanency to trade interrupted by the severity of winter. All these improvements have been undertaken with the twofold object of diminishing the cost to the consumer of what he imports, and of increasing the *net* result of the labor of the country when finally realized in Great Britain. ...

Finance Department, (Signed) A.T. Galt,
Quebec, 17th March, 1862. Minister of Finance

Fiscal policy was therefore directly linked to problems of transportation, and it is scarcely necessary to add that the link has been a permanent one.

Fiscal policy became involved not only in the improvement of transportation by providing funds according to Galt's explanation but also in developing manufactures, trade, and traffic. The development of industry contributed in turn to the growth of centres of large population and to an increase in traffic, a decrease in deficits, and a lighter burden for the government. The demands of transportation improvements were reflected directly and indirectly in fiscal policy. The fixed charges involved, especially in canals and the improvement of water transportation and in railways, led to a demand for new markets in the East and in the West. Expansion eastward and westward involved Confederation. The debates of the period suggest that the Intercolonial was not commercially feasible and that it was undertaken as a political measure, but it is difficult to conceive of its construction without reference to the demands for new markets. In any case, the results were evident. An excellent line was built at heavy initial cost, as is the custom with government undertakings, heavy interest charges followed, the line was operated at a loss, and goods were carried at unremunerative rates from the larger industrial centre to the Maritimes. The industrial area of central Canada strengthened its position with cheap water transport and access to the coal of the United States and Nova Scotia, and new markets were found in the Maritimes.

Sir Edward Watkin of the Grand Trunk regarded expansion to the West as the solution of its difficulties.[12] The interest of Sir Hugh Allan in the early plans for expansion westward, which occasioned the Pacific Scandal, is significant of the continued importance attached to the development of traffic to the West in relation to the St Lawrence route. The opening of the Intercolonial in 1876 gave the Allan line a Canadian winter port at Halifax, and the deepening of the St Lawrence ship channel from seventeen and a half feet in 1860 to twenty-two feet in 1878 and to twenty-seven and a half feet in 1887 completed an efficient ocean steamship connection to Montreal in summer and to Halifax in winter. The immediate effects were evident in such divergent results as the rapid growth of the live-stock industry in central Canada, the rapid decline of the wooden sailing vessel, the displacement of Quebec by Montreal, and the substitution of square timber by sawn lumber.

But of more striking importance was the demand for more rapid expansion westward to open markets for improved transport. From the standpoint of fiscal policy the outlay of capital in these improvements of transportation in canals and railroads contributed to the difficulties of the Mackenzie Administration and its free-trade policy in the depression of the seventies. The slow development of transportation to the West which followed from this policy was finally speeded up with the National Policy, which provided a guarantee of earnings on traffic carried within Canadian territory in case of success in keeping out goods and protecting the manufacturer, and a guarantee of revenue in case of failure to keep out goods with which to pay the deficit due to loss of traffic. The double-barrelled effectiveness of the policy was enhanced by recovery from the depression and the energetic construction of the Canadian Pacific Railway. Subsidies in money and in land and further protection of east-west traffic by the monopoly clause hastened the early completion of the line in 1885. It is only necessary to refer briefly to such additional developments as the establishment of the Pacific Ocean Services and the improvement of the line by the short line to Saint John in 1890 and the construction of the Crow's Nest Pass Railway after 1897.

The depression of the nineties was in part responsible for the delay in expected results, but the final expansion after 1900 was undoubtedly dependent on the deepening of the Sault Ste Marie Canal to nineteen feet in 1895, of the Welland Canal to fourteen feet in 1887, of the St Lawrence canals to the same depth by 1901, and the St Lawrence ship channel to thirty feet by 1906. The efficient transport system built up around the St Lawrence basin for the handling of wheat hastened the industrial development of eastern Canada, including the iron and steel industry of the Maritimes, and contributed to the development of minerals, lumber, and fish in British Columbia. Eastern Canada lost her position as an exporter of dairy products to England and became a producer largely for rapidly increasing urban population in the home market. Improved transportation, followed by the opening of the West, was responsible for the period of marked prosperity from 1900 to 1914.

An important result of the dependence of staple products on transportation has been the suddenness of the changes which followed. The St Lawrence canals were not available until the last lock had been built, and then the whole route was opened. Again the rapidity of construction of the railway from Skagway to Whitehorse revolutionized the placer mining of the Yukon. These sudden and unpredictable results were particularly important in the rapid accumulation of revenue from the tariff after 1900 and in the unexpected profitableness of Canadian Pacific Railway operations. These developments contributed in turn to the construction of two other transcontinental lines, the Canadian Northern Railway by guaranteed government bonds, and the Grand Trunk Pacific by the construction of the National Transcontinental Railway. The results included bankruptcy, the Drayton-Acworth report of 1917, and the Canadian National Railways and its problems.

The railway network has spread beyond the St Lawrence basin but no one can deny the pull of the Great Lakes in the failure of wheat to move over the National Transcontinental Railway to Quebec. Canada has become to an increasing extent amphibian, but is still powerfully affected by the St Lawrence basin. Nevertheless there are signs that the immense physical plant involved in transcontinental railways is beginning to have effects similar to those of the Northwest Company at the peak of its activities. The decline in importance of virgin natural resources has tended, with the railways as with the Northwest Company, to favour independent lines of growth. The Hudson Bay Railway, the opening of the Panama Canal, and the growth of trade through Vancouver to the Orient parallel the independent development on the Pacific coast and the supremacy of the Hudson Bay route in the fur trade. Even with the support of the industrial revolution there are signs in the growth of regionalism that the second unity of Canada is beginning to drift in the direction of the first and that the control of the St Lawrence waterway is slightly but definitely on the ebb. The increasing strength of the provinces in contrast to the Dominion parallels the increasing importance of railroads and the staples dependent on railroads – minerals, pulp, and paper. The seasonal fluctuations which characterize dependence on water transport tend to become less important with the continuous operation of industries linked to the railroads. The revolution which has followed the use of the gasoline engine as seen in the automobile, the truck, the tractor, the aeroplane, and the motor boat, and the opening of the north, appears to point in the same direction. We have been able to change the winter to the open season, and with electricity the sources of early difficulties to transportation have been converted into sources of power. All these tendencies point to an emergence from the amphibian to the land stage.

It is difficult to summarize the importance of transportation as a factor in Canadian economic history. We can suggest, however, the overwhelming significance of the waterways and especially of the St Lawrence. Cheap water transportation favoured the rapid exploitation of staples and dependence on more highly industrialized countries for finished products. It favoured the position of Canada as an exporter of staples to more highly industrialized areas in terms of fur, lumber, and finally wheat, pulp and paper, and minerals. The St Lawrence was important in the establishment of British power in Canada by its possibilities from a naval and military point of view, but even more from the standpoint of providing a basis for the economic growth of the Empire in the export of staple raw materials and the import of manufactured goods. We cannot in this paper describe the economic effects of dependence on these staple products other than to indicate the drain which they made in transportation costs on the energy of the community. We can suggest that each in its turn had its peculiar type of development and that each left its stamp on Canadian economic history. We can suggest that changes in technique, improvements in the waterways and in types of boats were responsible for rather violent fluctuations in economic development through the dependence on staple raw materials. It is scarcely necessary to describe the effects of dependence on water transportation on problems of finance involved in heavy expenditures which led ultimately to subsidies and government ownership. Water transportation and dependence on staples have been responsible for a variety of heavy overhead costs. Dependence on staple products and the difficulties of the waterway probably delayed improvement of transportation on the one hand and hastened it on the other by permitting the borrowing of mature technique from the United States. Railroads built at a later stage of development were completed more rapidly and the Canadian Pacific Railway was able to draw heavily on American experience in its early stage of development. Moreover, depreciation through obsolescence in American transportation hastened Canadian development, and steamboats, captains, and pilots, displaced on the Mississippi by railroads, moved up to the Red River, and the Saskatchewan, and the Fraser, as they did in turn in Canada from the Saskatchewan and the Fraser to the Mackenzie and the Yukon. The arrival of the first steamboat down the Red River to Winnipeg is surely the most dramatic event in Canadian economic history.

We have traced the evolution of transport in the fur trade, which reached its height in the expansion from the St Lawrence following the development of vessels on the Great Lakes in combination with canoes on the rivers. This transport system disappeared with competition from the York boat from Hudson Bay. The disappearance of the fur trade from the St Lawrence was followed by the rise of the lumber trade. Lumber tended to emphasize the efficiency of downstream traffic on the large rivers, whereas fur tended to emphasize the efficiency of upstream traffic on smaller rivers. The growth of settlement which accompanied the development of the lumber trade led to a demand for efficient upstream transport. This demand became more effective with the introduction of steamboats on the St Lawrence from Quebec to Montreal, and on Lake Ontario and the upper lakes, especially after the completion of the Welland Canal. Pressure from Upper Canada for improved upstream traffic led to the completion of the St Lawrence canals by 1850.

The St Lawrence route, as improved by canals, was further strengthened by the completion of the Grand Trunk Railway and its connections with the seaboard in the following decade. These developments were in turn responsible for the completion of the Intercolonial to Halifax in 1876, and the deepening of the St Lawrence to Montreal to twenty-two feet in 1878, and for the construction of the Canadian Pacific Railway completed in 1885. Finally the deepening of the Sault Ste Marie, the Welland, and the St Lawrence canals, and the St Lawrence ship channel paved the way for the opening of the West, the export of wheat, and the addition of two transcontinental railways.

Again, we have suggested the relationship between the importance of the St Lawrence waterway and Canadian fiscal policy. The Act of Union was a prerequisite to the financial support adequate to completion of the St Lawrence canals, and in turn Confederation was essential to the financial support necessary to round out the policy inaugurated in canals and supplementary railways, by further improvements and extensions to the east with the Intercolonial Railway and to the west with the Canadian Pacific Railway. The policy necessary to provide financial support was outlined by Galt, and whether or not his explanation was one of rationalization after the fact, or of original theoretical analysis, reliance on the customs was undoubtedly the only solution. In the main this policy provided the basis for the elaboration under the National Policy of 1878. According to Galt's argument, the payment of duties actually reduced protection in so far as they were employed in reducing the cost of transportation on imports and exports. But the growing importance of railways, after the construction of the Intercolonial Railway, favoured the addition of the protection argument as a means of increasing traffic, especially in manufactured products. The National Policy was designed not only to increase revenue from customs from the standpoint of the waterways but also to increase revenue from traffic from the standpoint of railways. The increasing importance of railways has tended to emphasize the position of protection rather than revenue.

We can trace in direct descent from the introduction of steam on the St Lawrence waterways, the Act of Union, the completion of the St Lawrence canals, the Grand Trunk, Galt's statement, Confederation, the Intercolonial, the National Policy, the Canadian Pacific Railway, improved St Lawrence canals, the new transcontinentals, and the drift toward protection. The overwhelming importance of the St Lawrence waterways[13] has emphasized the production and export of raw materials, and in the case of wheat the extraordinary effects of a protective tariff during a period of expansion contributed to the construction of two new transcontinentals, and to the emergence of the Canadian National Railways. The problem of the railways is essentially one of traffic to enable them to increase earnings without excessive cost to the producers of exports. The problem of protection is therefore that of increasing the traffic of manufactured goods and thereby increasing earnings, with the result that railroad costs may be decreased to the producers of raw materials to an amount equal to or more than the rise in the price of manufactured goods as a result of protection. Dependence on the application of mature technique, especially in transport, to virgin natural resources must steadily recede in importance as a basis for the tariff. It will become increasingly difficult to wield the tariff as the crude but effective weapon by which we have been able to obtain a share of our natural resources.

NOTES

1 See S.A. Cudmore, *History of the World's Commerce with Special Relation to Canada* (Toronto, 1929).

2 H.P. Biggar, *Early Trading Companies of New France* (Toronto, 1901); H.A. Innis, "The Rise and Fall of the Spanish Fishery in Newfoundland," *Transactions of the Royal Society of Canada,* 3d. ser., 25, sec. 2 (1931): 51–70.

3 M.I. Newbigin, *Canada: The Great River, the Lands and the Men* (New York, 1926).

4 Champlain in 1608 went from Tadoussac to Quebec in pinnaces.

5 In 1932, as a result of construction of the railway to James Bay, the voyage conducted annually for over two and a half centuries through Hudson Straits to Charlton Island was abandoned.

6 See A.R.M. Lower, "Lumbering in Eastern Canada" (doctoral thesis, Harvard University, 1929).
7 Milo M. Quaife, ed., *John Askin Papers* (Detroit, 1931), 2:343; also H.A. Innis and A.R.M. Lower, eds., *Select Documents in Canadian Economic History, 1783–1885* (Toronto, 1933), 138ff.
8 The Lachine Canal was also begun as a private enterprise. See J.L. McDougall, "The Welland Canal to 1841," (master's thesis, University of Toronto, 1923).
9 D.A. MacGibbon, *Railway Rates and the Canadian Railway Commission* (Boston, 1917).
10 William Smith, *History of the British Post Office in British North America, 1639–1870* (Cambridge, 1920), chaps. 17–18.
11 Report of the Minister of Finance on the Reciprocity Treaty with the United States, (*Canada, Sessional Papers*, 1862, no. 23).
12 Sir E.W. Watkin, *Canada and the States* (London, 1887).
13 The proposed improvement of the St Lawrence waterways has not been given adequate consideration from the standpoint of the position of the St Lawrence in the economic development of Canada. The valuable work done by antagonists and proponents of the scheme in terms of neatly calculated estimates has in the main tended to leave out of account the historical background and various incalculable items. This paper cannot undertake a detailed analysis but it does suggest that the tremendous investments of capital built up around the St Lawrence system in terms of ships, canals, terminal facilities, harbours, and railroads, from the standpoint of the export of wheat from the West will suffer materially from drains in other directions. Improvement of the St Lawrence will contribute toward reducing the overhead costs of these tremendous investments. The strains of the political and economic structure built up largely in relation to the St Lawrence would be lessened accordingly.

CHAPTER EIGHT

Unused Capacity as a Factor in Canadian Economic History

The significance of navigation in the economic development of a region penetrated by the St Lawrence to the south and by Hudson Bay to the north has been evident in concentration on production of raw materials for consumption in the highly industrialized area of Europe,[1] and in problems which have arisen with intense specialization, such as unused capacity in terms of vessel space as a result of inability to secure a balanced two-way cargo. The green fishery as conducted from French ports on the banks and along the coast required heavy outbound cargoes of salt to balance return cargoes of fish, but the dry fishery, which became important with the development of Spanish trade at the beginning of the seventeenth century, required smaller quantities of salt and equipment on the outgoing voyage and made necessary the carrying of ballast.[2] The English dry fishery in Newfoundland involved a further lack of balance in that crews necessary to carry on the industry were larger than those necessary to man the vessels, and, because of the seasonal fluctuations and agricultural limitations of that area, men were carried back at the end of the season. Sale of fish in the markets of Spain and the Mediterranean necessitated the dispatch of vessels to England with the men necessary to carry on the fishery, and additional larger vessels (sack ships) with cargoes of fish to market. The addition of sack ships lowered the cost of provisions and facilitated the beginnings of a settlement in which men remained over the winter. Consequently, competition between sack ships and fishing ships for cargoes of fish and for profitable return cargoes of salt, tropical

From *Canadian Journal of Economic and Political Science* 2 (1936): 1–15; reprinted in *Political Economy in the Modern State* (Ryerson, 1946), 201–17.

tropical products, and specie from Spain and the Mediterranean to England, contributed to the long severe struggle which dominated the history of Newfoundland and placed severe restrictions on the introduction of political institutions. New England, with a winter fishery and a favourable area for the development of agriculture, lumbering, and shipbuilding, offered possibilities of year-round operation. Settlers rather than ballast, therefore, were brought to New England. Expansion of settlement contributed to more effective exploitation of the fishery, shipbuilding, and trade and to the decline of control of fishing ships from England. Numerous small New England vessels extended the fishery to the banks and the shores of Nova Scotia, participated in the coastal trade to Newfoundland in spring and summer, and carried products to the West Indies to exchange for sugar and molasses in winter when these products came on the market and there was freedom from hurricanes. Relative absence of unused capacity in New England shipping meant low costs and contributed to rapid economic development which facilitated control over Nova Scotia after its loss to France in the Treaty of Utrecht in 1713. The expansion of New England involved a continued drain of labour from Newfoundland and weakened the position of settlement in that area.

The concern of French fishing ships with the home market and the green fishery led to a late development of the dry fishery in more distant areas not occupied by the English, such as Gaspé. An unbalanced cargo facilitated the addition of trading goods on the outward voyage for development of trade on the St Lawrence in furs, which with small bulk and high value added little to the cargo of the home voyage. The importance of the Precambrian formation, and its limitations as to agricultural development, accentuated dependence on the fishing industry in the Maritime regions and on the fur trade in the area drained by the St Lawrence. Severe competition of fishing ships for the fur trade made monopoly control impossible in the Maritimes and inevitable in the restricted areas of the St Lawrence. Monopoly control in the fur trade and an unbalanced cargo were accompanied by attempts to reduce outbound cargo from Europe, to restrict settlement, and to increase return cargo by expansion of the fur trade. Similar effects were evident in the trade of the Dutch to New Amsterdam and up the Hudson and by the Iroquois to the Richelieu and to Lake Ontario. Competition between two routes characterized by long ocean voyages and unbalanced cargoes caused serious losses which culminated in the destruction of the villages of Huron middlemen north of Lake Simcoe. Severe losses in the fur trade, which accompanied monopoly under private enterprise, accentuated restriction of settlement. Intense competition between drainage basins necessitated direct control on the part of the French government in 1663 and active promotion of immigration and settlement and successful war against the Iroquois.

Groseilliers and Radisson attempted to avoid the difficulties of the St Lawrence by developing trade through Hudson Bay, but they were discouraged by the French who were opposed to the additional costs of maintaining control over two routes.[3] They turned to the English who founded the Hudson's Bay Company. To meet competitive attacks from this alternative route, the French ruthlessly checked that Company's activities prior to 1713. Not only was possible competition checked in the north, but efforts continued to extend the St Lawrence trade by the construction of military posts at Fort Frontenac, Niagara, and Detroit to prevent competition from the English, successors to the Dutch after 1664 to the south. The success of these efforts was followed by rapid increase in the number of lower grade southern furs brought on the market, a rapid decline in price, and attempts to increase prices by valorization schemes, which failed, particularly because of declining consumption caused by the lowering of the quality of materials used in the manufacture of beaver hats. The results accompanying the activities of the government in strengthening the position of the St Lawrence by heavy military expenditures were evident in the development of inflation and in the loss of Hudson Bay and Nova Scotia in the Treaty of Utrecht. The persistent effects of unused capacity were evident under private enterprise in restriction of settlement and the necessity of governmental intervention. The consequent increased settlement in turn necessitated expansion of the fur trade to the interior. Inability to control the rate of expansion was particularly serious with a luxury product.

The Hudson's Bay Company, handicapped by limitations of agriculture in Hudson Bay, was similarly compelled to restrict a heavy outbound cargo, and to limit population, with the result that it was in a weak position to resist inroads from the French. The difficulties of combating the smuggling of a light, highly valuable commodity such as fur necessitated a highly centralized organization similar to that attempted by the Spanish in the handling of precious metals. (Possibilities of smuggling in the St Lawrence checked efforts at centralization such as matured in the Hudson's Bay Company.) The problem of restricted population was eventually solved in part by governmental intervention in the form of military and naval campaigns, the success of which led to the reoccupation of Hudson Bay in the Treaty of Utrecht.

The penetration of the French to the interior and increasing dependence on the fur trade accentuated the weakness of agriculture in the St Lawrence, with its limitations of soil, climate, and technique, to the extent that New France was not even self-sufficient and was unable to provide support to the fishing regions, particularly of Cape Breton after 1713, or to the French West Indies, or to compete with lumber and fish from New England and agricultural products – especially flour – from New York and Philadelphia. Moreover, the long closed season of the St Lawrence restricted the possibilities of developing a satisfactory trade to the West Indies. The hurricane season coincided with the open season of the St Lawrence and the sugar season with the closed season. Inability to link up the St Lawrence with the fishing industry and the West Indies weakened the French Empire, in contrast with the economic integration of settlement in New England and expansion of the fishing industry and trade to the West Indies and Newfoundland which strengthened the English Empire. Expansion of the fur trade and the fishing industry in New France weakened the French, while integrated development increased the strength of the regions under British control on the Atlantic. After 1713, New England advanced to the fishing regions in the vicinity of Canso and extended trade to Newfoundland and the West Indies. Expanding trade involved exports to, and imports from, the foreign West Indies in spite of such legislation as the Molasses Act of 1733. From the south, New York, with cheap supplies of rum from the West Indies, began to compete more effectively in the interior with the French transatlantic, St Lawrence trade with its dependence on brandy. To the north, the Hudson's Bay Company re-established its position on Hudson Bay, although the problem of unbalanced cargo continued; settlement was restricted and exploration and penetration to the interior were limited. Indians were encouraged to bring their furs down to Hudson Bay. Continued competition from the north and the south necessitated continued extension westward of the French fur trade of the St Lawrence. La Vérendrye and his successors took advantage of the weakness of the Hudson's Bay Company on Hudson Bay by pushing trade to the Saskatchewan and making visits of the Indians to Hudson Bay unnecessary; but increasing costs of transportation weakened the position of the French Empire and contributed to its collapse. Renewed efforts to increase control over the fur trade by expansion westward, and over the fishing industry by fortification of Louisburg in Cape Breton, were again defeated and followed by the collapse of the French Empire in 1763.

That collapse facilitated the expansion of British colonial trade, as shown in the penetration of Albany traders to the St Lawrence and to the upper lakes, but the problem of unbalanced cargo in the European Atlantic trade in furs by the St Lawrence route remained, and with it the necessity for westward expansion. The divergence between the New York and the St Lawrence trade was recognized in regulations permitting extension of trade beyond the posts in 1768, and in the Quebec Act of 1774, which attempted, by a boundary line down the Ohio, to re-establish control by Montreal over territory occupied by the French. Penetration to the northwest followed lines worked out by the French. On the Atlantic, expansion of integrated colonial trade increased the tension incidental to the restriction of West Indies trade through enforcements of the Sugar Act. Pressure in the interior and on the Atlantic contributed to the Revolution.

After the Revolution, England was scarcely more successful than the French had been in developing an empire based on the St Lawrence, the Maritimes, and the West Indies. The West Indies lost their influential position for Great Britain, and although Britain paid heavy penalties to build up the Maritimes as a substitute for the American colonies, they were unable to provide adequate supplies of foodstuffs for their own needs. The fur trade of the St Lawrence continued as a drain on agriculture in that area. Fur traders continued to solve their problems by expansion to the Saskatchewan, the Churchill, the Mackenzie, and the rivers draining to the Pacific. Reorganization in the formation of the Northwest Company, support of West Indies rum, use of vessels on the Great Lakes, and organization of food supply in the interior with reliance on pemmican and the potato, contributed to the achievement. The Hudson's Bay Company, with its persistent problem of unbalanced cargo to Hudson Bay, was again weakened by expansion from the St Lawrence and was compelled to make determined efforts to overcome its handicaps and penetrate to the interior, in part by reorganization, and in part by settlement in the Red River district under Lord Selkirk as a means of reducing costs of imported provisions and supplies. The inevitable severe competition between rival organizations – on the one hand from the St Lawrence with expansion to new territory with unexploited resources as a means of mitigating the increasing cost of transportation, and on the other from Hudson Bay with the necessity of penetration to the interior to meet traders from the St Lawrence – was followed by outbreaks of hostilities and amalgamation in 1821. Continued expansion from the St Lawrence and the increasingly difficult problem of an unbalanced cargo, accentuated not only by distance but also by the necessity of travelling upstream with heavy outbound cargo, eventually weakened the Northwest Company as they had the French. The significance of unbalanced cargoes was evident in the intensity of competition, in the rapid extension westward from the St Lawrence, in restriction in Hudson Bay, and in the clash which brought amalgamation.

The drain of the fur trade and its opposition to settlement in the St Lawrence were ended temporarily in the French régime by the active intervention of government, and similarly in the English régime. Restricted settlement on the St Lawrence, as a result of the characteristics of the fur trade, was overcome not only by active encouragement to migration of the Loyalists, particularly to Upper Canada, by military settlements, and by strong military support in the War of 1812, but also by determined efforts of Great Britain through an extremely high preference to build up the timber trade in order to offset the effects of dependence on European and American supplies during the Napoleonic Wars. The disappearance of the fur trade in the St Lawrence was followed by exploitation of softwood (white pine) timber. As a bulky commodity with low specific gravity it could be floated down the long continental rivers, and with the manufacture of ships provided its own means of transportation to Great Britain. With a heavy return cargo and empty space on the outbound voyage, its effects were the reverse of the fur trade, and large numbers of settlers were brought out in preference to ballast. Rapid increase of settlement, particularly after 1820, was followed by rapid expansion of agriculture, especially in Upper Canada. Increased agricultural production, wheat and flour, in the newly settled regions of Upper Canada led to demands for construction of canals across the Niagara Peninsula and on the upper St Lawrence. The difficulties of obtaining financial support for canal construction in newly settled regions, and increasing demands for cheaper transportation, contributed, together with the depression of the 1830s and the pronounced cyclical fluctuations of an economy largely dependent on the timber trade, to the outbreak of the Rebellion in 1837, Lord Durham's *Report*, the Act of Union, and creation of a financial structure capable of supporting rapid construction of canals. Concentration on the timber trade, with its unbalanced cargo and the indirect effect on increasing emigration and settlement, was followed by governmental intervention not only in the form of improvements of transportation but also of changes in land policy. The unwholesome conditions of immigration in dilapidated ships suited only to the timber trade, shown in outbreaks of cholera which spread through the continent, necessitated governmental regulation. The timber trade was encouraged by the development of settlement, as costs of transportation were lowered by securing immigrants for the outbound voyage, but as it expanded in these circumstances, the problems of settlement became more acute. The period of shifting from dependence on the timber trade to dependence on agriculture was essentially a period of difficulty.

After 1821 the fur trade as conducted from Hudson Bay continued to be involved in problems of unbalanced cargo, though they were less acute on account of settlement of Red River, more efficient transportation, and increasing possibilities of regulation. Continued expansion to new territory in the Yukon and Labrador was accompanied by attempts to lower costs by reducing the heavy incoming upstream cargo. New England traders, restricted by the British Navigation Acts on the Atlantic, were free from the restraints of the East India Company on the Pacific, and could take advantage of the discoveries made by Captain Cook towards the prevention of scurvy during long voyages, and of the new resources of furs. On the other hand, Canadian traders expelled from American territory after the Jay Treaty and the Embargo Act of 1807, pushed into the Pacific coast drainage basin and displaced Astor's establishment on the Columbia in the War of 1812. After amalgamation in 1821, the Western Department by virtue of its distance and its interest in the Pacific, tended to develop along lines independent of the Northern Department. Exhaustion of new territory for the fur trade accentuated economies of operation, particularly in transportation, and contributed to the development of settlement and agriculture, particularly on the Columbia and the Red River. Settlement eventually brought demands for new types of government, shown in the loss of Oregon and in the difficulties leading to the Riel Rebellion and the establishment of the province of Manitoba. The problem of unused capacity in the fur trade, and the necessity of reducing westbound upstream movements of bulky provisions and supplies, resulted in constant expansion westward to the Pacific and the organization of settlement in relation to production of food supplies. In turn agriculture and settlement hastened the decline of the fur trade and provided abutments for the railway bridge. Monopoly in the fur trade receded and new trade routes emerged in which the Hudson's Bay Company deserted the Hudson Bay route and imported goods from the south.

In the Maritimes continuous efforts were made to develop an integrated economy similar to that of New England in a struggle for control over the fishery, trade, and shipping. Concentration of trade in Halifax was followed after the middle of the century, particularly with the advent of steamships, by attempts to overcome the handicaps of the fishing industry, evident in scattered ports, through government construction of short stretches of railway to the Gulf of St Lawrence and the Bay of Fundy; and in Saint John by construction of short stretches of railway to the Gulf of St Lawrence. Competition of railways with shipping brought profound disturbances to an economy based on ships, and shifted interest from external to internal development. Decline of shipping and difficulties of the railways necessitated efforts to extend traffic to the interior by linking the railways to continental systems. An attempt was made to solve the problem of unused railway capacity by Confederation and construction of the Intercolonial Railway.[4]

On the St Lawrence, the inadequacy of canals as a solution to the problems of agriculture in Upper Canada, the difficulty of securing traffic from the western states in competition with the Erie Canal, improved upper lakes steamboats, and railways, necessitated further governmental intervention in the form of substantial assistance to the Grand Trunk from Sarnia to Montreal and Portland, and later to Rivière du Loup to connect with the Intercolonial to Halifax. Private enterprise with government support was able to build the short line to the American seaboard, but government ownership was essential to link up Maritime railways with the Grand Trunk by the Intercolonial and to supplement water transportation to Montreal during the summer season. As the Act of Union was a financial prerequisite to the St Lawrence canals, so Confederation was a financial prerequisite to the Intercolonial. A more balanced cargo, which was available in New York and American ports, pulled American steamships – for example, the Cunard line – from Canadian ports. In spite of attempts to increase traffic by construction of through lines, the problems of unused capacity became more serious. Construction of a railway to the Pacific offered possibilities of relief.

On the Pacific coast the sudden economic expansion precipitated by the gold rush in the late fifties and early sixties was followed by rapid decline and serious financial difficulties accompanying heavy interest charges on the debt incurred in construction of roads to the interior.[5] Construction of a transcontinental railway as a condition on which British Columbia joined Confederation was expected to solve problems of debt in relation to existing transportation facilities in British Columbia and in the St Lawrence. Substantial governmental support necessitated construction of a road through Canadian territory north of Lake Superior and precluded participation by the Grand Trunk Railway, insistent on building up traffic for its main line to the western states.[6]

The anxiety of the government to solve the problems of public finance, which followed the severe depression of the seventies, by development of traffic for existing transportation facilities enabled Montreal financiers, who had gained materially from the first line from Minneapolis to Winnipeg and from reversal of the flow of traffic from Hudson Bay on the north to the south, to obtain the contract for construction of the Canadian Pacific Railway. Rapid construction of the main line in the prairie regions, adoption of a southern route in spite of recommendations of Sandford Fleming in favour of the northern route, encouragement of immigrants, acquisition of feeders in the industrialized St Lawrence region, completion of the line to a winter port at Saint John, and extension of ocean services were part of a policy incidental to the overwhelming importance of developing traffic on a transcontinental line. "It was the Oriental traffic that helped to save the Canadian Pacific from the disaster which sunk a hundred and fifty-six American railroads in the depression of 1893–95 and might well have overwhelmed a new railway through Canada depending for its existence on local business."[7] Oriental traffic during the depression was supplemented by economic expansion of British Columbia, particularly in the construction of the Crow's Nest Pass line, in the mines of the Kootenay region, in lumbering, in fishing, and in the gold rush to the Klondike. The tariff designed in the National Policy to support east-west traffic and the monopoly clause (cancelled 1888) supported the policy of following a southern route across the prairies to check competition from American roads for long-haul traffic.

Determined efforts to maintain control over traffic were accompanied by rapid increase in profits at the turn of the century, and release of contractors after completion of the main line led to the construction of a second main line from Winnipeg northwest to the Yellowhead Pass, with government support from the provinces in protest against the burden of monopoly from a transcontinental line supported by a federal government. Control by the Canadian Northern of a line carrying traffic from the prairies to the head of the lakes necessitated extension westward to Vancouver and eastward from the head of the lakes to the St Lawrence. In eastern Canada the Grand Trunk was compelled by encroachment from the Canadian Pacific to secure control of local traffic by amalgamation with the Great Western, and to search for means of supplementing through-line traffic. Protection encouraged transcontinental lines and weakened the position of the Grand Trunk main line to the United States. Montreal became the apex of an angle of which one side – the main line of the CPR – extended to British Columbia and the other – the main line of the Grand Trunk – to Sarnia and Chicago. Development of traffic on these lines, deepening of the upper St Lawrence canals to 14 feet and of the St Lawrence Ship Channel to twenty-five feet early in the century, and extension of wireless, enabled Montreal to compete more effectively with New York for grain and for ships. Inability to link up the Intercolonial as a government undertaking with railways under private enterprise which were anxious to take the shortest cut to seaboard, decline of Quebec as contrasted with the rise of Montreal, attempts to tap the clay belt extending westward to Winnipeg in order to provide for possible expansion in northern Quebec and in northern Ontario, and increasing revenue from the tariff led to the construction of the National Transcontinental Railway from Winnipeg to Quebec and its extension to Maritime ports. The more distant Grand Trunk Pacific line, extending from Winnipeg, as the terminus of the National Transcontinental, to Prince Rupert, appeared as a possibility of developing through long-haul traffic to the Orient, British Columbia, and western Canada, and as a further means of checking the effects of monopoly from the Canadian Pacific under the National Policy. Attempts to link the Grand Trunk in the East and the Canadian Northern in the West were destined to defeat through the insistence of private enterprise in the Canadian Northern on a line to the Great Lakes and industrial areas of the St Lawrence, and of the federal government in the National Transcontinental on a line opening new territory and recapturing lost ground for the Intercolonial and the Maritimes.

The enormous outlay of capital in canals and transcontinental railways accentuated problems of unused capacity, particularly because of the basic importance of the production and export of wheat from the prairie regions. Construction of elevators and of branch lines on a vast scale in the wheat-producing regions necessitated double tracking of lines to the head of the lakes and additions of lines from Georgian Bay ports to Montreal. Seasonal navigation implied rapid movement of grain and a pronounced peak load of east-bound traffic. Empty cars were distributed over a long period to points throughout the West in preparation for the harvest rush. Seasonal navigation on the lower St Lawrence facilitated storage of wheat in Buffalo elevators for shipment to New York.

The secular trend of expanding wheat production shown in long-run peak-load problems of transportation was accompanied by short-run problems of annual fluctuations of crop, and affected government policy. The tendency of costs incidental to peak-load operation, made more rigid by competitive rates with American lines and the importance of government debt, to fall on regions exposed to world competition in prices of wheat, has involved the struggle for control over elevators, lower rates, the cooperative movement, the Hudson Bay Railway, and shipment via Vancouver and the Panama Canal. Finally, the recent depression and sustained drought led to governmental support of wheat prices and establishment of a wheat board.

The burdens were less conspicuous during the period of rapid expansion from the middle nineties to the beginning of the war on account of increased immigration, branch- and main-line construction, expansion of wheat production, and the development of mining in the Cordilleran region, especially the Kootenay and the Klondike. Rapid increase in capital equipment in western Canada was accompanied by expansion of the industrial areas of the St Lawrence and of the Maritimes. Provincial government support of hydro-electric power in Ontario to utilize the enormous water powers of Niagara accompanied support by bonuses of the iron and steel industry of the Maritimes and the St Lawrence for the production of coal, railway cars, rails, and machinery. Similarly, rapid increase of population in the west involved provincial government support in the construction of telephone lines and extension of other social services. Decline in rate of expansion in western Canada brought a sharp decline in the demand for railway cars, rails, and other types of capital equipment, with particularly serious effects for more distant regions such as the Maritimes, and in turn necessitated increased government support in subventions.

The acute difficulties of new transcontinental railways in competition with an established line before traffic had been developed, and the freezing of capital markets with the outbreak of the Great War, led to the appointment of the Drayton-Acworth Commission and formation of the Canadian National Railways to include lines built by private enterprise – namely the Grand Trunk, and its subsidiary, the Grand Trunk Pacific, and the Canadian Northern – and by government – the Intercolonial and the National Transcontinental. These lines were merged, and determined efforts were made to build up long-haul traffic by steamship lines, hotels, and branch lines. The Canadian Pacific, in an attempt to maintain control and to extend traffic, engaged in construction of branch lines, hotels, steamships, and extension of external activities. The upward swing of the business cycle favoured extension of capital equipment by both organizations. The necessity of competing for long-haul traffic in mature economic areas with which private enterprise had been particularly concerned, accentuated the problem of lines built by the government. These lines were essentially developmental and, being undertaken by the government with ample supplies of credit, were built with heavy initial outlays of capital. Consequently, light traffic, as a result of competition from lines built under private enterprise and privately owned and of their essentially developmental character, involved heavy unit costs of operation and maintenance, which were accentuated by heavy sunk costs of construction. Expansion of mining and of the pulp and paper industry, and settlement in northern Ontario and northern Quebec, were of first importance in reducing costs and meeting the deficit of the Canadian National Railways and in offsetting the effects of competition within the Canadian National System with lines to Chicago, to the northwest, and from the northwest to Quebec and the Maritimes.

The effects of the depression on the Canadian Pacific and the Canadian National have been evident in the passing of dividends and in the extent of Canadian National deficits. The Canadian Pacific has been relatively barred from further participation in expansion and has even been seriously affected by decline in the southern drought areas, but, on the other hand, its entrenched position has served as a powerful bulwark and it has continued to develop external traffic through its steamship lines. The Canadian National has been restricted by competition from the Canadian Pacific and by financial stringency. A more aggressive developmental policy in new territory would ease its difficulties.

The basic importance of transportation in the economic history of Canada has been responsible for the profound effects of unused capacity. The restrictive effect on settlement of an unbalanced cargo from Europe, and of up-stream traffic for heavy goods in the fur trade, resulted in governmental intervention on an extensive scale and collapse in the French régime. On the other hand, the expansive effect of an unbalanced cargo in the timber trade, which followed governmental intervention in the form of high preferences and military settlements to overcome the restrictive influences of the fur trade, brought expansion of agriculture and the necessity of further government intervention to solve the problems of improved transportation.

The significance of water transportation in the export of fur and timber involved emphasis on commercial credit. In the fur trade governmental support to military and naval ventures brought problems of government finance and led to inflation. The severity of fluctuations in the timber trade brought disastrous losses to interests concerned. Production and export of wheat necessitated railways and canals and the introduction of long-term credit through corporate and government finance. Fixed interest charges accompanying extensive government support, and insufficient revenue, necessitated further governmental intervention with Confederation, and extension to the Maritimes and the Pacific. Government intervention took the form of ownership and operation of the Intercolonial to the Maritimes and strong support to private enterprise westward to the Pacific. The expansion westward from the St Lawrence which was typical of the fur trade was also essential to agriculture. The necessities of a transcontinental railway system were evident in the policies of the federal government – for example in tariff and immigration policy – and of the Canadian Pacific Railway; but they implied the development of competing lines to offset the effects of monopoly control, supported by the provinces of the prairie region and the metropolitan centres of Toronto, Quebec, and Halifax, and the emergence of control through the Board of Railway Commissioners, and of statutory rates such as the Crow's Nest Pass Rate Agreement and more recently British Columbia rate adjustment and the Maritime Freight Rates Act. The Hudson Bay Railway was a conspicuous illustration of the continued necessity for, and significance of, governmental intervention in relation to the problems of monopoly in western Canada. Ostensibly intended to provide relief from the problem of monopoly, it has been regarded as creating additional burdens of debt. Capital equipment essential to the production and export of wheat, in the form of a transcontinental railway, brought acute problems in non-competitive areas, which were temporarily solved, with the assistance of an upward swing of the business cycle and favourable prices of wheat, by further additions of capital equipment in two transcontinental railways. Decline in the rate of expansion, and the depression, emphasized the weight of overhead costs in relation to extensive capital equipment, and the heavy fixed charges involved in government ownership were evident in rigidities of railway rates and interest charges. These factors contributed to a decline in standards of living in the exposed areas and in turn to a reduction in demands for manufactured products from central Canada, to industrial unemployment, to numerous disparities and destructive eddies in the current of economic life – described in the evidence before the Royal Commission on Price Spreads – and to governmental intervention on a vast scale, ranging from the spate of federal legislation of the session 1935 to the cancelling of power contracts by the provincial government of Ontario. Dependence of the Prairie Provinces on wheat, and the tariff, are factors accentuating the burden on western Canada and are not offset by lower costs through competition for westbound traffic in manufactured products from eastern Canada. The sharp decline in prices of raw material, especially wheat, and low returns on bulk movements of grain and additional competition from motor transport in the competitive St Lawrence region compel the railways to search for more remunerative westbound traffic of manufactured products in the face of declining purchasing power in the wheat area. More exposed regions with rigidities of freight rates and interest charges and shrinking income through drought and falling prices, and without an integrated balanced economic structure, have been more seriously affected by political disturbance, as evident in the movement for social credit in Alberta. The inadequacy of methods of control, increasing unit costs with shrinkage of volume and plant built for peak-load operations, and limited possibilities of further expansion, have necessitated substantial federal support of the Prairie Provinces in a wide variety of relief measures during the depression, and have brought forth protests from the Maritimes and British Columbia in favour of readjustment of federal-provincial relations.[8]

Problems of unused capacity have had the effect of quickening and accentuating the long-run general trends of economic development and have necessitated governmental intervention as a steadying or remedial factor. In the main, problems have been solved by aggressive developmental measures but limitations have been apparent in the present depression. Governmental intervention as a means of solving problems during a period of expansion creates problems to be solved by new types of government intervention during a depression. Lower tariffs bring relief, particularly to the regions more distant from the St Lawrence and probably throughout the entire economy, but they do not solve the problems of reducing the violence of the swings incidental to the significance of unused capacity.

The long-run period of depression in the latter part of the last century was accompanied by continued determined efforts to enable the St Lawrence to compete with New York, and the long-run period of prosperity of a third of a century which followed was marked by the success of those efforts and by further efforts to swing the Canadian economy further to the north to support Quebec and the Maritimes. The failure of those efforts, shown in an enormous debt and heavy deficits, has been accompanied by a retreat. Heavy outlay incidental to government construction and ownership of the railways designed to support the lower St Lawrence and Maritime regions have accompanied lower rates incidental to water competition and statutory intervention. Narrowing of the range of the economy dependent on the St Lawrence as a result of the development of a competitive region on the Pacific coast, largely as a consequence of the Panama Canal, has complicated the problem. Drastic revision of debts, ranging from the passing dividends on the CPR to agricultural debt adjustment operations, has been inevitable. Transfers to more exposed regions have been gradually developed, but much remains to be done before the implications of unused capacity are understood.

NOTES

1 See H.A. Innis, *Problems of Staple Production in Canada* (Toronto, 1933), chap. 2.

2 Numerous regulations were enacted against the dumping of ballast in the harbours of Newfoundland.

3 See G.L. Nute, *Cæsars of the Wilderness* (New York, 1943).

4 "It is to be hoped that the folly of expecting any large results from local and isolated railways is already fully demonstrated to both Nova Scotia and New Brunswick, and that it has now become a first consideration with them to direct their attention to the means by which both may be relieved from the consequences of a large debt incurred for works not only unproductive of any directly remunerative results but also unattended by any substantial advantage to our trade or commercial importance. The conviction must have forced itself upon the public mind that we must extricate ourselves from these difficulties by obtaining connection with the railways of Canada and the United States by one or other of the routes proposed. Much has already been done towards achieving that result" (from a speech by Sir Charles Tupper at Saint John, 1860, quoted in Sir Charles Tupper, *Recollections of Sixty Years in Canada* [Toronto, 1914], 34–5). "There is a little over a hundred miles of railway in the province but owing to some cause which is unintelligible to an outsider and many less important reasons, which are easily understood, this undertaking has burdened the province with a heavy debt and consequently heavy taxation while it has irritated politicians, and been a cause of deferring ... perhaps for ever ... many important acts of local legislation. The primary error, undoubtedly, was the making it a government work, instead of leaving it to a company. Heavy sums raised at *six per cent.* on provincial debentures make sad havoc with revenue of the country. And the next great error ... patent to all ... is the custom too prevalent in our colonies under the system of representative government, of changing every official, however petty, at every change of government" (F. Duncan, *Our Garrisons in the West* [London, 1864], 100). "Provincial isolation and a blundering neglect to make railways which indi-

vidually are burdens but would become as a grand whole a source of revenue and profit, are among the features at present most apparent on our British American Railway system ... It is well said, by one of their own journals 'We cannot afford to bear the burden of our present incomplete road'" (ibid., 280).

5 "Although sentiment in Vancouver Island on the whole was unfavourable to Confederation, the entire mainland including Cariboo, then an important factor, was practically a unit in its favour" (Tupper, *Recollections*, 126).

6 Ibid., 140.

7 J.M. Gibbon, *Steel of Empire* (Toronto, 1935), 336.

8 See "A Note on Problems of Readjustment in Canada," *Journal of Political Economy*, Dec. 1935, for a discussion of the implications of W.A. Mackintosh's *Economic Problems of the Prairie Provinces* (Toronto, 1935).

CHAPTER NINE

Commerce and Industry in Canadian Economic Development, 1760–1935

Writing at the end of a long period of rapid expansion in the English colonies and at a time when such expansion threatened imminent revolt, Adam Smith concluded that "Plenty of good land, and liberty to manage their own affairs their own way, seem to be the two great causes of the prosperity of all new colonies."[1] The second cause was elaborated at great length. The colonies of England conducted their governments upon a much less expensive plan and with a much less expensive ceremonial than those of France, Portugal, and Spain. The colonies of the latter countries had even more serious difficulties to contend with:

> Such ceremonials are not only real taxes paid by the rich colonists upon those particular occasions, but they serve to introduce among them the habit of vanity and expence upon all other occasions. They are not only very grievous occasional taxes but they contribute to establish perpetual taxes of the same kind still more grievous; the ruinous taxes of private luxury and extravagance. In the colonies of all those three nations too, the

---

This paper was read before the economics section of the British Association for the Advancement of Science, Nottingham, 11 September 1937, and it follows in logical order: "Transportation as a Factor in Canadian Economic History," *Problems of Staple Production in Canada* (Toronto, 1933), 1–17; "Unused Capacity as a Factor in Canadian Economic History," *Canadian Journal of Economics and Policial Science* 2 (Feb. 1936): 1–15; "Introduction to the Canadian Economic Studies," *The Dairy Industry in Canada* (Toronto, 1937), x–xxvi, and editor's introduction to *Labor in Canadian-American Relations* (Toronto, 1937), v–xxxi. It is intended as a complement to C.W. Wright's "American Nationalism: An Economic Interpretation," *Facts and Factors in Economic History* (Cambridge, 1932), 357–80. It was published in the *Canadian Historical Review* 18 (Dec. 1937): 374–84, and first appeared as "Significant Factors in Canadian Economic Development."

ecclesiastical government is extremely oppressive. Tithes take place in all of them ... All of them besides are oppressed with a numerous race of mendicant friars, whose beggary being not only licensed, but consecrated by religion, is a most grievous tax upon the poor people, who are most carefully taught that it is a duty to give, and a very great sin to refuse them their charity. Over and above all this, the clergy are, in all of them, the greatest engrossers of land.

Fourthly, in the disposal of their surplus produce, or of what is over and above their own consumption, the English colonies have been more favoured, and have been allowed a more extensive market, than those of any other European nations. (541–2)

The first cause was linked to the second and was described more briefly: "... the engrossing of uncultivated land, though it has by no means been prevented altogether, has been more restrained in the English colonies than in any other" (539). "The labour of the English colonists, therefore, being more employed in the improvement and cultivation of land, is likely to afford a greater and more valuable produce, than that of any of the other three nations, which, by the engrossing of land, is more or less diverted towards other employments" (540). "The political institutions of the English colonies have been more favourable to the improvement and cultivation of this land, than those of any of the other three nations" (538–9), although good land was less abundant. "It has been the principal cause of the rapid progress of our American colonies towards wealth and greatness that almost their whole capitals have hitherto been employed in agriculture" (347). "Agriculture is the proper business of all new colonies; a business which the cheapness of land renders more advantageous than any other" (575). He knew that good land was not abundant in the English colonies and that agricultural technique was inefficient (223) and yet he concluded: "... through the greater part of Europe the commerce and manufactures of cities, instead of being the effect, have been the cause and occasion of the improvement and cultivation of the country. This order, however, being contrary to the natural course of things, is necessarily both slow and uncertain. Compare the slow progress of those European countries of which the wealth depends very much upon their commerce and manufactures, with the rapid advances of our North American colonies, of which the wealth is founded altogether in agriculture" (392).

One may venture to suggest that the two causes were closely interlocked, but that expansion in the North American colonies as in Europe was the "cause and occasion of the improvement and cultivation of the country." Adam Smith in his analysis of the division of labour and the extent of the market as determined by transportation, can be quoted in support of this suggestion: "In our North American colonies the plantations have constantly followed either the sea-coast or the banks of navigable rivers, and have scarce any where extended themselves to any considerable distance from both" (19). "As by means of water-carriage a more extensive market is opened to every sort of industry than what land-carriage alone can afford it, so it is upon the sea-coast, and along the banks of navigable rivers, that industry of every kind naturally begins to subdivide and improve itself, and it is frequently not till a long time after that those improvements extend themselves to the inland parts of the country" (18). The improvement of transportation facilitated the expansion of external and internal trade.

> Good roads, canals, and navigable rivers, by diminishing the expence of carriage, put the remote parts of the country more nearly upon a level with those in the neighbourhood of the town. They are upon that account the greatest of all improvements. They encourage the cultivation of the remote, which must always be the most extensive circle of the country. They are advantageous to the town, by breaking down the monopoly of the country in its neighbourhood. They are advantageous even to that part of the country. Though they introduce some rival commodities into the old market, they open many new markets to its produce. Monopoly, besides, is a great enemy to good management, which can never be universally established but in consequence of that free and universal competition which forces everybody to have recourse to it for the sake of self-defence. (147)

Cheap water transportation from Europe to North America stimulated commerce and brought "improvement and cultivation of the country." The fishing industry capitalized to the full the advantages of water transportation. The discovery of the abundance of fish in the New World was followed by the expansion of the industry from Europe to meet the demands of countries predominantly Catholic and with a limited production of meat products. France prosecuted the industry in relation to her own demands. England was attracted to the Spanish market by the specie obtained from the New World, and occupied Newfoundland, and later New England, as a base for the production of dry fish for that market. The expansion of trade from France to Spain was followed by the occupation of Nova Scotia and the Gulf of St Lawrence. As a result of contact with the hunting Indians of the interior by the St Lawrence and its tributaries, the fur trade emerged to meet the demands of metropolitan Paris for luxuries and of the aborigines for European goods. Fur, being a commodity of small bulk and high value, supported a trade carried on over increasing distances to the interior. In the more tropical regions, Spain and Portugal were concerned with treasure, England and France with tobacco and later, in the West Indies, with sugar (156ff, 162ff).

The technique of production of these various commodities involved sharply differentiated economies. Slaves were taken by English ships from Africa to the West Indies, and supplies and provisions for the consumption of slaves and the production of sugar were carried by colonial ships from the north temperate colonies. New England became an active commercial region with its prosperity based on the fishing industry and shipping to Europe, the West Indies, and Newfoundland. France had an expanding fur trade which handicapped the production of agricultural products on the St Lawrence and in turn accentuated dependence of the French West Indies and the French fishing industry on the English colonies. Attempts on the part of France to check dependence on the English colonies helped to make a vicious circle in which the costs of production were increased and the necessity of overcoming restrictions enhanced. England had the advantage of a relatively coordinated empire, but the principle of exporting staples to the home market was violated to an increasing extent, especially as a result of the expansion of New England. The British Empire competed with the French Empire on all fronts – in the West Indies, in Europe, and in North America through the Hudson's Bay Company by Hudson Bay and through New York by the Hudson River. Adam Smith explained the weakness of the French Empire as due to its organization rather than to the character of its trade. "Of all the expedients that can well be contrived to stunt the natural growth of a new colony, that of an exclusive company is undoubtedly the most effectual" (542). "The French colony of Canada was, during the greater part of the last century [seventeenth], and some part of the present, under the government of an exclusive company. Under so unfavourable an administration its progress was necessarily very slow in comparison with that of other new colonies; but it became much more rapid when this company was dissolved after the fall of what is called the Mississippi scheme" (538). Recent investigation has shown that government policy, supplemented by the principle of commercial monopoly, the seigniorial system, and the dominance of the Roman Catholic church, was moulded and designed to strengthen control over the fur trade and was successful in resisting encroachments of the English until the fall of New France.[2] The prosperity of the colony noted by Adam Smith coincided with the extension of the trade from the St Lawrence to the Saskatchewan, and its collapse with the inability to compete with the British Empire.

The resistance of the French contributed to the unity of the British Empire, and the collapse of the French Empire was followed by the collapse of the British Empire in North America. The first British Empire eventually failed to coordinate the aggressive commercialism of the colonies, especially New England, with the demands of Great Britain that the colonies be primarily staple-producing regions. The commercial organization of New England became competitive with that of Great Britain. After the American Revolution, with the elimination of New England, the second British Empire proved more efficient than the French Empire in co-ordinating the interests of staple-producing regions. The success of the second British Empire was dependent on commercial organization which increased the value of land.

The fur trade on the St Lawrence was extended beyond the boundaries reached by the French and eventually to the Pacific, as a result of the more efficient industrial and commercial organization of Great Britain, of the migration of technique from the United States as illustrated in the effective development of navigation on the Great Lakes, and of the efficiency of the co-partnership of the Northwest Company. Increasing costs of transportation, due to the extension of the fur trade over greater distances, combined with Scottish clannishness and nepotism to defeat the Northwest Company and to lead to its amalgamation with the Hudson's Bay Company and to the abandonment of the St Lawrence in favour of the shorter route by Hudson Bay.

In the fishing industry of the Maritime Provinces, as in the fur trade of the St Lawrence, migration of technique from the United States combined with the extension of commercial organization from the Channel Islands[3] to enable Great Britain to occupy territory vacated by the French in the Gulf of St Lawrence, Cape Breton, and Nova Scotia. Nova Scotia attempted to reoccupy the place vacated by New England in the trade of the first Empire with the West Indies. The increasingly aggressive commercialism of Nova Scotia succeeded in excluding the United States from the British West Indies, but such exclusion compelled the United States to support expansion of trade in the South American republics. With the growth of their independence, and enunciation of the Monroe Doctrine in 1822, substantial modifications in the British colonial system were demanded by Nova Scotia and secured in the Trade Acts of 1825.

The decline of Britain's supply of timber from the American colonies as a result of exhaustion and of the American Revolution, and from Europe as a result of the continental system, led to the adoption of substantial imperial preferences on timber from the colonies as a means of hastening the exploitation of the resources of the St Lawrence and the rivers of New Brunswick. British timber merchants from the ports on the west coast of Great Britain, such as Liverpool and Glasgow, established branch houses in British North America and purchased ships and timber to meet the demands of industrialism in the rise of urban communities and the construction of railways.

The disappearance of the fur trade on the St Lawrence in 1821 was followed by the rise of the timber trade. The fur trade had involved concentration of a French Catholic population at Montreal at the junction with the Ottawa as the route to the northwest, and on the lower St Lawrence. The timber trade, on the other hand, hastened the coming of English-speaking immigrants, who crossed the Atlantic in empty timber ships returning to Canada. Many of them were unemployed, displaced by the effects of the industrial revolution on handicrafts and agriculture, and they were compelled to settle the unoccupied regions of the upper St Lawrence. The military and political organization which had been developed in the upper and lower St Lawrence valley in the last decades of the eighteenth century, with the purpose, especially under the United Empire Loyalists, of resisting encroachments from the south, now came into conflict with the aggressive commercialism of Montreal which emerged as a result of increasing exports of grain from the newly settled areas of the upper St Lawrence. The demands of the new commercial class for lower costs of transportation by roads and canals for imports and exports involved a reorganization of the political structure, which followed as a result of the outbreak of revolt in 1837, Lord Durham's *Report*, and the Act of Union in 1840. The decline of the British preference on grain and timber and the increasing effectiveness of improved transportation from New York, especially by the Erie Canal, necessitated the union of the governments of Lower and Upper Canada to provide a financial base for a competitive transportation route by the St Lawrence.[4] But in spite of the completion of the St Lawrence canals, the chagrin at the loss of the preferences was marked by the annexationist manifesto and the burning of the parliament buildings in 1849.

In Nova Scotia the defeat of attempts to exclude the United States from the British West Indies in 1830 was followed by a policy of rigid exclusion of American trade by tariffs and of American ships from British waters by a narrow interpretation and strict enforcement of the Convention of 1818. The retaliatory policy in Nova Scotia against American tariffs, and the effort to obtain a large share of traffic from the western states for the St Lawrence route in Canada, led to the Reciprocity Treaty of 1854[5] which admitted Canadian fish duty free and arranged for increasing traffic on the St Lawrence. In Canada, the competition of the St Lawrence with New York was strengthened by the construction of the Grand Trunk Railway to provide transportation from the western states to Portland.

The demands of industrial Britain for foodstuffs and the significance of capital equipment for the transportation of grain involved a shift from commercialism to capitalism, from dependence on short-term credit to dependence on long-term credit. The commercial class, supported by the mother country in the French and British empires and with their chief interests in the fur trade and the timber trade, tended now to be displaced by the capitalist class. The earlier appeals on the part of commercial groups for continuations of the preferences were replaced by the appeals of Hincks and Galt for capital support from the houses of Baring and others. The autonomous capitalist state replaced commercial colonialism. Adam Smith's arguments, which had contributed to the decline of the colonial system, were now used to support the claim for Canadian fiscal autonomy. In his pamphlet *Canada 1849 to 1859*,[6] Galt wrote that in 1849 "the only hope lay in the fact that the people had at last the management of their own affairs." They had the right to impose a tariff on British goods to secure revenue to meet the demands of British capitalists for interest on loans spent on public works to reduce costs of transportation. "As the expence of carriage ... is very much reduced by means of such public works, the goods, notwithstanding the toll, come cheaper to the consumer than they could otherwise have done; their price not being so much raised by the toll, as it is lowered by the cheapness of the carriage," wrote Adam Smith (683), and "It might very easily be shown that any increase of duty which has been placed on English goods is quite indemnified by the decreased cost at which our canals, railways and steamships enable them now to be delivered throughout the province," wrote Galt.

The emergence of fiscal autonomy as a basis of support for large-scale improvements of transportation necessitated further readjustment in the political structure. The Grand Trunk Railway, controlled from London through British capital support, unfortunately illustrated Adam Smith's comments on joint stock companies and was hampered by government-supported competition in canals. The imposition of tariffs for revenue involved tariffs for protection and led to the abrogation of reciprocity in 1866 and in turn to demands for measures of defence against the United States. The interests of the government and private capital in increasing traffic and in reducing the burden of fixed charges demanded the extension of the Grand Trunk Railway by the Intercolonial to Nova Scotia, the extension westward to the Prairie Provinces and the Pacific coast, and the creation of a new credit structure in Confederation under the British North America Act. The provinces of Quebec and Ontario were restored and Nova Scotia and New Brunswick were added. Cultural areas with their special interests of language, religion, and political and economic organization were given assurance of permanence by the federation. The position of the provinces under the British North America Act is a recognition of the differences in cultural characteristics: of Nova Scotia based on the fishing industry, of New Brunswick on the timber trade, of Quebec on the fur trade and later on agriculture and the timber trade, and of Ontario on the timber trade and agriculture. On the other hand, the influence of the new capitalism, which was essential to the completion of improvements in transportation by railway and canal, left its stamp on the Dominion government. This distinction is evident when we examine the creation of the new provinces in the prairie regions and on the Pacific coast.

The demands of private capitalism as represented by the Grand Trunk diverged from those of state capitalism. The Grand Trunk[7] became concerned with the extension of its line to Chicago to tap the traffic of the western states. The federal government engaged itself in a program of extension to the east, marked by the Washington Treaty which admitted Canadian fish to the United States duty free from 1871 to 1885, and by the completion of the Intercolonial Railway in 1876, and to the west by the strong support given to the construction of the Canadian Pacific Railway which was completed in 1885. The National Policy was designed in 1878 to secure revenue to pay deficits and to increase traffic to reduce deficits. Loss of population, especially from Ontario to the United States, during the long depression from the seventies to the nineties, was finally checked by continual efforts extending from the deepening of the St Lawrence canals to 14 feet to a program of intensive propaganda to attract immigrants from Europe and the United States. Competition from New York was eventually offset by improvements of the St Lawrence, and by the boom which followed the turn of the century and which was hastened by the occupation of the Prairie Provinces and the development of mining in British Columbia and the Yukon and of lumbering and fishing on the Pacific coast. Two additional transcontinental lines of railway were completed by 1914 with substantial government support. With the outbreak of war, the transcontinental railways constructed after 1900 were forced into bankruptcy and acquired by the federal government.

Throughout the economic history of Canada, the dominance of water transportation in the Maritime Provinces and the St Lawrence has accentuated dependence on Europe for manufactured products and for markets of staple raw materials. The fur trade was followed by the timber trade and agricultural products. Concentration on staple commodities was accentuated by the migration of technique from the United States. As the export trade in staples from the United States to Great Britain declined in importance, the Canadian trade in staples was encouraged. The fur trade was strengthened by American aggressiveness and technique, the timber trade shifted from New England to New Brunswick and the St Lawrence, the fishing industry migrated from New England to Nova Scotia, agriculture, in the production of wheat in Ontario and the Prairie Provinces and in dairying, benefitted from the contributions of the United States. The dependence of Canada on Great Britain was accentuated by the United States indirectly and by British and Canadian policy directly. European markets and European capital dominated Canadian economic development through the background of water transportation.

In the postwar period and during the depression, the St Lawrence has contracted in influence as a transcontinental factor. The Panama Canal attracted wheat from territory as far east as the western boundary of Saskatchewan. The end of expansion in western Canada for the export of wheat has come in sight, and regions which contributed to rapid expansion in Canada have, by virtue of sustained drought, contributed to sharp depression. The iron and steel and coal industries of Nova Scotia and the St Lawrence, and industrialism based on expansion in western Canada, have felt the effects of the end of a long-run secular trend. Another element in the decline of the St Lawrence has been the growing insecurity of Canadian trade in the European markets which has made American capital and American markets increasingly important. The mining and pulp and paper industries have emerged as a result of the increasing population and the declining resources of the United States. With changed conditions, the activities and powers of the provinces have assumed a new importance. For example, as a result of the automobile and tourist trade, roads have been built on a large scale by the provinces, while the Dominion government continues primarily to be concerned with railroads and transcontinental traffic.

The end of the period of expansion based on the St Lawrence and trade with Great Britain coincided roughly with the achievement of dominion status which followed the Great War and which was marked by the Statute of Westminster. The end of the struggle for control over external policy has been followed by problems of internal policy; and the decline of the St Lawrence as a factor contributing to the centralization of the Dominion has been accompanied by the increasing importance of regionalism evident in the growth of the powers of the provinces. The cultural features in terms of language, religion, metropolitan and political organizations based on the peculiarities of staple trades from various regions of Canada to Europe, which provided the basis of the provinces in the British North America Act, have hardened and been strengthened by the decline in the influence of the St Lawrence as a centralizing factor in the Canadian system. The expansion of provincial powers, conspicuous in New Brunswick, Ontario, and Quebec, has been scarcely less evident in Manitoba, Alberta, and British Columbia. The decline in commercialism which accompanied the rise of free trade advocated by Adam Smith and his disciples, left a structure which moulded the growth of capitalism (sponsored by those who paid lip service to Adam Smith) and hastened the growth of protectionism. The extension of the American empire, the decline of its natural resources, and the emergence of metropolitan areas, supported capitalist expansion in Canada and reinforced the trend of regionalism. The pull to the north and south has tended to become stronger in contrast with the pull east and west. The British North America Act and later decisions of the Privy Council have strengthened the control of the provinces over natural resources such as minerals, hydro-electric power, and pulpwood on Crown lands, resources which have provided the basis for trade with the United States and for investment of American capital. The problem of transportation – itself made possible by Dominion support to the construction of transcontinental railways – and problems of drought and depression in western Canada, have compelled the appointment of a federal Royal Commission, which must run the race between the Charybdis of increasing provincial powers and the Scylla of railway amalgamation masquerading as national unity. The energy and genius of Adam Smith have been replaced by a multitude of counsel and it is significant that the Commission has been announced, with regional representation, to consider a revision of financial and taxing powers in a year in which the Anglo-Saxon population of Canada ceases to be a majority.

NOTES

1 Adam Smith, *An Inquiry into the Nature and Causes of the Wealth of Nations* (Modern Library ed., New York, 1937), 538. For a reference to the continued influence of the physiocrats and the interest in land as a basis of wealth, see J. Bonar, *Malthus and His Work* (London, 1885), 246–7.

2 See W.B. Munro, *The Seigniorial System in Canada* (Cambridge, 1907); also A.G. Bailey, *The Conflict of European and Eastern Algonkian Cultures* (Saint John, 1937).

3 See J.B. Brebner, *The Neutral Yankees of Nova Scotia* (New York, 1937).

4 See D.G. Creighton, *The Commercial Empire of the St. Lawrence* (Toronto, 1937).

5 See D.C. Masters, *The Reciprocity Treaty of 1854* (Toronto, 1937).

6 London, 1860. The influence of Adam Smith on Canadian political thought is extensive, as a sampling of newspaper editorials, letters to the editor, and the works of Howe and Mackenzie will indicate. He was quoted to suit their purposes.

7 See G. de T. Glazebrook, *A History of Transportation in Canada* (Toronto, 1938).

CHAPTER TEN

The Place of Land in North American Federations

Professor Hedge's volume is the most recent of a number of studies on the administration of land in Canada[1] and the United States, and the opportunity to review his book suggests a discussion of the significance of land in American economic and political development. It was a thesis of the late Professor Max Handman[2] that the impact of Spanish and Portuguese feudalism on the highly developed Indian civilization of Central and South America brought concentration on imports of precious metals to Europe and the transfer of feudal institutions to America with their emphasis on military conquest and land. In contrast, an Anglo-Dutch trading culture prevailed in North America. Its development weakened the feudalistic control of France and contributed to the breakdown of the French Empire and to the French Revolution. In turn, the feudalistic communities of Central and South America were affected by Anglo-Dutch trade and by the ideologies of the French Revolution which led to the collapse of the Spanish and Portuguese empires.

The pouring of specie into Spain and Portugal hastened the organization of trade by the Dutch and the English as a means of securing a share of it. The fishing industry developed from the West Country at Newfoundland as a basis for trade to Spain brought a decisive defeat to feudalism in Newfoundland with the result that ownership of land was unimportant until the beginning of the nineteenth century. The possibilities of settlement on the continent, however, supported a fishing industry in the new world which with

From *Canadian Historical Review* 21 (1940): 60–7, a book review of James B. Hedges's *Building the Canadian West: The Land and Colonization Policies of the Canadian Pacific Railway* (New York and Toronto, 1939).

a widely extended trade fostered the occupation of land and defeat of the companies. In New France the more conspicuous feudalistic character of the mother country left a stronger feudalistic stamp. The feudal organization of France supported a demand for furs, and expansion of trade in that commodity to the interior necessitated the entrenchment of feudalism as a basis for defence[3] of the St Lawrence. In New France companies were replaced by direct supervision under the crown in 1663 and in the English colonies by the crown and assemblies representing settlement. "In the plenty of good land the English colonies of North America, though, no doubt, very abundantly provided, are, however, inferior to those of the Spaniards and Portuguese, and not superior to some of those possessed by the French before the late war. But the political institutions of the English colonies have been more favourable to the improvement and cultivation of this land than those of any of the other three nations. First the engrossing of uncultivated land, though it has by no means been prevented altogether, has been more restrained in the English colonies than any other."[4]

The growth of settlement in the English colonies and the decline of feudalism (as reflected in the control by companies or the crown over land) strengthened the power of the Assemblies and weakened the power of the Executive by depriving it of sources of revenue from land.[5] While the power of the crown through control over land declined, the power of Parliament through the control over trade increased. After the restoration, Parliament insisted on a coronation oath in which the King was "to govern the people of the kingdom of Great Britain and the dominions thereunto belonging according to the statutes of parliament agreed on and the respective laws and customs of the same" but it resisted efforts such as those of the Board of Trade to persuade it to encroach on prerogatives of the crown concerned with land rather than trade. The colonies[6] conceded demands of Parliament in the mercantilism of the Navigation Acts, which followed the decline of companies, but they opposed the imposition of internal direct taxes as an interference with the rights of the Assemblies which had grown up under the crown. The Stamp Act was accordingly withdrawn and the Townshend Acts which imposed duties on external trade were passed. At the same time Parliament extended its control by the Declaratory Act insisting on supremacy. The Massachusetts Assembly in its *answer* to Governor Hutchinson on 2 March 1773, insisted on the continued importance of the crown and opposed the extension of the control of Parliament. It stated that upon the principles advanced, the Lordship and dominion, later that of the lands in England, was in the king solely, and a right from thence accrued to him, of disposing such territories under such tenure, and for such services to be performed, as the king or lord thought proper. We conceive that upon the feudal principles all power is in the king; they afford us no idea of parliament. We have said that our ancestors considered the land, which they took possession of in America, as out of the bounds of the kingdom of England, and out of the reach and extent of the laws of England; and that the king also, even in the act of granting the charter, considering the territory as not within the realm; that the king had an absolute right in himself to dispose of the lands and that this was not disputed by the nation; and that, therefore, our ancestors received the lands, by grant from the king; and at the same time compacted with him, and promised him homage and allegiance not in his public or politic, but natural capacity only.[7]

The declaration of Congress in 1774 conceded the right of Parliament to regulate external trade, asserting

that the foundation of English liberty, and of all free government, is a right in the people to participate in their legislative council; and as the English colonists are not represented, and from their local and other circumstances, cannot properly be represented, in the British parliament, they are entitled to a free and exclusive power of legislation in their several provincial legislatures, where their right of representation can alone be preserved, in all cases of taxation and internal policy, subject only to the negative of their sovereign, in such manner as has been heretofore used and accustomed. But, from the necessity of the case, and a regard to the mutual interest of both countries, we cheerfully consent to the operation of such acts of the British parliament, as are bona fide, restrained to the regulation of our external commerce, for the purpose of securing the commercial advantages of the whole empire to the Mother Country, and the commercial benefits of its respective members; excluding every idea of taxation, internal or external, for raising a revenue on the subjects in America, without their consent.[8]

The Colonial Tax Repeal Act[9] (18 Geo. III, 112), 1778, in turn conceded the following clause:

From and after the passing of this Act the King and Parliament will not impose any duty, tax, or assessment whatever, payable in any of his Majesty's colonies, provinces or plantations in North America or the West Indies, except only such duties as it may be expedient to impose for the regulation of commerce; the net produce of such duties to be always paid and applied to and for the use of the colony, province, or plantation in which the same shall be respectively levied in such manner as other duties collected by the authority of the respective general courts or general assemblies of such colonies, provinces or plantations are ordinarily paid and applied.

In the second empire this Act served as a guarantee to Nova Scotia with its Assembly but not to the province of Quebec which had not been granted an Assembly in the Quebec Act partly because of the possibility of losing control over revenue and trade especially following the decision of Lord Mansfield in *Campbell v. Hall*[10] with regard to Grenada. Duties were continued from the French régime but these were replaced by others in the Quebec Revenue Act[11] (14 Geo. III, c. 88), 1774. The grant of an Assembly in 1791 introduced and extended the guarantee provided by the Colonial Tax Repeal Act of 1778 to Upper and Lower Canada[12] but it did not deprive the Executive of substantial support from the Earlier Quebec Revenue Act.[13] "The net produce of such duties" from acts passed after 1778 was paid to the Assemblies, but revenues from the Quebec Revenue Act of 1774 remained under the control of the Executive to 1831 and with them the revenue from lands. The seigniorial system continued from the French régime in Lower Canada and substantial returns from trade enabled the Executive to evade control of the Assembly. As a result of its geographic position, control of the Executive and of the Assembly over revenue from trade limited the revenue of Upper Canada, led to continuous friction, and compelled the latter to impose taxes on land.[14] The attempt to extend and consolidate control by the St Lawrence against possible attacks from the United States was accompanied by the alienation of large quantities of land. Professor N.A. MacDonald[15] has vividly described the ill effects of the management of lands by the Executive under the crown and Parliament and their contributions to the outbreaks in 1837–8, and the struggle for control under responsible government.

In the ninety-two resolutions of the Assembly of Lower Canada in 1834 it was stated[16] "that the executive government has endeavoured by means of the arbitrary regulations ... and particularly by the sale of the waste lands of the Crown and the timber on the same, to create for itself out of the revenue which this house only has the right of appropriating, resources independent of the control of the representatives of the people." While Glenelg insisted in his dispatch to Gotsford of 17 July 1835, that "the office of settling and alienating the uncleared territory properly belongs to the executive government," he prepared the way for the handing over of the public lands in return for a civil list.[17] In the Act of Union (3 and 4 Vic., c. 35) this was "carried into effect."[18]

Revenue[19] from timber and lands increased materially under the control of United Canada but control over revenues from trade continued the centre of interest. The trend toward free trade in the United Kingdom hastened the decline of revenues under the colonial system, and the increase of revenues from tariffs imposed by the provinces. Canals were constructed with loans guaranteed by Great Britain based on revenues from tariffs on imports obtained chiefly by exports of staple products. Revenue was obtained indirectly from imports rather than directly from exports. In the old empire control over land by Parliament was resisted and control over trade admitted, but in the new empire control over trade was resisted and pressed forward to control over land.

A study of land policy in Canada and the Maritime Provinces under responsible government prior to Confederation would indicate the methods by which the problems inherited from the previous period were solved. The Clergy Reserves Act and the Seigniorial Tenures Act in 1854 disposed of these controversial questions and liquidated major difficulties of feudalism. Lower costs of transportation by canals and railways hastened settlement and by the early sixties "the best lands of the Crown" had passed into private hands. Increasing distance and higher transportation costs lessened the possibility of securing returns from sales of land, and the Homestead Act of 1862 in the United States was a recognition of this trend. The competition of free land finally removed land as a basis of revenue in the United Province of Canada. The accumulated debt emerging from the construction of canals, railways, and roads and competition from American transportation development contributed to the demand for a larger governmental structure in Confederation and to increasing interest in the prairie regions.

The importance of tariffs rather than direct taxes was in part a result of competition from the United States. Prior to the Revolution, grants of land in the various colonies which placed the landowner in an increasingly powerful position, and increase in trade which strengthened the merchants in the Assemblies, led to resistance to direct taxation and in turn to indirect taxation. The emphasis of the colonies on a feudal relationship to the crown rather than to Parliament weakened their position in relation to federation. As they withdrew from the first empire they were compelled to substitute for the centralized control from Great Britain, a federal constitution which protected their individualistic background, and provided for the regulation of interstate and foreign commerce,[20] for continuation of the power of the common law in the Supreme Court, and for control over land outside the states as a basis for revenue and expansion. Colonies along an extended coast line were not in a position to exercise central control[21] over trade and they were impelled to concentrate on land in the interior as a means of securing revenues.[22] Centralized control over land and the persistent difficulties in disposing of it as a source of revenue necessitated encouragement of settlement, which involved competition with the provinces remaining under British control and contributed to the discontent which led to the collapse of the system. The American federation was compelled to rely on land as a basis of finance but the difficulties favoured tariffs as a source of revenue. Consequently United Canada and later the Canadian federation were unable to rely on land and compelled to rely on the tariff. Revenue was obtained to improve transportation to meet competition in the expanding market of the Western States through tariffs on imports. The importance of centralization on the St Lawrence facilitated the collection of revenues from trade under the Act of Union and Confederation. Land, forests, and minerals[23] were of relatively minor importance and revenue from trade and tariffs became the basis for subsidies[24] paid by the federal government to the provinces and for the payment of interest on debt transferred by the provinces to the federal government.

Apparently in return for the construction and operation of the Intercolonial Railway as provided for by the Act, the imperial government,[25] regarded it as a defence measure, guaranteed a substantial loan and arranged for the handing over of lands belonging to the Hudson's Bay Company.

The charter of the Hudson's Bay Company and the dependence of the Company on trade in furs discouraged settlement and the establishment of an Assembly as had been the case on the St Lawrence in the French régime. Land was returned by the Company to the crown and in turn to the Canadian Parliament under the British North America Act and the Rupert's Land Act. Monopoly control in the interests of the fur trade delayed the growth of settlement but construction of the railway reversed the trend and settlement was encouraged. Increase in the tariff under the national policy and other monopoly devices enabled the Canadian Pacific Railway to reap the full advantages of this reversal. The management of land in western Canada was directed primarily to the growth of trade from eastern Canada and of traffic eastbound and westbound for the railway. Professor Martin in his work on *"Dominion Lands" Policy*[26] and Professor Hedges in his *Federal Railway Land*

Subsidy Policy of Canada[27] and in his more recent work have described the policies of the government and of the Canadian Pacific Railway in the exploitation of their monopoly position. Retention of natural resources by the provinces entering Confederation and the establishment of separate provincial departments necessitated the creation of a new department by the federal government for the administration of lands in western Canada. This department was forced to compete with the United States and was strongly influenced by American practices in administration. Both authors indicate the importance of land in relation to government and railway policies but they do not stress sufficiently the significance of monopoly control in Canada. Both authors emphasize (this reviewer thinks unduly, as the resources were of slight consequence at that time) implications of control over natural resources by the old provinces, including British Columbia, in the necessity of making large grants of land "fairly fit for settlement" in the prairie region to an alert syndicate for the construction of a transcontinental railway.

Professor Hedges in his recent work *Building the Canadian West* has concentrated on the land and colonization policies of the Canadian Pacific Railway. He has had access to the archives of the Company and as a foil has used the files of the *Manitoba Free Press.* It provides a valuable supplement to Professor Morton's work with its dependence on the records of the Hudson's Bay Company and on settlers' accounts, and to Professor Martin's work with its dependence on the material made available in the evidence presented to the Royal Commissions on natural resources in the Prairie Provinces. In the latter work it is suggested that the policy of the CPR was advantageous to settlement partly on the basis of low prices of land as compared to those of the Hudson's Bay Company and school lands. Professor Hedges points to the policy of the CPR in holding its sections until the alternate sections were disposed of as homesteads by the government and to the policy of selling land tributary to its own railway and holding it or selling with a view to speculation where it was tributary to other railways. He suggests that a policy concerned with railway traffic favoured conservative prices and acted as a stabilizing factor. School lands and Hudson's Bay lands were scattered over a large area and sold at a later stage of economic development with emphasis on speculation rather than on railway traffic. Neither Professor Martin nor Professor Hedges discusses the full implications of this policy. While the CPR held land for sale in territory not tributary to its railway and possibly with other large landholding organizations increased costs of settlement in terms of schools and community organization, its withholding of such land permitted the concentration of the settler on grain production from his own land and livestock production on the open range or on the adjoining CPR sections. The sale of these sections, when it took place, tended to force the settler to concentrate still further on wheat.

In the period immediately following incorporation, the Company developed a land policy based on American experience of selling land and townsites adjacent to the main line, and pouring the returns into hotels, and an immigration policy designed to attract settlers from eastern Canada, the United States, and Europe. With the upward swing after 1896, settlers, encouraged by the activities of colonization companies, moved from the higher priced land of the United States. The frontal wave of wheat miners which swept across the continent was speeded up. The account of the technique of propaganda is illuminating. Schools, churches, markets, postal facilities, newspapers by advertising and editors' excursions, harvester excursions, and steamship agencies were among the devices by which the immigrants, their families, and religious groups[28] were shaken from their communities and moved to western Canada.

The location of the main line to the south, according to Professor Hedges, involved building up traffic in this region by concentration on settlement, a reduction in the amount of land "fairly fit for settlement," and dependence on northern reserves and on acquisition of government sections to develop an irrigation block tributary to the railway. From 1905 to 1914 policy was marked by "the disposal of the land in a manner which would best serve the larger interests of the railway" (293). Following the success of the Alberta Railway and Irrigation Company, the Canadian Pacific Railway Company invested enormous sums in opening the irrigation block to settlement. From dependence on a colonization company it built up an elaborate sales organization. The Canadian Pacific Irrigation colonization Company was taken over by the Canadian Pacific Railway in 1908. A Department of Natural Resources was formed in 1912 and was followed by a Department of Colonization and Development in 1916 with a view, it was said, to building up the rural areas to support the urban areas. Terms were steadily improved for the settler. In 1908 payment plans were introduced and assisted settlement schemes were initiated by the use of loans. A twenty-year payment plan was introduced in 1912 but changed to a thirty-four year amortization plan in 1923. Various adjustments were made after the depression.[29] These adjustments suggest that monopoly advantages had steadily declined. The organization built up with its headquarters at Calgary to colonize the irrigation block turned after the war to the disposal of the reserves in the Edmonton, Battleford, and Lloydminster areas. Rise in land values through construction of competitive lines to the north and construction of its own branch lines was expected to offset the difficulties to the south. Competition in this region was a part of the struggle between the two railways in the twenties. Professor Hedges has given a most valuable account of the policy of the CPR, largely the policy of J.S. Dennis, in settlement of the West.

Both Professor Martin and Professor Hedges point to the waste of human and natural resources which marked the policy of monopoly resulting from concentration on rapid settlement by the government and the Company. The balance still remains to be struck as to the results of settlement and land policies in the occupation of North America by European peoples. President Bowman,[30] as becomes a geographer, has discussed at length the role of land as a factor in political history and his interest has sponsored the publication of the "Frontiers of Settlement" series. Henry George seized upon land as the key to reform. Turner emphasized the importance of free land in his frontier thesis. Professor Andrews has written that "in no single particular have the customs of the past been more tenacious and persistent than in the domain of real property, for even today the laws governing descent, contract, conveyance, and tenure bear marks of their feudal origin." Even in these days the importance attached to land is evident in struggles to adjust national boundaries. A policy of restriction of trade and of specialization increases the importance of policies concerned with land. Adam Smith made his attack on the companies and on mercantilism, and Ricardo paved the way for release of the control of the landowner over trade by stressing the importance of trade to the value of land. The interest in land persists as a relic of feudalism. Refusal to recognize the supremacy of Parliament in the American colonies created difficulties which left their stamp on the constitution of the United States and in turn on the constitution of Canada. Recognition of the supremacy of Parliament in Canada provided an escape the significance of which has not been thoroughly appreciated because of the strength of colonial and American precedents.

The history of land policies in North America indicates the role of feudalism in the constitutional framework but it suggests primarily the importance of trade and the increasing importance of money and credit. The competition of free land on the frontier operated as a powerful deterrent to effective control over settlement by governments. Inability of feudal institutions such as federal constitutions to secure support from land (except in the case of the monopoly of the Hudson's Bay Company and its transfer to the monopoly of the federal government and of the Canadian Pacific Railway and even here large dividends have been followed by cessation) compelled reliance on revenue from tariffs on trade. Finally the inefficiencies of the latter device have led to taxes on incomes. Land[31] has ceased to differ in any fundamental way from capital but it will be long before our constitutions are adapted to this fact and it will be long before the iniquities attributable to them are overcome.[32]

NOTES

1 The volumes in the "Canadian Frontiers of Settlement" series contain a great deal of valuable material. Of particular interest in this connection is the volume by Professor A.S. Morton and Professor Chester Martin, *History of Prairie Settlement* and *"Dominion Lands" Policy* (Toronto, 1938; reviewed in *Canadian Historical Review* (March 1939, 71–2). See also N. Macdonald, *Canada, 1763–1841: Immigration and Settlement* (Toronto, 1939; reviewed Dec., 1939, 435); and two articles by R.G. Riddell, "A Study in the Land Policy of the Colonial Office, 1763–1855," *Canadian Historical Review* 18 (Dec. 1937): 385, and "The Policy of Creating Land Reserves in Canada," *Essays in Canadian History Presented to George Mackinnon Wrong*, ed. R. Flenley (Toronto, 1939).

2 "The Bureaucratic Culture Pattern and Political Revolution," *American Journal of Sociology* 39 (1933): 301–15.

3 W.B. Munro, *The Seigniorial System in Canada* (New York, 1907).

4 Adam Smith, *An Inquiry into the Nature and Causes of the Wealth of Nations* (Modern Library ed., New York, 1937), 538–9.

5 See B.W. Bond, *The Quit-rent System in the American Colonies* (New Haven, 1919); also J.E. Howe, "Quit-rents in New Brunswick," *Report of the Canadian Historical Association*, 1928, 55–61.

6 See C.P. Nettels, *The Money Supply of the American Colonies before 1720* (Wisconsin University Studies in the Social Sciences and History, no. 20, 1934); A.M. Schlesinger, *The Colonial Merchants and the American Revolution* (New York, 1917); C.L. Becker, *The History of Political Parties in the Province of New York, 1760–1776* (Madison, 1909).

7 Cited by C.H. McIlwain, *The American Revolution: A Constitutional Interpretation* (New York, 1923), 130.

8 Ibid., 115–16.

9 W.P.M. Kennedy, ed., *Statutes, Treaties and Documents of the Canadian Constitution, 1713–1929* (Toronto, 1930), 167.

10 Ibid., 89.

11 Ibid., 140–1; see also 15 Geo. III, c. 40, 153. See G.S. Graham, *British Policy and Canada, 1774–1791* (London, 1930), chap. 6.

12 Kennedy, *Statutes, Treaties and Documents,* 204; see also 1 and 2 Wm. IV, c. 23, 262–3.

13 See D.G. Creighton, "The Struggle for Financial Control in Lower Canada, 1818–1831," *Canadian Historical Review* 12 (June 1931): 120–44.

14 D.G. Creighton, *The Commercial Empire of the St. Lawrence, 1760–1850* (Toronto, 1937), 129.

15 Macdonald, *Canada, 1763–1841: Immigration and Settlement.*

16 Kennedy, *Statutes, Treaties and Documents,* 284. "The irresponsible manner in which the land granting department is conducted, the salary disproportioned to the duties performed, which is attached to the office and other abuses connected with the Woods and Forests, demand revision" (ibid., 294).

17 Ibid., 307, also 343.

18 Ibid., 440, 444, also 17–18 Vic., c. 534; see Chester Martin, "Lord Durham's Report and Its Consequences," *Canadian Historical Review* 20 (June 1939): 178.

19 See "A History of Crown Timber Regulations" (*Report of the Department of Lands, Forests and Mines,* 1907); R.G. Albion, *Forests and Sea Power* (Cambridge, 1926).

20 A.C. McLaughlin, *The Foundation of American Constitutionalism* (New York, 1932), 157.

21 V.G. Setser, *The Commercial Reciprocity Policy of the United States, 1774–1829* (Philadelphia, 1937).

22 See Merrill Jensen, "The Creation of the National Domain," *Mississippi Valley Historical Review* (Dec., 1939): 323–42; also P.J. Treat, *The National Land System, 1785–1820* (New York, 1910); B.H. Hibbard, *A History of the Public Land Policies* (New York, 1924); Thomas Donaldson, *The Public Domain* (Washington, 1884).

23 Under the British North America Act the provinces controlled "the management and sale of the public lands belonging to the province and of the timber and wood thereon" (subsection 5, section 92). "All lands, mines, minerals, and royalties belonging to the several provinces of Canada, Nova Scotia and New Brunswick at the union and all sums then due or payable for such lands, mines, minerals or royalties shall belong to the several provinces of Ontario, Quebec, Nova Scotia and New Brunswick in which the same are situate or are subject to any trust existing in respect thereof and to any interest other than that of the province in the same" (section 109).

24 The reviewer has accepted with approval the statement that "at Confederation it was decided to make of the natural resources the corner-

stone of finance" made in the Report of the Royal Commission on the Transfer of the Natural Resources of Manitoba in 1929 in the *Report of the Royal Commission, Provincial Economic Inquiry* (Halifax, 1934), 208, but he now feels that this cannot be regarded as satisfactory. Recognition of the *supremacy of Parliament* destroys the dominance of feudalism and the common law. While insistence on the position of land in the feudal structure served as an effective argument in the American Revolution and in adjustments of the Canadian constitution, it introduces rigidities of a serious character. No acceptable formula has been developed by which compensation for the use of lands by the Dominion can be determined, and the search for such a formula obscures the demands for adjustments based on need. Not only are adjustments hampered in western Canada but the difficulties of adjustment are increased so far as the provinces which have had control over natural resources since Confederation are concerned. The enormous gains in hydro-electric power sites, minerals, and the pulp and paper industry which have emerged from the advance of technology in a region which was a northern waste must be regarded under the feudalistic approach as the inherent property of the old provinces. Natural resources were given to the Prairie Provinces after a large portion of the most valuable land had been alienated. See Chester Martin, *The Natural Resources Question* (Winnipeg, 1920).

25 D.G.G. Kerr, "Edmund Head, Robert Lowe, and Confederation," *Canadian Historical Review* 20 (Dec. 1939): 409.

26 Toronto, 1938.

27 Cambridge, 1934; reviewed in *Canadian Historical Review* 16 (March 1935): 86.

28 See C.A. Dawson, *Group Settlement: Ethnic Communities in Western Canada* (Toronto, 1936).

29 See C.S. Burchill, "The Eastern Irrigation District," *Canadian Journal of Economics and Political Science* 5 (May 1939): 206–16.

30 Isaiah Bowman, *The New World* (New York, 1928).

31 See F.H. Knight, "The Ricardian Theory of Production and Distribution," *Canadian Journal of Economics and Political Science* 1 (Feb. 1935): 18–19.

32 See G.E. Britnell, *The Wheat Economy* (Toronto, 1939), xii–xiv; also A.R.M. Lower, *The North American Assault on the Canadian Forest* (Toronto, 1938), xvii–xviii and *passim.*

CHAPTER ELEVEN

Organized Labour and Living Standards in Canadian Economic History

Organization of farmers and labour thrives on achievement and emerges in industries and regions providing a suitable environment for the formation of associations and during periods in which wages can be increased or maintained by pressure. They have necessarily been less concerned with industries and regions in which organization has been restricted and in which standards of living are on a lower level and subject to wider fluctuations. Studies of these standards are being published elsewhere.[1]

PROBLEMS OF DEFENCE AGAINST THE UNITED STATES

The European economy first touched North America in the development of the fishing industry in the maritime regions, an industry characterized by the mobility typical of sailing vessels. Fishing ships were quick to exploit the industry on the coasts of New England in the seventeenth century, and expansion in that area attracted labour on a large scale from the restricted industry of Newfoundland. The French settlements in the Bay of Fundy traded with New England rather than with France. Attempts to develop a sedentary fishery on Cape Breton after 1713 were defeated by an inevitable dependence on the English colonies for food and ships. Penetration to the interior by the St Lawrence and extension of the fur trade involved competition from New York, and French traders carried furs

From Norman J. Ware and H.A. Logan, *Labor in Canadian-American Relations*, ed. H.A. Innis (Ryerson, 1937), v–xxxi; first appeared as "Labour in Canadian Economic History."

to Albany. The establishment of forts at points along the Great Lakes designed to check trade to the English colonies, and extension to the Northwest to check trade to Hudson Bay, brought collapse because of burdens imposed on the colony, evident in the outbursts of inflation, and because of the barrier imposed against the English colonies in the interior, which contributed to the difficulties leading to the expulsion of the Acadians and the occupation of Nova Scotia. The retreat of the French Empire from North America was a reflection of the inability of France to maintain a standard of living comparable to that of the English colonies.

Resistance to the expansion of the New England colonies involved not only misery and hardships for the French population but also increasing organization. New France was an efficient armed camp and regimentation was reflected in policies of immigration, settlement, industry, and trade. Protestants were severely discouraged, lands were occupied in relation to strategic military sites, industry was regulated in the interests of mercantilism, and trade was supported by extensive fortifications. In Quebec the guild system was introduced, as in the case of the tanning industry;[2] and wages reflected the influence of government regulation, extensive government intervention in industry, and scarcity of skilled labour. In Cape Breton the share system continued in fishing ships from France, but wages were controlled in the interests of a sedentary fishery. Great Britain assumed control of a thoroughly disciplined population in the lower St Lawrence: a foundation had been hammered out which was destined to support an increasingly powerful and coherent cultural group in North American history.

The conquest of New France and the consequent displacement of French by English government and of French trading organizations by Anglo-American merchants accentuated the importance of the Church as a factor providing continuity and a cohesive institution. It became the shield and sword of a race and language exposed to foreign domination. The French-Canadian population supplied the labour for Anglo-American enterprise in reconstruction of the fur trade. With the outbreak of the American Revolution and the closing of the Albany route demand for labour increased, and as early as 1778 governmental authority was invoked by employers to decide disputes.[3] The co-ordination of Great Lakes shipping with the Ottawa route, the efficiency of the Montreal route in relation to British manufactured goods, and the power of the British navy, together with a disciplined population, enabled Great Britain to succeed where France had failed, in maintaining control over the St Lawrence when the thirteen colonies withdrew. Efficient business organization in the Northwest Company facilitated extension of the fur trade to the Mackenzie River and the Pacific, but not without indications of protests from French labour.[4] Wage contracts were drawn up in detail for men engaging with the Northwest Company and in 1789 each employee was required to produce "a certificate from his curé." Encouraged by the hesitancy of magistrates in enforcing punishment for breaking contracts, voyageurs struck for higher wages at Rainy Lake in 1794 only to have the ringleaders sent back to Montreal.[5] Competition with the Hudson's Bay Company and its shorter route by Hudson Bay, and a rigid discipline at its ports on the Bay, and later in the interior, involved a decline in standards of living for all concerned and the clash of organization in the massacre of Seven Oaks. After the amalgamation of 1821 Sir George Simpson "ruled with a rod of iron" in western Canada.

The Northwest Company was based not only on French labour but also on the expansion of agriculture by the United Empire Loyalists in Upper Canada. Following the outbreak of the American Revolution and the Treaty of Versailles in 1783 United Empire Loyalists were encouraged to occupy strategic military regions along the Great Lakes and in the Maritimes. On the principle "divide and rule," New Brunswick was organized as a separate province in 1784[6] and Upper Canada in 1791. They served as fortified outposts which guaranteed control over the French and resisted encroachment from the United States. Like New France in the wars with England, Upper Canada was a disciplined military community in the War of 1812 with the United States. Competition of Nova Scotia with New England after the Treaty of Versailles involved measures to check New England trade with the British West Indies, and insistence on the restrictions involved in the Convention of 1818 and on modifications of the colonial system. But privateering and smuggling were indications of the limitations of restrictive measures. The pressure on standards of living in Nova Scotia was accentuated by migration from areas with lower standards such as Newfoundland, during the disturbed years of the Napoleonic Wars. On the other hand, the United Empire Loyalists in New Brunswick gained from the substantial preference given by Great Britain to colonial timber.

After 1821 British America was divided into compact units – western Canada dominated by the Hudson's Bay Company from Hudson Bay, Upper Canada by a strong official class supported by military organization, Lower Canada by the Church, Nova Scotia by Halifax mercantile interests, Prince Edward Island by landlords, and New Brunswick by Loyalist control.[7] The policy of defence implied in the military settlements, the construction of the Rideau Canal, and encouragement of immigration, particularly in Upper Canada, involved a centralization of control which contrasted sharply with the outlook of immigrants pouring into Canada after the Napoleonic Wars. Large numbers of settlers displaced by the industrial and agrarian revolution in Great Britain and fleeing from the intolerance of the period[8] were quick to resent the restrictions of centralized control evident in land policy, public finance, and transportation handicaps. Immigrants supported by the timber trade poured into areas unprepared to absorb them. Unfavourable contrasts with the expansion in the United States, and the development of the competitive route by the Erie Canal, supported the demands for reform which culminated in the outbreak of rebellion in 1837, Lord Durham's *Report*, the Act of Union, the achievement of responsible government, the construction of canals, and numerous reforms.[9] The demands of farmers for lower costs of transportation for exports and imports coincided with the demands of commercial interests in Montreal and Upper Canada.[10] In Lower Canada English commercial interests were opposed by the French. The Church protested against the exploitation of dispossessed Acadians employed by Channel Island firms which had become entrenched in the fishery on the Gaspé coast and in Cape Breton after the Treaty of Paris.[11] In both Lower and Upper Canada the problems of commercial interests were met by the Act of Union. In Nova Scotia the increasing importance of commercial and agricultural interests contributed to the early development of responsible government. New Brunswick and Prince Edward Island followed. In western Canada the control of the Hudson's Bay Company clashed with settlement and increasing trade to the south. Adam Thom, who had stoutly resisted the French in Lower Canada, continued to pursue his role in the employ of the Hudson's Bay Company. Concessions to freedom of trade in 1849 were followed by increasing difficulty with French Canadians. On the Pacific coast, the settlement of the Oregon boundary dispute compelled the Hudson's Bay Company to retreat from Fort Vancouver on the Columbia River to Victoria. The movement toward responsible government was a corollary to the movement toward abolition of the colonial system in Great Britain. It was hastened by the aggressive development of newspapers under such leaders as Mackenzie and Howe, by the cohesiveness of the clan, strengthened by military organization, which continued among Scottish immigrants,[12] and by the solidarity of religious groups.[13]

The weakening of centralized control, through the Colonial Office, from Great Britain tended to strengthen rather than weaken opposition to the United States in the units involved. In Nova Scotia the Hovering Act of 1836 followed the admission of the United States to the West Indies trade in 1833. Indeed, the restraining hand of Great Britain was imposed to keep the zeal of Nova Scotia from causing international disturbance. In 1854 an attempt was made in both the Canadas and the Maritimes to capitalize the increasing division in the United States by securing entry to the American market through the Reciprocity Treaty. Increase in the tariff in 1858 in the Canadas, the problems of debt which followed the depression in the late fifties, difficulties with the United States during the Civil War, and the victory of the north were factors contributing to abrogation of the treaty by the United States in 1866. Survival of the Union in the United States increased the necessity of union in British North America.[14]

The stress of organization which characterized the separate provinces in their resistance to the United States continued in these areas and was reinforced by the formation of a federal government including first the four provinces and later extending to the Pacific. The St Lawrence area again divided into separate cultural groups in Ontario and Quebec. The Intercolonial was built as a government undertaking with Imperial Support to provide a military railway between the Maritimes and the St Lawrence. Tariffs were imposed to increase the consumption of Nova Scotia coal and interprovincial trade. Confederation was extended to include Manitoba and British Columbia on the basis of railway construction. The Hudson's Bay Company, faced with increasing competition from the United States to the south following steady improvement of transportation facilities, finally abandoned the Hudson Bay route. In 1859 a report on insubordination of freighters at York Factory stated that "The Red River freighters had agreed among themselves to make the company pay a much higher freight, in which they were disappointed in seeing it taken out of their hand via St. Paul's and I doubt not in a short time will rue the day of their abuse to the Company."[15] Displacements of labour by a change of routes and the introduction of steamboats contributed to the unrest, marked by the Riel Rebellion, which accomplished the sale of Rupert's Land to Canada by the Hudson's Bay company. The death of Thomas Scott in the Rebellion of 1870 accentuated the bitterness in Ontario which led to the execution of Louis Riel in 1885. The division between French and English in Quebec and Ontario was deepened and extended to Manitoba.[16] With the retreat of the Hudson's Bay Company to Victoria, and the gold rush to the Fraser River and its tributaries in the late fifties, Crown colonies were established in Vancouver Island and the mainland, and they were united and brought under Confederation. Rigid opposition to American encroachment, evident in regions adjacent to the United States, particularly in Nova Scotia, New Brunswick, Ontario, Manitoba, and British Columbia, was consolidated, particularly through the influence of such individuals as Tupper and Macdonald, in the route of the Canadian Pacific Railway on Canadian territory close to the American boundary in western Canada and British Columbia, especially with the construction of the Crow's Nest Pass line. The line of defence was supported by the monopoly clause, substantial government support in land and cash, the tariff, and government ownership of the Intercolonial Railway.

RESISTANCE TO THE BURDENS OF DEFENCE

The burden of defence measures prior to and after Confederation changed with the stage of economic development in Great Britain, Canada, and the United States and was evident in the movement of population and of goods. Competition for labour in the United States and the movement of population from Canada set up a vicious circle in which the resistance and burden of organization opposed to the United States increased as population emigrated from Canada. On the one hand rebellion broke out in the thirties, and on the other hand extensive public works in canals and railways became inevitable. As an example, as a refuge for rebels, and as a source of technical innovations, the United States exerted a modifying influence in the earlier period, an influence accentuating later economic trends.

In the period dominated by commercial activity and water transportation preceding 1850 farmers merged their protests in opposition to centralized control or they migrated to the United States. Even the French habitants offered resistance to the demands of the government in the French régime. "Although the common people in Canada have not the docility of the French peasant, they are quite willing to do what is asked of them if the project always suits their taste. They consider that the governors and intendants come and go but that they will only disappear with the disappearance of the country."[17] Their refusal to obey the government was evident in their insistence on raising horses rather than cattle. In the French régime "They [the French] say among themselves Lesse enrages les merchands pour trouver en bon prix."[18] Papineau became the centre of activity in support of the interests of the farmers while Mackenzie was supported by the farmers of Ontario. In Nova Scotia agricultural societies were promoted by John Young to reduce dependence on agricultural products from the United States;[19] but agriculture was limited by the demands of the fishing industry and the lumbering industry. Fishermen from Nova Scotia joined the mackerel fleet of the United States and labour continued to move from Newfoundland to Nova Scotia and from Nova Scotia to New England. Labour and agriculture, concerned more directly with the timber trade in New Brunswick and on the St Lawrence, were affected by the wide fluctuations of the industry arising from the business cycle, imperial preferences, and exhaustion of resources. They accepted sharp fluctuations in the standard of living or migrated.

The organization of skilled labour was limited by the character of urban and industrial growth. A printers' union was formed in Quebec City in 1827, in Toronto in 1832, and in Montreal and Hamilton in 1833. Journeyman carpenters organized in Montreal in 1833, and stone cutters, coopers, and shipwrights were represented by unions by 1850. A tailors' riot broke out in Montreal in 1830 and shoe-making had an organization by the middle of the century. William Lyon Mackenzie wrote that "Dutcher's foundry-men and Armstrong's axe-makers all ... could be depended on" in the outbreak in 1837.[20]

Construction of railways and canals was followed by rapid growth of settlement, and by an increase in the number of small towns and in the size of urban centres. The development of the livestock industry and of exports of agricultural products was accompanied by a decline of a relatively self-sufficient economy and the rise of small domestic industries such as flour and grist milling, lumber milling, woollen mills, boot and shoe and harness plants, wagon and cart making, agricultural implements, and blacksmith shops. Construction of railways and shipbuilding brought demands for labour in the St Lawrence and the Maritimes. The depression which followed the prosperity of the early fifties was marked by an aggressive agitation among farmers led by the Honourable George Brown and the Toronto *Globe.*[21]

While increased tariffs and the rise of industrial towns, marked by the shift from wood, water, and sail to iron and coal, brought protests from agriculturalists, they encouraged the expansion of the factory system and the rise of organized labour. In 1851, as a result of the increase in the number of vessels and the demand for labour in Montreal, "the labourers now dictate to the trade in what manner the vessels shall be discharged and loaded and during what hours the work shall be continued – On several occasions of late the captains and crews of American vessels have been grossly maltreated in addition to having been compelled to pay for the work in the expensive manner insisted on by the labourers."[22] They resisted the introduction of horses. In 1852 the journeymen tailors in Toronto organized to resist the introduction of the Singer Sewing Machine. The prosperity of 1854 led to a successful strike by the printers in the same city. British technique and capital involved in the construction of railways were accompanied by labour organization. The English Amalgamated Society of Engineers was introduced in 1854 and the Amalgamated Society of Carpenters and Joiners followed.

The impact of machine industry on labour in the United States was felt in Canada, particularly during the period of the Reciprocity Treaty and the Civil War. The end of the Civil War and abrogation of the Reciprocity Treaty were accompanied by the migration of skilled labour and establishment of additional international unions. In 1861 the International Iron Moulders Union entered Canada and in 1865 the International Cigar Makers Union established a branch at Montreal. It was followed by the International Journeymen Coopers' Association and the International Typographical Society. The Brotherhood of Locomotive Engineers established branches in 1864 and the Brotherhood of Railway conductors in 1868. In the iron and nail works in Montreal in 1866 "the greatest proportion of the skilled labor comes from the United States, the workmen there being accustomed to the peculiar tempering of the steel required for our cold climate."[23] At the same time it was claimed that "our American friends would find plenty of excellent openings for skilled workmen" in the boot and shoe industry.[24] The Knights of St Crispin, which began in the shoemaking industry in Milwaukee in 1867, spread rapidly into Massachusetts and into Canada where it had seventeen unions in 1870.

The organization of unions provided a basis for the formation of city assemblies (in Toronto in 1871, and in Ottawa and Hamilton shortly afterward) and for the spread of labour movements from the United States and Great Britain. In the spring of 1872 the Typographical Union led a concerted demand for a nine-hour day in Toronto,[25] which capitalized the hostility of the Honourable George Brown and the Toronto *Globe* by securing the passage in the federal house by the Conservatives under Sir John A. Macdonald of an Act based on British legislation in 1871 legalizing unions. The success was followed by further activity, with British precedent in the British Trades Union Congress of 1858, and with American precedent in the National Labor Union, which resulted in the formation of the Canadian Labour Union in 1873.

FARMER AND LABOUR ORGANIZATIONS IN THE LONG DEPRESSION

The success of labour organization in the early seventies was paralleled by the rapid spread of farmers' organizations from the United States. The depression was marked by collapse of the labour movement and rapid spread of the farmers' movement. The Patrons of Husbandry[26] spread from Vermont to the Eastern Townships in Quebec and Ontario in 1872–3, to the Maritimes in 1875, and to Manitoba in 1876. The movement in Canada became independent of the United States with the formation of the Dominion Grange (1875), which increased to a peak in 1878. While opposed to intervention in politics, it supported the National Policy in a tariff on agricultural products from the United States.

The stimulus to industry which followed the completion of the Intercolonial Railway, and the increase of tariffs and of railway construction under the National Policy, coincided with recovery in the early eighties. The depression "caused the entry into the Dominion of large numbers of the mechanic class" from the United States.[27] At Hamilton in 1878 "the demand for cotton operatives has been largely in excess of the supply and in some instances this class of hands has been imported from the mills in New England by our mill owners owing to the increased capacity of the mills and the demand for this class of goods."[28] The increasing importance of machine industry and its impact on Canada[29] involved support not only to craft unions but also to the organization of unskilled labour. In 1881, under the leadership of the International Typographical Union, the Toronto Trades and Labor Council was organized and was followed by similar organizations in other centres. In the same year the Knights of Labor swept across the boundary from the United States and district assemblies were formed at various centres in Ontario and Quebec. It was conspicuously successful in penetrating the province of Quebec, which had scarcely been influenced by the earlier development of international unions, and reached its peak in the late eighties. The Trades and Labor Congress of Canada was organized in Toronto in 1886 to include representatives from both international unions and the Knights of Labor. The completion of the Canadian Pacific Railway was followed by industrial development in Manitoba and British Columbia, and by representation from these areas in 1895. The Maritime Provinces sent delegates in 1901. Increasing specialization in industry was evident in the formation in Toronto of the Federated Council of Building Trades in 1886, the Allied Printing Trades Council in 1895, and the

Federated Metal Trades Council in 1901. In the United States and Canada the Knights of Labor declined and the increasing strength of international unions in the American Federation of Labor finally brought the expulsion from the Trades and Labor Congress in 1902 of twenty-three unions, in part representing the Knights of Labor and chiefly from Quebec. These unions formed the Canadian Federation of Labour which in turn expelled the Knights of Labor in 1908.

As labour organizations became entrenched following the growth of industrialism, the farmers' movement declined in the long depression of the eighties and nineties and shifted from a position favourable to the tariff to one of opposition. The Patrons of Industry started in Michigan. With the enthusiasm of the populist movement it swept across the border, entered Canada in 1889, was incorporated in Ontario in 1890, and became independent of the United States in 1891. The short-lived Manitoba and Northwest Farmers Protective Association (1883–6) and the Farmers Alliance (1890–2) paved the way for the establishment of branches in western Canada. It spread to Quebec and the Maritimes and reached a peak with the election of seventeen members in Ontario in 1894. Defeat in the federal election of 1896 brought collapse of the movement.

FARMER AND LABOUR ORGANIZATIONS AND THE OPENING OF THE WEST

With the turn of the century improved transportation, disappearance of free land in the United States, higher prices, a marked increase in immigration, and the opening of the West brought a rapid advance of industrialism in the St Lawrence region. Increasing industrialism was accompanied by concentration on export staples such as wheat in western Canada, and minerals, lumber, and fish in British Columbia and the Maritimes. Labour and farmers' organizations reflected the character of industrial growth. The Maritimes had felt the full impact of industrialism in the decline of shipbuilding, the disappearance of industries through competition from the St Lawrence region, and the shift to concentration on coal and iron.[30] Coal miners in Nova Scotia were organized in the Provincial Workmen's Association in 1879 and, following the development of the iron and steel industry, it became aggressive in strikes in 1904 and later years. It affiliated with the Canadian Federation of Labour, but the inevitable weak support facilitated the entry of the United Mine Workers in 1908 and amalgamation with that organization in 1917.

In British Columbia the high rate of wages, which characterized the gold rush, attracted Oriental labour[31] with low standards of living, and involved constant friction. A strike at the Wellington colliery in 1883 and other labour difficulties were followed by an extended investigation and by legislation which became increasingly restrictive to Oriental immigration. The extension of metal mining from the western states to the Kootenay was followed by migration of organized labour. The Western Federation of Miners entered the Rossland district in 1895 and, with the completion of the Crow's Nest Pass Railway and the opening of the coal mines in the Crow's Nest region, extended its range by the formation of District Union Number 7 in 1902. It severed affiliation with the American Federation of Labor in 1898 and joined the American Labor Union. The aggressiveness of industrial unionism under the American Labor Union in British Columbia and Alberta was evident in the formation of the United Brotherhood of Railway Employees, in the withdrawal of the Vancouver Trades Council from the Trades and Labor Congress in 1902, and in numerous strikes. The difficulties led to the appointment of a Royal Commission by the Dominion government, which recommended that foreign radical unions and foreign leadership of strikes should be declared illegal and that investigation of trade disputes and arbitration in "public service industries" be compulsory.[32] Continued difficulties in Alberta coal mines in 1906 led to the Industrial Disputes Investigation Act in 1907.[33] Radical unionism had declined and the United Mine Workers had displaced the Western Federation in the Crow's Nest coal region in 1903. A working arrangement was reached between the two organizations in 1908 and the Western Federation joined the American Federation of Labor in 1910. The United Mine Workers extended control over Vancouver Island mines in 1911, but disappeared in 1915. The Western Federation of Miners supported the Industrial Workers of the World in 1906 and a strike developed on the Grand Trunk Pacific Railway in 1912.[34]

Labour organizations with English-American traditions were unable to penetrate French Quebec effectively. The Knights of Labor disappeared, the Canadian Federation of Labour held its position with difficulty, and the Trades and Labour Congress was restricted. Migration of French-Canadian labour, particularly to the shoemaking and textile centres of New England, facilitated the spread of labour organization from the United States, but insistence of the Church on compliance with the encyclical *Rerum Novarum* (1891) necessitated independent growth. Language and religion were effective bulwarks against English-American unions. Catholic unions[35] spread persistently in the early part of the century and particularly during the war and post-war period. In 1912 the Féderation Ouvrière de Chicoutimi was formed, in 1915 the Western Federation was displaced in Thetford Mines, in 1918 the National Central Trades Council was formed in Quebec City, and in 1922 the Federation of Catholic Workers was organized.

The divergence of cultural and regional factors accentuated by the character of the spread of industrialism in Canada affected farmers' organizations as well as labour organizations. In Ontario the shift from wheat to the livestock and dairy industries, and from the export to the domestic market during the prosperous period after 1900 involved severe strains on the farmers' movement. The Farmers' Association of Ontario was formed in 1902 but amalgamated with the Grange in 1907. The increasing importance of an expanding urban market weakened the opposition of farmers to protective tariffs. The Reciprocity Treaty of 1911 obtained slight support in the rural areas of industrial Ontario.

In western Canada, on the other hand, the dominance of the Canadian Pacific Railway, rapid expansion, and dependence on exports of wheat implied efforts on the part of the farmers to combat high railway rates, elevator and marketing charges, and tariffs. The Territorial Grain Growers' Association was formed in 1902, and was divided with the formation of the provinces into the Saskatchewan Grain Growers' Association and the Farmers' Association of Alberta in 1905, the Manitoba Grain Growers' Association being formed in 1903. The migration of American farmers of the western states to western Canada was followed by the penetration of American organizations. The American Society of Equity penetrated Alberta in 1905 and was amalgamated with the Farmers' Association in the United Farmers of Alberta in 1908. An interprovincial council was formed in 1907. Opposition to the Winnipeg grain exchange was responsible for the emergence of the Grain Growers' Grain Company in 1907. Attempts on the part of Alberta and Manitoba to support a scheme of government ownership of elevators led to the acquisition of Manitoba elevators in 1912 and of Alberta elevators in 1917 by the Grain Growers' Grain Company, which became the United Grain Growers. Saskatchewan built up an independent organization, the Saskatchewan Co-operative Elevator Company. Increasing opposition to the tariff led to the formation of the Canadian Council of Agriculture in 1910, which linked organizations in western Canada to the Grange in Ontario.

FARMERS' MOVEMENTS AND THE WAR

Rising prices during the pre-war period and the outbreak of the war supported a rapid expansion of farmers' organizations. The United Farmers Co-operative Company, formed in 1914, expanded rapidly in Ontario. The United Grain Growers and the Saskatchewan Co-operative Elevator Company flourished with high grain prices and the introduction of the Wheat Board. Political movements emerged from a background of financial success. The weakness of the Liberal party following the defeat of the Reciprocity Treaty, the establishment of the Union Government and the isolation of Laurier and the French population led to the emergence of Progressive groups in western Canada. Opposition to conscription was accompanied by opposition to high tariffs. The Canadian Council of Agriculture was reorganized with ample financial resources and the new National Policy formulated. With the end of the war farmers' governments succeeded in capturing control of the provinces on a wide scale. In Ontario the United Farmers of Ontario formed a government in 1919. In western Canada the influence of the Non-Partisan League spread to Saskatchewan and Alberta. Mr Henry Wise Wood advocated, with striking effect, group government with adequate representation of farmers, and the United Farmers of Alberta secured control in 1921. The United Farmers of Manitoba were elected to office in the following year. This success of the farmers' movement in the provincial field was accompanied by the election of sixty-five Progressive members in the federal field in 1921 (Prairie Provinces, thirty-nine; Ontario, twenty-four). But the anchorage of tradition held in the older provinces of Quebec and Nova Scotia, and the strength of the farmers' movement soon began to recede.[36] In Ontario the power of urban influence became evident in the divergent views of Premier Drury, who advocated a "broadening out" policy, and of Mr J.J. Morrison, who insisted on the occupational basis, and in the collapse of the government in 1924. The persistence of the influence of the Progressive movement continued and was shown in the inclusion of the Honourable Mr Nixon in the Liberal cabinet in 1934. In Manitoba the Farmers' Government continued under Mr Bracken, first by amalgamation with the Liberals and later by agreement with Social Credit; in Alberta the United Farmers were defeated by Mr Aberhart in 1935; in Saskatchewan the dominance of wheat and the relative absence of metropolitan development implied basic dependence of party organization on agriculture, with the result that the provincial government continued under the control of Liberals until the election of 1929. The religious issue contributed to their defeat. The significance of group government as developed in Alberta was evident in the break-up of party organization and the necessity during a depression of choosing other alternatives such as that of Social Credit. Like the philosophy of group government, that of Social Credit has swept into Saskatchewan and Manitoba and the federal house. The increasing strength of the Conservatives contributed to a decline of Progressive representation in the federal house to twenty-four members in 1925. Alberta federal representation following the independent development of Alberta provincial politics became the nucleus of a more aggressive group (while Progressives from the remaining provinces became increasingly concerned with the broader policies of the old parties, particularly the Liberal), and suffered the fate of the provincial party, in the victory of Mr Aberhart when Social Credit members were elected in 1935.

Cooperative organizations reflected the influence of the war and post-war difficulties. The disappearance of the Wheat Board and a sharp decline in the price of wheat led to demands for the introduction of pooling methods. Owing to the aggressive interest of Mr H.W. Wood and the dominance of the farmers' movement in Alberta politics, a pool was organized in Alberta in 1923. The enthusiasm of Mr Aaron Sapiro, who had been conspicuously successful in the cooperative movement in California and elsewhere, was enlisted to support extensions of pools to Saskatchewan and Manitoba. The strength of the old parties in Saskatchewan concentrated the influence of the pool movement and intensified its activities. The pool acquired the assets of the Saskatchewan Co-operative Elevator Company. In Manitoba the strength of private elevator companies and of the United Grain Growers limited the extent of pool activities. In Ontario and the older provinces agriculture became increasingly specialized, with the result that cooperation has developed along specialized lines. In Quebec the influence of cultural factors was in evidence in the formation of "Les Fermiers de Québec" in 1917 and the Catholic Farmers' Union in 1924, and in the success of credit unions.[37] In Nova Scotia the success of the cooperative movement[38] directed from St Francis Xavier University has been strengthened by religious factors.

Similarly, specialization with increasingly complex problems has supported the formation of associations. In Ontario and Quebec the dairying and livestock industries, fruit farming, and tobacco farming, and in the Maritimes potato and apple growing and fur farming, illustrate the general trend. Geographic limitations in

British Columbia have strengthened organizations concerned with the marketing of dairy products and fruit. With these trends the importance of broad movements has declined. The dairying industry has tended to develop along protective lines in contrast with wheat and apples, which depend on the export market. The Canadian Council of Agriculture disappeared in 1924. The sharp decline in prices during the depression has accentuated the problem of marketing as seen in the introduction of the short-lived Natural Products Marketing Act and in the formation of the Canadian Chamber of Agriculture in 1935, followed by provincial organizations in Manitoba in 1936 and Ontario in 1937. The Canadian Dairy Farmers' Federation[39] has become an important rival to the National Dairy Council.

THE WAR AND LABOUR ORGANIZATION

The effect of the war was as evident in the labour movement as in the farmers' movement. In western Canada protests arose against the more conservative policies of the Trades and Labor Congress dominated by the craft organizations of the industrial areas of the St Lawrence. Agitation which centred about the Winnipeg strike contributed to the election of members to the provincial and federal governments. Labour organization reflected the unrest in the formation of the One Big Union in 1919, as an attempt to meet the problems of radical unionism. In 1927 it was merged with unions not affiliated with the Trades and Labour Congress or the American Federation of Labor, nor influenced as in the case with the Catholic unions by cultural factors, to form the All-Canadian Congress of Labour. The Canadian Federation of Labour served as a nucleus to which was added the Canadian Brotherhood of Railroad Employees, which had its origin among workmen of the Intercolonial Railway and was extended to include chiefly the industrial workers on Canadian railways not under the jurisdiction of Railway Brotherhoods affiliated with American unions. The depression imposed a severe strain on an organization including divergent groups, and in 1936 the Canadian Federation of Labour withdrew from the All-Canadian Congress. Industrial unionism became increasingly important during the depression, as shown in the growth of the Workers Unity League and in the extension of activities of the CIO from the United States. The wave of industrial unionism with political implications which swept from the United States to British Columbia early in the century and led to the Royal

Commission of 1903, was followed by the CIO, which at Oshawa met with the determined opposition of the provincial government of Ontario. The Industrial Disputes Investigation Act, which emerged from a background of strikes in Alberta and British Columbia, was declared *ultra vires* in 1923, and subsequent legislation of the same kind has not been introduced in the province of Ontario. Consequently the task of directing labour disputes has fallen more obviously on the shoulders of the provincial government.

GENERAL RÉSUMÉ

The impact of American influence on farmer and labour movements in Canada has become increasingly direct with westward expansion. Competitive routes from the interior to the seaboard early necessitated constant efforts to secure adjustment in the St Lawrence region which took the form of smuggling, in the French régime, and later of lower standards of living except in so far as the St Lawrence permitted dependence on the highly efficient industrialized area of Great Britain, and offset the disadvantages of dependence on raw materials with wide fluctuations in yield and prices. The advantages were evident in the migration of traders from Albany to Montreal and in the extension of the Northwest Company. They were not evident in the difficult period after the Napoleonic Wars, when population was released with the inroads of industrialism in Great Britain, transported by returning empty timber ships, and settled in the virgin forest areas of Upper Canada, and when prices of lumber and wheat fluctuated in relation to imperial preferences, the business cycle, and changes in price and yield. The results were apparent in the outbreak of rebellion, and the difficulties were met by lowered costs of transportation as a result of the construction of railways and canals, and the reorganization of government following Lord Durham's *Report.* The attempt to capitalize the advantages of lower costs of transportation through the Reciprocity Treaty by extension of traffic to the western states were offset by a more rapid lowering of costs in the United States. The financial burden of transportation improvements and depreciation through obsolescence meant that an increase was needed in the tariff against goods from the United States and Great Britain; and the abrogation of reciprocity and the depression were followed by Confederation, and extension to the Maritimes and the Pacific coast by the Intercolonial and the Canadian Pacific railways. The effect of the burdens imposed by the tariff and transportation costs were evident during the depression in the last half of the century, in a realignment of agriculture in the St Lawrence region toward dairy and livestock industries facilitated by improved transportation to Great Britain and borrowing from the United States, in extensive migration to the United States, and in the spread of farmers' organizations from the United States. Expansion of industry and further reorganization of agriculture in the St Lawrence increased after the opening of the West. The burden of the monopoly of the Hudson's Bay Company (which contributed to the Riel Rebellion) was followed by the burden of railway rates, tariffs, and marketing charges, leading to organized opposition from western farmers. Extensive migration from the United States, especially to Saskatchewan and Alberta, and heavier burdens which accompanied increasing costs incidental to distance from Montreal, contributed to the success of protest movements which spread from the grain-producing areas of the northwestern states. Alberta became a centre of disturbance which contributed to the success of the farmers' movement in the war and post-war periods. The burden of debt of the recent depression was again most vigorously resisted in Alberta. Opposition movements to the burdens of a northern transcontinental structure have developed persistently through the proximity and competitive influence of the United States. Protest movements have proved the centre of greatest stress to be the weakest point in the impact of American influence. In the East and the West the United States has exercised constant pressure in bringing the adjacent Canadian structure into line. Compensation to the Maritimes and to western Canada to meet the burdens of the tariff and railway rates has been compelled by American competition. While the contributions of American technique have helped to accentuate upward swings in the Canadian economy, contributions of American protest have hastened adjustments during the downward swings.

The wide swings of Canadian economic development, which have coincided with improvements of transportation on the upper St Lawrence and across the Precambrian formation, have largely determined the character of American influence. Extension of the fur trade under the Northwest Company to the Pacific was supported by technique and personnel from the United States. The collapse of the fur trade and the problem of transportation on the upper St Lawrence accentuated the importance of protests, built up on British radicalism and Jacksonian democracy, which led to the rebellion. The completion of the canals, the railways, and Confederation increased the importance of technique and personnel from the United States. The long depression which followed brought protests in the form of dominance of Ontario politics by

Liberals, attempts to secure reciprocity and agitation for commercial union which were offset by the National Policy, construction of canals and the Canadian Pacific Railway, and the astute political activity and Scottish birth of Sir John A. Macdonald and his appeals to imperial connection. "A British subject I was born, a British subject I will die." The success of the Liberals was eventually built on a strong cultural group, such as the French Canadians under Laurier or the Scots under the two other Liberal Premiers of Canada of the Mackenzie clan.[40] The defeat of Laurier in 1911 was to prove again the limitations of possible attachments to American influence. The achievement of Dominion status and the growth of Canadian nationalism have facilitated agreements with the United States, but imperialistic sentiment remains a factor of major political and economic importance. Periods of depression accompanied by migration to the United States have been accompanied by a hardening of the central structure and appeal to imperialist sentiment, and this in turn has increased the importance of governmental intervention during periods of prosperity. Government ownership in Canada is based on a hard core of defence against the United States.

The necessity of deodorization in political protest movements has accentuated American influence on protest organizations eschewing politics. American influence in political movements has been indirect. So far as the present writer is aware, no one of American birth has ever become premier of a province. Whether Mr H.W. Wood might have been premier of Alberta is a question for academic discussion, but it is sufficient to say that he did not, and that his influence was strengthened because he stressed organization rather than political movements. The success of the pools was accentuated by the insistence of Mr Sapiro on the avoidance of politics. The results were evident in strengthening the position of the Liberal party in Saskatchewan and weakening the Farmers' party in Alberta. Farmer and labour organizations have become powerful factors with American support, partly because they have been compelled to avoid political activities. Political organizations in Canada have in turn become more sensitive to the pressure of organized groups. The success of these organizations has led to a counter movement in the United States – the Canadian pools stimulated the interest of American farmers in similar organizations.

Labour organizations have occupied a more strategic position through their more direct relations to the more rigid price structure of industry sheltered by the tariff. The success of labour organizations accentuates the necessities of political movements of farmers. While the farmers' movements have taken political form supported by American influence, labour organization[41] has been more effectively supported by American development, with the result that political movements have been of minor importance. The success of the affiliations of the American Federation of Labor has been partly a result of the policy of non-political intervention of Mr Gompers. Labour movements with political possibilities have been resisted vigorously in Canada, to cite British Columbia in the strikes of 1902 and the Oshawa strike of 1937, partly because the relations of labour in Canada and the United States have been immediate and direct. Financial support from the United States has been important in winning strikes,[42] and the necessity of such dependence compels Canadian labour to avoid political movements and concentrate on indirect influence.

The development of separate governments as nuclei of defence against the United States, the addition of Confederation as a means of concentrating defence measures, and the formation of new provinces in western Canada as a continuation of the "divide and rule" principle have provided the basis for provincial rights as protected under the British North America Act and developed under decisions of the Privy Council. The provinces have served as compartments tending to reduce the effects of American influence, and have tended not only to weaken the political influence of the United States in the growth of farmers' movements in the federal field, but also to accentuate it in isolated provinces. The influence of farmers' movements has been weakened further by the concentration of industrialism. The character of agriculture increases the difficulties of cooperation with western Canada. The character of industry is reflected in labour organizations which by virtue of age, tradition, language, similarity of development, and proximity to the United States are linked to American influence. Labour organizations in exposed areas in the Maritimes and in western Canada tend to diverge in policy from those in Ontario. They are not only necessarily more closely associated with the production of raw materials such as lumber, coal, and minerals and more closely concerned with industrial unionism, but also more closely associated with American influence because of the cultural factors involved in the province of Quebec and, in turn, in Ontario. Labour organizations reflect the regional and cultural background. The more strongly organized industrial region involves more rigid wages, particularly with increasing dependence on the United States. Since 1918 railway wages in Canada have paralleled closely railway wages in the United States.[43] Organized labour in the pulp and paper industry attempts to maintain wages on a par in Canada and the United States. American branch plants as in Ford and International

Harvester extend labour policies developed in the United States to Canada.[44]

Rigidity in prices tends to be strengthened by increasing dependence on the United States in eastern Canada. Prices of pulp and paper and gold serve as illustrations of the increasing importance of the American market. As prices and wages tend to become more rigid the fluctuations in income from products such as wheat exported to the extra continental markets become more severe. Producers of staple exports subject to wide fluctuations are penalized by the increasing rigidities which accompany the increasing importance of the United States. Unorganized groups of labour in the industrial areas are squeezed between the depressed income of exporters of raw material and rigidity of prices, as the evidence of unemployment and sweated labour has shown.[45] Professor Logan has attempted to give greater precision to the character of the burden of defence[46] against the United States, as shown in a lower standard of living which suggests an even greater disparity in less organized groups and less sheltered areas.

The importance of staple products in terms of fish, fur, lumber, and wheat for export to Europe implied extensive credit facilities, with wide fluctuations in price and yield, distance from the market, dependence on the share system, the truck system, intensive self-sufficiency, and marked fluctuations in the standards of living. The increase of industrial development and the growth of urban centres, the development of the mining and pulp and paper industries, and the tourist trade and consequent dependence on American capital have involved increasing efficiency and extension of the monetary structure. These developments have been accompanied by increasing flexibility and increasing mobility.[47] On the other hand the shift from commercial capitalism to industrial capitalism has been striking in a country dependent on transcontinental railways and canals, hydro-electric power development, mines and smelters, and roads, and has led to a later stage of state capitalism with the attendant rigidities of capital structure. The impact on Canada of the business cycle in the highly integrated industrial system of the United States varies directly with the importance of American capital and of the American market, and with the character of the industrial structure in Canada. In the mining and pulp and paper industries, distant from the more highly integrated industrial structure, standards of living are influenced directly by American prices and by the character of labour organization. Isolation increases the importance of capital control, as shown in company towns. Regions exporting products to Great Britain are subject to the more intense competition of world markets and the greater rigidities of transportation costs. The conflict between a price structure dominated by Great Britain and a price structure increasingly dominated by the continent has serious implications for the Canadian economy in the inequalities between groups and regions. The influence of the United States has been, in part, to increase the rigidities of wages. It has contributed to the solution of difficulties involved in the depressed regions but such contributions have been inevitably limited in scope. The importance of these regions necessitates the elaborate machinery, peculiar to Canada, providing for compensation in railway rates, railway deficits, subsidies, and grants in aid. The tariff, immigration quotas, and other restrictions accentuate the significance of transfer devices.[48] The tourist trade, the pulp and paper industry, gold mining, and capital movements provide rough balances in which mobility increases in response to fluctuating exchange rates.

The machinery of adjustment has emerged from a background peculiar to Canada in her relations with Great Britain and the United States. The significance of cheap water transportation to the St Lawrence system has been evident in the export of staple products to Europe.[49] The migration of technique from the United States has supported the trend toward specialization on staple products for Great Britain. Concentration on staple products has involved maturity of development which in turn has had repercussions on the United States. Astor attempted the adoption of Northwest Company organization and temporarily occupied the Columbia region. Marquis wheat spread through Canada to the United States. But on the whole the migration of technique has been from the United States and has been hastened by the absence of political attachments. Political organization in Canada has thrived on importation of technique from the United States through support of extensive capital improvements. Political support of capitalism characteristic of the production of staple exports has contrasted with the demands of the industrial areas of the United States for labour. The immobility of labour described by Adam Smith was not applicable to a frontier population habituated to migration.[50] The problem of political organization in Canada has been that of restricting emigration to the United States.

NOTES

1 See G.E. Britnell, "Saskatchewan, 1930–1935," *Canadian Journal of Economics and Political Science* 2 (May 1936): 143–66. A series of studies

on standards of living in western Canada, British Columbia, and the Maritimes has been planned under the auspices of the Institute of Pacific Affairs. See also a study of Winnipeg in 1915, *Board of Inquiry into Cost of Living in Canada Report* (Ottawa, 1915), 2: 1018–19, and "Family Living Expenses in the Red River Valley of Manitoba," *Economic Annalist* 3 (1933): 51–3. Throughout, the term, standards of living, is given the narrow meaning of standards of expenditure.

2 See H.A. Innis, ed., *Select Documents in Canadian Economic History, 1497–1783* (Toronto, 1929), 301–2, 393–4, 402, and *passim.*

3 H.A. Innis, *The Fur Trade in Canada* (New Haven, 1930), 221.

4 G.L. Nute, *The Voyageur* (New York, 1931).

5 Innis, *Fur Trade in Canada,* 245.

6 See M. Gilroy, "The Partition of Nova Scotia, 1784," *Canadian Historical Review* 14 (Dec. 1933): 375–92; also ibid., 16 (March 1935): 91–3, and J.B. Brebner, ibid., 15 (March 1934): 57–9.

7 H.E. Conrad, "The Loyalist Experiment in New Brunswick" (doctoral thesis, University of Toronto, 1934).

8 See *The Narrative of Gordon Sellar, Who Migrated to Canada in 1825* (Huntingdon, 1915), chap. 3; also R.A. MacKay, "The Political Ideas of William Lyon Mackenzie," *Canadian Journal of Economics and Political Science* 3 (Feb. 1937): 1–22.

9 See H.M. Morrison, "The Principle of Free Grants in the Land Act of 1841," *Canadian Historical Review* 14 (Dec. 1933): 392–408.

10 D.G. Creighton, "The Commercial Class in Canadian Politics, 1792–1840," *Proceedings of Canadian Political Association,* 1933, 43–58; and *The Commercial Empire of the St. Lawrence* (Toronto, 1937).

11 F. de Saint Maurice, *De Tribord à Babord* (Montreal, 1877), 361.

12 W.S. Wallace, "Some Notes on Fraser's Highlanders," *Canadian Historical Review* 18 (June 1937).

13 See C.B. Sissons, *Egerton Ryerson* (Toronto, 1937).

14 See C. Martin, "The United States and National Nationality," *Canadian Historical Review* 18 (March 1937): 1–11.

15 Innis, *Fur Trade in Canada,* 230.

16 G.F.G. Stanley, *The Birth of Western Canada: A History of the Riel Rebellion* (London, 1936).

17 Innis, *Select Documents in Canadian Economic History, 1497–1783,* 35.

18 Ibid., 525. "1 Jan, 1773. Mr. Stuart arrived here a few days ago; seems dissatisfied with his progress, as he expected a great deal not only from the rum and dry goods but from the influence of his brother in law who married the priest's niece, and if it were possible that his mother and sister were married to the priests themselves would not hinder the inhabitants to buy cheap and sell dear" (ibid., 526).

19 John Young, *The Letters of Agricola* (Halifax, 1922).

20 C. Lindsey, *The Life and Times of W.L. Mackenzie* (Toronto, 1862), 2: 55.

21 See F.H. Underhill, "Some Aspects of Upper Canadian Radical Opinion in the Decade before Confederation," *Canadian Historical Association Report,* 1927, 46–61; also G.W. Brown, "The Grit Party and the Great Reform Convention of 1859," *Canadian Historical Review* 16 (Sept. 1935): 245–65. On the decline of rural population and industries, see C. Shott, *Landnahme und Kolonisation in Canada* (Kiel, 1936), 245ff and 274ff.

22 H.A. Innis and A.R.M. Lower, eds, *Select Documents in Canadian Economic History, 1783–1885* (Toronto, 1933), 453.

23 Ibid., 598.

24 Ibid., 612.

25 B. Ratz, "United Front in Toronto – 1872," *New Frontier,* 1936.

26 See L.A. Wood, *A History of Farmers' Movements in Canada* (Toronto, 1924), *passim*; also S.J. Buck, *The Grange Movement* (Cambridge, Mass., 1913), and H. Mitchell, *The Grange in Canada* (Kingston, 1914).

27 Innis and Lower, *Select Documents in Canadian Economic History, 1783–1885,* 622.

28 Ibid., 611.

29 Ibid., 619ff; also *Report of the Royal Commission on the Relations of Labor and Capital in Canada* (Ottawa, 1889), E. Young, *Labor in Europe and America* (Washington, 1875), and H.B. Ames, *Incomes, Wages and Rents in Montreal* (US Dept. of Labor Bulletin, 1898), 39–51.

30 See E.A. Forsey, *Economic and Social Aspects of the Nova Scotia Coal Industry* (Toronto, 1928); *Report of the Royal Commission, Provincial Economic Inquiry* (Halifax, 1934); *The Maritime Provinces, 1867–1934* (Dominion Bureau of Statistics, Ottawa).

31 See Cheng Tien-Fang, *Oriental Immigration in Canada* (Shanghai, 1931); P.C. Campbell, *Chinese Coolie Immigration in the British Empire* (London, 1923); *Report of the Royal Commission on Chinese Immigration* (Ottawa, 1885); W.L.M. King, *Industry and Humanity* (Toronto, 1918).

32 *Report of Royal Commission on Labor Disturbances in British Columbia* (1903).

33 See B. Selekman, *Postponing Strikes* (New York, 1923).

34 See E.W. Bradwin, *The Bunkhouse Man* (New York, 1928), and J.B. Bickersteth, *The Land of Open Doors* (Toronto, n.d.), for a description of labour conditions in railway construction. See also *Report on Immigration of Italian Laborers to Montreal and Alleged Fraudulent Practices of Employment Agencies* (1905).

35 See A.B. Latham, *The Catholic and National Labor Unions of Canada* (Toronto, 1930); also A.S. Lortie, "Compositeur Typographe de Québec [1903]," *Les Ouvriers des Deux Mondes,* 1908, 61–132.

36 See E.M. Reid, "Canadian Political Parties: A Study of the Economic and Racial Bases of Conservatism and Liberalism in 1930," *Contributions to Canadian Economics*, University of Toronto Studies, History and Economics (Toronto, 1933), 6: 7–39.

37 On the success of A. Desjardins, see H. Michell, *The Problems of Agricultural Credit in Canada* (Kingston, 1914); see also an account of the self-sufficient character of rural life, M. Gauldrée-Boileau, "Payson de Saint-Irénée (Bas-Canada-Amérique-du-Nord), [1861–1862]," *Les Ouvriers des Deux Mondes*, 5 (1885): 51–108.

38 For a description of cooperative stores in Nova Scotia, H. Michell, *The Cooperative Store in Canada* (Kingston, 1916).

39 See J.A. Ruddick et al., *The Dairy Industry in Canada* (Toronto, 1937), *passim.*

40 It is an interesting speculation as to how far the inevitable choice of a vigorous English-speaking leader as a means of rebuilding the Liberal party after the war has been responsible for the withdrawal of Quebec and as to how far this necessitated increasing dependence on western Canada. The present Liberal Administration includes Mr T. Crerar, Mr J. Gardiner, Mr W.L. Mackenzie King, and Mr C.A. Dunning – the first three representing western constituencies and the latter a former premier of Saskatchewan. Mr Crerar and Mr Dunning, as former prominent members of the two large farmers' organizations, the United Grain Growers and the Saskatchewan Co-operative Elevator Company, indirectly reflect the influence of the pool movement in their withdrawal from the farmers' organizations. The success of the Liberals in Ontario contributed further to the decline of the Liberals in Quebec. Politically the two provinces have proved difficult to drive in double harness.

41 The Canadian Federation of Labour and the All-Canadian Congress are at once tributes to the importance of national influence and indications of the importance of the non-political activities of the Trades and Labour Congress.

42 See H.S. Ephron, "A Study of the Internal Workings of the International Typographical Union during the Forty-four-Hour Strike" (master's thesis, University of Toronto, 1924).

43 G.M. Rountree, *The Railway Worker* (Toronto, 1936), 57ff; the Baltimore and Ohio plan of management was adopted by the Canadian National Railways. See H.A. Stark, "Industrial Democracy in Canada" (master's thesis, University of Toronto, 1928); L.A. Wood, *Union Management Cooperation on the Railroads* (New Haven, 1930).

44 See *Canadian-American Industry* (New Haven, 1936), 206. For an account of labour policies in part influenced by the United States, see

H. Michell, *Profit Sharing and Producers' Co-operation in Canada* (Toronto, 1918), and *Report of the Royal Commission on Industrial Relations* (Ottawa, 1919).

45 See *Report of Royal Commission on Price Spreads* (Ottawa, 1935); also H.M. Cassidy and F.R. Scott, *Labour Conditions in the Men's Clothing Industry* (Toronto, 1935); H.A. Innis and A.F.W. Plumptre, *The Canadian Economy and Its Problems* (Toronto, 1934); and the Fessenden Report submitted to the *Royal Commission on the Textile Industry* (Ottawa, 1938). According to the latter, actual wages in American mills for weavers were Northern, \$16.46; Southern, \$14.78; and in Canadian mills a range from \$11.21 to \$15.37; for spinners, Northern, \$14.55; Southern, \$12.08, and a range from \$9.11 to \$17.56; for doffers, Northern, \$16.20; Southern, \$13.09, and a range from \$5.30 to \$9.11; for all operatives, Northern, \$15.38; Southern, \$12.98; Canadian, \$11.62. On unemployment, see R.W. Murchie, W.H. Carter, and F.J. Dixon, *Seasonal Unemployment* (Manitoba, 1928); H.M. Cassidy, *Unemployment and Relief in Ontario, 1929–32* (Toronto, 1932); Rountree, *The Railway Worker.*

46 For a description of the defence in terms of attitudes, see H.F. Angus, ed., *Canada and Her Great Neighbor* (Toronto, 1938).

47 For an excellent account of the decline of barter and the spread of the wage system and its implications to mobility, see J. Davidson, *The Bargain Theory of Wages* (New York, 1898).

48 See *Commerce Journal Annual Review*, Feb. 1936, 24ff.

49 The general argument has been developed in Ruddick et al., *The Dairy Industry in Canada*, v–xxvi.

50 See L. Hémon, *Maria Chapdelaine* (Toronto, 1921).

CHAPTER TWELVE

The Economics of Conservation

The spate of literature[1] on conservation in the United States issuing from federal departments and from publishing houses and written by authors or groups of authors ranging from the expert to the popularizer is a reflection of the growth of nationalism[2] during the depression. The attractive appearance of much of the material has been a result of improved technique of communication and more efficient propaganda. "The Plough That Broke the Plains" is a significant motion picture. Apologists have written of the interest in conservation as part of a long-run secular trend, in which natural resources have been depleted, that has been accentuated by the effects of the war and the depression; but it has emerged during a period in which resources are being utilized far less than during the preceding boom of the twenties, when the interest in conservation was slight. An extensive governmental program of "recovery" included a large-scale construction of public works[3] for the employment of labour and price-raising policies of a far-reaching character. All this has involved research, publication, and propaganda; and limitations of time have precluded a thorough and extended analysis of the implications in spite of the government's enlistment of the resources of educational institutions. An intensely critical review of this literature would be unfair. The publications that have the authority of expert opinion are on the whole justifiably guarded in their conclusions, and those that do not have such authority are dogmatic enough to warrant scepticism on the part of even the casual reader. Moreover, as this is part of a nationalistic trend during the depression linked with protection, monetary policy, and

From *Geographical Review* 28 (1938): 137–9.

other devices, it would perhaps not be a neighbourly act to indulge in obvious criticism of this literature. The difficulties of reaching agreement on international conservation measures such as the St Lawrence waterway, the Pacific-coast salmon fisheries, and the ever present Trail smelter compensation suggest that Canada is not less nationalistic than the United States, the Migratory Birds Convention Act, scientific research on the fisheries, the halibut treaty, and the work of the International Joint Commission notwithstanding.

The fundamental criticism is the lack of a philosophy. Take, for example, "Our Natural Resources and Their Conservation," a symposium by 22 geographers, a useful volume that should find its way into every college library. An economist can find enlightenment on numerous points in its various informative articles; but the whole question of conservation is begged by its definition as "wise use."[4] Attempts to answer the question are implied in the sane discussion of irrigation and of transportation as regards expenditures on railways and waterways and also in Dr O.E. Baker's article on the importance of family life and the philosophical outlook of rural life, but even this is a matter of faith. The issue of "scant means in relation to given ends" has been largely avoided.

We are compelled to inquire about the preconceptions of conservation. Is the enlistment of the state in the interest of "conservation" in the interests of a bureaucracy, of publishing houses and paper plants, of authors, or of "the people"? Is it in the interest of modern industrialism, to support it beyond the limits of private capitalism by direct contribution to large undertakings or by securing a more rapid transfer of funds to consumers? What is a "better" standard of living? Does the conception arise from changes in the kind of goods consumed, i.e. "progress" that follows from a change in technique, with all its accompaniment of waste through obsolescence? Does the technique change as a result of relative accessibility of natural resources, of consumers' demands (or are these changed by advertising?), or of the advance of invention through trial and error or subsidized and unsubsidized scientific research? When does a product become or cease to be a natural resource under changing conditions of technique? Are the "ends" determined by industrialism, and does the character of the "means" change with industrialism?

It is this conspicuous absence of a philosophical approach to conservation that makes the task of a reviewer in raising questions comparatively simple and the task of answering them extremely difficult. Reforestation has perhaps been the object of attention[5] on the part of conservationists for a longer period than most subjects and has had the advantage of extensive practice by older civilizations. The bulkiness of the commodity and high costs of transportation and substantial state control have stimulated an interest in the planting of trees and the care of forests in denuded areas adjacent to large metropolitan markets. The widespread production and the demands of construction industries, on the other hand, have exposed it to wide fluctuations in price as a result of the business cycle, improvements in transportation and technology, and competition from metal products. In North America agriculture displaced hardwood forests, with great loss of trees, but agricultural products rather than hardwoods were adaptable to prevailing transportation facilities. White pine was exhausted and was followed by spruce and balsam and other trees, and paper products displaced lumber for package material. The opening of the Panama Canal brought competition to Eastern forests from the Pacific coast. Southern pine and the radio threaten to reduce the demands for Canadian spruce and northern paper mills. Governments may support education, scientific investigation, and improved ways for transportation such as the Panama Canal at the expense of government expenditure to support reforestation.

Agricultural development has been fostered by governments through encouragement to railways and land policy. Land has been occupied during a period of improved methods of production, high prices, and heavy rainfall, and then farmers have been forced to meet the effects of intensive cultivation, low prices, and drought. Should the government support removal of farmers and abandonment of farms and equipment, or should it engage in large-scale public works of irrigation and maintain farmers on relief pending a return of a period of heavier rainfall and higher prices? What are the implications to wheat-producing regions in a similar situation in Australia, Canada, and elsewhere and to relief problems in urban centres of migration from rural areas? The policy adopted may depend on short-run problems of public finance, on long-run intangibles such as the belief in the importance of maintaining a stable rural population,[6] and on such factors as the decline in consumption of wheat.

The fishing industry[7] of the North Atlantic expanded rapidly with the governmental support of bounties and duties and encouragement to steamships and trawlers, thus contributing to the circumstances under which fishing villages of France, Newfoundland, Nova Scotia, and New England based on the wooden sailing vessel have faced migration and conditions of extreme poverty such as brought about the disappearance of responsible government in Newfoundland and St Pierre. In the latter case the difficulties were added to by the abolition of prohibition as a recovery measure in the United States.

Mining[8] has been greatly affected by monetary policy during the depression. Abandoned plants and towns have been reoccupied on a vast scale and new deposits developed as a result of the increase in the price of gold. Higher prices of other metals have had similar but less conspicuous results. Conservation has been important for labour and capital equipment, and higher prices and lower costs resulting from improved transportation and technology accentuate the rate of exhaustion and depletion on the one hand and facilitate the mining of lower-grade ores on the other hand. The extreme difficulty of accurate appraisal of resources and the dominance of private enterprise in exploitation make an estimate of the influence of governmental policy impossible except in very general terms. How far does extensive hydroelectric-power development with governmental support involve a reduction in the demand for coal and aggravate the complicated problems of the coal-mining industry? The crucial position of the mining industry in modern industrialism has been evident in attempts to increase production in the heavy industries by public works, armaments, and housing projects. The widely scattered locations of the diverse minerals demanded by modern industrialism have led to demands of highly industrialized nations for control over resources beyond their boundaries.

The place of the state in the development of conservation policies is largely a reflection of the demands of modern industrialism. Should the state withhold natural resources from private enterprise and thereby increase the prices of commodities, as has been charged in the case of Alaska?[9] Should it encourage increased production by stimulating invention and thereby endeavour to maintain the essentially dynamic character of modern industrial society? Emphasis on large-scale public works involves rigidities of location of industry and labour. In any case, has the state any alternative other than to meet the demands of industrialism as expressed through "standards of living"?[10] Migration to urban centres contributes to declining birth rate and to stability and possibly decline of population. Should this be the aim of the state? The drive of modern technology with the modern pecuniary economy involves exhaustion of natural resources and getting on to something else. Depletion of pulpwood enables hydroelectric power to be turned from paper plants to other industries in the interests of "progress" and "higher standards of living." The problems of conservation are concerned with restricting technology as well as with improving it and utilizing it to capacity.

All this is not to question the importance of the conservation movement but rather to suggest the conflicting elements that enter into it and to inquire into the causes of its development as a phase of nationalism. There is little room for philosophical inquiry when the waste of resources includes extensive publication and discussion of conservation.

NOTES

1 The following works may be instanced here: A.E. Parkins and J.R. Whitaker, eds, *Our Natural Resources and Their Conservation* (London, 1936); *The Future of the Great Plains*, Report of the Great Plains Committee, 75th Congr., 1st Sess., House of Repr. Doc. 144, 1937; "Headwaters Control and Use: A Summary of Fundamental Principles and Their Application in the Conservation and Utilization of Waters and Soils throughout Headwater Areas" (paper presented at the Upstream Engineering Conference, Washington, D.C., 22 and 23 September 1936), Soil Conservation Service and Forest Service, U.S. Dept. of Agriculture, with the cooperation of Rural Electrification Administration (Washington, 1937); Stuart Chase, *Rich Land, Poor Land: A Study of Waste in the Natural Resources of America* (New York and London, 1936).

2 H.A. Innis and A.F.W. Plumptre, eds, *The Canadian Economy and Its Problems* (Toronto, 1934), chap. 1.

3 J.M. Clark, *Strategic Factors in Business Cycles* (New York, 1934) and *Economics of Planning Public Works* (Washington, 1935).

4 Parkins and Whitaker, *Our Natural Resources*, 19.

5 B.E. Fernow, *Economics of Forestry* (New York, 1903); C.R. Van Hise, *The Conservation of Natural Resources in the United States* (New York, 1910); W.F. Ogburn, *Social Change with Respect to Culture and Original Nature* (New York, 1922; London, 1923).

6 V.W. Bladen, "The Economics of Federalism," *Canadian Journal of Economics and Political Science* 1 (1935): 348–51.

7 H.A. Innis, *The Atlantic Fishing Industry in North America* (in press).

8 Harold Hotelling, "The Economics of Exhaustible Resources," *Journal of Political Economy* 39 (1931): 137–75; A.R.M. Lower and H.A. Innis, "Settlement and the Forest and Mining Frontiers," *Canadian Frontiers of Settlement*, 9 (Toronto, 1936).

9 J.A. Hellenthal, *The Alaskan Melodrama* (New York, 1936).

10 F.H. Knights, *The Ethics of Competition, and Other Essays* (New York, 1935).

PART THREE

Metropolitanism, Nationality, and the Crisis of Industrialism

CHAPTER THIRTEEN

Economic Nationalism

This paper cannot do more than pretend to indicate the drift of economic nationalism and it must remain content with an outline of the indications which seem to point in a certain direction. I shall proceed from the following conclusion of a careful student of subject:

Peculiarly basic has been the development of large scale machine industry, with the impetus it has afforded to the growth of middle class and proletariat, to the improvement of means of transportation and communication and to the rivalry of peoples for economic advantage. In the main nationalism has flourished most abundantly in national states which have been most industrialized and the advent of the industrial revolution among "oppressed" nationalities has been the most potent factor in arousing their national consciousness and in enabling them to create national states of their own. It has been naturally so. For, while industrialization favors commercial intercourse between peoples, it is even more conducive to commercial intercourse within each nation. It is easier and more natural to do business with persons who speak and read one's own language than with others. Exports and imports of an industrialized nation do not equal in value what it buys and sells at home. Credit and banking function nationally far more than internationally. Labor is organized by nations and if it has international affiliations it subordinates them to what it considers to be its particular national interests. There is much more travel by people within a nation than between nations. There is more news in the public press about one's nation than about others.[1]

From *Papers and Proceedings of the Canadian Political Science Association* 6 (1934): 17–31.

The trend of industrialism has strengthened the trend of nationalism. Industrialism based on coal and iron and on all the year round water transportation implied a world dominated by the Atlantic basin and by areas with ample reserves of these basic commodities. Population density in the coal producing regions assumed transportation and finance for the movement of raw materials inward and of manufactured products outward. Areas with access to cheap all the year round water transportation became dominant as termini of ocean routes and of land routes and were supported by nuclei of economic activity developed in smaller metropolitan centres. These centres have gradually emerged to a position of relative financial independence and metropolitan stature.

The twentieth century and especially the post-war period has witnessed an expansion of new areas, beyond the territory dominated by cheap water transportation and abundant supplies of coal, to territory in which hydro-electric power and oil have played an important role. Oil and electric power have contributed to the flexibility and expansion of metropolitan centres based on coal and to the widening of the whole base to areas formerly handicapped by a lack of cheap supply of that commodity[2] – for example the opening of the Pacific, or Russia and northern Canada. The last regions of expansion have been staked.

The marked realignment of the post-war period was in large part a result of the contributions to mechanistic improvement of the war period, of the application of new sources of power to transportation, for example the aeroplane, and of a major technological transport improvement the Panama canal. The expansion of mining, and of wheat production, and the Ottawa agreements may be cited as results of interest to Canada. The Hochkapitalismus of Sombart reached immediately before the war and based on coal and coke and iron and steel was rounded out in the post-war period by oil, hydro-electric power and the new industrial metals.

Hydro-electric power development implies a geographic background of adequate rainfall and uneven topography and a region relatively inaccessible to coal in which its competitive advantage is enhanced. Regions formerly under a decided handicap from the standpoint of industrialism as dependent on coal become endowed with decided advantages. Power sites involve enormous initial investments of capital in many cases requiring support of the state. The significance of overhead costs necessitates expansion of power consumption to capacity and in turn the development and encouragement of exploitation of natural resources in the growth of basic industries, such as mining and pulp and paper, and of more highly integrated industries. Whereas hydro-electric power development is strongly characterized by regionalism and tends to be concentrated in a few areas, oil is essentially a basis of mobility since it is widely available and provides its own means of transport. Its impact has been primarily on transportation and distribution. Areas with emphasis on labour rather than on supplies of coal and iron have succeeded, as in the case of Japan in the production of textiles, in expanding the range of markets. Production of raw materials dependent on cheap supplies of power has increased materially for example in the case of wheat as it has been influenced by the tractor, the truck and mechanization generally. In conjunction with the Panama canal, oil burning vessels have increased the range of markets for Pacific countries and introduced disturbances of far-reaching proportions.

New sources of power strengthened tendencies emerging from the war. Emphasis on the iron and steel industries and on the wide range of industries linked to war demands brought fresh impetus to post-war industrialism. The peace consolidated the gains of industrialism of the war. New nations were carved out and industries which had grown up during the war were supported by nationalism and tariff barriers. Competition from highly industrialized areas with industries stimulated by the war was checked in areas more recently industrialized. Nationalist sentiment and organization developed during the war provided support for tariffs to protect new industries. In turn competition from more recently industrialized areas based on hydro-electric power and the drive of overhead costs, and on oil, on improved technique, and on less exhausted natural resources was followed by tariffs imposed by highly industrialized regions; to protect older industries based on coal and iron, more exhausted natural resources; less tractable labour, and plant affected by depreciation through obsolescence; and to stimulate new industries based on new sources of power as in Great Britain. Nationalism becomes cumulatively more intense. Migration of improved technique and the shift from primary production to secondary production has been hastened by expanding purchasing power and a wider range of markets in the large number of new industrial areas. Increased mobility through transportation facilities particularly evident in the completion of road systems in the last decade and the advantages of new plant and equipment working on lower cost raw materials contributed to the movement in these areas.

The pressure of industrialism based on new sources of power has been most striking in continental regions and large political organizations. Freedom of trade, diversified resources, mature industrial equipment (including the Panama canal), enormous supplies of capital and skilled labour contributed to the expansion of the United States in the boom of the twenties. Centralized political control, and in turn concentration on the development of natural resources through application of mature capital equipment and skilled labour imported from highly industrialized countries culminating in five year plans in the second large continental region, Russia, combined with expansion in the United States to give capitalism a final strong upward swing which collapsed in 1929. State activity in Europe supported restoration of the devastated areas and credit organization characteristic of the boom in the United States contributed to reconstruction of the capital equipment of Europe following inflation. The marked expansion of credit and of capital equipment in the twenties assumed the efficiency of private enterprise and the support of weaker economic and political organizations to mention only the guarantees of the Canadian government of borrowings of the Canadian National Railways, and loans to Australia, South American republics and to Russia. The pressure of continental industrialism during a period of expansion was followed by resistance on the part of more recently industrialized areas in the form of protection to infant industries. Moreover, the importance of state support for capital borrowings strengthened this trend through reliance on tariffs as a source of revenue to meet interest on loans. United States tariffs accentuated this trend by making it difficult to export goods in payment. More recently industrialized areas, more dependent on production and export of raw materials have been subjected to the effects of the more rapid decline in prices of raw materials and have found it more difficult to meet the burden of fixed charges of capital borrowed during the boom period. They have been subjected as a result of extensive state intervention to heavy fixed charges partly through more rapid decline of prices of raw material and partly through depreciation from obsolescence which accompanied the introduction of new sources of power. In Canada motor competition in areas with heavy traffic density and competition of the Panama canal have been partly responsible for larger railway deficits to be borne by the government.

Nationalism fostered by the war and the boom period became more intense as a result of depression. Dumping from more highly industrialized countries presents serious problems to industries of recent growth in weaker industrial regions particularly in the form of unemployment and is followed by increased tariffs and anti-dumping legislation. The national policy of 1878 in Canada followed the long period of depression in the seventies, and the present Canadian tariff belongs to the present depression. Relative lack of governmental machinery in weaker industrial regions tends to throw increased burdens on customs administration which becomes in turn a means of controlling exchange, of relieving unemployment, of producing revenue and of maintaining railway rates. Difficulties become evident in internal rigidities and unequal spreading of the burden. Prices of raw materials for exports exposed to world competition crush the primary producer between declining returns and relatively stable costs in terms of prices of manufactured products, of interest on debts, and of railway rates.

Within national boundaries the effects of these strains have been evident in the increasing strength of metropolitan centres. New sources of power and increasing industrialism have been responsible for increasing urbanization and increasing dominance of the city. Democratic institutions accentuate the influence of urban population and metropolitan centres and in turn mechanization strengthens the position of centralized control. Improved communication such as the press and the radio, improved transportation, and the development of modern architecture, for example, the skyscraper, tend to stress similarities of language and ideas. Expansion of the pulp and paper industry has supported intensive advertising and revolutions in marketing essential to the demands of the city. It has coincided with the decline of editorials and of freedom of speech, and the emergence of headlines and the modern newspaper with its demands for excitement including wars and peace to appeal to a large range of lower mental types. The coincidence with the advent of radio of dictatorship in Russia, Germany, Italy, Great Britain, the United States, or Canada is not accidental. Mechanization moreover implies more effective utilization of physical force. Machine guns are effective keys to the city. Metropolitan centres have continued to play increasingly important roles in the war, the peace, and the post-war period. The peace set its seal on the ambitions of older European metropolitan centres in the breakup of large political units. New nations brought into existence by the Treaty of Versailles reflected the demands of Prague and other centres in opposition to Vienna. Further realignments in the post-war period have continued in the increasing control of metropolitan centres, the weakening of competitors, the decline or disappearance of powers of subsidiary units such as the state or the province in Germany, Italy, the United States, and Canada.

Nourished in a friendly fashion by the state, the metropolitan region, without any formal sort of constitution and until recently without plan, has grown to be a potential rival of the state. Born of a mixture of physical and economical convenience it promises to take on a measure of cultural unity. Under the guidance of business men of large calibre, it is likely in America to develop a policy that leads at once to the conservation of regional interests and the advancement of general social welfare. Rooted as it is in the facts of nature rather than in political expedience, it promises to have vitality and endurance.[3]

Metropolitan centres in recently industrialized regions which are still important producers of raw materials are strengthened in part by new sources of power[4] and lower prices of raw materials in contrast with metropolitan centres in highly industrialized regions which have been weakened by higher prices of raw material incidental to protection and economic self-sufficiency, and particularly in relation to wheat. The trend of modern industrialism has been toward the more recently industrialized regions with new sources of power, and less exhausted natural resources, but this trend has been strengthened by cumulative forces in economic nationalism. The results have been evident in the increasing disparity between standards of living of urban and rural population – a disparity accentuated by the increasing strength of established metropolitan centres as opposed to more recently developed centres. The political strength of metropolitan areas implies support of the depressed classes in unemployment relief and the forging of political weapons to operate more effectively to advance metropolitan demands. Recent legislation in the United States tends to reflect the interests of large manufacturers through its emphasis on price fixing arrangements and in spite of determined efforts to relieve agriculture and the exposed industries. The struggle between miner and peasant which has characterized the industrial revolution becomes progressively more intense. Relief through the application of science and closer integration holds little promise, since scientific advance has been particularly important in the production of raw materials. Pressure of technological innovations particularly in large political units with free trade, a large market, and adequate resources tends to be restricted with the growth of nationalism to internal development and in turn leads to the development of internal resistances which take the form of regionalism. Internal pressure again supports attempts to restrict imports of goods produced by lower cost producing regions and reinforces the demand for higher tariff barriers. The results have been evident in the growth of regionalism in the United States, in the recent legislation of British Columbia and Alberta, and the unrest of the maritimes and threats of secession in western Australia. Failure to accept the St Lawrence waterway may be interpreted in part as a reflection of the increasing strength of New York and of Chicago as metropolitan areas and of the increasing difficulty of political organizations in breaking the grip of rigidities characteristic of rail transport.

The development of rigidities has strengthened the growth of nationalism and in turn of regionalism. Large political organizations adapted to periods of expansion become inefficient with the decline in importance of virgin natural resources, and metropolitan areas become increasingly significant. The position of the state in the more recently industrialized areas especially in relation to guarantees of loans to transportation implies ability to rely on general taxing power rather than direct returns and involves a lower interest rate, but this is offset by larger capital outlay than is involved by reliance on private enterprise. Guaranteed fixed interest rates on large capital outlay creates serious rigidities in an economy dependent on raw materials subject to wide fluctuations in price and yield. Governmental guarantees imply an intensification of nationalism on the part of the borrower and the lender. The post-war business cycle has been enormously influenced by the rigidities which have emerged with nationalism.[5] Rigidities of labour costs in Great Britain and Australia have paralleled rigidities of capital charges, railway rates, and interest levels in Canada. The importance of fixed capital equipment characteristic of modern industrialism and particularly in recent industrialized continental countries with emphasis on transportation, on hydro-electric power, and on the expansion of metropolitan centres has emphasized the increasing significance of overhead costs. Heavy fixed charges and overhead costs particularly in continental countries were responsible for policies favouring marked increase in the production of raw materials. These policies became more effective with the addition of motor power notably in the production of wheat[6] and of minerals. The impact of overhead costs in increased production of raw materials and declining prices has coincided with the extension of fixed charges. Increased specialization in production of raw materials and decline of self-sufficiency involved further extension of a monetary economy and additional burdens with the depression. The low price of raw materials necessitated additional support of the state in relief measures and in market control in various forms. Within the political units involved, metropolitan areas have gained with lower prices of raw materials and have been forced less quickly to adjust prices of finished products particularly with the coincident existence of demand from raw material producing regions which have gained in importance as a result of the depression[7] – gold mining in Northern Ontario. Prices of foodstuffs (wheat) have been held down further by the spread of nationalism in more highly industrialized regions and the trend toward self-sufficiency. As a result of the importance of overhead costs, in its effects on inelastic supply and especially joint supply, the price level has become an uncertain and far from delicate indicator in adjusting supply and demand. The state has been concerned either with attempts, as in Canada, to restrict production and to maintain railway rates, interest levels and other indications of rigidity in order to avoid the vicious circle of inflation on the ground of attracting capital, or with attempts to reduce interest rates and to eliminate rigidities rather than to restrict production as in the case of Australia. Canada with inadequate, badly coordinated machinery stands on the one hand in danger of being burned at the stake of natural resources and on the other hand of being boiled in the oil of unrestricted competition. It is only necessary to mention the writings of J.M. Clark and the pronounced swing of economic theory to problems of monopoly rather than competition to note the reflection of recent trends in economic development.

The implications of the increasing importance of overhead costs are significant to capital and to labour. Increasing intervention of the state may involve a marked improvement in efficiency and offset in part the stifling effects of rigidities. The pronounced swing from gold and the shift to a commodity basis for the value of the monetary unit is evidence even of the possibility of weakening rigidities! But the difficulties which have involved these developments, as well as the developments themselves, tend to restrict capital movements. Extensive borrowings of recently industrialized countries for purposes of transportation, urbanization, and the war have involved a long term burden of fixed charges at a relatively high level and marked increase in production of raw materials for export with consequent lower prices with which to meet heavy charges payable abroad. The effect of uncertain prices of raw materials has been evident in the freezing of short term credit shown in the insistence of the banks on governmental guarantees for the handling of wheat and the decline of speculative activity. Governmental control weakens speculative interest in commodities and securities. Internal control and the shift on the part of new countries from capital importing to capital exporting regions or the marked decline of capital movements between countries implies increasing internal absorption of surplus capital and with determined financial control may be followed by lower interest rates. Increased taxation as a result of the war either directly or by inflation has wiped out capital reserves and the capital supporting middle classes. The emergence of urban centres to metropolitan status assumes not only financial independence but with the demands of modern democracy the absorption of capital surplus in government services. Increasing complexity facilitates bureaucracy and dictatorship. Financial institutions such as insurance companies or investment trusts engaged as capital distributing organizations tend to become more concerned with internal investments which promise greater security. Skill and technique are moved more easily than commodities. Henry Ford prefers to establish plants in other countries rather than export automobiles from the United States.

Population like capital has declined in mobility. Democracy, nationalism, and regionalism are involved in vicious circles which imply lowering of the standard of living and protection in unemployment relief and restrictions on immigration. Restriction of immigration is followed by more rapid distribution of population within nations and in turn by the growth of metropolitan regions at the expense of regions producing goods for export. Increasing industrialization and urbanization implies higher standards of living for urban than for rural labour and inability to promote readjustments by back to the land movements or immigration of agricultural labour from European countries. The effects are evident in areas formerly supporting substantial migration such as Italy and the activity of the state in developing industrialism to absorb population and in areas such as Japan which has attempted to combine industrialism with population increase and an improved standard of living. In highly industrialized countries, restrictions on immigration and urbanization have been accompanied in the main by a decline in the birth rate. Lowering of the death rate and decline of the birth rate imply larger numbers of the population in advanced age levels and less flexibility. The war accentuated the contrast between upper and lower age limits and in the youth movements contributed to dictatorship.

The rapid strides of technological improvement which accompanied the war and the use of new sources of power have involved relative exhaustion of the last virgin natural resources. The disappearance of free land has coincided with the rise of nationalism.[8] The pressure of population on the land has been interpreted as a basic factor in the marked emigration of the last century and the discontent which has characterized the trend toward nationalism in older agricultural regions for example Ireland, Russia, Germany, and other countries.[9] Rise in cost of production, especially transportation, in the agriculture of new countries strengthens the position of agriculture in old countries. Consequently demands for more adequate domestic wheat supply become less difficult to meet and restricted imports involve less serious burdens on the general economy. Pressure of natural resources and sudden disturbances which accompanied new developments will tend to be less severe. The determining factors in recently industrialized countries have spent their force and flexibility has declined. The trust movement has solidified industrial development. Inventions are patented and placed in cold storage. The metal industries have been influenced to an increasing extent by the market for scrap and to a lesser extent by new ore production. The costs of protecting established industries based on more exhausted resources tend to decline. On the other hand demand tends to become saturated and stable. We have begun the process of abandoning rather than constructing railways, of restricting rather than increasing wheat production, of closing down pulp and paper plants rather than opening them. We avoid saturation in the automobile industry by new models. We protect obsolescence in the iron and steel industry by substantial tariffs. The enormous impetus of the war to iron and steel industries and the relatively light demands, of armaments following the peace treaty, and of railroads with the competition of motor transport, created a surplus of steel for the construction of skyscrapers, bridges, and motor cars. But the vital relationship of militarism to capitalism and the modern state which has become to a large extent a collector and distributor of funds for war purposes persists. The depression closed these new outlets for iron and steel products and has led to search for new possibilities which have been satisfied in part by minor wars, the manufacture of beverages following the repeal of prohibition, and the cleaning of slums. Armaments and housing supported by the state appear at the moment the more promising outlets and these strengthen nationalism and metropolitan growth. Russia remains as a possible safety valve for capitalism. The enormous increase in production of raw materials which followed the pressure of the iron and steel industries and new sources of power, whether it is fish or wheat has so disorganized the price structure that it restricts the possibility of financial support to further expansion of iron and steel.

Continental areas with emphasis on capitalistic types of development in terms of heavy equipment, mass production, and overhead costs have through mature metropolitan regions witnessed the emergence of rigidities. Maritime areas characterized by increasing density of population without relief by immigration and with access to new sources of power such as Italy and Japan have concentrated on types of industrialism which stress the importance of labour – for example the textile industry. Low prices of raw materials and accessibility to wheat and wool as in the case of Australia, and to products of the Atlantic basin in the case of the Panama Canal have supported strong competition with established textile industries in England and the United States. Retreat from the markets of Pacific areas by Atlantic basin industries accentuated competition between nations in this area and in turn substantial protective duties as in the case of Canada. Continental areas characterized by rigidities tend to be exposed to competition from maritime regions characterized by flexibility.

In conclusion, we have reached the stage in which natural resources in the form of free land have relatively disappeared. In continental countries the importance of fixed capital especially as to transportation, and in turn, of overhead costs, and the importance of new sources of power – oil and hydro-electric power – have involved a marked increase in the production of raw materials and a decline in price.[10] Cheap raw material, new sources of power, and the opening of the Panama Canal have hastened the development of the Pacific and particularly the industrial growth of Japan. Competition from cheap raw materials involved depreciation through obsolescence on a wide scale particularly in established industrial regions based on coal. The rigidity of the credit structure in the coal regions and depreciation through obsolescence has necessitated the introduction of protection and in turn of the complex machinery of economic nationalism. We are faced with the problems of overhead cost on a vast scale, prices have become less satisfactory as indicators, the solution depends on the introduction of economic intelligence which avoids monopoly and perfect competition – nationalism with intelligence – an intelligent dictator (e.g. civil service) preferred. Democracy in its attempt to force governments to meet the difficulties of an increasingly complex economic development has been met with the loss of leadership during the war and the rise of the youth movement, and has been forced to emphasize centralization of control and various forms of dictatorship.[11] Political duplicity has become an asset of first importance in democratic countries. The stakes are not the downfall of western civilization and the beginning of the new middle ages but a standard of living.

The implications of the struggle for Canada are serious.[12] Canada developed at the latest stages of modern industrialism and is among the first to feel the effects of the turn. The importance of the state, reliance on production of raw materials for export particularly wheat and the rigidities of continental development create serious problems of internal maladjustment as shown by quotas, bonuses, unemployment relief, the breakdown of provincial-federal relations, and the like. The sheltered metropolitan areas tend to impose burdens on regions exposed to world fluctuations. These problems have already contributed to a marked extension of governmental machinery and governmental machinery involves more machinery. It would appear probable as has been suggested that areas producing a surplus of raw material may be forced to extend the two price system by which world market price becomes a price of dumped goods and domestic prices are increased by protection.[13] The resulting disturbances can be prevented only by recourse to the new devices which have already made substantial advances. Exchange controls, quotas, dumping legislation, empire agreements, regional arrangements may endanger or offset the implications of the decline of the most favoured nation clause, Elliotism, economic autarchy, and the new weapons which have grown up to take the place of war, according to the wisdom with which they are designed. "The new internationalism is upon us."[14] No country stands to gain or lose more than Canada.

NOTES

1 C.J.H. Hayes, "Nationalism," *Encyclopedia of the Social Sciences* (New York, 1933), 11: 231–48. See also C.J.H. Hayes, *The Historical Evolution of Modern Nationalism* (New York, 1931), and *The State and Economic Life* (Paris, 1934).

2 "The pre-war development of extreme specialization has been not merely arrested but even reversed ... pre-war production was based upon steam power and the use of steam gave the coal-bearing regions of the world so great an advantage that the benefits of geographic concentration were obvious and of extreme importance. Post war production has been based largely, and to a rapidly increasing extent, upon oil and electricity which favor a wider distribution of industry not only within a country but also between different countries. Natural advantages tend to diminish in respect of a large group of industries: differences in real costs tend to be reduced. For this reason the penalty suffered from the pursuit of a policy of economic nationalism is not so severe as of old" (J.H. Jones, "A Policy for Sterling," *Lloyds Bank Monthly Review*, Feb. 1934). "Over an increasingly wide range of

industrial products and perhaps of agricultural products also, I become doubtful whether the economic cost of national self-sufficiency is great enough to outweigh the other advantages of gradually bringing the producer and the consumer within the ambit of the same national economic and financial organization ... As wealth increases, both primary and manufactured products play a smaller relative part in the national economy compared with houses, personal services and local amenities which are not the subject of international exchange; with the result that a moderate increase in the real cost of the former consequent on greater national self-sufficiency may cease to be of serious consequence when weighed in the balance against advantages of a different kind" (J.M. Keynes, "National Self-Sufficiency," *New Statesman and Nation*, 8 July 1933, 36–7). See also the *Yale Review* 22 (Summer 1933): 755–69, and E.A. Robinson in the *New Statesman and Nation*, 22 July 1933, 102, pointing out that the size of the national market has increased so greatly that for some products no considerable economy would be likely to be obtained from adding foreign markets and further increasing the scale of production. The trend has been toward exhaustion of economies of specialization; see also a criticism of N. Kaldor, ibid., 5 August 1933, 158.

3 N.S.B. Gras, "Regionalism and Nationalism," *Foreign Affairs* no. 3 (April 1929): 466. The problem of government following metropolitan expansion has become acute – for example, conflicts with suburban areas.

4 See R.D. McKenzie, *The Metropolitan Community* (New York, 1933), with reference to the effects of motor transportation.

5 See W.A. Mackintosh, "Gold and the Decline of Prices," *Papers and Proceedings of the Canadian Political Science Association* 3 (1931): 88–110.

6 See J.F. Booth, "Some Economic Effects of Mechanization of Canadian Agriculture with Particular Reference to the Spring Wheat Area," *Proceedings of the World's Grain Exhibition and Conference* (Regina, 1933); A. Stewart, "The Economy of Machine Production in Agriculture," *Essays on Canadian Problems*, Royal Bank of Canada Essay Competition 1930–31, vol. 4 (Montreal, 1931).

7 E.A. Forsey, "Equality of Sacrifice," *Canadian Forum*, Nov. 1933.

8 See C.R. Fay, "Adam Smith and the Doctrinal Defeat of the Mercantile System," *Quarterly Journal of Economics* 48, no. 2 (Feb. 1934): 304–16.

9 Isaiah Bowman, *The New World* (London, 1929).

10 M.T. Copeland, *Raw Material Prices and Business Conditions*, Business Research Studies, no. 2 (Cambridge, Mass., 1933).

11 J. Coatman, "Economic Nationalism and International Relations," *Political Quarterly* 4, no. 4 (October–December 1933): 561–74.

12 See "Canadian Trade Policy in a World of Economic Nationalism," *Queen's Quarterly* 41, no. 1 (Spring 1934): 81–98.
13 See also C. Schrecker, "The Growth of Economic Nationalism and its International Consequences," *International Affairs* 13, no. 2 (March–April 1934): 208–25.
14 C. Foreman, *The New Internationalism* (New York, 1934).

CHAPTER FOURTEEN

The Canadian Economy and the Depression

The papers in this volume are concerned with the immediate problems of the depression in Canada, but they are also intended to suggest the importance of problems peculiar to the secular trend which have accentuated the decline characteristic of the business cycle. The type of expansion which has characterized this century, namely, railroad construction and the opening of the West, the installation of hydro-electric power and pulp and paper plants, the development of mines and the construction of roads and hotels which have accompanied the increasing use of motor transport, will very materially decline. While the readjustment in economic life which this decline implies is taking place, the markets for our products have been narrowed partly as a result of competition from similar activity in other countries. The effects have been evident in the extension of defences such as are involved in economic nationalism which has intensified the depression. We are faced with the far-reaching results of the technological drift of modern industrialism. The success of measures designed to solve the problems of the depression is necessarily determined by their relation to problems of the secular trend. An analysis of the factors peculiar to a long-run development is essential to an understanding of immediate difficulties. ...

We may accept the losses incidental to economic nationalism as inevitable and beyond relief, or we may attempt to divert the drift of international development along lines which involve the least

---

From *The Canadian Economy and Its Problems*, ed. H.A. Innis and A.F.W. Plumptre (Ottawa, 1934), 3–24; edited to remove material that appears in chapter 13, "Economic Nationalism."

possible difficulty; but assuming the most favourable results from such a policy we are forced to consider the possibility of internal readjustment in the interests of a more efficient economy and of the relief of human misery. The dangers of introducing badly designed machinery in a country susceptible to the slightest ground-swell of international disturbance are as obvious as the necessity of introducing machinery correctly designed. The policy of economic nationalism which attempts to create a self-sufficient economy in order to obtain stability and security at the expense of the production of goods has grave consequences for an economy which rides on the crest of modern industrialism and has been concerned with the demands of an international market. Industrialism has provided an abundance of goods but not the first luxury of security.

We lack vital information on which to base prospective policies to meet this situation. The emphasis on speculative discussion as to the probable effects of certain proposals, the reliance on works dealing with the economics of countries other than Canada, for example Australia, and the absence of finality are indications of our weakness. The causes of the weak position of the social sciences in Canada are varied and numerous, but in part they are linked to the phenomenal expansion which has characterized Canadian development during this century and which has absorbed the energies of a small population. The effects have been evident in the "solutions" which have been proposed during the present depression and in the phenomena which are described as election campaigns. On the other hand a demand for a systematic and sympathetic understanding of Canadian problems has become increasingly urgent during the depression.

The outstanding characteristics of Canadian problems have been clearly outlined, but the details are relatively obscure and the obscurity makes prescription difficult. The importance of a relatively small group of raw materials and in particular of wheat in Canadian income is accentuated by dependence of these raw materials on enormous investments of capital which imply problems of overhead costs and of fixed charges. The pressure of overhead costs involved in transcontinental railway lines and capital equipment essential to the handling of wheat[1] is evident in immigration policies, construction of branch lines as feeders, and intense competition between the railways. Additional capital equipment introduced as a result of overhead costs implies additional overhead costs and more intense competition. Finally, the costs of abandoning capital equipment, assuming the vicious circle of expansion to have exhausted itself, increase overhead costs. Meanwhile, in spite of a decline in price and particularly with a slight decline in price which accompanies speculative activity in a boom period, production of the raw material is increased with lower costs of transportation accompanying the enormous advantages of railroads[2] and particularly with the introduction of new sources of power such as gasoline. The economics of overhead costs introduces a serious disturbing factor in the automatic adjustments incidental to changes in price. The results are evident in a sharp decline in prices during a period of depression, in the accumulation of debts, in the passing of dividends by the Canadian Pacific Railway, in Canadian National deficits, in election turnovers, in relief measures, in letters to editors, in a marked reduction in standards of living, and in a slow readjustment such as is involved in the migration of population, the production of hogs and livestock, empire agreements, and wheat agreements. The effects are far reaching. It might be expected that a decline in the price of wheat would involve reduced costs of living in the urban industrial centres so far as bread is concerned but again overhead costs and fixed charges are implied in the enormous capital investment peculiar to the flour milling[3] and bread baking industries and in the emergence of monopoly control, with the result that the price of bread has declined very slightly during the depression. In competitive industries overhead costs stimulate production whereas in industries with monopoly possibilities the drive is toward restriction and control. The vicious effects of overhead costs on production have been checked in part by industries that have evaded the Combines Investigation Act, with serious results for competitive industries such as farming which have been at a disadvantage, not to forget the pools.

The newsprint industry again implies enormous capital equipment in mills and power plants, heavy fixed charges, and serious problems of overhead costs. A vast range of accessible raw materials in spruce forests and available power sites, an immediate large market, ample financial resources, and government policy with embargoes on exports of pulpwood from Crown lands caused rapid expansion in the production of newsprint. The heavy initial outlay and important overhead costs necessitated continuous operation in spite of a decline in price and during the depression involved further attempts to increase production and further decline in price. The results have been evident in bankruptcy and receiverships, financial amalgamations, abandoned mills and towns with wholesale migration of labour and futile attempts to check the downward spiral by price agreements. But whereas in the case of agriculture the impact tended to fall with greatest severity on the farmer, in the pulp and paper industry it tended to fall on the security holder.

The mineral industry, with particular reference to gold and the base metals, copper, lead, zinc, and nickel, is characterized similarly by heavy capital equipment and large overhead costs. Relatively low costs of production with freshly opened ore bodies and improved methods of extraction contribute to the general effects of overhead costs in maintaining production in spite of a decline in prices. In the production of gold, low prices of supplies characteristic of the depression have been responsible for marked expansion of activity. The effects have been evident in the closing down of weak marginal mines, reduction of earnings, and the weakening of the position of capital and labour, but the character of ore reserves has served as a cushion to prevent the more drastic effects shown in wheat production and newsprint.

Minerals and newsprint are affected not only directly by overhead costs but also indirectly through the overwhelming importance of hydro-electric power. A conspicuous determining factor as to the extent and character of power sites is the geographic background. The relative scarcity of suitable power sites and the extremely heavy initial cost of installation result in a powerful thrust toward utilization to capacity of power production on the part of predominant consumers such as the mining and newsprint industries. The character of price arrangements which favour the large consumers, and long-term contracts for power indicate the type of pressure applied.

The problem of overhead costs incidental to the production of staple products has been rendered more acute by the cyclical trend. Plants of the most recent design, installed during the boom period, came into production during the depression. The Welland Canal, the Hudson Bay Railway, the Abitibi Canyon power project, and smelters at Noranda and Flin Flon illustrate the general development.[4] Mining activity at Bear Lake has expanded throughout the depression. Moreover, the rapidity and unpredictability of development on a continental scale has seriously reduced the value of the price mechanism as an effective means of adjusting supply to demand.

The basic position of overhead costs in the production of a small group of important staple commodities has involved the Canadian economy in a nose dive during the depression which has cut income in half. Each staple has its own peculiar developments and its peculiar relations with other staples. The gold mining industry, for example, has gained from the low price of raw materials and has tended to serve as a cushion by contributions to railroad earnings and increasing demand for supplies. The effects of the depression are determined in part by the character of competition from other producing areas. More effectively organized economies become stronger competitors and can be met in part by similar effective organization which implies an elimination of inequities and an adjustment of the burden in relation to the whole economy and the staple industries of the economy. Under conditions of production which involve highly specialized equipment such as railways, canals, and elevators for handling wheat, or newsprint mills, mining equipment, and hydro-electric plants, output to capacity represents the most efficient basis. With mature development, capacity is based largely on relatively inelastic limiting geographic factors such as power sites, ore bodies, or areas of land with a suitable climate. The effectiveness of the drive of overhead costs toward that point in competition with other areas will imply concentration on the most effective unit within each basic industry and in turn very serious losses to less effective units in terms of owners of farms or pulp and paper mills, or of farmers, capitalists, and labourers. Attempts to avoid the consequent maladjustment have been evident in the newsprint industry, the wheat pools and wheat agreements, the arbitration board of the railroads, amalgamation of banks, and evasion of the Combines Act. The peculiar character of the Canadian economy with its emphasis on overhead costs has been largely responsible for a persistent trend toward unity. Success has been haphazard and combinations in one field have caused increased severity of competition in others. The essential problem in the Canadian economy is to introduce limits to the vicious spiral. Mitigation of severe costs to exposed groups by enhancing the burden of sheltered groups and reduction of the burden to the whole economy to a minimum are among the tasks involved.

The difficulties of bringing the economy out of a nose dive are very great. Panic generally prevails and the most courageous pilots with no experience with such disasters can do little more than apply nostrums used in other economies and possibly do more harm than good. Royal commissions, investigating committees, and the persistent search for scapegoats break out in a burning rash on the body politic. The political quack is ever alert to capitalize public fears.

It will be apparent that no single remedy can be recommended. Adjustment by arbitration or the scaling down of debts, which has already gone far, the application of direct control over individual industries, and monetary policy have been discussed and their limitations suggested. Dependence on exports and on capital borrowed abroad implies a widely fluctuating income beyond control of domestic policies. Exports are sold in competition with products produced under similar conditions of overhead costs on a world market. Important costs of production such as transportation are beyond control because of competition with the United States. The Canadian railway rate structure is based, as a result of geographic competition, on the American rate structure. Proximity to the United States places a severe handicap on control of capital movements. The character of our development results in rigidities such as those governing ownership. Assuming these limitations it is obvious that mechanism designed to remove inequities must be flexible and capable of rapid adjustment in response to economic changes in the United States and Great Britain and in other parts of the world. Such flexibility assumes a strong and unified control over income and expenditure. It assumes an appreciation of the economy of Canada as a whole sufficiently strong to support unified control. These considerations limit the importance of any single institution such as a central bank or a loan council. Controls of wages, agricultural returns, corporation finance, monetary policy, and public finance[5] must be linked together to provide an equitable adjustment of burdens.

The effects of reliance on a single method of control have been evident during the depression in the dominance of the tariff as a means of providing unemployment relief, protection, and control of exchange. The results have been evident in the innumerable devices which it has been necessary to introduce as a means of stopping leaks. Reliance on monetary policy would have had similar results. Extensive manipulation of monetary policy is particularly dangerous under conditions which involve large overhead costs and has the effect of pouring oil on fire. The close alignment of our competitive price structure with the United States (e.g., railway rates) would imply disturbances throughout the economy. We have built up in Canada in competition with the United States a delicately balanced economy which has more than once crashed through ill-designed machinery. Devices must be used with a view to creating the least possible disturbance and must involve important supplementary controls. Taxation machinery is most obvious and most important in achieving redistribution of income but difficulties of development necessitate emphasis on measures which are preventative and which will contribute toward equality of income.

The depression has illustrated the inevitable introduction of more elaborate machinery. The constitutional problem threatens to become a barrier of major difficulty and revision of the British North America Act an urgent task. Failing the introduction of more responsive machinery we are left with the alternative of the cumulative difficulties of the present depression with disaster breeding disaster. We need more information designed to throw light on specific problems and in turn to reinforce the demand for co-ordination of controls in more effective fashion than can be achieved under the cabinet system.

The specific character of the Canadian economy demands specific types of control. General remedial measures applied to the economy as a whole are limited because of the varying characteristics of basic elements of the economy. Measure suited to the improvement of conditions in western agriculture will tend to be advantageous to Canada as a whole but the effect of those measures on other staple products such as newsprint and minerals must be taken into account. Adequate control implies adaptation not only to the demands of the economy as a whole but also to the specific interests of each of a small group of basic commodities. The methods adopted to check the effects of overhead costs or to bring industry out of the nose dive of a depression will vary with conditions in each industry. Those who object to proposals for control must present the case for an economy responsible for the present unfortunate conditions. They will find the farmer, the labourer, and the capitalist difficult to convince. On the other hand the state of the social sciences will not support the arguments of those who favour the introduction of strait jackets.

NOTES

1 Professor V.W. Bladen prefers the terms rents and quasi-rents in his article in emphasizing the specific and specialized character of Canadian equipment: "The Theory of Cost in an Economy Based on the Production of Staples: Canada and Wheat," *The Canadian Economy and Its Problems.*

2 See W.A. Mackintosh, *Prairie Settlement: The Geographical Setting* (Toronto, 1934), 56.

3 A.C. Oakhurst, "The Staff of Life Supports the Millers," *Canadian Forum,* June 1933.

4 See H.A. Innis, "Economic Recovery in Canada in 1933," *Commerce Journal,* Feb. 1934 (mimeograph; publication of the Commerce Club of the University of Toronto).

5 See "A Submission on Dominion-Provincial Relations and the Fiscal Disabilities of Nova Scotia within the Canadian Federation," Royal Commission of Economic Enquiry (Nova Scotia), 1934.

CHAPTER FIFTEEN

Some Problems of Adjustment in Canada

In the volumes reviewed in the October number of this *Journal*,[1] Professor W.A. Mackintosh raises problems of fundamental importance to the Canadian economy which warrant emphasis and comment. He expresses the hope that the whole series of studies "will make some contribution toward the development of economic and social planning in a field where the costs of planless development are peculiarly heavy." "The need for the systematic planning and control of settlements, if heavy financial and human costs are to be avoided, is likely to be greater in the future than it has been in the past." The problems of planning are suggested in the concluding sentence of Volume IV. "In both public and private finance this region adapts itself to the most important economic characteristic; its highly variable income." And again, "The combination of highly fluctuating gross incomes with relatively fixed expenses lies at the centre of the economic problems of the prairie regions" – and he might have added of Canada. He has placed before Canadian economists the dilemma of the Canadian economy in the conflict between variability and systematic planning.

The volumes proceed from a discussion of the broad geographical background of the prairie provinces and long-run price changes in relation to the secular trend in the opening of the West, to short-run fluctuations with such disturbances as the World War, and to a detailed analysis of immediate problems. The studies included in Volume IV are concerned chiefly with statistical material for the years ending in 1931.

From *Journal of Political Economy* 43 (1935): 800–7; first appeared as "Notes on Problems of Adjustment in Canada."

Stress is laid on the inadequacy of institutions to equalize burdens and gains as between fringe areas and mature centres:

> The districts which required most assistance because education placed on them the heaviest comparative burden, received the smallest grants from the province. The weight of providing necessary community service tends to become heavier as the power to carry the load declines. During the decade as a whole the burden of taxation has rested more heavily on the pioneer than on the established communities. In truth the latter have had at their command more excellent and various local government services than were available to the other municipalities and at less cost.

The difficulty of developing more efficient machinery in relation to variability, particularly in the fringe areas, is enhanced by the uncertainty of objectives. Social costs – "In too many instances taxes, interest or mortgages, and other obligations have so burdened the farmer as to place the health and happiness of his family in jeopardy" – are difficult to balance against pecuniary costs; and "however desirable the extension of social services, including the health program may be, they should be kept strictly within the limits of the taxpaying capacity of the people."

The continuation of the depression and the drought years has enhanced the difficulties of immediate adjustment. Decline in wheat prices and relatively inelastic support from natural resources shown in retreat from drought areas and in advance in the park-belt areas emphasize rigidities shown in transportation costs and debt charges. "By 1932 the decline of wheat prices had been so great that in some cases half of the Liverpool price of wheat was absorbed in tonnage charges" – without allowing for the effects of the tariff and transportation on costs of manufactured products and on costs of production. The results have been evident in a wide range of expedients including relief, debt adjustment, and substantial governmental support of the wheat market; and of proposed expedients including lower tariffs, amalgamation of the railways, and social credit. The problem is not only one of adjustment between fringe areas and mature centres within the prairie provinces, but also between the prairie provinces and other parts of Canada. The problems of planning in Canadian federalism are extremely complex and alternatives or expedients are difficult to discover.

The problem has been raised in other regions such as British Columbia and the maritime provinces in the form of demands for compensation for burdens imposed by the tariff[2] and for readjustment of the subsidies. While no formula can probably be devised which will avoid expedients, nevertheless basic considerations are essential to any approach to the subject. Subsidy arrangements are conceded as unsatisfactory, partly because of their rigid character. Not only has it been constantly necessary to struggle for, and to grant, revision, but numerous shifts have been necessary and have taken the form of additions to capital equipment such as railways, ports, and canals, statutory reductions in railway rates such as the Manitoba rate agreement, the Crows Nest Pass rate agreement, the British Columbia rate agreement, the maritime freight-rates act, and concessions of various sorts. Major adjustments as to natural resources of the provinces have been completed within the last year and the ground has been cleared for a general overhauling of the problem.

Enormous expenditures on the part of the government in improvement of navigation, particularly on the St Lawrence River, the transcontinental railways (the Canadian National, besides assistance to the Canadian Pacific) and in port facilities, and the relative rigidity of interest rates on government borrowing to secure this equipment, especially with large amounts held abroad, implies inability to meet these changes directly from earnings and the necessity of relying on payments from revenues obtained chiefly from customs. The effect of the tariff has been partly to provide revenues to meet these charges and partly to prevent imports, and in turn to force areas most distant from the industrial centres of the St Lawrence region to purchase from that region and to pay the freight on the manufactured goods involved. In so far as the tariff is not successful in keeping out goods and the railways are not used, customs are collected to meet the loss involved in not hauling the goods. The burden of transportation charges, either direct as railway rates, or indirect through the tariff, tends to be thrown on the more distant regions. These regions are, in the main, producers of raw materials, chiefly for export, and the weight of the burden varies with fluctuations in prices and in yield and with other factors.

The burden tends to fall more severely on an old region with relatively exhausted raw materials than on a new region with abundant and rich natural resources. A sudden improvement in transportation such as the Panama Canal may lower costs and consequently reduce the burden. An upward swing of the business cycle will tend to alleviate its severity, particularly in a region where lumbering is important. The character of the commodity produced and the character of economy involved will affect the weight of the burden. It follows that mathematical calculations as to the weight of the tariff, although suggestive, are of limited value and that adjustments should be made annually rather than over a long period of time.

Devices for achieving adjustments are limited in scope. Statutory reduction of railway rates has been a favourite device, but it involved rigidities. Statutory rates generally applicable to raw materials tend to force railways to rely on the higher rates of manufactured products and in turn on the tariff. Moreover, rates are compelled, to an important extent, to meet competition from American lines and this compulsion restricts not only Canadian manipulation of rates, but other possible lines of policy. Control over exchange rates involving wide variation between prices of Canadian and American funds creates difficulties in Canadian railway finance. Again, transcontinental railway systems become unwieldy and rate adjustments and railway policy tend to be developed in relation to long-haul traffic. These factors necessitate emphasis on the principle of charging what the traffic will bear, or increasing rates in non-competitive areas to meet losses in competitive areas. The advantages of water competition are evident in the growth of industrialism; and the development of truck competition again involves losses to the railways in heavy-traffic areas and accentuates reliance on higher rates in non-competitive raw material producing areas. Lowering of the tariff and further statutory reduction of rates in non-competitive areas which are generally raw material producing areas would in part solve the problem, particularly if these measures increased the revenue of the railroads through increased traffic.

Increased traffic in the crucial wheat-producing regions of the prairie provinces is dependent on the weather. A marked increase in volume of traffic following a good harvest – assuming a policy on the part of the government favourable to export – enormously increases gross earnings with a smaller proportional increase in expenses; and, conversely, a bad crop is followed by a marked decrease in volume and by a marked decline in receipts with a smaller decline in expenses. The accentuated character of depression and recovery incidental to the problem of overhead costs is reflected alternately in reduced or expanded earnings of the railways or in the passing or payment of dividends on the Canadian Pacific and the contraction or increase of deficits in the Canadian National. In the former case shareholders bear part of the loss and in the latter chiefly those who are compelled to bear the burden of the tariff, depending on the proportion of customs revenue going to the railway. Depression tends to accentuate the burden of those least able to bear it. Control over railway finance may, of course, reduce the burden, but the possibilities of such reductions are limited.

The difficulties involved in restricting crop acreage and volume of production are apparent. The relative inelasticity of railway rates[3] during a period of depression is accompanied by difficulties of shifting labour to alternative occupations or to new land, in spite of the terrific pressure.[4]

These circumstances provide the background for attempts to provide assistance to farmers in creditor-arrangement acts and direct relief for the more exposed groups of farmers, and bonuses on wheat and pegging of wheat prices of particular interest to less exposed groups. Again the losses tend to fall on those particularly exposed to the burden of the tariff. A policy of holding wheat, while it may reduce overhead costs incidental to elevators, leaves the railroads and transportation generally subject to fluctuations in traffic and earnings and thereby involves the government not only in the direct losses on wheat but also in indirect losses on transportation. Again, a policy of protection accentuates the necessity for these devices but they may flatten out the decline to the advantage of farmers in the acute stages of depression, even though the farmer pays for it from his own pocket.

As a result of these limitations on public action widespread relief tends to wait upon developments in other countries, particularly the United States. Recent monetary adjustments in the United States have been accompanied by material improvement in Canada but the Canadian economy, with its relative inelasticity, tends to suffer as a result of a lag in American adjustment. British policy unfortunately was too far in advance of American policy, with the result that Canada was pulled between low prices in the British market and heavy interest charges on loans to the United States.

The difficulties of Western Canada contributed to and were accompanied by difficulties of a similar but divergent character in the maritime areas of the Atlantic and the Pacific, depending in part on the character of the commodities involved and on the geographic background. In British Columbia[5] high transportation costs from the industrial areas of the St Lawrence have been offset partly by lower statutory rates, by abundant natural resources in base metal and gold mining, forests, and fishing, and by the effects of the Panama Canal shown in imports, and in increasing exports of wheat from Alberta. But heavy transcontinental transportation costs, except in so far as the railroads are forced to meet water competition, tend to stress coastal rather than internal development and to warp the economic life of the area into specialization in raw materials, particularly lumber.[6] Aside from the interrelations between British Columbia and the prairie provinces and the long-run effects of the burdens of protection, short-run fluctuations as shown in the present depression have peculiar effects on the coastal region. Lumber is particularly susceptible to price fluctuations but losses have been offset by the low cost and accessibility of raw materials. Metal mining (lead and zinc) has had the advantage of abundant raw material and the region covered has been assisted by heavy investments of capital in by-product industries such as fertilizers, and by the direct interest of a transcontinental railway. Gold mining has responded to the influence of the depression and to monetary policy. Agricultural exports, especially apples, have been handicapped by low prices and high costs of supplies. The fishing industry has been similarly burdened. In contrast to the effects of the depression, particularly in the coastal region with its severe problems of topography, heavy outlays of government expenditure on such items as bridges, roads, and railroads have involved fixed charges, deficits, lower standards of living, and unemployment.

The maritime provinces, with their dependence on lumbering, fishing, and agriculture, have been similarly exposed to sharp declines in export prices, have had less of the cushion of natural resources on which to rely, and have been directly affected by competition from commodities brought in from relatively unexploited areas on the Pacific Coast through the Panama Canal. Although nearer to the European market, they have been forced to meet more intense competition. Coal mining has gained from protection and subventions, but, as in the case of British Columbia and the prairie provinces, these concessions and statutory rates tend to be paid for by the regions concerned or/and at the expense of other regions similarly exposed.

The effects of the distribution of the burden of the fall in prices of raw materials have been evident in turn in the central provinces. Sheltered industries have been unable to dispose of their products and unemployment has been a result. The bankruptcy of municipalities has been conspicuous in this region as in other regions. Relief has perhaps been more generous and decline in the standard of living less conspicuous. But weaker groups have suffered here as elsewhere. The pulp and paper industry has suffered drastic capital reorganization. Gold mining has increased even more than in British Columbia. The advantages of the St Lawrence region in cheap water transportation with an outlet for its own agricultural products and for those of the prairie provinces, with lower rates by rail, water, and motor truck as a result of competition, with cheap supplies of hydroelectric power, with important resources of mineral wealth, particularly nickel and gold, have been evident in a highly integrated economy with relatively high population density, with political power, and with possibilities of rapid shiftability of resources enabling the region to take advantage of low prices of raw materials in other parts of Canada, to break down possible industrial development of such regions which threaten competition, and to capitalize on advantages available in export markets, as, for example, through the Empire trade agreements.

A policy of protection increases the advantages of the St Lawrence region by facilitating the establishment of additional industries and contributing to further integration. Manufactured products demanded by raw-material-producing regions are produced at higher costs and carried at high rates over long hauls. Railway rate policy favourable to development of long-haul traffic further weakens the industrial possibilities of raw-material-producing areas. The relative unshiftability of resources in raw-material-producing regions and consequent specialization, the emphasis on capital equipment in production of raw materials, subject to relatively inelastic demand, and possibilities of monopoly prices, slow up the adjustment of prices between raw materials for export and prices of manufactured goods for the sheltered market. Regions with advantages of natural resources, soil, climate, and the like, gain from the fact that industries are compelled to concentrate, to an increasing extent, in more efficient areas or firms. The contraction weakens the position of more marginal areas or firms and compels them to shift the burden particularly to labour in lower wages or unemployment. Credit difficulties imply bankruptcy or involve increases in government assistance. For example, automobiles produced in the St Lawrence region and sold at higher prices than in adjoining areas in the United States are used in smaller numbers than they might be in the raw-material-producing regions, with the result that financial problems of roadbuilding become more acute, expenditures of provincial government and municipalities are increased, and taxes on automobiles and gasoline are higher. Attempts to build up Canadian industries in relation to the demands of raw-material-producing regions tend to raise costs not only directly but also indirectly, by providing less efficient equipment than could be obtained abroad.

The impact of this background on the fundamental financial principle of confederation is evident in the contraction of the value of natural resources on which provincial finance was based. "At Confederation it was decided to make of the natural resources the cornerstone of provincial finance." The financial basis of the provinces is weakened by reduction of exploitable natural resources and by additions to their burdens. The regional problem indicated by

Professor Mackintosh has been accentuated, since not only the raw-material-producing regions are affected, but also the municipalities or subregions. Taxation rests with greater weight "on the pioneer than on the established communities" and the burden is accentuated during a period of depression with relative exhaustion of resources.

The limited possibilities of tariff reduction as a solution to these problems consequent upon the extent of fixed charges, and the inevitable significance of government ownership of railways, canals, and ports necessitates consideration of other alternatives.[7] Expediency has necessitated contributions of relief from the federal government and assistance in various forms to the provinces. Suggestions that costs of social services should be transferred to the dominion neglect the complexity of the problem and probably would involve greater assistance to the provinces of the industrialized area than the raw-material-producing regions. It is of first importance that continued thorough investigation should be made by such bodies as economic councils in the separate provinces and the economic council of the Dominion. The character of the problem shifts in each region with phases of the business cycle and necessitates constant readjustment of provincial and federal relations. Increasing dependence on sources of revenue other than the tariff, such as the income tax, is inevitable. The depression has shown clearly the haphazard character of existing machinery and the necessity for continued application of economic intelligence. The development of new machinery must be such as will take into account problems of the Canadian economy as a whole and will rapidly adjust burdens and returns through the economy in relation not only to pecuniary but also to social costs. In some such way the dilemma propounded by Professor Mackintosh may be attacked.

NOTES

1 W.A. Mackintosh, *Prairie Settlement: The Geographical Setting* (Toronto, 1934); W.A. Mackintosh et al., *Economic Problems of the Prairie Provinces* (Toronto, 1935).

2 See *Canadian Journal of Economics and Political Science* 1 (August 1935), passim.

3 Proposals to reduce railway costs by amalgamation have been widely urged. These tend to neglect the problem of overhead costs and to apply a short run pecuniary test calculated on an insufficient accounting basis. For example, proposed abandonment of branch lines tends

to neglect the contribution of traffic by branch lines to the main lines and in turn the reduction of overhead costs on the main line, and also the continued debt charge of the branch line plus the cost of abandoning it (minus the salvage). Moreover it neglects the unpaid costs to settlers left stranded by abandonment of the line.

4 See V.W. Bladen, "The Theory of Cost in an Economy Based on the Production of Staples," *Canadian Economy and Its Problems* (Toronto, 1934), 135–43; also W.B. Hurd and J.C. Cameron, "Population Movements in Canada, 1921–31," *Canadian Journal of Economics and Political Science* 1 (May 1935); also *Proceedings of the Canadian Political Science Association,* 1934, 220–37.

5 See W.A. Carrothers, "The Barter Terms of Trade between British Columbia and Ontario and Quebec, 1935," *Canadian Journal of Economics and Political Science* 1 (Nov. 1935).

6 Violation of the long- and short-haul clause accentuates these effects.

7 See *Complementary Report of the Royal Commission of Provincial Economic Enquiry* (Halifax, 1934), 133 ff.

CHAPTER SIXTEEN

"For the People": The Intellectual State of Canada

A REVIEW[1]

That "insidious and crafty animal vulgarly called a statesman or politician" – the description is Adam Smith's – knows the necessity of appearing intellectual if he is to capture votes. This fact has already been noticed in the *Quarterly* (for April 1934) in a review of lectures delivered to political summer schools. As the federal election approached, this necessity became more urgent, and an appeal to books was sustained. Commenting in parliament on Mr Bennett's program as outlined in the radio-broadcast of January (1935), Mr King retaliated by a recital of his own long and sustained activity in the interests of social legislation, and indicated that he had even written a book on the subject. Members of the government and the press tried to turn this fact to his disadvantage by implying that anyone who had written a book was discredited from further participation in governmental activities (even the Liberals were worried); but Mr Bennett, unwilling to join the attempt to discredit intellectual interest as evinced in books, stated that he himself had read, and been influenced by, Mr Bready's on *Lord Shaftesbury*.

We know, however, that Mr Bennett was directly concerned with, and far more deeply influenced by, the production of a book which was destined to have far-reaching effects on political life in Canada, namely, the *Report of the Royal Commission on Price Spreads*. Even more than Mr Bennett, Mr Stevens had been concerned with the initiation of the work, with its progress, and with the publicity involved.

From *University of Toronto Quarterly* 5 (1936): 278–87; first appeared as "For the People."

The volume had but slight interest for the general public, and the ensuing legislation came too late to be of political assistance; but the significance of extensive publicity over a long period was sufficient to evoke and support Mr Bennett's own program, to warrant general agreement with the legislation on the part of Mr King, to lead Mr Stevens to form an additional party, to encourage a provincial party led by Mr Aberhart, to strengthen the Communist party, and to steal the scant clothing of the loosely-knit organization associated with Mr Woodsworth. No bolder attempt than the price-spreads investigation has ever been made to repair the political damage of a sustained depression.

The intense political activity which characterized the federal election has been an inevitable result of the depression. But an older and very interesting political document from an intellectual point of view (though of least political effectiveness, as seen in the haste and determination with which all parties dissociated themselves from it), the *Communist Manifesto,* has an illuminating comment: "In every historical epoch, the prevailing mode of economic production and exchange, and the social organization necessarily following from it, form the basis upon which it is built up and from which alone can be explained the political and intellectual history of that epoch." Certainly much light is thrown on the intellectual state of Canada by some of the volumes under review.

A re-reading of Mr King's book and a survey of his work since its publication suggest a consistency in outlook which is impressive. A student of the social sciences with academic distinction, he has been actively engaged in the field of social legislation since the late nineties. His contributions include the establishment of the Department of Labour, his work as deputy minister and as minister, his development of technique in conciliation in the United States, and the legislation attributable to him as prime minister. These are a testimony to industry and administrative capacity of a high order. His record of work in the federal field is difficult to match. It has coincided almost exactly with the period of expansion which began in the latter years of the nineteenth century and ended in 1929. His long training in parliament and in the political arena has given him a mastery of parliamentary strategy and of political tactics. Against almost overwhelming odds he dominated the decade of the twenties. Party irregularities, conflict with old-line party-leaders and regional representatives, with its inevitable accompaniment of weak appointments, were probably a result of circumstances rather than of personal defects which have been attributed to academic exclusiveness. His political philosophy, outlined in his *Industry and Hu-*

manity, has striking similarities to that of the Price-spreads Report and *Social Planning for Canada*, and dissimilarities to that of the members of his own party who subscribe to *laissez-faire*. But, as might be expected, there is in his book little appreciation of economic complexities which have, for the most part, emerged in a period of depression coinciding with a relative decline of natural resources. He belongs to an old and important school of economics, whose precepts Canadians can never neglect, and not to the new school faced with modern complexities.

Mr Bennett has emerged from a similar background in time, but his training in the Maritimes, and his concern with business, law, and politics, in the rough school of Western Canada, have strengthened his forcefulness and accentuated his courage and decisiveness. He vigorously met the problems of the depression as they arose, and commanded – or should have commanded – universal admiration and respect. His dominating personality, which contrasted with the weakness of his cabinet, enabled him to procure the ablest men available for the numerous commissions and boards which were a feature of his *régime*. The haste with which much of the work was done, the urgent character of the political situation, and the weak position of the social sciences in Canada (with consequent reliance on men brought in from outside), will necessitate material revision. But the years of Mr Bennett's *régime* will stand out as the turning point of the century in the history of Canadian legislation. As would be expected, the outstanding contribution to the economic literature of the depression in Canada is to be found in the Price-spreads Report. But even here the enormous body of evidence, together with political exigences, prevented an elaborate and thorough analysis of economic problems in Canada during a depression. Mr Bennett's reference to Lord Shaftesbury suggests a broader philosophy of evangelical bourgeois meliorism, which Halévy, Clapham, and others regard as a basic factor in the social legislation of the nineteenth century, but even this was probably incidental to his task of meeting the problem of the moment. The prestige, wealth, and discipline of the Conservative party provided strong support to his herculean efforts, but even this support has shown signs of strain. An immediate task of the party is to repair the damages by reorganization and by the encouragement of younger men.

Mr Stevens, as a product of the Pacific frontier and the political instability of that area, has found discipline irritating. Throughout his career industry and initiative have carried him through numerous investigations and have enabled him to capture ground which other characteristics have prevented him from holding and consolidating. Nevertheless, as the centre of interest in the last two sessions of parliament, as a man with intimate knowledge of the problems he attacks, and with evangelical fervour and executive capacity, Mr Stevens succeeded in developing an organization on a national scale, supported by obvious wealth and influence and votes.

Mr Aberhart worked with greater effectiveness in a narrower region and an environment better adapted to new parties. This region, by virtue of location, has been subjected to sharp fluctuations in income, has felt more acutely the problems of freight rates, debts, and drought, and has been less subject to the steadying effects of strong metropolitan growth. It deserted the old parties in the depression after the War, and it substituted loyalty to individuals for loyalty to parties. Consequent instability followed the declining influence of Henry Wise Wood through age, and of other leaders through attacks on personal conduct. Individuals who have broken relations with parties are compelled to rely on new policies, and the United Farmers of Alberta flirted in turn with left-wing Labour elements, and with monetary schools. Mr Aberhart emerged as an individual who capitalized the radio and built up religious enthusiasm to repair the losses of established ecclesiastical organizations after church-union. Then, turning to politics, he secured an overwhelming victory by skilful political strategy, particularly in his choice of candidates and use of literature.

His small low-priced manual, supported by numerous advertisements, represents an attempt to modify theories worked out by Major Douglas and other engineers who have become interested in monetary problems. The general arguments emphasize the dangers of the centralization of wealth (as evident in debts), the vital importance of inventions, and the plenty-scarcity paradox referred to as the problem of distribution. The engineer has had a dominant influence in the history of capital equipment in Canada: he has planned for, and committed government to, enormous expenditures in canals, railways, elevators, and the large-scale type of capital equipment which characterized the Canadian structure. The pressure of modern industrialism in iron and steel, gasoline, and electricity, has been evident in government ownership of railways, roads, and power-plants, and in governmental intervention in housing and armaments. The inevitable clash between the engineer and the financier has been described in detail elsewhere, and it will be sufficient here to deal with Mr Aberhart's philosophy as part of a general struggle which has become increasingly acute during the depression, and which, in the main, has involved advances on the part of the engineer in the form of numerous monetary devices. In a sense Mr Aberhart is right in suggesting that economists do not understand social credit. Nor does Mr Aberhart. But the protest can be understood. The old parties, the UFA, the bankers, and the Socialists, united in opposition, were swept to defeat.

Mr Aberhart owes much in Alberta, in Saskatchewan, and possibly in British Columbia, to the groundwork prepared by the new parties which capitalized the evidence of the Price-spreads Report and assiduously broke down loyalties to the old parties. Moreover, Alberta is a province on the height of land of Canadian trade from the East and the West, and has been more closely associated with the Pacific coast. Its political and economic structures have been more closely united, and with dependence on individuals the possibility of migration upwards from rural areas, and from the younger generation, has been less conspicuous than in other areas, with the result that political revolutions are more pronounced.

The particular types of appeal which will influence "the exploited and downtrodden masses"– in the rural areas apparently differ vastly from those which characterize "the pecuniary industrial culture pattern" if the volume on *Social Planning for Canada* is an indication. The size, weight, price, and lack of paid advertising, present a striking contrast to Mr Aberhart's manual. The academic gloss is more conspicuous, but the absence of self-confidence is possibly less effectively concealed. Ostensibly outlining the Socialist point of view, it has fundamentally the philosophy of Mr King and the Price-spreads Report. There is a significant omission of reference to works on socialism such as G. Myers, *History of Canadian Wealth* (Chicago, 1914).

Social Planning for Canada is obviously intended to influence the more opulent middle class with its pecuniary concern in prestige-values. To quote the *Communist Manifesto* once more, "To this section belong economists, philanthropists, improvers of the condition of the work class, organizers of charity, members of societies for the prevention of cruelty to dumb animals, temperance fanatics, hole-and-corner reformers of every imaginable kind." The present reviewer is not competent to judge as to the effectual character of this type of appeal to this class; but he cannot refrain from referring to the kindly, well-meaning interest of a large group (more than twenty) who have been concerned in restoring clothes which had been snatched by old and new parties, and in searching for further supplies by rummaging through the baskets not only of Canada, but also of numerous classes and countries, to cover nakedness exposed to the cold blasts of the depression in Canada. It would be ungracious and grossly unfair to ask why extremely valuable pieces of homespun clothing had been left behind, or to raise questions of any kind. To an economist the ways of politicians are past finding out. The result may not appeal to fastidious tastes, and careful scrutiny will show many ill-fitting pieces, many pieces designed for one purpose and used for another, and many ill-secured pieces, which will certainly fall off if the subject moves about unduly or if the winds blow. The tailors have not agreed as to the design; but they have been apprenticed in London and Oxford, and it may appeal to more exclusive tastes insistent on imported styles. An attempt is made to assert self-confidence and self-assurance by insistence on the "intellectual" (quotation marks Mr Woodsworth's) approach, but apparently there were sufficient intellectuals involved to defeat this object. The insistence "that we are not just another political party" is defeated by the presence of innumerable political devices, such as the *cliché* "that statistics absolutely prove," and a constant application of the principle *suggestio falsi, suppressio veri.* Artistic effects have not been neglected and will strike many as the most significant feature of the work. To change the metaphor, theme-songs run through the volume: "The capitalist system is breaking up" (to the tune of "London bridge is falling down"); "The Big Bad Wolf of St. James Street" (with some reference also to the nicer wolf who is chancellor of McGill University; for these "wolves," it would seem, are largely responsible for this nasty depression); and "Sectionalism, the curse of the Canadian economy, shall not prevail" (to the tune of "Curfew must not ring to-night"). It would be quite unfair, and out of place here, to subject the most pretentious of these political documents to detailed examination in the light of those standards accepted by students of economics. The concern of this review is limited to the effects of the depression on economic intelligence in Canada, and the reasons for its evident decline.

In the art of propaganda political parties have much to learn from, and some things to avoid in, the publicity work of the Canadian Pacific Railway, particularly as evinced in *Steel of Empire,* a volume from the skilled hand of its director of publicity. Numerous photographs, reproductions of cartoons, maps, and paintings, together with the general attractiveness, interest, and information of the book, carry one through its theme of the place of the railway as a culmination of the quest for a Northwest Passage, to the inevitable conclusion that amalgamation under the Beatty plan is the end towards which the whole creation should move. And this it does with a skill and effectiveness certainly absent from the effort of *Social Planning for Canada* to lead by a huge compilation of material to its much vaguer conclusion. But *Steel of Empire* constitutes further proof that it is more difficult to keep the CPR out of politics than to keep politics out of the CNR. And the convincing logic of the book tends to defeat its own end. For no people will knowingly submit itself to such perpetual and efficient propaganda as would apparently reign if the Beatty Plan were adopted!

A reading of the volumes under review raises searching questions as to the position of the social sciences in Canada during the depression. The very small proportion of valid economic thinking which has been associated with recent political activities is offset by important work in the social sciences, such as that being published in the "Canadian Frontiers of Settlement" series, the Canadian-American Relations project, and the McGill Social Research series, and that done by numerous unsubsidized individuals. But allowing for this work, the abysmal ignorance of the economic structure in Canada, with the accompanying volume of political talk, suggests that we are still suffering grievously from the loss of large numbers of able men during the War. In a lecture to the London School of Economics, Professor Pigou indicated difficulties in England, which are much more acute in Canada:

> To a young man the ambition to play a part in great affairs is natural: and the temptation to make slight adjustments in his economic view so that it shall conform to the policy of one political party or another, may be severe. As a Conservative economist or a Liberal economist or a Labour economist he has much more chance of standing near the centre of action than he has as an economist without adjectives. But for the student to yield to that temptation is an intellectual crime. It is to sell his birthright in the household of truth for a mess of political pottage. He should rather write up for himself and bear always in mind Marshall's weighty words: "Students of social science must fear popular approval; evil is with them when all men speak well of them. If there is any set of opinions by the advocacy of which a newspaper can increase its sales, then the student ... is bound to dwell on the limitations and defects and errors, if any, in that set of opinions, and never to advocate them unconditionally even in an *ad hoc* discussion. It is almost impossible for a student to be a true patriot and to have the reputation for being one at the same time."[2]

Professor Pigou would have noted that in a new country in which the rewards of scholarship are small and without prestige, in which intellectual strength has been weakened by the War and by losses to other countries, and in which economic activity is subject to wide fluctuations as a result of dependence on raw materials for export, foot-loose adventurers in universities turn in some cases to business and its profits during booms, and in others to political activity and popular acclaim during depressions.

Universities, unable to provide for the protection of social scientists through lack of traditions of, or respect for, scholarship, have been forced to compromise and have reflected the stress of economic pressure in Canada during the depression. Particularly in the newer universities the construction of buildings, during a boom period, and the installation of equipment incidental to the emphasis laid on industrial, or agricultural, and professional activity, have been accompanied, in the following depression, by inflexible charges of maintenance, operation, and interest, to the detriment of more intangible assets such as libraries and staff. Universities have been further weakened by the loss of abler members of the staff, through competition and through the necessity of participation in political activity directly and indirectly, to secure adequate support. In both old and new universities, administrations have increasingly competed for financial support and staffs. Extension courses follow their usual trend during depression and have expanded as a means of bringing the universities to the public and strengthening their political position. Misguided attempts to offset decline in prestige[3] have been evident in the importation of university presidents from abroad, and in efforts to prevent dismissals of members of the faculty, even in cases of obvious incompetence. There is sufficient truth in the statement that it is impossible to leave a Canadian university except by death or resignation, to evoke general recognition of its accuracy. Incompetence, erratic behaviour (often confused with brilliance), external activities, even to the point of writing party-platforms and bank-letters – nothing will avail. Distrust and suspicion are inevitable with the breakdown of morale and the spread of politics. Universities can survive only by the principle, *united we fail, divided we stand*; but the necessities of politics require union rather than division.

Outside the universities and schools, the depression has also brought into prominence weaknesses in our cultural life. The attractions of the state in politics have increased with the lowering in prestige of our universities, the declining power of our ecclesiastical bodies, and the weakened state of our business organizations. The severity of the depression on the last-named has involved reduced salaries and payrolls and an inability to absorb able and energetic young men. Decline in business morale has accompanied decline in morale in other institutions, as the evidence leading to the Price-spreads Report has shown. The low cultural level of Canadian business, conspicuous in speeches, architecture, the standard of living, and in an inconceivable narrowness of outlook, together with the relative inability of the large corporate organization characteristic of transcontinental development, to meet problems of adjustment during periods of depression – these have not been things pleasant to contemplate.

Disappearance of loyalties to groups and associations has accompanied the weakened position of individuals during the depressions. The law loses respect, and prophets reign in the land. Geographic handicaps have been suggested by Dennis Ireland: "I am oppressed by the atmosphere of provinciality which hangs over Canada like a cloud – due, I suppose, to the fact that there are so few Canadians to people this enormous country."[4] Elections in a depression are not conducive to high standards in the discussion of the complex problems of the social sciences in volumes written for political purposes. New catch-calls suited to new conditions, such as an appeal to youth, or an exploiting of "justice and equity," are not indications of profound thought. Nor are the pleas of academicians for more education, more ethics, more philosophy, or more economics, of striking significance. The confusion of volubility with intellectual interest, and of symptoms with cures, are reflections of the fundamental effects of the depression. That the intelligentsia begin to think they are thinking because of what the intelligentsia thought they thought somewhere else; that they refuse to conform to standards of workmanship; that they discuss planning with the vehemence of those who are opposed to planning – these things may be signs of the breakup of Capitalism. But we are told that they are the signs of the *existence* of Capitalism. Even the case for Communism, and the logic and vigour with which it has been advanced, become for some observers a further symbol of the breakup of Capitalism or, paradoxically, of its continuation. But of more significance is the sign they give of the possibility of an intellectual approach, without which no modern civilization can survive. Marx contributed much in building the ladder to escape from his enemies, his followers, and himself. Meanwhile the people ask for bread and are showered with books.

NOTES

1 *Report of the Royal Commission on Price Spreads* (Ottawa, 1937); J. Wesley Bready, *Lord Shaftesbury and Social-industrial Progress*, with introduction by Sir Josiah Stamp (London, 1926); W.L. Mackenzie King, *Industry*

and Humanity: A Study in the Principles underlying Industrial Reconstruction (Toronto, 1935); William Aberhart, *Social Credit Manual: Social Credit as applied to the Province of Alberta* (Calgary, n.d.); Research Committee of the League for Social Reconstruction, *Social Planning for Canada* (Toronto, 1935); J.M. Gibbon, *Steel of Empire: The Romantic History of the Canadian Pacific* (Toronto, c.1935).

2 A.C. Pigou, *Economics in Practice* (London, 1935).

3 How far can professorial demands for an "academic freedom" which has little basis in the needs of scholarship (not freedom to teach your subject, but freedom to carry on propaganda for your own opinions) be described as one more attempt to develop and support prestige? And local readers will not forget the heroic gesture of Toronto's "sixty-eight."

4 Dennis Ireland, *Life and Letters,* April 1935.

CHAPTER SEVENTEEN

The Rowell-Sirois Report

Three large volumes and a large number of appendices were presented to the Prime Minister on 3 May 1940, by a Royal Commission appointed on 14 August 1937 at the request of the Prime Minister "with the concurrence of the Minister of Finance and the Minister of Justice." The Commissioners apparently regarded themselves, however, as subject to instructions from the Department of Finance.[1] The Royal Commission included Commissioners acceptable to a government controlled by the Liberal Party, and representing five regions.

The Commission planned to secure the cooperation of the governments of the separate provinces in the presentation of briefs and in the consideration of arguments, but the political atmosphere was not favourable. Two members of the Commission were *personae non gratae* to the Premier of a province, the government of which refused to present a brief. The resignation of the Honourable Thibaudeau Rinfret who represented the region of Quebec on 18 November 1937, was followed by the appointment of Dr Joseph Sirois. The Chairman of the Commission, the Honourable N.W. Rowell, representing the region of Ontario, became seriously ill in May 1938, before the public hearings at Quebec and New Brunswick had been held, and on 22 November Dr Sirois was appointed Chairman in his place. Distinguished representation from Ontario was followed by its complete absence. The Premier of Ontario, in a letter of 13 July

---

From *Canadian Journal of Economics and Political Science* 6 (1940): 562–71. The full title of the report is *Report of the Royal Commission on Dominion-Provincial Relations*, vol. 1, *Canada: 1867–1939*; vol. 2, *Recommendations*; vol. 3, *Documentations* (Ottawa, 1940).

1938, refused to cooperate further. The administration of the Province of Quebec was politically hostile to the federal administration and declined cooperation. The illness of Mr Rowell was a tragedy to Canadian life and had disastrous consequences for the political plans of the Commission. The removal of his hand was surely responsible for the political tactlessness, if not offensiveness, of the suggestion by the Commission that the brief of the Edmonton Chamber of Commerce could be regarded as a satisfactory substitute to a brief from the government representing the people of the Province of Alberta. His political tact would scarcely have permitted publication of this and other acerbities in the Report. In the final hearings the provinces took less interest. "We were obliged to continue without inquiry without having to consider how far our proposals would be acceptable to any of the ten governments" (1: 17).

Preoccupation with the political approach reinforced the unfortunate effects of other restrictions. The Commission followed the unfortunate precedent of other commissions in not admitting evidence from individual Canadians and confining it to that presented by a representative of organizations and by individuals of other nationalities. These restrictions may not have been serious as individual Canadians exercised considerable ingenuity in donning the necessary apparel of various organizations, political and otherwise, which had clothing to spare. The practice may have reduced the work of the Commission by excluding individual Canadians with peculiar tastes in clothes, but the varied livery of innumerable organizations can scarcely have been less hideous. It should be possible for Canadians to appear before Royal Commissions in their own clothing.

The failure of its political plans and the exclusion of individual Canadians necessitated increased emphasis on the development of a research program and the employment of a large staff. On 15 September 1937, provision was made for the appointment of Mr Alex Skelton, the Secretary of the Commission (on leave of absence from the position of economic adviser to the Bank of Canada) as director of research, and of Mr J.J. Deutsch (also a member of the research staff of the Bank of Canada) as assistant director. The work of the large staff of the Commission was paralleled by work of a smaller staff in each of most of the separate provinces. Social scientists throughout Canada and some from the United States were enlisted by the federal government or the provinces, and at least one social scientist by both. The work of the Commission's research staff was made available in the form of published and mimeographed appendices, and of the provinces, in the less accessible evidence as well as in the published briefs. The extensive demands inevitably revealed the limitations of the supply. The work ranged through a gamut of good, mediocre, and bad, as a rapid glance through the appendices and the briefs even by an unpractised eye will show. Research like Mesopotamia is a blessed word. Volumes written by those already interested in research in the field with which they were concerned can be recognized as contributions, to mention specifically those of the authors of the income study and those of Messrs Corry, Creighton, Knox, Mackintosh, and Saunders. Volumes written by those with limited training or with little previous knowledge of, or interest in, the field tend to be much less important. The best of the contributions would not be regarded by their contributors as finished work. The time was short and the conditions unavoidably unfavourable.

The uneven character of the work provides no solid uniform base for the Report of the Commission, with the exception of book I, which is based largely on work by those previously interested in the period of Confederation and after, and is a high tribute to the skill of the research staff, and, one suspects, of its secretaries. It will provide a stimulus to the study of economic history in Canada for which all academic students will be grateful. Its chief defect, indeed, is its pretence at final thoroughness and the danger of supporting the dogmatic fallacy. It is almost necessary to write that there is no last word in the writing of economic or of other history except in totalitarian states. The volume has minor inconsistencies and some repetition which suggest that a single mind has not dominated the material for a sufficient length of time. The arrangement might be simplified and the bulk reduced. Insufficient attention is given to economic developments in the United States and in Great Britain, particularly in the discussion on the depression after 1929. Self-sufficiency in the Confederation period and later is overemphasized, and the effects of severe depressions on unemployment is not stressed enough. Export trade has been fundamental to the economic life of Canada since its discovery. The attack on Mr Bennett's tariff policy and his neglect of monetary policy (184) is partially retracted (186). This reviewer was sensitive to a feeling of superficiality in the later part of the book and unfortunately in chapter VIII. But these are trivialities in an important volume.

The failure of its political plans and the necessity of relying on the extensive work of the research staff have had less happy effects on the extent and character of the other publications of the Commission. The size of the Report, the number and the diverse quality of the appendices, and the extensive literature in the form of articles and reviews written by members of the Commission and of the research staff since its publication have hampered reading of the material by any appreciable number and have made criticism difficult. Gladstone's comment regarding such inquiries that they were "well fitted for overloading every question with ten or fifteen times the quantity of matter necessary for its consideration,"[2] if not apt, at least comes to one's mind. The Report is in danger of being damned by loud praise. The critic is terrified at the prospect of questioning the recommendations of a report arrived at through agreement which "reflects a sincere unanimity of judgment on the great issues which confront the nation. Its significance is enhanced by the fact that the four Commissioners are men from different regions of Canada, who differ widely in background and training, as well as in general outlook; and it is also significant that the conclusions which they have reached are far from being the views which any one of them held at the outset of the inquiry" (2: 269).

"All one body we," and yet it is precisely this paraded unanimity arising from such a diversity of material which must arouse suspicion. One is astonished that no Commissioner ventured any form of protest – even a "memorandum of dissent" in the manner of the MacMillan Commission. Would a representative of Ontario have agreed? Has the sovereignty of economists been finally established in Canada? Is this a further indication of the menace of the economists in the decline of political alertness? Unable to meet the political horn of the dilemma has the Commission become impaled on the economic horn? The student of political subtlety may argue that a unanimous decision is an important political argument, and that even if it leads to dissent by separate provinces it may enable a federal party to appeal for election on the grounds of providing unity. Divide and rule is still a maxim of government. This reviewer cannot pretend an ability to appraise these arguments. He is compelled to throw down the gauntlet to large numbers of friends and colleagues and even to expose himself to the charge that he is employed by a university supported by the funds of a province which has seen fit to criticize the Report, that he is "destructive" and not "constructive." A belief[3] in the democratic state and in the necessity of distinguishing between the welfare of a party and the welfare of the community makes criticism imperative. At the risk of aiding those who "invite disaster" by refusing to accept the recommendation of the Report, but supported by the comment of Adam Smith that a nation will stand a lot of ruin, this review must be critical.

The Commission may be pardoned for its relative neglect of the political activities incidental to the working of a federal structure and of the position which it occupies in these activities. It included expert politicians in its personnel who might have thrown light on these activities, but it was inevitable that the political implications of the Commission should be suppressed. But it is scarcely probable that the political implications have not been obvious to them. The academic footnotes, and the emphasis on economic and constitutional aspects and the financial problems of constitutional entities, and the neglect of religious organizations, trade unions, and parties will not obscure the political features of the Report to those trained to detect them, of whom the reviewer is not one. But an arm-chair academic critic can start on the assumption that the Commission was appointed for political purposes. He is aware that political activities since Confederation have been characterized by antagonisms[4] between the provinces and the Dominion. The Cabinet system of responsible government in a country of such diversities as Canada stresses the position of leaders and in turn of organizations which respond to leadership. Federal government since Confederation has been dominated by as few as four Prime Ministers, three of Scottish descent. Social institutions facilitate effective party organizations as the Macdonald and Mackenzie clans attest. The long régimes of federal Prime Ministers have been paralleled by long régimes of provincial Premiers. The comment of Joseph Chamberlain on meeting Oliver Mowat and being told of his long term as Premier of Ontario. "Is there no public opinion in that province?" is to the point. In the United States the difficulty of third and fourth terms necessitates continuous readjustment within parties and a continuous succession of leaders. Third parties are consequently under a serious handicap. Royal Commissions are a part of the machinery of government in Canada by which leaders of parties dominate administrations over long periods. Parties which neglect the contributions of leadership in Canada and insist on a leader winning elections have a notoriously difficult history as the Conservative party[5] since the war must appreciate. The necessity of long years of service on the part of a leader requires dependence on every possible device. A Royal Commission strengthens the hands of a leader with a large as well as a small majority.

In a democracy the existence and activity of parties are of crucial importance. Parties must live either by patronage in the civil service or by subscription from various interests. With the decline of party newspapers and the emergence of amalgamated neutral newspapers, the influence of a government-owned radio, the increasingly bureaucratic character of the civil service, and the increasing costs of elections, the importance of subscriptions is enhanced. Third parties may offer to live more cheaply but their proposals generally involve more jobs in the civil service. The jealousy of the constituent members of a federal state leads to the choice of sites for capitals at points remote from large centres. Bureaucracy has little of the leavening influence of finance, trade, or education. Patronage becomes an inside job. Appointments and promotions in the upper income brackets of the civil service depend on the favour of civil servants rather than of party influence, by no means to the advantage of effective government. The results have been evident in part in the change of political activities. Strengthening of the party in the provinces gradually brought about the success of the federal party in the election of 1896 and the appointment of provincial Premiers to the federal Cabinet. The Opposition party in the provinces gradually increased in strength and eventually captured the federal administration. In turn the political complexion of the provinces changed and liberal and farmers' parties brought return of the Liberal party to Ottawa. The strain of the war reduced the elasticity of the mechanism. The legacy of bitterness in Quebec limited the possibilities of Conservative support and in Western Canada favoured the continued withdrawal of Alberta from control by the old parties. The federal government attempted to restore the balance and increased in power. If Alberta was sour, efforts were redoubled to keep Saskatchewan sweet. Mayor Houde is reported after the last provincial election in Quebec to have said that provincial governments could not afford to be out of step with the party in power in Ottawa.

In this sordid world does the Commission envisage an increase of control by the federal administration and a reversal of the trend in which the provinces assumed the lead in political change? Will business interests find it advantageous to converge on Ottawa and to concentrate their attention on parties in the federal field? Will parties in the provinces look to the federal party for patronage or will they be forced to concentrate on the provincial field for patronage and the federal field for funds? What form will co-operation between parties in the provincial and in the federal fields assume? The significance of parties and patronage to the relative efficiency of the civil services of the provinces and the Dominion was an untouchable subject for the Commission, particularly with the failure of its political approach, and it does not appear to an academic armchair student to have been adequately kept in mind in spite of the fact that it must have been considered. Duplication of services is discussed, particularly in the case of agriculture (2: 174–5), but there is an almost complete disregard, at least to a superficial reader, of the dominance of politics and patronage in an industry in which large numbers of votes are involved. A distinction of a very flimsy character is drawn between mines and forests as a basis for recommending extension of federal control over mines but not over forests. The fundamental division of the British North America Act which placed natural resources under the provinces and trade and commerce under the federal government ought perhaps to be abolished, but the efficiency of the civil service of the provinces chiefly concerned with natural resources cannot be disregarded. The federal government has not been happy in carrying out intensive developmental programs and the branches of the civil service concerned with natural resources, with a few notable exceptions, have not been of a character to command general confidence.

The proposal to place unemployment under the federal administration which occupies a more crucial position in the recommendations of the Report suffers from the same neglect of the efficiency of the civil services. The allocation of social services between different governments appears to illustrate the exercise of dialectical ingenuity which mars sections of the Report and to neglect the fundamental unity of the problem. The civil services in the provinces concerned with the social services have improved beyond recognition since the beginning of the depression and further improvement will take the line of further coordination of administration of the social services. It is probable that the provinces and municipalities have shown greater capacity for administrative improvement than the federal government. Local administration is immediately concerned with local problems, and burdens of taxation have contributed powerfully to efficiency in an exceedingly difficult administrative problem.

The burden which the Commission proposes should be carried by the federal civil service is disquieting. A "national minimum standard of social services" (2: 10, 86) is recommended but not adequately discussed. Assuming that difficulties of securing a statistical average pattern for a country with diverse regions and standards of living such as Canada are overcome, does the establishment of a "national minimum" involve restrictions on migration between provinces? Restrictions on immigration in the United States necessitate mobility of population within Canadian borders. Are the provinces to be regarded as static institutions – the sacred kin of the federal structure and supported to resist economic adjustments? Are we to have a new constitutional Procrustean bed? Provincial equity may imply a rigid framework checking economic adjustments. Vast differences in economic and political strength and efficiency, historical background and tradition, and political structure suggest that proposals to make provinces equal *de facto* as well as *de jure* may involve serious handicaps. Frequent references to marginal industries are not extended to a discussion of economic equilibrium, especially in relation to problems of imperfect competition. How far was the evidence submitted to the Royal Commission on Price Spreads[6] taken into account in an attempt to understand the significance of rigid prices in manufacturing centres to the fluctuating prices of raw materials?

The stress of the Report on the principle of subsidies in relation to need and on problems of expenditure and national income has contributed to the general disregard of problems by which income may be increased. The Report strengthens the expensive popular interest in national income and neglects the important interest in trade. Much is written on the inequities of income and inheritance taxes and little on the inequities of the tariff. It will be argued that federal policy was beyond the terms of reference, but the background of the Commission appointment and much important evidence presented to the Commission, particularly by the Province of Manitoba, was concerned with the tariff. The late Norman Rogers once expressed to the reviewer his keen dissatisfaction that the terms of reference of the Duncan Commission as outlined by the Meighen administration made no reference to the burdens of the tariff on the Maritime Provinces. He was largely instrumental in securing the appointment of the Jones Commission in Nova Scotia and prepared and presented the brief[7] suggesting the extent of the tariff burden. He attempted to apply the technique used in Australia, and his work was given extensive notice in the Canadian press. His estimates were subjected to criticism[8] and substantial progress had been made in their refinement. And yet all this was elbowed out of the Report with a footnote reference to a statement by Dr Carrothers (2: 232n8). On the other hand, cautious references are made to the possibilities of federal policy in using monetary devices to check the effects of business cycles. The emergence of acute financial difficulties, particularly in the prairie provinces, has completely overshadowed the basic problem of the tariff.

The attempt to escape from the problems of the tariff involves a break between book 1 in which its role in the National Policy has been outlined and book 2. The significance of federal policy in registering and accentuating disequilibrium can scarcely be disregarded. Disequilibrium which followed consolidation of the Hudson's Bay Company in western Canada after 1821 through concentration on the Hudson Bay route, with the Precambrian Shield as a line of defence against the St Lawrence route, and in turn the destruction of that defence by construction of the Canadian Pacific Railway and the rapid occupation of the prairie region with its unwise settlement and land policies and its problems of debt adjustment, has been a striking feature of Canadian development. The National Policy reflected the disequilibrium and accentuated it through land, tariff, and railway policies and bonuses indirectly and directly to the steel and coal industries of Nova Scotia. Readjustment has been extremely painful and has necessitated the assumption of burdens by the provinces which have been shared only under great pressure by the Dominion. The regions particularly concerned should be recognized as having grievances, incidental to disequilibrium registered in deliberate federal policy, and assisted accordingly. The substantial proportion of revenues paid by Ontario and Quebec should be distributed not only on the basis of need but also with a view to increasing the efficiency of the Canadian economy and increasing income. Bonuses to inefficiency would inevitably follow neglect of intensive study of the problems of each region and of the country as a whole. Failure to appreciate the importance of such study is evident in the deplorable recommendation to abolish the prairie quinquennial census which provided basic information on the difficulties of an area with acute problems.

Contrary to the suggestion of the Commission that the Report paralleled the British North America Act (2: 274), the latter enabled the federal government to assume debt burdens of the provinces largely represented by expenditures on transportation. A logical extension of the policy would suggest the assumption of expenditures on transportation in roads as formerly it had assumed expenditures on canals and railways. Such a program would facilitate coordination of transport facilities on a national scale and enable the federal government to contribute effectively to increased income. The attempts to introduce regional tariffs, deplored by the Commission, including that of the federal government under the Maritime Freight Rates Act, might be more effectively checked. Even the Commission's mistake of suggesting that provincial regulation of milk was without significance to the federal government with its interest in butter and cheese might be avoided. The British North America Act was concerned with developmental policy whereas the Report is concerned largely with needs.

The criticisms which have been advanced are to the effect that the reviewer favours plan II of the Commission or adjustments within the present structure rather than plan I with the artificial divisions of the social services. They are made in the hope that discussion of the Report may become more effective and that the suggestions of the Report should not be buried in its own bulky contents. In contrast with most important commissions, its members were native Canadians and the Report deals effectively with a vast number of minor points which have been a source of friction. The work is characterized by breadth and boldness and should be read by all students of government in Canada. Book 3 contains the results of the invaluable work of the staff in presenting governmental accounts on a uniform basis. Its value will depend on the interpretation placed on it in the light of the fact that in the social sciences one and one rarely make two. The reviewer cannot but feel that the adoption of plan I at the present time would be an abuse of power under "the peace, order, and good government" clause of the constitution, and would leave a legacy of bitterness in some provinces comparable to that which was left in Nova Scotia after the adoption of the British North America Act. Peace is essential to effective discussion.

NOTES

1 See a letter from the deputy minister of finance, 22 Nov. 1938, *Report of the Royal Commission on Dominion-Provincial Relations,* vol. 2, *Recommendations,* 2: 234n4.

2 Cited in H.M. Clokie and J.W. Robinson, *Royal Commissions of Inquiry* (Stanford University, 1937), 80.

3 "The enemies of this object – the people who want to act quickly – see this very distinctly: they are forever explaining that the present is 'an age of committees,' that the committees do nothing, that all evaporates in talk. Their great enemy is parliamentary government: they call it, after Mr. Carylyle, the 'national palaver'; they add up the hours that are consumed in it and the speeches which are made in it, and they sigh for a time when England might again be ruled, as it once was, by a Cromwell, – that is, when an eager absolute man might do exactly what other eager men wished, and do it immediately. All these invectives are perpetual and many-sided; they come from philosophers each of whom wants some new scheme tried, from philanthropists who want some evil abated, from revolutionists who want some old institution destroyed, from new era-ists who want their new era started forthwith: and they all are distinct admissions that a polity of discussion is the greatest hindrance to the inherited mistake of human nature, – to the desire to act promptly, which in a simple age is so excellent, but which in a later and complex time leads to so much

evil" (Walter Bagehot, "Physics and Politics," *The Works of Walter Bagehot* (Hartford, 1889), 4: 569.

4 J.A. Maxwell, *Federal Subsidies to the Provincial Governments in Canada* (Cambridge, 1937). The author deplores the tactics involved but fails to appreciate the importance of political activity.

5 See also the difficulties of party leaders after 1896 and the problems of Sir Robert Borden as described in *Robert Laird Borden: His Memoirs* (Toronto, 1938).

6 See also L.G. Reynolds, *The Control of Competition in Canada* (Cambridge, 1940); H.A. Logan, "Labor Costs and Labor Standards," *Labor in Canadian-American Relations* (Toronto, 1937).

7 *A Submission on Dominion-Provincial Relations and the Fiscal Disabilities of Nova Scotia within the Canadian Federation* (Halifax, 1934).

8 See D.C. MacGregor, "The Provincial Incidence of the Canadian Tariff," *Canadian Journal of Economics and Political Science* 1 (1935): 384–95; also W.A. Mackintosh, app. 3, chap. 7.

CHAPTER EIGHTEEN

Recent Trends in Canadian-American Relations

The general argument of this paper is to the effect that American policies are destined to affect the policies of Canada, and the policies of North America as a whole, to an increasing extent, and that it is to the interest of all concerned that the probable effects of American policies on Canada should be considered before they are finally formulated.

It is significant that I should be asked by an American committee of arrangement to prepare a paper of a popular character on economic trends in Canadian-American relations. A Canadian committee would, I hope, have been less certain about economic trends and would certainly have implied that political trends were included. I propose to follow the usual procedure by disregarding the title of the paper and presenting a compromise between the Canadian and American point of view, by adopting the Canadian approach or by attempting to indicate the background between the two points of view. We are in danger, particularly in the maritime regions, of taking for granted a common point of view, since it is from these regions that similarities have spread throughout the continent. The emphasis on regionalism which characterizes a long coastline has been sharpened on the Atlantic coast by the growth of the fishing industry dependent on the sea and by the development of trade in commodities produced from regions with a wide range of climate and geology. As has been pointed out elsewhere,[1] it is not an accident that four sovereign bodies are represented in the Atlantic fishing regions, Newfoundland, France, Canada, and the

---

An address delivered at the Conference on Educational Problems in Canadian-American Relations, at the University of Maine, Orono, Me., 21–3 June 1938; first appeared as "Economic Trends in Canadian-American Relations."

United States, and it is not an accident that the particularism of New England and the Maritimes, of Massachusetts and Nova Scotia, has been indelibly stamped in the character of the federal constitutions of Canada and the United States. Sir John A. Macdonald attempted to avoid the difficulties of the American Constitution which became evident in the Civil War, by emphasizing federal power but the position of Nova Scotia limited federal power in the constitution and in its later development.

But we are being carried into the whirlpool of common points of view. The particularism of the maritimes was reflected not only in the constitutions of the Untied States and Canada but also in the sharp differentiation between the United States and Canada, and to that we must turn our attention. Separatist Nova Scotia and New England accentuated differences between the northern and the southern parts of the continent. The emergence of two nations in North America reflected the profound influence of geological structure and topography, with a large number of short rivers along the southern part of the Atlantic seaboard, a long river, the St Lawrence, along the southern edge of the Precambrian formation to the heart of the continent, and a vast bay to the north. Penetration from Europe along the southern part of the Atlantic seaboard was slow and consolidated, by the St Lawrence rapid and far-flung, and by Hudson Bay reluctant. Increase in population, trade, and industry in the English Atlantic colonies brought conflict with French control over the St Lawrence and defeat of the French, and a sharp break with English control in the American Revolution and the emergence of the United States. In the final break Nova Scotia and the St Lawrence remained under English control. The economy built up by the St Lawrence reflected the continuous political influence of Europe, in contrast with the southern Atlantic coast. The export of staple products of the St Lawrence to an increasingly industrialized Europe involved defence of a long thin line of settlement. The fur trade shifted to the short route by Hudson Bay and the timber trade responded to the urban demands of Great Britain and the definite encouragement of imperial preferences.

Emigration was stimulated by various devices. Capital equipment in canals and railways was designed to strengthen the St Lawrence and to check the influence of routes to New York and other United States ports. The Grand Trunk was followed by the Intercolonial to the east and the Canadian Pacific to the west. The tariff was increased to strengthen the position of transportation facilities concentrating on the St Lawrence. With this development, wheat succeeded lumber as a staple export by the St Lawrence to Europe.

The structure of the Canadian economy was an extension of the European or British economy, with a consequent increase in efficiency guaranteed by cheap water transport, imperial preferences, and the opening of new resources. It was handicapped by the extent of government intervention, the rigidity of government indebtedness, railway rates and tariffs, and dependence on a commodity subject to wide fluctuations in yield and price. Increase in urban population in the United States was accompanied by a decline in exports of staple products to Europe and by the shift of this trade to Canada. In turn exports from Canada have been forced to retreat in the face of competition from other parts of the Empire as well as from Argentina, Denmark, and Holland. Rapidity of expansion in Canada and concentration on staple products, such as wheat, have accentuated rigidities imposed by competition from other wheat producing areas. In the face of this competition Canada has retreated behind tariffs and concentrated on other forms of production. Precluded by tariffs from exporting to the United States, Canada has imposed tariffs and secured empire preferences and agreements compelling the establishment of branch factories from the United States. Urbanization of the United States has meant not only the retreat of exports to Europe, the shift to Canada, retreat of Canada, and the development of exports of manufactured products, but also the pull of raw materials and finished products in which depletion of American resources has been conspicuous, such as pulp and paper, or of which Americans have deprived themselves by changes in the constitution, such as liquors, or of which they feel they have special need in cases of emergency, such as gold.

Canada is facing to an increasing extent the effects of contrast between two systems. An old system linked her to Europe by a geographic background dominated by the St Lawrence and provided for the efficiency of specialization under free trade. The character of defence was apparent in the constitutional set-up of the federal system – a tariff along the international boundary and a series of compartments in the provinces built up on control over natural resources and designed to save the ship through the closing of bulkheads, as evident in the recent Saskatchewan elections. As the burden increases, the strain on the bulkheads increases. The costs of defence and of supporting those who hide behind it, as in the case of protected industries, become too heavy. The character of the defence is evident not only in the tariff but also in the development of government ownership, as in the case of hydro-electric power in Ontario and the Canadian Broadcasting Corporation, in the Canadian railway problem, the talk of nationalism, and bursts of oratory about the long undefended international boundary line, the long period of peace, and the work of the International Joint Commission. These are witnesses to the efficiency of defence as much as to the continuation of peace. The new system links Canada to the United States and is evident in the increasing importance of exports from Canada to the United States, such as pulp and minerals, and in the rapid spread of inventions from the United States to Canada and the consequent decline in efficiency of defence. The radio crosses boundaries which stopped the press.

The conflict between the two systems has cumulative effects. Nationalism becomes more intense. The influence of the radio is canalized through the Canadian Broadcasting Corporation and interest in national culture is intensified. The intensification of nationalism increases the burden of tariffs and fixed charges, precipitates regionalism, and enhances the importance of the provinces. Particularism leads to decline in national loyalties and to increase in imperial loyalties. The instability of the Canadian political and economic structure offsets the effects of rigidities and reflects the conflict between the European and the American systems. It increases the weakness of Canada as a political unit in relation to Europe.

The burden of defence in Canada is made more severe by the character of the conflict between the two systems. The economic structure in relation to Great Britain and Europe implied an east-west haul on a transcontinental scale of raw materials for export and of manufactured products chiefly within Canada. The highly industrialized and urbanized character of Great Britain and its demand for foodstuffs, particularly from western Canada, necessitated railways, elevators, canals, ports, and steamships. The Panama Canal, and Churchill to a slight extent, have encroached on the St Lawrence system but the effects have been offset by the increasing demands of the United States for pulp and paper and minerals and, indirectly, hydro-electric power. The stage of industrial development and the proximity of the United States create a demand for bulky cheap commodities of a non-agricultural character from non-agricultural regions. The contrast between western Canada and its relations with Europe, and eastern Canada and its relations with the United States, involves strains between the Dominion, concerned with federal problems of transportation, and, on the one hand the provinces in the west, coinciding in their interests with the federal government, and on the other hand the provinces in the east, opposed to the federal government through the background of tradition and the possibility of depending on their own resources for export to both the United States and Great Britain. These strains accentuate Canadian instability and the strengthening of imperial rather than national loyalties.

The nuisance value of Canada in Anglo-American relations, as a subject of investigation, has been neglected because of the importance attached by after-dinner speakers to the long "undefended" boundary line. It was Great Britain and the United States that had the "will to peace," and Canada cannot escape the accusation of playing the role of the small boy anxious to stick pins in either when there was something to be gained by it. We had muddied the water, and the sentiment expressed by a typical Britisher is too generally applicable. He said, "Now I know why Americans and Englishmen are not too friendly. You think we are like these damn Canadians."[2] It was inevitable in an adolescent colony that Great Britain should find it necessary to step in, on various occasions, and call a halt to Canadian pin-pricking lest it should endanger Anglo-American relations.

A few examples must suffice. Nova Scotia badgered Great Britain into restricting American trade to the West Indies until 1830. She began with the Hovering Act of 1834, a policy of exclusion of the United States from British waters, which in 1840 compelled great Britain to restrain her. She became such a nuisance with her protective system that reciprocity was welcomed as a relief. Canada was not less difficult. She fought for preferences on timber and on wheat, and when they were cut off, the disgruntled element stuck a vigorous pin in Great Britain in the annexationist manifesto of 1849. Here, too, reciprocity was welcomed. With the end of reciprocity, Nova Scotia compelled Canada and Great Britain to adopt a vigorous policy of exclusion, which led to the Washington Treaty as a way of escape. With the end of the Washington Treaty, Canada again became offensive and pursued vindictiveness to the point of preventing a treaty between the United States and Newfoundland. In Ontario export taxes were levied on lumber going to the United States, and in retaliation against American tariffs an embargo on lumber cut on Crown lands was introduced in 1898. Canada spurned the rising tariffs of the United States and introduced imperial preferences in 1896. We played our cards with effect and secured the free entrance of newsprint in the reciprocity arrangements of 1911 and the tariff of 1913. But largely because of our annoyance with Great Britain and the United States over the settlement of the Alaska boundary dispute, we refused in a very striking fashion the reciprocity treaty as a whole.[3] In spite of friendships arising from the war, we were annoyed with the Fordney-McCumer tariff and we countered the Hawley-Smoot tariffs with the Ottawa agreements. It is scarcely necessary for this paper to elaborate on Canadian tactics. The politician is quick to seize upon the possibility of capitalizing hostility to either the United States or Great Britain, and Canadian nationalism flourishes under these conditions, but it is nationalism in the interest of the short run rather than the long run. It is only with maturity that Canada can be expected to play a role in which pin-pricking ceases to be a policy, in which we will cease fishing in troubled waters, and in which we will take advantage of the "will to peace" between Canada and the United States.

The weakening of nationalism, the strengthening of regionalism, and the stress on imperialism leaves Canada as the weak link in the North American structure – the Achilles heel to North American isolation. Outbreak of war in Europe involving Great Britain involves Canada and in turn, sooner or later, the United States. We turn, therefore, to the problem of possible contributions of the United States which might strengthen Canadian unity, render the voice of Canada more effective in the League of Nations and in the British Commonwealth of Nations, and enable her to take a stronger stand in the interests of world peace.

The Siamese twin relationship between Canada and the United States – a very small twin and a very large one, to be exact – is evident not only in the exports from Canada and the United States but also in the establishment of branch plants in Canada, important wage levels, for example in railway labour, competitive railway rates, movement of liquid capital, ownership of government securities, and the temporary migration of tourists, to mention significant relationships. The exchange rate between the Canadian dollar and the American dollar does not depart from par for any great length of time and then chiefly as a result of the importance of fluctuations in returns from agriculture in terms of price and yield.

It is scarcely necessary to stress the obvious significance of American economic policies to Canada and to point out the existence of an American empire without the desire to assume responsibilities which go with imperialism. This is not to say that any implicit statement as to responsibilities by the United States would not be regarded with hostility by Canada, that Canadians prefer to look upon vagaries of American policy as acts of God and Mr Roosevelt over which they have no control, and that the United States would not resent any suggestion that Canada should plead for consideration of the effects of an American policy on her. But it is to suggest that the United States in her own interests must consider particularly the effects of any policy on Canada, which is without benefit of political representation. Lest I should become involved in any breach of hospitality on these subjects, may I plead the indulgence of such courtesies as these conferences make available. The emergence of governmental control on a large scale in the United States, evident in tariffs and monetary policy, makes the question increasingly acute. Whether the United States agrees or not, its monetary and tariff policies are largely the monetary and tariff policies of the North American continent, including Canada. It is not surprising that devices should have been developed to prevent changes of too drastic a character. The Canadian legation at Washington has become a more efficient clearance channel. An exhaustive discussion of treaty possibilities and the work of such bodies as the International Joint Commission enable both countries to obtain an appreciation of the implications of policy in one country to that of the other. American branch plants in Canada ensure representation of the American point of view in Canada and possibly the Canadian point of view in the United States. Areas such as Detroit and the border cities register immediately the effects of changes of policy. These devices are defective because of lack of information, and because of the narrowness of interest in which it may be advantageous for branch plants to support a high Canadian tariff against the United States or for American interests to prevent measures which may lead to conservation of resources, as in the British Columbia salmon fishery.

The tariff is a crucial point of conflict because it reflects the interests of definite industries and is part of a background of traditional policy. The American tariff is designed to check imports of goods produced by groups in control of strategic voting power, which because of the demands of increasing industrialism in the United States are threatened by competition from imports. The application of the cost of production principle was particularly adapted to defend this group. Agricultural products were protected in the United States partly through the efforts of organized interests and partly as a means of relief to rural areas and at the expense of urban areas. While these products from Canada are excluded, the monetary policy of the United States, and in turn of Canada, prevents their export from Canada to Europe. Canada can compete with difficulty with the Argentine, Australia, New Zealand, Holland, and Denmark, and, failing attempts to secure preferences in the markets of Great Britain, as a defence measure is forced to engage in protection for the dairy industry and to accept low prices for such exports as wheat. In Canada as in the United States the voting strength of the agricultural industry, particularly of the highly organized dairy industry, is sufficient to support measures of retaliation in the form of higher tariffs and preferences to Great Britain. These high tariffs encourage the establishment of American branch factories – for example, automobiles – and increase the costs of Canadian agriculture. Lower prices for agricultural products exported to Europe and higher costs for manufactured goods precipitate the difficulties of Canadian agriculture and the strains of debt which have necessitated the appointment of the Royal Commission on Dominion-Provincial Relations and have led to the outbreak of provincialism.

Monetary policy, as has been suggested, cannot be confined to the United States and is particularly important to Canada. It immediately affects the production of gold and influences the prosperity of the St Lawrence region, notably Ontario. The sharp difference in its effects on the regions of Canada accentuates the importance of regionalism and the difficulties of federation in Canada.

This paper was labelled "Economic Trends," and it may be expected with the more rapid growth of population in the United States and the continued decline of natural resources that Canada will become increasingly dependent on the United States and that the problem will become more, rather than less acute. All that can be asked is that consideration should be given to the implications of policy on a next-door neighbour. We can hope that closer cooperation between the United States and Great Britain automatically solves numerous problems of disequilibrium in Canada, but we can also hope that some curb may be placed on the influence of powerfully organized groups and, that democratic government may function more effectively. There are certain strategic points which can be carefully watched but they are strategic because they are difficult to control.

I can best sum up the argument by an extract from A.A. Milne's *Winnie the Pooh* (117–18), with which I hope all of you are familiar.

"I think," said Christopher Robin, "that we ought to eat all our Provisions now, so that we shan't have so much to carry."

"Eat all our what?" said Pooh.

"All that we've brought," said Piglet, getting to work.

"That's a good idea," said Pooh, and he got to work too.

"Have you all got something?" asked Christopher Robin, with his mouth full.

"All except me," said Eeyore. "As usual." He looked round at them in his melancholy way. "I suppose none of you are sitting on a thistle by any chance"

"I believe I am," said Pooh. "Ow!" He got up, and looked behind him. "Yes, I was. I thought so."

"Thank you, Pooh. If you've quite finished with it." He moved across to Pooh's place, and began to eat.

"It don't do them any Good, you know, sitting on them," he went on, as he looked up munching. "Takes all the Life out of them. Remember that another time, all of you. A little Consideration, a little Thought for Others, makes all the difference."

NOTES

1 See R.F. Grant, *The Canadian Atlantic Fishery* (Toronto, 1934), 7.

2 W.R. Curtin, *Yukon Voyage* (Caldwell, 1938), 249–50.

3 J.W. Dafoe, *Clifford Sifton in Relation to His Times* (Toronto, 1931).

CHAPTER NINETEEN

Great Britain, the United States, and Canada

Canadians have reason to remember industrial cities in the Midlands for their protests against the imposition of a protective tariff in Canada in 1858 and later dates, following the introduction of free trade in England in the forties. Free trade was accompanied by factory legislation at home and by protective tariffs in the colonies. Thorold Rogers wrote that "a protective tariff is to all intents and purposes an act of war,"[1] and its introduction in Canada undoubtedly appeared to Nottingham and other cities as an act of war on the part of the colonies against the mother country. The complaints led Canadians such as A.T. Galt to present arguments showing that the protective tariff was not an act of war but was adapted to the demands of a new country and that it was a fiscal device by which improvements in navigation and transportation could be financed, and the cost of moving industrial goods from Great Britain to new markets, and raw materials to Great Britain, could be lowered. British investors were thus insured of a return on capital loans. According to Galt, "The fiscal policy of Canada has invariably been governed by considerations of the amount of revenue required." Moreover, he insisted, "Self government would be utterly annihilated if the views of the imperial government were to be preferred to those of the people of Canada." But the arguments probably made little impression on England. Robert Lower is stated to have said to Lord Dufferin following his appointment as Governor-General of Canada in 1872, "Now you ought to make it your business to get rid of the Dominion."[2]

A revision of the twenty-first Cust Foundation Lecture delivered at the University of Nottingham, 21 May 1948; printed in *Changing Concepts of Time* (Toronto, 1952), 109–33.

I

Throughout the history of Canada, the St Lawrence River has served as an outlet from the heart of the continent for staple products and as an entrance for manufactured products from Europe. Consistently, political and economic considerations have directed its improvement by the construction of canals and the building of railways. The constitution of Canada, as it appears on the statute book of the British Parliament, has been designed to secure capital for the improvement of navigation and transportation. Railways have been extended from the St Lawrence to the Atlantic and to the Pacific, and canals have been deepened as a means of increasing the commercial importance of the river. Reliance on the tariff in the Galt tradition has become a crude instrument in the use of which there has been some waste, particularly in duplication of railways, and constant friction over the adjustment of the burden, evident in controversies about freight rates and subsidies to provinces.

To an important extent the emphasis has been on the development of an east-west system with particular reference to exports of wheat and other agricultural products to Great Britain and Europe. However, since the turn of the century, the United States has had an increasing influence on this structure. The construction of the Panama Canal, through the energetic efforts of Theodore Roosevelt, has been followed by the development of Vancouver as a port competitive with Montreal and by a weakening of the importance of the St Lawrence.[3] The exhaustion of important industrial raw materials in the United States has been followed by the growth of the mineral industry and of the pulp and paper industry in Canada. The Precambrian Shield, which has been a handicap to a system built up in relation to Europe, has become a great advantage as a centre for the development of hydro-electric power and for the growth of a pulp and paper and of a mineral industry in relation to the United States. American imperialism has replaced and exploited British imperialism. It has been accompanied by a complexity of tariffs and exchange controls and a restriction of markets, with the result that Canada has been compelled to concentrate on exports with the most favourable outlets. Newsprint production in Canada is encouraged, with the result that advertising and in turn industry are stimulated in the United States, and it becomes more difficult for Canada to compete in industries other than those in which she has a distinct advantage. Increased supplies of newsprint accentuate an emphasis on sensational news. As it has been succinctly put, world peace would be bad for the pulp and paper industry.

II

The dangers to Canada have been increased by the disturbances to the Canadian constitutional structure which have followed the rise of new industries developed in special relation to the American market, and to imperial markets notably for the products of American branch plants. The difficulties have been evident in the central provinces, Ontario and Quebec, and in provinces which continue to be largely concerned with the British market. A division has emerged between the attitude of provinces which have been particularly fortunate in the possession of natural resources in which the American market is interested and that of provinces more largely dependent on European markets. This division has been capitalized on by the politicians of the respective provinces and by those of the federal government. American branch factories, exploiting nationalism and imperialism in Canada, were in part responsible for agitation in regions exploited by the central area and for regional controversies.

The strains imposed on a constitution specially designed for an economy built up in relation to Great Britain and Europe have been evident in the emergence of regionalism, particularly in western Canada where natural resources were returned to the provinces in 1931, and in regional parties such as Social Credit in Alberta and the CCF in Saskatchewan. In regions bearing the burden of heavy fixed charges and dependent on staples which fluctuate widely in yield and price, political activity became more intense. Relief was obtained by political pressure. A less kindly critic might say that currents of hot air flowed upwards from regions with sharp fluctuations in income. Regional parties have gained from the prestige which attaches to new developments. They have arisen in part to meet the demands of regional advertising, which in turn accentuates regionalism. They have also enjoyed the prestige which attaches to ideas imported from Great Britain, notably in the case of Social Credit and of socialism. The achievement of Canadian autonomy has, then, been accompanied by outbursts of regional activity. Small groups have emerged to combine, disband, and re-combine in relation to protests against the central provinces, notably in the matter of railway rates. Large parties have found it extremely difficult to maintain an effective footing and have tended to break up into provincial parties or into small back-scratching, log-rolling groups within the party.

Provincial regional parties have been in part also a reflection of the influence of new techniques in communication. The radio station, the loud speaker, and the phonograph record enormously increase the power of the regional politician. The radio, for instance, proved a great advantage to skilful preachers in the political field in both Alberta and Saskatchewan. In Alberta, with its vast potential resources, the late William Aberhart, during the period of severe depression and drought, built up a large audience throughout the province using this medium. The influence of Social Credit in Saskatchewan is said to have varied directly with distance from Alberta, the strength of receiving sets, and the power of broadcasting stations. Its success warrants detailed consideration since it points to the elements responsible for the breakup of large political parties. As a teacher Aberhart had acquired an extensive vocabulary. Graduates from his school were scattered throughout the province and his influence persisted as a factor facilitating effective appeal. His Bible Institute and appeals to the Bible and to religion were used with great effect. Bible texts and hymns and semi-biblical language were designed to attack usury, interest, and debts. The conversations and parables of the founder of Christianity were repeated with great skill, notably in attack on the money changers. Audience's throughout the province were held together by correspondence. Large numbers wrote in and subscribed small amounts. Their names were read over the radio and comments were made on their letters. There were attacks on older types of communication such as the chain newspapers dominated by eastern control. The Calgary *Albertan* was purchased as a means of carrying these attacks into the newspaper field itself.

In the East, Nova Scotia had regarded Confederation as a device for opening American markets, whereas the St Lawrence region thought of it as a basis of protection against American goods. The Maritimes felt the full impact of capitalism in the destruction of wooden shipbuilding and in expensive transportation to central Canada. Their iron and steel and coal industries, developed to answer the demand for rails and the needs of industrial expansion in Canada, were among the first to feel the effects of a decline in the rate of that expansion. With strong political traditions, born of a maritime background, it might be expected that the Maritimes would be among the first to voice complaint against injustice. Newfoundland has entered Confederation with a great instrument for political intrigue in the federal system, namely, admission without responsible government.

The appearance of a large number of small parties in Canada suggests an obvious incapacity of a party or of two parties to represent effectively the increasing number of diverging interests.

Provincial boundaries have become important considerations in determining party growth: to mention Social Credit in Alberta, CCF in Saskatchewan, coalitions in British Columbia and Manitoba, Liberals in the Maritime provinces, Mr Frost in Ontario, and Mr Duplessis in Quebec. The consequent complexity suggests a new type of politics or the disappearance of an old type of politics.

The effects of this complexity have been evident in the federal field. At one time government was said to be determined by the longevity of the Walpole Administration. The length of life of one administration became an argument for the greater length of life of another. As evidence of the futility of political discussion in Canada, there were Liberals who deplored the activities of the federal administration in no uncertain terms but always concluded with what was to them an unanswerable argument – "What is the alternative?" In one's weaker moments the answer does appear conclusive, but what a comment on political life, that no one should vote against the administration for fear of worse evils to come! One forgets that it probably matters little how one votes so long as one votes against the government or for the party one expects to see defeated in order to secure a healthy minority. All this is in part a result of the exhaustion which accompanies a long term in office, particularly in a trying period, and in the demands of provincial politics. A distinguished federal civil servant once told me that no administration should be in office more than five years. At the end of that time members have ceased to have new ideas or at least are not expected to have any ideas. The exhaustion becomes evident not only among members of the administration but also in the body politic generally.

A further evidence of political lethargy has appeared in an infinite capacity for self-congratulation. Invariably we remark on the superiority of Canadian institutions, Canadian character, and Canadians generally, over Americans. This, of course, is our common North American heritage but in Canada it appears to lead to little more than a congenital tendency toward long arms with which we can slap our own backs. It is a commonplace, of course, that we are encouraged in this by our polite friends from the United States and Great Britain.

III

Our constitution has proved inadequate in the face of the demands made upon it. The Senate, that unique institution, has lent itself to political manipulation. As a guarantee of maritime rights the Maritime provinces were given a substantial number of senators. They have supported the growth of a strong party organization. Politicians have before them as their reward for activity an appointment to the Senate for life. The active part of a politician's life is guaranteed to the party by postponement of appointment. It may be that the Liberal party will fear an eventual revival of political life and appoint senators who are younger in age so that in case of a political reverse the Senate will continue to be filled for a reasonable length of time with senators loyal to the cause. A careful medical check could be made of senatorial possibilities; the late W.L. Mackenzie King favoured only a general convention that an appointee must be under seventy and have fought an election.

The relation of the Senate to party organization has been inadequately studied. The Senate not only provides a useful anchorage for the Liberal party in the Maritimes but also a support to party organizations throughout Canada. A federal party organizer can be appointed to the Senate and the cost of secretarial expenses charged to services to the country. The procedure has disadvantages in that once senators are appointed they may lose interest in party work since they cannot easily be dislodged, but another senator can be appointed and may bring in new blood. A senatorship is also a reward for journalists[4] who have been active in the party's interest and who will presumably continue active after their appointment. A senator stands as a guard over the party's interest and is expected to be continually alert to the improvement of the party's position in the region from which he is appointed. The entrenched position of the party in the Senate contributes to inflexible government, makes political instruments less sensitive to economic demands, and possibly contributes to the rise of new provincial parties.

Parties are held together to an important extent by patronage and the judicious (not a pun) use of patronage. For the legal profession there remains control over appointment to the bench. Ample salaries, security, retiring arrangements, and prestige tend to make the judiciary a preferred alternative to the Senate. The legal profession and to some extent the medical and other professions are handicapped by professional ethics which prohibit advertising, and the political field is admirably designed to offset this handicap. Lawyers presumably are expected to be concerned with law and it seems eminently fitting that lawyers should be selected by the party to run as members. The substantial advertising developed during the course of a campaign may be followed by the most coveted of all political positions, that of a defeated candidate. The lawyer will not be forgotten by the party when it becomes necessary for the government to select individuals to handle the enormous amount of its legal business. The position of the legal profession in and out of Parliament provides great opportunities for the distribution of patronage. Lawyers will do well, however, to support the party discreetly and strongly since a fanatical loyalty may weaken their prospects of appointment to the bench.

The lack of industrialism in French Canada has meant an emphasis on the church and the law. "Of all the roman provincials the French have been the ones who inherited most of that organizing capacity of the Romans." "It was the French culture of the English ruling caste that made England's power possible."[5] British governors took over the French bureaucratic administration after the conquest of New France and installed members of the English aristocracy in the civil services. The struggle for responsible government was essentially a struggle for jobs for the native born, a struggle which still continues in Ottawa in the interest of positions for French Canadians in the civil service. To an important extent the history of Canada has been that of a struggle between French and English, and the struggle over patronage has been particularly intense in the legal profession in Quebec.

The importance of the legal profession to party strength necessitates discussion of the calibre of men attracted to it and of legal education, which is hampered in Canada by the broad division of common law and code law, and more seriously by divisions between the universities and educational institutions controlled by the profession, particularly the bench. It is difficult to build up great law schools such as are to be found in the United States, Great Britain, or even Australia. Great legal philosophers have been conspicuously absent. Appointments to important positions such as the deanship of a law faculty have been determined by political prejudices. Consequently the legal profession has lacked confidence and there has been reluctance to take final measures for abolishing appeals to the Privy Council. A strong supreme court is essential to the effective operation of written constitutions, but this has proved to be difficult to obtain, partly because of the necessity of appealing to the Privy Council and partly also because of the handicaps imposed by the British North America Act on systems of legal education through placing education under the jurisdiction of the provinces.

As a result of its lack of prestige political parties have been able to exploit the legal profession in a fashion which has been the subject of much discussion in legal literature. Legal patronage has been described as "injurious to the independence of both bench and bar." Members of the Supreme Court have been selected to act on Royal Commission on subjects in which the government finds itself in an embarrassing position, such as the Hong Kong investigation, the Halifax investigation, and the Communist trials. This use of members of the Supreme Court has fortunately not always met with success, to cite only Mr Drew's attacks on the Hong Kong investigation, and the failures to secure conviction in the spy trials. Embarrassment to the rights of Canadian citizens has been obvious. A Canadian citizen whose rights may be imperilled by the report of a Royal Commission which includes members of the Supreme Court will not feel happy about the prospect of appearing before the Supreme Court in a possible appeal from lower courts. The citizen's rights against police interference have been seriously weakened. The use of the legal profession to whitewash political activities of the government is only possible in a country in which the profession has suffered in prestige. The Supreme Court ought not to be in a position in which the government can use it as a doormat on which to wipe its muddy feet.

The lowering of the prestige of the legal profession has implied a heightening of the prestige of the academic profession, with unhappy results for both. The tradition begins perhaps with the late Prime Minister, W.L. Mackenzie King, who came into his position armed with that great academic weapon, a doctorate from Harvard. It would be tedious to trace the steps by which various parties have enlisted the prestige of the academic profession but we can note that members of it were employed on a large scale during the depression, conspicuously with the appointment of the late Norman Rogers as Minister of Labour, and that the trend reached a great climax in the report of the Sirois Royal Commission and in the great trek of the academic profession to the Ottawa salient during the war. Royal Commissions have become a device for exploiting the finality characteristic of academic pronouncements as well as of legal statements. The Sirois Report with its length and the number of its appendices was calculated to bring to a focus all the light and leading of the legal and the academic professions in order to produce the great solution to the Canadian problem, and to guarantee the life of the Liberal Administration in Ottawa for an indefinite period. It has been used with devastating effect to divide what are called the have-nots and the haves among the provinces and to strengthen the Liberal party in English-speaking regions. The use of the class struggle as an instrument of politics has been developed to a high point and we could possibly show the Russians a few details in the higher dialectics. The other parties have been paralysed by a situation in which large numbers of voters support Liberals in the federal government, notably in Ontario and Quebec, and at the same time another party in the provincial government, in order that the dominance of any one group may be checked and that a strong opposition may be maintained against the bureaucracy.

During the war period large numbers of the academic profession joined the civil service. Government became extremely complex and the academic profession thrives on complexity. Complexity was suited to patronage, particularly after the war. We may well be concerned with the change in the attitude toward government in Ottawa, since general appeals are made to it for the solution of every conceivable problem, reflecting a belief that governments are omnipotent. We are again thrown back on the limitations of the legal profession in that legislation itself has been used to an enormous extent to strengthen the position of the party and to extend the one-party system in the federal administration.

IV

Heinrich Brueing, former Chancellor of Germany, has described basic changes in government and their causes.

> I think that the greatest hindrance to constructive political action in the last thirty years has been the influence on final decisions of experts, especially of experts obsessed with the belief that their own generation has gained a vantage point unprecedented in history. No quality is more important in a political leader than awareness of the accumulated wisdom and experience handed down not only in written documents but also by word of mouth from generation to generation in practical diplomatic, administrative and legislative work. ... The more we work with mass statistics and large schemes the more we are in danger of neglecting the dignity and value of the human individual and losing sight of life as a whole.[6]

Increasing centralization and control by federal civil servants, which have accompanied political difficulties, explain the violation of British traditions of the civil service by which civil servants make pronouncements which are perhaps taken more seriously than those by members of the Cabinet. During the war new civil servants, unaccustomed to these traditions, were apparently encouraged to abandon anonymity and to draw fire away from the government. Such pronouncements have been made in the field of foreign policy and reflect the increasing influence of conventions of the United States, particularly as centralization facilitates cooperation or collaboration with that country.

The emergence of the civil service to authoritarian control or, to use the German expression, development of *Gruppenführer* and

Übergruppenführer has had an important influence on politics. The press is compelled to change its attitude in the news since the facts of governmental intervention are inconceivably dull. Nor is the dullness alleviated by the unrelieved monotony of photographs. Complexity compels the press to emphasize nonsensical subjects or to retreat to issues of the utmost simplicity. The hypothesis may be suggested that the tendency has also made for mediocrity in political leadership. It would be interesting to learn whether calculated stupidity has become a great political asset, but a careful study of the political leaders of Canadian parties leaves little doubt of the existence of the appearance and of the reality. Perhaps political talent is inadequate to the demands of a large number of parties. In any case it would be difficult to find greater political ineptitude than exists in Canadian parties. I must ask to be excused from giving specific examples. Cabinet-making becomes "a thoroughly unpleasant and discreditable business in which merit is disregarded, loyal service is without value, influence is the most important factor, and geography and religion are important secondary considerations." Sir John A. Macdonald regarded the ideal cabinet as one over which he held incriminating documents such as might place each member in the penitentiary. Broderick referred to the "malicious credulity of Canadian party spirit and the extreme lengths to which party warfare is carried at the instigation of a most virulent and unscrupulous press."[7] "Comprehensive representation ... has deprived and will continue to deprive the Dominion of the possible maximum of efficiency in its growing bodies."[8] The demands of the present century have contributed to the exhaustion of political capacity. During World War II the conscription issue destroyed the Liberal party in Ontario since Mr Hepburn, the leader of the provincial Liberals, was compelled to oppose Mr King in the hope of securing Conservative votes. In Quebec the provincial Liberal party was destroyed by supporting conscription. Political parties have become bankrupt in regionalism.[9]

Provincial parties, or, in the words of Professor C.B. Macpherson, quasi-parties, hampered in the federal field, have been compelled to undertake measures in their respective provinces which are unacceptable to the federal government. Disallowance of provincial legislation has been a measure of the political necessity felt by the provinces to intensify friction between themselves and the federal government. The difficulties of the British North America Act have been met over a long period by appeals to the Judicial Committee of the Privy Council. The British North America Act has produced its own group of idolators and much has been done to interpret the views and sayings of the fathers of Confederation in a substantial body of patristic literature. But though interpretations of decisions of the Privy Council have been subjected to intensive study and complaints have been made about their inconsistency, inconsistencies have implied flexibility and have offset the dangers of rigidity characteristic of written constitutions.

V

The change from British imperialism to American imperialism has been accompanied by friction and a vast realignment of the Canadian system. American imperialism lacked the skill and experience of British imperialism and became the occasion for much bitterness. American foreign policy has been based on conditions described by Mahan, who quoted the advice of a member of Congress to a newly elected colleague, "to avoid service on a fancy committee like that of foreign affairs if he wished to retain his hold upon his constituents because they cared nothing about international questions." In the Alaskan boundary dispute Canadians felt that they had been exploited by the United States and Great Britain, with results that were shown in the emphatic rejection of the reciprocity proposals of the United States in 1911. But the tide had turned to the point where even those gestures against the United States operated to the advantage of American capital. Branch plants of American industries were built in Canada in order to take advantage of the Canadian-European system and British imperialism.[10] As part of her east-west program, Canada had built up a series of imperial preferential arrangements in which Great Britain had felt compelled to acquiesce and which proved enormously advantageous to American branch plants. Paradoxically, the stoutest defenders of the Canadian tariff against the United states were the representatives of American capital investors. Canadian nationalism was systematically encouraged and exploited by American capital. Canada moved from colony to nation to colony.

The impact of American imperialism was eventually felt by Great Britain. It began with the spread of American journalism in the latter part of the nineteenth century, and continued notably in the campaign of R.D. Blumenfeld and Lord Beaverbrook in the *Daily Express* for British imperial preference. The campaign was supported with great vigour by the late Viscount Bennett when he became Prime Minister of Canada, and ended in a compromise, as British resistance was gradually mobilized and stiffened.

Participation of the United States in the First and Second World War has greatly increased the power of American imperialism and given it a dominant position in the Western world. The shift of

Canadian interest towards the United States and the influence of this on Great Britain were brought out sharply in the work of the Right Honourable Arthur Meighen, then Prime Minister of Canada, in persuading Great Britain to abandon the Anglo-Japanese alliance. Canada has had no alternative but to serve as an instrument of British imperialism and then of American imperialism. With British imperialism, she had the advantage of understanding a foreign policy which was consistent over long periods and of guidance in relation to that policy. as she has come increasingly under the influence of the United States, she has become increasingly autonomous in relation to the British Empire. Her recently acquired autonomy, marked conspicuously in the first instance by the signing of the Halibut Treaty, has left her with little time in which to develop a mature foreign policy, with the result that she has necessarily felt the effects of the vacillating and ill-informed policy of the United States.

Autonomy following the Statute of Westminster has been a device by which we can cooperate with the United States as we formerly did with Great Britain. Indeed the change has been most striking. We complained bitterly of Great Britain in the Minto affair, the Naval Bill, and the like, but no questions are asked as to the implications of joint defence schemes with the United States or as to the truth of rumours that Americans are establishing bases in northern Canada, carrying out naval operations in Canadian waters, arranging for joint establishment of weather stations, and contributing to research from funds allocated to the armed forces of the United States under the direction of joint cooperative organizations.

The ease with which such cooperation is carried out is explained in part by the opposition to socialistic trends in Great Britain. Central and eastern, in contrast with western, Canada have had essentially counter-revolutionary traditions, represented by the Untied Empire Loyalists and by the church in French Canada, which escaped the influences of the French Revolution. A counter-revolutionary tradition is not sympathetic to socialistic tendencies and is favourable to the emphasis on private enterprise which characterizes the United States. Opposition to socialistic devices has been particularly important because large sectors of Canadian economic life have come under government ownership, notably the Hydro-Electric Power Commission of Ontario and the Canadian National Railways. Indeed the large-scale continental type of business organization in private enterprise reflects the influence of governmental administration, in its emphasis on seniority rules and the general sterility of bureaucratic development. Large administrative bodies are compelled to recognize the importance of morale as essential to efficiency. Mobility within the hierarchy can be achieved only with an enormous outlay of energy devoted to the appraisal of capacity. A large number of private enterprises and organizations assume constant attention to the capacities of individuals and are stoutly opposed to the restriction of choice involved in the expansion of large-scale organization. Their concern with private enterprise is reinforced by the views of American branch plants and facilitates American domination.

The abolition of titles has perhaps reflected American influence. The remarks of E.L. Godkin, a native of the north of Ireland, "the most intellectual among American journalists," have been to the point.

> To a certain class of Canadians, who enjoy more frequent opportunities than the inhabitants of the other great colonies of renewing or fortifying their love of the competition of English social life, and of the marks of success in it, the court, as the fountain of honour, apart from all political significance, is an object of almost fierce interest. In England itself the signs of social distinction are not so much prized. This kind of Canadian is, in fact, apt to be rather more of an Englishman than the Englishman himself in all these things. He imitates and cultivates English usages with a passion which takes no account of the restrictions of time or place. It is "the thing" too in Canadian society, as in the American colony in Paris, to be much disgusted by the "low Americans" who invade the Dominion in summer, and to feel that even the swells of New York and Boston could achieve much improvement in their manners by faithful observance of the doings in the Toronto and Ottawa drawing rooms.[11]

"There is nothing in the universe lower than the colonial snob who apes the English gentleman." "These fellows are the veriest flunkies on earth; they are always spouting loyalty and scrambling for small titles and all the crumbs that fall to them from the tables of the aristocracy" (Goldwin Smith). The weakening of the position of these symbols, unfortunate as their effects may have been, has not been without implications for American influence.

American imperialism has been described as "latent and fundamentally political." It has been made plausible and attractive in part by the insistence that it is not imperialistic. Imperialism which is not imperialistic has been particularly effective in Canada with its difficulty in dealing precisely and directly with foreign problems because of division between French and English.

A commercial society in a newspaper civilization is profoundly influenced by the type of news which makes for wider circulation of newspapers – "For God, for country and for circulation." Advertising, particularly department store advertising, primarily demands circulation. Circulation becomes largely dependent on the instability of news and instability becomes dangerous. Effective journalists are those most sensitive to emotional instability. Lack of continuity in news is the inevitable result of dependence on advertisements for the sale of goods. The influence of advertising in the United States spread to Europe, notably to Germany, before the First World War. Bertrand Russell has said with much truth that "the whole modern technique of government in all its worst aspects is derived from advertising."[12] "The intellectual level of propaganda is that of the lowest common denominator among the public. Appeal to reason and you appeal to about four per cent of the human race."[13] "*You cannot aim too low.* The story you present cannot be too stupid. It is not only impossible to exaggerate – it in itself requires a trained publicist to form any idea of – the idiocy of the public."[14] The radio has tended to dominate the news presented in the newspaper, selecting spot news and compelling the newspapers to write it up at greater length because of the feeling that people will wish to know more about the items even though they are not news.

American foreign policy has been to a large extent determined by domestic politics. Publishers of newspapers were rewarded in the patronage system with appointments to ambassadorial posts. The secretary of state has generally played an active role in party politics. An attempt under the second Roosevelt to establish a bi-partisan basis for foreign policy has given greater stability, but foreign issues are all too apt to be dominated by the immediate exigencies of party politics. Under these circumstances a consistent foreign policy becomes impossible and military domination of foreign policy inevitable. The limitations of American foreign policy are largely a result of its lack of tradition and continuity and its consequent emphasis on displays of military strength.

Partly because of the instability of its political system,[15] the United States has shown considerable partiality for generals as presidents throughout its history. The sword has been mightier than the pen, to cite only the defeat of Greeley by Grant. Even in the United States there have been complaints of the pervasive influence of the armed forces, but no signs of abatement are in evidence. Conscription implies a strengthening of their influence. George Ticknor, an American writing in the latter part of the nineteenth century, stated: "Nothing tends to make war more savage than this cruel, forced service, which the soldier who survives it yet claims at last as his great glory because he cannot afford to suffer so much and get no honour for it. It is a splendid sort of barbarism that is thus promoted, but it is barbarism after all; for it tends more and more to make the military character predominate over the civil."[16] De Tocqueville described military glory as a scourge more formidable to republics than all other evils combined. An American has described Washington as becoming the centre for those impelled by the power rather than the profit motive. Bureaucracy assumes a hierarchy, and thus the problem of power.

Formerly it required time to influence public opinion in favour of war. We have now reached the position in which opinion is systematically aroused and kept near boiling point. Strong vested interests in disagreement overwhelm concern for agreement. With control by military men and the difficulties of a constitution which places power in the hands of the public it may become difficult to check the swings of public opinion. American "candour, good temper, immediate and fearless experimentation, sense for fact, etc., is the positive role of their incapacity for discussions and ideas." "Any fact interests them and *no idea* except as it can be shown to be in direct relation to fact" (Lowes Dickinson). The United States has been described by John Gunther as "the greatest, craziest, most dangerous, least stable, most spectacular, least grown up and most powerful and magnificent nation ever known."[17] Her attitude reminds one of the stories of the fanatic fear of mice shown by elephants.

The Department of Economic Affairs of the United Nations in *A Survey of the Economic Situation and Prospects of Europe* described the trade problem in these words: "The European import-surplus problem is essentially the same as the export-surplus problem of the United States, and the alternatives facing the United States are those facing Europe with the signs reversed; sooner or later the United States must either increase its imports or decrease its exports or do both. But the danger exists that if adequate remedial measures are not taken to work out a tenable balance, the economic structure of both Europe and the United States may become so adjusted to the disequilibrium as to create strong pressures tending to perpetuate it." As suggested by the *Economist* there is a prospect of a "United States dollar shortage forever."[18] Nor does Europe gain much comfort from the United States. Professor J.H. Williams, a judicious observer, writes: "Deep-seated in the whole process has been the growing predominance of the United States: resting on the cumulative advantages of size and technological progress and expressing itself in the so-much discussed chronic dollar shortage ... We must think of the objectives of the Marshall Plan in terms of reshaping the European economy and adjusting it to its changed world position, and of making the necessary adjustments in our own. We must also regard it as the beginning rather than the end of the adjustment process."[19]

The tariff is an important instrument in American imperialism, described, in the words of Mr Dooley, as taking up the white man's burden and handing it to the coon. "The mind that thinks in terms of the protectionist symbol is equally at home in the imperialistic symbol."[20] It is as much a contradiction in terms "to speak of protective tariffs as instruments of free enterprise as to speak of militarism or imperialism as instruments of free enterprise."[21] Trade barriers and monopolies become deadly enemies of free enterprise capitalism.[22] Reduction in the American tariff which might widen an outlet for European goods and alleviate the problem have been proposed on a limited scale, but discussion of the tariff in general will not be raised even to the high level of the argument advanced by Mr Dooley. "The tariff! What difference does it make? Th' foreigner pays th' tax anyhow. He does," said Mr Dooley, "if he ain't turned back at Castle Garden." There is little prospect of discussion of the tariff in the United States and Canada since European countries cannot expect to have much influence on this subject and, again in the words of Mr Dooley, "Them that the tariff looks after will look after the tariff."

European countries feel more directly exposed to American influence and to the threat that "the cumulative advantage of size and technological progress" of the United States may enforce uniformity and standardization with disastrous implications for the artistic culture of Europe and for Western civilization. The effects have been evident in the emergence of developments which reflect a profound determination to maintain the supremacy of European culture against the threats of Americanization and communism. Civilization can hardly survive a dumbbell arrangement with its energies drawn to two centres of power, nor an arrangement dominated by one or other power group. Yet is it exceedingly difficult for an Anglo-Saxon trained in a common law tradition to understand the point of view of a European trained in the Roman law tradition.

Canadians can scarcely understand the attitude of hostility of Europeans towards Americans because of the overwhelming influence upon them of American propaganda.[23] Americans are the best propagandists because they are the best advertisers.[24] Whatever hope of continued autonomy Canada may have in the future must depend on her success in withstanding American influence and in assisting the development of a third bloc[25] designed to withstand the pressure of the United States and Russia. But there is little evidence that she is capable of these herculean efforts and much that she will continue to be regarded as an instrument of the United States. The tariff has long since been forgotten in Canada. We too have our mild imperialist ventures, as shown in our acquisition of Newfoundland. "War is self-defence against reform."[26] Neither a nation, nor a commonwealth, nor a civilization can endure in which one half in slavery believes itself free because of a statement in the Bill of Rights,[27] and attempts to enslave the other half which is free. Freedom of the press under the Bill of Rights accentuated the printed tradition, destroyed freedom of speech, and broke the relations with the oral tradition of Europe.

We may dislike American influence, we may develop a Canadian underground movement, but we are compelled to yield to American policy. We may say that democracy has become something which Americans wish to impose upon us because they say that they have it in the United States; we may dislike the assumption of Americans that they have found the one and only way of life – but they have American dollars. It may seem preposterous that North America should attempt to dictate to the cultural centres of Europe, France, Italy, Germany, and Great Britain how they should vote and what education means – but it has American dollars. Yet loans or even gifts are not a basis for friendship. The results are expressed in the remark: "I cannot understand why he is so bitterly opposed to me. I have never done anything for him." Even in the United States a slight appreciation of the definition of gratitude, as a keen sense of favours to come, exists.

In our time we have seen the overrunning of Czechoslovakia by Germany with the concurrence of the Allies and on a larger scale the overrunning of Europe in spite of their opposition. But culture and language have proved more powerful than force. In the Anglo-Saxon world we have a new mobilization of force in the United States, with new perils, and all the resources of culture and language of the English-speaking peoples, including those of the United States, will be necessary to resist it. In the crudest terms, military strategy dominated by public opinion would be disastrous.

The future of the West depends on the cultural tenacity of Europe and the extent to which it will refuse to accept dictation from a foreign policy developed in relation to the demands of individuals in North America concerned with re-election. American foreign policy has been a disgraceful illustration of the irresponsibility of a powerful nation which promises little for the future stability of the Western world. In the words of Professor Robert Peers, Canada must call in the Old World to redress the balance of the New, and hope that Great Britain will escape American imperialism as successfully as she herself has escaped British imperialism.

NOTES

1 J.E. Thorold Rogers, *The Economic Interpretation of History* (New York, 1888), 339.

2 Herbert Paul, *The Life of Froude* (London, 1906), 253. "The Canadians, or rather the Maritime provinces, seem likely to give some trouble, and the British Government may perhaps have an illustration of the difficulties and dangers incident to the retention in diplomatic dependence of communities which are otherwise independent, and which, naturally enough, look to no interest but their own" (Goldwin Smith to Gladstone, 14 May 1871, *A Selection from Goldwin Smith's Correspondence* [Toronto, n.d.], 39). In the United States, Sumner intended to press "every possible American claim against England, with a view of compelling the cession of Canada to the United States" (*The Education of Henry Adams* [New York, 1931], 275). Motley as American ambassador in London in 1870 opposed construction of the Canadian Pacific Railway (Allan Nevins, *Hamilton Fish: The Inner History of the Grant Administration* [New York, 1936], 421). "Our relations with England are of far greater importance to us than those with Germany – there being more points at issue, more chances of friction and greater difficulty in almost every question that arises on account of the irresponsibility and exacting temper of Canadian politicians" (Whitelaw Reid to President Roosevelt, 19 June 1906, cited by Royal Cortissoz, *The Life of Whitelaw Reid* [London, 1921], 2: 331).

3 See H.A. Innis, "Economic Trends," *Canada in Peace and War*, ed. Chester Martin (Toronto, 1941), 58–85.

4 Mackenzie King prided himself on journalistic appointments to the Senate. See Arthur Ford, *As the World Wags On* (Toronto, 1950), 175–6.

5 Wyndham Lewis, *The Art of Being Ruled* (New York, 1926), 371.

6 R.B. Heywood, ed., *The Works of the Mind* (Chicago, 1947), 116–17.

7 Hon. G.C. Broderick, *Memoirs and Impressions, 1831–1900* (London, 1900), 287.

8 Paul Bilkey, *Persons, Papers and Things* (Toronto, 1940), 100.

9 Sir Wilfrid Laurier argued that the calibre of members of the House had declined as business attracted men from politics and law but that the Maritimes continued to send able individuals because of the small character of business there (Ford, *As the World Wags On*, 126).

10 The older type of craft unionism avoided politics and facilitated an

international labour movement, but in the newer types of industrial unionism direct intervention in politics in the United States is paralleled by direct intervention in Canada.

11 *Reflections and Comments* (New York, 1895), 270.

12 Cited by Denys Thompson, *Voice of Civilization* (London, 1943), 180.

13 Ibid., 201.

14 Lewis, *The Art of Being Ruled*, 91.

15 "By the Constitution, the Executive may recommend measures which he may think proper, and he may veto those he thinks improper, and it is supposed he may add to these certain indirect influences to affect the actions of Congress. My political education strongly inclines me against a very free use of any of these means by the Executive to control the legislation of the country. As a rule I think that Congress should originate as well as perfect its measures without external bias" (Lincoln in a speech at Pittsburgh, 15 Feb. 1861, as recorded in D.A.S. Alexander, *History and Procedure of the House of Representatives* [Boston, 1916], 358).

16 *Life, Letters and Journals of George Ticknor* (Boston, 1880), 2: 475.

17 William James referred to "the exclusive worship of the bitch-goddess success" (Lloyd Morris, *Postscript to Yesterday* [New York, 1947], 330). The vices were "swindling and adroitness, and the indulgence of swindling and adroitness, and cant, and sympathy with cant – natural fruits of that extraordinary idealization of 'success' in the mere outward sense of 'getting there' and getting there on as big a scale as we can, which characterizes our present generation."

18 See F.A. Knox, "The March of Events," *Canadian Banker*, Autumn 1948, for a most useful discussion.

19 "The Task of Economic Recovery," *Foreign Affairs*, July 1948, 14–15.

20 E.M. Winslow, *The Pattern of Imperialism: A Study in the Theories of Power* (New York, 1948), 203.

21 Ibid., 234.

22 Ibid., 237.

23 "Says the New York Times' Hansen Baldwin: 'Canada must arm.' " *Time*, 3 Jan. 1949, 20, section on Canada – an illustration of the crude effrontery of American imperialism.

24 G.S. Viereck, *Spreading Germs of Hate* (New York, 1930), 168.

25 See B.S. Keirstead, "Canada at the Crossroads in Foreign Policy," *International Affairs*, Spring 1948, 97–110. The problem has not been simplified by the change in the position of the Canadian exchange rate.

26 Emery Neff, *Carlyle and Mill* (New York, 1930), 168.

27 See M.L. Ernst, *The First Freedom* (New York, 1946); also O.W. Riegel, *Mobilizing for Chaos: The Story of the New Propaganda* (New Haven, 1934).

CHAPTER TWENTY

Business and Government

This title suggests a sharp division between the two subjects and compels a discussion at the beginning of its background. If we adopt the British tradition of the absolute supremacy of parliament, it will not be possible to claim the existence of a sharp division whereas the American tradition specifies a constitution in which encroachments on common law are definitely checked. For this reason business and government can be regarded as separate entities. It would be surprising if American influence was not evident in Canada. One can cite not only the title of the subject which has been assigned to me but a general attitude on the part of both government and business to regard each other as separate entities. Much of the hostility between government and business in Canada can be attributed to our neglect of legal education and to American influences. Socialistic legislation has been possible in England and to some extent in Canada but the place of property in the constitution of the United States restricts its development.

Nevertheless British tradition has been powerfully reflected in the decisions on appeals to the Privy Council, in the control of parliament over natural resources, in the development of large scale public ownership and in other activities. The British tradition was strengthened by the necessity of large scale capital undertakings which could enable Canadians to compete with the United States. Canals in the United States, especially the Erie, compelled Canadians with the assistance and encouragement of great Britain to undertake improvements of the St Lawrence waterways, and railways necessitated construction of the Grand Trunk, of the Intercolonial

---

From a paper read at the first Management Conference at the University of Toronto, 23 June 1949; printed in *Commerce Journal*, 1950, 36–9.

and of the Canadian Pacific Railway. The union of upper and lower Canada, and Confederation were to an important extent a result of these demands. They provided a new credit base by which capital could be obtained at low interest rates in competition with the United States. The problem of cheap capital was evident in later railway and other transportation activities, provincial and federal, and in the development of hydro-electric power.

Capital acquired under these circumstances has presented problems which in spite of extended experience have not yet been solved. Cheap capital hastened the development of facilities such as the Intercolonial railway which were essentially political in character and not to be operated at a profit. It facilitated the construction of large scale capital undertakings on a more pretentious scale than would have been possible under private enterprise. These and other features have contributed to problems of management in government ownership. Ostensibly government owned ventures are responsible to parliament which provided cheap supplies of capital. But parliamentary bodies are not skilled in the management of operations which are highly technical in character. Consequently parliament must be content to be reasonably certain of the competency of those placed in charge and must accept their recommendations. The enormous responsibility placed on the shoulders of those appointed to such positions and the unstable character of parliament have had the effect of compelling them to rely on public opinion and of being tempted to rely on public opinion as reflected by the power of the party in power. As a result a shift in the strength of political parties in parliament has led to tragic dismissals and appointments to mention the names of Sir Henry Thornton and of officials of the Hydro-Electric Power Commission. Control has been clumsy and inefficient and involves a sort of terrorism of which the effects are evident throughout the administrations concerned.

The inadequacies of control are evident not only in the summary dismissals of heads of organizations but also in the mechanisms which have been worked out by parliament. It is scarcely necessary to do more than refer to the parliamentary committee. It is only necessary to glance through the proceedings of its meetings to appreciate its limitations. Nor can we expect guidance from a series of boards with regional or class representation. The departments concerned with administration are necessarily sensitive to the influence of public opinion and of parliament. The press can scarcely be expected to present a balanced or a considered view of the operations of highly technical works. Suggestions have been made to the effect that independent boards should be set up but these neglect the responsibility of parliament for the provision of funds and for the care over funds which it has provided.

We can scarcely overestimate the interest of the businessman in the efficient organization of these large scale vital operations and yet the businessman has tended to be rather narrow in his interests; to rest content with the statement that government ownership is a bad thing and that it is not in his short run interests to improve it. The dangers of this attitude from a short and a long run point of view need scarcely be emphasized. Not only may he suffer because of the inefficiency of these undertakings in a direct fashion but he will suffer from increased taxes to meet the deficit of inefficient operation and from the prospect that the inefficiency of a government undertaking may very well be followed by public extension of government ownership. There can be very few questions to which businessmen might more profitably direct their attention than that of developing an efficient administrative system in government owned operations. "The more business in politics and the less politics in business, the better for both" (Sir Horace Plunkett).

It may be that one of the most unfortunate effects of government ownership has been the narrow point of view of businessmen. This becomes evident in the tendency of businessmen to think of government as a particular individual in a department who can act influentially on the government in terms of interpretation of administrative regulation, of orders-in-council or of legislation. The heavy traffic of passenger trains to Ottawa is a tribute to the concern of businessmen with governmental regulations. Regulations have become an essential part of business activity and bureaucratic tendencies emerge from the interest of businessmen as well as of civil servants.

The important extent to which bureaucratic tendencies have developed during and since the war and the role of governmental regulations in business activity has compelled businessmen to become extremely cautious in their attitude toward changes in government. A change in government introduces a vast number of unpredictabilities which business has neither the energy nor the time to meet and which warrant a concern with relative stability and a continuance of the status quo. Businessmen may dislike bureaucracy but they dislike rather more an unpredictable bureaucracy.

As Professor Easterbrook has suggested the most serious menace to the position of the businessman is the obsession of the businessman with his own immediate short run interests. To some extent this has been accentuated by the large scale character of business organizations evident in the railways, banks, department stores and various industries. It has been said that the greatest single price fixing factor in Canada is the mail order catalogue and that price control would have been very much more difficult without two large department stores. In large organizations it becomes possible to develop a long run point of view and to emphasize a broader approach but it is probably for this reason that smaller businesses are compelled to take a narrower view. This narrow view is reflected in the difficulties in forming associations and in the incredibly stupid pronouncements of such associations.

Many of the difficulties between labour and business are a result of this narrowness of view. Many of the statements about education can be traced to the same source. In the social sciences in the universities one is apt to see these tendencies at their worst. An economist cannot be a good economist and have a business point of view. Not even in the interests of business can he appear to have a business point of view. Businessmen with a broad outlook are fully aware of this and even advise students to take classics. Unfortunately other businessmen, and I am afraid universities are not guiltless, hold the view that an economist must have a business point of view and that he must develop courses with a business point of view. Fortunately for universities, members of the staff with a business point of view are attracted by the high salaries paid by business organizations which want economists with a business point of view and the threat is more apparent than real.

It may be that I speak with some prejudice on this subject since my desk, in common with the desks of social scientists, seems to be the target for every bit of propaganda put out not only by cranks of every conceivable sort but also by every type of business and I am afraid it must be said that with a few notable exceptions it is difficult to detect the difference. Unfortunately my desk is not well polished, and I have the sort of primitive belief in the printed word, so clear to the individuals who send this material, which makes me reluctant to destroy it. Consequently, my desk becomes piled with literature and reaches the point which fills my colleagues with concern and at which something must be done. I am able then to convince myself that time has elapsed and that most of its pleas are outdated and that I can fill waste paper baskets without losing a wink of sleep.

I must speak therefore of what I know and you must allow for my prejudices. Nevertheless I suspect that these antics have been responsible for a considerable distrust of business on the part of the public. As a mere member of that public I think I can say that we are not taken in by this nonsense and that we resent these impositions on our intelligence. These feelings have reached the point at which one is reminded of the dialogue between the two black crows of some years past in which one remarked after hearing the other playing some music "Even if that was good, I wouldn't like it." Much play for example has been made of the word "service" but I think most of us regard it as the last attack on consumer resistance. All this explains to some extent why the public distrusts governments which seem to be favourable to business and why politicians are able to exploit such distrust so effectively.

This paper is a plea for a broader and more intelligent approach on the part of businessmen to government and a suggestion that much remains to be done in the short run and long run interests of business itself to enable it to overcome its obsession with its own immediate interests. The university is a very old institution and has been concerned throughout its history with long run problems. It is anxious to see its point of view recognized and to assist in any effort toward its achievement. On the other hand, the university must avoid in its own interests and in the interests of those with whom it cooperates contacts which give rise to suspicion. In this conference the University of Toronto has been glad to take the initiative and it welcomes your cooperation.

PART FOUR

Political Culture, the Bias of Communication, and Economic Change

CHAPTER TWENTY-ONE

On the Economic Significance of Cultural Factors

I

In discussing the limitations of economic history or of the social sciences or more specifically of the framework of the price system, we can improve our perspective regarding the place of the field of economic history and in turn of the social sciences in Western civilization. We need a sociology or a philosophy of the social sciences and particularly of economics, an economic history of knowledge or an economic history of economic history. Economic history may enable us to understand the background of economic thought or of the organization of economic thought or of thought in the social sciences. The influence of the Greeks on philosophy and in turn on universities compels us to raise questions about the limitations of the social sciences.

We must somehow overcome what Leslie Stephen calls the "weakness for omniscience which infects most historical critics."[1]

The Walrus and the Carpenter
Were walking close at hand:
They wept like anything to see
Such quantities of sand:
"If this were only cleared away,"
They said, "it *would* be grand."

"If seven maids with seven mops
Swept it for half a year,
Do you suppose," the Walrus said,

From *Political Economy in the Modern State* (Ryerson, 1946), 83–107.

"That they could get it clear?"
"I doubt it," said the Carpenter,
And shed a bitter tear.

Economics implies the application of scarce means to given ends, and the vast range of social phenomena compels a similar strategy of approach.

Within the broad subject of the social sciences we can see clearly the use of obvious strategies. The impact of the natural sciences and machine industry has been evident in the emphasis on pecuniary phenomena which are particularly suited to mathematics and mechanical devices developed in relation to mathematics. As slot machines have been built up around the sizes and weights of various denominations of coins so there has been a tendency for economics to be built up around the monetary structure. Walter Leaf wrote of three main causes disposing men to madness – love, ambition, and the study of currency problems, with the last named as the worst. Bamberger wrote that people go mad because of love and bimetallism. Sorokin has described the importance of the quantitative approach in modern society, fittingly enough in four large volumes, and has deplored the emphasis on economic questions as peculiar to the approach.

Left to themselves all find their level price,
Potatoes, verses, turnips, Greek, and rice, ...[2]

The pecuniary slant of economics is as evident in Veblen's elaboration of the pecuniary economy of North America as in the discussion by monetary theorists of liquidity preference. I need hardly refer to the work of the committee on price studies and the important contributions of those working under its directions, mentioning only the studies of Bezanson, Cole, and Hamilton.

The widespread interest in prices reflected in economics and in economic history has effectively broadened the approach to history and corrected the bias which emphasized military exploits or political activities. The state and other organizations of centralized power have had a vital interest in records of their activities and have given powerful direction to the study of political, legal, constitutional, and ecclesiastical history. The mechanics of archival organization have given enormous impetus to the writing of history from the standpoint of centralized power. Administrative machinery and preservation of records have impressed on historical writing the imprint of the state and fostered the bias which made history the handmaid of politics. In the eighteenth century rigid censorship fostered evasions in the form of histories written as political weapons. An interest in history is still fostered as a means of strengthening the church or the state, and the demands of particular groups are reflected even in economic history. The honorific position of military, legal, and ecclesiastical groups is evident in the history textbook, a form of historical writing which is extremely sensitive to political demands and to nationalistic interests. Scholarship is harassed by the demands of pressure groups. Even though price history has a bias of its own, it can check tendencies favourable to power groups. Economic history can point to the dangers of bias and the necessity for a broader perspective.

On the other hand, the pecuniary approach, when all pervasive, tends to obscure the significance of technology and workmanship. It has threatened to make economics a branch of high accountancy.

> The modern tendency to find mental satisfaction in measuring everything by a fixed rational standard, and the way it takes for granted that everything can be related to everything else, certainly receives from the apparently objective value of money, and the universal possibility of exchange which this involves, a strong psychological impulse to become a fixed habit of thought, whereas the purely logical process itself, when it only follows its own course, is not subject to these influences, and it then turns these accepted ideas into mere probabilities.[3]

Concentration on the price system, driven by mathematics, involves neglect of the technological conditions under which prices operate. The use of liquidity preference as a concept in the study of economic history emphasizes short-run points of view acceptable to the price system rather than long-run points of view which necessitate perspective. An equilibrium of approaches to the study of economic phenomena becomes exceedingly difficult to achieve with the insistence on short-run interests and the obsession with the present. There is in the social sciences a liquidity preference for theories concerned with the present which is more dangerous in its implications than liquidity preference is to monetary stability. Marx and his followers sharpened awareness of pressure groups and emphasized the importance of the study of technology and the means of production. While Schumpeter has attempted to bridge the pecuniary and the technological approaches and to void the danger of concentrating on the price system and the profit motive and on technology, his efforts have meant the sacrifice of too much in both approaches and particularly in the technological. Moreover he deliberately neglects the important work of political historians. The late N.J. Silberling made a more successful attempt to coordinate the political, pecuniary, and technological approaches but his work was limited by national boundaries. In part, the weakness of the technological approach has been a result of the restricted knowledge of technical development. The work of Nef on coal, of Usher on mechanical inventions, and of a large number of students in the field must be supplemented extensively. Such work must emphasize not only technical changes but their significance to economic and political institutions. The interest in legislation, court decisions, and legal systems shown by Commons should be integrated with the work of the historian of prices, technology, and government. Sir Henry Sumner Maine made a comment of profound significance when he pointed to the interrelation of legislation, prices, and technology and the mathematical bias.

> Experience shows that innovating legislation is connected not so much with Science as with the scientific air which certain subjects, not capable of exact scientific treatment, from time to time assume. To this class of subjects belonged Bentham's scheme of Law-Reform, and, above all, Political Economy as treated by Ricardo. Both have been extremely fertile sources of legislation during the last fifty years.[4]

The vast range of studies of business cycles and their significance to unemployment would gain perceptibly by the integration of basic approaches. The conflict between technology and the price system described by Veblen in *The Engineer and the Price System,* in which the restrictions on technology have been of primary concern, can be resolved more easily with a broader perspective. A broader synthesis would enable us to counteract the regression in thought shown by Schumpeter and Polanyi who regard monopoly as a means of resisting the effects of obsession with the short run. In technology as in the price system, advance has been supported by mathematics, but the effectiveness of the application of mathematics varies in the two fields and may make for divergence rather than convergence in the study of economic phenomena as a whole. Since there has been a very perceptible lag in the spread of mathematics in relation to the price system, engineers and scientists such as Douglas and Soddy, social-credit theorists, technocrats, and others have taken advantage of the gap. But it is possible that God is not a mathematician as some philosophers would have us believe.

The intensive demands of technology on students in the social sciences have contributed to the narrowness of its approach and such narrowness has been intensified by the emphasis that political and military history put on nationalism. The important contributions of geography have been restricted to studies of localization such as those of Alfred Weber and of Usher. The significance of basic geographic features has been suggested by Mahan from the standpoint of the sea and by Mackinder from the standpoint of continental land masses but they have not been incorporated effectively in economic history. Nor do we have an effective study of air. In a general way we are familiar with the influence of the sea on the development of democratic institutions in Greece and of the land on the centralizing tendencies of Rome. Although we can trace the influence of Roman institutions in the codified law of Europe and in the Roman Catholic Church as adapted to a continent, and can see the growth of parliamentary institutions and Protestantism in the Anglo-Saxon world in relation to the demands of the sea, it may be doubted whether we appreciate their significance to economic history. But the effects of geography may be offset by technology in that the development of defensive tactics led to the growth of feudalism and the use of gunpowder brought a return to efficient offensive tactics and to increasing centralization in the Western world. Geography provides the grooves which determine the course and to a large extent the character of economic life. Population, in terms of numbers and quality, and technology are largely determined by geographic background, and political institutions have been to an important extent shaped through wars in relation to this background.

II

Geography has been effective in determining the grooves of economic life through its effects on transportation and communication. The lower costs of tonnage by sea than by land strengthened the position of Great Britain in the development of trade in more bulky commodities suited to industrial growth and expansion. France, Spain, and Portugal with a continental background developed connections with the continental hinterlands of the New World. As the late Max Handmann suggested, the Anglo-Dutch trading systems expanded in relation to the sea, continental feudalism in relation to the land. The expansion of Great Britain was in terms of the migration of Englishmen and the development of industries, either, as in the northern colonies, by using English labour in the production of bulky commodities or, in the tropical regions, by organizing imported labour on a large scale for the production of sugar and cotton. Spanish feudalism and militarism exploited native labour primarily for precious metals, and French feudalism for furs. British expansion linked trade with naval strength and limited financial burdens, whereas French expansion meant trade and military strength and enormous demands on finance for the construction of forts and the maintenance of garrisons and bureaucracies. But British maritime expansion meant parliamentary institutions and decentralization characteristic of the Anglo-Saxon world. Federalism became an important feature. In Canada feudalism continued in the ownership of natural resources by the provinces and produced the dual mixture of a capitalistic federal government and feudalistic provincial governments.

The advantages to Great Britain of maritime expansion and of access, with low costs of navigation, to cheap supplies of bulky goods were accompanied by the development of coal mining and industry. Coal began to pull raw materials from the fringes of the Atlantic basin and beyond, and to provide the power for conversion of the raw materials into finished products for export. The effectiveness of the pull began to vary with distances, and distances changed with improvements in manufacturing and particularly in transportation. Timber and cotton from the northern and southern parts of North America could be transported to Great Britain, and penetration to the interior with canals and railways brought steadily expanding trade first in wheat and then in the products of animal husbandry. Successive waves of commodities responded to the lowering of costs of navigation across the Atlantic and of transportation to the interior. As wheat production moved to the interior, older areas became concerned with the production of other commodities. England shifted her fields from arable land to pasture. In these broad trends we see the basis of the stages outlined by Gras and his students in the description of the growth of the metropolitan economy. In the general migration and shift in production of raw materials and, in turn, of semifinished and finished products, we can see the problems that the late Frederick Turner described in his work on the frontiers. Disturbances to these more or less regular trends were a result of sudden developments in which costs were lowered, of geographic factors such as access to the great plains and obstruction by mountains, of cyclonic activities such as accompanied the gold rushes around the fringes of the Pacific, and of the development of new sources of power in the opening up of the coal regions of North America.

The emergence of a complex industrial and trading structure centring about the coal areas of the Anglo-Saxon world assumed not only improvements in transportation but also in communication. Correspondence between individuals and firms with slow navigation, on which Heaton has thrown much light, was inadequate to meet the demands of large-scale industry and large-scale consumption. The rapid and extensive dissemination of information was essential to the effective placing of labour, capital, raw materials, and finished products. Oscar Wilde wrote that "private information is practically the source of every large modern fortune,"[5] and the demand for private information hastened the development of communications. The application of steam power to the production of paper and, in turn, of the newspaper, followed by the telegraph, and the exploitation of human curiosity and its interest in news by advertisers anxious to dispose of their products created efficient channels for the spread of information. The state, acting through subsidies, the post office, libraries, and compulsory education, widened the areas to which information could be disseminated. Democratic forms of government provided news and subsidies for the transmission of news. As Carlyle wrote, "He who first shortened the labour of copyists by device of *movable types* was disbanding hired armies and cashiering most kings and senates, and creating a whole new democratic world: he had invented the art of printing."[6]

With the rise of a vast area of public opinion, which was essential to the rapid dissemination of information, and the growth in turn of marketing organizations, the expansion of credit, and the development of nationalism, the vast structure previously centring about religion declined. Eric Gill wrote, "Where religion is strong, commerce is weak," but religion played an important role in the growth of commerce. The significance of religion to civilization has been described by Max Weber, Tawney, Toynbee, and others. Centralized religious institutions checked fanaticism but their limitations were evident in the emergence of dissent. Leslie Stephen wrote that "the full bitterness which the human heart is capable of feeling, the full ferocity which it is capable of expressing is to be met nowhere but in religious papers." Adam Smith in his comments on religious instruction noted the handicaps of the established church in England. The clergy had

> ... many of them become very learned, ingenious, and respectable men; but they have in general ceased to be very popular preachers. The methodists, without half the learning of the dissenters, are much more in vogue. In the church of Rome, the industry and zeal of the inferior clergy are kept more alive by the powerful motive of self-interest, than perhaps in any established protestant church. The parochial clergy derive, many of them, a very con-

siderable part of their subsistence from the voluntary oblations of the people; a source of revenue which confession gives them many opportunities of improving. The mendicant orders derive their whole subsistence from such oblations. It is with them, as with the hussars and light infantry of some armies; no plunder, no pay.[7]

The restraining influence of religious institutions has limitations, and dissenting groups and philosophical systems emerge on their fringes. Centralization is followed by decentralization.

The printing press and commerce implied far-reaching changes in the role of religion. In Victor Hugo's famous chapter in the *Notre Dame de Paris* entitled "This Has Killed That," he writes: "During the first six thousand years of the world ... architecture was the great handwriting of the human race." Geoffrey Scott has described the effects of printing:

Three influences, in combination, turned Renaissance architecture to an academic art. They were the revival of scholarship, the invention of printing, the discovery of Vitruvius. Scholarship set up the ideal of an exact and textual subservience to the antique; Vitruvius provided the code; printing disseminated it. It is difficult to do justice to the force which this implied. The effective influence of literature depends on its prestige and its accessibility. The sparse and jealously guarded manuscripts of earlier days gave literature an almost magical prestige, but afforded no accessibility; the cheap diffusion of the printing press has made it accessible, but stripped it of its prestige. The interval between these two periods was literature's unprecedented and unrepeated opportunity. In this interval Vitruvius came to light, and by this opportunity he, more perhaps than any other writer, has been the gainer. His treatise was discovered in the earlier part of the fifteenth century, at St. Gall; the first presses in Italy were established in 1464; and within a few years (the first edition is undated) the text of Vitruvius was printed in Rome. Twelve separate editions of it were published within a century; seven translations into Italian, and others into French and German. Alberti founded his great work upon it, and its influence reached England by 1563 in the brief essay of John Shute. Through the pages of Serlio, Vitruvius subjugated France, till then abandoned to the trifling classicism of François I.; through those of Palladio he became supreme in England.[8]

The book destroyed the edifice, and in the religious wars and the French Revolution it destroyed social institutions as well. Brooks Adams wrote:

That ancient channel [the church] once closed, Protestants had to open another, and this led to deification of the Bible, ... Thus for the innumerable costly fetishes of the imaginative age were substituted certain writings which could be consulted without a fee. The expedient was evidently the device of a mercantile community.[9]

Leslie Stephen in a letter to Charles Adams wrote:

I always fancy that if one could get to the truth, the Puritan belief in the supernatural was a good deal feebler than Carlyle represents. The man-of-business side of them checked the fanatic, and the ironsides beat the cavaliers as much because they appreciated good business qualities as because they were "God-fearing" people.[10]

"'We that look to Zion,' wrote a gallant Anabaptist admiral of the age, 'should hold Christian communion. We have all the guns aboard.'"[11]

It is scarcely necessary to elaborate on the significance to the economic development of European civilization of the emphasis which Calvinism put on the individual. This significance was reinforced by the adaptability of the alphabet to the printing press, private enterprise, and the machine, and by the consequent spread of literacy, trade, and industrialism. The Chinese were handicapped by a language ill adapted to the printing press except through support of the state, and there was consequently no expansion of commerce adequate to defeat the demands of religion. We are told of the handicaps of a religion with innumerable devils and gods in contrast with the efficiency of Christianity which reduced their numbers and enhanced economic efficiency. On the other hand, Burckhardt has described the tyranny of religions which emphasized otherworldliness, established a hierarchy to guard the entrance to other worlds, and participated in the most bitter warfare. Morley wrote of "the most frightful idea that has ever corroded human nature – the idea of eternal punishment" and of its deadening effects on the interest in social reform. The terrifying threats of a single organization which inspired Lord Acton to write that "all power corrupts and absolute power corrupts absolutely" were evaded by the printing press and commerce.

Religion has been vitally related to the mysteries of life and death and to the family. The decline of the Church in Europe reflected the impact of birth control on the confessional. The importance of the biological background stressed by Knight in his discussion of the sociological significance of the family was evident in feudal societies with or without primogeniture based on land and military power. Religious sects have fostered the accumulation of wealth over long periods by intermarriage of families. Whereas the Church in its fight for sacerdotal celibacy as a means of preventing the dispersion of wealth left itself open to the looting of its monasteries, the Jews and other sects have been persecuted because of the building up of large fortunes. One needs only to point to the studies of the Jews in relation to trade and economic development and to the peculiarities of economic organization in various sects, for example the interest of the Quakers in developing industries around nonintoxicating beverages, to appreciate their significance. We have no clear understanding of the economics of death and bequest (with apologies to Wedgwood) in relation to the redistribution of wealth among groups and sects.

In the United States the importance of religion to the growth of trade is shown in the large numbers of denominational periodicals and their promising returns to advertisers in a national market. Significantly, among the first advertisers who were alert to these possibilities were those large-scale dealers in human credulity, the patent-medicine firms. Sir William Osler wrote that "the desire to take medicine is perhaps the greatest feature which distinguishes man from animals."[12] Patent medicine capitalized an age of faith in miracles by emphasizing cures and led to the growth of advertising, trade, and scientific development. The railroad and the telegraph steadily increased the efficiency of advertising media – chiefly weeklies, monthlies, and quarterlies – which created a national market. In a country of vast extent the dailies expanded in relation to metropolitan markets and flourished by sensational appeals to larger numbers. After the invention of the electric light and the reduction of fire losses, the department store provided the advertising essential to their success.

The newspaper, with the technological advances evident in the telegraph, the press associations, the manufacture of paper from wood, the rotary press, and the linotype, became independent of party support and became concerned with an increase in circulation and with all the devices calculated to bring about such an increase to meet the demands of advertising. The phenomenal increase in the production of goods and the demands for more efficient methods of distribution stimulated the expansion of newspaper production, and newspapers stimulated production by widening and intensifying the market.

By the beginning of the twentieth century the new journalism directed by Pulitzer, Hearst, and Northcliffe had become entrenched in the Anglo-Saxon world. The Spanish-American War and the

South African War were the preludes to its supremacy. Bismarck, even before 1900, spoke of the power of the press. It had done a great deal of harm.

> It was the cause of the last three wars, ... the Danish press forced the King and the Government to annex Schleswig; the Austrian and South German press agitated against us; and the French press contributed to the prolongation of the campaign in France.[13]

On 28 January 1883, he said:

> You have only to look at the newspapers and see how empty they are, and how they fish out the ancient sea-serpent in order to have something to fill their columns. The feuilleton is spreading more and more, and if anything sensational occurs, they rush at it furiously and write it to death for whole weeks. This low water in political affairs, this distress in the journalistic world, is the highest testimonial for a Minister of Foreign Affairs.[14]

Bagehot wrote, "Happy are the people whose annals are vacant but woe to the wretched journalists that have to compose and write articles therein." Sir Wemyss Reid, editor of the Leeds *Mercury*, claimed that the interest of the English public in foreign affairs began with *The News*'s agitation over the Bulgarian atrocities in 1876 and Gladstone's shrewdness in capitalizing the agitation. From that time public opinion never returned to its interest in domestic problems. As the "ancient Gothic genius, that sun which sets behind the gigantic press of Mayence" was crushed by the book, so the book was crushed by the newspaper. In turn the newspaper was destined to feel the effects of the radio. With Victor Hugo we can say, "It is the second tower of Babel of the human race."

III

In all this we can see at least a part of the background of the collapse of Western civilization which begins with the present century. The comparative peace of the nineteenth century is followed by a period in which we have been unable to find a solution to the problem of law and order, and have resorted to force rather than to persuasion, bullets rather than ballots. "I know only two ways in which society can be governed – by public opinion and by the sword," wrote Macaulay. But Croker, representing the Conservative position, claimed that we govern by the law saving us from extremes of government by public opinion or by the sword. The rule of law became less effective. Where Bismarck had been able to use *The Times, The Daily Telegraph,* and *the Pall Mall Gazette* and say, "It was easier, cheaper, more humane to supply the English journals with news that to fight England,"[15] his master hand was gone, and the newspapers had grown beyond control. They had become something more than his description of "just printer's ink printed on paper." Where diplomacy by paragraphs had reached the point that a reference in *The Times* served as a check to French debates, *The Times* was now in other hands. Northcliffe had control of a power which could break the Asquith cabinet during the war. President Theodore Roosevelt and the big stick had been created by the American press. This vast new instrument concerned with reaching large numbers of readers rendered obsolete the machinery for maintaining peace which had characterized the nineteenth century. Guizot wrote of the great evil of democracy. "It readily sacrifices the past and the future to what is supposed to be the interest of the present," and that evil was accentuated by the reign of the newspaper and its obsession with the immediate. But to paraphrase Hilaire Belloc we must say of democracy,

Always keep a hold of nurse
For fear of finding something worse.

Lipmann's desertion of the study of rationalizing processes as developed with Graham Wallas, following the emergence of Freudian concern with the irrational, was a significant step. It would scarcely be decent in this gathering to refer to the implications to the social sciences, but one notes with alarm the changing fashions in economics. The breakup of the classical tradition of economics is an indication of the powerful influence of fashions in our times. At one time we are concerned with tariffs, at another with trusts, and still another with money. As newspapers seldom find it to their interest to pursue any subject for more than three or four days, so the economist becomes weary of particular interests or senses that the public is weary of them and changes accordingly. And this paper will be cited as an obsession with the obsession with the immediate. There is need for a study of economics and insanity supporting that of Durkheim on religion and suicide.

The inability of the twentieth century to find a solution to the eternal problem of freedom and power is basically significant to the study of economic history. When the climate of opinion makes impossible any concern with the past or the future, the student finds it exceedingly difficult to discover an anchorage or a point of view from which to approach the problem of European civilization. A recognition of factors affecting irrationality is a beginning. The church, the army and the police, industry, and possibly the drink trade have been powerful forces affecting fanaticism. A study of the drink trade cannot be undertaken here, but the coffee houses in England after the Puritan revolution in the middle of the seventeenth century weakened the position of the tavern and provided centres of discussion which undermined the position of the Stuarts. The encouragement to sugar production in the West Indies which followed the increase in consumption of coffee, tea and chocolate had its unfortunate consequences in the increased production of molasses and rum. Puritanism in England meant decline in the taverns but a rise in the rum trade of the new world. A change of the whole drinking habits of the United States followed the dumping of tea in Boston harbour, and it may be that the devotion to coffee has had important political results. The relation between beverages and intelligent discussion offers an interesting bridge between economic history and political history. The drink trade has been significant for trade and war. The economic history of North America might be written around the struggle of brandy supported by the French against rum supported by the English. It was the considered view of C.C. Buell, who in the 1880's edited the reminiscences of generals of the Civil War for *Century,* that it "was a whiskey war. With few exceptions, like Howard, all the union generals kept themselves going with hard liquor. The men who came through and succeeded were the ones who could stand up to their drink."[16]

The fundamental problem of civilization is that of government or of keeping people quiet, or following Machiavelli "to content the people and to manage the nobles." All politicians will echo the words of Lord Melbourne, "Damn them! Why can't they keep quiet?" We are aware of the devices of oriental empires and of the empires of Central America through the linking of religion to the state. The Jewish and Mohammedan religions persisted by virtue of discipline and the use of force. Greece used the army and navy as sources of resistance to external domination, and Rome used the army and the road as means of domination. Countries with a revolutionary tradition acquired adaptability and a belief in the power to accomplish change by individual efforts, but the right and ability to protest is not paralleled by an ability to accept responsibility. Vitality assumes the ability to reorganize efficiently. But a revolutionary tradition is safer in the state than in religion. In Germany as the home of the printing press a revolutionary tradition in religion was supported by the state. In England the religious revolution followed the revolution of the state and facilitated the outbreak of Puritanism and the growth of trade. In Canada the revolutionary tradition missed the French in the church, and in turn the English in the state, with the migration of Loyalists after the Revolution, and provided the basis for mutual misunderstanding. Weakening of the Church as a device to destroy fanaticism by the invention of printing, the rise of Protestantism, and the emergence of philosophy in the Age of Enlightenment left commerce as the great stabilizer. Its influence was evident in the comparative peace of the nineteenth century. Samuel Johnson said that there were "few ways in which a man can be more innocently employed than in getting money."

Rationality which accompanies the price system brings its own handicaps in the formation of monopolies. Large-scale effective mechanization of distribution necessitated a single price and the search for devices to prevent outbreaks of competitive warfare. The price system weakens the profit motive by its emphasis on management. Cartels and formalism in commerce paralleled ecclesiasticism in religion and in both cases initiative in thought was weakened. Volumes of economic history were written about business firms, epitaphs in two volumes (George Moore), as part of the literature of the new scriptures. Ecclesiasticism and the devastating effects of the depression brought an acute paralysis of thought and the rush to such illusions and catchwords as security and full employment. The price system brought not only rationality in business but also luxury and freedom from work. The intellectual snob who exploits by telling others how they are exploited and luxurious discussions of the class struggle have been evident enough. We need an economic interpretation of the class struggle, but, as Troeltsch has pointed out, the objectivity of the price mechanism supports the plausible finality of the Marxian interpretation. The price system with its sterilizing power has destroyed ideologies, and broken up irreconcilable minorities by compelling them to name their price. Unrestrained, it has destroyed its own ideology since it too has its price. In a sense religion is an effort to organize irrationality and as such appears in all large-scale organizations of knowledge. Commerce follows the general trends of organized religious bodies as does thought in the social sciences. "Most organizations appear as bodies founded for the painless extinction of the ideas of their founders."[17] Alexander Murray wrote to Archibald Constable, the Edinburgh publisher, on 7 July 1807:

It will be no wonderful occurrence if, in this age of constitution making and universal improvement, the nations which have long been unscientifically free shall become scientifically servile – for it is only when people begin to want water that they think of making reservoirs; and it was observed that the laws of Rome were never reduced into a system till its virtue and taste had perished.[18]

As in organized religion, dissent appears on the fringes bringing the sceptic and philosopher, or bringing into being the Economic History Association which springs up on the fringes of large ecclesiastical academic organizations.[19] The principle that authority is taken, never given, begins to emerge. Or there may be a palace revolution such as that started by Lord Keynes. "Dost thou not know my son, with how little wisdom the world is governed?" (Count Oxenstierna).

The outbreak of irrationality, which in the early part of the twentieth century became evident in the increasing interest in psychology following the steadying effects of commerce in the nineteenth century, is the tragedy of our time. The rationalizing potentialities of the price system and its importance in developing powers of calculation in the individual have failed to prevent a major collapse. It has been argued that man as a biological phenomenon has been unable to sustain the excessive demands of rationalism evident in the mathematics of the price system and of technology. Charles Dickens wrote to Charles Knight (30 January 1854):

My satire is against those who see figures and averages, and nothing else – the representatives of the wickedest and most enormous vice of this time – the men who, through long years to come, will do more to damage the really useful truths of political economy, than I could do (if I tried) in my whole life – the addled heads who would take the average of cold in the Crimea during twelve months, as a reason for clothing a soldier in nankeen on a night when he would be frozen to death in fur – and who would comfort the labourer in travelling twelve miles a-day to and from his work, by telling him that the average distance of one inhabited place from another on the whole area of England, is not more than four miles. Bah! what have you to do with these![20]

How far does the spread of mathematics and the intensity of modern life create demands for irrationalism and fanaticism? Is the emergence of Freud and the psychologists a result of the spread of irrationalism or an effort to meet the problems of irrationalism? Has commercial development been effective in destroying religious centralization as a stabilizing influence to the point that new sources of power such as nationalism and autarchy with subordination to militarism have taken their place? Morley described the stubborn sentiment of race and the bitter antagonism of the church as the two most powerful forces affecting civilized society. In weakening the church, commerce has been unable to check nationalism, although religious institutions can be more effective than industrialism or commercialism in crushing intelligence. The breakdown of the press shown in the sharp decline in influence of the editorial in the twentieth century points in the direction of nationalism.[21] The printing press and new methods of communication have been developed as methods of division rather than cooperation. National and linguistic differences have been accentuated and internationalism weakened. The mechanization of art intensified nationalism. Where the stage meant an international interest, the movies and the talkies were subject to customs duties. Following its concentration on the problems of the immediate, commerce has lost its control as a stabilizer of power.

IV

The significance of economic history in all this is shown in its concern with long-run trends and its emphasis on training in a search for patterns rather than mathematical formulae. It should compel the study of interrelationships between the social sciences and between nations. It should rescue the social sciences from the charge of producing books "each with a hundred methods of distributing the fruits of productive labour among those whose labour is unproductive."[22] It should weaken the position of the textbook which has become such a powerful instrument for the closing of men's minds with its emphasis on memory and its systematic checking of new ideas. Biases become entrenched in textbooks which represent monopolies of the publishing trade and resist the power of thought. Machine industry through printing dispenses with thought or compels it to move in certain channels. The dispersion of thought through the printing industry makes attacks on monopoly increasingly difficult. In emphasizing a long-range approach to social phenomena, economic history should contribute to stability. Not only should it supplement political and social history, it should in supplementing them check the tendency in itself and in them to bias and fanaticism. Within the narrower range of the social sciences it should provide a check against the specialization of mathematical systems peculiar to a monetary and a machine age and should indicate the extent and significance of the irrational as contrasted with the rational. It should offset the superficiality in the mathematical approach of which Wesley Mitchell complains. This is to recognize that the subject is more difficult than mathematics and to insist that tools must be used, and not described, if interpretation is not to be superseded by antiquarianism. In the words of Cobden, political economy is "the highest exercise of the human mind, and the exact sciences require by no means so hard an effort."[23]

Economics tends to become a branch of political history and it is necessary to suggest alternative approaches and their limitations, to emphasize sociology with its concern with institutions, geography, and technology. By drawing attention to the limitations of the social sciences and of the price system it can show the importance of religion and of factors hampering the efficiency of the price system. Not only does it introduce a balance to constitutional and legal history, it draws attention to the penchant for mathematics and for other scientific tools which have warped the humanities. Economic history may provide grappling irons with which to lay hold of areas on the fringe of economics, whether in religion or in art, and with which, in turn, to enrich other subjects, as well as to rescue economics from the present-mindedness which pulverizes other subjects and makes a broad approach almost impossible.[24] Economic history demands the perspective to reduce jurisdictional disputes to an absurdity. The use of economic theory as a device for economizing knowledge should be extended and not used to destroy other subjects or an interest in them. Goldwin Smith wrote, "Social science if it is to take the place of religion as a conservative force has not yet developed itself or got firm hold of the popular mind."[25] Economic history can contribute to the fundamental problem of determining the limits of the social sciences. Without a solution to this problem there can be no future for them. "There is no use in printing in italics when you have no ink."

The circulation of printed matter cheapened thought and destroyed the prestige of the great works of the past which were collected and garnered before the introduction of movable type. Rational thought and art consequently had more influence. European civilization lived off the intellectual capital of Greek civilization, the spiritual capital provided by the Hebrew civilization, the material capital acquired by looting the specie reserves of Central American civilizations, and the natural resources of the New World. Crozier wrote with regard to England:

> It pays her better to buy her intellect, penetration, originality, invention and so on, when she wants them and where she wants them, than to breed them. ... Germany and France and other continental nations supply her with nearly all the new departures that have to be made in science and

philosophy in medicine, in scholarship and the higher criticism, in the art of war; in new chemical and industrial processes; and in enlargements of the scope of music and of art.[26]

He might have extended the argument to Western civilization.

The enormous capacity of Western European civilization to loot has left little opportunity for consideration of the problems which follow the exhaustion of material to be looted. But this civilization has shown continual concern in the common man and in the distribution of loot. Perhaps economic history can begin from this point to make its contribution in the building up of spiritual, intellectual, and material capital, since it is not concerned with the belief in the common man but with the common man himself.

NOTES

1 *History of English Thought in the Eighteenth Century* (London, 1876), 1: 438.

2 Cited in A.S. Collins, *The Profession of Letters: A Study of the Relation of Author to Patron, Publisher, and Public, 1780–1832* (London, 1928), 120.

3 Ernst Troeltsch, *The Social Teaching of the Christian Churches* (London, 1931), 1: 408. For a suggestive account of the far-reaching implications of objectivity reflected by the mathematics of the price system, see the description of baseball in Victor O. Jones, "Box Score!" *Newsmen's Holiday* (Cambridge, 1942), 162–82: "The one thing which distinguishes baseball from all other sports and which has been the main reason for 'organized baseball's' hold upon the public is its development of a statistical side" (165–6). For a discussion of the importance of statistics in political propaganda, see F.C. Bartlett, *Political Propaganda* (Cambridge, 1940), 93–4. "When a statement is 'quantified' it seems to convey to the majority of persons a superior certainty, and it passes without question" (94). The Gallup poll has possibly made politics more absorbing. But statistics has been particularly dangerous to modern society by strengthening the cult of economics and weakening other social sciences and the humanities.

4 *Popular Government* (London, 1885), 146.

5 *An Ideal Husband,* act 2.

6 *Sartor Resartus* (London, n.d.), 128.

7 Adam Smith, *An Inquiry into the Nature and Causes of the Wealth of Nations* (Modern Library ed., New York, 1937), 791–2.

8 Geoffrey Scott, *The Architecture of Humanism: A Study in the History of Taste* (New York, 1924), 194–5.

9 *The Law of Civilization and Decay: An Essay on History* (London, 1895), 150–1.
10 F.W. Maitland, *Life and Letters of Leslie Stephen* (London, 1906), 448–9.
11 John Morley, *Oliver Cromwell* (London, 1919), 478.
12 Harvey Cushing, *The Life of Sir William Osler* (Oxford, 1925), 1: 342.
13 Moritz Busch, *Bismarck: Some Secret Pages of His History* (New York, 1898), 2: 175.
14 Ibid., 2: 346.
15 John Russell Young, *Men and Memories: Personal Reminiscences,* ed. M.D.R. Young (New York and London, 1901), 271.
16 Will Irwin, *The Making of a Reporter* (New York, 1942), 146.
17 G.P. Gooch, *Life of Lord Courtney* (London, 1920), 416.
18 Thomas Constable, *Archibald Constable and His Literary Correspondents* (Edinburgh, 1873), 1: 261.
19 See Troeltsch, *Social Teaching of the Christian Churches*; also S.D. Clark, "Religious Organization and the Rise of the Canadian Nation 1850–85," *Report of the Canadian Historical Association,* 1944, 86–97.
20 Charles Knight, *Passages of a Working Life During Half a Century* (London, 1865), 3: 188.
21 Oswald Garrison Villard, *The Disappearing Daily: Chapters in American Newspaper Evolution* (New York, 1944).
22 Henry Holt, *Garrulities of an Octogenarian Editor* (Boston, 1923), 104.
23 John Morley, *The Life of Richard Cobden* (London, 1887), 1: 323.
24 Alec Lawrence Macfie, *An Essay on Economy and Value: Being an Enquiry into the Real Nature of Economy* (London, 1936).
25 *Essays on Questions of the Day, Political and Social* (New York and London, 1893), 39. "It was this youthful religion – profound, barbaric, poetical – that the Teutonic races insinuated into Christianity and substituted for that last sigh of two expiring worlds. In the end,with the complete crumbling away of Christian dogma and tradition, Absolute Egotism appeared openly on the surface in the shape of a German speculative philosophy. This form, which Protestantism assumed at a moment of high tension and reckless self-sufficiency, it will doubtless shed in turn and take on new expressions; but that declaration of independence on the part of the Teutonic spirit marks emphatically its exit from Christianity and the end of that series of transformations in which it took Bible and patristic dogma for its materials. It now bids fair to apply itself instead to social life and natural science and to attempt to feed its Protean hunger directly from these more homely sources" (George Santayana, *Reason in Religion* [London, 1906], 3:125–6).
26 John Beattie Crozier, *History of Intellectual Development on the Lines of Modern Evolution* (London, 1901), 3: 166–7.

CHAPTER TWENTY-TWO

Industrialism and Cultural Values

We must all be aware of the extraordinary, perhaps insuperable, difficulty of assessing the quality of a culture of which we are a part or of assessing the quality of a culture of which we are not a part. In using other cultures as mirrors in which we may see our own culture we are affected by the astigma of our own eyesight and the defects of the mirror, with the result that we are apt to see nothing in other cultures but the virtues of our own. During the twentieth century machine industry has made it possible to amass enormous quantities of information evident in encyclopaedias, histories of civilization, and quiz programs. The concern with the study of civilization in this century is probably a result of the character of our civilization. Certainly such studies reflect our civilization. Spengler in *The Decline of the West* could not have been unaffected by the position of Germany, nor could Toynbee free himself from the traditions of English-speaking countries, nor could Kroeber escape the influence of the United States and the obsession with the objective qualities of science. I shall assume that cultural values, or the way in which or the reasons why people of a culture think about themselves, are part of the culture.

It is perhaps a unique characteristic of civilization that each civilization believes in its uniqueness and its superiority to other civilizations. Indeed this may be the meaning of culture – i.e., something which we have that others have not. It is probably for this reason that writings on culture can be divided into those attempting to weaken other cultures and those attempting to strengthen their

From a paper read at the meetings of the American Economic Association, Chicago, 30 Dec. 1950; printed in *The Bias of Communication* (Toronto, 1951, chap. 5, 132–41.

own. The emphasis of St Augustine on original sin implied an attack on those representing the secular state, as the emphasis of John Locke on the *tabula rasa* was the basis of an attack on ecclesiastical hierarchy, and the work of Spencer on progress was the basis for the claim to supremacy of Anglo-Saxons. "Reason is and ought only to be the slave of the passions and can never pretend to any other office than to serve and obey them" – a statement as true of this quotation and of Hume's writings as of others. Perhaps the obsession of each culture with its uniqueness is the ultimate basis of its decline. Dean Inge has remarked that civilization is a disease almost invariably fatal unless the cause is checked in time. The Hindus and the Chinese have survived by marking time.[1]

A brief survey of cultural development in the West may indicate the peculiarity or uniqueness of culture and elements which make for duration and extension. Cultures will reflect their influence in terms of space and in terms of duration. How large an area did they cover and how long did they last? The limitations of culture, in point of duration, are in part a result of the inability to muster the intellectual resources of a people to the point where stagnation can be avoided and where boredom can be evaded. The history of boredom or stagnation has yet to be written but it might well include the story of the ostracism of Aristides the Just on the ground that the Greeks became weary of hearing him called the Just. Hume wrote that "when the arts and sciences come to perfection in any state, from that moment, they naturally or rather necessarily decline and seldom or never revive in that nation where they formerly flourished." Intense cultural activity is followed by fatigue.

The capacity to concentrate on intense cultural activity during a short period of time and to mobilize intellectual resources over a vast territory assumes to an important extent the development of armed force to a high state of efficiency. Cultural activity, evident in architecture and sculpture, capable of impressing peoples over a wide area, is designed to emphasize prestige. It becomes an index of power. A concern for continuity, the biological limitations of the patriarchal system as a basis for dynasties, and the difficulties of maintaining a high cultural level over a long period of time will involve an emphasis on types of architecture calculated to reflect a control over time as well as over space. The pyramids were an index of power over time but dynasties represented by them were displaced and in turn new dynasties concentrated on new monuments to enhance their prestige. Old capital sites scattered along the Nile Valley are a memorial of the demands of successive dynasties for prestige. The Egyptian Empire was a tribute to their success. But such monuments as capitals with tombs, palaces, temples, and sculpture were expensive and did much to bring the Empire to an end. Political power reflected in capitals was supported by such cultural activities as writing evident in successive bureaucracies.

Civilization in the Tigris and Euphrates valleys developed along lines similar to that in the Nile but solutions to the problem of time appear to have been reached before the problem of space and organized force became acute. Religious communities with hierarchical organizations characterized Sumerian civilization. Though architecture dependent on bricks made from the clay of the delta regions became important, writing on clay was a basis for communication, administration, and trade. Organized force represented by Sargon of the Akkadians brought religious communities under control and with access to writing made possible a vast empire. With religion based on writing Sumerian culture proved sufficiently strong to throw off control of a foreign ruler and to support a capital at Ur for a limited number of dynasties. In turn this culture came under the control of fresh conquerors and a new capital of palaces and temples emerged at Babylon. The effectiveness with which control over time reflected in religion was fused with control over space was evident in the long period in which Babylon persisted as a capital under the Kassite dynasty.

The success of organized force was dependent in part on technological advance, notably, in early civilizations, in the use of the horse, the crossing of the light African horse with the heavier Asiatic horse, the introduction of horse riding and cavalry to replace horse driving and chariots, and the use of iron as a substitute for bronze. The Hittites with the use of iron succeeded in building an empire with a capital which emphasized sculpture and architecture but it was checked on the south by Babylon and on the north and west by the Greeks with their control over the sea at Troy. They were followed by the Assyrians who exploited technological advance in warfare and made fresh contributions to its development. With a new capital at Nineveh they succeeded in offsetting the prestige of the Nile and of Babylon and establishing an empire to include the civilizations of both. Prestige was secured not only by architecture and sculpture but also by writing. The library became a great instrument of imperial power and set an example which has influenced the history of the West until the present time. The concern of the Assyrian Empire with the collection of Sumerian documents for the library at Nineveh has been paralleled at Alexandria, Rome, Paris, Berlin, London, Moscow, and Washington. In Canada we are attempting to follow in our own way at Ottawa. The Assyrians attempted to maintain their prestige not only by libraries but also by development of a reputation for warlike ferocity, paralleled in this century. Failure of the Assyrian Empire was in part a result of the tenacity and diversity of civilization in Babylon and Egypt.

Persia succeeded where Assyria had failed by emphasizing the importance of a single capital by architecture and sculpture and of small capitals of districts or satrapies governed from a centre. The beginnings of the principle "divide and rule" were evident in recognition of the religions of Babylon and Egypt and encouragement of the religion of the Hebrews at Jerusalem. But as in the case of Assyria the political organization of Persia was unable to meet the demands of continuity.

Political organizations determined to an important extent by the limitations of armed force and characterized by centralized power emphasized the capital city and left their impress on cultural activity in architecture and sculpture. They emerged in land areas, from the Nile valley to Asia Minor. They provided a shelter for the development of communication facilities and for the growth of trade such as that of the Aramaeans on land and of the Phoenicians on the Mediterranean. Communication was subordinated to the demands of centralized power in religion and in political organization; it was characterized by the use of the eye rather than the ear. The scribe occupied a strategic position in centralized bureaucracies.

In attempting to use other civilizations as mirrors by which we may understand our own we are exposed to much greater dangers in studying Greek culture and its successors since our own culture has been profoundly influenced by it. Civilizations of the Nile and Asia Minor had a limited influence on peoples along the north shore of the Mediterranean. Minoan civilization was an attempt to encroach on the sea which failed in the face of opposition from the north. Mycenean civilization on the mainland proved more adaptable but in turn succumbed. The Greeks escaped the centralizing tendencies of river civilizations with their effects on capitals, architecture, and sculpture and on writing with its implications for bureaucracy. In their settlements on the islands and along the coast, the Greeks emphasized cultural aspects suited to their needs. The oral tradition rather than writing provided a basis for the epic and for literature designed to unite scattered groups in a consciousness of Greek culture. The alphabet borrowed from the Phoenicians was given vowels and adapted to the demands of speech. The ear replaced the eye. With the spread of writing the oral tradition developed fresh powers of resistance evident in the flowering of Greek culture in the sixth and fifth centuries. A concern with the Eastern concept of the capital was apparent in the age of tyrants in the sixth century notably in Athens and in the fifth century notably in the Athenian Empire. But as the epic and tragedy reflected the character of Greek civilization so too did architecture and sculpture. "The statues of the classic artists are the relics of ancient dancing" (S.H. Butcher). "After art had been toiling in India, in Persia, and in Egypt to produce monsters, beauty and grace were discovered in Greece" (Sir James Mackintosh). "Nothing over-much" was a maxim which implied distrust of specialization in all phases of cultural life. Greek culture was destroyed in the growth of writing and of individualism in the latter part of the fifth century.

The vitality of Greek culture was evident finally in the flowering of military skill in the conquests of Philip and Alexander. Greek culture with its political organization reflected in the city state came in contact with concepts peculiar to early civilizations and compromised with them in the Hellenistic kingdoms. The capital to a limited extent was restored. In Egypt the Ptolemies established a new capital at Alexandria and created a new deity to destroy the influence of the old capital at Thebes, and built up a library to exploit the limitations of Athens and to offset the influence of Babylon. At Pergamum, the Attalids developed a capital with a library designed to offset the prestige of Alexandria. The Seleucids were eventually defeated by a revival of Persian civilization.

In the east, along the north coast of the Mediterranean, Rome came under the cultural influence of Greece, and after destroying Carthage, which had inherited the commercial traditions of Phoenicia, extended her influence to the Hellenistic kingdoms to the east, and to Spain and Gaul in the north and west. The influence of Egypt was evident in the deification of the ruler, in the decline of the Roman Republic and the emergence of the Roman Empire, and in the increasing centralization of a bureaucracy. The attempt to offset the influence of Persian civilization was evident in the orientalization of the emperors and eventually in the establishment of Constantinople as a capital to take advantage of the support of Hellenistic culture including Christianity. The inroads of the barbarians were followed by the decline of Rome and the rise of Constantinople as a political centre. The difficulty of subordinating cultural capitals with their roots in earlier civilizations reflected in the religious controversies of the period led to the emergence of Rome as the religious capital of the West, and to the spread of Mohammedanism in the East. With Mohammedanism new capitals arose at Baghdad and at Cordova in Spain. Access to a medium other than papyrus and parchment, namely paper, enabled these centres to build up libraries and compelled Constantinople to take a fresh interest in learning. In the West the Holy Roman Empire became an institution designed to strengthen the prestige of Rome. In turn the political influence of Rome led to the increasing prestige of Paris as a theological centre. The attempt of the papacy to recapture Jerusalem and the Eastern church in the Crusades was followed by the growth of small Italian city republics notably at Venice, Florence, and Genoa. The final collapse of Constantinople and of the Byzantine Empire in 1453 following the use of artillery brought new efforts to regain prestige in the East at Kiev and in the West at Paris.

The capitals of the northern Mediterranean and Europe while reflecting the influence of the capitals of the Nile and the Tigris and Euphrates valleys were dominated by the oral tradition of Greece. The absolute monarchy of Egypt and the East became the Roman emperor, the English Tudors, Louis XIV, and the czars of Russia, and its influence was evident in the courts of Rome and Constantinople, London, Paris, and St Petersburg. The city state of Greece was revived in the city republics of Italy and Germany and in the Renaissance, and its influence softened the tyranny of the courts. In some sense the culture represented by the courts had solved the problem of time and space. The Byzantine Empire persisted as a unique achievement in duration, and while the size of its territory fluctuated, its achievement in the solution of problems of space was scarcely less remarkable. Paris became the cultural centre of the West notably under Louis XIV and the influence of the French court was evident in the England of Charles II, in the courts of Russia, and indeed wherever culture in the Western sense raised its head. Antwerp, Amsterdam, London, Berlin, St Petersburg, Moscow, and Washington were influenced directly and indirectly by the dominance of Paris. French culture persisted after the Revolution and after the occupation of the recent war, and survived the state. Like Paris, London became more dependent on cultural influence than on political organization as is evident in the British Commonwealth of Nations.

After this brief survey of earlier civilizations we can attempt an appraisal of the possibilities in terms of duration and extent of our own civilization. We have emphasized the significance of communication in determining the characteristics of earlier civilizations and of changes in methods of communication. The discovery of printing in the middle of the fifteenth century implied the beginning of a return to a type of civilization dominated by the eye rather than the ear. With printing and an increase in the use and manufacture of paper German cities strengthened their position and facilitated a break from the church in Holland, Germany, and England. Their advance was registered in the concern for the word of the Bible, the Reformation, and the rise of Protestantism. The full impact of printing did not become possible until the adoption of the Bill of Rights in the United States with its guarantee of freedom of the press. A guarantee of freedom of the press in print was intended to further sanctify the printed word and to provide a rigid bulwark for the shelter of vested interests. Printing assumed mass production or reproduction of words and once it escaped from the pattern of the parchment manuscript it compelled the production of vast quantities of new material including material to meet the demands of science and technology. Improvement of communication hastened the development of markets and of industry. The Industrial Revolution followed the printing industry and in turn in the nineteenth century, with the use of steam power in the manufacture of paper and of printed material, supported rapid expansion of the printing industry.

We are perhaps too much a part of the civilization which followed the spread of the printing industry to be able to detect its characteristics. Education in the words of Laski became the art of teaching men to be deceived by the printed word. "The most important service rendered by the press and the magazines is that of educating people to approach printed matter with distrust."[2] But there are unmistakable signs that ours is a civilization which partakes of the character of all civilizations in its belief in its uniqueness and superiority over other civilizations. We are all familiar with the claims of the printing industry to the effect that it has ushered in a new and superior civilization. No other civilization, we are told, has enjoyed our advantages. Democracy, education, progress, individualism, and other blessed words describe our new heaven. At this point the water becomes swift and we are in grave danger of being swept off our feet by the phenomenon we are describing. We are in danger on the one hand of losing our objectivity and on the other hand of being placed under arrest. Freedom of the press has been regarded as a great bulwark of our civilization and it would be dangerous to say that it has become the great bulwark of monopolies of the press. Civilizations have their sacred cows. The Middle Ages burned its heretics and the modern age threatens them with atom bombs.

In contrast with the civilization dominated by Greek culture with its maxim "nothing in excess," modern civilization dominated by machine industry is concerned always with specialization which might be described as always in excess. Economics, beginning with Adam Smith, and indeed other social sciences have an obsession with specialization. Specialization and industrialism support an emphasis on equality. An interest in material goods which characterized the Scottish people, represented notably in Adam Smith, has been followed by an attitude described by Samuel Butler: "All progress is based upon a universal innate desire on the part of every organism to live beyond its income." The concern with specialization and excess, making more and better mousetraps, precludes the possibility of understanding a preceding civilization concerned with balance and proportion. Industrialism implies technology and the cutting of time into precise fragments suited to the needs of the engineer and the accountant. The inability to escape the demands of industrialism on time weakens the possibility of an appraisal of limitations of space. Constant changes in technology particularly as they affect communication, a crucial factor in determining cultural values (for example, the development of radio and television), increase the difficulties of recognizing balance let alone achieving it.

The cultural values of an industrial society are not the cultural values of other societies. The equation of ethical values between cultures is possibly more difficult than the equation of other values, though Professor V. Gordon Childe has described the implications of cultural change in such fields of abstraction as mathematics. The outburst of rich artistic activity in Greece coincided with a decline in the status of women. Dean Inge has reminded us that the extreme sensitivity of modern civilization, for example in the attitude toward cruelty to animals, and the extreme insensitivity toward unbelievable cruelty to human beings have synchronized with the complete collapse of spontaneous and unconscious artistic production.[3] The ugliness of English and American towns and the disappearance of beauty accompanied the invention of machinery and great industries. Von Eicken's thesis that the master key to history lies in the conclusion that human movements provoke violent reactions has much to support it. Roman imperialism created by intense nationalism ended by destroying the nationality of rulers and subjects. The nationalism of the Jews left them without a country. The Catholic church renounced the world and became the heir of the defunct Roman empire. Universal suffrage heralded the end of parliamentary government. The more successful a democracy in levelling population the less the resistance to despotism. The interest of the French Revolution in humanity kindled the fire of patriotism, and nationalism in Spain, Germany, and Russia.[4]

Anthropologists, notably Pitt-Rivers, have explored the dangers of the intrusion of one culture on other cultures. Historians have commented on the unsatisfactory results which followed the importation of the parliamentary system to the European continent. The disasters which overtook North American civilization following the coming of Europeans have been described at length. The disturbances which have characterized a shift from a culture dominated by one form of communication to another culture dominated by another form of communication whether in the campaigns of Alexander, the Thirty Years' War, or the wars of the present century point to the costs of cultural change. The impact of Point Four on other cultures, the clash of so-called "backward" and so-called "forward" countries involve such unpaid cost as the enormous loss of life directly through war and indirectly through cultural change. The spread of communism from France to Russia and China is a further illustration of the instability of Western civilization. Stability which characterized certain periods in earlier civilizations is not the obvious objective of this civilization. Each civilization has its own methods of suicide.

NOTES

1 W.R. Inge, *Diary of a Dean, St. Paul's 1911–1934* (London, 1950), 195.
2 *Further Extracts from the Note-Books of Samuel Butler,* ed. A.T. Bartholomew (London, 1934), 261.
3 See his essay in *The Legacy of Greece,* ed. R.W. Livingstone (Oxford, 1923), 40.
4 Inge, *Diary of a Dean,* 208, 210.

CHAPTER TWENTY-THREE

The Bias of Communication

The appearance of a wide range of cultural phenomena at different periods in the history of Western civilization has been described by Professor A.L. Kroeber in *Configurations of Cultural Growth* (Berkeley, 1946). He makes suggestive comments at various points to explain the relative strength or weakness of cultural elements but refrains from extended discussion. I do not propose to do more than add a footnote to these comments and in this to discuss the possible significance of communication to the rise and decline of cultural traits. A medium of communication has an important influence on the dissemination of knowledge over space and over time and it becomes necessary to study its characteristics in order to appraise its influence in its cultural setting. According to its characteristics it may be better suited to the dissemination of knowledge over time than over space, particularly if the medium is heavy and durable and not suited to transportation, or to the dissemination of knowledge over space than over time, particularly if the medium is light and easily transported. The relative emphasis on time or space will imply a bias of significance to the culture in which it is imbedded.

Immediately we venture on this inquiry we are compelled to recognize the bias of the period in which we work. An interest in the bias of other civilizations may in itself suggest a bias of our own. Our knowledge of other civilizations depends in large part on the character of the media used by each civilization in so far as it is capable of being preserved or of being made accessible by discovery as in the case of the results of archaeological expeditions.[1] Writing on

From a paper presented at the University of Michigan, 18 April 1949; printed in *The Bias of Communication* (Toronto, 1951), chap. 2, 33–60.

clay and on stone has been preserved more effectively than that on papyrus. Since durable commodities emphasize time and continuity, studies of civilization such as Toynbee's tend to have a bias toward religion and to show a neglect of problems of space, notably administration and law. The bias of modern civilization incidental to the newspaper and the radio will presume a perspective in consideration of civilizations dominated by other media. We can do little more than urge that we must be continually alert to the implications of this bias and perhaps hope that consideration of the implications of other media to various civilizations may enable us to see more clearly the bias of our own. In any case we may become a little more humble as to the characteristics of our civilization. We can perhaps assume that the use of a medium of communication over a long period will to some extent determine the character of knowledge to be communicated and suggest that its pervasive influence will eventually create a civilization in which life and flexibility will become exceedingly difficult to maintain and that the advantages of a new medium will become such as to lead to the emergence of a new civilization.

Egyptian civilization appears to have been powerfully influenced by the character of the Nile. Utilization of its periodic floods depended on the unified control of an absolute authority. It has been claimed that the discovery of the sidereal year as early as 4241 BC made it possible to work out a calendar avoiding the difficulties of a year dependent on the moon. The discovery and the adoption of a calendar with the certainty of dates for religious festivals facilitated the establishment of an absolute monarchy and the imposition of the authority of Osiris and Ra, the Nile and the Su, on upper Egypt. Success of the monarchy in acquiring control over Egypt in terms of space necessitated a concern with problems of continuity or time. The idea of immortality strengthened the position of the monarch. Mummification and construction of the pyramids as devices for emphasizing control over time were accompanied by the development of the art of pictorial representation as part of the funerary ritual and by the emergence of writing. The spoken word, by which the orders of the monarch were given, in itself possessed creative efficiency which in turn was perpetuated in the written word in the tomb. Pictorial decorations became hieroglyphic script. Writing gradually developed toward phoneticism and by the time of Menes (about 3315 BC) many picture signs had a purely phonetic value and were regularly spelled out. Autocratic monarchy developed by divine right culminated in the pyramids of about 2850 BC. Private property disappeared and all arable land became the king's domain.

The monopoly of knowledge centring around stone and hieroglyphics was exposed to competition from papyrus as a new and more efficient medium. Royal authority began to decline after about 2540 BC and its decline was possibly coincident with the discovery of the solar year by the priestly class as a device to overcome the deficiencies of the sidereal year in which a day was gained each year. The king was lowered from the status of the Great God to the son of Ra. The chief priest of the Ra cult was exalted to the rank of chief god and Heliopolis became the centre of priestly power. Oligarchy succeeded an absolute monarchy. After about 2000 BC the masses were admitted to religious rites and immortality and to political rights. The gates of heaven and the jaws of hell were opened and a "most powerful instrument for the domination over men's unruly wills" devised.[2] The increasing use of papyrus and the brush was accompanied by the development of the hieratic character and the emergence of the profession of scribes. Writing and thought were secularized. Administration was extended following the spread of writing and reading. The social revolution involved in a shift from the use of stone to the use of papyrus and the increased importance of the priestly class imposed enormous strains on Egyptian civilization and left it exposed to the inroads of invaders equipped with effective weapons of attack. The Hyksos or Shepherd Kings captured and held Egypt from 1660 to 1580 BC. The strength of Egyptian cultural elements facilitated reorganization, and mobilization of resources was directed to expulsion of the invaders. The introduction of the horse and light four-spoked chariots enabled Egyptian rulers not only to expel the Hyksos but also to conquer vast new territories and to build an empire.

An extension of political organization to include peoples of different races and religions reflecting a temporary solution of problems of space in government compelled the king to attempt a solution of problems of continuity. Worship of the solar disc was designed to provide an imperial religion which would overrule distinctions between Egyptians and foreigners. Failure to overcome the hostility of the entrenched priestly class in Egypt was followed by imperial decline and eventually by the subjugation of Egypt by the Assyrians and the Persians. A monopoly of knowledge supported by a difficult script resisted demands for change and brought the Egyptian Empire to an end. With abundant supplies of papyrus and the conservative influence of religion on writing, pictographic writing was maintained and the emergence of consonantal signs was largely a result of the introduction of foreign names and words. The spoken word tended to drift away from the written word in spite of the efforts of Ikhnaton to bring them into closer accord.

In contrast with the civilization of the Nile that of the Euphrates and the Tigris lacked the necessity of unity and was characterized in its early development by a number of small theocratic city states in which the chief priest of the temple was direct representative of the god. Rivers were subject to irregular and incalculable flooding. The growth of city states assumed continuity in time and the development of writing and reading by which the complex systems of accounting could be made intelligible to individuals and to their successors.

Alluvial clay as the medium for writing had implications for Sumerian civilization in the difficulties of transport and the tendency to encourage the development of a decentralized society. The difficulties of writing on moist clay led to the disappearance of pictographs and the emergence of conventional signs or formal patterns of cuneiform. The stylus was developed in relation to the demands of clay. With a language which was largely monosyllabic, signs were introduced to meet the demands of economy and the necessity of uniformity to establish communication between scattered cities. The administration of temple properties and trade implied an emphasis on mathematics in the early development of writing and in turn an emphasis on abstractions.

Accumulation of wealth in temple organizations involved rivalry, warfare between city states, the emergence of a military leader and an army. The problems of control over space in contrast to the success with which problems of time were met in a religious organization necessitated centralization in the hands of a king. Control over large stretches of territory meant delegation of authority and an emphasis on law as a means of offsetting religious jealousies. To the same end old capitals were destroyed and new capitals were built to strengthen the prestige of the king, and the deities of conquered cities were arranged in hierarchies under the deity of the conqueror. The difficulties of political organization were evident in the ultimate breakdown of Sumerian empires and in the success of Semitic invaders, as the advantages of cultural organization were evident in the tenacity of Sumerian institutions under alien rule. Semitic invaders rearranged the position of the chief gods of city states.

The eventual success of Semitic peoples was marked by the ascendancy of Babylon as a new capital and by the reforms of Hammurabi. The centralized power of a monarchy favoured the architecture of palaces, and the use of stone in sculpture and as a medium of writing, particularly of laws designed to establish uniformity over vast empires. The language of the conquerors could not be united to that of the conquered but the signs of the latter were used by the former. The Semitic language was made official by Hammurabi. The spoken word was Semitic but the written word was in the non-Semitic forms of the Sumerians. The conventionalization of written language was hastened by the demands of the conquerors. "The basis of the Sumerian system of writing was word-values, while that of the Accadian method was syllable-values."[3] Sumerian became a fossilized sacred language of priests. Hammurabi developed the territorial state with a centralized system of administration, a common collection of written laws, a common capital, and a common calendar. Trade over a vast territory was facilitated by the use of fixed standards of weights and measures. Mathematics was developed in the use of the sexagesimal system with its enormous advantages in the handling of fractions, advantages still exploited in the currency system of Great Britain, and in the twenty-four hour system which has persisted in the reckoning of time.

A centralized system of administration persisted with modification under peoples speaking Aryan languages. Equipped with more efficient instruments of warfare, particularly the horse and the chariot, the invaders captured and dominated Babylon from about 1740 BC to the end of the thirteenth century. Political organizations in northern regions without an abundant supply of writing material such as clay were built up but were unable to find an effective solution to problems of time. The Hittites worked out a highly organized central administration with a strong imperial capital and a system of radiating communications but were unable to capture Babylon in their attack about 1150 BC. The Assyrians succeeded in disrupting the Hittite federation and eventually dominated the Aramaeans by the use of heavier horses which made possible the introduction of cavalry, and the use of iron which had been developed by the Hittites. Their imperial organization was based on the establishment of provincial governments placed under governors who exacted tribute. Babylonia was captured in 729 BC and the religious pantheon subjected to rearrangement under Ashur as the Assyrian god. The power of Babylonian religion and culture was apparent in the difficulties of governing Babylon evident in its destruction in 689 BC and in the attempt to develop the prestige of the capital at Nineveh by the building of a library of Sumerian documents. Egypt was invaded and made an Assyrian province in

674 BC but the task of governing two powerful and divergent religious centres proved insuperable, and Nineveh was destroyed in 612 BC.

Expansion of the Assyrian Empire was accompanied by the subjugation of peoples of different languages, races, and cultures, the destruction of Aramaean city states, and the practice of deportation on a large scale to stamp out narrow local cultures. As a result of these measures trade increased greatly. In the twelfth century the camel was domesticated and caravan trade was extended. An enlarged empire facilitated the growth of trade and industry. In turn these developments assumed a more efficient system of writing shown in the increasing dominance of Aramaic.

Monopolies of knowledge to an important extent dominated by priestly organization and protected by complex types of script such as the cuneiform and the hieroglyphic checked the growth of political organization. Escape from these monopolies came from the fringes of Babylonian and Egyptian civilizations in which new languages among primitive peoples demanded simplicity. Semitic peoples in contact with Egypt before 1500 BC apparently invented an alphabet in Palestine and perfected it on the Phoenician coast. Access to supplies of papyrus from Egypt and acquaintance with the reed pen enabled marginal peoples to borrow the simplest signs of the Egyptian system and to abandon its complexities. Invasion of the Hyksos apparently created a barrier between the south and the north of Arabia and led to a divergence between Aramaic and Phoenician writing. Aramaic script developed in relation to the demands of an extensive land trade for a concise conventional alphabet and possibly in relation to the use of parchment. The Phoenician script developed as a result of the demands of an extensive maritime trade for an alphabet in relation to the use of papyrus. Sounds of human speech were analysed into primary elements represented by twenty-two consonants.

A flexible alphabet favoured the growth of trade, development of the trading cities of the Phoenicians, and the emergence of smaller nations dependent on distinct languages. Hebrew was probably spoken in Palestine after 1200 BC. The oral tradition was written down and the sacred character of writing emphasized by the Egyptians was reflected in the writing of the Hebrews. The importance of sculpture to large-scale political and religious organizations was shown in the prohibition of images by the Hebrews. The written letter replaced the graven image. Concentration on the abstract in writing opened the way for an advance from blood relationship to universal ethical standards, to the influence of the prophets in opposition to the absolute power of kings, and to an emphasis on monotheism. Laws were collected and written down in codes. Literature such as is presented in the Old Testament took root and flourished. Destruction of local sanctuaries by Sennacherib was followed by an emphasis on Jerusalem as the single sanctuary after 621 BC.[4] After the fall of the Assyrian Empire the Babylonians extended their control and captured Jerusalem in 586 BC.

With the advantage of new instruments of war such as the long bow and the long pike and of an improved alphabet, the Persians rapidly built up an empire to take the place of the empire of the Assyrians. As a result of support from the priests Cyrus became king of Babylon in 536 BC. Cambyses added Egypt to the Empire in 525 BC. The problems of the Assyrians in dominating two divergent religious centres were inherited by the Persians. They were solved in part by a policy of toleration in which subject peoples were allowed to keep their gods and their religions. The Jews were released from captivity in Babylonia in 539 BC and Judah became the centre of an effective religious organization. The Persians developed an elaborate administration based on a system of roads and the use of horses to maintain communication by post with the capital. Satrapies were created and three officials, a satrap, a military governor, and a secretary of state, each acting independently of the other and directly responsible to the capital, were appointed. But centralization of power in the hands of the king quickly brought to the fore the problem of administrative capacity and of continuity or the problem of time. Difficulties increased with the tenacious religious centres of Babylonia, Egypt, and Jerusalem and with peoples such as the Greeks located on the fringe of the Empire. The introduction of new tactics of warfare enabled Alexander to overthrow the Empire in the decisive battles of 333 BC and 331 BC. Oriental empires succeeded in organizing vast areas and in solving territorial problems but failed to find a solution to problems of continuity and of time. The empires of Assyria and Persia emphasized control over space but were unable to solve the problems of time in the face of the monopolies of religion in Babylonia and Egypt.

The Phoenician Semitic consonantal alphabet was taken over by the Greeks on the north shore of the Mediterranean. Unlike the peoples of Aryan speech in Asia Minor the Greeks escaped the full effect of contact with the civilizations of Egypt and Babylonia. The necessity of crossing water enabled the Greeks to select cultural traits of significance to themselves and to reject others. Without a script they had built up a strong oral tradition centring about the courts of conquering people from the north. The Homeric poems were the work of generations of reciters and minstrels and reflected the demands of generations of audiences to whom they were recited. This powerful oral tradition bent the consonantal alphabet to its demands and used five of the twenty-four letters as vowels. As vowels were equal in value to consonants they were used in each written word. The written language was made into an instrument responsive to the demands of the oral tradition. Introduction of the alphabet meant a concern with sound rather than with sight or with the ear rather than the eye. Empires had been built up on communication based on sight in contrast with Greek political organization which emphasized oral discussion. Greece escaped the problem of worship of the written word which had embarrassed oriental empires. The delay in the introduction of writing until possibly as late as the beginning of the seventh century, the difficulties of securing large and regular supplies of papyrus from Egypt, and the limitations of stone as a medium combined to protect the oral tradition. No energy was lost in learning a second language and monopolies of knowledge could not be built around a complex script.

The significance of the oral tradition and its vitality in Greek civilization became evident in its influence on the later history of the West. Its power has been such that it becomes impossible for modern Europeans who have participated in the heritage to approach it from an objective point of view. The impact of writing and printing on modern civilization increases the difficulties of understanding a civilization based on the oral tradition. We can perhaps remain content in quoting Renan, "Progress will eternally consist in developing what Greece conceived."

The power of the oral tradition was evident in the Homeric poems and in the adaptability of the hexameter to a wide variety of content. Hesiod's poetry was in sharp contrast with that of Homer. It facilitated the break of the individual from the minstrel tradition. The demands for greater sensitivity were met by the development of elegiac and iambic poetry. With accessibility to papyrus from Egypt in the late seventh and sixth centuries and the use of the lyre as a musical instrument, the position of professional minstrels was weakened. Lyric poetry developed on an impressive scale.

Not only did the strength of the oral tradition bend the alphabet to suit its needs, it also adapted other contributions of earlier civilizations. In the Homeric poems the gods became anthropomorphic deities. The supernatural was replaced by a concern with nature and science. The Ionian philosopher was able to reject the implications of the words as implying a creative act. "And God said" of the Hebrews ceased to be the symbol of creation. The contributions of the Chaldeans after the introduction of an exact system of chronology in 747 BC which facilitated a study of the periodic character of celestial phenomena were apparently used by Thales of Miletus to predict the eclipse of 28 May 585 BC. The Olympian tradition which assumed fixed limits to the power of gods and men emphasized spatial concepts and in turn geometry. The science of nature dominated by geometry involved a concern with the internal properties of things rather than their relations with other things.

A concern with geometry and spatial relations was reinforced by the place of land and the search for land in colonization in Greek life. The results were evident in the evils which followed attempts to monopolize land. The growth of written laws in the colonies and in Athens in the seventh century threatened to impose a heavy load on debtors. But the power of the oral tradition was evident in the effectiveness of a search for means by which freedom might be achieved. It was possible to give individuals such as Draco, Solon, and Cleisthenes power to set up machinery adapted to continuous adjustment. Solon in the tradition of Ionian philosophy sought for universal truths and expressed the conviction that violation of justice involved disruption of the life of the community. The individual became responsible for his actions and the root of authority was destroyed. The rights of creditors engraved on ward stones erected on property were destroyed and the enslavement of labour as a disruptive force avoided. Solon discovered the secret of democracy in "the constitution of the judicial courts out of the whole people" (Bury).

Solon's reforms reflected the increasing significance of trade in contrast to land but their inadequacy became evident in the rise of a commercial class and in turn of tyrants in the sixth century. The Apollonian religion and Ionian philosophy were offset by encouragement of the worship of Dionysus. The tyrants encouraged the arts and in 537 BC assembled a collection of oracles to offset the prestige of the temple of Delphi. Increased trade and a concern with money suggested the limitations of an interest in geometry and spatial relations and the necessity of an interest in arithmetic and time. The philosophy of spatial externality involved discreteness and neglected the importance of continuity. The religion of Dionysus was probably modified by the influence of Mithraism from the East and by the Orphic revival. In turn Pythagoras developed a philosophy of numbers rather than geometry. As a result of these refinements a reconciliation between the Dionysian religion and the Apollonic became possible and the road was opened leading to the overthrow of the tyrants and the reforms of Cleisthenes. Solon had been largely concerned with problems incidental to the importance of land, space, and geometry and Cleisthenes was concerned with problems incidental to the importance of trade, time, and arithmetic. He rescued control over time from the nobles and introduced a solar calendar which governed a definite system of rotation in elections to the councils. The family state was replaced by the city state.

The effectiveness of the oral tradition in the development of the state became evident in the success with which the Greeks checked the expansion of the Persian Empire and in the cultural flowering of Athens in the fifth century. A powerful stimulus was given to philosophical speculation by the arrival of Ionian refugees from Miletus. The Dionysiac ritual and the choral lyric as perfected by Pindar provided the background for the development of the drama[5] under Aeschylus, Sophocles, and Euripides. In the second half of the fifth century writing began to make its encroachments on the oral tradition. Nietzsche has pointed to the significance of music, in which the joy of annihilation of the individual was understood, to tragedy. Disappearance of the spirit of music was followed by the decline of tragedy.[6] An increase in laws reflected an interest in prose. Literature in prose increased rapidly after the beginning of the Peloponnesian War. Plays were widely read in the time of Euripides. By the end of the fifth century the *boustrophedon* style had been abandoned and changed to writing from left to right. The Ionic alphabet was adopted in Athens with the codification and republication of the laws in 403–2 BC.[7]

An increase in writing in Athens created divergences in the Greek community and accentuated differences particularly with Sparta. The Athenian Empire proved unable to meet the strains imposed by diverging cultures. Athenian courts were unable to escape charges of favouritism to democratic states. Interstate cooperation imposed demands which could not be met. The end came with the outbreak of war and the defeat of Athens.

In the fourth century Plato attempted to save the remnants of Greek culture in the style of the Socratic dialogues which in the words of Aristotle stood half way between prose and poetry. In the seventh epistle he wrote, "no intelligent man will ever be so bold as to put into language those things which his reason has contemplated, especially not into a form that is unalterable – which must be the case with what is expressed in written symbols." The interest of Aristotle in science was reflected in prose. But neither Aristotle nor Plato thought of a library as a necessity to the city state. It was significant that a library was founded by Aristotle in 335 BC and a public library started in 330 BC. The written tradition had brought the vitality of the oral tradition to an end. In the words of Nietzsche, "Everyone being allowed to read ruineth in the long run not only writing but also thinking."

The role of the oral tradition in providing the milieu for the cultural activity of Greece had a profound significance for the history of the West and immediately for the history of Rome. The success with which the problems of time and space were solved had its implications for Roman culture. Greek culture awakened the native forces of Rome. Greek gods and Greek architecture were introduced in the latter part of the sixth century. The struggles for reform in Greece culminating in the work of Draco, Solon, and Cleisthenes were paralleled at a later date in Rome in the decemvirs' code of the Twelve Tables in 451 and 450 BC and in the increasing powers of the plebeians culminating in the appointment of the first plebeian pontifex maximus in 253 BC.

The comparative isolation of Roman culture from Greece in the fifth and fourth centuries was followed by a fresh invasion of Greek influence in which the rich development of Greek culture checked that of Rome and compelled the latter to concentrate on its own capacities notably in law. Flexibility inherent in the oral tradition was evident in the rise of the plebeians, and in constitutional changes, in the activity of lawyers, and in the creation of machinery designed to meet the increasing demands for adjustment. In 242 BC the position of a second praetor, *peregrinus*, was introduced to reflect the importance of an expanding trade with alien peoples. Formulae were made more flexible in spite of the spread of writing. Praetors issued new edicts at the beginning of their years of office adapted to changing demands. The *patria potestas* was broken down to make way for the individual, and the contract, that "greediest of legal categories," developed. the concept of property was isolated. *Res privata* necessitated a concern with *res publica* and an interest in the legal concept of the state. By the middle of the first century BC the influence of writing became evident in the demand for codes. Laws and precedents in the oral tradition had been largely in men's minds to the time of Cicero. In the senate the introduction of an official gazette in 54 BC compelled speakers to consider a wide public and created a demand for a matter-of-fact style. Limitation of time for pleas in court in 52 BC reinforced the tendency. Latin prose which had developed in relation to the demands of the republic in the speeches of the Gracchi, of Cato, and of Cicero was subjected to the influence of writing.[8] The oral tradition absorbed the philosophy of teachers of Stoicism from the East and law was subjected to the demands of universality. Custom was criticized, the religious and ceremonial character of law was weakened, equality was promoted, harshness mitigated, and the factor of intent emphasized.

The adaptability of Roman law in the oral tradition facilitated the extension of the Roman Empire which followed the success of Roman arms. Wars with Carthage brought Rome into conflict with Hellenistic kingdoms and into contact with Greek culture. The Antigonids who succeeded Alexander in Macedonia gradually changed Greek city states into municipalities but continued difficulties enabled Rome to destroy the Achaean League in 168 BC and to dominate Greece and Macedonia. The Ptolemies inherited the problems of political control in Egypt. They created a new capital at Alexandria, a large library, and a new god Serapis to offset the influence of the priestly class at Thebes. The demotic system and the use of the pen were encouraged at the expense of the hieratic system and the brush. As Rome acquired control over Egypt she adopted the policies of the Ptolemies. The Attalids built up a library at Pergamum to offset the prestige of the Ptolemies and, prevented from using papyrus by prohibitions on export, began the use of parchment on a large scale. Friendly relations with Rome were evident in the transfer of the *Magna Mater* in 204 BC. The Seleucids, inheriting the problems of the Persian Empire of dominating the Persian, Babylonian, and Hebrew religions, attempted to introduce the city state as an instrument of government but failure was evident in the ultimate collapse of the kingdom. Rome fell heir to the unfortunate legacy.

As a result of expansion to the east Rome felt the full effects of Greek cultural achievements. Libraries were brought from Greece. Supplies of papyrus were available from Egypt. A book trade was developed and public and private libraries constructed. The spread of writing brought an interest in the codification of laws. Bureaucratic administration emerged. The Republic was replaced by the Empire. The emperor began to face the problems of empire which had been faced by earlier civilizations and to rely on solutions which had been developed in the East. Emperor worship gradually became more important. The dynastic problem which had menaced the attempts of former absolute monarchs to establish control over time strengthened the position of the army and a bureaucratic administration. New dynasties relied to an increasing extent on the prestige of Greece.

Under the influence of law the individual had been separated from the family. With the increasing rigidity of codes in the Empire the individual turned to Eastern religions. Efforts to exclude alien religions gradually broke down. The scrupulous fear of the gods which according to Polybius kept the Roman Empire together was no longer adequate.[9] Attempts of the nobility to maintain the traditional religion of the state against new tendencies meant leading a class against the masses and conflict with the "religious feelings of those lacking social privilege" (Max Weber).[10] Military campaigns in the east were followed by the spread of Mithraism and in 274 AD Aurelian dedicated a shrine to the god *Sol Invictus.* Recognition of an Eastern religion as a basis of political support brought a revival of the hostility of Hellenism and compelled the emperor to accept the support of a religion more acceptable to Greek demands. Unable to provide a link between Greece and Persia since the Greeks refused to accept an absolute emperor Rome was compelled to set up a model similar to that of Persia in Constantinople. In turn the demands of bureaucracy were reflected in the division of the Empire between the Latin West and the Greek East. The Illyrian mountains prevented the establishment of a capital linking the Latin and the Hellenic provinces as the Alps were later to prevent the establishment of a capital uniting the German and Italian divisions of the Holy Roman Empire.[11]

The bureaucratic development of the Roman Empire and success in solving problems of administration over vast areas were dependent on supplies of papyrus. The bias of this medium became apparent in the monopoly of bureaucracy and its inability to find a satisfactory solution to the problems of the third dimension of empires, namely time. A new medium emerged to meet the limitations of papyrus. The handicaps of the fragile papyrus roll were offset by the durable parchment codex. With the latter the Christians were able to make effective use of the large Hebrew scriptures and to build up a corpus of Christian writings. The contributions of Alexandrian scholars in translating the Hebrew scriptures into Greek and the development of a Christian centre of learning at Caesarea after 231 AD checked the influence of a Babylonian priesthood, which had been encouraged by the Seleucids to check the influence of Persian religion, and which had been reconciled with Persian religion after the fall of Babylon in 125 AD. Support of these religions for the Sassanid dynasty after 228 AD hindered the spread of the Roman Empire and compelled Constantine to select a new capital in Constantinople in 330 whence he could command the interest of a Christian population. The problem of the Roman Empire in relation to time was solved by the support of religion in the Christian church. The cumulative bias of papyrus in relation to bureaucratic administration was offset by an appeal to parchment as a medium for a powerful religious organization. Recognition of Christianity was followed by the drastic suppression of competing pagan cults.

The attempt of emperors to build up Constantinople as the centre of the civilized world especially after the fall of the Western Empire in 476 AD by establishing a large library and producing a code of civil law created friction with Rome and with Alexandria. Justinian's *Digest* carried in its prefix a description of law identical with that of Demosthenes, namely, an invention and gift of the gods, the opinion of sensible men, the restitution of things done amiss voluntary and involuntary, and a general compact of a state in accordance with which it is proper that all in that state should live.[12] But geographical separation reinforced differences in religion and exposed the Eastern Empire to the attacks of the Persians and in turn of the Arabs.

The spread of Mohammedanism cut off exports of papyrus to the east and to the west. The substitution of parchment in the West coincided roughly with the rise of the Carolingian dynasty and the decline of the Merovingians. Papyrus was produced in a restricted area and met the demands of a centralized administration whereas parchment as the product of an agricultural economy was suited to a decentralized system. The durability of parchment and the convenience of the codex for reference made it particularly suitable for the large books typical of scriptures and legal works. In turn the difficulties of copying a large book limited the numbers produced. Small libraries with a small number of large books could be established over large areas. Since the material of a civilization dominated by the papyrus roll had to be recopied into the parchment codex, a thorough system of censorship was involved. Pagan writing was neglected and Christian writing emphasized. "Never in the world's history has so vast a literature been so radically given over to destruction."[13] "Whatever knowledge man has acquired outside Holy Writ, if it be harmful it is there condemned; if it be wholesome it is there contained" (St Augustine).[14] The ban on secular learning gave a preponderance to theological studies and made Rome dominant.[15] The monopoly of knowledge centring around parchment emphasized religion at the expense of law.

Parchment as a medium was suited to the spread of monasticism from Egypt throughout western Europe. St Benedict founded a monastery at Monte Cassino about 520 AD and emphasized rules which made the preservation of books a sacred duty. His work followed by that of Cassiodorus gave "a scholarly bent to western monasticism." In spite of these efforts learning declined in Europe. Revival came on the fringes of the West in the independent and self-governing monasteries of Ireland. Missionary zeal led to the establishment of monasteries in Scotland and northern England and early in the seventh century on the Continent. The revival gained impetus with the support of Charlemagne and the migration of Alcuin from York. England and northern France were exposed to Danish raids but European monasteries had acquired transcriptions from English codices and supplemented them with those from Rome. Durable parchment books could be moved over long distances and transferred from regions of danger to regions of safety.

In the Byzantine Empire attempts to check the spread of Mohammedan influence were made by appeals to monophysite influence in the proscription of image worship and in attacks on the drain of monasticism on economic life. Resistance to Mohammedanism in the East strengthened the pressure of Mohammedanism in the West but the dangers were checked by the success of Charles Martel in 732 AD. The ultimate effects were evident in the division between the East and the West. Encouraged by the success of resistance in the west, the papacy allied itself to the Carolingian line and anathematized the iconoclasts of the East. To recapture the West the Byzantine emperors abandoned the iconoclastic controversy in 775 AD. In turn Charlemagne forbade the worship of images. The accession of the Empress Irene to the Byzantine throne in 797 enabled Charlemagne and the papacy to regard the throne as vacant under Salic law. Charlemagne was accordingly crowned emperor. The concern of Charlemagne for an efficient administration was reflected in efforts to improve educational institutions under control of the church and in his success in encouraging the development of an efficient uniform script, the minuscule.[16] His contributions toward the unification of Europe were destroyed by recognition of the Teutonic principle of equal division among the heirs. A nucleus of power emerged in Paris following attempts to check the influence of the Danes and in Germany following attempts to defeat the Magyars. Encroachments of the Holy Roman Empire on the papacy were followed by reforms in the church and the development of a powerful ecclesiastical organization. Parchment became the medium through which a monopoly of knowledge was built up by religion.

This monopoly of knowledge invited the competition of a new medium, namely paper from China. Discovery of the technique of making paper from textiles provided a medium with which the Chinese, by adaptation of the brush for painting to writing, were able to work out an elaborate system of pictographs. A system of four to five thousand characters were used for ordinary needs "enabling those who speak mutually unintelligible idioms to converse together, using the pencil instead of the tongue."[17] Its effectiveness for this purpose meant the abandonment of an attempt to develop an alphabet system.

An elaborate development of writing supported the position of the scholarly class in administration of the empire. In turn a wide gap between a limited governing class and the mass of the people led to the spread of Buddhism from India. The monopoly of knowledge of the Brahmins in India based on the oral tradition and the limitations of communication had led to the spread of Buddhism with its emphasis on writing and its appeal to the lower classes. After Alexander, Buddhism had been encouraged but decline of Macedonian power brought a revival of the power of the Brahmins and migration of Buddhism to China. Access to supplies of paper in China enabled Buddhists to develop block printing on a large scale. Confucianism gained by the influence of the state and the reproduction of the classics. A script which provided a basis for administration in China and emphasized the organization of an empire in terms of space proved inadequate to meet the demands of time and China was exposed to dynastic problems and to the domination of the Mongols from 1280 to 1368.

The spread of Mohammedanism to the east was followed by introduction to the technique of paper production. After establishment of a capital at Baghdad by the Abbasids paper manufacturing expanded and became the basis for an intense interest in learning. The Nestorians excommunicated from the church had established schools in which Greek and Latin works were translated into Syriac. Closing of the schools in Athens by Justinian in 529 AD had been followed by the migration of scholars to Persia. From this background of learning Baghdad became a centre for translators of Greek, Syriac, and Persian works into Arabic.

The prestige of Baghdad provoked a revival of Greek learning in Constantinople and of Latin learning in the West in the ninth century.[18] Revival of Greek learning was followed by the hostility of Rome. Rivalry between the Eastern and the Western church was accompanied by missionary activity and extension of the activities of the Eastern church to Bulgaria. The scriptures were translated into the Slavic vernacular on the one hand in the East, and translations from Latin into the vernacular were discouraged on the other hand in the West. The Cyrillic and the Glagolitic alphabets were invented to represent the sounds of the Slavonic language and to provide the basis for a richer expression.[19] An emphasis on secular learning in Byzantine education widened the breach with Rome and led to final separation of the churches of the East and West in 1054. Decline of the Abbasids was accompanied by activity of the Seljuk Turks and the capture of Jerusalem in 1070. The papacy refused to meet the requests of the Byzantine emperor for assistance and organized the Crusades. Ultimate failure to maintain control over Jerusalem led Crusaders to turn to Constantinople. It became subject to Latin states from 1204 to 1261 when it was recaptured by the Greeks.

Paper production spread from Baghdad to the West. After the capture of Baghdad by the Mongols in 1258, manufacturing was confined to western centres. With its development in Italy in the latter part of the thirteenth century new processes were introduced and a much better quality of paper produced. The art of paper making spread to France in the fourteenth century. Since linen rags were the chief raw material and the large cities provided the chief market for paper, production was determined to an important extent by proximity to cities with access to supplies of water and power. The commercial revolution beginning about 1275 paralleled increasing production of paper. The activity of the commercial cities of Italy weakened the Byzantine Empire. Religious prejudice against a product of Arabic origin was broken down and the monopoly of knowledge held by the monasteries of rural districts was weakened by the growth of cities, cathedrals, and universities.

The effects of the introduction of paper suggested by the rise of Baghdad were evident also in the concern with learning among the Mohammedans in Sicily and Spain. Large libraries were collected in Spain and following the recapture of Moorish cities by the Spaniards their contents in philosophy, mathematics, and medicine were made available to Europe. Acquaintance with the writings of Aristotle led to attempts such as those of St Thomas Aquinas (1227–74) to reconcile classical with Christian teaching. Aristotle as a creator of formal logic could be absorbed in orthodoxy. Attempts of the church to dominate learning in the universities were paralleled by attempts to check the spread of the scriptures in the vernacular. Persecution of the Waldensians and other heretics and the Albigensian crusades were followed by the creation of new preaching orders, the Dominican and the Franciscan, and the establishment of the Inquisition. Revival of an interest in the study of Roman law in the twelfth century strengthened the position of the emperor but it was offset by the codification of canon law. In spite of this activity the increased use of paper and the growth of trade favoured the development of cities and the position of monarchies. The increasing importance of the vernacular and the rise of lawyers strengthened the position of political at the expense of ecclesiastical organizations. The power of France was evident in the migration of the papacy to Avignon (1307–78) and in the hostility of England. Roman law made little impression in England and the influence of the common law was shown in the jury system and in parliament. Again as a result of the war with France the court encouraged the vernacular. Decline of the monopoly of knowledge based on parchment in which an ecclesiastical organization emphasized control over time followed the competition of paper which supported the growth of trade and of cities, the rise of vernaculars, and the increasing importance of lawyers, and emphasized the concept of space in nationalism.

Monopolies of knowledge controlled by monasteries were followed by monopolies of knowledge controlled by copyist guilds in the large cities. The high price for large books led to attempts to develop a system of reproduction by machine and to the invention of printing in Germany which was on the margin of the area dominated by copyists. The centralized control of France was less adapted to evasion than the numerous political divisions of Germany. The coarse brown parchment of Germany led to an interest in the use of paper. The beauty of Gothic script in manuscript[20] and its adaptability to printing were other factors emphasizing an interest in the invention with its numerous problems of ink, production of uniform type on a large scale, and a press capable of quick operation. Abundance of paper in Italy and political division similar to that of Germany led to the migration of printers to Italian cities and to the development of Roman and italic types. Printing in Paris was delayed until 1469 and in England until even later.

Manuscripts which had accumulated over centuries were reproduced and by the end of the fifteenth century printers became concerned with the possibilities of new markets. Commercialism of the publisher began to displace the craft of the printer. The vernacular offered new authors and new readers. The small book and the pamphlet began to replace the large folios. In England, Caxton avoided the competition of Latin books produced on the Continent and attempted to widen his own market. He wrote in the Prologue to the *Eneydos*: "And that comyn englysshe that is spoken in one shyre varyeth from another. ... I haue reduced and translated this sayd booke in to our englysshe, not ouer rude ne curyous, but in suche termes as shall be vnderstanden. ..."[21] In Germany opposition of the German language to scolasticism as it had developed in Paris in the French language implied an emphasis on mystical teaching and the vernacular. The attack on the pride of scholastic philosophy was evident in the words of Thomas à Kempis, "But what is the good of wisdom without the fear of God?"[22] "For lack of training the mind turns to reason" (Henry Adams). German music protected by the Hohenstaufens resisted encroachments from the church. An interest in the vernacular was supplemented by the concern of scholars such as Reuchlin and Erasmus with Hebrew and Greek and led to the translations of Luther and Tyndale of the Bible in German and English. Publication of the scriptures in the vernacular was followed by new interpretations and by the intensive controversies conducted in pamphlets and sheets which ended in the establishment of Protestantism. Biblical literalism became the mother of heresy and of sects.

Printing activity incidental to the Reformation in Germany was accompanied by repressive measures against heretical publications in France. The authority of the University of Paris stood in contrast to the Frankfurt Book Fair and the rise of Leipzig as a publishing centre. Printers migrated from France to adjacent countries such as Switzerland and the Netherlands and published books to be smuggled back to France. Learning declined in France in the sixteenth century but the vernacular found fresh support in printers shown in the writings of Montaigne and Rabelais. French became an official language after 1539. Its influence in the Huguenot controversies was evident in the Edict of Nantes of 1598, the first acknowledgment of a Roman Catholic country that heretics should be accorded civil rights. A policy of restrictions on publications paralleled a policy encouraging exports of paper. Countries encouraging a free press were subsidized by French mercantilist policies and the difficulties of restricting the smuggling of prohibited literature were increased. In the Empire repression in Antwerp was followed by the migration of printers such as Plantin to Holland and by an intensive development evident in a large-scale type-founding industry. Printing was accompanied by the production of printed sheets and postal services and by the growth of a financial centre at Antwerp. After the destruction of Antwerp in 1576 Amsterdam increased in importance. The Union of Utrecht in 1579 with ample financial resources was able to withstand the demands of the Empire and of France.

In England the absolutism of the Tudors involved suppression of printing but encouragement of the Renaissance and of the Reformation. Abolition of the monasteries and disappearance of clerical celibacy were followed by sweeping educational reforms. The printing press became "a battering-ram to bring abbeys and castles crashing to the ground."[23] Freedom from the Salic law made it possible for women to ascend the throne and to encourage the literature of the court. Restrictions on printing facilitated an interest in the drama and the flowering of the oral tradition in the plays of Shakespeare.

By the end of the sixteenth century the flexibility of the alphabet and printing had contributed to the growth of diverse vernacular literatures and had provided a basis for divisive nationalism in Europe. In the seventeenth century France continued to implement a mercantilist policy in suppression of publications and encouragement of exports of paper. Revocation of the Edict of Nantes in 1685 was followed by migration of skilled paper makers and the growth of paper making in England and Holland. Inefficiency in paper making incidental to state interference in France was paralleled by the introduction of more efficient methods in Holland. Refugees from France such as Pierre Bayle and Descartes developed a critical literature and a philosophy which had repercussions in the later criticism of the eighteenth century. In Holland type founding became an industrial enterprise and publishing activity by such firms as the Elzevirs built up markets throughout Europe. In England suppression of printing contributed to the outbreak of civil war. Increase in numbers of booksellers who encouraged printers as a means of reducing costs of publication led inevitably to the production of seditious literature, to renewed suppression, and finally to the outburst of controversial literature of the civil war.[24] Emphasis on the Bible accompanied restrictions on printing and facilitated an attack on Aristotelianism and scholastic philosophy and contributed to an interest in the moderns, the emergence of science, and deism. The Royal Society founded in 1662 was concerned with the advancement of science and the improvement of the English language as a medium for prose. It demanded a "mathematical plainness of language" and rejection of "all amplifications, digressions and swellings of style."[25]

Suppression of printing limited the attention to language which characterized France. Dictionaries were gradually developed but the English language was not adequate to the precision of the law codes of the Continent. Printing and improved communication strengthened a representative system in parliament. Suppression was met by newsletters and the rise of coffee-houses. The absolute power of parliament emerged to offset the absolute power of monarchy and annihilated the claims of common law which persisted in the colonies. It became the basis of public credit. The revolution of 1689 was followed by establishment of the Bank of England in 1694. Again, the revolution brought an end to the Licensing Act in 1694.

Immediately large numbers of papers were printed and the first daily appeared in 1701. In the Augustan age, Addison and Steele reconciled "wit and virtue, after a long and disastrous separation, during which wit had been led astray by profligacy and virtue by fanaticism." Limitations of the hand press led to a political war of pamphlets and to the imposition of a stamp tax in 1712. The excessive burden of a tax on a commodity selling at a very low price compelled printers to undertake compendious works such as weeklies and monthlies and Ephraim Chambers's *Universal Dictionary of Arts and Sciences* which appeared in 1728. Restrictions on political writing hastened the development of other types of literature such as the novel and children's books and the establishment of circulating libraries. The Copyright Act of 1710 gave protection to publishers but a legal decision of 1774 denying the right to perpetual copyright under common law destroyed control over publications, encouraged large numbers of small publishers to engage in the production of reprints, supported a large second-hand book trade, and compelled large publishers to concentrate on expensive publications. Scottish writers who had not been hampered by the Grub Street of English writing in the early part of the eighteenth century and who had the support of universities and a background of Roman law concentrated on such philosophical speculations as those produced by Hume and Adam Smith. Scottish publishers exploited the limitations of English publishing.[26] Constable was concerned with publication of the work of Sir Walter Scott and the *Edinburgh Review.*

The decline of political censorship after the fall of Walpole, an increase in the production of paper, escape from the monopoly of Dutch type foundries in the work of Caslon, and increased reliance on advertising following legislation against bill posters were followed by an expansion of newspapers. Resistance of the city of London against the absolute supremacy claimed by parliament supported the activities of Wilkes and Junius in the demand for the right to publish debates. Alderman Oliver, a member of parliament, stated that "whenever King, Lords or Commons assume unlimited power I will oppose that power."[27] The press attacked "the triple union of Crown, Lords and Commons against England." The newspaper article displaced the editorial and the essay in the writings of Junius who chose anonymity as it was "by no means necessary that he should be exposed to the resentment of the worst and most powerful men in the country." In spite of the achievement, taxes and threats of libel suits restricted expansion of newspapers and contributed to an interest in romantic literature. The position of deism which had been strengthened by the problems of the church during the revolution was weakened by the attacks of Hume and the way was opened to romanticism and to the religious revivals of Wesley and Whitefield.

The interest in literature which paralleled suppression of newspapers checked the growth of literature in the colonies and compelled an emphasis on newspapers. In the colonies a demand for printers for the publication of laws of the assemblies was followed by an interest in newspapers and in the post office. Printers were concerned with an agitation against restrictions and followed the arguments imported from England. The enormous burden of the stamp tax in 1765 on a low-priced commodity led to successful demands for repeal. Protests of Wilkes and Junius against the supremacy of parliament were elaborated in the colonies and the role of the newspapers in the Revolution was recognized in a bill of rights guaranteeing freedom of the press. Reliance on the common law implied a refusal to accept the principle of supremacy of parliament. Inability to find a middle course between absolute dependence and absolute independence broke the first empire. The influence of Roman law evident in an absolute parliament implied a conflict with an emphasis on common law in the colonies.

In France increasing centralization imposed heavy burdens on the administrative capacity of the monarchy. The increasing disequilibrium which followed attempts to export paper and to restrict publications led to increased development of printing in Holland and Switzerland and to continued smuggling of books into France. Attacks of French writers on restrictions became more aggressive in the writings of Voltaire, Diderot, Montesquieu, Rousseau, and others. The *Encyclopaedia* based on Chambers's work in England became a storehouse of ammunition directed against the monarchy. With the outbreak of revolution newspapers became the artillery of ideas. After the Revolution Napoleon introduced a system of censorship. Throughout the nineteenth century the long struggle for freedom of the press was marked by advance culminating in the revolution of 1830, by recession under Louis Napoleon, and by advance under the republic. Journalists played an active role as politicians with disturbing effects on the political history of France.

Fear of the effects of the French Revolution in England was evident in the severely repressive taxes on the press.[28] Introduction of machinery in the manufacture of paper and in the printing press and restrictions on newspapers led to an emphasis on media concerned with material other than news. Periodicals, magazines, and books increased in importance and brought a demand for the reduction of taxes and cheap postage. The moderation of the French revolution of 1830 preceded the bloodless revolution of the Reform Acts.[29] In the second half of the century the monopoly of *The Times* protected by taxes disappeared and newspapers increased in number and circulation in London and in the provinces. The monopoly of London strengthened by the railway was destroyed by the invention of the telegraph which encouraged provincial competition after 1868.[30] The success of German education, regarded as responsible for the defeat of Austria in 1866 and of France in 1870, led to the Education Act of 1870 and the creation of a large number of new readers. Newnes and Northcliffe exploited the new market in the new journalism. The monopoly of the circulating library disappeared before the new periodicals, cheap editions of novels, and literary agents.

An emphasis on literature in England in the first half of the nineteenth century incidental to the monopoly of the newspaper protected by taxes on knowledge and absence of copyright legislation in the United States compelled American writers to rely on journalism.[31] Publishers in New York such as Harper after the introduction of the steamship line drew on the vast stores of English literature and made them available to the enormous reading public of the United States.[32] Publishers and paper dealers such as Cyrus W. Field and Company opposed proposals for international copyright in 1852.[33] The emphasis on news which consequently characterized American journalism protected by the Bill of Rights supported the development of technological inventions in the fast press, the stereotype, the linotype, and the substitution of wood for rags. As in England the telegraph destroyed the monopoly of political centres and contributed, in destroying political power, to the outbreak of the Civil War. Technological development had its effects in the new journalism in England and on the Continent. The varying effects of technological change spreading from the United States destroyed the unity of Europe and contributed to the outbreak of the First World War. The British according to Bismarck were unable to participate in the work of the intimate circle of European diplomacy because of responsibility to parliament, and the inability increased with the new journalism.[34] The attitude of Bismarck expressed in the remark, "Never believe a statement until you see it contradicted,"[35] was in contrast with Anglo-American journalism. The great pioneers of intellectual life in Germany left a legacy of leadership assumed after about 1832 by the state culminating in a deadening officialdom.[36] Northcliffe in the search for news made unprecedented use of cables and private wires and exploited

Paris as a vast and cheap source of journalistic wealth with the result that French influence became more powerful.[37] The diplomatic institutions and techniques of an age of dynastic cabinet politics failed to work in a situation characterized by the press, electrical communications, mass literacy, and universal suffrage.[38] The Treaty of Versailles registered the divisive effects of the printing industry in its emphasis on self-determination. The monopoly of knowledge centring around the printing press brought to an end the obsession with space and the neglect of problems of continuity and time. The newspaper with a monopoly over time was limited in its power over space because of its regional character. Its monopoly was characterized by instability and crises. The radio introduced a new phase in the history of Western civilization by emphasizing centralization and the necessity of a concern with continuity. The bias of communication in paper and the printing industry was destined to be offset by the bias of the radio. Democracy which in the words of Guizot sacrificed the past and the future to the present was destined to be offset by planning and bureaucracy.

NOTES

1 See the complaint that archaeologists have been unduly concerned with objects of art, in S. Clarke and R. Engelbach, *Ancient Egyptian Masonry, the Building Craft* (London, 1930), vi.

2 V. Gordon Childe, *What Happened in History* (New York, 1946),150.

3 See G.R. Driver, *Semitic Writing from Pictograph to Alphabet* (London, 1948), 59.

4 J.M.P. Smith, *The Origin and History of Hebrew Law* (Chicago, 1934), 55.

5 J.E. Harrison, *Prolegomena to the Study of Greek Religion* (Cambridge, 1908), 568.

6 F. Nietzsche, *The Birth of Tragedy from the Spirit of Music* (Edinburgh, 1923), 120–7.

7 W.S. Ferguson, *The Treasures of Athena* (Cambridge, Mass., 1923), 178.

8 "The build of the Roman sentence was but another consequence of Rome's battles which in giving her conquests forced her people as a nation to think administratively" (Spengler).

9 T.R. Glover, *The Conflict of Religions in the Early Roman Empire* (London, 1932), 17.

10 Franz Altheim, *A History of Roman Religion* (London, 1938), 330.

11 Vaughan Cornish, *The Great Capitals: An Historical Geography* (London, 1923), 140.

12 J.L. Myers, *The Political Ideas of the Greeks* (New York, 1927), 308–16.
13 T.K. Osterreich, *Possession Demoniacal and Other, among Primitive Races, in Antiquity, the Middle Ages, and Modern Times* (London, 1930), 160.
14 Benjamin Farrington, *Science and Politics in the Ancient World* (London, 1939), 46.
15 P.H. Lang, *Music in Western Civilization* (New York, 1941), 46.
16 The minuscule was a descendant of papyrus cursive writing which had been submerged by the vellum uncials after the fourth century. See F.G. Kenyon, *The Palaeography of Greek Papyri* (Oxford, 1899), 124–5.
17 Edward Clodd, *The Story of the Alphabet* (New York, 1913), 182.
18 Werner Jaeger, *Humanism and Theology* (Milwaukee, Wisc., 1943),24.
19 D. Diringer, *The Alphabet: A Key to the History of Mankind* (London, n.d.), 475.
20 A.W. Pollard, *Early Illustrated Books* (New York, 1927), 7–8.
21 Cited G.M. Trevelyan, *English Social History* (New York, 1942), 82.
22 Jaeger, *Humanism and Theology*, 14.
23 Trevelyan, *English Social History*, 58.
24 H.R. Plomer, *A Short History of English Printing, 1476–1900* (New York, 1927), 169.
25 M.M.Lewis, *Language in Society* (London,1947), 38.
26 See L.E. Gates, *Three Studies in Literature* (New York, 1899), 50 ff.; also J.A. Greig, *Francis Jeffrey of the Edinburgh Review* (Edinburgh, 1948). On the influence of Roman law on Adam Smith, see the Rt. Hon. Lord Macmillan, *Two Ways of Thinking* (Cambridge, 1934), 28–30.
27 Michael MacDonagh, *The Reporters' Gallery* (London, n.d.),236.
28 See A. Aspinall, *Politics and the Press, c. 1780–1850* (London, 1949); and W.H. Wickwar, *The Struggle for the Freedom of the Press, 1819–1832* (London, 1928).
29 Emery Neff, *A Revolution in European Poetry, 1660–1900* (New York, 1940, 110.
30 James Samuelson, ed., *The Civilization of Our Day* (London, 1896), 277.
31 E.L. Bradsher, *Mathew Carey, Editor, Author and Publisher: A Study in American Literary Development* (New York, 1912), 79; and L.F. Tooker, *The Joys and Tribulations of an Editor* (New York, 1924), 3–10.
32 J.H. Harper, *The House of Harper* (New York, 1912), 89.
33 Ibid., 108.
34 J.A. Spender, *The Public Life* (London, 1925), 48.
35 Harold Spender, *The Fire of Life: A Book of Memories* (London,n.d.), 36.
36 Viscount Haldane, *Selected Addresses and Essays* (London, 1928),22.
37 Max Pemberton, *Lord Northcliffe: A Memoir* (New York, n.d.), 62.
36 O.J. Hale, *Publicity and Diplomacy, with Special Reference to England and Germany, 1890–1914* (New York, 1940), 209.

CHAPTER TWENTY-FOUR

The Mechanization of Knowledge

Mechanization has emphasized complexity and confusion; it has been responsible for monopolies in the field of knowledge; and it becomes extremely important to any civilization, if it is not to succumb to the influence of this monopoly of knowledge, to make some critical survey and report. The conditions of freedom of thought are in danger of being destroyed by science, technology, and the mechanization of knowledge, and with them, Western civilization.

My bias is with the oral tradition, particularly as reflected in Greek civilization,[1] and with the necessity of recapturing something of its spirit. For that purpose we should try to understand something of the importance of life or of the living tradition, which is peculiar to the oral as against the mechanized tradition, and of the contributions of Greek civilization. Much of this will smack of Marxian interpretation but I have tried to use the Marxian interpretation to interpret Marx. There has been no systematic pushing of the Marxian conclusion to its ultimate limit, and in pushing it to its limit, showing its limitations.

I propose to adhere rather closely to the terms of the subject of this discussion, namely, "a critical review, from the points of view of an historian, a philosopher and a sociologist, of the structural and moral changes produced in modern society by scientific and technological advance." I ask you to try to understand what that means. In the first place, the phrasing of the subject reflects the limitations of Western civilization. An interest in economics implies neglect of

---

Extracts from a paper presented to the Conference of Commonwealth Universities at Oxford, 28 July 1948; printed in *The Bias of Communication* (Toronto, 1951), chap. 8, 191–5, where it appeared as "A Critical Review."

the work of professional historians, philosophers, and sociologists. Knowledge has been divided to the extent that it is apparently hopeless to expect a common point of view. In following the directions of those responsible for the wording of the title, I propose to ask why Western civilization has reached the point that a conference largely composed of university administrators should unconsciously assume division in points of view in the field of learning and why this conference, representing the universities of the British Commonwealth, should have been so far concerned with political representation as to forget the problem of unity in Western civilization, or to put it in a general way, why all of us here together seem to be what is wrong with Western civilization. Some of you may remember James Thurber's story of the university professor pointing to a student and saying to him: "You are what is wrong with this institution."

In the remainder of this paper, I shall be concerned with an interest in the economic history of knowledge in which dependence on the work of Graham Wallas will be evident. He pointed to the danger that knowledge was growing too vast for successful use in social judgment, since life is short and sympathies and intellects are limited.[2] To him the idol of the pulpit and the idol of the laboratory were hindrances to effective social judgment, arising, as they do, from the traditions of organized Christianity and the metaphysical assumptions of professional scientists.[3] He assumed that creative thought was dependent on the oral tradition and that the conditions favourable to it were gradually disappearing with the increasing mechanization of knowledge. Reading is quicker than listening and concentrated individual thought than verbal exposition and counter-exposition of arguments. The printing press and the radio address the world instead of the individual. The oral dialectic is overwhelmingly significant where the subject-matter is human action and feeling, and it is important in the discovery of new truth but of very little value in disseminating it. The oral discussion inherently involves personal contact and a consideration for the feelings of others, and it is in sharp contrast with the cruelty of mechanized communication and the tendencies which we have come to note in the modern world. The quantitative pressure of modern knowledge has been responsible for the decay of oral dialectic and conversation. The passive reading of newspapers and newspaper placards and the small number of significant magazines and books point to the dominance of conversation by the newspaper and to the pervasive influence of discontinuity, which is, of course, the characteristic of the newspaper, as it is of the dictionary. Familiarity of association, which is essential to effective conversation, is present but is not accompanied by the stimulus which comes from contacts of one mind in free association with another mind in following up trains of ideas. As Graham Wallas pointed out, very few men who have been writing in a daily newspaper have produced important original work. We may conclude with the words of Schopenhauer, "To put away one's thoughts in order to take up a book is the sin against the Holy Ghost."

The impact of science on cultural development has been evident in its contribution to technological advance, notably in communication and in the dissemination of knowledge. In turn it has been evident in the types of knowledge disseminated; that is to say, science lives its own life not only in the mechanism which is provided to distribute knowledge but also in the sort of knowledge which will be distributed. As information has been disseminated the demand for the miraculous, which has been one of the great contributions of science, has increased. To supply this demand for the miraculous has been a highly remunerative task, as is evidenced by the publications of firms concerned with scientific works. Bury described the rapidly growing demand in England for books and lectures, making the results of science accessible and interesting to the lay public, as a remarkable feature of the second half of the nineteenth century. Popular literature explained the wonders of the physical world and at the same time flushed the imaginations of men with the consciousness that they were living in the era "which, in itself vastly superior to any age of the past, need be burdened by no fear of decline or catastrophe but, trusting in the boundless resources of science, might surely defy fate."[4] "Progress itself suggests that its value as a doctrine is only relative, corresponding to a certain not very advanced stage of civilization, just as Providence in its day was an idea of relative value corresponding to a stage somewhat less advanced."[5] The average reader has been impressed by the miraculous, and the high priests of science, or perhaps it would be fair to say the pseudo-priests of science, have been extremely effective in developing all sorts of fantastic things, with great emphasis, of course, on the atomic bomb. I hoped to get through this paper without mentioning the atomic bomb, but found it impossible.

Geoffrey Scott has stated that the romantic movement gave nature a democratic tinge. The cult of nature became a political creed with the theory of natural rights. The worship of nature supplanted a more definite and metaphysical belief. The creed of nature meant emphasis on representation, a fidelity to natural fact, and a prejudice against the Renaissance, order and proportion.[6] We may well heed his words: "It is thus the last sign of an artificial civilisation when Nature takes the place of art."[7]

The effects of obsession with science have become serious for the position of science itself. It has been held that the scientific mind can adapt itself more easily to tyranny than the literary mind, since "art is individualism and science seeks the subjection of the individual to absolute laws,"[8] but Casaubon was probably right in saying that "the encouragement of science and letters is almost always a personal influence." The concept of the state in the Anglo-Saxon world has been favourable to the suppression or distortion of culture, particularly through its influence on science. Under the influence of the state, communication among themselves has become more difficult for scientists with the same political background and practically impossible for those with a different political background, because of the importance attached to war. Mathematics and music have been regarded as universal languages, particularly with the decline of Latin, but even mathematics is a tool and has become ineffective for purposes of communication in a highly technical civilization concerned with war.

I can refer only briefly to the significance of mechanized knowledge, as affected by science, to the universities. Reliance on mechanized knowledge has increased with the demands of large numbers of students in the post-war period. Henry Adams wrote: "Any large body of students stifles the student. No one can instruct more than half a dozen students at once. The whole problem of education is one of its cost in money."[9] We have been compelled in the post-war period, with the larger number of students, to depend on textbooks, visual aids, administration, and conferences of university administrators such as we have here. They imply increasing concern with the written mechanized tradition and the examination system, of which Mark Pattison remarked that "the beneficial stimulus which examination can give to study is in an inverse ratio to the quality of intellectual exertion required."[10] We can subscribe to his reference to "the examination screw, which has been turned several times since, till it has become an instrument of mere torture which has made education impossible and crushed the very desire of learning."[11]

Finally we must keep in mind the limited role of universities and recall the comment that "the whole external history of science is a history of the resistance of academies and universities to the progress of knowledge." Leslie Stephen, referring to the period in the late eighteenth and early nineteenth centuries in England, when there was no system of education, said: "There is probably no period in English history at which a greater number of poor men have risen to distinction." "Receptivity of information which is cultivated and rewarded in schools and also in universities is a totally different thing from the education, sometimes conferred even by adverse circumstances, which trains a man to seize opportunities either of learning or of advancement." One need mention only the names of Burns, Paine, Cobbett, William Gifford, John Dalton, Porson, Joseph White, Robert Owen, and Joseph Lancaster.[12] Compulsory education increases the numbers able to read but does not contribute to understanding. Some of you may remember the comment in a discussion on literature by university graduates: "Literature? Sure; we took it in the senior year. It had a green cover."[13] Education is apt to become "merely the art of reading and writing, without training minds to principle of any kind, and destitute of regard for virtue and even decency."[14]

We are compelled to recognize the significance of mechanized knowledge as a source of power and its subjection to the demands of force through the instrument of the state. The universities are in danger of becoming a branch of the military arm. Universities in the British Commonwealth must appreciate the implications of mechanized knowledge and attack in a determined fashion the problems created by a neglect of the position of culture in Western civilization. Centralization in education in the interests of political organization has disastrous implications. This becomes one of the dangers of a conference of British Commonwealth universities, since, as Sir Hector Hetherington pointed out, the search for truth is much broader than that which can be undertaken by any political organization. Referring to the dangers of centralization, Scott wrote over a century ago: "London licks the butter off our bread, by opening a better market for ambition. Were it not for the difference of the religion and laws, poor Scotland could hardly keep a man that is worth having."[15] The problem is perhaps even more acute for the broader English-speaking world, with its common law tradition. The overwhelming influence of the United States as the chief centre of power points to the serious limitations of common law in making politics part of law and of emphasizing the position of the state, particularly in those nations with written constitutions. In Roman law countries, notably France, culture has had an opportunity to expand, politics have become less of an obsession, and leadership has been given to Western civilization. Culture survives ideologies and political institutions, or rather it subordinates them to the influence of constant criticism. Constant whining about the importance of our way of life is foreign to its temper.

The universities should subject their views about their role in civilization to systematic overhauling and revise the machinery by which they can take a leading part in the problems of Western culture. For example, we should extend our scholarships to universities on the Continent. Lecturers should be encouraged to write books as a means of compelling them to give new lectures. The universities must concern themselves with the living rather than with the dead.

NOTES

1 See S.H. Butcher, "The Written and the Spoken Word," *Some Aspects of the Greek Genius* (London, 1891); also V.H. Galbraith, *Studies in the Public Records* (London, 1949).

2 Graham Wallas, *Social Judgment* (London, 1934), 29.

3 Ibid., 161.

4 J.B. Bury, *The Idea of Progress: An Inquiry into Its Origin and Growth* (London,1920), 345–6.

5 Ibid., 352.

6 *The Architecture of Humanism: A Study in the History of Taste* (London, 1924), 75–80.

7 Ibid., 92.

8 Albert Guérard, *Literature and Society* (Boston, 1935), 80.

9 *The Education of Henry Adams* (Boston, 1918), 302.

10 *Essays by the late Mark Pattison* (Oxford, 1889), 1: 491.

11 Mark Pattison, *Memoirs* (London, 1885), 303.

12 A.V. Dicey, *Lectures on the Relations between Law and Public Opinion in England during the Nineteenth Century* (London, 1930), 113, 114.

13 H.W. Boynton, *Journalism and Literature and Other Essays* (Boston, 1904).

14 Cyrus Redding, *Fifty Years' Recollections* (London, 1858), 3: 316.

15 *The Journal of Sir Walter Scott* (Edinburgh, 1890), 2: 256.

CHAPTER TWENTY-FIVE

A Plea for Time

I must plead the bias of my special interest in the title of this paper. Economic historians and indeed all historians assume a time factor and their assumptions reflect the attitude towards time of the period in which they write. History in the modern sense is about four centuries old[1] but the word has taken on meanings which are apt to check a concern with facts other than those of immediate interest and its content is apt to reflect an interest in immediate facts such as is suggested by the words "all history proves." As a result history tends to repeat itself but in the changing accents of the period in which it is written. History is threatened on the one hand by its obsession with the present and on the other by the charge of antiquarianism. Economic history is in a particularly exposed position as is evident in the tendency to separate it from economics or to regard it as a basis of support for economics. "Knowledge of the past is at all times needed only to serve the present and the future, not to enfeeble the present or to tear the roots out of the vigorous powers of life for the future" (Nietzsche). The danger that knowledge of the past[2] may be neglected to the point that it ceases to serve the present and the future – perhaps an undue obsession with the immediate, support my concern about the disappearance of an interest in time.

Perhaps the exposed position of economic history may strengthen the urge to discover a solution of the difficulty, particularly as it becomes imperative to attempt to estimate the significance of the attitude towards time in an analysis of economic change. The economic historian must consider the role of time or the attitude to-

---

From a paper presented at the University of New Brunswick in 1950; printed in *The Bias of Communication* (Toronto, 1951), chap. 3, 61–91.

wards time in periods which he attempts to study, and he may contribute to an escape from antiquarianism, from present-mindedness, and from the bogeys of stagnation and maturity. It is impossible for him to avoid the bias of the period in which he writes but he can point to its dangers by attempting to appraise the character of the time concept.

It has been pointed out that astronomical time is only one of several concepts. Social time, for example, has been described as qualitatively differentiated according to the beliefs and customs common to a group and as not continuous but subject to interruptions of actual dates.[3] It is influenced by language which constrains and fixes prevalent concepts and modes of thought. It has been argued by Marcel Granet that the Chinese are not equipped to note concepts or to present doctrines discursively. The word does not fix a notion with a definite degree of abstraction or generality but evokes an indefinite complex of particular images. It is completely unsuited to formal precision.[4] Neither time nor space is abstractly conceived; time proceeds by cycles and is round; space is square.[5]

The linear concept of time was made effective as a result of humanistic studies in the Renaissance. When Gregory XIII imposed the Julian calendar on the Catholic world in 1582 Joseph Justus Scaliger following his edition of Manilius (1579) published the *De emendatione temporum* and later his *Thesaurus temporum* (1606) "probably the most learned book in the world."[6] With his work he developed an appreciation of the ancient world as a whole and introduced a conception of the unity of history at variance with the attitude of the church. While Scaliger assisted in wresting control over time from the church he contributed to the historical tradition of philosophy until Descartes with his emphasis on mathematics and his unhistorical temper succeeded in liberating philosophy from history. The ideal of mathematical sciences dominated the seventeenth century. It was not until the Enlightenment that the historical world was conquered and until Herder and romanticism that the primacy of history over philosophy and science was established. Historicism was almost entirely a product of the nineteenth century.[7] In geology the precise date of the earth's formation advanced by Bishop Ussher was destroyed. "The weary series of accommodations of Genesis to geology was beginning."[8] In archaeology a knowledge of earlier civilizations implied a vast extension of time. In the hands of Darwin the historical approach penetrated biology and provided a new dimension of thought for science. In astronomy time was extended to infinity. Laws of real nature became historical laws. Even in mathematics arithmetic escaped from its bondage to geometry and algebra as "the science of pure time or order in progression" (Sir William Hamilton) came into its own.

The effects on history were evident in a recognition of the limitations of the written and the printed record. Mommsen made politics proper the subject-matter of historical knowledge but in the last decades of the nineteenth century the limitations of political historiography were evident. Burckhardt and to some extent Lamprecht approached the study of civilization through fine art. The highest value of art as of all free intellectual activity was to provide release from subservience to the will and from entanglement in the world of particular aims and individual purposes.[9] Taine held that intellectual development was the moving force behind political affairs and that the classical spirit was responsible for the French Revolution.[10] Fustel de Coulanges emphasized the myth[11] as a device for studying periods before writing had developed. Worship of the dead was regarded as the inner bond uniting divergent expressions of faith.

I have attempted to show elsewhere[12] that in Western civilization a stable society is dependent on an appreciation of a proper balance between the concepts of space and time. We are concerned with control not only over vast areas of space but also over vast stretches of time. We must appraise civilization in relation to its territory and in relation to its duration. The character of the medium of communication tends to create a bias in civilization favourable to an overemphasis on the time concept or on the space concept and only at rare intervals are the biases offset by the influence of another medium and stability achieved. Dependence on clay in Sumerian civilization was offset by dependence on stone in Babylon and a long period of relative stability followed in the reign of the Kassites. The power of the oral tradition in Greece which checked the bias of a written medium supported a brief period of cultural activity such as has never been equalled. Dependence on the papyrus roll and use of the alphabet in the bureaucracy of the Roman Empire was offset by dependence on parchment codex in the church and a balance was maintained in the Byzantine Empire until 1453. "Church and Army are serving order through the power of discipline and through hierarchical arrangement" (Metternich).[13] On the other hand in the West the bias of the parchment codex became evident in the absolute dominance of the church and supported a monopoly which invited competition from paper as a new medium. After the introduction of paper and the printing press, religious monopoly was followed by monopolies of vernaculars in modern states. A monopoly of time was followed by a monopoly of space. A brief survey of outstanding problems of time will perhaps assist in enabling us to understand more clearly the limitations of our civilization.

The pervasive character of the time concept makes it difficult to appreciate its nature and difficult to suggest its conservative influence. The division of the day into 24 hours, of the hour into 60 minutes, and of the minute into 60 seconds suggests that a sexagesimal system prevailed in which the arrangement was worked out and this carries us immediately into Babylonian history.[14] The influence persists in systems of measurement and more obviously, for example, in Great Britain where the monetary system is sexagesimal. The advantages of the sexagesimal system are evident in calculations which permit evasion of the problem in handling fractions and have been exploited effectively in the development of aviation with its demands for rapid calculations.

In a system of agriculture dependent on irrigation the measurement of time becomes important in predicting periods of floods and the important dates of the year, seed-time and harvest. A concern with time was reflected in the importance of religion and in the choice of days on which festivals might be celebrated. The selection of holy days necessitated devices by which they could be indicated and violation of them could be avoided.[15] Dependence on the moon for the measurement of time meant exposure to irregularities such as have persisted in the means of determining the dates for Easter. Sumerian priesthoods apparently worked out a system for correcting the year by the adjustment of lunar months but the difficulties may have contributed to the success of Semitic kings with an interest in the sun, and enabled them to acquire control over the calendar and to make necessary adjustments of time over the extended territory under their control.[16] With control over time kings began the system of reckoning in terms of their reigns; our present statutes defy Anno Domini and date from the accession of the king in whose reign they are enacted. Control over time by monarchies, on the other hand, in addition to the human limitations of dynastic and military power, was limited by the continuity of priesthoods and the effectiveness of an ecclesiastical hierarchy.

In Egypt and Babylonia the principal changes in nature were accompanied by appropriate rituals which were part and parcel of cosmic events. Time was a succession of recurring plans each charged with peculiar value and significance.[17] In a sense it was a biological time with a sequence of essentially different phases of life. In Egypt as in Babylonia the importance of the Nile floods and dependence on irrigation were linked with the celebration of religious festivals and the importance of determining an exact date. It is possible that the absolutism of Egyptian dynasties was dependent on the ability of kings to determine the sidereal year in relation to the appearance of the star Sirius. Recognition of the first dynasty by the Egyptians implied a recognition of time as dating from it. The joining of the two lands in Egypt apparently coincided with kingship and implied an emphasis on religious ceremony and ritual. The power of absolute kings over time and space was reflected in the pyramids which remain a standing monument to justify their confidence, in the development of mummification, a tribute to their control over eternity, and in the belief in immortality. The power of the absolute monarchy may have been weakened by the priesthood which discovered the more reliable solar year. Absolutism passed with control over time into the hands of the priesthood and checked expansion over space in the Egyptian Empire.

In Egypt the power of the absolute monarchy reflected in the monumental architecture of the pyramids and in sculpture was offset by the power of the priesthood based on a complex system of writing and the use of papyrus. The emphasis of a civilization on means of extending its duration as in Egypt accompanied by reliance on permanence gives that civilization a prominent position in periods such as the present when time is of little significance. In Babylonia the power of the priesthood was dependent in part on a mastery of complex cuneiform writing on clay tablets, and an increasing power of the monarchy on the creation of new and elaborate capitals emphasizing sculpture and architecture. Relative stability was gradually established over a long period by compromises between political and religious power. In turn the Kassites, the Assyrians, and the Persians recognized the power of the Babylonian priesthood. In Egypt the power of the priesthood checked the possibilities of political development of the monarchy and prevented effective conquest by conquerors such as the Hyksos and later the Assyrians and the Persians. Monopolies of control over time exercised by the priesthoods of Babylonia and Egypt made the problems of political organization in the Assyrian and Persian empires and indeed of later empires insuperable.

The Babylonian priesthood in its concern with time contributed to the study of astrology and astronomy by the introduction of a system of chronology at the era of Nabonassar in 747 BC. It possibly followed the discovery that every 18 years and 11 days the moon returned almost to the same position in relation to the sun.[18] The discovery of the periodic character of celestial phenomena and the possibility of prediction gave Babylonia an enormous influence on religious cults and led to the domination of fatalism based on scientific knowledge.

The limited possibility of political organizations expanding their control over space incidental to the control of priesthoods in their monopolies of knowledge over time facilitated the development of marginal organizations such as those of the Jews in Palestine. Periods of expansion and retreat in political organization centring on Egypt or Babylonia weakened an emphasis on political organization and strengthened an emphasis on religious organization. The marginal relation to cultures with monopolies of complex systems of writing favoured the development of relatively simple systems of writing such as emerged in the alphabet of the Phoenicians and the Aramaeans. In these marginal cultures religious organization emphasized a system of writing in sharp contrast with those of Egypt and Babylonia, and in compensation for lack of success in political organization with control over space built up an elaborate hierarchy with control over time. The latter emphasized the sacred character of writing and drew on the resources of Egyptian and Babylonian civilizations to an extent obvious to students of the Old Testament. There was "no engrossment in the moment but full recognition that human life is a great stream of which the present is only the realized moment. ... It was no accident that the supremely religious people of all time were likewise our first great historians" (W.A. Irwin). History emerged with the Hebrews as a result of the concern with time.

Contact of barbarians on the north shore of the Mediterranean with older civilizations was followed by the emergence of Greek civilization. An emphasis on problems of space incidental to a concern with conquest of territory was evident in the Homeric poems developed in the oral tradition. Geometry with its bias toward measurement and space imposed restrictions on a concern with time. The spread of a money economy strengthened an interest in numbers and arithmetic and in turn in mystery religions in conflict with the established Apollonic religion. The flexibility of an oral tradition enabled the Greeks to work out a balance between the demands of concepts of space and time in a city state. In the reforms of Cleisthenes control over time was wrested from religion and placed at the disposal of the state. The results of a balanced society were evident in the defeat of the Persians and the flowering of Greek culture in the fifth century. But such a balance was not long maintained.[19] Cleisthenes created a senatorial year with ten prytanies of 36 or 37 days in each solar year averaging 365¼ days over a period free from cycles and intercalations, but the old civil calendar sanctioned by religious observance continued. The Metonic cycle[20] of 19 years, 30 days in each month, was introduced on 25 June (Julius) 432 BC and became a norm for the accurate measurement of time. A change was made to a new senatorial year probably in the year of anarchy 404–3. When democracy was re-established the senatorial year was made to conform to the civil year. The Callippic cycle was introduced in the first summer solstice 27–8 June 330 BC with 30 days to each month and every sixty-fourth day dropped.

The spread of writing in the latter part of the fifth and in the fourth centuries accentuated strains which destroyed Greek civilization. Following the collapse of Greece and the success of Alexander, the East was divided in the Hellenistic kingdoms. In Egypt in a new capital at Alexandria the Ptolemies attempted to offset the influence of the priesthood at Thebes and of Babylonian science by the creation of a new religion and the encouragement of research in libraries and museums. Aristotelian influence was evident in the concern with science and in developments in astronomy. The names of the planets and constellations remain as testimonials to the interest of antiquity in astronomy. Leap year was introduced in 239 or 238 BC but was later abandoned until taken up by the Romans.

After the conquest of Egypt by the Romans Julius Caesar employed Sosigenes, an Egyptian astronomer, to work out an accurate calendar and it is probably significant that the new calendar recognized the festivals of Isis and contributed to the spread of Egyptian and other religions in the Empire. Exploitation of the irregular measurement of time for political purposes[21] and demands for regularity and the power of Julius Caesar in enforcing the new calendar led to a change from the beginning of the new year on 1 March to 1 January in 46 BC, or 708 years from the date of the foundation of Rome, and to a year of 365¼ days. A fixed date of reckoning, that of the founding of the city, reflected the interest of Rome in the unique character of a single day or hour and the belief that continuity was a sequence of single moments. An emphasis on specific single acts at a unique time contributed to the growth of Roman law notably in contracts in which time is of the essence. Alternate odd months were given 31 days and even months 30 days excepting February which had 29 days but 30 every fourth year. The month following that named for Caesar, July, was called Augustus and was given the same number of days. A day was taken from February and given to August. September and November were reduced to 30 days and October and December increased to 31 days to avoid three months in succession with 31 days.

A powerful bureaucracy at Rome and at Constantinople maintained control over time. Toward the end of the third century a 15-year cycle was introduced for tax purposes and after 312 AD the Egyptian date of indiction was changed from 29 August to 1 September the beginning of the Byzantine year. As a result of the influence of astronomy each day became sacred to a planet and the liturgy of the mysteries of Mithra contributed to the substitution of the seven-day week for the Roman eight days about the time of Augustus. 25 December as the date of the birth of the sun in the worship of Mithra was replaced by Christmas Day between 354 and 360 AD.[22] Easter probably took the place of festivals celebrating Attis at the vernal equinox.[23] The Christians used 1 March as the beginning of the year following the Mosaic ordinance as to the Passover.

Following the collapse of the Empire in the West the church supported the system of dating events from the supposed year of the birth of Christ. The concern of religion for the domination of time evident in stories of the flood designed to show that a past had been wiped out and that a new era began, in the beginnings of Egyptian time, in the history of Greece and Rome continued in the Christian era. St Cyril was reputed to have drawn up a table of 95 years (five cycles of 19 years each) to be based on the accession of Diocletian in 284 AD. The base was changed to the Incarnation and the table introduced into the calendar of the West by Dionysius Exiguus in 525 AD. St Wilfrid secured adoption of the system to celebrate Easter on or after 15 March at Whitby in 664 AD in opposition to the Celtic system which allowed the celebration of Easter on the 14th and calculated the moon on a cycle of 84 years. From the time of Bede, in England the year was reckoned from the Incarnation. The system was carried by missionaries to the eastern regions of the Franks and the Incarnation became the official date in 839. Under the influence of Otto the Great it was adopted in the papal chancery in 963.[24] Use of the imperial year and indiction had apparently begun in the papal chancery in 537 and had become general practice in 550. They were never used after 781 AD.[25] Charles the Great visited Rome in that year and under Hadrian the Frankish practice of using a double form of dating documents was used, the pontifical year replacing the regnal of the emperor at Constantinople.

By at least the last quarter of the ninth century Frankish emperors reckoned from Christmas Day as the beginning of the New Year. Religious movements stimulating devotion to the Virgin Mary led to the establishment of Lady Day (25 March) as the beginning of the year in the French chancery after 1112 and in England in the latter part of the twelfth century. After the middle of the thirteenth century, possibly as a result of the study of Roman law and the increasing use of almanacs, there was a gradual return to the Roman system in which the year began on January 1. It was not until 1752 that the beginning of the year was moved from 25 March to 1 January in England.[26] The pagan form of reckoning was gradually restored by the modern state. As in Egypt and in Rome control over time by the church was emphasized by architecture notably in the enduring monuments of the Gothic cathedral.

Gregory XIII introduced a calendar reform in 1582 in which the cumulative inaccuracies of a year based on 365¼ days were corrected and 5 October reckoned as 15 October. While the Roman Catholic church exercised a dominant control over time other religions Jewish and Protestant asserted their rights notably in the determination of holidays. This division weakened the state in the creation of friction and strengthened it by compelling an insistence on unity. Significantly Protestant states grudgingly conceded the advantage of the change but it was not until 1750 that Great Britain ordered 2 September 1752 to be followed by 14 September. It was only after the overthrow of the Tsarist régime in Russia that the Julian calendar was superseded by the Gregorian.

The Christian system followed Roman religion in giving a fixed year, that of the birth of Christ, a unique position. Control over time was not only evident in chronology but also in its place in the life of the Middle Ages. Spread of monasticism and the use of bells to mark the periods of the day and the place of religious services introduced regularity in the life of the West. Sun-dials, whose usefulness was limited in the more cloudy skies of the north, gave way to water clocks and finally to devices for measuring time with greater precision.[27] The modern hour came into general use with the striking clock in the fourteenth century.[28]

Regularity of work brought administration, increase in production, trade, and the growth of cities. The spread of mathematics from India to Baghdad and the Moorish universities of Spain implied the gradual substitution of Arabic for Roman numerals and an enormous increase in the efficiency of calculation.[29] Measurement of time facilitated the use of credit, the rise of exchanges, and calculations of the predictable future essential to the development of insurance. Introduction of paper, and invention of the printing press hastened the decline of Latin and the rise of the vernaculars. Science met the demands of navigation, industry, trade, and finance by the development of astronomy and refined measurements of time which left little place for myth or religion. The printing press supported the Reformation and destroyed the monopoly of the church over time though the persistence of its interest is evident in feast days. The church recognized at an early date the threat of astronomers to the monopoly over time and treated them accordingly.

The struggle between church and state for control over time had centred about a series of measures in the states in the West and the iconoclastic controversy in the Byzantine Empire in the East. The fall of Constantinople in 1453 which followed the perfection of artillery came as a profound shock to Europe. A bulwark of opposition to the absolute supremacy of the papacy had been removed and new states became attracted to the problem of duration and to the possibility of devices which had contributed to the solution of problems of longevity in the Byzantine Empire. The experiment of the Tudors[30] had many parallels with that of the Byzantine Empire – notably the emphasis on a sort of Caesaropapism by Henry VIII in becoming head of the Anglican church, on the destruction of monasteries paralleling the iconoclastic controversy, and on the position of women on the throne in contrast with the prohibitions of Salic law. As the Tudors assumed the mantle of divine right from the papacy they laid the foundation for internal struggles for control over time evident in the contention over monopolies[31] under Elizabeth and James I, and in the absolute supremacy of parliament. The interest of parliament in time was evident in the statute of limitations, restrictions on the period for patents and copyright, the rule against perpetuity in wills, and abolition of entail. The interest of the state in the subject of mort-main has been followed by estate taxes to check control over time beyond life itself. It was not until 1774 that perpetual copyright in common law was destroyed by a decision of the courts following the refusal of Scottish courts to recognize the pretensions of English common law and London booksellers. The concern of the Crown in the problem of time and in the permanence of dynasties was evident in the choice of names for monarchs, to mention only the four Georges. A growing interest in problems of permanence of the British Empire was evident in Gibbon's *Decline and Fall of the Roman Empire.* The struggle over control of time on the Continent led the French to start a new era at the birth of the republic on 22 September 1792. Names descriptive of the seasons, such as Thermidor for the summer, were introduced. The arrangement was brought to an end in 1805 following the Concordat of 1802. Holidays determined by the church were suppressed and new holidays were created by the modern state. Economic inefficiencies incidental to the growth in numbers of religious holidays were paralleled by industrial controversies over shorter working weeks.

Weakening of control over time by the church and limited control by the state left a vacuum which was occupied by industry. The church, particularly in the monastic orders, had introduced a rigorous division of time for services following the spread in the use of clocks and the bell. But industrial demands meant fresh emphasis on the ceaseless flow of mechanical time. Establishment of time zones facilitated the introduction of uniformity in regions. An advance in the state of industrialism reflected in the speed of the newspaper press and the radio meant a decline in the importance of biological time determined by agriculture. Demands for the reform of the calendar and daylight saving schemes follow the impact of industrialism. The persistence of Easter as a movable feast points to the conservative character of time arrangements.

The demands of industry on time have been paralleled by the demands of business. Family concerns extending over generations were followed by more flexible and permanent arrangements in partnerships and corporations. Certain types of industries such as communication, particularly newspapers, were apparently suited to family control, partly because of the need for advertising and use of the same name over a long period to give an appearance of permanence where permanence and dependability were important. The length of life of corporations has been dependent on concern of management with policies affecting duration and with the character of an industry. Centennial volumes are published to reflect the element of permanency and as a form of institutional advertising. The long history of the Hudson's Bay Company was perhaps in part a result of the necessity of conducting operations extending over a period of five or six years between the date of purchase of goods and the date of the sale of furs. Periods of expansion and consolidation imply an alternative interest in time and place.

Conflict between different groups over monopolies of time hastened the intervention of the state. Devices emphasizing rapid turnover of goods, whether technological (for example, in the substitution of buses for street railways), or commercial (for example, in the introduction of pennies to secure newspaper sales and in an emphasis on changing fashions as in the case of motor cars or the publication of books by popular authors), tend to conflict with long-term investment supported by savings voluntary or compulsory, whether insurance or old age pensions. Competition between consumers' goods with rapid turnover and durable goods implies conflict within an economy and conflict between nations emphasizing the durable character of goods, such as England, and those emphasizing a less durable character, such as North America. As a result the state intervenes with policies ranging from the breaking of trusts to the devices of socialism. In fields concerned with durable goods and involving long-term investment of capital, such as railways, electric power, forests, and steel, state intervention has been marked. The ultimate steps are taken in a concern with long-term budgets and long-term capital arrangements and with five-year plans. The need for a sane and balanced approach to the problem of time in the control of monopolies, and in the whole field of interest theory and in other directions, is evident in the growth of a bureaucracy in a totalitarian state. The static approach to economic theory has been of limited assistance in meeting the problems of time.

A balanced civilization in its concern with the problem of duration or time and of extent or space is faced with several difficulties. Systems of government concerned with problems of duration have been defeated in part by biology, when dynasties fail to provide a continued stream of governing capacity, and by technology,[32] when invaders are able to exploit improvements in the methods of warfare at the expense of peoples who have neglected them. Writing as a means of communication provides a system of administration of territory for the conquerors and in religion a system of continuity but in turn tends to develop monopolies of complexity which check an interest in industrial technology and encourage new invaders. "For where there is no fear of god, it [the state] must either fall to destruction, or be supported by the reverence shown to a good Prince; which indeed may sustain it for a while, and supply the want of religion in his subjects. But as human life is short, its government must of course sink into decay when its virtue, that upheld and informed it, is extinct" (Machiavelli). A balanced concern with space or extent of territory and duration or time appears to depend on a dual arrangement in which the church is subordinate to the state and ensures that the mobilization of the intellectual resources of the civilization concerned, by religion or by the state, will be at the disposal of both and that they will be used in planning for a calculated future in relation to the government of territory of definite extent. If social stratification is too rigid and social advancement is denied to active individuals as it is in plutocracies a transpersonal power structure will be threatened with revolt.[33]

The tendency of a monopoly over time in religion to lead to an accumulation of wealth invites attacks from the state with demands for redistribution evident in the embarrassments of the church in the Middle Ages, and in the attacks on monasteries in England and in the Byzantine Empire, and in confiscation of the property of the Jews. The linking of church and state in an absolute monarchy and the accumulation of wealth may lead to revolution as it did in France and Russia. This implies a fundamental break with a concept of time increasingly out of line with the demands of a bureaucracy centring on space. The bias of communication in space or in time involves a sponge theory of the distribution of wealth which assumes violence.

It is beyond the bounds of this paper to enumerate the inventions for the measurement of time or to suggest their implications in the various developments of modern industrialism. It is concerned with the change in attitudes toward time preceding the modern obsession with present-mindedness, which suggests that the balance between time and space has been seriously disturbed with disastrous consequences to Western civilization. Lack of interest in problems of duration in Western civilization suggests that the bias of paper and printing has persisted in a concern with space. The state has been interested in the enlargement of territories and the imposition of cultural uniformity on its peoples, and, losing touch with the problems of time, has been willing to engage in wars to carry out immediate objectives. Printing has emphasized vernaculars and divisions between states based on language without implying a concern with time. The effects of division have been evident in development of the book, the pamphlet, and the newspaper and in the growth of regionalism as new monopolies have been built up. The revolt of the American colonies, division between north and south, and extension westward of the United States have been to an important extent a result of the spread of the printing industry. In the British Empire the growth of autonomy and independence among members of the Commonwealth may be attributed in part to the same development. In Europe division between languages has been accentuated by varying rates of development of the printing industry. Technological change in printing under constitutional protection of freedom of the press in the United States has supported rapid growth of the newspaper industry. Its spread to Anglo-Saxon countries has sharpened the division between English and languages spoken in other areas and in turn contributed to the outbreak of the First World War. Not only has the press accentuated the importance of the English language in relation to other languages, it has also created divisions between classes within English-speaking countries. Emphasis on literacy and compulsory education has meant concentration on magazines and books with general appeal and widened the gap between the artist concerned with improvement of his craft and the writer concerned with the widest market. The writing of history is distorted by an interest in sensationalism and war. The library catalogue reflects an obsession of commercialism with special topics, events, periods, and individuals, to mention only the names of Lincoln, Napoleon, Churchill, Roosevelt, and others.

Large-scale production of newsprint made from wood in the second half of the nineteenth century supported large-scale development of newspaper plants and a demand for effective devices for widening markets for newspapers. The excitement and sensationalism of the South African War in Great Britain and of the Spanish-American War in the United States were not unrelated to the demands of large newspapers for markets. Emergence of the comics[34] coincided with the struggle for circulation between Hearst and Pulitzer in New York. Increased newspaper circulation supported a demand for advertising and for new methods of marketing, notably the department store. The type of news essential to an increase in circulation, to an increase in advertising, and to an increase in the sale of news was necessarily that which catered to excitement. A prevailing interest in orgies and excitement was harnessed in the interests of trade. The necessity for excitement and sensationalism had serious implications for the development of a consistent policy in foreign affairs which became increasingly the source of news. The reports of MacGahan, an American newspaper man, on Turkish activities were seized upon by Gladstone and led to the defeat of Disraeli.[35] The activity of W.T. Stead in the *Pall Mall Gazette* was an important factor in the fiasco of Gordon's expedition to Egypt. While it would be fatal to accept the views of journalists as to their power over events it is perhaps safe to say that Northcliffe played an important role in shifting the interest of Great Britain from Germany to France and in policy leading to the outbreak of the First World War.

Technological advance in the production of newspapers accompanied the development of metropolitan centres. In the period of western expansion "all these interests bring the newspaper; the newspaper starts up politics, and a railroad."[36] A large number of small centres were gradually dwarfed by the rise of large cities. In turn the opinion of large centres was reflected in their newspapers and in an emphasis on differences. "No," said Mr Dooley, "They've got to print what's different."[37] Large centres became sources of news for distribution through press associations and in turn press associations became competitive with an emphasis on types of news which were mutually exclusive. The United Press became a competitor of the International News Service (Hearst) and of the Associated Press. The limitations of news as a basis of a steady circulation led to the development of features and in particular the comics and photography. Improvements in the reproduction of photographs coincided with the development of the cinema. News and the cinema complemented each other in the emphasis on instability. As a result of the struggle between various regions or metropolitan centres political stability was difficult to achieve. "It is one of the peculiar weaknesses of our political system that our strongest men cannot be kept very long in Congress."[38] While Congress was weakened the power of the president was strengthened. Theodore Roosevelt appealed to the mass psychology of the middle class and significantly gave the press a permanent room in the White House.[39] Oswald Garrison Villard claimed that "Theodore Roosevelt did more to corrupt the press than anyone else."[40]

The steadying influence of the book as a product of sustained intellectual effort was destroyed by new developments in periodicals and newspapers. As early as 1831 Lamartine would write: "Le livre arrive trop tard; le seul livre possible dès aujourd'hui, c'est un journal." The effect of instability on international affairs has been described by Moltke: "It is no longer the ambition of princes; it is the moods of the people, the discomfort in the face of interior conditions, the doings of parties, particularly of their leaders, which endanger peace."[41] The Western community was atomized by the pulverizing effects of the application of machine industry to communication. J.G. Bennett is said to have replied to someone charging him with inconsistency in the *New York Herald*, "I bring the paper out every day." He was consistent in inconsistency. "Advertisement dwells [in] a one-day world."[42]

Philosophy and religions reflected the general change. In the words of *Punch*: "It was the gradually extended use of the printing press that dragged the obscure horrors of political economy into the full light of day: and in the western countries of Europe the new sect became rampant." Hedonism gained in importance through the work of Bentham. Keynes has described his early belief by stating that he belonged to the first generation to throw hedonism out the window and to escape from the Benthamite tradition. "I do now regard that as the worm which has been gnawing at the insides of modern civilisation and is responsible for its present moral decay. We used to regard the Christians as the enemy, because they appeared as the representatives of tradition, convention, and hocus-pocus. In truth it was the Benthamite calculus, based on an over-valuation of the economic criterion, which was destroying the quality of the popular Ideal. Moreover, it was this escape from Bentham, joined with the unsurpassable individualism of our philosophy, which has served to protect the whole lot of us from the final *reductio ad absurdum* of Benthamism known as Marxism."[43] But Keynes was to conclude "we carried the individualism of our individuals too far" and thus to bear further testimony to the atomization of society. In religion "the new interest in the future and the progress of the race" unconsciously undermined "the old interest in a life beyond the grave; and it has dissolved the blighting doctrine of the radical corruption of man."[44] We should remind ourselves of Dean Inge's remarks that popular religion follows the enslavement of philosophy to superstition. The philosophies of Hegel, Comte, and Darwin became enslaved to the superstition of progress. In the corruption of political science confident predictions, irritating and incapable of refutation, replaced discussion of right and wrong.[45] Economists (the Physiocrats) "believed in the future progress of society towards a state of happiness through the increase of opulence which would itself depend on the growth of justice and 'liberty'; and they insisted on the importance of the increase and diffusion of knowledge."[46] The monopoly of knowledge which emerged with technological advances in the printing industry and insistence on freedom of the press checked this development.

The Treaty of Versailles recognized the impact of printing by accepting the principle of the rights of self-determination and destroyed large political organizations such as the Austrian Empire. Communication based on the eye in terms of printing and photography had developed a monopoly which threatened to destroy Western civilization first in war and then in peace. This monopoly emphasized individualism and in turn instability and created illusions in catchwords such as democracy, freedom of the press, and freedom of speech.

The disastrous effect of the monopoly of communication based on the eye hastened the development of a competitive type of communication based on the ear, in the radio and in the linking of sound to the cinema and to television. Printed material gave way in effectiveness to the broadcast and to the loud speaker.[47] Political leaders were able to appeal directly to constituents and to build up a pressure of public opinion on legislatures. In 1924 Al Smith, Governor of the State of New York, appealed directly by radio to the people and secured the passage of legislation threatened by Republican opposition. President F.D. Roosevelt exploited the radio as Theodore Roosevelt had exploited the press. He was concerned to have the opposition of newspapers in order that he might exploit their antagonism. It is scarcely necessary to elaborate on his success with the new medium.

In Europe an appeal to the ear made it possible to destroy the results of the Treaty of Versailles as registered in the political map based on self-determination. The rise of Hitler to power was facilitated by the use of the loud speaker and the radio. By the spoken language he could appeal to minority groups and to minority nations. Germans in Czechoslovakia could be reached by radio as could Germans in Austria. Political boundaries related to the demands of the printing industry disappeared with the new instrument of communication. The spoken language provided a new base for the exploitation of nationalism and a far more effective device for appealing to larger numbers. Illiteracy was no longer a serious barrier.

The effects of new media of communication evident in the outbreak of the Second World War were intensified during the progress of the war. They were used by the armed forces in the immediate prosecution of the war and in propaganda both at home and against the enemy. In Germany moving pictures of battles were taken[48] and shown in theatres almost immediately afterwards. The German people were given an impression of realism which compelled them to believe in the superiority of German arms; realism became not only most convincing but also with the collapse of the German front most disastrous. In some sense the problem of the German people is the problem of Western civilization. As modern developments in communication have made for greater realism they have made for greater possibilities of delusion. "It is curious to see scientific teaching used everywhere as a means to stifle all freedom of investigation in moral questions under a dead weight of facts. Materialism is the auxiliary doctrine of every tyranny, whether of the one or of the masses."[49] We are under the spell of Whitehead's fallacy of misplaced concreteness. The shell and pea game of the country fair has been magnified and elevated to a universal level.

The printing industry had been characterized by decentralization and regionalism such as had marked the division of the Western world in nationalism and the division and instability incidental to regions within nations. The radio appealed to vast areas, overcame the division between classes in its escape from literacy, and favoured centralization and bureaucracy. A single individual could appeal at one time to vast numbers of people speaking the same language and indirectly, though with less effect, through interpreters to numbers speaking other languages. Division was drawn along new lines based on language but within language units centralization and coherence became conspicuous. Stability within language units became more evident and instability between language units more dangerous.

The influence of mechanization on the printing industry had been evident in the increasing importance of the ephemeral. Superficiality became essential to meet the various demands of larger numbers of people and was developed as an art by those compelled to meet the demands. The radio accentuated the importance of the ephemeral and of the superficial. In the cinema and the broadcast it became necessary to search for entertainment and amusement. "Radio ... has done more than its share to debase our intellectual standards."[50] The demands of the new media were imposed on the older media, the newspaper and the book. With these powerful developments time was destroyed and it became increasingly difficult to achieve continuity or to ask for a consideration of the future. An old maxim, "sixty diamond minutes set in a golden hour," illustrates the impact of commercialism on time. We would do well to remember the words of George Gissing: "Time is money – says the vulgarest saw known to any age or people. Turn it round about, and you get a precious truth – money is time."[51]

May I digress at this point on the effects of these trends on universities. William James held that the leadership of American thought was "passing away from the universities to the ten-cent magazines."[52] Today he might have argued that it had passed to the radio and television. But it is still necessary to say with Godkin in the last century: "there is probably no way in which we could strike so deadly a blow at the happiness and progress of the United States as by sweeping away, by some process of proscription kept up during a few generations, the graduates of the principal colleges. In no other way could we make so great a drain on the reserved force of character, ambition, and mental culture which constitutes so large a portion of the national vitality."[53] By culture he meant "the art of doing easily what you don't like to do. It is the breaking-in of the powers to the service of the will."[54]

If we venture to use this definition we are aware immediately of the trends in universities to add courses because people like to do them or because they will be useful to people after they graduate and will enable them to earn more money. In turn courses are given because members of the staff of the universities like to give them, an additional course means a larger department and a larger budget and, moreover, enables one to keep up with the subject. These tendencies reflect a concern with information. They are supported by the textbook industry and other industries which might be described as information industries. Information is provided in vast quantities in libraries, encyclopedias, and books. It is disseminated in universities by the new media of communication including moving pictures, loud speakers, with radio and television in the offing. Staff and students are tested in their ability to disseminate and receive information. Ingenious devices, questionnaires, intelligence tests are used to tell the student where he belongs and the student thus selected proceeds to apply similar devices to members of the staff. A vast army of research staff and students is concerned with simplifying language and making it easier for others to learn the English language and for more people to read and write what will be written in a simpler language. In the words of Santayana, "It doesn't matter *what* so long as they all read the *same* thing." Ezra Pound quotes the remark of an American professor: "The university is not here for the exceptional man."[55] Henry Adams in a discussion of teaching at Harvard summarized the problem in the remark, "It can not be done."[56] I have attempted to use the word information consistently though I am aware that the proper word is education. George Gissing has referred to "the host of the half-education, characteristic and peril of our time." "[E]ducation is a thing of which only the few are capable; teach as you will, only a small percentage will profit by your most zealous energy."[57] "To trumpet the triumphs of human knowledge seems to me worse than childishness; now, as of old, we know but one thing – that we know nothing."[58]

The relative adaptability of various subjects to mechanical transmission has threatened to destroy the unity of the university. "The University, as distinct from the technological school, has no proper function other than to teach that the flower of vital energy is Thought, and that not Instinct but Intellect is the highest form of a supernatural Will."[59] It tends to become a congeries of hardened avid departments obsessed with an interest in funds in which the department which can best prove its superficiality or its usefulness is most successful. Governments have been insensitive to the crucial significance of a balanced unity in universities and have responded to the pleas of specific subjects with the result that an interest in unity has been distorted to give that strange inartistic agglomeration of struggling departments called the modern university. The University of Oxford has recognized the threat and has set up a committee on the effects of university grants on balance in university subjects. It will probably be argued that social scientists have lost out in this race for government grants or that they should suffer for views as to the dangers of direct government intervention in the social sciences to the political health of the community. But I am afraid that just as with other subjects if the federal government should provide grants the social sciences will be on hand with the most beautifully developed projects for research that federal money can buy.

Under these circumstances we can begin to appreciate the remarks of an Oxford don who said after solving a very difficult problem in mathematics, "Thank God no one can use that." There must be few university subjects which can claim immunity or few universities which will refrain from pleading that their courses are useful for some reason or other.[60] The blight of lying and subterfuge in the interests of budgets has fallen over universities, and pleas are made on the grounds that the universities are valuable because they keep the country safe from socialism, they help the farmers and industry, they help in measures of defence. Now of course they do no such thing and when such topics are mentioned you and I are able to detect the odour of dead fish. Culture is not concerned with these questions. It is designed to train the individual to decide how much information he needs and how little he needs, to give him a sense of balance and proportion, and to protect him from the fanatic who tells him that Canada will be lost to the Russians unless he knows more geography or more history or more economics or more science. Culture is concerned with the capacity of the individual to appraise problems in terms of space and time and with enabling him to take the proper steps at the right time. It is at this point that the tragedy of modern culture has arisen as inventions in commercialism have destroyed a sense of time. "Our spiritual life is disorganized, for the over-organization of our external environment leads to the organization of our absence of thought."[61] "There is room for much more than a vague doubt that this cult of science is not altogether a wholesome growth – that the unmitigated quest of knowledge, of this matter-of-fact kind, makes for race-deterioration and discomfort on the whole, both in its immediate effects upon the spiritual life of mankind, and in the material consequences that follow from a great advance in matter-of-fact knowledge."[62] "In the long run, utility, like everything else, is simply a figment of our imagination and may well be the fatal stupidity by which we shall one day perish" (Nietzsche).

The limitations of Western culture can perhaps be illustrated by reference to the subject with which I pretend some acquaintance, namely the social sciences. Enormous compilations of statistics confront the social scientist. He is compelled to interpret them or to discover patterns or trends which will enable him to predict the future. With the use of elaborate calculating machines and of refinements in mathematical technique he can develop formulae to be used by industry and business and by governments in the formulation of policy. But elaboration assumes prediction for short periods of time. Work in the social sciences has become increasingly concerned with topical problems and social science departments become schools of journalism. The difficulty of handling the concept of time in economic theory and of developing a reconciliation between the static and dynamic approaches is a reflection of the neglect of the time factor in Western civilization. It is significant that Keynes should have said that in the long run we are all dead and that we have little other interest than that of living for the immediate future. Planning is a word to be used for short periods – for long periods it is suspect and with it the planner. The dilemma has been aptly described by Polanyi, "laissez-faire was planned, planning is not." The results have been evident in the demand for wholesale government activity during periods of intense difficulty. The luxury of the business cycle has been replaced by concerted measures directed toward the welfare state and full employment. Limited experience with the problem has involved expenditures on a large scale on armaments.

The trend towards centralization which has accompanied the development of a new medium of communication in the radio has compelled planning to a limited extent in other directions. Conservation of natural resources, government ownership of railways and hydro-electric power, for example in Canada and by T.V.A. in the United States, and flood control are illustrations of a growing concern with the problems of time but in the main are the result of acute emergencies of the present. Concern with the position of Western civilization in the year 2000 is unthinkable. An interest in 1984 is only found in the satirist or the utopian and is not applicable to North America. Attempts have been made to estimate population at late dates or the reserves of power or mineral resources but always with an emphasis on the resources of science and with reservations determined by income tax procedure, financial policy, or other expedients. Obsession with present-mindedness precludes speculation in terms of duration and time. Morley has written of the danger of a "growing tendency to substitute the narrowest political point of view for all the other ways of regarding the course of human affairs, and to raise the limitations which practical exigencies may happen to set to the application of general principles, into the very place of the principles themselves. Nor is the process of deteriorating conviction confined to the greater or noisier transactions of nations. ... That process is due to causes which affect the mental temper as a whole, and pour round us an atmosphere that enervates our judgment from end to end, not more in politics than in morality, and not more in morality than in philosophy, in art, and in religion."[63]

Concern of the state with the weakening and destruction of monopolies over time has been supported by appeals to science whether in an emphasis on equilibrium suggested by the interest of the United States in a balanced constitution following Newtonian mathematics or in an emphasis on growth, competition, and survival of the fittest of Darwin. Attempts to escape from the eye of the state have been frustrated by succession duties, corporation laws, and anti-combine legislation. The demands of technology for continuity have been met by rapid expansion of the principle of limited liability and devices such as long-term leases guaranteeing duration but these have provided a base for active state intervention in income taxes. Little is known of the extent to which large corporations have blocked out the utilization of future resources other than in matters of general policy. A grasping price policy sacrifices indefinite possibilities of growth. A monopolist seeks expanding business at a reasonable profit rather than the utmost immediate profit.[64] Organization of markets and exchanges facilitates the determination of predictions and the working-out of calculations which in turn have their effect on immediate production as an attempt to provide continuity and stability, but limitations progressively increased as evident in business cycles and their destruction of time rigidities. The monopoly of equilibrium was ultimately destroyed in the great depression and gave way to the beginnings of the monopoly of a centralized state. The disappearance of time monopolies facilitated the rapid extension of control by the state and the development of new religions evident in fascism, communism, and our way of life.

The general restiveness inherent in an obsession with time has led to various attempts to restore concepts of community such as have appeared in earlier civilizations. The Middle Ages have appeared attractive to economic historians, guild socialists, and philosophers, particularly those interested in St Thomas Aquinas. "The cultivation of form for its own sake is equally typical of Romanticism and Classicism when they are mutually exclusive, the Romantic cultivating form in detachment from actuality, the Classicist in subservience to tradition" (Fausset).[65] It is possible that we have become paralysed to the extent that an interest in duration is impossible or that only under the pressure of extreme urgency can we be induced to recognize the problem. Reluctance to appraise the Byzantine Empire may in part be a result of paralysis reinforced by a distaste for any discussion of possible precursors of Russian government. But the concern of the Byzantine Empire in the Greek tradition was with form, with space and time. The sense of community built up by the Greeks assumed a concern with time in continuity and not in "a series of independent instantaneous flashes" (Keynes) such as appealed to the Romans and Western Christianity.

"Immediacy of presentment was an inevitable enemy to construction. The elementary, passionate elements of the soul gave birth to utterances that would tend to be disconnected and uneven, as is the rhythm of emotion itself."[66] There was a "parallel emergence, in all the arts, of a movement away from a need which, whether in the ascendant or not, was always felt and honoured: the craving for some sort of continuity in form."[67] The effort to achieve continuity in form implies independence from the pressure of schools and fashions and modes of expression. In the words of Cazamian the indefinite duration of productive vitality in art and letters requires that the individual writer or reader be reinstated in the full enjoyment of his rights.[68]

Wyndham Lewis has argued that the fashionable mind is the time-denying mind. The results of developments in communication are reflected in the time philosophy of Bergson, Einstein, Whitehead, Alexander, and Russell. In Bergson we have glorification of the life of the moment, with no reference beyond itself and no absolute or universal value.[69] The modern "clerks" "consider everything only as it exists *in time,* that is as it constitutes a succession of particular states, a 'becoming,' a 'history,' and never as it presents a state of permanence beyond time under this succession of distinct cases." William James wrote: "That the philosophers since Socrates should have contended as to which should most scorn the knowledge of the particular and should most adore knowledge of the general, is something which passes understanding. For, after all, must not the most honourable knowledge be the knowledge of the most valuable realities! And is there a valuable reality which is not concrete and individual."[70] The form of mind from Plato to Kant which hallowed existence beyond change is proclaimed decadent. This contemporary attitude leads to the discouragement of all exercise of the will or the belief in individual power. The sense of power and the instinct for freedom have proved too costly and been replaced by the sham independence of democracy.[71] The political realization of democracy invariably encourages the hypnotist.[72] The behaviourist and the psychological tester have their way. In the words of one of them: "Great will be our good fortune if the lesson in human engineering which the way has taught us is carried over, directly and effectively, into our civil institutions and activities" (C.S. Yoakum).[73] Such tactlessness and offence to our good sense is becoming a professional hazard to psychologists. The essence of living in the moment and for the moment is to banish all individual continuity.[74] What Spengler has called the Faustian West is a result of living mentally and historically and is in contrast with other important civilizations which are "ahistoric." The enmity to Greek antiquity arises from the fact that its mind was ahistorical and without perspective.[75] In art classical man was in love with plastic whereas Faustian man is in love with music.[76] Sculpture has been sacrificed to music.[77]

The separation and separate treatment of the senses of sight and touch have produced both subjective disunity and external disunity.[78] We must somehow escape on the one hand from our obsession with the moment and on the other hand from our obsession with history. In freeing ourselves from time and attempting a balance between the demands of time and space we can develop conditions favourable to an interest in cultural activity.

It is sufficient for the purpose of this paper if attention can be drawn on the occasion of the 150th anniversary of a university of this continent to the role of the university in Western civilization. Anniversaries remind us of the significance of time. Though multiples of decades are misleading measures as the uniform retiring age of 65 is inhuman in its disrespect of biological differences they draw attention to a neglected factor. The university is probably older than Hellenistic civilization and has reflected the characteristics of the civilization in which it flourished, but in its association with religion and political organization it has been concerned with problems of time as well as of space. I can best close this paper by an appeal to Holy Writ. "Without vision the people perish."

NOTES

1 The use of the letters AD and BC apparently dates from the eighteenth century. Hellenic rationalism might be said to have persisted for 700 years and to have been obscured for 1,200 years. "The longest period of consecutive time in human history on which we can found inductions is, upon the whole, a period of intellectual and moral darkness" (Julien Benda, *The Great Betrayal* [London, 1928]), 159.

2 History "threatens to degenerate from a broad survey of great periods and movements of human society into vast and countless accumulations of insignificant facts, sterile knowledge, and frivolous antiquarianism" (Morley in 1878). See Emery Neff, *The Poetry of History* (New York, 1947), 193.

3 P.A. Sorokin and R.K. Merton, "Social Time: A Methodological and Functional Analysis," *American Journal of Sociology* 42, 1936–37.

4 "In general, the rigidity of the Japanese planning and the tendency to abandon the object when their plans did not go according to schedule

are thought to have been largely due to the cumbersome and imprecise nature of their language, which rendered it extremely difficult to improvise by means of signalled communication" (Winston Churchill).

5 R.K. Merton, "The Sociology of Knowledge," *Twentieth Century Sociology*, ed. G. Gurvich and W.E. Moore (New York, 1945), 387–8.

6 H.W. Garrod, *Scholarship, Its Meaning and Value* (Cambridge, 1946), 42.

7 Ernst Cassirer, *The Problem of Knowledge: Philosophy, Science, and History since Hegel*, trans. W.H. Woglom and C.W. Hendel (New Haven, Conn., 1950), 170–3.

8 Leslie Stephen, *History of English Thought in the Eighteenth Century* (London, 1876), 1: 458.

9 Cassirer, *The Problem of Knowledge*, 277.

10 Ibid., 251.

11 See H. Frankfort et al., *The Intellectual Adventure of Ancient Man: An Essay on Speculative Thought in the Ancient Near East* (Chicago, 1946).

12 H.A. Innis, *Empire and Communications* (Oxford, 1950).

13 Cited by Alfred Vagts, *A History of Militarism* (New York, 1937), 16.

14 See J.T. Shotwell, "The Discovery of Time," *Journal of Philosophy, Psychology, and Scientific Methods*, 1915, 198–206, 254–316. It is argued that mathematics made the use of time possible. See F. Thureau-Dangin, "Sketch of a History of the Sexagesimal System," *Osiris* 7. The Sumerian system was developed by crossing the numbers 10 and 6. Babylonian science was weak in geometry whereas the Greek science was strong. The Greeks learned the sexagesimal system through astronomy and discovered the Hindu system with a zero.

15 J.T. Shotwell, *An Introduction to the History of History* (New York, 1922), 43–4.

16 The calendar was apparently organized by Marduk and was under the control of the ruler of Mesopotamia (Frankfort et al., *The Intellectual Adventure of Ancient Man*, 181).

17 Ibid., 23–5.

18 Shotwell, *An Introduction to the History of History*, 45.

19 A new concern with time was evident in Herodotus, who presented a history "that neither the deeds of men may fade from memory by lapse of time, nor the mighty and marvellous works wrought partly by the Hellenes, partly by the Barbarians, may lose their renown." See also Thucydides' reasons for writing history.

20 See J.K. Fotheringham, "The Metonic and Callippic Cycles," *Monthly Notices of the Royal Astronomical Society* 84: 384; also B.D. Meritt, *The Athenian Calendar in the Fifth Century* (Cambridge, Mass., 1928), 72, 102, 122, 126.

21 The calendar was controlled by the college of pontifices. Of 192 days in a year on which people could be called together only 150 were left after ruling out days falling on market days, the last day of the Roman eight-day week, and days of seasonal games. An intercalary month was inserted in February every two years to bring the linear year into harmony with the solar year but in the early second century BC the pontifices obtained the right to insert it at will. The magisterial year for purposes of litigation, public contracts, and the like was changed according to their interests. These abuses were brought to an end by Caesar and the days added to the year by him as *dies fasti* were possibly intended as meeting days. See L.R. Taylor, *Party Politics in the Age of Caesar* (Berkeley, Calif., 1949), 79–80.

22 Franz Cumont, *Astrology and Religion among the Greeks and Romans* (New York, 1912), 162–5.

23 J.G. Frazer, *Adonis, Attis, Osiris: Studies in the History of Oriental Religion* (London, 1906), 200.

24 R.L. Poole, *Chronicles and Annals: A Brief Outline of Their Origin and Growth* (Oxford, 1926), 26.

25 R.L. Poole, *Lectures on the History of the Papal Chancery Down to the Time of Innocent III* (Cambridge, 1915), 38.

26 See R.L. Poole, "The Beginning of the Year in the Middle Ages," *Proceedings of the British Academy* 10.

27 A.P. Usher, *A History of Mechanical Inventions* (New York, 1929); also Lewis Mumford, *Technics and Civilization* (New York, 1934).

28 M.P. Nilsson, *Primitive Time-reckoning* (London, 1920).

29 L.T. Hogben, *From Cave Painting to Comic Strip* (London, 1949), 103ff; see also Etienne Hajnal, "Le rôle social de l'écriture et l'évolution européenne," *Revue de l'Institut de Sociologie,* 1934.

30 Byzantine policy also had implications for the French. The Edict of Nantes was supported by an illustration of tolerance told by Jacques Auguste de Thou (1533–1617) in *Continuation of the History of His Time,* to the effect that the Pope visited Constantinople in 526 to plead against the persecution of Arianism. See A.A. Vasiliev, *Justin the First: An Introduction to the Epoch of Justinian the Great* (Cambridge, Mass., 1950), 220–1.

31 C.H. McIlwain, *Constitutionalism, Ancient and Modern* (Ithaca, NY, 1940), 124.

32 See Benjamin Farrington, *Head and Hand in Ancient Greece: Four Studies in the Social Relations of Thought* (London, 1947).

33 N.S. Timasheff, *An Introduction to the Sociology of Law* (Cambridge, Mass., 1939), 207.

34 Coulton Waugh, *The Comics* (New York, 1947).

35 Archibald Forbes, *Souvenirs of Some Continents* (London, 1894).

36 Matthew Josephson, *The Robber Barons: The Great American Capitalists, 1861–1901* (New York, 1934), 27.
37 Cited by L.M. Salmon, *The Newspaper and the Historian* (New York, 1923), 29.
38 Brand Whitlock, *Forty Years of It* (New York, 1925), 157.
39 Matthew Josephson, *The President Makers, 1896–1919* (New York, 1940), 145.
40 Oswald Garrison Villard, *Fighting Years: Memoirs of a Liberal Editor* (New York, 1939), 151.
41 Vagts, *A History of Militarism*, 173.
42 Wyndham Lewis, *Time and Western Man* (London, 1927), 28.
43 John Maynard Keynes, *Two Memoirs* (London, 1949), 96–7.
44 J.B. Bury, *A History of Freedom of Thought* (London, 1928), 227.
45 W.R. Inge, *Diary of a Dean, St. Paul's 1911–1934* (London, 1950), 193–8.
46 J.B. Bury, *The Idea of Progress: An Inquiry into Its Origins and Growth* (London, 1920), 175.
47 William Albig, *Public Opinion* (New York, 1939), 220.
48 S. Kracauer, *From Caligari to Hitler* (Princeton, NJ, 1947), 297–8. "The camera's possibility of choosing and presenting but one aspect of reality invites it to the worst kinds of deceit" (*The Journals of André Gide*, trans. Justin O'Brien [New York, 1951], 4: 91).
49 Amiel, *Journal intime*, 17 June 1852.
50 Ilka Chase, *Past Imperfect* (New York, 1942), 236. For a reference to the breath-taking feats of tight-rope walking to avoid any possible offence by the major networks see ibid., 234.
51 George Gissing, *The Private Papers of Henry Ryecroft* (London, 1914), 287.
52 Norman Hapgood, *The Changing Years: Reminiscences* (New York, 1930).
53 E.L. Godkin, *Reflections and Comments, 1865–1895* (New York, 1895), 157.
54 Ibid., 202.
55 *The Letters of Ezra Pound, 1907–1941*, ed. D.D. Paige (New York, 1950), xxiii.
56 Ibid., 338.
57 George Gissing, *The Private Papers of Henry Ryecroft*, 70.
58 Ibid., 178.
59 Henry Adams, *The Degradation of the Democratic Dogma* (New York, 1919), 206.
60 For example, the teaching that "intellectual activity is worthy of esteem to the extent that it is practical and to that extent alone ... the man who loves science for its fruits commits the worst of blasphemies

against that divinity" (Benda, *The Great Betrayal,* 121). The scholar's defeat "begins from the very moment when he claims to be practical" (ibid., 151).

61 Albert Schweitzer, *The Decay and the Restoration of Civilization* (London, 1932), 32.

62 Thorstein Veblen, *The Place of Science in Modern Civilization and Other Essays* (New York, 1919), 4.

63 John, Viscount Morley, *On Compromise* (London, 1921), 6.

64 J.M. Clark, *Alternative to Serfdom* (New York, 1948), 65.

65 E.E. Kellett, *Fashion in Literature* (London, 1931), 282.

66 Louis Cazamian, *Criticism in the Making* (New York, 1929), 72.

67 Ibid., 64.

68 Ibid., 129. The novelists Smollett, Fielding, Sterne, Richardson, Defoe, and the cockney artist Hogarth all had "an intimate connection with early journalism, sharing its time-sense as a series of discrete moments, each without self-possession, as well as its notion of the 'concrete' as residing in the particular entity or event sensorily observed" (Milton Klonsky, "Along the Midway of Mass Culture," *Partisan Review,* April 1949, 351).

69 Lewis, *Time and Western Man,* 27.

70 Benda, *The Great Betrayal,* 78–80.

71 Lewis, *Time and Western Man,* 316.

72 Ibid., 42.

73 Cited in ibid., 342.

74 Ibid., 29.

75 Ibid., 285.

76 Ibid., 295.

77 Ibid., 299.

78 Ibid., 419. For a discussion of the effects of printing on music, see Constant Lambert, *Music Ho! A Study of Music in Decline* (London, 1934).

CHAPTER TWENTY-SIX

The Concept of Monopoly and Civilization

I am taking advantage of this opportunity to put before you questions which have worried me in research on the character of civilizations[1] and to solicit your advice. I have been concerned with the possible extension of concepts in the special field of economics and in particular the concept of monopoly, notably in knowledge. Since the First World War the study of civilization has been threatened by two monopolies, the first in Germany represented by Spengler, and the second in Great Britain or possibly the English-speaking world represented by Prof. A.J. Toynbee.

In the United States Sorokin, a Russian exile, and Kroeber of German descent have developed elaborate approaches. In France you have been critical – I refer particularly to Prof. Lucien Febvre – of such monopolies. As has been the case in the past, we look to you for criticism of inclusive systems.

I am under special obligation to such criticism and to special studies in attempting to develop an approach to the study of civilizations through the subject of communications and of monopolies in relation to them. I shall not refer to special studies such as those in the history of civilization series, but my remarks will indicate my debt to them. In confining my comments to political organization, I shall restrict my attention to two dimensions – on the one hand the length of time over which the organization persists and on the other hand the territorial space brought within its control. It will be obvious in the case of the second consideration that organization will be dependent to an important extent on communications in a

A paper read at a meeting under the chairmanship of Professor Lucien Febvre, Paris, 6 July 1951.

broad sense – roads, vehicles of transmission, especially horses, postal organization, and the like for carrying out orders. It will be less obvious that effective communication will be dependent on the diffusion of a knowledge of writing or in turn a knowledge of an alphabet through which orders may be disseminated among a long number of subjects.

A discussion of the other dimensions of a political organization, namely, duration, raises numerous problems. Examples of organizations which have persisted over a long period such as the Roman, late Roman, and Byzantine empires suggest that attention must have been given not only to the administration of territorial space but also to ways and means by which survival was achieved. Obvious devices involved with the problem of duration were the organization of force, notably in defence and the encouragement of industry and trade essential for the support of defence. Force in itself implies a hierarchical arrangement but also an arrangement which permits of the rapid advancement of ability to the top. Every soldier must carry a marshal's baton in his knapsack.

The problem of force arises from its inability to emphasize its limitations and from its tendency to make increasingly heavy demands on the resources of the country it is concerned in protecting. The Byzantine army seems to have been built up with a view to using the smallest possible resources with the greatest possible effectiveness. Changes in dynasties suggest that it was not too difficult for able soldiers like Justin and others to reach the position of emperor. It assumes that the necessity of employment of force is sufficiently continuous to maintain an effective demand for ability at higher levels in the army and that a military bureaucracy does not become stale. The dangers of a dynasty, in which able leadership tends to die out with successive generations, are avoided by the pitiless demands of force.

The limitations of force in maintaining continuity may be offset by reliance on religion. Belief resting on ritual with an emphasis on the oral tradition and on hierarchical organization, is adapted primarily to a concern with duration and with control over time. Death itself as an obvious permanent phenomenon was used as a concept emphasizing continuity, particularly in relation to immortality.

Religion linked to force as in the Byzantine empire following Constantine's recognition of Christianity made it possible to enlist the support of culture and in particular the arts. In architecture a capital city designed to reinforce the prestige of force may be supplemented by ecclesiastical buildings as in the case of St Sophia. Imperial ceremonial may be joined to religious ritual. Sculpture will reflect the demands of religion and of the state – so too will painting. It has been said that religion is a good servant but a bad master, but there is evidence that it may not be the best servant. The conservative and rigid character of belief restricts its adaptability to the demands of force, and an effective hierarchy which enlists the ablest minds and places them at its head may insist on a position which will embarrass if not threaten the state as in the case of iconoclastic controversy.

I have ventured these remarks by way of illustrating the problem of political organization in relation to territorial space and duration in time. I shall now attempt to discuss the problem of a political organization in relation to monopolies which develop in relation to space and in relation to time. In Babylon and in Egypt it appears that the problem of spatial organization was more or less effectively worked out in Babylon, and the problem of time organization in Egypt. In Mesopotamia, religious organization centring in the City state was concerned with the development of knowledge, particularly in language and mathematics essential to economic organization and determined to an important extent by the character of its medium, namely clay. Sumerian culture provided a nucleus of organized knowledge and an emphasis on continuity in religious organization which supported the development of political organizations in the empire of Sargon, in the restoration of dynasties centring on Ur, in the empire of Hammurabi and of its successor under the Kassites. In turn the Hittite, the Assyrian, and the Persian empires paid Sumerian culture the tribute of recognition or of imitation. While the monopoly of knowledge and the control over time reflected in the persistence of Sumerian culture contributed to the effectiveness of political organization, it was in turn a source of weakness to successive empires and contributed to their disappearance.

In Egypt religious organizations emerged in relation to the king or to political organization possibly on the occasion of the joining of two kingdoms, the north and the south. The power of the combination was evident in the pyramids of stone and in the development of the concept of immortality. Death became a support to continuity. The burden of the demands became evident in a decline in the absolute position of the king, in the emergence of a religious organization, and in the development of an oligarchy in which immortality was extended to the people. Decline of political organization was evident in the success of the invasion of the Hyksos. But the tenacity of religion supported a reorganization of force, expulsion of the Hyksos and the extension of control over space in the Egyptian empire. Again, its demands were responsible for a succession of dynasties and for their collapse in the face of extension of the Assyrian, the Persian, and the Alexandrian empires. The monopoly of knowledge controlled by religion was determined to an important extent by the character of writing, namely hieroglyphics and its medium, namely papyrus and the brush.

The limitations of monopolies of knowledge in Babylonia and in Egypt shown in the instability of political organizations were evident in the emergence of simpler forms of writing centring around the alphabet which developed among peoples who were marginal to the influence of the two regions. The alphabet responded to the demands of a spoken language by linking sound to letter. The Greeks carried the adaptability of the alphabet to the point of developing certain letters as vowels. An escape from the limitations of the monopolies of knowledge of Egypt and Mesopotamia and the adaptation of the alphabet to the demands of a powerful oral tradition were evident in the freshness and flexibility of Greek culture in the fifth century and its emergence as the basis of Western civilization as contrasted with civilizations of the Far East and of the Americas.

The adaptability of the alphabet to the spoken language created new problems of monopoly in that spoken languages which differed materially were crystallized in a written language and great effort was necessary to develop understanding over a vast area and with different languages. In the Alexandrian empire and the Hellenistic kingdoms the limitations of language were evident in the necessity of relying on a religion based on the deification of kings, in problems of continuity of political organizations, and in their absorption by the Roman empire. With the extension of control over territorial space, including diversity of languages and dependence on organized force in the Roman empire, religion proved an inadequate support. The choice of Constantinople for defensive purposes as a capital of the Empire was accompanied by an acceptance of Christianity which would enlist the cooperation of eastern Hellenistic populations. As we have suggested, a balance of control over monopolies of time and monopolies of space explained the success evident in the duration of the Byzantine empire.

In the West decline of control over territorial space in the face of barbarian invasions led to an emphasis on control over time and religion. In the words of Gibbon it was characterized by the rise of barbarism and religion. In this monopoly, emphasis was placed on Latin as a language and as a device to offset the divisive influence of several languages. A monopoly was built up through dependence on a limited body of scriptural writings on a relatively permanent medium namely parchment. A hierarchical organization was strengthened by development of ritual, a concern with monasticism and celibacy, and the emergence of Gothic architecture. The effects of the monopoly were evident in the position of the papacy and its control over knowledge and in the inquisition.

A monopoly over time invited competition such as that which followed a spread in the use of paper from China through the Mohammedans at Baghdad and Cordova and in the recognition of new sources of learning, notably in Greek science and philosophy represented especially by Aristotle filtered through Arabic or coming direct from Constantinople. In the competitive strife the monopoly of Latin as a language was destroyed and increasing supplies of cheap paper supported the growth of a literature of the vernacular as in Italy and France and the Reformation as in Germany, the Netherlands, and England. It would be instructive to trace the influence of paper on the development of writing and of printing, particularly in Germany on which the Roman Empire had made little impression and which was marginal to France in which copyists exercised an important monopoly, and in Italy which had witnessed an expansion of the paper industry. In any case, the vernaculars emerged in different regions and became an ultimate determinant of political boundaries.

The modern state with political boundaries influenced by the paper and printing industries has been profoundly affected by the industrial revolution and the application of steam power to the paper and printing industries, especially in the latter part of the nineteenth century. The divisive influence of these industries has been evident in the division of regions speaking the same language, as in the separation of the United States from the British Empire, in the emergence of the British Commonwealth of Nations, and in the growth of regionalism centring around large metropolitan areas. Freedom of the press has been given constitutional guarantees as in the United States or guarantees in other forms as in other countries and has provided bulwarks for monopolies which have emphasized control over space. Under these circumstances the problem of duration or monopoly over time has been neglected, indeed obliterated. Time has been cut into pieces the length of a day's newspaper. The tyranny of monopoly over space in its emphasis on change and instability has assumed graver threats to continuity than the tyranny of monopoly over time in the Middle Ages to the establishment of political organization. It may be that the concept of progress arises from the effects of a swing from a type of monopoly concerned with control over time to a type of monopoly concerned with control over space and that we favour this type of change in contrast with a civilization which assumes control over space and time which seems to us to favour stability and possibly stagnation.

NOTES

1 See H.A. Innis, *Empire and Communications* (Oxford, 1950), being the Beit Lectures for 1948.

CHAPTER TWENTY-SEVEN

The Problem of Space

"Space and time, and also their space-time product, fall into their places as mere mental frameworks of our own constitution."[1] Gauss held that whereas number was a product of the mind, space had a reality outside the mind whose laws cannot be described *a priori.* In the history of thought, especially of mathematics, Cassirer remarked, "at times, the concept of space, at other times, the concept of numbers, took the lead."[2]

A concern with problems of space and time appears to have marked the beginnings of civilization in Egypt and Mesopotamia. A change from a pre-dynastic to a dynastic society, or a precise recognition of time, in both regions appears to have coincided with writing, monumental architecture, and sculpture. In both regions surplus supplies of labour appear to have been the result of the pronounced seasonal character of agriculture incidental to floods.

The flow of the long Nile river to the north and dissipation of its regular floods in the numerous channels of the delta provided a background for the development of artificial canals and dykes by which the valley might be widened and the water held at the height of the flood for irrigation. The length of the river with the downward flow and the delta, and a shifting economic development incidental to dependence on a single line of transportation militated against a compact government and a stable political organization.[3]

A kingship probably emerged to meet the demands for a uniform system of administration.[4] Its power was possibly strengthened with the beginnings of the measurement of time on 19 July 4241 BC when Sirius arose at sunrise and prediction of time became more

From *The Bias of Communication* (Toronto, 1951), chap. 5, 92–131.

certain with recognition of a year of 365 days. After 3400 BC the importance of the south became evident in its conquest of the north by a king, leader of the Falcon clan, and in the selection of a capital at Thinis under Menes to mark the consolidation of the two lands north and south. The growing importance of the delta and the north was reflected in the displacement at the end of the second dynasty, early in the thirtieth century BC, of Thinis by Memphis as a capital with its location at a distance from Heliopolis, a centre of religious influence. As a means of increasing the prestige and power of the king in response to the demands of a vast increase in territory and of maintaining continuity of dynastic power, provision was made for the development of a state religion with elaborate temple endowments, rituals, priesthoods, and an increasing emphasis on the dead. With a new capital at Memphis[5] the pyramids were built by the fourth dynasty "to furnish a vast, impenetrable and indestructible resting place for the body of the king" and to reflect the "power of a far-reaching and comprehensive centralization effected by one controlling mind."[6] The permanency of death became a basis of continuity through the development of the idea of immortality, preservation of the body, and development of writing in the tombs by which the magical power of the spoken word was perpetuated in pictorial representation of the funeral ritual. The tombs of courtiers were placed around the pyramid of the king; they shared his divine glory and had ultimate consubstantiality with him, partly derived from him and partly inherent in themselves. Control over large bodies of organized labour was tangibly indicated in a monument with a square base of 755 feet to each side, covering 13 acres, 481 feet in height, and involving the handling of 2,500,000 blocks of stone of 2½ tons each, without the advantage of pulleys.

The enormous economic drain of the pyramids enabled the priests of Ra or the sun cult at Heliopolis to exploit discontent. In this they were strengthened by the neglect of Horus, the god of the pre-dynastic kings. The fourth dynasty collapsed and in the fifth dynasty beginning about 2750 BC the king was regarded as the bodily son of Ra. The limitations of an hereditary family as a basis of continuity in spite of reliance on such devices as the pyramids pointed to the efficiency of a religious cult as a centre of control over time and in turn over space. Without the absolute power of kings of the fourth dynasty, the fifth and sixth dynasties were characterized by decentralization and a marked increase in the independence of local nobles. Civil servants, masters of the art of hieratic writing and supported by a papyrus industry, had brought agriculture to a high level over a period of five centuries but a highly centralized bureaucracy introduced a division of class between the learned and the unlearned. In a decentralized bureaucracy, the demands of administration increased, the art of writing was encouraged, a system of uniform orthography was established, and the civil service was opened to the middle class. In the twelfth dynasty of the middle kingdom the rights and privileges of the nobles were adjusted to the centralized authority of the king.

The official supremacy of Amon-Ra, the solar god, in the twelfth dynasty and decline in the power of the king accompanied a shift in power to the south and migration of the capital from Memphis to Thebes about the middle of the twenty-second century. Osiris, as a judge in the next world, god of the dead, and king of the realm of the blessed, achieved a victory among the people. Immortality was shared by the king with the people. Rights for the masses meant rites for the masses.[7] A belief in immortality became a source of strength in the army in Egypt, as it did later with the Druids and the Mohammedans. A stable organization emerged about 2000 BC. The middle kingdom replaced the old kingdom.

A decline of centralized bureaucratic power and a shift from an emphasis on control over space reflected in the pyramid to a decentralized bureaucratic power with an emphasis on continuity and religion to be seen in the spread of writing and the use of papyrus, the extension of magical formulae from the hieroglyphic of the pyramids to that of papyrus, from the king to the people weakened control over space and invited the invasions of the Hyksos from the north. By mobilizing new resources, notably the horse[8] and the chariot, Ahmose I about 1580 BC expelled the Hyksos and restored control over space by making Egypt his personal estate and extinguishing the decentralized bureaucracy of the middle kingdom. In the eighteenth dynasty a concern with the problem of time was accompanied by the subordination of all priestly bodies to the high priest of Amon. A priest of Amon became Thutmose III in 1501 BC and destroyed the Hyksos army at Megiddo in 1479. Use of the horse meant success in attack and consolidation of control over space through improved communication. An attempt to build up an empire as an organization concerned with problems of duration or of time and of space was carried out through a powerful priesthood and marriage alliances with alien peoples, for example, the marriage of the daughter of Mitanni to Thutmose IV.

Extension of the empire to the north and organization of space, and inclusion of new peoples, imposed strains on a bureaucracy built up around Thebes, a southern capital, and brought an attempt at compromise in the decision of Amenhotep IV to gain support from the suppressed Ra cult, to establish a more northerly capital at Akhetaton, and to change his name to Ikhnaton. He attempted to destroy the magical properties of the hieroglyphics and to bring the written and spoken languages into close accord but the power of the Amon priesthood prevailed. His successor Tutenkhaton changed his name to Tutenkhamon and returned to Thebes.

With the end of the eighteenth dynasty about 1350 BC and the restoration of the Amon priesthood at Thebes the handicaps of a southern capital became more obvious. Harmhab, a military leader, as king attempted to eliminate inefficiency in the administration. His successors through treaties and marriage alliances arranged a *condominium* with the Hittites similar to the earlier arrangements with the Mitanni from 1280 BC to 1260. The Amon priesthood became more effective in its control over time. It was estimated that one of every five persons and almost a third of the cultivable land were controlled by the temples. Control over space was weakened, the empire contracted, and from 945 BC to 745 BC Egypt was ruled by Libyan invaders. Ethopians gained control in 712 BC and the Assyrians sacked Thebes in 668 BC Egyptian civilization failed to establish a stable compromise between a bias dependent on stone in the pyramids and a bias dependent on papyrus and hieroglyphics in the face of difficulties imposed by dependence on the Nile.

In contrast with the centralizing tendencies of the Nile, the two rivers of the Tigris and Euphrates dominated Mesopotamia and flooding was irregular and incalculable. Clay was predominant and fertile. Single enduring monuments of stone such as the pyramids in Egypt were absent. The land was centrifugal in its influence and the economy was separated. Each city developed as a community in relation to its tall brick temple and though strongly democratic was essentially a theocratic communism. The gods symbolized divine powers and the communities. Several temple communities, each the estate of god, made up a city state under a god who owned one of the largest temple communities of which his high priest was governor charged with the integration of the component parts. The communities were organized in relation to the problem of continuity and time. With increased population, improved equipment, and greater use of metal, fields became contiguous, conflict developed, problems of space emerged, and a kingship was established,[9] first temporary and then permanent. With the high priest of the powerful temple the king provided the essential vigorous leadership.[10] He was a mortal endowed with a divine freedom, receiving his authority in divine election from the city god, acting in agreement with divine authority. Conflicts between the city states or between divine owners were settled by an assembly of the gods which assigned temporary rule of land to one city after another.[11]

The military limitations of a society concerned with problems of time and the importance of unification in developing an elaborate canal system were evident in the subjugation of Sumerians by the Akkadians, a Semitic people, and the temporary solution of problems of space in the development of an empire under Sargon. Under a monarchy and a vast empire the local customs of religious city states were replaced by personal legislation. Sumerian was displaced by Akkadian as a spoken language but the power of religion was evident in the persistence of Sumerian in the written word.[12] The two tongues became vehicles of profoundly different cultures and the friction between them provided the flexibility essential to political stability.

The economic advantage and vitality of a large political organization were indicated in a new artistic freedom: the abrupt appearance of modelling in relief as a vehicle of expression of physical reality and the escape by seal cutters from the limited outlook of a theocratic régime or the excessive demands of the market.[13] Problems of continuity of political organization appeared in the tenacity of religious city states and the difficulties of maintaining a dynastic line. It disappeared in the face of bands of invaders from Gutium and was eventually replaced by a Sumerian dynasty at Ur supported by a culture represented in temples, libraries, and schools. Theocratic Sumerian city states were brought under the control of native kings who had learned the advantages of political organization in a civil service from former conquerors. The effects of monopoly over time and continuity exercised by religion were offset by the development of a system of administration of justice. About 2450 BC Urukagina rescued classes of the population from the exactions of priests.

The solution of problems of administration was influenced by the character of the medium of communication, namely clay. It compelled an early shift from pictographic writing to the symbol and the cuneiform. In turn these were adapted to the demands of mathematics and accounting and the development of writing essential to the economic organization of the temple community. A civilization dominated by monopolies of time had its own peculiarities, notably in abstractions implied in the development of mathematics. The interrelation between writing and arithmetic in the conduct of affairs stimulated mathematical speculation and the land of Sumer and Akkad became the cradle of algebra. Limitations were reflected in problems of political organization and of control over space and it was significant that in the second half of the third dynasty of Ur innumerable contracts, receipts, and agreements were in evidence, that written documents increased "one thousand fold,"[14] and that seal cutters lost interest in a variety of designs and emphasized the ritual scene as a predominant pictorial element.

Again the political organization proved unable to withstand the attacks of invaders; a new empire was built up under Hammurabi, with Babylon as a capital. Babylon was destroyed by the Hittites about 1600 BC and in turn relative stability was reached in the Kassite dynasty. Marduk became the god of Babylon, chosen by divine assembly through Anu, the god of the sky[15] and influencing the whole universe as an organized society, and Enlil, god of the storm representing force and defining society as the state.[16] The gods of the various city states were bound in a higher unity and the tendency toward political unification was sanctioned by the most violent measures. The successful conqueror as Enlil's representative on earth became the moderator and judge between the city states.[17] He stood at the head of the clergy[18] and appointed the high priest, was the chosen servant of the gods, absolute master whom man was created to serve,[19] and interpreted their will.[20] In New Year celebrations the main actors were the gods but participation of the king was essential.

A more stable political organization accompanied more effective control over space in the use of horses and the replacement of heavy solid wheels by light spoked wheels.[21] Control over time was strengthened by the practice of reckoning in terms of the years of the reign of the king. The Sumerian language became sacred and a source of strength to religion and continuity in contrast with the language of the conquerors concerned with problems of space and administration of law. The king and the god became the joint sources of law and order but law freed itself from religion and the judge became a secular authority. The scribe drew up contracts and acted as a professional notary without a necessary connection with the temples.[22] The code of Hammurabi was inscribed on stone. A large, effective political organization provided a powerful stimulus to commerce.

The power of the Babylonian priesthood was evident in the establishment of the era of Nabonnasar in 747 BC with the discovery that every 18 years and 11 days the moon returned to almost its original position with reference to the sun.[23] The discovery of periodicity in the heavens enormously strengthened the position of religion in its control over time and continuity. In 729 BC Tiglath-Pileser III became King of Babylon; Ashur assumed the leading position in the pantheon succeeding Marduk[24] and Assyrian kings made annual visits to take part in the ceremonies of Babylon.[25] After Sargon seized the throne in 722 BC and built a palace at Dur-Sharukin an attempt was made to offset the influence of the Babylonian priesthood by construction of a library. Its resources were extended by his son who also built a new palace. Difficulties with the Babylonian priesthood led Sennacherib to destroy Babylon in 689 BC but his son Esar-haddon was compelled to restore it. After the successful conquest of Egypt the royal library and archives were rapidly extended at Nineveh under Ashur-bani-pal (668–626 BC). In 625 BC Nabopolassar, of a native dynasty in Babylon, threw off the Assyrian yoke. He was followed by Nebuchadrezzar (605–562 BC). Finally opposition of the priesthood to Nabonidus who attempted to introduce new gods in Babylonia encouraged invasion by the Persians in 539 BC and was followed by the consecration of Cyrus as king in 536 BC. The apparatus by which the Mesopotamian ruler was set aside as an intermediary between society and the divine process continued.[26]

In contrast with an absolute king in Egypt who cultivated an interest in the next world and immortality, Sumerian and Babylonian priests by virtue of the importance of religion had little interest in the hereafter but were concerned with the systematizing of knowledge[27] and an emphasis on a sense of order and law. The significance of religion in Mesopotamia enabled the priesthood to withstand the effects of sudden change and to compel conquerors concerned to recognize the importance of continuity. The importance of systematized knowledge in Babylonia forced the Assyrians to emphasize libraries in a new capital. On the other hand the adaptability of the priesthood to the demands of conquerors made religion malleable and laid the foundations essential to the development of an enduring empire. Compromises between the demands of a monopoly of space and of a monopoly of time, between a monopoly emphasizing capitals and a Semitic language and a monopoly emphasizing architecture and writing determined by clay and the Sumerian language, between barbarian invaders and an earlier culture, implied ultimate instability and adjustments. The maintenance of separate languages checked the encroachment of cultures on each other and facilitated political and technological adjustment.

The written tradition has left a powerful stamp on knowledge regarding the civilizations of Egypt and Babylonia. An oral tradition may be presumed from the emphasis in Egypt on the spoken word. The systematic revision of documents in the Near East by cuneiform scribes to eliminate archaic spelling and grammar points to an extended familiarity with writing.[28] Sacred and profane documents were copied with great care. Semitic peoples between the civilizations of Egypt and Babylonia adapted elements of Egyptian writing to the demands of an extensive oral tradition and the alphabet was developed and spread in Phoenicia and Palestine.[29] Devices had been used to facilitate continuous repetitions and to strengthen memories, including the knot.[30] Aids to memory began with constant diligent repetition and developed form in metre and rhyme, in knot symbols as mnemonics, and finally in writing.[31] As a most radical innovation the latter was undertaken with religious sanction. Moses introduced the art of writing at the command of God. According to the rabbis,[32] shortly before his death he reduced the Torah to writing on thirteen scrolls, one for each tribe and one for the tribe of Levi, the latter to serve for collation, to prevent the possibility of disappearance of the oral tradition through the death of elders. The Torah was not intended for practical use and was practically a sealed book until the discovery of the Book of the Law under Josiah about 622 BC. Even five hundred years after its official publication in the time of Ezra about 444 BC men were able to recite the whole Bible from memory. By the time of Ezra Jews spoke Aramaic but portions of the Pentateuch were recited in Hebrew, which had become sacred and continuing the oral tradition contained divine revelation in oracles and prophecies. Each word was full of deep meaning with mysteries and magic powers. Language recited and preserved with the use of metre and rhyme to support the memory became poetry.[33] Writing became sacred after it was associated with the sacred book and the written word became the principle of authority.

Ancestors of some of the Israelites had probably lived several centuries in Egypt before migrating to Palestine.[34] After the conquest of Canaan an epic nucleus was probably extended to include the story of Moses and the combined narratives recited by Levites or rhapsodists. The Hebrew alphabet was written in ink and used in the fourteenth and thirteenth centuries. Writing was practised in the early eleventh century. Quantities of papyrus were exported from Egypt to Phoenicia about 1100 BC. After the break-up of the amphictyonic organization of Israel by the Philistines in the eleventh century the epic was written down separately as J in the south and E in the north before 750 BC; was combined in the JE recension of the eighth or seventh century.[35] The oral as compared with the written transmission of tradition was inherently more consistent and logical in its results because of the constant sifting, refining, and modifying of what did not fit into the tradition.[36] In the cumulative effects of the oral tradition the pieces of an edifice were carried to another site and worked into the structure of a different novel. Fact shifted into legend, legend into myth. Facts worked loose and became detached from their roots in space and time. The story was moulded and remoulded by imagination, passion, prejudice, religious presumption, or aesthetic instinct.[37] The oral tradition probably transmitted the Song of Deborah, Amos, Hosea, Isaiah and much of Joshua, Judges, and Samuel, part of Kings, and the prophetic books. Some of the contents of Joshua and Judges were probably written in the tenth century though the form belongs to the seventh century.[38] Most of the prophetic books were anthologies attributed to certain prophets, circulating in written and oral form, and brought together by collectors. The apodictic laws of Israel with commands not to sin because Yahweh so wills were unique and original. The introduction of writing was an important factor in unifying the people and the power of the scriptures was reinforced by the selection of a fixed capital at Jerusalem at the expense of local sanctuaries.

The oral tradition and its relation to poetry implied a concern with time and religion. "The artist represents *coexistence in space*, the poet *succession in time*" (Lessing at the University of Berlin, 1810).[39] The oral tradition reflected the positive influence of Egypt in the name of Moses, the doctrine that God is the sole creator and the formula from which his name Yahweh derived, the concept of a single god and the establishment of doctrine based on monotheism, and the recognition of the international, cosmic character of the reigning deity. The negative influence appeared in the revolt against "virtually every external aspect of Egyptian religion," the complex, grotesque iconography, the dominance of magic over daily life evident in the nineteenth dynasty, and the materialistic absorption in preparation for a selfish existence in the hereafter. Distinctive Hebrew elements included a close association between God and his worshippers illustrated by the giving of personal names and by sacrificial rites, a contractual relation or covenant between the deity and his people, and the association of terrestrial manifestations of deity with storms and mountains.[40] As a migratory people, the Hebrews were compelled to abandon a god attached to a site and to develop a bond between Yahweh and a chosen people.

In the face of attacks from the Philistines who had the advantage of a monopoly of iron, the amphictyonic principle of confederation of the Israelites was replaced by the selection of a king, Saul, from Benjamin, the weakest and most central tribe, and in turn of David (about 1000–960).[41] The burdens of Solomon's lavish régime led to revolt of the northern tribes after his death and division of the monarchy about 925 BC. In the reaction against centralization of secular and religious government and to offset the appeal of Solomon's temple which contained the Ark of the Covenant, Jeroboam I built sanctuaries to Yaḥweh at Bethel and Dan.[42]

Empires which had achieved relative equilibrium between religious organization with its emphasis on time and political organization with its emphasis on space were subjected to disturbance with technological change incidental to a shift from dependence on bronze to dependence on iron. The horse-drawn chariot which displaced the wheel cart about 1500 BC was followed by horse training in North Syria after the fourteenth century. The command of a mobile army which could be dispatched quickly in war and used to maintain contact over wide areas with officials and overseers contributed to the expansion of the Egyptian empires.[43] Discovery of iron by the Hittites and its greater abundance and cheapness brought the Bronze Age to an end about 1200 BC. With the use of iron and the crossing of light Libyan horses with heavy Asiatic horses, the Assyrians developed the cavalry arm with horse-riding rather than horse-driving units. Their attempts to build up new organizations of space in relation to an organization of time were defeated by the entrenched organizations of time in Babylon and Thebes. The Assyrian Empire collapsed with the fall of Nineveh in 612 BC.

In the political realignments which followed the fall of the Assyrians the Babylonians held Jerusalem from 587 to 539 BC and the Persians re-established a political organization comparable to that of the Assyrians by conquering Babylonia and, in 525 BC, Egypt. With improved communication, the building of roads, the organization of posts, the simplification of script, an increase in the use of papyrus after the conquest of Egypt, and with a system of decentralization implied in the use of satrapies, the Persians established a more efficient empire. Toleration of religious organization was evident in the return of the Jews to Palestine from 538 to 522 BC and the building of the Temple from 520 to 515. In 444 BC, under Artaxerxes I, Nehemiah, the autonomous governor of Judaea, made the official practice of the Temple in Jerusalem, embodied in the priestly code, standard for Judaism. In 397 BC Ezra as priest and scribe had special royal authority to reorganize the ecclesiastical administration of Judaea; he "ushers in the period of the autonomous theocratic state of Judah."[44]

The early Persian religion was substantially identical with the faith of the Rig-Veda. The Avesta was transmitted orally for from five to eight centuries and probably reduced to writing in the first century AD and to canonical form in the third century AD. In the seventh or sixth century BC Zoroaster preached a new gospel in favour of one supreme being, Ahura-Mazda, which abolished blood sacrifices and purified worship and relegated the old Iranian gods to the ranks of demons. The religion involved a dualism of the god with an organized angelic hierarchy and a personal antagonist and a belief in the last judgment and rewards and punishment after death. Its influence on Judaism became apparent after the second century BC. About 400 BC Mazdayasnian phraseology was abandoned by Artaxerxes II.[45] The problem of organization of time contributed to the difficulties of the Persian Empire and to its disappearance at the hands of Alexander in 331 BC.

As in Palestine the oral tradition in Greece implied an emphasis on continuity. It created recognized standards and lasting moral and social institutions;[46] it built up the soul of social organizations and maintained their continuity;[47] and it developed ways of perpetuating itself. The oral tradition and religion served almost the same purpose. Language was the physiological basis of oral traditions, and religion was the sociological mechanism through which traditions were established, directing and enforcing the cooperation of individuals in the interest of the community, maintaining group life, and creating a lasting organization of society independent of a living leader.[48] Education involved training, cultivating, and strengthening the memory. The specialized reciter was the carrier of social traditions. The memory took the place of logical process in writing and supported an immense burden of vocabulary and grammatical complexity with the help of verse, metre, rhyme, and proverbs. "Poetry is the chain of the stories" (Arab saying).[49] What was once well said was not to be changed but repeated in the very words of its original author. In oral intercourse the eye, ear, and brain, the senses and the faculties acted together in busy cooperation and rivalry each eliciting, stimulating, and supplementing the other.[50]

A concern with communication by the ear assumes reliance on time. Persistence of the oral tradition in Greece implied an emphasis on poetry intimately associated with music and a time art.[51] Verbal poetry goes back to the fundamental reality of time. The poetic form requires a regular flexible sequence as plastic as thought, reproducing a transference of force from the agent to the object which occupies time and requires the same temporal order in imagination. Migration and conquest weakened the influence of place on religion, accentuated the importance of the oral tradition, and enhanced the adaptability of religion to the demands of new areas. The emotional colour of localities faded and primitive concepts and concrete orientations were destroyed. The oral tradition in the Homeric epics reflected the character of early Greek society.[52] The *Iliad* reflected a monarchy and the *Odyssey* an oligarchy. The Olympian tradition and its influence on philosophy was evident in its emphasis on the *Moirai* and spatial relationships. Among peoples accustomed to migration, the position of the religious sanctuary was weak and priesthoods had limited influence compared with their standing in communities with relative permanence and the possession of writing.

The use of armed force in conquest and defence emphasized the spatial concept and organization of the society in terms of space rather than time and continuity. It meant demands for more effective control over space and for more efficiency than was implied in a religious organization. In Greece, a country with poor pasturage and unsuited for horse breeding, military strength depended on the hoplites; this revolution in tactics in the eighth century compelled the Eupatrids to rely on the non-Eupatrids.[53] As a result of military compromise Eleusis was joined to Athens about 700 BC, and the Eupatridae in two sections of Attica, and the Eleusinian sanctuary, represented three regions with three annual archonships. In the struggle against the Eupatridae as a privileged caste Draco published a code of laws and set up a council with a majority of non-Eupatrid hoplites in addition to the Areopagus.[54] The time element represented by the Eupatridae and representatives of the Eleusinian sanctuary was compelled to compromise with the space element. Solon recognized the time or religious element by making the tribe a political unit to cut across regional sectors.[55] His abolition of the personal security of the debtor favoured urban migration and encouragement of industry was followed by immigration of alien elements.[56] The highlands and the rural classes represented by Pisistratus, the tyrant, were temporarily defeated by a coalition of the men of the coast and of the plain, but were finally successful through a personal alliance between Pisistratus and Megacles, the Alcmaeonid leader of the coastal region. Dionysus was favoured by a new religion. The Tyrants in Athens as in other Greek cities, for example, in Corinth (657–586 BC), emerged between periods dominated by old methods of government and newer powers more closely adapted to economic and social difficulties incidental to problems of spatial organization. Later the Alcmaeonidae with the aid of the Spartans expelled the tyrants, and Cleisthenes, the Alcmaeonid, with ex-slaves and immigrants of the urban areas of the coast enroled in the citizen body, defeated Isagoras. Solon had left the great families too strong and Cleisthenes attempted to neutralize politically the historical division into three regions by rearranging the tribes in artificial units. He avoided the odium of interfering with religious customs and obtained sanction from Delphi to offset the religious sanctions of the system discarded.[57] The artificial units broke up regionalism and destroyed control over time.

Draco's publication of the code broke the Eupatrid monopoly of the interpretation of the laws and Solon their monopoly of political office. Cleisthenes destroyed their hold over the electorate and prevented the state falling into the hands of the rural classes which had supported the tyrants. The democratic reforms of the fifth century implied the capture of the Areopagus from the Eupatridae. The decline of the oral tradition and its monopoly over time evident in the weakening of the Eupatridae and the Areopagus under Draco, Solon, and Cleisthenes reflected an increasing importance of problems of space, the rise of the Demos, and the spread of writing. With the appointment of official exegetes by the end of the fifth century, the space element became dominant. Apollo proved adaptable to the demands of Rome.

The change in military tactics which accompanied the revolution at the close of the eighth century and in which the polis emerged, saw the epic tradition developed in the art of recitation sink to the level of the cycle. The danger of the insertion of lines which might prove advantageous to contemporary interests led to a demand for protection against infiltration.[58] The carriers of the oral tradition, the rhapsodes and minstrels, resisted the threats of the written tradition by the use of writing as a means of guaranteeing accuracy. Writing and accuracy were religious necessities. Their success has been evident in the continued dominant influence of the great religious books, the Bible, the Vedas, the Koran, the New Testament, and Homer. After about 675 BC the schools for training rhapsodes became concerned for the preservation of the epics and the oral tradition, and resisted pressure for change. The demand for an exact rendering paralleled an interest in the seventh and sixth centuries in Egypt and western Asia in the recovery of ancient religious literature in its true wording and in the restoration of ancient cult forms. Scribal groups in Judah turned back to the Mosaic tradition, collected and wrote down the material for JE. The search for Mosaic traditions led to the Book of Deuteronomy. A revival of interest in the past was evident in the seventh century in Phoenicia and a flood of allusions to Canaanite literature appeared in Hebrew works from the seventh to the third centuries. In Assyria and Babylonia, Sargon II (722–705) filled his inscriptions with archaisms. A library was collected by Sardanapalus (668–626) and his brother Saosduchinus, King of Babylonia, had official inscriptions in the Sumerian tongue. Nabonidus was concerned with religious revivals. The Libyan princes of Sais, the Saite kings (660–526 BC), the twenty-sixth dynasty, deliberately attempted to revive the ancient gods and forms of cult and to restore the pyramid age.[59]

Possibly the examples of Egypt and Babylonia supported the interest in the appearance of written copies of Greek poems during the religious movement in Athens in the sixth century and in transference from the spoken to the written word. Hesiod had promoted religious legalism and the severe ritualism of the sixth century. Influenced also by examples of the Saite kings, Solon possibly proposed the preparation of a state copy of the ancient religious literature with exact wording. Pisistratus, as a tyrant without religious sanction, was probably concerned with an accurate writing down of texts. At the great Panathenaea festival in 566 BC a musical contest between the rhapsodes provided a means of collecting the text of Homer. The great bulk of the oracular literature from the archaic period was presented in the form of hexameter.[60] The corpus of ancient verses of Orpheus and Musaeus, or *chresmoi*, the inspired utterances of oracles and wandering prophets with ritual prescriptions and predictions of future events, collected and written out, was interpreted by individuals of Eupatrid descent or *chresmologoi* who could thus tie the ancestral law into the framework of the polis.[61] It was significant that their disappearance should have been linked to their inability to adapt themselves to military demands or to problems of space. The failure of the Sicilian expedition destroyed their unlimited pretensions to expert knowledge. They were under continued attack from the old comedy poets from 410 to 400 BC and following revision of the laws of Solon in 399 BC were probably replaced by official exegetes who were given limited but undisputed authority to expound the non-statutory sacred law. The Eupatridae were stripped of the last tool by which they could exert pressure on political life. Their right to authoritative exegesis was put on a clear basis but their special influence was restricted to the religious and moral fields.[62]

The changing position of spatial organization became apparent not only in relation to political structure but also to art. Geometrical design on the vases of Athens and the province of Attica from 900 to 700 BC was finally replaced by pictorial representation which under the influence of literature reflected the fundamental principle of progressive narration[63] especially in the black figured vases. The ear and the concern with time began to have its influence on the arts concerned with the eye and space. The painter attempted to create an impression of a single scene in which time was not fixed but transitory and in which several actions took place at the same time. In the fifth century this device was rapidly displaced by a method emphasizing unity of time and space and in the fourth century a single action represented in a picture became dominant.[64] A mono-scenic method concentrated on a single action within the limits of one scene.[65] Similarly in the drama the unseen supernatural action paralleled by human action on the stage was represented in pictorial scenes at upper and lower tiers on vases.[66] Literature was adapted to the demands of space in an emphasis on unity with time.

The philosophical implications of the growing importance of spatial organization were evident in the field of mathematics. In Egypt geometry had developed as an empirical art of mensuration but in Greece it was seized upon as the very centre of the true philosophical sort of knowledge. Mathematics was recognized as something which could be reduced to general laws with a scientific content.[67] The Ionians were under the spell of an undissolved relation between man and nature but saw the possibility of establishing an intelligible coherence in the phenomenal world. For Thales "all things are full of gods" but he was concerned with coherence of the things. The passionate concern for consistency involved a disregard of the data of experience but a recognition of the autonomy of thought. For Anaximander the infinite was boundless. The ground of all determinate existence could not itself be determinate. Opposites were separated out from the boundless. The power of abstraction reached new levels when Heraclitus concentrated attention on the knowing of things rather than the thing known. As thought constitutes the thinker it controls phenomena. Since thought controls all things the universe was intelligible. The whole was a perpetual flux of change. The cosmos was the dynamics of existence. Being was a perpetual becoming. In attempting to meet the problem of correlating being and becoming or space and time Parmenides declared the two to be mutually exclusive and that only being was real. His philosophical absolute was "the unshaken heart of well-rounded truth."[68]

Pythagoras was anxious to determine existence quantitatively. From his time there was an intimate association, "not to say an indissoluble correlation between the theory of numbers and the theory of extension: between arithmetic and geometry."[69] In the boundless sphere of Anaximander and Anaximenes he represented numbers by patterns of dots arranged in geometric figures. The void distinguished their nature in blank intervals between the units or in gaps separating the terms in a series of natural integers. Units of number were identified with geometrical points having a position in actual space and an indivisible magnitude.[70] The mathematical void was invoked to separate units of number. From about 450 BC geometers realized that they needed space which was continuous and of infinite extent and not a space made up of points that could be identified with units of number separated by intervals of emptiness as in the discontinuous arithmetical void of Pythagoras. Geometry detached itself from arithmetic. Leucippus and Democritus accepted the framework of geometers and maintained the existence of an unlimited void. They ascribed to the physical void the infinite extent of geometrical space. Atoms were unlimited in number and demanded an unlimited extent in space. Infinite space, postulated for the construction of geometrical figures, was paralleled by recognition of an unlimited void in nature by the atomists or physicists. The ancient boundaries of spherical space were broken down and space robbed of circumference and centre.[71] The static shapes discovered by Greek mathematics supported the Platonic concept of the theory of ideas. Geometry influenced in turn by Plato was codified and brought to completion by Euclid at Alexandria about 300 BC. For a brief period the Greeks escaped from the oral tradition and from the written tradition. The oral tradition was sufficiently strong to check complete submergence in the written. The oral tradition supported Greek scepticism and evaded monopolies of religious literature.

The increasing importance of problems of space was accompanied by improvements in the efficiency of military tactics leading to the conquests of Philip and Alexander. With an abundance of good horses and a numerous and hardy nobility in Macedonia, they developed effectively the support of light armed troops and cavalry to the hoplites. The phalanx became a more heavily armed and a more immobile body in the interests of solidarity and rigidity and the heavy cavalry force the striking arm. Military success depended on the co-ordination of various kinds of troops. The Persian Empire was followed by the Alexandrian Empire.

The Persian Empire had succeeded in part through the possession of an organization of continuity in religion and through a recognition of the existence of other organizations in Babylon, Judaea, and Egypt. Alexander had no comparable organization other than that of the divine king, a concept tempered by the Platonic doctrine of wisdom to govern, and, with his death, the Empire broke up into the Hellenistic kingdoms. The Seleucid dynasty attempted to exploit possible division between Babylonian religion and Persian religion but the latter became the basis of expansion of the Parthian Empire. Babylon fell in 125 BC and the Seleucid kingdom retreated and disappeared. Hellenizing priests, Jason and Menelaus (175–165 BC) proposed a reorganization of Judaism as a Syro-Hellenic religion in the interests of the Seleucids but pious Jews supported the Maccabees and under Simon (143–135 BC) secured the autonomy of Judaea and the purification of Jerusalem.[72] The Ptolemies established a new capital at Alexandria and attempted to offset the religious influences of Thebes and of Babylonia by a new religion and the organization of knowledge in a university, a library, and a museum. Recognition of problems of space was shown in the work of Euclid and of time in the study of astronomy and in the revisions of the texts of Homer and the Old Testament.

The trend of development in Rome paralleled roughly the trend described in Athens. A monarchy was followed by an aristocracy of patricians and the laws were controlled by four colleges of priests. The struggle against the Eupatridae in Athens for control of the oral tradition in law was not dissimilar to the struggle against the patricians in Rome. The appointment of exegetes in Athens in the latter part of the fifth century or early in the fourth century and the influence of Greece on Rome probably contributed to the early development of a specialized class in Rome when ancestral law still had great importance. The Roman pontiffs acquired enormous influence in contrast with the Athenian exegetes.[73] The oral tradition and religion provided an organization of continuity which persisted through the republic. With Scipio the idea emerged that religion could be used by the government but with this development religion lost significance among the people. Polybius wrote: "A scrupulous fear of the gods is the very thing which keeps the Roman commonwealth together." As problems of organization of space incidental to the success of Roman arms in Italy, North Africa, Spain and Gaul, and the eastern Mediterranean became more pronounced, the problems of religious organization and continuity increased. Following the defeat of Roman arms in 9 AD by Arminius, an attempt was made to consolidate the territory of the empire behind lines of defence such as the Rhine and Danube rivers and to solve the problem of continuity by reliance on constitutionalism and dynasties. Augustus attempted to revive a dying religion to support morality and the state. "The alliance of throne and altar dates from that time." The tendency of Caesarism toward absolute monarchy necessitated increasing dependence on oriental clergy.[74] An interest in problems of space was evident in Strabo's geography, an attempt to present a unified view of the universe, and in the work of Ptolemy in collecting all the known geographical information and in constructing a cartographical map of the earth. Force became increasingly important and the dynastic problem more acute. Dependence on war and organized force weakened the possibility of extended dynasties, increased dependence on successful leaders of the army, and involved lack of continuity. The deification of emperors, following the acquisition of Egypt, development of the legal concept of adoption, an emphasis on architecture especially in Rome, the capital, propaganda devices in literature, gladiatorial games, coins, and columns, and effective control over the calendar especially in the names July and August, were designed to strengthen the position of various dynasties. Roman religion as a basis of continuity became less effective and the significance of the bureaucracy increased. Its demands required a division of the empire between east and west, and the necessity of establishing a new capital in the East at Constantinople weakened the influence of the sacred place in Roman religion.

Expansion to the East and contact with Eastern religions compelled the Roman Empire to face the problems of earlier empires, namely the problems of control over religion and organized time. Elements of the Persian religion which had been transmitted orally were written down and became the basis of expansion of the Parthian Empire. The Sassanid dynasty of 228 AD selected a new capital at Ctesiphon, supported a ruling hierarchy in charge of revived Mazdaism, and gave the Avesta a place as a sacred book. In the struggle between Rome and Persia, Rome extended the policy of exploiting religions and Mithraism spread rapidly throughout the armed forces of the Empire.

An attempt to meet the problems of Persia led to difficulties with Judaism. In the last two centuries BC the influence of Iran on Judaism was pronounced.[75] The dualistic conception of Iranian religion had an important triumph in solving the problem of evil. The idea of the seven chief angels was taken from Iranian sources. After the translation of the Bible from Hebrew into Greek in Alexandria, the influence of Hellenistic thought on Judaism became pronounced. In the strife between the Sadducees and the Pharisees from 130 BC to 70 AD, the Sadducees held that a belief in a future life, a divine judgment, bodily resurrection, and an angelic hierarchy was unscriptural and insisted on freedom of the human will, in opposition to the Stoic doctrine of predestination; the Pharisees recognized a duality, predestination or the providence of God and the free action of man's will. Under the influence of Hellenism, the Pharisees developed ritual law by exegetic and dialectic methods, emphasized the study of law and the formation of schools of disciples.[76] The scope of canonical legislation was extended by hedging the rules of Torah with new regulations protecting the observance of the original rules. As rigorous legalists the Pharisees aimed to perpetuate the Torah in the purest form.[77] They favoured the oral tradition and appealed to popular support in contrast with the Sadducees who were chiefly aristocratic and insisted upon the written Bible and Greek speculation. The oral tradition checked the possibility of translation and left the Pharisees in exclusive possession. The Talmud and the Mishnah were kept from being written down, translation and transmission to others was prevented, and religion was protected.[78] The early Christians repudiated the Pharisaic content. "The strength of sin is in the law." They developed their own oral tradition, traced back through the disciples to the apostles. The Greek Gospels were possibly based on an Aramaic substratum of an oral tradition. Mnemotechnic devices were essential to oral transmission; the first and third Gospels, which reveal these, were developed from related oral sources.[79] The oral tradition of early Israel had been associated with an anthropomorphic god; the hardening effects of a written tradition had necessitated a return to the oral tradition and an anthropomorphic god in Christianity.[80] The Gospels and Acts, narratives of the life of Christ and the work of the apostles, were compiled for purposes of dissemination. In the face of persecution, transcription and circulation were difficult and the variety of readings increased.[81] About the end of the fourth century, the Byzantine received text was given recognition in the church of Constantinople. Increasing recognition of other texts led to the Revised version of 1881.[82] As compared with the accurate, authoritative texts of the classics transmitted through Alexandria and Constantinople the New Testament emerged from a variety of texts, the work of comparatively illiterate scribes.[83]

Cheap copies of works suited to Christians as a persecuted sect were probably written on papyrus in the form of a codex in the second century AD.[84] The codex form carried more material and was more convenient. Use of the roll would restrict content to single Gospels or the Acts. Vellum had an advantage over papyrus in that it could be carried without fraying. It was fully developed as a writing material at the beginning of the second century BC and was used at Pergamum and later for notebooks and books of second grade at Rome, Athens, and Alexandria. With recognition of Christianity in the Empire, papyrus was displaced by vellum. The demand for authoritative Christian scriptures led to a determination of the canon of the New Testament and the production of complete Bibles. A marked increase in the demand for copies of the scriptures following the end of persecution probably hastened the revolution in the change from papyrus to vellum. The narrow two- to three-inch column of the papyrus roll was continued in the early vellum manuscripts, which contained three or four columns to a page.[85]

The transformation from the papyrus roll to the parchment codex in the fourth century AD presented the miniaturist with a durable material, papyrus being generally limited to a life of three generations, with a surface more suited to delicate techniques. Book illumination was raised to a high artistic level. The artist on papyrus was limited to line drawing and water colouring and parchment prevented the use of thick layers of paint. While the parchment roll persisted as it permitted an intimate connection between picture and text, the proportions of a single page of the codex led the painter to adjust the picture to the new format.[86] With the change from a square format to one in which height is greater than width, the number of columns was reduced to two and to one. Libraries were recopied on vellum, that of Pamphilus at Caesarea having vellum copies by 350 AD. The Vaticanus and Sinaiticus vellum codices belong to the same period.

Mithraism proved unacceptable to the Hellenistic population of the eastern Mediterranean and it became necessary for an administrative bureaucracy to give more direct attention to the wealthier portions of the Empire and for the emperor to choose a more defensible site for the capital. Constantinople was chosen and Christianity became the official religion. It had syncretistic elements and included with other religions the virgin birth of a god, his astral associations, birth among cattle, imprisonment, death, descent to the underworld, disappearance for three days, resurrection, and exaltation to heaven.[87] The holidays of other religions, such as the 25th of December of Mithraism, were taken over by Christianity. The element of time had been organized in relation to religion to meet the demands of an organization of space in relation to the Empire. "We must regard as altogether divine that which alone and really exists and whose power endures through all time" (Constantine). A bureaucracy built up in relation to papyrus and the alphabet was supplemented by a hierarchy built up in relation to parchment. The consequent stability was evident in the continuity of the Byzantine Empire to 1453. The success of the Ptolemies in Egypt in adapting a religion to their needs had not been lost on the Roman emperors.

The development of the church in relation to the New Testament, the writings of the Fathers, and the oral tradition was accompanied by heresies centring about the spelling and interpretation of words and the problem of continuing powerful religious organizations in Egypt. Constantine became concerned to secure the support of a unified Christianity.[88] With the summoning of a universal council of the whole church to settle the Arian controversy, Constantine secured acceptance of an inclusive formula, proposed by Western bishops but derived from the concept of consubstantiality of Egyptian religion, that "homoiousios" or "of one essence" should describe the Father and Son whereas the East, possibly continuing Babylonian tradition, held that the Son cannot be in the same sense God.[89] The importance of unity on the other hand and the strength of Arianism in the East and among the Goths explained the return of Constantine to the Arian faith and the persistence of its influence until 381.

The imposition of the Trinity on the Christian world by a small number of bishops from the West was followed by the Pelagian, Nestorian, and other heresies. The precedent set for the Eastern church by Constantine that only an emperor could call a general council left the initiative in the settling of heresies with the emperor. The attempts of Gregory of Nazianzus and Basil of Caesarea to temper the doctrine to the East failed to meet the demands of monophysitism. Rejection of the latter in the Council of Chalcedon in 451 was followed by discontent in Syria and Egypt. The position of the church in the West was strengthened as the political position of the Empire was weakened. Establishment of Constantinople in itself probably weakened the Empire and hastened its collapse, as it controlled the wealthy provinces of Asia Minor and the best recruiting ground, the Illyrian provinces.[90] Since the Roman religion did not permit a priestly caste and the pontifices and augurs were lay experts on religion,[91] the way was open for the growth of the papacy.

The fundamental bases of the unwritten constitution of the Byzantine Empire were the senate, the army, the demes, and the church.[92] The emperor was the central figure in religion and in politics. The effectiveness of organized force in the Byzantine Empire arose in part from the ruthless recognition of military capacity in the army. "Every man in the Byzantine army had an imperial sceptre in his hands." Justin, for example, was born in Thrace, of peasant stock, and became Emperor to be succeeded by his nephew, Justinian. The capacity of Justinian was evident in his administration. They strengthened the position of the Chalcedonians and weakened the position of the monophysites. Acacius, Patriarch of Constantinople, had attempted to reconcile Chalcedonians and monophysites in the Edict of Union in 482 under the

Emperor Zeno, but had been anathematized by the pope. The Egyptian tradition in religion, which had been strengthened by Alexandrian theologians, first in opposition to Babylonian religion, resisted pressure from Constantinople. The first breach between the Eastern and the Western churches was brought to an end with Justin's accession on 9 July 518. A Chalcedonian policy implied opposition to Theodoric, the Ostrogoth, an Arian, in Italy and the West. Arian religion provided no central organization of time to maintain political power and he attempted to maintain independence of the Eastern Empire by matrimonial alliances with his German neighbours.[93] The weakness of political organization based on these alliances led Justinian to press toward the West, as did his difficulties with Persia and with Egypt. The papacy attempted to check persecution of Gothic Arians in the Eastern Empire, but John I, who succeeded Pope Hormisdas in 523, went to Constantinople in 526 and crowned Justin Emperor of the Orient. The papacy came under the domination of the Byzantine Empire until Pope Zacharias (741–52), the last Greek on the papal throne.[94]

Control over the papacy in Rome was acquired at the expense of increasing difficulty with the monophysites in Egypt. This weakness of the Empire was the opportunity of Mohammedanism. Among the Arabs poetry contributed to the rise of a standard, national language and later to political unity.[95] It was sacred and linked to the pagan religion, but at the time of Mohammed both were on the decline. In the four sacred months, when war was forbidden, rival poets declaimed their verses at the fairs which were centres of social and literary life.[96] Mohammed began by oral recitals (Koran=recital) inspired by God through the angel Gabriel. After the death of Mohammed and the loss of many reciters at the battle of al-Yemama in 633, steps were taken to write down the tradition and to provide an official written text. The memory was the seat of the book. A final recension was established in 651.[97]

Restriction of writing to the sacred book and the limitations of legal and ritual matter in the Koran were followed by the growth of an oral tradition in the Hadith, a new saga, which replaced the old prose sage of the Arabs. It gained the force of law and the authority of inspiration and became a system of law and religion. Writing slowly extended its influence to the Hadith. The late recognition of writing was due in part to the cost and effort of writing down a large volume like the Koran. Disapproval of writing compelled Mohammedans to concentrate on the Koran and kept them from other books. Professional memorizers whose repetitions depended on memory and not on what they committed to writing, opposed the writing down of the Hadith. As the Jews had forbidden the composition of fresh books in addition to the Old Testament so the Mohammedans opposed possible rivals to the Koran.

The earlier pagan religion began to return in the secular antireligious reaction of the Umayyad dynasty (651–750) and Islam made a compromise with the old poetry. In turn the supporters of the poetry of tradition developed hostility to the Umayyads as descendants of the pagan aristocracy which had persecuted Mohammed and were joined by the Abbasid revolutionaries who came into power in 750.[98] The capital was moved from Damascus to Baghdad, and the Umayyads set up an independent capital at Cordova in Spain.

The Byzantine Empire with its close relation between church and state was an absolutism which was always in danger of being tempted to the persecution of heresy.[99] Heretics became a source of strength to enemies of the Empire. The Nestorians expelled by Zeno were welcomed in the Sassanid Empire.[100] "It was by the genius of Muhammad that Nestorius' doctrine was to be restored to the realm of religion" (F.W. Buckler).[101] Athenian scholars migrated to Persia after the closing of the schools in 529. Extension of Byzantine interests to the West was at the expense of conciliation with Persia. Disaffection of the monophysites facilitated the conquest of Palestine and Egypt by the Persians. Though territory was reconquered by Heraclius, the struggle between Persians and Byzantines and continued religious disaffection enabled the Mohammedans with the zeal of a new religion to extend their conquests from Palestine to Spain. The failure of Nestorius in the Christian church made restoration outside in Islam inevitable. Byzantine Christianity as monophysitism became one of the main foundations of Islam and the early caliphates followed the methods and system of Byzantium and Sassanid Persia.[102] They were eventually checked by Leo III at Constantinople in 718 and by Charles Martel in the West in 732. This resistance increased the difficulties of Mohammedanism as a political organization and contributed to the revival of Persian influence evident in the rise of the Abbasids and the break between Baghdad and Cordova. The limitations of the organization of space in relation to the demands of religion and of the organization of time and continuity persisted in the weakness of Mohammedanism.

Retreat of the Byzantine Empire in Egypt weakened its position in the West particularly as the Franks had defeated the Mohammedans. The attempts of the Church in the East to strengthen its power at the expense of the emperor through monasticism had led to the resistance of the latter and had created difficulties for it in the iconoclastic controversy from 730 to 787. In the Byzantine Empire as in the principate "the imperial power is an autocracy tempered by the legal right of revolution" (Mommsen). An organization adapted to problems of space and of time such as the Byzantine Empire was faced with difficulties of balance which were met by contraction in space. "Belief and unbelief never follow men's commands" (Hobbes). The precedents of the coronations of Anastasius I by the Patriarch Euphemius in 491, by which the appearance of encroachment on the omnipotence of imperial power was scrupulously avoided but in which the Patriarch participated on condition that the Emperor would "introduce no innovations into the holy Church of God,"[103] and of Justin by Pope John I in 526, ultimately had sinister results for the Eastern Empire. The patriarch participated in the coronation as a representative of the people who cooperated with the army and the senate in the election of the emperor. The papacy in the West made coronation one of the most important rights of the church.

As a result of Byzantine weakness Pope Zacharias approved the consecration of Pippin as King of the Franks by Boniface in 751 and enabled him to dispossess the Merovingian dynasty. In turn the Frankish church was reformed and Frankish rulers were brought into close relation with the papacy. The Carolingian renaissance was accompanied by the crowning of Charlemagne[104] by the pope. Friendship between Haroun-al-Raschid and Charles the Great eventually compelled the Byzantine Empire to recognize Charles as Emperor in 812.[105]

The independence of the papacy and its relation with the Franks had unfortunate implications because of the number of bad popes from the ninth to the eleventh centuries. The papacy fell into slavery whereas the Eastern patriarchs retained their independence conscious of their strength, dignity, and privileges.[106] The political organization of Europe after the invasion of the barbarians lacked a significant basis of continuity. Monasticism had been introduced in Gaul by Athanasius and had spread rapidly. As Roman organization was submerged by the invaders, the Roman aristocracy became the hierarchy of the Roman church.[107]

The Roman conquests and extension of political organization had involved destruction of the oral tradition of the conquered and the imposition of writing. The oral tradition of the Druids reported by Caesar as designed to train the memory and to keep learning from becoming generally accessible had been wiped out. In Ireland and in Germany, beyond the bounds of the Roman conquest, the oral tradition persisted. In Ireland the oral system was retained with the native secular education while the official religion was recognized in foreign schools with writing. With the introduction of Christianity the Druids were eliminated, but the fili, or official poets attached to a central monarchy, renounced paganism and made peace with the church, thus preserving the mythological heroic literature in the oral tradition in spite of Christianity with writing and books.[108] The file was replaced by the bard with the fall of the central monarchy. By 575 the rapacity of the bards became intolerable and measures were taken against them. After the eleventh century, official secular and ecclesiastical scribes collected stories and genealogical tales which had persisted in the oral tradition. Assemblies of poets or of the learned were held as late as 1351 and were of political significance.[109] The insistence of the Pharisees on the oral tradition of native religion in opposition to Greek writing was paralleled by the insistence of Irish poets on the oral tradition in contrast with Christian writing and led, on the one hand, to Jewish, and, on the other, to Irish nationalism.

In Germany heroic poems were of courtly origin. Minstrels recited metrical speeches accompanied by the harp.[110] Court poems became the basis of epic and narrative poems from the fourth to the sixth centuries. In the heroic age bonds of kinship were disintegrating, the primitive sanctity of the family was giving way.[111] Tribal obligations broke down.[112] The Teutonic poems, like the Homeric poems of the heroic age, were a characteristic of a period of long-standing relations between semi-civilized people and civilized people.[113] On the other hand the Greeks maintained their language intact whereas the Teutons were exposed to the influence of Latin. Indeed the Greek oral tradition in surviving the impact of oriental civilizations influenced Rome, and destroyed the oral tradition of the Franks. Charlemagne attempted to collect existing poems and in the twelfth and later centuries they came into favour with the upper classes. They continued as testimony of freedom from Roman conquest and became a support to German nationalism. It has been significant that the national propaganda of the small nations of Europe has been largely in anthologies of poetry as the media best designed to protect them from the influences of "products of pure intelligence."[114] Plato's concern with expulsion of the poets was perhaps not unrelated to his appreciation of their role.

The limitations imposed on Christianity in Ireland by the persistence of the oral tradition released its energies for missionary activity to Scotland and England and to the Continent. Christian missions to the Continent gave momentum to the Carolingian renaissance and strengthened the position of the empire in the

West, in which the papacy at Rome occupied a position parallel to that of the patriarch of Constantinople in the Byzantine Empire. The Carolingian revival of ancient Latin literature in the ninth century paralleled the revival of Greek at Constantinople in the same period and followed the outburst of activity in learning at Baghdad. These revivals did much to enable the classics to survive.[115] But the Byzantine Empire had no dark ages such as had followed the invasions of the barbarians for the Western church. The Western church had become independent of the Eastern church and of the Byzantine Empire but had allied itself with a new emperor who had not been disciplined by a church.

The Western Empire had the elements of a Caesaropapism in its capacity for organizing space and its relations with the church for organizing time and securing continuity. But it lacked elements of political strength. After the death of Charlemagne the Teutonic principle of division among the heirs was preserved and the vast area controlled by Charlemagne was divided. Nuclei of force were organized to meet the invasions of the Norsemen and of the Magyars. At Paris resistance to the invaders led to the emergence of the Capet family which followed the hereditary principle and became the basis of a dynastic kingship. In Germany the principle of election meant that the emperor was not attached to any one region and that dukedoms broke into small municipalities.[116] The church escaped from political influence and, as a step toward independence, in 1059, organized a school of cardinals which selected popes and in turn the cardinals. Control over time and continuity was wrenched from the state. A monopoly over time was built up centring around the name of Rome, the use of Latin, celibacy of the clergy, freedom from the state, and a monastic system. The church sponsored the Crusades and extended the decentralizing forces which accompanied the barbarian invasion in the West to the East and in 1204 erased "the last vestige of Rome's unification."[117]

A monopoly over time stimulated competitive elements in the organization of space. The introduction of paper from China to Baghdad and to Cordova and to Italy and France contributed to the development of cursive writing and to the organization of space in relation to the vernaculars. Venice, Pisa, and Genoa exploited the growing weakness of the Byzantine Empire. Uniformity in writing followed the work of Charlemagne in the development and spread of the Carolingian minuscule to Italy. Arabic numerals displaced the cumbersome Roman numerals and facilitated calculation. In Italy writing[118] continued as an instrument of secular life after antiquity. Florence led in the practical aspects of writing in domestic industry and as a means of organizing trade in the twelfth century. Wool became an industrial and commercial product introducing profound transformations in Europe. Life could be organized legally and politically over vast territories. Toward the end of the twelfth century Florence had about six hundred notaries employed in industrial and commercial work and early in the thirteen century a guild was formed with masters to whom children were apprenticed. Notaries specializing in commercial law were sent to distant countries where they acted as collaborators with banks and brought Florence in touch with the business and politics of Europe and of foreign countries. The notariat was transformed in a practical sense. Manuals of commercial calculation were produced. With a knowledge of reading, writing, and calculation artisans could become masters. About 1330, 8,000 to 10,000 children in Florence knew how to read, of whom 1,000 to 1,200 had a knowledge of the abacus and 500 to 600 a knowledge of grammar and logic. Schools were conducted as private enterprise and studies had a practical purpose. The corporations of Florence were based on a system of writing in Italian, accounts, central control of "boutiques," matricules, registers, scribes, and postal services. Writing compelled the individual to reflect more intensively. Discipline brought greater aptitude for expression. Calculability had intellectual consequences. Commercial property developed with contracts and economic relations lost their personal colour. Great artists and individuals rose from the ranks of the notaries. Writing played a decisive role in the intellectual and artistic revolution.

In Flanders and the low countries a civilization similar to that of Tuscany emerged. The Dutch language had an existence separate from Germany because it was fixed early in writing. Outside Italy only Flanders had an original renaissance.[119]

The impact of paper and writing on the monopoly over time exercised by the church was evident in the growing importance of the vernacular and the development of industry and trade. In defence against the stubborn and varied assaults on the most precious beliefs of Catholic Christianity, the apostolic rule of faith and the apostolic order of bishops had been developed as a guarantee of truth in addition to reliance on the Old and New Testaments.[120] Limits were set to the compass of Holy Scripture; baptism and the Lord's Supper were given the form of mysteries; it was forbidden to put the baptismal symbol in writing and part of the public worship was forbidden to profane eyes. Bible reading was emphasized and the church became a great elementary school. Every Christian must know what he believed.[121] The Greek church pressed on to the translation of the Bible into other tongues and laid the foundations of national literature among other peoples. Cyrillic and Glagolitic alphabets, developed to make the scriptures and liturgy available to the Slavs, more adequately represented the sounds of the Slavonic language and provided a more effective bridge between the oral and the written traditions.[122] Christianity as the daughter of Judaism had defended the sacred writings from the encroachment of a priesthood in a world of mystery religions.[123]

In the church of Rome, monasticism and monastic theology had become established before the elements of a mystery religion became important. In the struggle against barbarism, the church emphasized exclusion by concentrating on Latin and supported its position by monastic orders (notably the friars), architecture (notably the Gothic cathedrals), and manuscripts (notably in the work of illumination) and music. Stone in architecture and scripture emphasized permanence and durability. In the thirteenth century "Tout ce que' les théologiens, les encyclopédistes, les interprètes de la Bible ont dit d'essentiel a été exprimé par la peinture sur verre ou par la sculpture."[124] Psalm singing created, in the words of Ambrose, "a great bond of unity when the whole people raise their voices in one choir."[125] Music was handicapped by limitations of writing "for if music is not retained by man's memory, it is lost, since it cannot be written down."[126] Early in the eleventh century Guido wrote regarding his system of notation: "For since I have undertaken to teach this method to my boys, certain of them have succeeded, easily, within three days, in singing melodies previously unknown to them; a result which formerly, by the other methods, could not have been brought about in many weeks."[127] Counterpoint in which the aim is "to perform several melodies simultaneously and bind them together by good and well-regulated consonances" developed about 1300.[128]

The manufacture of paper near urban centres because of demand and of cheap supplies of linen rags as raw material hastened the shift of writing from the monasteries to urban communities. The writing master emerged in the fourteenth and fifteenth centuries and in turn printing in the trend toward urbanization.[129] Machine industry, of which printing was an early and conspicuous illustration, made effective inroads on a society dominated by the manuscript. The interrelation and unity of the arts in which the production of manuscripts meant writing and painting, which in turn were influenced by sculpture and architecture, was destroyed. The perfection of the sculpture of Michelangelo supported by the wealth of Italian cities and the papacy and combining Christian and pagan traditions was the last gesture of a society destined to fall with the Italian city state, following the French invasions and the influence of the book. The horrors of the Bible illustrated by the statues of the cathedrals were offset by classical influence. The painting of the Last Judgment reflected the doom of a culture based on stone, parchment, and painting. Stone was a medium of expression of immortality for the artist and the culture. The attack of Savonarola was based on the book and it was symbolic of an end of a period that Michelangelo should have designed the Vatican library.

That the sacred character of the scriptures in the Middle Ages was expressed in sculpture and architecture had disastrous implications following the expansion of printing with its emphasis on the scriptures. Greek scriptures following the translations of Erasmus and a concern with the possibility of translation into the vernaculars destroyed the monopoly of the church as expressed in Latin. In the Reformation print was used to overwhelm sculpture and architecture as interpreters of the scriptures. Translations into the vernaculars gave them a sacred character and gave a powerful drive to nationalism. Milton was concerned with the production of an epic in English which would combine nationalism and Christianity.

The printing industry made rapid advance in regions in which the effects of the Roman conquest were limited such as Germany and England or in regions marginal to areas dominated by a bureaucracy based on papyrus. Regions in which Latin was strong or regions of the Romance languages developed opposition to mechanized print partly through other arts including literature. In England the strength of the oral tradition was evident in Shakespeare, and in Germany in the absence of a uniform dialect until after Luther's Bible was printed. In these regions Protestantism made rapid headway and supported the growth of the state. New monopolies of space began to emerge as the monopoly over time was weakened.

A new interest in space was evident in the development of the mariner's compass and the lens.[130] Columbus discovered the New World, Magellan proved the earth a sphere, and in astronomy the Ptolemaic system was undermined especially after the invention and improvement of the telescope. The architect Brunelleschi has been credited with first constructing a scene according to a focused system of perspective. Dürer advanced from the empirical to mathematical construction.[131] In Florence the new conception of space was translated into artistic terms as a counterpart of the modern notion of individualism.[132] Its immediate effect on architecture was evident in the baroque. In philosophy Leibniz was the first to explain space as pure form, an order of existence, and time as an order of succession.

The paper and printing industries supported the development of monopolies of space in nationalism and the state. Printing emphasized vernaculars, reduced the speed of movement of ideas, and divided the European mind. Formerly philosophy directed scientific knowledge but an increase in printed material has compelled science to go now in one direction and now in another. Germany became more isolated from England in part because of the difficulty of its language as compared with that of France. It would be interesting to conjecture as to the history of Europe in the nineteenth century if Newman and Comte had known German. The vested interests of the printing industry tend to check the movement of ideas and to contribute to the building-up of monopolies, and, ultimately, to the breaking-over into other languages and to the ebb and flow of movements. The delay in the industrial development of Germany followed by its rapid development after 1870 described by Veblen is in part an illustration. Even science with its emphasis on a common vernacular and on translations has come under the influence of monopolies of knowledge in patents, secret processes, and military "security" measures. Science had gained in the escape from the monopoly of knowledge in terms of time but eventually lost in the development of knowledge in terms of space. An obsession with monopolies of space has been evident in the effects of militarism on geography. As a military instrument it was especially effective in propaganda in its adaptations to regionalism and nationalism. "We must know about our own country." Geopolitics was developed in Germany by seizing on Mackinder's thesis and attempting to create an impression of fatalism and inevitability. But, as Cornford remarked, when war is described as inevitable, its causes are not known.

The destruction of time and the increasing importance of monopolies of space were evident in the writings of Hegel for whom progress was perpetual movement and strife or of Marx who regarded time as "formless inevitability."[133] For Schopenhauer music was the highest because the most irrational form of art, the most naked unreflected expression of the essence of life, of the will.[134] Wagner expressed in music the resistance to Rome and Christianity. "What I have never forgiven Wagner is his condescending to Germany" (Nietzsche).[135] The destruction of Germany's contribution to Western civilization based on the book and on music was followed by attempts at recovery from the standpoint of militarism and the state and the aberrations of German culture incidental to the effects of war.

The increasing influence of print has been reflected in republicanism with the bias toward constitutions and documents and guarantees of freedom of the press and of the right of the individuals. Demands for control over time were reflected in the separation of church and state. George Washington wrote in a statement to Tripoli: "The government of the United States is not in any sense founded upon the Christian religion." More significant perhaps have been the varying attitudes of peoples toward the state, as between East and West, between common law countries and Roman law countries, and between countries at different stages of industrial development. The concept of the state as an economic factor has become an indication of economic activity. Without religion as an anchorage the state has become more dependent on cultural development. With cultural maturity as in France the state becomes a cloak to put on and off at will during periods of emergency in the form of constitutional changes. In nations without cultural maturity such drastic changes become unthinkable and the statute books become cluttered with constitutional amendments and legislation. The totalitarian state or the welfare state with rigid constitutions is compelled to resort to endless administrative activity.

The oral tradition implies the spirit but writing and printing are inherently materialistic. The influence of the oral tradition through resort to writing and printing and a stress on its sacredness – thus paralysing its possible rivals, turning the weapons of its enemies against them – persisted in the Bible and Homer. The accumulation of poetry under the oral tradition dominated the history of the West. Greece and Rome kept their respect for the oral tradition.[136] A decline of the oral tradition meant an emphasis on writing (and hence on the eye rather than the ear) and on visual arts, architecture, sculpture, and painting (and hence on space rather than time). The significance of time persisted in the character of materials notably in the use of stone in architecture and sculpture because of their permanence and durability. The emphasis on capitals in Egypt, Babylonia, Assyria, Persia, Greece, Rome, Constantinople, Paris, Berlin, London, Washington, and Moscow reflected a concern with the problems of control over time and over space. The burden of capitals on the peoples concerned has not been unrelated to their decline and to revolutions, for example in France and Russia. Religious monopolies concerned with time relied on the oral tradition. It had resort to the support of architecture in its sacred places as in Rome, Jerusalem, and Mecca. Again revolutions were in part protests against the burden of capitals, as in the case of Protestantism. The destruction of the Temple in Jerusalem by the Romans accentuated the importance of the oral tradition among the Jews and made Judaism unadaptable to political demands. The rise of Palestine has been a tribute to the persistence of the oral tradition as a basis for the organization of time on the one hand and to the increasing pressure of the written and printed tradition toward the organization of space on the other.

In the clash between types of monopoly, an unpredictable freedom has been achieved. The Roman Catholic church, with its control over time, absorbed elements of administration of the Roman Empire essential to control over space and attempted to maintain a balance comparable to that of the Byzantine Empire. In a sense they supported each other and destroyed each other. The spread of paper and printing from China and the Mohammedan world upset the balance and compelled new adjustments. Germany's escape from the discipline of Rome permitted the clash of ideas between France and the Holy Roman Empire and between England and Germany. In the West the demands of faith – it is certain because it is impossible (Tertullian) – when disseminated by translation into different languages were too heavy. The fanaticism of faith and the fanaticism of reason tore Europe apart and intensified the problem of adjustment between obsession for the state and obsession for the church and led to the growth in the name of science of new monopolies to exploit faith and incredibility.

NOTES

1 President of the British Association, 1934. Cited by F.M. Cornford, "The Invention of Space," *Essays in Honour of Gilbert Murray* (London, 1936), 216.

2 Ernst Cassirer, *The Problem of Knowledge: Philosophy, Science, and History since Hegel*, trans. W.H. Woglom and C.W. Hendel (New Haven, Conn., 1950), 98.

3 J.H. Breasted, *A History of Egypt, from the Earliest Times to the Persian Conquest* (New York, 1912), 7.

4 For a description of the transition from the egalitarian and undivided totemic clan to territorially organized and individualized sovereign power, from matriarchal to patrilinear relationships, see A. Moret and G. Davy, *From Tribe to Empire* (London, 1926), 1–106. V. Gordon Childe has argued that writing was necessitated by economic demands and that its development was generally connected with the change from kinship to a territorial basis of social organization; see *Man Makes Himself* (London, 1951) and *Progress and Archaeology* (London,

1945), ii. On the effects of political expansion on writing, see W.F. Albright, *The Vocalization of the Egyptian Syllabic Orthography* (New Haven, Conn., 1934).

5 Significantly Ptah, the god of Memphis, was the god of art and of all handicrafts. The high priest of Ptah was the chief of stone workers and artist to the king. Architecture as the chief force in the artist's life meant that sculpture became part of the decorations and subordinate. See M.A. Murray, *Egyptian Sculpture* (London, 1930), xvii–xxiii.

6 Breasted, *History of Egypt*, 117, 119.

7 V. Gordon Childe, *What Happened in History* (New York, 1946), 149. In the social revolution illusory gratifications were substituted for changes in social order. See Abram Kardiner, *The Psychological Frontiers of Society* (New York, 1945), 427.

8 The significance of the horse in the chariot and in the cavalry has been generally underestimated. It compelled an improvement in the standard of intelligence in the armed forces and probably led to the rise of humanitarianism. E.J. Dillon remarked concerning a mounted policeman that he was always surprised by the look of intelligence on the horse's face. The greater stability of the oriental empires of the second millennium as compared to those of the third has been attributed to the acceleration of official journeys by the use of chariots. The horse supported development of a separate military class. See Childe, *Progress and Archaeology*, 68.

9 See Henri Frankfort, *Kingship and the Gods: A Study of Ancient Near Eastern Religion as the Integration of Science and Nature* (Chicago, 1948), 217–19.

10 Ibid., 218–23.

11 Ibid., 237–44.

12 Ibid., 225.

13 See Henri Frankfort, *Cylinder Seals: A Documentary Essay on the Art and Religion of the Ancient Near East* (London, 1939), 93.

14 Ibid., 12.

15 H. Frankfort et al., *The Intellectual Adventure of Ancient Man: An Essay on Speculative Thought in the Ancient Near East* (Chicago, 1946), 139.

16 Ibid., 43.

17 Ibid., 192–5.

18 Frankfort, *Kingship and the Gods*, 252.

19 Ibid., 309.

20 Ibid., 258.

21 Childe, *What Happened in History*, 245.

22 L.R. Farnell, *Greece and Babylon: A Comparative Sketch of Mesopotamian, Anatolian and Hellenic Religions* (Edinburgh, 1911), 132.

23 See J.T. Shotwell, *An Introduction to the History of History* (New York, 1922), 45.

24 Frankfort et al., *The Intellectual Adventure of Ancient Man*, 169.
25 Frankfort, *Kingship and the Gods*, 327.
26 Ibid., 338.
27 W.F. Albright, *From the Stone Age to Christianity: Monotheism and the Historical Process* (Baltimore, 1940), 146–9.
28 Ibid., 45–6.
29 It was known to the Canaanites between 1700 and 1500 BC (ibid., 43).
30 Solomon Gandz, "The Knot in Hebrew Literature, or From the Knot to the Alphabet," *Isis* 14 (1930): 190–214.
31 Solomon Gandz, "Oral Tradition in the Bible," *Jewish Studies in Memory of George A. Kohut, 1874–1933*, ed. S.W. Baron and A. Marx (New York, 1936), 254–5.
32 Ibid., 286.
33 Solomon Gandz, "The Dawn of Literature: Prolegomena to a History of Unwritten Literature," *Osiris* 7 (1939): 290–1.
34 Albright, *From the Stone Age to Christianity*, 184.
35 Ibid., 190.
36 Ibid., 209.
37 F.M. Cornford, *Thucydides Mythistoricus* (London, 1907), 131.
38 Albright, *From the Stone Age to Christianity*, 209.
39 Sir John Edwin Sandys, *A Short History of Classical Scholarship from the Sixth Century BC to the Present Day* (Cambridge, 1915), 294.
40 Albright, *From the Stone Age to Christianity*, 206.
41 Ibid., 221–2. For the emphasis on a written constitution by the priests to limit the authority of the king, see Deuteronomy 17:18–20.
42 Albright, *From the Stone Age to Christianity*, 228.
43 Childe, *What Happened in History*, 167.
44 Albright, *From the Stone Age to Christianity*, 248.
45 Ibid., 277–8.
46 Gandz, "The Dawn of Literature," 274.
47 Ibid., 261.
48 Ibid., 294.
49 Ibid., 306.
50 S.H. Butcher, "The Written and the Spoken Word," *Some Aspects of the Greek Genius* (London, 1891), 167.
51 Ernest Fenollosa, "An Essay on the Chinese Written Character," *Instigations* of Ezra Pound (New York, 1920), 360–1.
52 F.M. Cornford, *From Religion to Philosophy: A Study in the Origins of Western Speculation* (London, 1912), 143. See also Frankfort et al., *The Intellectual Adventure of Ancient Man*, on the significance of Babylonian epics for an understanding of Sumerian society.
53 J.H. Oliver, *The Athenian Expounders of the Sacred and Ancestral Law* (Baltimore, 1950), 67.
54 Ibid., 68.

55 Ibid., 69.
56 Ibid., 70.
57 Ibid., 71.
58 H.L. Lorimer, "Homer and the Art of Writing: A Sketch of Opinion between 1713 and 1939," *American Journal of Archaeology*, 52 (1948): 22.
59 See Albright, *From the Stone Age to Christianity*, 242.
60 Oliver, *The Athenian Expounders of the Sacred and Ancestral Law*, 1–4.
61 Ibid., 17.
62 Ibid., 30.
63 See Kurt Weitzmann, *Illustrations in Roll and Codex: A Study of the Origin and Method of Text Illustration* (Princeton, NJ, 1947), 12–13.
64 Ibid., 14.
65 Ibid., 16. See also F.H. Robinson, "The Tridimensional Problem in Greek Sculpture," *Memoirs of the American Academy in Rome* 7 (1929): 119–68.
66 Cornford, *Thucydides Mythistoricus*, 196.
67 Cassirer, *The Problem of Knowledge*, 47.
68 Frankfort et al., *The Intellectual Adventure of Ancient Man*, 378ff.
69 Cassirer, *The Problem of Knowledge*, 37.
70 Frankfort et al., *The Intellectual Adventure of Ancient Man*, 230.
71 Cornford, "The Invention of Space," 224.
72 Albright, *From the Stone Age to Christianity*, 271–2.
73 Oliver, *The Athenian Expounders of the Sacred and Ancestral Law*, 121. On the effects of the introduction of the phalanx from Greece on Roman political development, see G.W. Botsford, *The Roman Assemblies from Their Origin to the End of the Republic* (New York, 1909), 58–71.
74 Franz Cumont, *The Oriental Religions in Roman Paganism* (Chicago, 1911), 39.
75 Albright, *From the Stone Age to Christianity*, 278–80.
76 Ibid., 272–3. See also E.R. Goodenough, *By Light, Light: The Mystic Gospel of Hellenistic Judaism* (New Haven, Conn., 1935).
77 Albright, *From the Stone Age to Christianity*, 301.
78 Gandz, "The Dawn of Literature," 447.
79 Albright, *From the Stone Age to Christianity*, 296–7.
80 Ibid., 303–4.
81 F.G. Kenyon, *The Text of the Greek Bible* (London, 1949), 245–7.
82 Ibid., 165ff.
83 F.G. Kenyon, *Ancient Books and Modern Discoveries* (Chicago, 1927), 42–3.
84 Ibid., 40.
85 Ibid., 56–9.
86 Weitzmann, *Illustrations in Roll and Codex*, 77–84.

87 Albright, *From the Stone Age to Christianity*, 306. See also L.G. Rylands, *The Beginnings of Gnostic Christianity* (London, 1940), and W.B. Smith, *Ecce Deus: Studies of Primitive Christianity* (Chicago, 1913).
88 See N.H. Baynes, "Constantine the Great and the Christian Church," *Proceedings of the British Academy* 4 (1929): 367.
89 A.H.M. Jones, *Constantine and the Conversion of Europe* (London, 1948), 140–62.
90 Ibid., 237.
91 Ibid., 250.
92 A.A. Vasiliev, *Justin the First: An Introduction to the Epoch of Justinian the Great* (Cambridge, Mass., 1950), 75.
93 Ibid., 321.
94 Ibid., 216.
95 Gandz, "The Dawn of Literature," 485.
96 Ibid., 491.
97 Ibid., 498.
98 Ibid., 512.
99 N.H. Baynes and H.St.L.B. Moss, eds, *Byzantium: An Introduction to East Roman Civilization* (Oxford, 1948), xxv.
100 Ibid., 117.
101 Cited in ibid., 309.
102 Ibid., 310.
103 Vasiliev, *Justin the First*, 78–80.
104 F.M. Stenton, *Anglo-Saxon England* (Oxford, 1943), 170.
105 F.W. Buckler, *Harunu'l-Rashid and Charles the Great* (Cambridge, Mass., 1931), 27.
106 Baynes and Moss, *Byzantium*, 123.
107 See Theodore Haarhoff, *Schools of Gaul: A Study of Pagan and Christian Education in the Last Century of the Western Empire* (Oxford, 1920); also C.E. Stevens, *Sidonius Appollinaris and His Age* (Oxford, 1933).
108 Gandz, "The Dawn of Literature," 353–60.
109 Ibid., 368.
110 H.M. Chadwick, *The Heroic Age* (Cambridge, 1926), 93.
111 Ibid., 347.
112 Ibid., 443.
113 Ibid., 458.
114 Julien Benda, *The Great Betrayal* (London, 1928), 64.
115 Werner Jaeger, *Humanism and Theology* (Milwaukee, Wisc., 1943), 24.
116 See H.M. Chadwick, *The Nationalities of Europe and the Growth of National Ideologies* (Cambridge, 1945), 94–7.
117 Baynes and Moss, *Byzantium*, 32.
118 Etienne Hajnal, "Le rôle social de l'écriture et l'évolution européenne," *Revue de l'Institut de Sociologie*, 1934, 255–9.

119 Ibid., 266.

120 Adolf von Harnack, *Bible Reading in the Early Church*, trans J.R. Wilkinson (New York, 1912), 48–9.

121 Ibid., 85–6.

122 D. Diringer, *The Alphabet, a Key to the History of Mankind* (London, n.d.), 476.

123 Von Harnack, *Bible Reading in the Early Church*, 145–8.

124 Emile Mâle, *L'Art religieux du XIIIe siècle en France* (Paris, 1910), 3.

125 P.H. Lang, *Music in Western Civilization* (New York, 1941), 43.

126 Ibid., 85.

127 H.E. Woolridge, *The Oxford History of Music* (Oxford, 1929), 1: 281.

128 Lang, *Music in Western Civilization*, 162.

129 Hellmuth Lehmann-Haupt, *Peter Schoefler of Gernsheim and Mainz* (Rochester, NY, 1950), 9; also S.H. Steinberg, "Medieval Writing Masters," *The Library*, 4th ser., 22 (1942).

130 M.S. Bunim, *Space in Medieval Painting and the Forerunners of Perspective* (New York, 1940), 105.

131 Ibid., 187–91.

132 Sigfried Giedion, *Space, Time and Architecture: The Growth of a New Tradition* (Cambridge, Mass., 1941), 31.

133 Hans Kohn, *The Twentieth Century: A Mid-Way Account of the Western World* (New York, 1949), 55.

134 Ibid., 47.

135 Cited by Benda, *The Great Betrayal*, 47.

136 Albright, *From the Stone Age to Christianity*, 46.

PART FIVE

The Intellectual as Citizen

CHAPTER TWENTY-EIGHT

The Role of the Social Scientist

The disquieting character of the conclusions of two articles in the first number of the *Canadian Journal of Economics and Political Science* by the heads of the two largest Departments of Political Science and Economics in Canada, and of the point of view of Professor Knight,[1] the author of the first article, warrants further consideration. Alert to the dangers of rushing in where older economists fear to tread and of the prospect of being exposed to the psychoanalyst – who will point to the two articles as representative of age and maturity in a major depression after a world war and to this "further consideration" as representative of youth and immaturity searching for hope where none exists, and as a further effect of the War, the depression, and the winter season – the writer is convinced that more needs to be said even if only by way of a note.

The argument as to the difficulties, if not impossibility, of a social science may be repeated and extended. In elaboration of the impossibility of building a science on a basis on which the observer becomes the observed, it may be suggested that not only is the individual subject to neuroses in terms of age, sex, height, health, family, and personal characteristics generally, but also that these characteristics are played upon by the infinite variety of circumstances of the modern world. A social "scientist," who must be presumed to have made some attempt to allow for the errors of particular biases arising from his institutional surroundings, is continually haunted by the dangers of exaggeration or understatement.

From *Canadian Journal of Political Science* 1 (1935): 280–6; first appeared as "The Role of Intelligence: Some Further Notes."

The social scientist in the university[2] may be regarded as relatively free from major sources of bias, but the dangers are numerous and subtle. At least one university president in Canada has urged that he should be expected to engage in activities outside the university and thereby make up a deficient salary in a long vacation. Important recent work in economics, as suggested by Professor Knight, has centred about the market, and an appreciation of the machinery and operation of the market may be obtained by participation in its activities; this may seem desirable, particularly if the social scientist is paid for obtaining such an appreciation. The most serious dangers arise possibly from the lowering of prestige among his fellow social scientists which accompanies participation in outside activities (offset possibly in the eyes of the social scientist concerned by a rise of prestige in other circles), and from the growing lack of confidence in his conclusions. But whether the social scientist succeeds in advancing the interests of any single enterprise or any group of enterprises by contributing to the solution of any problem, or whether he is employed by such an enterprise or group of enterprises for honorific purposes, his contribution is assumed by those who pay for it to have advanced their interests, probably at the expense of other interests and not necessarily to the advantage of the community as a whole – whatever that may mean. In any case, the social scientist is apt to develop strong vested interests in the prospects of an enterprise or of a group or of a society. He becomes concerned in many cases with the increasing profits and the increasing sale of products irrespective of the wants of the community, and acts largely in a predatory capacity.

Increasing attention by social scientists to the limitations of the price system tends to suggest that there is increasing danger of the social scientist placing his weight on the balance and giving estimates, without making due allowance. A state university is more apt to frown upon such activities than a privately endowed university, but it is apt to encourage activity, which involves similar assistance to the state, partly because this may in turn react favourably through encouraging support by the state to the university, but perhaps largely because of the conviction that assistance to the state implies assistance to the community as a whole. Limitations to the implication are numerous. As has been said, the state is a number of baldheaded men living in offices and most of these men have a strong political, i.e., party, sense. A politician succeeds by detecting and using to his advantage the weaknesses of others, and the others include the social scientist. Social scientists of reputable standing are known as nationalists or imperialists or internationalists or protectionists or free traders. Support to both or all parties to offset the disadvantages of support to any is not necessarily effective and involves considerable agility on the part of the social scientist concerned.

Assistance to ecclesiastical organizations is perhaps the most dangerous, not, as will be argued, because the remuneration is negligible, but because it appeals to the ecclesiastical bias of the university and of the social scientists. Large numbers of social scientists have been interested in ecclesiastical if not political organizations and have become social scientists because of their belief in the possibility of achieving their objectives more effectively. Objectives are more dangerous than politicians and it is fatal to attempt a study of society with definite views as to the direction society should take. The control or planning bias arises in part directly from this background.

A further danger to social science has arisen from foundations to subsidize research, because of the statement of objectives and of the extent of the subsidies. Social scientists with a bias toward a living, accentuated because of possible inefficiency and inability to obtain a living in more exacting employments, are attracted to the prospects of remuneration from foundations with standards of research adaptable to the achievement of an objective.

Institutions act as channels through which civilization bears with persistent corroding effects on the position of the social scientist. The enormity of the task of withstanding the effects of corrosion, and of interpreting the complexity of social phenomena, has led to the emergence of schools of thought in which definite advance is made by an individual, to be followed by the work of others in merging the conclusions of separate schools or in testing the validity of assumptions and rounding out the details of schemes of thought. The mental limitations of social scientists and the pervasiveness of a pecuniary economy lead to the writing of texts which simplify the conclusions of schools, and to the creation of vested interests on the part of publishing houses, of departments, and of professorial chairs. The importance of vested interests and of rigidities in thought in the social sciences weakens the position of the social scientist in relation to impacts of cultural importance. For example, the current belief in progress reinforces the importance of *change* in the thinking in the social sciences. New departments and new countries as well as old departments and old countries capitalize the possibilities of new developments in the social sciences. Vested interests are implied in the resistance to *change* and the demand for *change*. The adjustment of social science to current demands has been facilitated by improved methods of communication, such as the radio, which strengthen the influence of lower levels of intelligence. An attempt to escape the difficulties by resort to history has led to the simplification of thinking in the social sciences in terms of the Marxian analysis and the class struggle.

With these difficulties increased by a depression following a great war, with the end of an era of rapid expansion, and with human misery on every hand, there is the temptation, with perhaps some justification, to cut the Gordian knot by resort to immediate action. The temptation and the activity are indications of the inadequacy of social thought which accompanies depreciation of cultural support following periods of strain. According to Professor Leacock's paper, classical economics is valuable as a discipline of the classroom and we must "faire faire," – make things happen. One prominent economist in a recent book has suggested the task of undoing things which have been done and of energetically setting out to do nothing. The emergence of this school from the circumstances of the present depression coincides with the demands of democracy as reflected in the appeals of the politician. It is in part a form of whistling in the dark to keep up one's courage, and is closely related to the school of thought which insists that something is going to happen, or else. ... Its effectiveness is shown in the determined efforts of modern governments to stop leaks and to repair damages as they occur, and has a close parallel in the fable of the fly on the chariot wheel which was surprised at the dust it was raising.

Ceaseless wrestling with the beasts of Ephesus tends to leave the social scientist intellectually exhausted. The task of attempting to become a social scientist may be regarded as beyond human endurance. He may take comfort in the argument that thought in the social sciences grows by the development and correction of bias. On the other hand, he will receive small thanks and possibly much contempt and persecution for attempting to tear the mask from innumerable biases which surround him. It is not in the best taste to bare one's views, certainly in a Scottish protestant community, which prefers the weak and "sound" to the strong, or to criticize one's elders or one's ancestors. The first duty of the social scientist is to avoid martyrdom. As a tribute to that duty the writer hereby brings to an end a list of biases which can be illustrated, or extended, or interpreted to illustrate the bias of the writer to the reader's content.

The innumerable difficulties of the social scientist are paradoxically his only salvation. Since the social scientist cannot be "scientific" or "objective" because of the contradiction in terms, he can learn of his numerous limitations. The "sediment of experience" provides the basis for scientific investigation. The never-ending shell of life suggested in the persistent character of bias provides possibilities of intensive study of the limitations of life and its probable direction. "Introspection" is a contradiction, but what is meant by the word is the foremost limit of scientific investigation in a range extending back to geological time. The difficulty if not impossibility of predicting one's own course of action is decreased in predicting the course of action of others, as anyone knows who has been forced to live in close relations with one other person over a considerable period of time. The exasperating accuracy with which such prediction is possible has been the cause of more than one murder in northern Canada and the dissolution of numerous partnerships. The habits or biases of individuals which permit prediction are reinforced in the cumulative bias of institutions and constitute the chief interest of the social scientist.

The economist as suggested in Professor Urwick's paper has possibly been fortunate in having at his command measurable data arising from the activities of the market, but he has undoubtedly lost much through his failure to attempt a study of factors underlying the market and to resist the fatal attraction of analogies with the physical sciences and particularly with the possibilities of mathematics. The spread of industrialism and of the price system has stressed physics and chemistry and mathematics and the development of these subjects has had its effect on biology in the emergence of such fields as biological chemistry and biometrics. The price system has presented material admirably adapted to the *penchant* for mathematics with the result that enormous numbers of studies in mathematical tabulations and small numbers of advanced mathematical arguments have been published; the possibilities of proliferation are endless. "Scientificismus" in the social sciences has been in part a result of the extensive development of statistical elaboration. The overhead costs of plant and equipment in terms of calculating machines have given a drive in the same direction. Moreover, the limitations of language, illustrated in the problem of Marshall, who attempted to write for businessmen but who has been understood with great difficulty by social scientists, have contributed to the introduction of mathematics. This is not to deny the importance of studies of price phenomena or of statistics but to emphasize their limitations and inadequacies and their position as an introduction to social science. They are comparable in contributions to social science to studies of the palaeontologist or the archaeologist or the anthropologist or the geographer. Price phenomena are only a part of the "sediment of experience" and throw light on its character similar to that of the study of architecture, literature, or other evidences of cultural activity. Incidentally, the significance of a classical training to the social scientist should rest in the breadth of the approach and its emphasis on the range of human activity, but unfortunately, like the social sciences, it tends to concentrate on aspects which appeal to individual interests and to be even more barren.

The fundamental limitations outlined by Professor Urwick involve the salvation and the despair of the social sciences. Habits and institutions, even stupidity, are the assets of the social scientist. Relative capacities of social scientists for observing, in contrast to being observed, extend his range. Institutions such as professional associations, office hours, and a reputation for curtness may serve as defences in improving the position of the observer, but like all the paraphernalia and equipment of modern scholarship they have their advantages and limitations. The significance of discussion has been emphasized, but organized discussion is a contradiction in terms and other types of discussion involve the dominance of a relatively small number or the outbreak of violence, such as is implied in signs which hang in dining halls of lumber camps, "No talking during meals." Nor are treatises on the art of thinking particularly illuminating except as indices of the shallow thinking of the authors.

The decline of intelligent discussion has been indicated in its persecution on the part of interests which profit most from freedom of discussion. The news value of intelligent discussion has practically led to its suppression or to its restriction to circumstances in which the press is not admitted. A fundamental difficulty even under favourable conditions continues in the complexity of the social sciences. Discussion through debates which imply oratory and chicane practically excludes contributions to the solution of problems of the social sciences. Conferences arranged for discussion in the social sciences, and not including the large majority arranged definitely for the prostitution of social science to an avowed objective, are faced with innumerable and obvious handicaps. The emphasis has been to an increasing extent on publication as a medium of discussion – the *Canadian Journal of Economics and Political Science* being a case in point.

Intelligence in the social process is, therefore, seriously confined in its attempts to predict general trends, but in so far as the "sediment of experience" becomes deeper its task becomes at once easier and more difficult. Its range may be narrowed and its data may be increased. Intelligence in the social sciences tends to be absorbed in the abstruse and abstract tasks of adjustment and to be lost in specialization, with the result that it is unable to participate in the endless and complex and possibly fruitless search for trends. The elements of the curricula of the social sciences conflict, in emphasis on the "scientific" aspect, and in attempts to meet the demands of social organization (especially economic) for trained workers. The technician may be engaged in loosening or remoulding the clutches of outworn institutions or even in tightening and repairing the breaches. The chances of the existence of surplus energy to be directed to the extremely complex task of determining trends of development are slight. The possibility that a discovery of trends may involve a change in the direction of institutional growth is slight since at best intelligence will be slow in detecting the prevailing drift and will tend to reflect rather than to predict.

The periods and regions with sufficient stability to support freedom of inquiry in the social sciences have been short and small and surrounded with hazards, but death is persistent and the removal of dictators inevitable. The elusiveness of life involves change. Contributions to an understanding of social trends have been made from a great number of approaches. Illustrations of contributions which have been significant include the studies on technology as outlined by Marx and elaborated by Sombart, Veblen, and others; on metropolitan growth as described by Gras; on economic theory by Adam Smith; on overhead costs by Clark; on geographic influences by Vidal de la Blache. These indicate determining factors in the drift of social development. They have involved intensive study on the dead shells of human life but have indicated in an extremely rough way the general background to the development of modern life; to mention them is to indicate the extent of the gaps which remain before even that which is possible has been mastered. Neglect of these contributions is an indication of a decline in the role of intelligence in the social process.

A NOTE ON UNIVERSITIES AND THE SOCIAL SCIENCES*

The university may be regarded as at least an active centre in strengthening the position of the natural and social sciences, but limitations to its possible assistance are numerous. The social scientist is concerned with departmental

* From *Canadian Journal of Political Science* 1 (1935), 286–7; first appeared as an appendix to the preceding article.

routine: discussion with colleagues and students on subjects which imply salary, promotion, popularity, and things other than the search for truth. The presence of "leaders," of "strong" men, and of the frictions which accompany them (*odium academicum*) is sufficient evidence of the pervasiveness of intellectual handicaps. The natural sciences, on the other hand, impose few restrictions on the "scientist" other than the discipline which may be acquired in the laboratory, and consequently permit him to indulge in all the biases from which the social scientist is barred. (It may be argued that the prevalence of these biases at close range should provide the social scientist with an excellent laboratory but it is seldom regarded as such.) The inhibitions of the social scientist tend to weaken his position in the university in the prevailing competition for staff and equipment, but these dangers may be offset by alertness on the part of the governing authorities. Equipment and buildings are tangible indications of "scientific" work and of the importance of more equipment and buildings, whereas a social scientist is just another social scientist. The appearance of solidity and certainty and the possibilities of display attract the interest of the supporting public and actually encourage the "scientist" to advance from statements in his own field, about which he may have private doubts, to statements of certainty in the field of the social scientists, about which he has no doubts. This situation has been met in part during the depression by demands for pronouncements from social scientists, and the latter, encouraged by university authorities, have responded to the warmth of popular acclaim with statements of certainty about which privately they must entertain grave doubts. The social sciences tend to become the opiate of the people. Statements of certainty made by social scientists, without encouragement from university authorities, have raised the problem of academic freedom. In the main the statements have done little more than reveal the poverty of the social sciences, but university authorities have been concerned unfortunately with other grounds. Whereas they have been absorbed with questions of freedom of expression, the fundamental problem is that of standards in the social sciences. Discussions of academic freedom in Canada on the part of the university authorities and the staff are little more than indications of the irritableness which accompanies a high wind.

The cultural background of the university is of fundamental importance. The war and the post-war periods have involved serious disturbances in Russia, Italy, and Germany and far-reaching changes in Great Britain, France, the United States, and other countries. Periods of profound disturbance create difficulties. The character of phenomena with which the social sciences purport to deal becomes more refractory and the mental distress of the observer greater. (This article is, of course, a product of such a background.) The university can protect the social scientists in part. Even in countries which have witnessed the most serious disturbances, apparently work in the social sciences can continue without serious interruption, chiefly because the complexity of the subject renders conclusions of little value to those in control of policy, and terminology becomes a defence against the inquisitive. Moreover, universities with centuries of tradition serve as a defence. In countries in which traditions are less conspicuous, in which an old generation of university presidents is being replaced by energetic young men guaranteed to do things, and where the development of the social sciences is so weak that conclusions are understood by those in control of policy, difficulties become serious even though the cultural background has been less seriously disturbed. The defence of the social scientist, a defence which is important in communities without sufficient mental acumen to perceive its weakness, follows the fallacy of the *argumentum ad hominem.* Because conclusions are reached by scholars in universities with long-established traditions, they are held to be valid and applicable universally. The more subtle of the social scientists will proceed by careful study to discover the weak points in the intellectual armour of the community and to utilize the conclusions with effect, and consequently they say that because Great Britain has a certain type of machinery therefore Canada should have it, that capitalism is a good thing, that we should produce for use and not for profit, and that we should read our Bibles. There are apparently advantages and profits to be gained by advocating any one or more of these "remedies," including production for use and not for profit. The natural scientist, of course, cannot be criticized as he has not had a training intended to make him aware of the fallacies of his statements. It would be cruel to single out special illustrations, and mention of controversies over Genesis and evolution, over pronouncements of geologists and physicists on immortality and on the existence of a Divine Being, and of the prevalence of reference to science in Canada or in the Empire, must suffice. The problem of the social scientist is the problem of the university.

NOTES

1 See F.H. Knight, "Social Science and the Political Trend," *University of Toronto Quarterly,* July 1934, 407–27.

2 See a note on universities and the social sciences, at the end of this essay.

CHAPTER TWENTY-NINE

The Passing of Political Economy

In 1937 there was published by Prof. W.R. Scott, Adam Smith Professor of Political Economy in the University of Glasgow, a volume called *Adam Smith as Student and Professor* dedicated "to my colleagues in the court and senate of the University of Glasgow on the two hundredth anniversary of Adam Smith's matriculation there." Singularly in a request to write an article for the *Commerce Journal* it was suggested that I should write not on that event but rather on some practical matter such as the Royal Commission on Dominion Provincial relations which would be of interest to businessmen as readers or as advertisers. The coincidence in the appearance of the volume and the request is a sign of the passing of political economy.

It is not necessary to say that the volume is a model of scholarship and erudition and adds immensely to our knowledge of the life of Adam Smith to 1763 when he gave up his professorship to become tutor to the Duke of Buccleuch. Chapters are included on his boyhood (1723–1737), on his student days at Glasgow and Balliol College, Oxford (1737–1746), on his lectures at Edinburgh (1748–1751), and on his professorship at the University of Glasgow (1751–1764). A final chapter traces the evolution of his thought at Glasgow and demonstrates conclusively the independent origin of *The Wealth of Nations.* In the appendices are included an early draft of part of *The Wealth of Nations* (1763) discovered recently in the papers of the Duke of Buccleuch, a wealth of material on his academic career at the University of Glasgow, and numerous letters "from, to, or relating to Adam Smith."

From *Commerce Journal,* 1938, 3–6.

We have had nearly the last word on the background of *The Wealth of Nations.* The work of Prof. Scott, Edwin Cannan, and John Rae trace clearly the emergence of the Mount Everest of political economy. These students have thrown light not only on Adam Smith but also on the range of peaks which surrounded and supported him. In Scotland there was his very close friend David Hume, in England Gibbons and Johnson, and in France Turgot and Quesnay. This epoch in thought was accompanied by major political events, in the breaking away of the American colonies, and the French revolution. Professor Scott has traced the breaking of the mercantilist crust in Scotland by reference to the life and times of Adam Smith senior and the importance of the union of England and Scotland in 1707. Scotland was admitted to the advantages of the English colonial system which expanded rapidly after the Treaty of Utrecht in 1713 and the Treaty of Paris in 1763. *The Wealth of Nations* was written during the years of major expansion of the Empire from 1763 to the beginning of the decline in 1776. No one can read it and the commentaries without appreciating the significance of increased trade to Scotland and particularly to Glasgow. With union had come also a break in Scottish institutions which Hume and Adam Smith were quick to note had been deterrents to, rather than supports of, economic growth. Adam Smith witnessed the attempts of the Church of Scotland to ex-communicate Hume. *The Wealth of Nations* was "an inquiry in to the nature and causes" of a broad cultural character.

Adam Smith had the advantages of the cultural life of Scotland, at Glasgow and Edinburgh, during a period in which economic activity had witnessed marked expansion with the extension of free trade in an expanding colonial system. He stood at a focal point of cultural adjustment in Scotland after the union. The intellectual life of the University of Glasgow reflected the change in the introduction of lectures delivered in English rather than in Latin. The consequent stimulus to thought in philosophy and theology was in striking contrast to the intellectual impotence of Oxford described by Adam Smith. Life in the two universities at a crucial age left no doubts as to the advantages of the one and the disadvantages of the other. His training as a student provided the advantages of the classics and of current trends in philosophy. He saw the contrasts between the civilizations of Greece and Rome and of Scotland and England. His lectures at Edinburgh were in English literature and he thought of *The Wealth of Nations* as a work in letters rather than in economics. As a professor of logic and moral philosophy at Glasgow he published his *Theory of Moral Sentiments* in 1759 and then began *The Wealth of Nations.* Completion of the latter required ample leisure and freedom to travel. His acceptance of the tutorship to the Duke of Buccleuch and his resignation as professor at the University of Glasgow were followed by a visit to France from February 1764 to October 1766. On this extensive visit to the continent he was struck with the contrasts between the institutions of France, England, and Scotland. After his return he worked on *The Wealth of Nations* chiefly in Scotland and it was published in 1776.

If his broad training, his acute observation, his life amid striking contrasts, his activity at the University of Glasgow, his opportunities as a student in Great and Britain and France, and his leisure at Kirkaldy were responsible for *The Wealth of Nations*, what can be said of the mist which hovers over the whole mountain range and obscures it from commerce students, or of the lack of interest in the highest peak and even in the foothills which stand in the foreground in the nineteenth and twentieth centuries with single peaks by the names of Bentham, Malthus, Ricardo, Senior, Mill, Jevons, and Marshall?[1] In the nineteenth century philosophy and theology became less conspicuous and biology more important. Economists were concerned with the details of realignment in the political structure ending in reciprocity with the United States and the Cobden treaty. The school to which laissez-faire was attributed included its most active governmental interventionists. Darwin and Huxley extended the contributions of Malthus on population to animal and plant life. Public interest shifted to the struggle over evolution. The social scientist, notably the economist, retreated from the public gaze and became concerned with mathematics. Adam Smith could write "I have no great faith in political arithmetic"; Marshall began as a philosopher and at the University of Cambridge, with its background of the natural sciences and mathematics, built up with great care a mathematical frame-work, but advised that the mathematics should be burned after the argument had been written down; the young economists of the post-war period are unable to go beyond the minutiae of the mathematical foundations; and those who fail to understand mathematics become institutionalists.

The end of the nineteenth century and the twentieth century were marked by the extension of industrialism dependent on minerals, new sources of power, physics and chemistry and mathematics. These have led to the decline in freedom of trade and the hardening of political entities in the intensity of nationalism. With these has come the end of political economy, the emergence of specialization in the social sciences, and its subordination to nationalism. The political scientist has emerged with an interest in government, federal, unitary and municipal, or in fascism, communism, democracy; the economist in occultism, or in practical affairs, public and private finance, money and banking, national, international, general and particular; transportation in general and particular; labour; and so on in the social sciences ad infinitum. New dogmas emerge to replace philosophy and theology. They carry conviction, and social scientists are in great demand at the prevailing rates among business firms, including publishers, governments, and political parties. The prevailing rates vary widely depending on the age and prestige of the branch of the social science. Political scientists have the advantage of relationship to the legal profession and probably command the highest returns. Economists can be had at appreciably lower rates, partly as a result of the larger supply, their lack of prestige in new countries, and the inability to attach themselves to established professions. Representing a later stage of development, they have been slower to command high fees. In those large feasts in which established professions participate, he is still confined, with the exception of a few forays, below the salt. Of some, Adam Smith's words would still apply "It is with them as the hussars and light infantry of some armies, no plunder, no pay." Others scorn cash, and take promissory notes on the revolution, or take both notes and cash; and still others, having found truth, have their own reward. But the sociologist does not despair. The creation of dogmas is a matter of time. The decline of philosophy and theology has brought demands for new temples and for new prophets. Churches have sensed the change and the social sciences have occupied an increasingly important place in their programs. The church has ceased to produce good heretics. It insists on losing its life and having it too. The accountant has penetrated the holy of holies and amalgamations have been in order in this as in secular organizations. Economics have displaced creeds. It may be said of the social scientist as Housman wrote in the "Epitaph on an Army of Mercenaries":

These, in the day when heaven was falling
The hour when earth's foundations fled,
Followed their mercenary calling
And took their wages and are dead;

Their shoulders held the sky suspended;
They stood and earth's foundations stay;
What God abandoned, they defended,
And saved the sum of things for pay.

It has been argued that the disappearance of political economy is an illusion and that it will emerge from behind the clouds. But the circumstances are not propitious for another great epoch of thought. The rise of literacy and improved communication promoted the rapid growth of groups, associations, and nations and reduced social scientists to a position as defenders with the zeal of proselytes of this and that particular cause. Under the influence of modern industrialism in the printing press and cheap paper, universities have become increasingly specialized, and increasing demands for space in the curriculum have enhanced the activity of administration and promoted the growth of vested interests. The leisure essential to intensive and sustained thought has been lost to the productivity of erudition at the expense of the essential broad philosophical approach. The breadth of reading of Adam Smith and of Marshall is evident on every page, but the latter required three large volumes to round out his system while Adam Smith had one. The amazing range of Spengler could only end with a volume called *Decline of the West*, and of Toynbee with periodic batches of three large volumes. We are faced with dilemma of the *Encyclopaedia Britannica* and Wells' *Outline of History*. The conditions which produced *The Wealth of Nations* do not appear in the foreground but nationalism has made them ripe for a Royal Commission on Dominion Provincial Finance.

NOTES

1 Perhaps Marshall should be thought of as part of a European plateau including Durkheim, Pareto, and Weber. See Talcott Parsons *The Structure of Social Action* (New York, 1937).

CHAPTER THIRTY

The "Common Man" and Internationalism: Myths in the Social Sciences

Failure to persist in the difficult task of attempting to understand the significance of the position of the "common man" has led the social scientist into strange paths. Internationalism has been a favourite fetish and has provided a theme for a large part of our oratorical and economic literature as a reference to world markets for wheat, fish, lumber, pulp and paper, and minerals will suggest. The League of Nations, the British Empire, Canadian-American relations are variants. There has been much said about the great role Canadians play in these matters. Toasts to a hundred years of peace, 3,000 miles of unprotected boundary line, the great North American experiment, our position as interpreter between the United States and England, and our part in Pacific affairs have been enthusiastically cheered. But the Prime Minister of England purchases a ticket direct to New York and we have 3,000 miles of respectable tariff walls manned by customs officials and immigration agents. American advertising is cherished for its effects on the newsprint industry and American tourists are welcomed for their benign influence in the balance of payments. Regionalism is a corollary of internationalism. Regions engaged in the production of raw materials for export are internationalist in outlook and the strength of internationalism is a rough indication of the strength of regionalism. Regionalism raises an unsightly head in the position of the provinces under the British North America Act and provides definite legal restrictions against a united Canada. Occasionally the regions most seriously affected by depressions talk in terms of secession. The effects have been evident in a great tangled mass of legislation involving railways, railway rates and hotels, ports, bonuses, the tariff, natural resources, labour, legislation, and other evidences of poli-

From *Commerce Journal*, 1936, 28–30.

tical pork barrels. In spite of its unfortunate effects regional pressure has been the only weapon available by which regions have been able to obtain a reasonable distribution of the burdens of Canadian nationalism.

The effect of the influence of these myths has been evident in the social sciences. Certain tribes never regard their own medicine man as having as much power as the medicine man of neighbouring tribes and in cases of severe illness prefer to call in two medicine men from such tribes, and in case of failure in such an event to refer wistfully to the extraordinary powers of a very distant medicine man whom they have never seen. In the case of extreme difficulty such as that which concerned the railways medicine men were brought in as commissioners from both Great Britain and the United States. In the case of the banks an extremely powerful medicine man was chosen and it is said carried great influence with all concerned. Difficulties in the grain trade were also overcome by a powerful economist. Medicine men from Great Britain tend to be regarded as more potent. Titles, the world's greatest travel system and its need for passengers and settlers, the demands of the increasingly large number of second rate medicine men for a hearing, and the ease with which it can be had, the vested interests of American branch factories in the Canadian tariff, and imperial markets are factors tending in this direction.

In the past a medicine man from abroad has been regarded as worth about six of the local product. But the depression has shown that we have an innate strength which has been largely neglected and the growth of nationalism as contrasted with internationalism and regionalism has brought forth a substantial crop. The great source has been the law but ancient history, history, the classics, physics, the sciences and the arts, and even economics have all made their contributions and I am told do very effective work – as why should they not. Our fellow citizens the Eskimo, it is said, often succeed in bringing back the caribou after a long period of starvation through the efforts of their medicine men, and the pronouncements of their more "educated" brethren are entitled to the same regard in curing the depression. Indeed they are entitled to a higher regard as they will gladly share their secrets if you have time to listen to them or you can buy them at a very moderate price.

We have had much of the exorcising of spirits during the present depression to refer only to what a colleague of mine has described as the extensive witch hunting of the royal commission on price spreads. I should like to refer personally, however, in a final word to the exorcising which has been conspicuous in youth movements particularly as to war and peace. The weakening control of age and the loss of a generation have been evident in the emergence of dictatorship in Germany and Italy strongly supported by the blind enthusiasm of youth. In a young country without a strong cultural background the dangers become more serious and it is doubtful whether as an individual I should be allowed to make any comment on the problems of war and peace because of the bias which arises from participation in the last war and the feelings which are stirred up annually by celebrations of the Armistice and by the misery of the depression. On the other hand it may be urged that fifteen years is ample time to permit of a sober analysis even by participants, and that to await a longer period would court the confusion which arises from the babblings of senility and the increasing lapses of academic memories. But the time is short, and it has not been long since most of us have been wakened by nightmares of intense shell-fire and even now the military bands played with such enthusiasm by young men are intolerable, and Armistice day celebrations are emotionally impossible.

But there is no reason to believe, speaking from an experience covering over a decade with students in this department that your generation is more brilliant than mine and realizing my own limitations and the loss of those who might have been your guides there is some reason for believing that you are less adequately equipped. It is doubtful, therefore, whether the response of your generation would differ from the response of mine in case of another war. The increasing power of the state and its conquest of the press, the church and the university, and of the tremendously improved system of communication, for example the radio, which have characterized the war and the post-war periods perhaps weighs more heavily against you than it did against us. You have been warned by the fate of your predecessors through every conceivable avenue and you have recognized the warnings in resolutions stating your refusal to serve the state but you have not seen the effects of mobilized propaganda. The bugle and drum count for more than your resolutions. To quote Houseman's *Shropshire Lad*, written on the occasion of the Queen's Jubilee in 1887.

Oh, God will save her, fear you not:
  Be you the men you've been,
Get you the sons your fathers got,
  And God will save the Queen.

Evil spirits are not exorcised by an appeal to other spirits. They die only with the scepticism which follows a persistent attempt to understand the problems of modern society.

CHAPTER THIRTY-ONE

The Intellectual in History

For a brief period I shall attempt to appear before you as an economist bewildered by the extent and range of discussion which deals in a final form with the problems of a subject in which he is particularly interested. It may seem strange that an economist should appear before you to admit that he does not see the answer to these problems, and I shall plead in extenuation that I am addressing a university audience interested in the pursuit of truth and in certain standards of intellectual integrity and honesty. This may be a bold assumption. But even universities, staff and students, have been known to advance solutions to world problems with conviction and sincerity and apparent logic.

University authorities have been particularly insistent in these days of Fascists, Communists, and the like that at least one certain cure of our ills may be said to rest with *freedom of discussion.* Heroic and mock battles have been fought in defence of freedom of speech and freedom of the press. It is the purpose of this paper to suggest that perhaps this assumption may be questioned. It is perhaps a comment on the character of present freedom of discussion that I should not care to discuss discussion to an audience of the younger university presidents, or to an audience insistent upon making constant speeches about the sanctity of freedom of speech. We should be free to discuss everything except discussion. I insist upon discussing even that. I propose to lay unholy hands on this white heifer of the sacred kine of liberalism.

A paper read before a meeting of the summer session of the University of British Columbia, 1935, and intended as complementary to "The Role of Intelligence," *Canadian Journal of Economics and Political Science,* May 1935, 280–7; printed in the *Dalhousie Review* 15 (Jan. 1936): 401–13, where it appeared as "Discussion in the Social Sciences."

As an economist, I am constantly faced with the extraordinary difficulty and complexity of the social sciences, and constantly forced to admit defeat. If an economist becomes certain of the solution of any problem, he can be equally certain that his solution is wrong. This is not to say that we cannot look back upon commendable achievements in the history of economic thought – beginning with Adam Smith and running through the classical economists Malthus, Ricardo, Mill, Marx, and Marshall, or with economic historians in Great Britain and the Anglo-Saxon world and in Europe. To acquire a knowledge of the writings of the masters of economic thought involves years of patient effort and study. The work continues, as a review of leading economic publications will indicate. Even in Canada, where our energies have been absorbed in the exploitation of virgin resources, the names of Shortt and Mavor may be mentioned, and with these, of living writers engaged in research over a wide field. The appearance of the *Canadian Journal of Political Science and Economics* is an indication of a widespread interest. With an appreciation of the work which has been done and of the work which remains to be done, what is one to say about the innumerable solutions propounded in this age of discussion?

Not only have there been important advances in economic thought, but in all countries, and particularly since the war and the depression, there have been advances in economic control and increasing efficiency of control. In Ottawa we have seen legislation rounding out a mechanism of control in the Central Bank, and a host of other devices. We have witnessed the appointment and activity of thoroughly trained and competent civil servants who played a predominant *role* in the framing and administering of legislation. It is probable that no federal administration has ever been manned by an abler group of civil servants. In the provinces we have seen the extension of control, and on the whole an improvement of the civil service. In spite of developments in the social sciences, and of increasing efficiency of application of scientific knowledge to modern problems, we have witnessed and are about to witness an outburst of discussion on incompetence such as has been seldom seen. The brutality and cruelty which we have already witnessed are a prelude of things to come. We may well ask as to the *role* of discussion in a complex society whose problems can be attacked only by patient continuous labour. We are faced with the problems of democracy. We are forced to recognize the increasingly difficult and complex character of social problems, and the necessity of applying the ablest intelligence to the solution of those problems. It has been said that phrenology was a substantial force in the spread of democracy in the nineteenth century, and it is apparent that tests of intelligence may play a similar *rôle* in the solution of the problems of the twentieth century. The phrenologist disregarded class and insisted on ability in relation to bumps, and the modern psychologist has advanced his claims along other lines.

But while our problems have become more complex, and the necessity of technical discussion chiefly in restricted conversations and in publications of limited circulation has become more acute, the possibilities of discussion have increased immeasurably. The character of discussion, like other forms of entertainment, has been tremendously influenced by recent industrialism and inventions. In the nineteenth century, with the development of the printing press, economic expansion, and the growth of literacy, discussion from the standpoint of the press was concerned with an attack on abuses which concerned those capable of reading or those capable of subscribing to the papers. It paid in the newspaper business to attack abuses, or to conjure up abuses and attack them. The reforms of Great Britain and the struggles for responsible government in the Dominion coincided with the emergence of the industrial press. William Lyon Mackenzie, Francis Hincks, and George Brown in Upper Canada, Joseph Howe in Nova Scotia and his disciple Amor de Cosmos in British Columbia, Buckingham and Coldwell in Manitoba, Frank Oliver in Alberta, and Eugene Allen in the Klondike were in the newspaper business, attacked abuses vigorously, and found it was a paying proposition. The struggle for cheaper rates on newspapers and a free press and for public education and public schools may have been a struggle for democracy, but incidentally it was a struggle for bonuses to literacy and indirectly to newspapers. No other industry has been so lavishly supported from public funds.

Newspapermen of the generation just passing never weary of commenting on the changes which have taken place within the industry in their time. News collection has been tremendously improved as a result of the telegraph and its successors, the telephone and wireless; distribution has been widened with improved transportation facilities; the press has been expanded in size and improved in accuracy and speed, and the raw material has been increased almost inconceivably by the shift from rags to wood. The pulp and paper industry is a fundamental development. With these epoch-making changes, the business of newspapers has changed as well. Circulation has become even more important with the increase in size and efficiency of the newspaper plant. The spread of literacy has provided a market. Moreover, the growth of urban centres and the complexity of marketing and distribution have accentuated the necessity for wider circulation. Advertising has become a basic source of revenues.

The contrast between literacy and intelligence implies a shift of emphasis from an attack on abuses to devices which will attract the interest of the largest possible number of readers. Constant emphasis on wars, watering down of editorials, the disappearance of editors and the emergence of owners, the tabloid, the chain newspaper, the comic strips, and the private lives of great men, are designed to increase and maintain circulation. Politics have dwindled to a position in which circulation is of first importance. The free press has proceeded to the point where freedom of expression has become important as news interest. Defence of freedom of speech has become an attractive means of attracting public attention. We are scarcely covering unfamiliar ground in all this. Recent improvements in facilities for discussion, particularly the radio, have tended to displace the newspaper, and it may be urged that improvements will overcome the difficulties. Unfortunately there is slight evidence to this effect, and much evidence to the contrary. Even government regulation and government ownership have failed to improve materially or to check the character of the discussion which dominates the air. Whether under government control or under private control, the appeal is to the largest number of possible listeners, and there are even more listeners than readers, or more people capable of listening than reading. The radio, like the newspaper, is concerned with marketing and distribution, and its discussion is probably on a lower level than that of newspapers. Fortunately one does not need to listen to lectures from the university on the radio, or to inter-university debates! A radio can be turned off, and there is always another program.

In Canada the difficulties are enhanced by the persistent trends toward centralization. Densely populated industrial areas in central Canada tend to dominate control over news and editorial policy in outlying regions. Magazines and periodicals and the high costs of publication in competition with American products necessitate centralization of production. Local expression is confined to letters written to the editor, or to letters written by the editor to himself. It is scarcely necessary to describe the results in either case.

Let us turn from these alternatives to the great centres of intelligent discussion in our numerous houses of parliament. Again there is the necessity on the part of members and parties of keeping in touch with the largest number of voters, which includes those who cannot read, see, or hear, and the results scarcely need elaborating. It would be unfair to single out the reports of parliamentary activities which appear in the press, as we know what to expect. But those of you who are particularly intelligent for political purposes, and who receive gratis copies of speeches by your local member or by your party leader, will be aware, or I hope you will be aware, of the sort of thing that passes for intelligent discussion. To read is to run. To make it worse, they all claim to be sincere. Would that we could call back the days of insincere politicians. To escape to the more serious aspects of discussion in our parliaments, if you have ever had occasion to read the enormous volumes of evidence collected by various select committees, as many of us unfortunately have been compelled to do, you will realize how much intelligence has been kept out of parliament and how little gets in. The valuable portions of the evidence are submitted in memoranda by experts called in from outside. Nor does a Royal Commission improve matters, and render parliamentary committees more valuable. A recent well known report of a Royal Commission may be cited as a case in point, and I am told on excellent authority that we should have seen it before it was shaped by the experts who were called in to do the work. The effective work of Royal Commissions has been done in the main by men from outside parliament and the ability evident even in their reports is not conspicuous.

Finally, we turn to the real source of intelligent discussion – that carried on by the "intellectual" – the most tragi-comic group in the history of discussion. In the main the intellectual has failed to realize the significance of the change which has so profoundly influenced discussion. He remains as a vestige of an era of discussion which has passed. He is valued by universities as a means of displaying to the public their continued belief in academic freedom – the steeplejack who dances about on the upper structures of the framework to demonstrate its soundness. No self-respecting university can afford to be without at least one. Discussions of academic freedom centre about inefficiencies in the social scientists, and academic freedom has become the great shelter of incompetence. The intellectual writes informatively for a respectable group of people who still believe they discuss the complex problems of society intelligently, and is employed by the paper accordingly, or failing the paper where his efforts are narrowed perhaps to a small column imprisoned as a memorial to freedom of the press, he writes for subsidized journals dedicated to the maintenance of the belief in the importance of freedom of discussion. Political parties find use for him, particularly new parties anxious to seize upon the intellectual limitations and sympathies of any group, and not cognizant of his limited value or even of his character as a liability. Intellectuals in large numbers will sink the raft of any party, and if allowed to write a program will kill it. In many cases a keen observer, the intellectual has the satisfaction of predicting the course of events with accuracy, and in his old age he begins to point to his influence on the course of events. The Fabians in England have been notorious examples of individuals who claim to have moulded the course of history. Mr Wells, like Roo in the expedition to the North Pole described by A.A. Milne, has fallen in the water, and drifting with the current, constantly shouts to those on shore "Look at me swimming." The intellectual's profound belief in his influence, his delight in believing that he lives dangerously, his pleasure at spinning ideologies, at amazing people with his knowledge, particularly of Aristotle and Plato, and at frightening them with bugaboos about the revolution and the breakup of capitalist society, are his consolations. Let us not disturb him.

It is only fair to add that we owe most to the intellectual for artistic discussion. Literature is perhaps the chief beneficiary. Conferences, subsidized and other sorts, for the discussion of problems of the social sciences would become intolerable with the platitudinous comments of important elderly men of affairs who grace them, and without the entertainment provided by a trained group of intellectuals designed to stimulate those anxious to think they are making important contributions to a solution of the world's problems and to amuse those who know better. The social sciences provide both the opiates and the stimulants to what passes for modern thought. The travelling comedians who masquerade as economists and prophets have fortunately done much to displace the meaningless outbursts of eloquence which delighted our fathers by at least a form of entertainment more suited to the taste of the present generation. We cannot complain of lack of variety. We are given alternately monologues on the gold standard, debates on the British North America Act, dramatics on the capitalist system and production for use and not for profit, and symphonies on social credit.

All this is not to question the change and character of discussion. We must recognize the inalienable right to be amused. The cost of discussion has been terrifically high and will continue to be high, but it is apparently worth it and more. I for one would not like to have missed the excitement of 1935. No one can say we have not solved the problem of circuses, whatever may be said as to the problem of bread. We should perhaps insist on more artistic discussion, since we pay so much for it, but that will come with time. But it has its dangers. The increasing cruelty of political life is a reflection of the increasing interest of the mobs. The struggle for position becomes more violent, and each accession to the political arena shrieks more loudly and vehemently. A tyranny of talk has ominous possibilities. Already raids are being made on the universities, and freedom from political control which universities have struggled to achieve is in danger. The enemy is becoming more vociferous, and the inner resistance is being weakened.

The effects have been most threatening to the social sciences. The possibility of achieving the conditions described by Alfred Marshall as important to the study of their complex problems decreases. He writes:

An epoch in my life occurred when I was, I think, about seventeen years old. I was in Regent Street and saw a workman standing idle before a shop window; but his face indicated alert energy, so I stood still and watched. He was preparing to sketch on the window of a shop guiding lines for a short statement of the business concerned, which was to be shown by white letters fixed on the glass. Each stroke of an arm and hand needed to be made with a single free sweep so as to give a graceful result; it occupied perhaps two seconds of keen excitement. He stayed still for a few minutes after each stroke, so that his pulse might grow quiet. If he had saved the minutes then lost, his employers would have been injured by more than the value of his wages for a whole day. That set up a train of thought which led me to resolve never to use by mind when it was not fresh, and to regard the intervals between successive strains as sacred to absolute repose. When I went to Cambridge and became full master of myself, I resolved never to read a mathematical book for more than a quarter of an hour at a time without break. I had some light literature always by my side, and in the breaks I read through more than once nearly the whole of Shakespeare; Boswell's *Life of Johnson*; the *Agamemnon* of Aeschylus (the only Greek play I could read without effort); a great part of Lucretius, and so on.

His wife wrote: "Alfred always did his best work in the open air. When he became a Fellow of St. John's, he did his chief thinking between 10 a.m. and 2 p.m. and between 10 p.m. and 2 a.m. He had a monopoly of the wilderness in the daytime and of the new court cloister at night." Such are the surroundings in which solutions to the problems of a complex society are advanced, and such surroundings are becoming more and more difficult to find.

It becomes apparent that discussion plays a minor if not negative *role* in the advance of social science. The results of such advance can be more satisfactorily placed before the world in writing than in discussion. Stimulation of mental activity follows perhaps more from walking than from talking, and more from lecturing than from discussion. The necessity of focusing the mind on the wider aspects of problems, and of grappling in a systematic way with the subject, which lecturing involves is important in the development of ideas. This will not sound convincing to students, but I assure them there is a grain of truth in it. But the dangers of lecturing to be bright always beset the path of the lecturer. Perhaps the danger of being confident is even more serious. The task of the social scientist is to discover, not to persuade. There are fewer and fewer people who will admit that they do not know, or who have the courage to say that they have not solved the problem. And yet that is what the social scientist must continually keep saying if he hopes to maintain any hold on intellectual life. Constant admission of ignorance is not popular in lecturing, to say nothing of its impracticability as a means of winning elections.

But the question will be raised, what is the hope of democracy? To which we must reply, what democracy? To an increasing extent it has become more dangerous to trust democracy to think out solutions to complex problems, and more necessary to rely on skill and intelligence. The complexity of economic life necessitates constant attention to detail such as only the civil servant can be expected to give. Policies must be formulated in relation to the work of the civil service. Improvements are essential, particularly in co-ordinating the policies of various departments, and formation of an economic council may do something to pool the resources of the civil service and the social scientist. Co-operation between economic councils set up by the provinces and the Dominion should go far in removing glaring injustices; but make no mistake, the peculiar and extraordinary difficulties of the Canadian economy necessitate long and arduous work on the part of the social scientist before serious injustice can be alleviated. A country built up in relation to export markets subject to violent fluctuations as a result of changes in prices and changes in yield, a country with diverse regional problems in relation to these fluctuations, is essentially one in which the politician thrives, in which scapegoats are essential, and in which, conversely, the difficulties of obtaining solutions to problems are increased. The number of cureall s varies directly with our difficulties, and indeed adds to them. Discussion has become a menace rather than a solvent to the problems of a complex society. The task is one of directing it so as to do the least possible damage. Freedom of discussion is of first importance as a means of preventing something worse. So long as attention is focused on circuses, on writing letters to the editor, on attending political meetings, or demanding a scapegoat, and getting one, provided it is not too costly, the civil servant and the social scientist have a chance of getting on with the problems. Our hope is in asking that discussion shall be louder and funnier, and in avoiding control by people with plans and blue prints who insist on interfering with the work of the civil servant and the social scientist, or by people who insist on making the civil servant and the social scientist the scapegoat.

Lest I run the risk of becoming a scapegoat, I shall not proceed further, but turn to a brief survey of the underlying problems as they appear to an economist, as a means of substantiating the account thus far. A major preliminary handicap is involved in attempting to see the problem as a whole. To quote from *A Discourse of Trade* (London, 1680) by N. Barton:

> The reasons why many men have not a true idea of trade is because they apply their thoughts to particular parts of trade, wherein they are chiefly concerned in interest, and having found out the best rules and laws for forming that particular part, they govern their thoughts by the same notions in forming the great body in trade, and not reflecting on the different rules of proportions betwixt the body and parts have a very disagreeable conception, and like those who have learnt to draw well an eye, ear, hand, and other parts of the body (being unskilful in the laws of symmetry) when they join together, make a very deformed body.

The difficulty of looking at Canada as a whole is almost insuperable. Emerging as a continental unit centring about the St Lawrence during the period of the fur trade, its relation to the disunity of the Atlantic Maritimes has been loose and tentative. Even control of the continental unit from the St Lawrence broke down as a result of competition from Hudson Bay after 1821, and from the Pacific coast. These divisions became sharper with the discovery of gold in the Fraser river and the disappearance of control of the Hudson's Bay Company on the Pacific coast and later in the prairie regions. A new unity was attained with the industrial revolution, the steamship, the railways, and the financial support provided in the Act of Union and the British North America Act or Confederation. The latter consisted of a set of agreements in which the provinces agreed, among other things, to give up control over customs and to hand over their debts to the Dominion in return for compensation in the form of subsidies, and of a railway to be built from the Maritimes to connect with the St Lawrence system and a railway to British Columbia. Later agreements have complicated and rounded out the structure. The prairie provinces have been carved out of the Northwest territories, with special arrangements as to subsidies. The Manitoba rate agreement, the Crowsnest Pass rate agreement, the British Columbia rate agreement, the Maritime freight rates Act and adjustments under the Duncan Commission are a part of the network which has been built up in relation to the British North America Act. The Board of Railway Commissioners, the Tariff Board, and the Central Bank may be cited as part of the permanent machinery installed to bring about readjustments. It would be difficult to find a reference to this complicated machinery in party programs dealing with amendments to the BNA Act.

The *British North American Act* is essentially a credit instrument designed to install capital equipment essential to the development of Canadian unity. If one includes the creations of the Act – federal, provincial, and municipal authorities – it would perhaps be safer to say credit instruments. The relation between the earning capacity of the capital equipment and the interest on the extent of the credit becomes of first importance. In the main, earning capacity in a country which emphasizes capital equipment rather than labour depends on exports, and these in turn fluctuate widely as a result of climate and yield in the case of wheat and as a result of world prices. Exports of lumber, pulp and paper, fish, minerals, and agricultural products such as wheat, livestock, and fruit, e.g. apples, are dependent on world prices and factors influencing world prices. Receipts are available to pay interest on the capital equipment and other costs. Capital equipment financed on government security in foreign markets has generally implied obligations which the country is loath to shirk, partly on moral grounds and partly because it may wish to borrow more capital, or it may wish to reduce the interest rate on capital already borrowed, or it may wish to avoid the appointment of a receiver, such as happened in Newfoundland. Foreign investors raise a tremendous howl in cases of threats to default, as you know. Since Canada has attempted to maintain her credit abroad, she has been reluctant to neglect interest payments, and the necessity of paying large sums as fixed charges has meant that large numbers of obligations which did not involve compulsory payments have not been paid. Owners of CPR stock will understand what I mean. Moratoria have been enacted, debts have been written down, and interest rates have been reduced. Moreover, governments being unable to borrow abroad have borrowed to a very large extent at home, partly with funds obtained by what amounts to compulsory saving, in the case of insurance companies, and partly with funds accumulating in the banks through inability to lend to industries restricted as a result of the decline in receipts from exports.

The complexity of the subject is only beginning. Fluctuations in receipts vary in relation to the character of exports, and consequently separate regions are affected differently. Apples in British Columbia may be compared to apples in Nova Scotia, but the fishing industry and the lumber industry are of an entirely different character, and these differ again from the western provinces producing wheat and from regions providing pulp and paper and minerals. Consequently it is extremely difficult to recommend a cureall, since an advantage to one industry may not be anything like as much of an advantage to another industry, and a gain for one region may not be a gain for another. And because of the interrelations between industries and regions it may not be anything like the gain it was thought it would be. Nor is this all. The cost of producing the article, which includes the interest paid by the government abroad and elsewhere, cannot change as rapidly as the prices of the exports or as the returns on exports, particularly if the capital equipment is involved in transportation and navigation, and if it is government-owned. Navigation and railway construction, as we have seen, have involved government ownership and operation. Moreover, the costs of navigation and transportation are *compelled*, and are forced to meet competition from United States transcontinental lines and the Panama Canal, and can be changed with difficulty, generally involving statutory rates or rates fixed by act of parliament. Costs of transportation of exports to the seaboard and to foreign ports tend to remain stable, except for statutory intervention, in which case the government pays the railway compensation. Costs of producers' goods in manufactured products used in the production of exports depend partly on costs of raw materials entering those goods, which may be higher than in other countries, costs of protection, possibly costs of monopoly and the cost of moving them from central Canada, in which they are chiefly produced and which pay a higher rate of transportation because they are manufactured products. The more distant regions tend to pay the higher rate. The tariff forces the most distant regions either to pay the cost of transportation directly, or, in case the purchaser still insists on buying from abroad and, therefore, not using the railway, to pay it indirectly in customs duties. Whether he imports from abroad or buys from central Canada, he pays the cost of transportation either for not using the railway or for using it. The revenues from the duties which he pays are used to pay the deficit on the railroad incurred by his not using it, or the freight is paid directly to the railroad for using it. The burden of transportation costs, through the tariff or through railway rates, tends to fall on the more distant regions, and it is a burden which can be carried without difficulty or complaint under certain conditions. When the railway is first completed, the burden would be very appreciable indeed if it involved higher costs of transportation than before the railway was built. Costs of transportation are reduced so sharply that no one notices the burden of railway rates or tariffs. With the opening up of new industries, tariffs and railway rates are not regarded as burdens, or during a period of boom no one notices additional costs. With the trend toward exhaustion of natural resources and during a period of depression with decline in rates of growth of population and absolute decline of population, attention is drawn to the burden in a very direct way, and particularly in the regions remote from the centres.

The province of Nova Scotia appointed last summer (1934) a Royal Commission of economic enquiry to consider the effects of the burden on its economy, and since that date the prairie provinces and the province of British Columbia have begun to enquire into the extent of the burden. It can be dodged – there are those who say the regions concerned can be bought off – by adding more capital, by building more railways, for example the railway to Hudson Bay, or by improving port facilities; but increased capital expenditure tends to become less remunerative, and adds additional debt charges, and each successive plunge tends to land one deeper in the mire. Sudden changes and improvements in transportation, such as the Panama Canal, may rapidly reduce the burden, or reduction may be obtained by statutory freight rate agreements such as have already been indicated, or you may even reduce the tariff; but if the tariff is reduced materially, freight may cease to travel on the railways, and deficits are increased. On the other hand, lowering of the tariff and consequent lowering of railway rates might actually increase revenue. This is not to say that tariffs are not too high, but rather that tariffs must be considered with railway rates, and to warn certain parties that tariffs are not the whole problem.

Transcontinental railway systems imply acute difficulties of management, and tend to lack flexibility and adaptability in relation to the demands of various regions at various times. The rigidity of the rate structure is in striking contrast with the variability, volume, and value of exports. Statutory rate agreements tend to perpetuate the rigidities they are enacted to avoid. Rate experts and railway policy and emphasis on capital equipment tend to emphasize long hauls, to reduce overhead costs, and to neglect traffic development from a local standpoint. It pays a railway to haul manufactured products from central Canada to British Columbia, but not to develop industry in British Columbia unless it has striking advantages over central Canada, when it may pay to carry goods eastbound to the prairie provinces or even to central Canada. But it is less remunerative to develop local industries for local traffic.

An attack on the problem based on expanding federal revenue, particularly from customs duties and payment of increased subsidies, or by lowering railway rates and paying compensation to the railway, implies that the region to which relief is given pays for it out of its own pocket. An income tax designed to tap the wealth of central Canada obtained as a result of protection, and expenditure in subsidies to assist the development of regions compelled to bear an undue share of the burden, would result in greater fairness. It is sufficient to say that collection and apportionment of the funds in relation to regions and to stages of the business cycle involves continual study on the part of provincial economic councils in cooperation with a federal economic council. I have only begun to hint at the complexity of the problem, and I venture to suggest that it cannot be solved by discussion.

The alternative to continuous study of the problem, by an organization supported by skill and intelligence and linking together federal and regional machinery, we have before us in the constant demand of the provinces for larger subsidies, in the appearance of numerous parties and Royal Commissions, in bonuses and subsidies in the form of support to the wheat regions, in freight rate acts, in relief and the extremely complex system by which Canada is governed. Regionalism becomes intensified, distorted, and involved in a constant scramble for more; or, programs for national government, for amalgamation of the railways, for social credit, for socialization of industry, appear on the horizon. Discussion runs riot and ceases even to be artistic.

CHAPTER THIRTY-TWO

The Church in Canada

Modern civilization, characterized by an enormous increase in the output of mechanized knowledge with the newspaper, the book, the radio, and the cinema, has produced a state of numbness, pleasure, and self-complacency perhaps only equalled by laughing-gas. In the words of Oscar Wilde, we have sold our birthright for a mess of facts. The demands of the machine are insatiable. The danger of shaking men out of the soporific results of mechanized knowledge is similar to that of attempting to arouse a drunken man or one who has taken an overdose of sleeping tablets. The necessary violent measures will be disliked. We have had university professors threatened with the loss of their positions for less than this. But I have little hope of making any impression with what I have to say.

I have made a slight study through unhappy experiences with meetings of this sort and I have always been impressed by the success which attends meetings addressed by Americans or Englishmen. Speakers of both groups are quickly made aware of our sensitiveness and spend much of their time commenting on how much better things are done in Canada than in Great Britain or the United States. Such speakers are very courteous, and are generally equipped with a great fund of stories carefully interspersed throughout the speech, and a peroration which emphasizes the absence of political boundaries between Anglo-Saxon peoples. The demand for this type of speech implies a lack of interest in a Canadian speaker who might say something distasteful about domestic affairs.

From *In Time of Healing*, Twenty-Second Annual Report of the Board of Evangelism and Social Service of the United Church of Canada (Toronto, 1947), 47–54.

THE CANADIAN CHURCH PROBLEM

The problem of the Church is the problem of Western civilization and for that reason is all the most dangerous to discuss. Our position in Canada is perhaps more serious because of our counter-revolutionary tradition. In Quebec the French population largely escaped the influence of the French Revolution and in the older English-speaking provinces immigrants arrived from the United States because of their definite hostility to the revolutionary tradition. The position of the Roman Catholic Church in Quebec is paralleled by the concern of Protestants and of Roman Catholics in English-speaking provinces with control over the activities of the state. Gibbon wrote that "the various methods of worship which prevailed in the Roman world were all considered by the people as equally true, by the philosopher as equally false and by the magistrate as equally useful," and this might be paraphrased by saying that "the various political groups which prevailed in Canada were all considered by the people as equally true, by the philosopher as equally false and by the Church as equally useful." Students of cultural development in Canada have failed to realize the extent to which religion in English-speaking Canada has been influenced indirectly by the traditions of the Gallican Church in Quebec. Nor do we appreciate the significance of the political background of the France of Colbert and Louis XIV. State and Church under an absolute monarchy in France was State and Church under an absolute monarchy in New France. Great Britain failed in the first Empire because Englishmen are alike, but succeeded in the second Empire to a greater extent than is generally realized because French bureaucracy had become solidly entrenched in New France. It was this bureaucracy which enabled the British to govern New France and which enabled Canadians through governmental activity to develop their natural resources by construction of canals, railways, hydro-electric power facilities, and other undertakings. It was this bureaucracy in Church and State which was reflected in the place of Quebec in Confederation and in turn of English-speaking provinces. Clemenceau once remarked that England was a French colony gone wrong. He might have felt that in Canada the French colony had followed expected traditions.

The absence of a revolutionary tradition in Canada assumes relative stability and continuous repression with the result, as Professor J.B. Brebner[1] has shown, that we have been largely concerned with the training of our best students for export to countries with a revolutionary tradition. The Erastian character of religion assumes that the Church has been largely concerned with the development of organization and in turn with ecclesiasticism and links with other interests notably in business. I am told that church union was to a very important extent a response to economic demands. Separate churches could not maintain activity in a large number of communities in the West, and it seemed wiser to follow the example of the banks, the railroads, and the elevators and to emphasize the branch system and avoidance of duplication. The results were evident in fact in the breaking away of radical elements, to cite only the case of the late J.S. Woodsworth and the rise of separate parties in the West. It is significant that the late William Aberhart seized on the relations between the Church and the money-changers in his speeches to his Bible Institute. It was a disturbing sight to see the United Church among the creditors who could lose through its position as a holder of Alberta's bonds.

The lack of a revolutionary tradition continually implies the dangers of compromise which have become conspicuous in Canadian life. In spite of the work of my friend Professor C.B. Sissons on the life of Egerton Ryerson it is difficult to evade the impression that his connection with education brought the school system of Ontario and of other provinces which followed its lead too close to the Prussian bureaucratic system. The results have been evident in an emphasis on the formalities of religious instruction in the schools and a neglect of the basic problem of character. We have been much concerned in academic circles with the decline of Greek, but I am afraid we do not realize that this is a symptom of an unwillingness to face the exacting demands implied in a study of Greek civilization. We have neglected the philosophical problems of the West and have not realized that the Greeks were fundamentally concerned with the training of character.

THE HAND OF PURITANISM

A counter-revolutionary tradition implies an emphasis on ecclesiasticism and the *ipsissima verba* of the Scriptures, particularly of the Old Testament with all the dangers of bibliolatry and of Puritanism. The hand of Puritanism is evident in our literature, in our art, and in our cultural life. This implies neglect of the interrelation between reason and emotion. Religion is a good servant but a bad master, or to cite Pattison: "Those periods when morals have been represented as the proper study of man and his only business have been periods of spiritual abasement and poverty."[2] Puritanical smugness has had a sterilizing influence on the cleansing effects of art and other expressions of cultural life.

The cause of this is, says Shelley, that statesmen and manufacturers have not learnt from the poets the art of recognizing and retaining the significance of that which they see:

The cultivation of poetry is never more to be desired than at periods when, from an excess of the selfish and calculating principle, the accumulation of the materials of external life exceed the quantity of the power of assimilating them to the internal law of human nature.[3]

Whilst the mechanist abridges, and the political economist combines labour, let them beware that their speculations, for want of correspondence with those first principles which belong to the imagination, do not tend, as they have in modern England, to exasperate at once the extremes of luxury and want. They have exemplified the saying, "To him that hath, more shall be given, and from him that hath not, the little that he hath shall be taken away."[4]

As one reads the last pages of the *Defence of Poetry* one begins to see light on that dark saying of Aristotle, "Poetry, therefore, is more philosophic and a higher thing than history, for poetry tends to express the universal and history the particular."[5]

The implications of ecclesiasticism to political life have been evident on every hand. We have had political leaders who have been notorious for breaking records for longevity in political life. When Oliver Mowat was introduced to a prominent statesman in England with a comment on the length of time he had been Premier of Ontario he was greeted with the comment, "Have you no public opinion in that province?" The late J.W. Dafoe is said to have stated that all great public questions in Canada were settled on the basis of personal prejudices, and that political leaders on the whole have lacked the virtue of magnanimity. Lord Acton's comment that "no public character has ever stood the revelation of private utterances and correspondence"[6] has particular significance for the fundamental corruption of Canadian public life.

THE VICISSITUDES OF AN ECONOMIST

Oscar Wilde wrote an essay on the decay of lying but I am not sure that it would bear reading in this country. We are all too much concerned with the arts of *suppressio veri, suggestio falsi.* "The inexorable isolation of the individual is a bitter fact for the human animal, instinctively so social, and much of his verbalizing reflects his obstinate refusal to face squarely so unwelcome a realization. The great maxims and social inventions are so drawn as to minimize this realization, and are often framed in terms which taken at their face value are operationally footless."[7] I am reluctant to make speeches in public for various reasons, and one reason for accepting your generous invitation was the feeling that this was an eminently suitable body to which I might present a personal dilemma. The Department of Political Economy, if I may judge from personal experience, is under constant surveillance by a wide range of individuals. If in the course of an article I make a reference to a large government department or a large business organization, I will receive in an incredibly short time after the article has been published a personal letter, possibly directly from the public relations officer of the organization concerned or indirectly from the president or head of the organization, explaining that my remarks are liable to misinterpretation and inferring that the head of such an influential department in a large university should be very careful about the way in which his views are expressed. I plan to leave in my estate a valuable collection of autographs of prominent men in this country. For these reasons I am largely compelled to avoid making speeches in public and to resort to the careful preparation of material to be made available in print. In most cases this involves writing in such guarded fashion that no one can understand what is written or using quotations from the writings of authors who stand in great repute. I have often envied the freedom of my colleagues in other subjects. On the rare occasions on which I read the reports of their speeches I am always impressed by the ease with which they make statements largely because no one will pay much attention to what they have to say, or because they speak about subjects which do not affect people's direct interests. I am unhappily too aware of the fact that I am the first Canadian to be appointed to the position which I have the honour to hold and that such an appointment coming at so late a date reflects the very great fear of pronouncements made by the holder of my chair. My predecessors have been regarded as safe since as non-Canadians they could not make statements on Canadian affairs which would be taken seriously. But even they, partly because they were not Canadians, were subjected from time to time to the most bitter attacks in the press. Members of the department have been harassed inside and outside the university by protests from representatives of various interests, including political parties.

CHURCH WEAKNESSES

The Church has been rather too intent on losing its life and having it too. It has not been sufficiently philosophical, nor raised sufficient questions as to its limitations. The following quotations are to the point:

This absence of a professional public, and not the restraints of our formularies, seems to me the true reason why a real theology cannot exist in England. Every clerical writer feels himself bound to decide every question of criticism or interpretation in favour of the orthodox view. It is demanded of him by public opinion that he shall be an advocate and not a critic. Science or knowledge cannot exist under such a system; it requires for its growth the air of free discussion and contradiction.[8]

As poetry is not for the critics, so religion is not for the theologians. When it is stiffened into phrases, and these phrases are declared to be objects of reverence but not of intelligence, it is on the way to become a useless encumbrance, the rubbish of the past, blocking the road.

Theology then retires into the position it occupies in the Church of Rome at present, an unmeaning frostwork of dogmas, out of all relation to the actual history of man. In that system, theological virtue is an artificial life quite distinct from the moral virtues of real life.[9]

The heresy trials which have littered the annals of the history of Canadian churches point in the same direction. The blood of the martyrs is the seed of the Church and the Church has apparently always demanded its share of blood. Over the doorway of one of your large colleges there are the words "the truth will make you free," but the heresy trials suggest that the search for truth may mean the loss of your job. The Church is always in danger of overstepping the bounds of moderation. Following Dean Inge, "In religion nothing fails like success."

The social sciences in which I happen to have an interest may be used as an illustration of the limitations of the Church. So, too, modern business has not been educated in terms of its limitations and responsibilities. The Church has been too apt in its acceptance of the claims of other interests because it has not been sufficiently critical of its own position. Instead of checking the pretensions of the social sciences it has accepted them and used them and even exaggerated them. Or it has regarded such subjects as sociology as dangerous and to be avoided, which in turn makes for over-emphasis on such subjects as economics and politics. The Church is in part responsible for a tendency in the social sciences to neglect the importance of training and character. With great pretentiousness they pronounce on questions of exceeding complexity in the social sciences and belittle the necessity of a long period of intense training and the development of character essential to an appreciation of the danger of interfering in other people's lives. They are very apt to assume an active role in the direction of education and in political and even military activity because of what appears to be their overwhelmingly Erastian character. While there is evidence of improvement in the attitude of the Church for example toward conscription in World War I and World War II, it has been all too supine in accepting the pretensions of bureaucracy in Ottawa to solve all problems and in its acceptance with little protest of the encroachments which have been made on civil liberties. Has the Church taken any active stand on the position of Jehovah's Witnesses? Has it given attention to the incipient totalitarian dangers of adult education programs in this country? Does it appreciate the significance of the interest of the totalitarian state in science and its abhorrence of philosophy?

SOME POINTS FOR DISCUSSION

I would like to present to the members of this body the problem not of telling the truth, because I am aware that I do not know what the truth is, but of presenting considerations which will lead to discussion and to a closer approximation to the truth without leading to bitter public controversy. The discussion of questions which affect people's lives must be carried on with great circumspection. I have had occasion recently to come in contact with two professions, the nursing and the medical profession, and to be impressed again with the assumption that a long period of intensive training is essential to the preparation of individuals who are to be concerned throughout their careers with the handling of problems affecting people's lives. I have been appalled on the other hand and by comparison with the cavalier fashion in which great numbers of people discuss the problems of managing people's lives with almost no intensive training. Dale Carnegie's *How to Win Friends and Influence People* is a symptom of a widespread interest in the technique of pushing people around. In universities the rise of the social sciences and in particular the emphasis on business subjects, personnel management, industrial relations, social work, applied anthropology, and so on point to the danger of forgetting that no one can undertake the task of pushing people around without adequate discipline and training, though in fairness it should be said that there is a widespread appreciation of this danger. But we would do well to follow the example of the medical profession based on centuries of experience and tradition in emphasizing the importance of respect for the individual, evident as early as the oath of Hippocrates, and to realize that decisions affecting the lives of individuals should be made only on the basis of intensive training and on character such as comes from a combination of work with the hands as well as the brain. The social sciences in the main suffer from the lack of physical training which is so important in medicine and are apt to become a part of that system of exploitation by which so-called brain workers exploit those who work with their hands. Socrates and Greek philosophers in general were profoundly impressed with the example of the medical profession and with the need for comparable selection and training in the social sciences.

I have sometimes wondered whether ecclesiastical Christianity has not tended to suppress the Greek point of view of the New Testament and to over-emphasize the Hebrew point of view of the Old Testament and to neglect an emphasis on training and character. In swinging from one point of view to the other and in allowing fanaticism to thrive, Christianity has tended to foster an anarchistic society. This view was expressed some years ago by Santayana, from whom I quote:

> Nothing is accordingly more patent than that Christianity was paganized by the early Church; indeed, the creation of the Church was itself what to a Hebraizing mind must seem a corruption, namely, a mixing of pagan philosophy and ritual with the Gospel. ... By this corruption it was completed and immensely improved, like Anglo-Saxon by its corruption through French and Latin; for it is always an improvement in religion, whose business is to express and inspire spiritual sentiment, that it should learn to express and inspire that sentiment more generously. Paganism was nearer than Hebraism to the life of Reason because its myths were more transparent and its temper less fanatical; and so a paganized Christianity approached more closely that ideality which constitutes religious truth than a bare and intense Hebraism, in its hostility to human genius, could ever have done if isolated and unqualified.[10]

> What was condemnable in the Jews was not that they asserted the divinity of their law, for that they did with substantial sincerity and truth. Their crime is to have denied the equal prerogative of other nations' laws and deities, for this they did, not from critical insight or intellectual scruples, but out of pure bigotry, conceit, and stupidity. They did not want other

nations also to have a god. ... What the moral government of things means when it was first asserted was that Jehovah expressly directed the destinies of heathen nations and the course of nature itself for the final glorification of the Jews.

No civilized people had ever had such pretensions before. They all recognized one another's religions, if not as literally true (for some familiarity is needed to foster that illusion), certainly as more or less sacred and significant. Had the Jews not rendered themselves odious to mankind by this arrogance, and taught Christians and Moslems the same fanaticism, the nature of religion would not have been falsified among us and we should not now have so much to apologize for and to retract.[11]

Yet what makes the difference is not the teaching of Jesus – which is pure Hebraism reduced to its spiritual essence – but the worship of Christ – something perfectly Greek. Christianity would have remained a Jewish sect had it not been made at once speculative, universal, and ideal by the infusion of Greek thought, and at the same time plastic and devotional by the adoption of pagan habits. The incarnation of God in man, and the divinization of man in God are pagan conceptions, expressions of pagan religious sentiment and philosophy. Yet what would Christianity be without them? It would have lost not only its theology, which might be spared, but its spiritual aspiration, its artistic affinities, and the secret of its metaphysical charity and joy.[12]

RELIGION AND FANATICISM

Denominationalism does not help to avoid this tendency toward fanaticism. It would be difficult to make any statement on the subject of religion which would not give rise to protests from a particular group. Newspaper editors are constantly aware of the increasing vigilance of various denominations and carefully avoid the subject, and it would not be wise for me to rush in where newspaper editors fear to tread. The churches must be regarded with other groups as always on the alert for an unguarded comment.

In universities one finds a reflection of this fanaticism in that individuals advance in all seriousness the proposition that civilization can be saved by having everyone take their specific subject. That such fanatical points of view can find expression in such an institution as a university points to very grave weaknesses in Western society, as Frederic Harrison in the following quotations makes plain:

This mania for special research in place of philosophic principle, for tabulated facts in lieu of demonstrable theorems and creative generalizations, attenuates the intelligence and installs pedantic information about details, where what man wants are working principles for social life. The grand conceptions of Darwin and of Spencer are too often used by their followers and successors as a text on which to dilate on microscopic or local trivialities which mean nothing. And even Spencer's Synthesis, the only one yet attempted by any English thinker, proves, on being closely pressed, to rest on a substructure of hypotheses, and to ignore two-thirds of the entire scale of the sciences viewed as an interdependent whole. The enormous accumulation of recorded facts in the last century goes on as blindly in this, quite indifferent to the truth that infinite myriads of facts are as worthless as infinite grains of sand on the sea-shore, until we have found out how to apply them to the amelioration of human life.

It was obvious that the literature of the first half of the nineteenth century greatly surpassed that of the second half. And it is sadly evident that literature in the twentieth century is far inferior even to that of the second half century.[13]

Historical study today is far more scientific, and is grouped and classified into elaborate sections, periods, and nations. But like almost every other study, it is overwhelmed with its infinite details, and its unity is lost in interminable special subdivisions, "periods," and subsidiary "ologies." Girls and lads in their teens are so deep in "diplomatics," numismatics, and the Manor system, that they are too learned to know anything of common things like the Punic Wars or the French Revolution. Science, too, suffers from the incoherent specialization which is bound up with modern research. The study of science, of course, must be said to be far more widely popularized today, and to be a much higher order of thought. But biography, the typical literature of our age, feels the reaction of the ceaseless multiplication of lives to record, until the best and the greatest lives are too often overwhelmed in the flow of the obscure and the commonplace.[14]

It is not only dangerous in this country to be a social scientist with an interest in truth but it is exhausting. You will remember the remarks of the Persian at a banquet in Thebes noted by Herodotus. "This is the most cruel pang that man can bear – to have much insight and power over nothing." On a wider plane it is a source of constant frustration to attempt to be a Canadian. Both Great Britain and the United States encourage us in assuming the false position that we are a great power and in urging that we have great national and imperial possibilities. From both groups we are increasingly subjected to pressure and in turn to bureaucratic tendencies dictated by external forces. We have no sense of our limitations. On the question of Russia we are constantly pushed into a position in which it is assumed that we take sides. We have little chance to raise questions as to the dominance of military authorities in the United States or as to the political needs of the Labour party in Great Britain. We seem destined to occupy in North America the place of Czechoslovakia as a show window in relation to Russia in Europe, first as to the British Empire and second as to the American Empire. But I am in danger of assuming that I may make an impression in what I have to say. I would conclude with an additional word about the Church.

I have attempted to underline certain facts. In common with many observers, I believe that the Church has ceased to have an intellectual interest for people because the Church has lost its curiosity for ideas. Failing to have an interest in ideas the Church has of necessity found an outlet for its energies in social action. This has led to a vast congeries of good works and a vast amount of planning for others and pushing others around. We have developed an amazing aptitude for knowing what the other fellow ought to be doing. If the Church can not return to an interest in ideas, and must therefore express itself exclusively in social action, we ought to insist upon a higher quality of discipline. I have indicated the physician and the nurse as types of special disciplines that are necessary, people who respect the individual and know when to leave him alone, but first of all they know their subject thoroughly. But skill and discipline are of little value unless the practitioners of good words are selected for their integrity and the high quality of their characters.

NOTES

1 *Scholarship for Canada* (Ottawa, 1945).
2 *Essays by the Late Mark Pattison* (Oxford, 1889), 2: 82.
3 Percy Bysshe Shelley, "Defence of Poetry," *Prose Works* (London, 1912), 31.
4 Ibid., 28–9.
5 Graham Wallas, *The Art of Thought* (London, 1926), 130–1.
6 Lord Acton, *Historical Essays and Studies* (London, 1919), 506.
7 P.W. Bridgman, *The Intelligent Individual and Society* (New York, 1938), 142–3.
8 Mark Pattison, *Memoirs* (London, 1885), 317.
9 *Essays by the Late Mark Pattison,* 2: 86–7.
10 George Santayana, *The Life of Reason,* vol. 3, *Reason in Religion* (London, 1906), 106–7.

11 Ibid., 76–7.
12 Ibid., 84–5.
13 Frederic Harrison, *Autobiographic Memoirs* (London, 1911), 2: 322–3.
14 Ibid., 1: 22–3.

CHAPTER THIRTY-THREE

Adult Education and Universities

The Manitoba Royal Commission on Adult Education has been concerned with the problem of adult education in relation to government and the dangers of propaganda. Propaganda has been described as "that branch of the art of lying which consists in very nearly deceiving your friends without quite deceiving your enemies";[1] unfortunately in a bureaucracy it effectively deceives the vast majority of people who are neither friends nor enemies. We have assumed that government in democratic countries is based on the will of the governed, that people can make up their minds, and that every encouragement should be given to enable them to do so. This implies that the state is concerned with strengthening intellectual capacity, and not with the weakening of that capacity by the expenditure of subsidies for the multiplication of facts. It also implies that adults have been so trained in the educational system that they can choose the facts and reach their own decisions. We should, then, be concerned like the Greeks with making men, not with overwhelming them by facts disseminated with paper and ink, film, radio, and television. Education is the basis of the state and its ultimate aim and essence is the training of character. "One of the aims of education is to break the strong hold of the present on the mind."[2] "To build up in every man and woman a solid core of spiritual life which will resist the attrition of everyday existence in our mechanized world – that is the most difficult and important task of school and university" (Sir Richard Livingstone).

Revised extracts from *Report of the Manitoba Royal Commission on Adult Education* (Winnipeg, 1947), 141–8; reprinted in *The Bias of Communication* (Toronto, 1951), app. 2, 203–14.

In the oft quoted remark of Lord Elgin, education "fits one for nothing and trains him for everything." Again, it is "the purpose of education not to prepare children for their occupations but to prepare them against their occupations" (C.G. Sampson).[3] It is not easy to focus on this broad objective. "The history of education is indeed a somewhat melancholy record of misdirected energy, stupid routine, and narrow one-sidedness. It seems to be only at rare moments in the history of the human mind than an enthusiasm for knowledge and a many-sided interest in the things of the intellect stirs the dull waters of educational commonplace."[4]

A major problem of society emerges in the development of institutions which enlarge the capacities of individuals and enable them to use such enlarged capacities to the greatest advantage of the individual and the institutions. In this the state occupies a crucial position. Education has been largely concerned with conservation of knowledge, and in turn becomes extremely conservative. This conservatism is evident in the lack of interest in educational philosophy and in the tendency of educational institutions, particularly those concerned with the teaching of Education as a subject, to avoid the major philosophical problems of Western civilization. Institutions thus concerned with the teaching of Education and their expanding activities are in themselves a comment on the poverty of education and may become obstacles to the attainment of broad objectives. "Educative discipline tends to preserve what has been acquired and presents very real obstacles to further advance."

The tendency towards conservatism has been accentuated by the mechanization of communication in print, radio, and film. They have tended not only to eliminate the personal factor but also to emphasize the factual and the concrete. Abstract ideas are less susceptible to treatment by mechanical devices.[5] Moreover, ideas must be ground down to a convenient size to meet the demands of large numbers. "Any purpose, any idea of training the mind itself, has gone out of the world. ... Those studies which produce no fruits obvious to the sense are fallen into neglect" (John Stuart Mill). Mechanical devices become concerned with useless knowledge of useful facts. Complaints of duplication and confusion are inevitable.

But I do see all the injury to the higher literature inflicted by the torrential multiplication of printed stuff coinciding with the legal enforcement of mechanical reading – absurdly misnamed *Education.* To teach boys and girls to read print, whilst leaving them sunk in the materialised state of mind and morals typical of modern anarchy, without beliefs, or ideals, or principles, or duties – this is to inaugurate a millennium of vapid commonplace and vulgar realism.[6]

... in spite of the vast increase of general education and of all forms of literary product ... literature is on the down grade. I hazard the paradox in good faith that the decline is not merely in spite of all this instruction, but is a result of the universal schooling. The incessant education drill, the deluge of printed matter, asphyxiate the brain, dull beauty of thought, and chill genius into lethargic sleep. ...

... I seriously maintain that a direct result of our mechanical schooling ... and that whether primary, middle, or highest; Board schools, high schools, academies, or universities – is the gradual deterioration of literature into dry specialism and monotonous commonplace. ...

The double effect of making life a race or a scramble, working with the ceaseless cataract of commonplace print, just good enough to occupy the average mind having a superficial school training, debases the general intellectual currency, and lowers the standard. Scientific and historical research piles up its huge record of facts with a sort of scholiast's attention to minute scholarship and inattention to impressive form. It would seem as if the higher order of literature were produced in inverse ratio to the number of the reading public and the volume of literary product. ... The printed book was the death of the cathedral. To-day we may say – the school has been the death of literature.[7]

The modern community of the Western world has been disciplined by the spread of machine industry. The vacuum created by the Industrial Revolution must be assiduously filled. Large-scale capital equipment has dominated the paper industry and the newspaper, the radio, the movie, and television, and each in turn has become monopolistic in character and concerned with reaching the largest number of people. The advertiser upon whom they have come largely to rely wishes to appeal to the largest possible number. He assumes an average age of twelve, and information in all media, to achieve the greatest possible results, is directed to that level.[8] The Anglo-Saxon world has become "distinguished for its lack of intellectual strenuousness."

This mania for special research in place of philosophic principle, for tabulated facts in lieu of demonstrable theorems and creative generalisations, attenuates the intelligence and installs pedantic information about details, where what man wants are working principles for social life. The grand conceptions of Darwin and of Spencer are too often used by their followers and successors as a text on which to dilate on microscopic or local trivialities which mean nothing. ... The enormous accumulation of recorded facts in the last century goes on as blindly in this, quite indifferent to the truth that infinite myriads of facts are as worthless as infinite grains of sand on the sea-shore, until we have found out how to apply them to the amelioration of human life.

It was obvious that the literature of the first half of the nineteenth century greatly surpassed that of the second half. And it is sadly evident that literature in the twentieth century is far inferior even to that of the second half century.[9]

Any community has only a limited number capable of sustained mental effort. According to biologists they may be found in all regions and in all strata. A democratic society can thrive only by the persistent search for its greatest asset and by constant efforts to conserve, to encourage, to train, and to extend it. Throughout the community assiduous interest must be taken in the discovery, conservation, and improvement of limited intellectual resources. In concentrating on the training of the best brains, it will be necessary to make certain that every device has been exhausted in the primary schools of rural and urban areas, the high schools, the colleges and the universities to detect and to encourage every sign of intellectual capacity. Every obstacle should be removed from the path of the brightest student particularly if he is found in the least advantageous circumstances. Scholarships on an extensive scale contribute to this end – the abolition of fees would contribute more – but even these would not be adequate.

The examination system by which students are selected from the schools for admission to universities reflects the worst evils of the mechanization of education. The results are evident in the success of students in large cities and of middle-class parents. Uniformity of examination systems over wide areas involves wholesale discrimination against districts which cannot attract the best teachers or command the best equipment. In large urban centres state schools are supplemented by private "cram" schools. An emphasis on uniformity of examinations is accompanied by an emphasis on uniformity of subjects. The matriculation system as an intelligence test has become a gigantic maze and the resources for training students to thread the maze have been built up in the large centres. A glance at the failure rate of small rural centres suggests the results. Similarly a careful study of the failure rate and of the success rate in the first year of university work brings out sharply the contrast between university teaching and high-school teaching. A large failure rate is accompanied by tremendous public pressure on the universities to adopt the standards of teaching of the high schools. The blight of mechanization spreads from the high schools to the universities. It has been said that "equality of educational opportunity is more essential to social justice than equality of fortune – and more easy of attainment"[10] but the difficulties can scarcely be exaggerated.

The universities must attempt to select the ablest students and must concentrate on the most efficient method of training them. They must be encouraged to achieve the objectives of an educational system in the most effective fashion. But universities are influenced by the mechanization of education, and hampered by tradition. "The academical establishments of some parts of Europe are not without their use to the historian of the human mind. Immovably moored to the same station by the strength of their cables and the weight of their anchors, they enable him to measure the rapidity of the current by which the rest of mankind is borne along."[11] The breaking down of ideas and the emphasis on factual information have been evident in the narrowing of professional education and of arts courses. Textbooks of systematized knowledge have been altogether too much in evidence. Courses have been carefully calculated with a view to the inclusion of all the relevant information during the three or four years of undergraduate work. The results have been a systematic closing of students' minds. Initiative and independence have been weakened. Factual material, information, classification, reflect the narrowing tendencies of the mechanization of knowledge in the minds of staffs and students. Professions become narrow and sterile. The teaching profession suffers perhaps most of all. A broad interest in the complex problems of society becomes almost impossible. The University graduate is illiterate as a result of the systematic poisoning of the educational system. Student and teacher are loaded down with information and prejudice. The capacity to break down prejudice and to maintain an open mind has been seriously weakened.

> The difference between the principles of this ancient education and our modern principles of education is rightly found in this, that to it the development of the aptitude and the possession of it counted for more than the work for which it was used and the fruitfulness of that work in result. Every individual was to be made a model example of his species: the species itself had nothing else to do but to exist and to enjoy the use of its powers. ... To this many-sided development, finding an end in itself, the spirit of modern education is no doubt less kind; it sets a higher value than it justly should on range of concrete knowledge in comparison with a general aptitude for knowing – on productive specialized labour in comparison with the free exercise of all the powers – on professional effort working in a groove in comparison with an interest in human relations generally [R.H. Lotze].

The traditions of the university in the Western world have centred around the direct oral method of instruction but these have been weakened by the impact of mechanization. "All originality is screened out of whatever is produced. Teaching, that noblest of all vocations, degenerates into pedantry. ... University lectures become infected with ... true moral cowardice, until the lecture-room style can be recognized and readily distinguished from the independent exposition of the original investigator. ... Along with the dwarfing effect of this state of things, there goes the further demoralizing influence of egotism and conceit."[12]

Universities must strive to enlist most active energetic minds to train most active energetic minds. "Education properly understood is little more, at best, than the creation of an artificial environment calculated to call into exercise all the latent talents of those who receive it. The number manifesting this kind of genius may, therefore, be greatly increased through a form of education which should be really adapted to calling it forth."[13] Students and staff should concentrate on the development of capacities to resist the influence of mechanization and to make fresh contributions to the solution of the age-old problems of Western civilization. The university should be concerned with the release of mental energy and with its training for an effective attack on these complex problems rather than with systematic destruction. It should produce a philosophical approach which will constantly question assumptions,[14] constantly weaken the overwhelming tendency, reinforced by mechanization, to build up and accept dogma, and constantly attempt to destroy fanaticism. Once the university, and in particular the arts faculty, becomes thoroughly seized of the vital significance of its role in Western society and staff and students realize the necessity of constant emphasis on training to produce the open mind, the whole educational system will begin to show signs of vitality. The university, in training the best intellectual resources and in developing a philosophical approach which assumes an open mind on the part of staff and student, can contribute powerfully to a solution of the problems of adult education. Society must regard the university as a community of scholars concerned with its vital problems.

The university tradition as developed in Europe and in Great Britain cannot find effective expression under the constitutional devices characteristic of North America. The institution of the board of governors in Canada is contrary to the European tradition which assumes the self-government of the university, which recognizes the capacity of scholars to govern themselves and thereby enhances their self-respect, their prestige, and their effectiveness. In the words of Lord Baldwin:

The University is an epitome of true democracy. Merit alone is the hallmark and freedom – ordered freedom – its birthright. Never must that freedom be bartered away. Universities need money; much of modern scientific research and teachings works through expensive tools; money has come to them generously from wealthy men or from the State. But let us never forget that the wealthy men and the State are honoured by being allowed to take part in the sacred work of education and, while their contributions are received with sincere gratitude, nothing gives a right either to the wealthy man or the State to interfere in any way with the freedom of the University itself. It must always be its own master, responsible to its conscience and sound tradition for what it teaches and how it teaches.[15]

In Canada there have been cases of harrying of individual members of staff by the community and by boards of governors. University professors are exposed to a continual sense of frustration. University presidents and administrative officers have been placed in intolerable positions by those who have no conception of the character of the university tradition. As a first step in adult education university statutes should be carefully studied and revised in the light of broad principles strengthening the university in the community.

It is probable that the university cannot bridge the gap between its level of intellectual training and that which characterizes the modern community under the influence of machine industry. It cannot yield to the obsession for information and instruction without neglecting education. The staffs of universities may be loaded down with abortive attempts to solve the problem by a direct attack. "New opinions, founded on a legitimate process of observation and inference, are generally worked out in solitude by persons of studious and reflective habits and they are, when once accredited and established among men of science, expounded, illustrated, and diffused, by popular writers. The two provinces of discovery and diffusion are usually divided; for the power of original thought, and the power of perspicuous elementary exposition, are often not combined in the same mind."[16] "Discovery of the great principles of nature demands a mind almost exclusively devoted to such investigations."[17] Large ideas can only be conceived after intensive study over a long period and through the direct and powerful device of the spoken word in small groups. It can be extended by small numbers of highly trained students of exceptional mental capacity.

... the name [university] has got to be associated with education of the highest type: to degrade the name of a University is therefore to degrade our highest educational ideal. ... It is natural and desirable ... that efforts should be made to diffuse knowledge and intellectual interests among all classes by means of evening lectures. The English Universities may well be proud of having taken the initiative in a movement of the most far-reaching social and political significance. But it would be a delusion, and a mischievous delusion, to suppose that evening lectures, however excellent and however much supplemented by self-education, can be the same thing as the student-leisure of many years, duly prepared for by a still longer period of regular school training. Examinations, too, and private preparation for them, are an excellent thing in their proper place: but it is a mistake to suppose that an Examining Board can discharge any but the very lowest of a University's real functions. The two most essential functions which a true University has to perform, and which all Universities have more or less discharged amid the widest possible variety of system and method and organization, hardly excepting even the periods of their lowest degradation, are to make possible the life of study, whether for a few years or during a whole career, and to bring together during that period, face to face in living intercourse, teacher and teacher, teacher and student, student and student. ... it behoves us not to lose or lower the ideal of the University as the place *par excellence* for professed and properly trained students, not for amateurs or dilettantes or even for the most serious of leisure-hour students; for the highest intellectual cultivation, and not merely for elementary instruction or useful knowledge; for the advancement of Science, and not merely for its conservation or diffusion; as the place moreover where different branches of knowledge are brought into contact and harmonious combination with one another, and where education and research advance side by side.[18]

Administrators may be attracted to the advantages of publicity from adult education as a means of influencing the public and the legislators and of securing funds, and may fail to appreciate the significance of advanced work in research. University aims are then obscured, a belief in stereotypes is developed, and it becomes impossible to maintain the freedom of the open mind. University administrators become exposed to new burdens and encroachments are made on the work of scholars. It is necessary to set up a buffer to avoid the misuse of funds for propaganda purposes. In the main, adult education has tended to fall into the hands of those who do not command the respect of scholars and looked upon with suspicion by them. Both scholars and the public look upon them as concerned with vested interests including parties, governments, or their own positions. Bringing the university to the people may become a pickpocket device which the public ought to suspect. As a part of the university machinery designed to impress legislators with the necessity of supporting the university, adult education may become a device to fool the public and the university administration. University extension courses may serve to relieve the pressure on other courses, but the cost must be carefully considered. Adult education is apt to involve the standardization of information and propaganda; the university has a special function to offset these tendencies.

Adult education, appealing to large numbers with limited training, can be disentangled with difficulty from the advertising of large organizations concerned with the development of goodwill. An agitation for the clearance of slums may be sponsored by organizations concerned with the sale of their products. Universities may engage in adult education programs on a large scale to build up their goodwill and to create new interest. The advertiser has created distrust[19] through his power of penetration in the field of education and in turn education has been the object of mistrust. To reach lower levels of intelligence and to concentrate on territory held by newspapers, radio, and films, adult education follows the pattern of advertising. "No adult education which we have at present seems to me much more than a puerile gesture. Nothing that I have seen does much more than continue the sort of instruction that was given in elementary schools, modified a little perhaps by the recognition that discipline becomes irksome and cannot be enforced when the enterprise on the part of the pupil is a voluntary one. Where is the scheme of adult education that recognizes that maturity has problems of its own and capacities of its own? ... The adult, then, has problems and capacities to solve them peculiar to himself, and adult education should be built around them."[20] The growing incompatibility between those who like to think, and those who do not has been described as characteristic of the Western world. "People who want to preserve to themselves the opportunity to think have got to do something about it as a matter of sheer self-interest."

On the other hand the increase in numbers of books and the growth of a book civilization contribute to the difficulties of the universities. There has developed a more extensive hierarchy of those who know more about books than others, and institutions to foster book knowledge and create hierarchies. It is difficult for adult education to make an impression on these and to develop new points of view. Freshness and vitality are lost. An indirect attack on the problem of adult education is essential. The graduates of the university in medicine, dentistry, law, theology, and teaching can play an important role in keeping the university closer to the public and preventing it from drifting beyond its range. The teacher can link books to conversation and oral education. He should be given refresher courses and courses in summer schools to enable him to serve as an effective link between the university and the community, between research and the public. He can provide the link between a written and an oral tradition. The graduate can fill a basic role in making the university available to the largest possible number.

NOTES

1 F.M. Cornford, *Microcosmograpia Academica: Being a Guide for the Young Academic Politician* (Cambridge, 1933), preface to 2nd ed.

2 *General Education in a Free Society: Report of the Harvard Committee* (Cambridge, Mass.).

3 Cited by E.B.Osborn, *Our Debt to Greece and Rome* (London, 1924), 16."Perfect good breeding consists in having no particular mark of any profession" (Samuel Johnson). "The outstanding mark of an education is the ability of a person to hold his judgement in suspense in unsettled questions" (Newton D. Baker).

4 Hastings Rashdall, *The Universities of Europe in the Middle Ages* (Oxford, 1895), vol. 2, pt. 2, 705.

5 "It is difficult to find a common ground for exact science and the public. The public craves immortality, and other miracles, and the Sunday papers murder science to meet the prevailing appetite. On the other hand, real science refuses to talk English, but instead writes a dialect of its own, and seems to believe that scientific ideas cannot be expressed accurately in English" (Norman Hapgood, *The Changing Years: Reminiscences* [New York, 1930], 285).

6 Frederic Harrison, *Autobiographic Memoirs* (London, 1911), 1: 23–4.

7 Ibid., 2:324–7.

8 "Psychologists have estimated that when the brain is receiving visual and aural impressions of a scene simultaneously about seventy per cent of the intelligence comes through the eyes and about thirty through the ears" (John Swift, *Adventure in Vision* [London, 1950], vi.

9 Harrison, *Autobiographic Memoirs,* 2: 322–3. See also W.R. Inge, *Diary of a Dean, St. Paul's 1911–1934* (London, 1950), 222–3: "I cannot doubt that the main cause of the decay is the pernicious habit of writing hastily for money. If we take the trouble to consult Mudie's catalogue of fiction, we shall learn to our amazement that there are several writers, whose names we have never heard, who have to their discredit over a hundred works of fiction apiece. They obviously turn out several books a year, just as a shoemaker manufactures so many pairs of boots. The great novelists have generally written rapidly, rather too rapidly; but such a cataract of ink as these heroes of the circulating library spill is

absolutely inconsistent with even second-rate work. Literature flourishes best when it is half a trade and half an art; and here again the Victorian Age occupies the most favourable part of the curve."

10 A.M. Thompson, *Here I Lie* (London, 1937), 39.

11 Sir Richard Jebb, *Essays and Addresses* (Cambridge, 1907), 601. See also Rashdall, *The Universities of Europe in the Middle Ages*, vol. 2, pt. 2, 710–11: "The very idea of the institution is essentially medieval, and it is curious to observe how largely that idea still dominates our modern schemes of education ... However much the modern mind may in certain directions be reverting to the ideas and spirit of the old world, education, like so much else in the modern world, will always exhibit a vast and incalculable difference from the education of ancient Greece or ancient Rome just because the Middle Ages have intervened ... Something of the life and spontaneity of old-world culture certainly seems to be gone forever. Universities have often had the effect of prolonging and stereotyping ideas and modes of thought for a century or more after the rest of the world has given them up. It is surprising how slowly an intellectual revolution affects the course of ordinary education. But educational traditions are marvellously tenacious, quite apart from institutional machinery such as that of the Universities: and education itself must always be, from the necessities of the case, a tradition."

12 L.F. Ward, *The Psychic Factors of Civilization* (Boston, 1906), 106–7.

13 Ibid., 205.

14 "It is difficult to see how ... a country can ... survive ... under the continual necessity of so controlling education that the people may not become aware of the meaninglessness of the whole elaborate superstructure. It constitutes a problem of probably superhuman difficulty to promote enough intelligence to enable the country to maintain its position in the race of material progress, without leaving open the possibility that that intelligence may sometime begin asking questions about the foundations of its own society" (P.W. Bridgman, *The Intelligent Individual and Society* [New York, 1938], 136).

15 Baldwin of Bewdley, *The Falconer Lectures, 1939* (Toronto, 1939), 27.

16 G.C. Lewis, *An Essay on the Influence of Authority in Matters of Opinion* (London, 1849), 286.

17 Charles Babbage, *On the Economy of Machinery and Manufactures* (London, 1841), 380.

18 Rashdall, *The Universities of Europe in the Middle Ages*, vol. 2, pt. 2, 714–15.

19 See H.M. McLuhan, *The Mechanical Bride: Folklore of Industrial Man* (New York, 1951).

20 Bridgman, *The Intelligent Individual and Society*, 202–3.

CHAPTER THIRTY-FOUR

Democracy and the Free City

Mr Chairman, Gentlemen, and friends. I am very grateful for the honour of being asked to speak at your annual meeting and for the opportunity of expressing my appreciation of the work of your organizations and of Dr Brittain. It is a work of deep concern not only to this city and to other cities in Canada but also to modern democracies and western civilization. I know of no more crucial problem in responsible government than that of governing cities. The solution of the problems of democratic government rests in the cities.

It will be unnecessary to emphasize the significance of this work to you but I am not sure that even you realize the role of the city in western civilization. You will remember that when the King visits the city of London he must be admitted at Temple Bar by the mayor. This is the continuation of a custom suggesting how very strongly the city held its privileges. It not only resented the intrusion of the Crown, it also insisted that even parliament had limitations. Wilkes would not have been able to win the great struggle for freedom of the press against parliament without the solid support of the city of London and its insistence on its rights.

The tradition of the city continued from Athens to the Roman empire, which was built on municipal institutions, and to the cities which survived the Roman empire and broke the power of feudalism by their ability to compel the concession of privileges. But aside from Florence according to Burckhardt "these later centres were

A paper read at the combined annual meeting of the Citizens' Research Institute of Canada and the Bureau of Municipal Research; printed in *The Importance of Local Government in a Democracy*, Citizen's Research Institute of Canada, Bulletin 84, 3 May 1945.

never anything but courts, residences, etc. Florence alone could vie with Athens." The glory of the city tradition reflected from Athens has never been more glowingly presented than in the funeral speech of Pericles in words which are particularly apt at this moment.

"For we have compelled every land and every sea to open a path for our valour, and have everywhere planted eternal memorials of our friendship and of our enmity. Such is the city for whose sake these men nobly fought and died; they could not bear the thought that she might be taken from them; and every one of us who survive should gladly toil on her behalf. I would have you day by day fix your eyes upon the greatness of Athens, until you become filled with the love of her; and when you are impressed by the spectacle of her glory, reflect that this empire has been acquired by men who knew their duty and had the courage to do it, who in the hour of conflict had the fear of dishonour always present to them, and who, if ever they failed in an enterprise, would not allow their virtues to be lost to their country, but freely gave their lives to her as the fairest offering which they could present at her feast. The sacrifice which they collectively made was individually repaid to them; for they received again and again each one for himself a praise which grows not old and the noblest of all sepulchres – I speak not of that in which their remains are laid, but of that in which their glory survives and is proclaimed always and on every fitting occasion both in word and deed. For the whole earth is the sepulchre of famous men; not only are they commemorated by columns and inscriptions in their own country, but in foreign lands there dwells also an unwritten memorial of them, graven not on stone but in the hearts of men. Make them our example."[1]

The free cities which emphasized commerce and peace included Venice, the members of the Hanseatic league, the cities of the Netherlands and finally London. Against the clergy, the army, the monarchy and the nobility, the burghers, the bourgeois, the traders tenaciously fought their way to compromises. So long as defence was stronger than attack the walled city became the oasis of freedom but with the invention of gun powder attack became stronger than defence and the city was dominated by nationalism and centralization. On the continent the traditions of the Roman empire persisted in Roman law and the strength of the army. In English-speaking countries the common law and the strength of the navy permitted the city to become the centre of commerce and finance. "Under Roman law the citizen exists for the benefit of the state. Under English law the state exists for the benefit of the citizen. Under Roman law the affairs of the people are an active concern of government.

Under English law the affairs of the government are an active concern of the people. Roman law is an institution of imperialism. English law is an institution of democracy. The best modern example of government under Roman law is Prussia ... These two conflicting systems cannot be permanently reconciled."[2]

London and New York as the great centres of Anglo-Saxon civilization supported by naval strength have become the great rulers in the interest of commerce and peace. A large number of cities have grown up in their tradition and western civilization finds its great bulwark in them. The dangers of democracy can be illustrated in their problems. London suffered because of its centralization of trade, and government. New centres became jealous and the rivalries of Europe, Paris of which Courier said "only Paris has laws" and in which the problem of centralization in Europe has always been acute, Berlin, Rome, and before the last war Vienna, as the centres of courts, created the atmosphere of new wars. New centres were created after the last war to offset the large centres of the continent including Prague, Buda-Pest, Warsaw. Leningrad and Moscow emerged farther east.

In the new world the jealousy of cities favoured the growth of federalism. Washington, Ottawa, Canberra were chosen at points distant from the large centres and each has built up its type of control over larger cities. The comment of an Australian that a fifth freedom should be added "Freedom from Canberra" will be echoed in the United States and Canada. The jealousies have brought their own problems including the growth of the political machine in large centres as a means of linking them up with the capitals. New York, Philadelphia, Chicago, illustrated what Lincoln Steffens called in his series of muckraking articles "The shame of the cities." I shall carefully avoid any reference to Canadian cities at least to machines in Canadian cities.

The power of cities in federal systems can however be shown very clearly in Canada. Montreal through the Bank of Montreal, took an active interest in the construction of the Canadian Pacific Railway – the first transcontinental railway. Toronto through the Canadian Bank of Commerce became actively concerned in the construction of a rival system the Canadian Northern, and Quebec City, with the support of Sir Wilfrid Laurier, in the construction of the National Transcontinental and the Grand Trunk Pacific. Halifax has contested with St John for a larger share of terminal traffic. In the new cities Winnipeg fought a valiant battle against Toronto, and in turn Regina and Saskatoon in the wheat pool days opposed the Winnipeg press and the Winnipeg grain trade. Calgary and Edmonton fostered the great revolt which broke out in social credit. Vancouver, without the initial independence of San Francisco, has been active in demanding such things as more favourable freight rates. The political divisiveness of Canada has been in part a result of the growth of new cities. I understand a questionnaire has been sent out asking why Toronto is hated. The answer in part is the same as why Winnipeg is hated and why each centre hates the other. But all these hatreds are somehow focused on Toronto. New areas strenuously endeavour to enhance their strength by exploiting grievances against Toronto and grievances persist so long as they are a vested interest and capable of exploiting.

The political problem of the modern city is the problem of democracy. Jealousy between cities enables central power groups to play one off against the other and to dominate. Divide and rule. Nationalism has become a great threat to the city and whether a solution can be found at San Francisco in the international field remains to be seen. With nationalism has come centralized military power and whether the problems of the army and the navy and air force, the problems of continents, oceans and air can be solved remains also for a solution at San Francisco. How far an enthusiasm for an international order can be expected to offset the fanaticism of nationalism remains to be seen. The fundamental problem of government is essentially that of law, order and freedom and in this specialized groups have their limitations. The lawyer plays an important part in government but his limitations are obvious.

"Of law-bred statesmen (if they have had practice at the bar) the peculiar merit is a more strenuous application of their minds to business than is often to be found in others. But they labour under no light counterpoise of peculiar demerit. It is a truth, though it may seem at first sight like a paradox, that in the affairs of life the reason may pervert the judgment. The straightforward view of things may be lost by considering them too closely and too curiously. When a naturally acute faculty of reasoning has had that high cultivation which the study and practice of the law affords, the wisdom of political, as well as of common life, will be to know how to lay it aside, and on proper occasions to arrive at conclusions by a grasp; substituting for a chain of arguments that almost unconscious process by which persons of strong natural understanding get right upon questions of common life, however in the art of reasoning unexercised.

"The fault of a law-bred mind lies commonly in seeing too much of the question, not seeing its parts in their due proportions, and not knowing how much of material to throw overboard in order to bring a subject within the compass of human judgment. In large matters largely entertained, the symmetry and perspective in which they should be presented to the judgment requires that some considerations should be as if unseen by reason of their smallness and that some distant bearings should dwindle into nothing. A lawyer will frequently be found busy in much pinching of a case and no embracing of it – in rooting and grunting and tearing up the soil to get at a grain of the subject; – in short, he will often aim at a degree of completeness and exactness which is excellent in itself, but altogether disproportionate to the dimensions of political affairs, or at least to those of certain classes of them."[3] The merchant is timid and by virtue of his training slow to see the broad implications of the problems of government and civilization. One has only to note the shortsighted, stupid, suicidal attitudes of some business men to party organization and to universities to realize how limited they are in the fields of government. Perhaps one is compelled to recognize the saying of Count Oxenstiern, "My son you little know with what little wisdom the world is governed." In such organizations as we have represented before us wisdom and rationality can be applied and the fanaticisms which dominate political problems can be checked. The support of citizens to these organizations tempers their own fanaticism. It was Talleyrand who said "Above all – no zeal." The fanaticism of party, religion, race, professions, nationalism, and militarism must somehow be met in the government of the city first and last and after that little is left of world problems. "The fault, dear Brutus, is not in our stars, but in ourselves that we are underlings."

NOTES

1 J.B. Bury, *A History of Greece*, trans. Jowett (New York, 1937).
2 John L. Heaton, *The Story of a Page* (New York and London, 1913).
3 Sir Henry Taylor, *Notes from Life: The Statesman* (Boston, 1853), 385.

Index